General Advisor to Palgrave: Professor Christian Pinson, INSEAD

Marketing Management

A value-creation process

Pierre-Louis Dubois

Alain Jolibert

Hans Mühlbacher

First published 2007 by
PALGRAVE MACMILLAN
Houndmills, Basingstoke, Hampshire RG21 6XS and
175 Fifth Avenue, New York, N.Y. 10010
Companies and representatives throughout the world

PALGRAVE MACMILLAN is the global academic imprint of the Palgrave
Macmillan division of St. Martin's Press, LLC and of Palgrave Macmillan Ltd.
Macmillan® is a registered trademark in the United States, United Kingdom
and other countries. Palgrave is a registered trademark in the European
Union and other countries.

ISBN-13: 978–0–333–77319–2
ISBN-10: 0–333–77319–5

This book is printed on paper suitable for recycling and made from fully
managed and sustained forest sources.

A catalogue record for this book is available from the British Library.

A catalog record for this book is available from the Library of Congress.

10   9   8   7   6   5   4   3   2   1
16 15 14 13 12 11 10 09 08 07

Printed and bound in China

Contents

List of figures

List of tables

Preface

Every student embarking on a course in marketing brings with them a rich personal view of marketing acquired through their own experience of being the target of marketing tools of companies and institutions. However, to be successful marketing managers, students must open their mind to a new 'view of marketing', in order to be able to make a thorough analysis of market opportunities, organizational capabilities, and marketing processes. A major goal of this book is to encourage students to think much more widely about markets and marketing.

Despite widespread complaints about malfunctions in marketing, most marketing managers view marketing from a functional perspective, that is as *one* function in a business organization alongside others such as purchasing, production, or financing, all of which are carried out by specialists. Yet, the importance of keeping customers satisfied in an environment where global competition has increased in a phenomenal way, the need to build lasting relationships with stakeholders whose goodwill is important for market success, the ever-rising pressure to launch new products successfully in ever-decreasing periods of time, and the increasing complexity of fulfilling promises to customers and stakeholders in a global market environment all require a marketing management approach that successfully integrates *various* functional areas of an organization. In the 21st century, marketing managers will have to apply a process perspective to be successful.

This book considers a company or an institution as the centre of a system of value creation and generation. Value is created and generated in a complex exchange with other agents such as customers, suppliers, intermediaries, public administrators, the media, or consultants. The objective of marketing is to clarify and influence processes of complex exchange to the benefit of all exchange partners involved. This textbook does not ignore the marketing mix tools covered in books focusing on transactional marketing in favour of tools that are used in the more fashionable relationship marketing. Instead, the reader is introduced to all of those tools in a process-oriented manner.

Marketing is conceived as a series of interrelated and largely cross-functional processes, including the strategic positioning of the company, its business units and products, market intelligence, value creation, and value generation. *Marketing Management: A Value Creation Process* is written for students and practitioners interested in marketing management from a general management perspective.

Philosophy

The underlying assertion of this book is that *any company or institution – regardless of size – has to manage four main processes: strategic positioning, market intelligence, value creation, and value generation.* Success is a function of perspective, opportunity, motivation, knowledge, skills, and luck. Market opportunities are plentiful. The challenge for today's marketing manager is to identify those opportunities that fit the capabilities of the firm, to develop an appropriate marketing strategy, and to build and sustain competitive advantages in cooperation with other members of the firm as well as external partners.

Approach and organization

The book's four sections, as illustrated in the Figure below, make the process-oriented approach to marketing accessible to students.

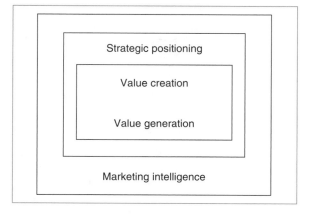

Figure 1 The central processes of marketing

- Building on an introduction to business organizations as the centre of a value creation system, Part I looks at *strategic positioning processes* to be conducted through assessing potential markets, the competitive position of the firm in those markets, and the potential for successful differentiation in them in order to determine and implement a planned strategic position.

- From the planned strategic position that then guides the application of marketing tools, Part II takes the student through the *process of market intelligence*. The most important steps in marketing research as well as useful knowledge on customer behaviour are presented here.
- Part III then discusses the implementation of strategic positioning decisions by the *process of value creation*. It shows how business organizations create new offers, and make potential customers as well as stakeholders aware of their benefits through product management, market communication, which involves advertising and other communication methods, and also through value negotiation.
- Part IV presents the elements of the *value generation process* once the offer exists and is known to potential customers and other stakeholders: distribution, merchandising and logistics, pricing, sales promotion, and direct marketing.

Why you should use this text

The turn of the century has been economically, socially, and politically turbulent. Fundamental changes in all parts of the world continue to occur. Although any textbook can become somewhat outdated through the speed of those changes, this book will remain useful because it provides a structured approach for *analysing* dynamic changes. The student is responsible for staying abreast of world affairs. Both the analytical framework, which addresses such issues, and the process-oriented marketing perspective in this book, will be valid even in rapidly changing environments. The process approach is necessary, not only to help a firm become aware of changes and their impact, but also to help it adjust successfully to such changes, which is the key to long-term survival.

To support this approach, this text offers several unique features:

- *Process perspective.* The cross-functional cooperation in business organizations to determine and implement a planned strategic position is a predominant theme.
- *Management orientation.* The book is organized in a way that it introduces students to marketing through the decisions that marketing managers must take.
- *Authors from two cultures.* The authors of the text have extensive experience in international marketing teaching, research, management, and consulting in

Eastern and Western Europe, Africa, Latin America, and Southeast Asia. This experience has resulted in an international outlook on marketing issues, in contrast to the more conventional US or European perspective.
- *Systemic approach.* Instead of a cursory discussion of relationship marketing, this book is written from a perspective that conceives business as a complex exchange taking place within networks of interrelated social units with more or less diverging interests. Forms of cooperation as well as confrontation are discussed in all parts of the book.
- *Current.* Every effort has been made to ensure that the material in the text is as current as possible in discussions of trends, environments, and relations. Where the developments are faster than the production process of a book, students are invited to update and compare latest developments with what has been said in the text.

Teaching and learning

The text has several features designed to motivate students' interest in the material, help them learn more efficiently, and make this text an effective teaching tool. Throughout, we have tried to present complex material in a straightforward manner, without oversimplifying the concepts. Various teaching and learning aids include the following:

- *Spotlight.* Every chapter begins with a Spotlight, a factual illustration of the chapter's content.
- *Boxes.* Boxed discussions highlight special issues and international aspects. In addition, specific boxes present tools that have been successfully applied in marketing processes.
- *Summary.* At the end of each chapter the main concepts and key points covered in each chapter are briefly reviewed.
- *End-of-Chapter Discussion Questions.* These questions provide a way for students to check their comprehension of the key issues discussed in the chapter. Some questions are appropriate for mini-projects, while others will stimulate class discussion. These questions also serve as an excellent vehicle for reviewing of all of the chapter material.
- *Suggested Further Reading.* The readings suggested at the end of each chapter allow the students to go into further details concerning some points of special interest discussed in the chapter.

Acknowledgments

The authors and publishers would like to acknowledge the following for special permission to reproduce copyright material:

Elsevier for the figure adapted from 'Exploring the Development of Store Images' by D. Mazursky and J. Jacoby in the *Journal of Retailing* 62(2): 145–165 (1986); and for the figure and table adapted from 'Servqual: a Multiple-item Scale for Measuring Consumer Perceptions of Service Quality' in the *Journal of Retailing* 64(1): 12–40 (1988).

The European Association of Communications Agencies (EACA) for the figure from the campaign 'Win a Donkey' created by the agency Billington Cartmell for GlaxoSmithKline (2005).

Pearson Education for the table adapted from *Marketing Channel Management: Strategic Planning and Tactics* by K.G. Hardy and A.J. Magrath (Scott, Foresman and Company, Glenview, Illinois 1988).

ACNielsen for the table: Private label market shares by country. Source: ACNielsen pour PLMA www.fcd.asso.fr/FCD/pub/secteur/marques.rtf (2005).

The Federation of European Direct and Interactive Marketing (FEDMA) for tables from the 'Survey on Direct and Interactive Marketing Activities in Europe' (2001).

McGraw-Hill Education for Figure 19.2 from *International Marketing*, 9th edition, by P. Cateora and J. Graham (1996).

The American Marketing Association for Exhibit 2: 'Scale of market entities' from the *Journal of Marketing* (April 1977), Table 3: 'Confirmatory sample of brands' from the *Journal of Marketing Research* (August 1997), and Figure 6: 'Average price elasticities at different stages of the life cycle' from the *Journal of Marketing Research* (November 1979).

Springer Science and Business Media for kind permission to use the table from 'A Cross Cultural Analysis of the Price Responses to Environmental Changes' by V.R. Rao and J.H. Steckel in *Marketing Letters* 6(1): 5–14 (1995).

The Market Research Society for figures from the *Journal of The Market Research Society* 37(1) (1995).

Cambridge University Press for the figure from 'Consumer involvement profiles' by L. Kapferer in the *Journal of Advertising Research* 25(6): 51 (1985).

The University of Chicago Press for the brief excerpt from 'The Nominal Group Technique: Its Potential for Consumer Research' by J.D. Claxton, J.R. Brent Ritchie and J.L. Zaichkowsky in the *Journal of Consumer Research* 7(3): 308–313 (1980).

University College Dublin for the figure: Sample Group Map of the Luxury Industry from A Note on the Global Luxury Goods Industry in 2000, Teaching Note (2001) by S. Duggan and E. O'Higgins.

John Wiley & Sons for the figure: The Core and Success Factors of an Organization from 'The Concept of Key Success Factors: Theory and Method' by K.G. Grunert and C. Ellegaard, in M.J. Baker (Ed.) *Perspectives on Marketing Management*, 3: 245–274 (1993).

Bertrand Bellon and Jean Marie Chevalier (eds) for the figure 'The Value-Chain of Textiles' from *L'industrie en France* (Flammarion, 1983).

Every effort has been made to trace all the copyright holders, but if any have been inadvertently overlooked, the publishers will be pleased to make the necessary arrangements at the first opportunity.

Part I
Strategic Positioning Processes

Creating value

1

Learning objectives

After studying this chapter you will be able to

1 Explain why a company may be conceived as the centre of a value-creation system
2 Discuss the importance of exchange processes and their results for the company and its stakeholders
3 Describe the ways value may be created through complex exchange processes
4 Discuss different kinds of competition in and among value-creation systems
5 Analyse the interests and power of stakeholders in a value-creation system
6 Discuss the influence of different layers of the environment on value creation
7 Define marketing and explain its constitutive processes
8 Understand the need for distinctive capabilities to sustain value-creation systems in dynamic environments.

SPOTLIGHT

Dell Computer Corporation, with its headquarters in Round Rock, Texas, near Austin, is the world's leading direct computer systems company and a premier supplier of technology for the Internet infrastructure. Dell is No. 1 and consistently the leader in liquidity, profitability, and growth among all major computer systems companies worldwide. The company has about 36,000 employees around the globe. Company revenue in the year 2000 totalled at about USD27 billion.

Dell is a trading hub. The company is committed to deliver highest value to their various groups of customers through excellent quality, leading technology, best service, and competitive prices. They do not produce any product components in-house. Dell is a brand and design specialist managing a network of relationships with carefully selected partners. Some of these partners

deliver just-in-time PC components needed by Dell to assemble customized products which are ordered by customers via telephone or the Internet. Using its production partners' capabilities, Dell has decreased its stock turnover to 11 days, compared to 80 days of its competitors. Other partners locally ensure the 24-hour technical support Dell guarantees to its customers. In house, a highly committed team of management leads the value-generation process from customer orders via supply logistics through assembly to distribution logistics. Delivery, again, is ensured by partners who have been selected for their punctuality, quality of service, and price competitiveness. As these facts show, the striking success of the company largely depends on the management of mutually satisfying relationships in a highly competitive value-creation system.

Value creation

Every day many new business organizations come into existence. The reasons why they are founded may be quite different. For example, an inventor may have found a new technical solution to a business problem, a craftsman may have specific skills allowing him to provide an attractive service to potential customers, a person may want to invest his capital into a productive venture, a manager may want to offer her experience to more than one firm, or a company may have decided to sell a newly developed product through a subsidiary. A substantial share of newly created companies, however, do not survive the first two years of their existence. In addition, every year a considerable number of established companies go out of business. The question is, why do some companies prosper – at least for some time – while others fail? A closer look at how a business organization basically functions may provide a tentative answer.

In this chapter we will analyse the functioning of business organizations from a value-creation perspective. Dependent as it is on the need for skills and resources to be able to fulfil its own purpose, every business organization must establish balanced exchange relationships with its stakeholders. Whether stakeholders consider their relationship with a business organization as balanced not only depends on the net value they receive from the total exchange offer, but also depends on the value offered by other suppliers and their value-creation systems.

Stakeholders' evaluation of a firm's total exchange offer is also shaped by continual changes in the environment. Management, therefore, must determine what elements of the general environment are relevant to the firm and how those elements interact. For that purpose, the general environment is split into the market environment, the macro environment, and the internal environment of the organization. The complexity and dynamics of these environments make management depend on techniques, methods, and approaches which enable them to master that challenge. As this chapter and the entire book will show, marketing thought and technology can make significant contributions to the establishment and maintenance of highly attractive value-creation systems.

Value-creation systems

Need for skills and resources

Whatever the productive purpose of a business organization, for example to lend money, to produce a crop, or to develop four wheel drive synchronization systems for car manufacturers, the organization needs various resources and skills to realize that purpose. Therefore, a company can be conceived as a resource transformation system, which needs a continual input of resources and skills to be able to transform them into an output of qualitatively different skills and resources.[1]

Resources procured, transformed, and redistributed by a company may be of various kinds. They may be tangible – such as financial, personal, technical, or property – or intangible – as for example time, knowledge, rights, norms and regulations, or goodwill. In many cases they are both, partly tangible and partly intangible at the same time. Resources are either held or owned by members of the company or by individuals, organizations, or institutions from outside the firm, such as investors, suppliers, competitors, the media, or public administration.

Skills are needed for the procurement of those resources, their transformation, and the distribution of the transformed resources. The skills of a company may be technical, professional, intellectual, or social. They may be acquired by hiring people who possess them, by using the service of trainers or consultants, by buying other firms, and also by cooperating with business partners.

Whatever the case, to fulfil its purpose a company must make sure it has the skills and resources available in time and in the quantity and quality needed for the intended kind and level of transformation and redistribution activities. The management of a business organization, therefore, has to determine who possesses the skills and resources needed to fulfil the company's purpose and what needs to be done to make those owners interested in providing their skills and resources to the firm.

Stakeholders

The owners of skills and resources needed by a business organization may be customers, competitors, suppliers, intermediaries, its potential work force, owners, shareholders, banks, the media, politicians, public administrators, trade unions, trade associations, and other agents interested in or concerned with the activities of the company, such as consultants, environmentalists, or human rights activists. They are called stakeholders because they are (groups of) individuals who have or may have aspirations and expectations concerning the company's activities. These aspirations and expectations are based on their own individual interests or stem from their roles in representing organizations or institutions.[2]

Because stakeholders may be more or less inclined to provide a company with their skills and resources, stakeholders can have a strong impact on a firm. For example, when Air France, the international air carrier of the country and one of the most important airlines in Europe, was running high deficits, its management planned to downsize the company to improve productivity, and its work force went on strike. Not only was air traffic from and to France heavily disrupted, but the company lost millions of dollars every day of the strike. Because of the firm's great importance to the country, the media covered the event closely, and in the end top French politicians intervened. The result, the president of Air France was changed and most of the planned measures were postponed.

Exchange

Stakeholders who possess the skills and resources needed by a company to fulfil its purpose will not be ready to provide their possessions to the firm if they do not receive some valuable compensation in exchange.[3]
Compensations may be goods, services, information, know-how, a symbol, a feeling, or combinations of these. For example, a donor to an organization such as the Red Cross may want to decrease its tax load, may want to know what the organization will do with its donation, or at the very least will want to feel good because of having donated some money for a rewarding purpose. Whether the compensations offered by a company are attractive enough to justify an exchange is subjectively determined by the stakeholders.

Balance of exchange

Stakeholders evaluate the offer of a potential exchange partner by comparing the benefits to be gained with the sacrifices to be made or the disadvantages to be tolerated in accepting the offer (Figure 1.1). Perceived benefits as well as sacrifices may stem from the exchange preparation process, the exchange itself, and the consequences of the exchange. Stakeholders will be ready to accept an exchange if the trade-off between benefits and sacrifices looks positive to them and no other exchange offer provides an even more attractive trade-off. For example, the potential buyer of a car may find the car dealer's personnel offensive, but the price to be paid for the selected car model as well as the prestige to be gained amongst friends by possessing the specific kind of car may seem so very attractive that the person decides to accept the offer.

As Figure 1.1 shows, there are various types of benefits and sacrifices a stakeholder may perceive. Toolbox 1.1

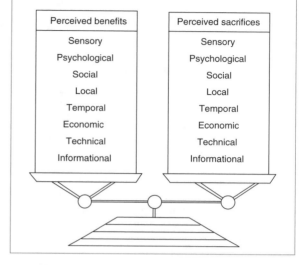

Confronted with an exchange offer by a company, stakeholders perceive various potential benefits to be gained and sacrifices to be incurred when accepting that offer. Depending on the result of the subjective trade-off among benefits and sacrifices, stakeholders will accept or decline the exchange.

Perceived benefits	Perceived sacrifices
Sensory	Sensory
Psychological	Psychological
Social	Social
Local	Local
Temporal	Temporal
Economic	Economic
Technical	Technical
Informational	Informational

Figure 1.1 The balance of perceived benefits and sacrifices
Source: Adapted from Lovelock, C. and C. Weinberg (1984) *Marketing for Non-profit Organizations*, New York: Wiley, p. 48.

describes a technique used to determine which benefits and sacrifices are (potentially) perceived by stakeholders in relation to an exchange process and its consequences. Potential benefits as well as sacrifices may be categorized into sensory, psychological, social, local, temporal, economic, technical, and informational. Sensory benefits or sacrifices are features of the exchange process or consequences thereof which can be sensed by the stakeholder, such as the design of a product or the atmosphere of the room where business negotiations take place.

TOOLBOX 1.1

SOPI: SEQUENCE-ORIENTED PROBLEM IDENTIFICATION

Sequence-oriented problem identification includes, first, "blueprinting" the sequence of steps that make up an exchange process from its preparation to its consequences as seen from an exchange partner's perspective. Second, exchange partners are asked to

provide accounts of critical incidents they may have experienced in each step of the exchange process.

"Blueprinting" is a term borrowed from movie production, where a story to be told is split up into a series of scenes that can be filmed apart from each other. In a similar manner, blueprinting an exchange process means defining a series of episodes from the first direct or indirect contact between potential exchange partners to an intended transaction and following episodes which are consequences of that transaction. Such a blueprint may be established through in-depth interviews with stakeholders reporting their view of "typical" interesting exchange processes. Blueprints may also be drawn up by people inside the company who have extended experience with the kind of exchange process under investigation.

With the help of a blueprint, a sample of (potential) stakeholders is guided through the entire exchange process in face-to-face, personal interviews. Respondents are requested to give an account of their experiences during the various episodes in individual exchange processes. Emphasis is placed on any particularly negative or positive incidents related to these episodes. The oral reports of interviewees are recorded, transcribed, and content analysed. The evaluation of the recorded incident reports results in the detection of process elements creating particular satisfaction or dissatisfaction of the stakeholders. These elements determine the value stakeholders perceive to gain when being offered the specific kind of exchange.

Source: Adapted from Botschen, G., L. Bstieler and A.G. Woodside (1996) "Sequence-Oriented Problem Identification Within Service Encounters", *Journal of Euromarketing*, 5(2), 19–52.

Psychological benefits or sacrifices mainly concern individual opportunities or risks resulting from a potential exchange. For example, the procurement manager of a company may perceive substantial functional as well as monetary risk when she has to buy a highly technical product, the quality of which she cannot fully evaluate. On the other hand, a journalist may perceive it to be a highly attractive opportunity when she is offered an exclusive story about a new luxury product that is to be launched by Hermés. A psychological benefit may also be the trust in a known potential partner offering an exchange, as contrasted by the sacrifice of feeling forced to trust a potential so far unknown exchange partner.

Social benefits and sacrifices are the perceived (potential) social consequences of an exchange. For example, it may be socially rewarding for a person to work for Mercedes Benz because their friends consider that firm highly reputable. Similarly, it may be socially degrading for a teenager to wear a certain brand of jeans because his peer group considers that brand outdated. Organizational procurement managers may either perceive a social benefit by having exchange relationships with partners that are well respected in their own firm, or encounter social sacrifices when their decisions for certain exchanges are internally questioned. For example, when the procurement manager of a firm in need of some new lathes considers buying from a new supplier, she may be aware of the risk of stirring up dissatisfaction and even passive resistance from workers used to the lathes of the usual supplier. Hold-ups or breakdowns due to misuse or lack of maintenance may be attributed to her "wrong" decision.

Local and temporal benefits may stem from the closeness and immediate availability of an exchange offer and its consequences, whereas local sacrifices result from distances to be covered in order to profit from the offered exchange. For example, a Portuguese engineer receiving a job offer from ABB in Sweden will consider carefully the distance between his home country and the new place of work. Purchasing managers of car manufacturing firms prefer offers from suppliers which have production sites nearby to ensure just-in-time delivery of parts or systems. Temporal sacrifices are waiting times before or during the exchange as well as time lost through the exchange. For example, people who consider waiting time in a restaurant as lost time will prefer a McDonalds to a French or Italian speciality restaurant.

Economic benefits may be the income generated by an exchange, cost reductions, a lower price compared with other offers, or access to less expensive sources of supply. Economic sacrifices are mainly the price to be paid as well as the cost incurred for the exchange and related processes and consequences. For example, a land owner who sells a lot of land to an oil company for the construction of a new gas station may receive an attractive amount of money for that land, but may incur taxes to be paid, may need to pay some specialists for surveying and developing the land, and later on, may need to invest in a noise barrier to be able to sell the rest of the land to a home construction firm.

Technical benefits may be based on the improvement of a stakeholder's technical processes, such as production, logistics, or information processing. Technical sacrifices arise, for example, from incompatibilities between existing installations and newly added systems. They are closely related to informational benefits, such as gains in know-how or technology transfer resulting from an exchange; and informational sacrifices such as the disclosure of internal information needed in the preparation phase of an exchange, or the training of personnel needed to fully profit from the potential consequences of the exchange. For example, both buyer and seller of specialist machinery need to exchange information about their production technologies in order to allow the development of a machine specifically needed by the potential buyer.

Stakeholders confronted with an exchange offer will consider the trade-offs among various benefits and sacrifices related to the potential exchange. Thus, a company interested in an exchange of skills and resources with a stakeholder must offer an exchange process and consequences of that process that make the stakeholder believe there is more to gain in benefits from the preparation of the exchange, the exchange and its outcomes, than will be lost in the sacrifices to be accepted in return. For example, a local benefit, such as convenience, may lower the related monetary sacrifice, thereby encouraging a purchase. Convenient Food Mart stores in the US, for example, offer a quick way to purchase groceries on the way home. In societies that value convenience highly, such as the US, consumers will pay a higher price to gain convenience; in other societies, such as Pakistan, convenience may be perceived as irrelevant or of low value. A lower price might be more important.

Aware of such trade-offs, managers who are responsible for the development of attractive offers to stakeholders will try to eliminate all perceived stakeholder sacrifices which do not contribute to a gain of skills or resources by their firm. But at the same time they will try to retain all stakeholder sacrifices which add to the skills and resources needed by their company. For example, investor relations managers will provide potential investors with well-presented information about their company's financial status and plans of activities for further improvements to minimize the perceived risk facing the shareholders. But they will try to avoid any reduction of those stakeholders' monetary sacrifices for shares in the company.

Voluntary versus imposed exchange

Not all exchange relationships are voluntary. Some exchange partners of a firm have only very limited or no choice in whom to supply with their skills and resources, and companies cannot freely select all of their suppliers of skills and resources. Imposed exchange relationships exist. But even in cases where the company is much more powerful than its exchange partner, for example, when the firm is the only big employer in the region, or when the exchange partner is forced by law to provide its skills and resources, such as a public agency responsible for issuing construction permits, company management is well advised to think about offering compensatory value in exchange.

Imposed exchange partners will be much more motivated to provide skills and resources of high quality in a timely fashion if they feel they are receiving an appropriate compensation. For example, a Dutch agency responsible for issuing business permits cannot choose its clients according to the value they offer. It must handle all applicants. On the other hand, when Royal Dutch Shell

plan to build a new cracker in one of their refineries in the Rotterdam area they are forced to deal with that agency. Nevertheless, both compulsory partners may try to provide value to each other in their own best interest. Shell may regularly inform the agency about latest technological developments, concerning for example potential measures in environmental protection, to ease (but also to influence) the agency's decision-making. The members of the agency, on the other hand, may do their work as fast and cooperatively as possible in order to keep the investor interested in the Rotterdam location (keeping jobs and tax income in the Netherlands).

Complex exchange

The value of an offer to a stakeholder may not directly emerge from a balanced one-to-one exchange. Attractive values may be subjectively derived from a complex exchange among various interacting stakeholders. That is, even if the value received from the direct exchange with a company is considered insignificant, an owner of skills or resources needed by that business organization may still provide such skills and resources because the stakeholder feels himself sufficiently rewarded through a third actor[4] (see Figure 1.2).

For example, when SOS-Kinderdorf, Austria, had to renovate the roofs of the homes of its oldest village at Imst (from where the idea of the organization has spread all over the world), they searched for a sponsor whose products and service would fit the given purpose and whose willingness to cooperate would not negatively

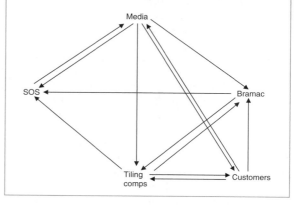

In a system of complex exchange, the value received by an agent from its direct relationship with another need not be totally compensatory. Through values received from other agents in the system the direct exchange relation may appear indirectly balanced.

Figure 1.2 Complex exchange

influence existing relations with other sponsors and donors. Bramac, one of the largest manufacturers of roof tiles in the country, was approached. The proposal was for Bramac to provide the tiles for all roofs of the village and additionally to identify some tiling companies to do the necessary work for free. In return, SOS-Kinderdorf would organize an event during which a large part of the village's roofs would be renovated in the presence of media representatives as well as important dignataries. Other major contributors and opinion leaders would be invited to join a closing party in the evening. Bramac accepted the deal. They expected an improvement in their image with those customers the media would reach and in their relations with regional tiling companies which are not closely associated with their customers. In addition, the decision makers in the company developed a personal interest in the project. Both the event and the accompanying campaign were successful. All Austrian news media reported on the activities of the sponsors. The event was covered by many interviews, and the sponsors received considerable public relations exposure in the trade press. The relations between Bramac and the participating tiling companies were strengthened. Local sales of tiles increased. Bramac's workers and employees involved in the event were highly motivated and personally satisfied with their contribution. SOS-Kinderdorf not only had the roofs renovated in time but also profited from the positive response to the event from other contributors and sponsors, representatives of important constituencies such as politicians and public administrators, and their own personnel. Media interest resulted in the appearance of additional public service messages about the importance of the organization. As the example shows, value-creation processes do not take place only in one-to-one exchanges. Most value-creation systems of business organizations consist of complex exchanges. Therefore, the management of a company are responsible for the establishment, development, and functioning of their entire value-creation system(s). At a certain point in time, none of the individual exchange relationships in such a system may be entirely balanced in terms of skills and resources provided and of benefits received in return.

As a consequence, stakeholders have a latent tendency to look for more attractive relationships. In order to stabilize the firm's value-creation system as a whole, company management must continually strive to augment the benefits directly or indirectly provided to their stakeholders and to reinforce their stakeholders' trust in the functioning of the complex exchange system. Management must be aware, however, that they can only lay the basis for the perception of attractive benefits by their stakeholders. What benefits those stakeholders become aware of and how they evaluate them is strictly subjective.

Value-creation system

Seen from an exchange perspective, a company may be conceived as the centre of a socio-technical value-creation system in which the skills and resources of various stakeholders are related to each other in a way that develops and maintains the capabilities needed to create value for those stakeholders (Figure 1.3).

To facilitate their business organization's exchange processes management must analyse what valuable compensatory offers they should make to individuals, organizations, or institutions in exchange for their skills and resources. In determining what offers stakeholders may perceive as most valuable, management may take various perspectives.

Product-orientation

Dominated by a product-oriented perspective, management focuses on the offer of goods and services. They tend to think that their company's stakeholders want to get a certain product in exchange for their skills and resources. The product can be a good, a service, an idea, information, a person, or a combination of these, depending on what is offered to the stakeholders. For example, a public relations manager thinks that the media representatives she is serving expect information from her. From a product-oriented perspective, the value offered to a stakeholder is best when the product has the highest technically defined quality. For example, a marketer of fuel is convinced that customers come to the petrol station because they want to buy fuel. Therefore, the technical quality of the product must be improved continually to remain attractive value to the customers. The public relations manager takes every effort to deliver complete information to the media. Logistics managers developing a new warehouse information system make sure that it contains all data combination possibilities provided by the latest level of technology. And product-oriented managers of insurance companies, as another example, are focusing on the technical quality of their insurance contracts. The question is, do customers and other stakeholders really search for specific products? Who goes to a petrol station because he or she wants petrol? What journalist is willing to work through a pile of complete information? And who is really interested in buying an insurance contract?

Benefit-orientation

Managers having a benefit-oriented perspective take a significantly different approach to exchange processes. They are convinced that stakeholders consider specific offers as ways to attain a certain benefit or as a solution to a problem. In their view, customers do not buy fuel because they want the product. They buy it to be mobile. Insurance contracts are not bought for their own sake, but for their effects, such as providing financial safety, for the

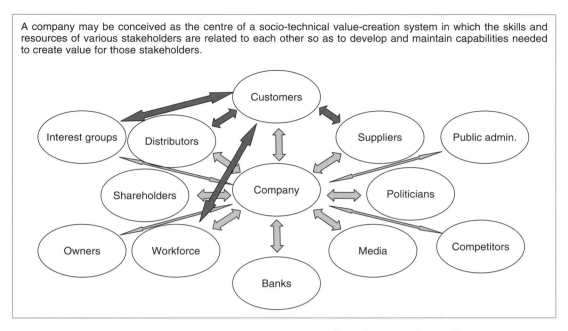

A company may be conceived as the centre of a socio-technical value-creation system in which the skills and resources of various stakeholders are related to each other so as to develop and maintain capabilities needed to create value for those stakeholders.

Figure 1.3 The company as centre of a value-creation system

replacement of possessions in case of an accident, or simply for the interesting rates of return on invested capital. Accordingly, managers with a benefit-oriented perspective try to enhance the value of their offerings to the company's stakeholders by improving the benefits they provide. For example, the public relations manager of an enduro-bike manufacturer such as Austrian KTM, will not only provide journalists of bike-related media with information about latest product developments and successes at international races, such as Paris–Dakar, but will also offer them the chance to ride the latest models in a trial camp on the Italian island of Elba together with some enduro sport champions.

To be able to offer attractive value to their stakeholders, managers need to understand what benefits stakeholders are looking for. Figure 1.4 shows a way of how to find potential benefits sought by a stakeholder group. The analysis is based on the idea that every decision of an individual or an organization to accept an offered exchange serves a certain purpose. It is a means to an end. Therefore, the process starts with the basic offer made to a stakeholder (group) and asks, why would the stakeholder(s) be interested in that offer. The product manager of Italy's Scheer, a marketer of specialty health food, for example, could ask the question, Why would a potential UK customer buy our new ready-to-serve meal? Buyers of such a meal hardly buy the product because they want to possess a ready-to-serve meal made by Scheer. Market research shows that the reasons British

customers give for their buying decision are product features such as freezability, reasonable price, tasty dish, or easy preparation. If asked why they look for easy preparation they answer, because it helps save time. But what do they need to save time for? In most cases the answer is to have time for other interests. And – as they say – having time for other interests, in turn, helps these consumers lead a satisfying life. That is, products possess certain features, which lead to certain consequences, which may have other consequences that lead to the fulfillment of a final goal or to reaching a certain value.

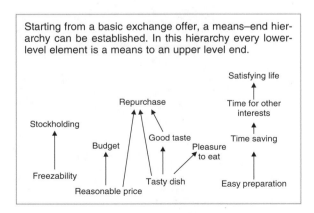

Starting from a basic exchange offer, a means–end hierarchy can be established. In this hierarchy every lower-level element is a means to an upper level end.

Figure 1.4 Example of a means–end hierarchy

Management may establish such a means–end hierarchy by simply trying to understand their stakeholders' expectations and aspirations. As the example has shown, however, there is more than one potential consequence to be reached by accepting an exchange offer. Thus, researching the means–end hierarchies existing in potential stakeholders' minds may help company management avoid misinterpretations. Toolbox 1.2 describes a market research technique called laddering, which allows analysis of the benefits stakeholders expect to gain by accepting a company's exchange offer.[5]

TOOLBOX 1.2

LADDERING

The laddering technique is based on the means–end theory that hypothesizes people doing things, such as buying a product, because that action leads to positive consequences, which in turn positively contribute to reaching attractive values.[i] Values are considered the ultimate source of choice criteria that drive exchange behaviour.[ii]

Personal oral or paper-and-pencil interviews are conducted in which first, features of an exchange offer which seem important to each individual respondent are determined. For that purpose questioning techniques such as dual comparison or triadic sorting can be applied. The individually important features are the basis for the laddering interview. In its oral version, this interview starts by picking up one of the features and asking the respondent why this feature seems important to him. As Exhibit A shows, the interviewee may respond by mentioning another feature of the exchange offer, but they may also mention a consequence resulting from the feature. By asking the same question, "Why is this important to you?", over and over again until the respondent is no longer able or willing to give a reason, the person is "laddered" up to the value(s) underlying the importance of the specific feature. Then the question sequence starts again at another feature of the exchange offer found to be of importance to the respondent.

In the written version of the laddering interview, respondents are asked first to note up to a maximum of five important attributes of the product under investigation in boxes aligned one above the other. Then the respondents are asked to write short statements about why they consider each of the listed attributes important in boxes next to the first column of boxes. The laddering goes on asking why the noted reasons are important to the respondents, as in the oral version above.[iii]

The data gathered by oral or written interviews are transcribed and content analysed. Content analysis of the interviews is based on a code book containing a categorization scheme developed by three researchers. For the purpose of developing the code book, additional data concerning the exchange context (for example, usage, exchange situation, personal environment) may be of help in interpreting and categorizing responses. Based on the categorization scheme, the researchers independently analyse the data and compare their findings. If there are differences, the researchers discuss the reason for these differences, and if needed ask another researcher for help as a kind of mediator. This process results in means–end chains for each of the respondents.

The next step is to aggregate the results across all respondents. Traditionally, a data matrix is established in which all identified attributes, consequences, and values act as the row and column elements. The cells of the matrix contain the frequency with which a particular column element is mentioned after a particular row element, aggregated across respondents and ladders. Usually only direct linkages between elements are entered.

Exhibit A Laddering

---

[i] Gutman, J. (1982), "A Means-End Model Based on Consumer Categorization Processes", *Journal of Marketing*, 46, 60–72.
[ii] Claeys, C., A. Swinnen and P. Van den Abeele (1995), "Consumers' Means-End Chain for 'think' and 'feel' products", *International Journal of Research in Marketing*, 12(3), 193–208.

[iii] Pieters, R., H. Baumgartner and H. Stad (1994), "Diagnosing Means-End Structures: The Perception of Wordprocessing Software and the Adaptive-Innovative Personality of Managers" in *Marketing, Its Dynamics and Challenges*, J. Bloemer, J. Lemnik and H. Kaspar (eds), EMAC: Maastricht, 749–763.

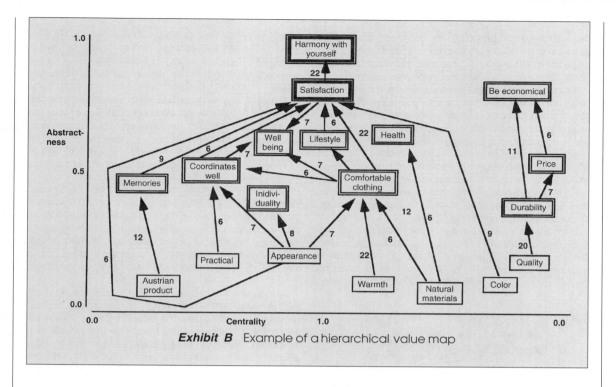

Exhibit B Example of a hierarchical value map

Finally, to allow better interpretation of the results, a map is constructed depicting the most important linkages in a graphical way. This Hierarchical Value Map not only shows the dominant contents of the exchange partners' means–end chains but also indicates the cognitive relations among various concepts and the strength of those relations (see Exhibit B).

In cases where stakeholders are confronted with a relatively new offer or where the exchange is of little importance to them, they may not have developed clearly structured means–end hierarchies concerning the exchange. Asking stakeholders to talk about their (non-existing) means–end structures would lead to results made up by the respondents during the interview. Toolbox 1.3 describes an alternative research technique, which may be applied when good reasons exist as to why potential stakeholders may not have developed means–end hierarchies about a potential exchange.

TOOLBOX 1.3

SITUATIONS-ALTERNATIVES-FEATURES ANALYSIS

A situations-alternatives-features analysis may be used when there is no good reason to presume that potential exchange partners have developed and stored in their minds hierarchical means–end structures concerning a certain kind of exchange offer. In addition, a situations-alternatives-features analysis provides richer material about the cognitive structures of (potential) exchange partners. A further advantage is the capability of the technique of providing for automatic information processing by eliciting top-of-mind choice alternatives, application situations, or features that spontaneously come to the minds of (potential) exchange partners.

Situations-alternatives-features analysis may confront respondents who are in a face-to-face interview or in a focus group interview, with either a certain consumption, usage, or application situation. Interviewees are asked to name the alternative exchange offers that come to their mind when they think of that situation, and then, to report their related experiences. In addition, respondents are led to talk about the specific features of each of the offers they are considering, how they compare to each other, and how they relate to the demands of specific application, usage, or consumption situations (see Exhibit A).

Interviews may also be started by presenting various exchange alternatives to the respondents, asking them to talk about the typical usage, consumption, or application situation which first comes to their mind when considering the selection of each individual offer, and then report their

experiences with these alternatives in the given situations. The choice alternatives may also be related to specific features which spontaneously come to the respondents' minds when thinking of given exchange offers.

Thirdly, the interviews could be started with certain features of competing exchange offers, asking the respondent to make comparisons, to indicate what exchange offers come to their mind when thinking of a specific feature, and to relate the features to certain consumption, usage, or application situations where those features seem to be most important.

One of these three approaches can be chosen depending on the information needs of a company – whether management is more interested in their (potential) exchange partners' expectations concerning a kind of exchange offer, or in the exchange partners' knowledge concerning competing exchange offers, or in the respondents' experience with existing exchange offers.

The answers of respondents are tape recorded, transcribed, and content analysed. First, researchers develop a categorization system. The categories should allow the researchers to analyse the transcribed interviews in a systematic way that is as independent of the perceptions of individual researchers as possible. Each category is characterized by a number of key words. Then the researchers read through the transcribed texts of the interviews and attribute the elements of the text to associated categories. The strength of associations among categories is measured by their relative distance in the text and the frequency of their relatedness. The more often two categories are related to each other and the closer to each other they occur in the text, the stronger their association.

Exhibit A

Source: Adapted from Grunert, K.G. (1990) *Kognitive Strukturen in der Konsumentenforschung*, Heidelberg: Physica Verlag.

The total exchange offer

Stakeholders derive value from more or less integrative value-creation processes and bundles of more or less intangible results of such processes (Figure 1.5). Both processes and results influence interactively the benefits stakeholders gain from an exchange. Staff in a company, for example, not only get a salary at the end of each month, they may also enjoy the prestige of working for a well-known company, the opportunity to enhance their personality, or an attractive working environment.

The result of a value-creating exchange process is constituted by the core-offer, features expected by the exchange partners, features added by the marketer to

increase the value provided to the stakeholders, and symbolic features (Figure 1.6).

The core-offer is the basis for a potential exchange. It can be a skill, a piece of information, a good, or access to another relationship, to name a few examples. In certain cases it might be sufficient to provide the core-offer. For example, when well-informed individuals search for an overview of potential forms of capital investment offered by an international bank, they may be satisfied with the information provided by the bank's homepage on the Internet. In most cases, however, potential exchange partners expect more than the core-offer to consider a potential exchange. The investor might, for example, firmly expect to be personally informed about the available choices.

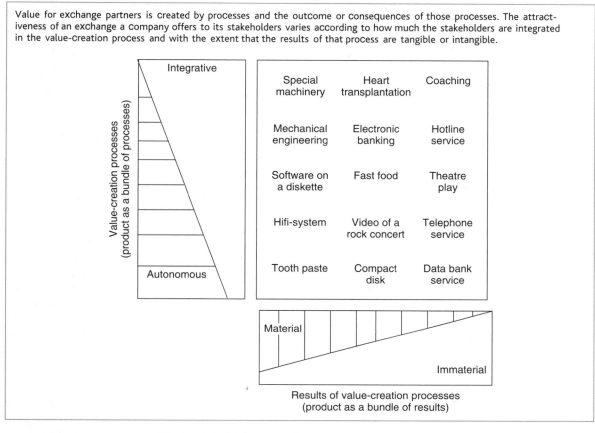

Value for exchange partners is created by processes and the outcome or consequences of those processes. The attractiveness of an exchange a company offers to its stakeholders varies according to how much the stakeholders are integrated in the value-creation process and with the extent that the results of that process are tangible or intangible.

Figure 1.5 Value creation as processes and results
Source: Adapted from Engelhardt, W.H.,M. Kleinaltenkamp, and M. Reckenfelderbäumer (1993), "Leistungsbündel als Absatzobjekte", zfbf, 45(5), 417.

Depending on their knowledge of and experience with existing offers, stakeholders tend to have different expectations concerning the results of an exchange as well as the process leading to these results. Management must decide how important it is to adapt their firm's offer to existing stakeholder expectations. The need for adaptation may depend on the stakeholders' willingness to trade off some expected features for unexpected "added" features (see Figure 1.6). When introducing its Lexus model in the USA, Toyota, for example, offered its potential customers a car looking very much like a Mercedes but not providing the same prestige. Toyota not only counteracted this lack of prestige with a lower price, they also offered two weeks of trials, delivered the ordered car to the home of the customers, and programmed the electronically adaptable driver's seat for various family members in advance. All these were added features not expected by but very welcome by the American customers. On the other hand, when Internorm, Europe's second largest manufacturer of doors and windows based in Austria, tried to convince its potential Spanish customers that higher technical standards and resulting energy savings – not expected by the customers – would justify a higher price for windows and doors, they failed.

Added features may be needed to attractively differentiate the company's offer to potential exchange partners from competitors' offers of the same skills and resources. Ermenildo Zegna, the Italian menswear maker, for example, offers clients who buy a Zegna suit an "idea card" that entitles them to all sorts of privileges: once a year for a two-year period, the suit will be cleaned and, if needed, repaired; should the suit be stolen or lost, the company will replace it at 50 per cent off and the client is entitled to a 50 per cent discount on his son's first Zegna suit.[6]

When the potential exchange partners tend to perceive existing offers as being largely similar, emotional attraction becomes more important in their decision about

The results of a value-creation process are constituted by the core-offer, additional features expected by the potential exchange partner, added features, and symbolic features the company provides to increase the attractiveness of the offered exchange.

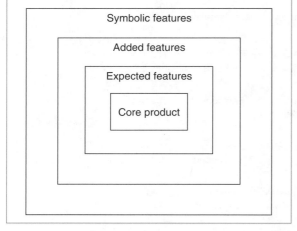

Figure 1.6   Results of a value-creation process

to whom they should offer their skills and resources. Symbolic features of a firm's exchange offer can become decisive. Car buyers all over the world, for example, will always watch the price category and will expect certain additional services. But when the decision for a price category has been taken, very often, symbolic features such as the brand, the country of origin, the status symbol, or the impression of belonging to a specific social group become important. For example, why would anybody buy a Ferrari given its high price if it were not for the emotional benefit of the product?

Tangible vs intangible results

Stakeholders may be attracted to an exchange by both tangible and intangible results of the value-creation process. They receive attractive value through a bundle of benefits, which they expect to enjoy during consumption or use of the total offer. For example, customers of an international advertising agency, such as U.S-based Grey Advertising, expect the agency to do more than produce international and local campaigns which fulfil their objectives. They also value personal contacts with a known partner in different parts of the world and the standard application of tools they have experience with. In addition, the name of the agency, its country of origin and special references may evoke positive associations with the managers who decide what partner to choose for market communication purposes.

In any case what a company offers to a stakeholder is more than what the stakeholder can touch or see. A vacation in a New Zealand ski resort, for example, contains elements such as the slopes, the hotel room, and the food in the restaurants, all of which can be physically experienced. At the same time the total vacation also consists of intangible elements such as the friendliness of service personnel, the waiting time at the lifts, the kind of "people around", or the impression it makes on friends and business colleagues who have taken skiing vacations at that resort.

Levels of stakeholder integration

From the stakeholder perspective, the results of a company's exchange offer are created by processes that more or less integrate the stakeholder (Figure 1.5). All value-creation processes can be positioned on a continuum ranging from highly integrative to highly autonomous. Depending on the kind of interaction with the stakeholder, where in the process the stakeholder is integrated, how often, and to what level of intensity, stakeholders will be more or less interested in establishing and maintaining an exchange relationship.

The integration of the stakeholder can take the form of personnel involvement, for example, when a specialist at Ochsner Hospital in New Orleans, Luisiana, transplants a kidney to a Brazilian customer. But stakeholder integration can also take place by the contribution of an object, such as a PC in the case of Otten, an Austrian producer of printed textiles, when using the hotline of its international production software provider. In other instances, stakeholders provide a right or some information to the value-creation process. For example, when the Boston Consulting Group gets the order to develop a new organizational structure for Basler Versicherungen, one of the biggest internationally operating Swiss insurance companies, the outcome of their work depends very much on the information provided by the company's personnel.

Parts of the value-creation process which take place in the presence of the stakeholders are above their line of visibility. They strongly influence the exchange partners' perception of created value and their level of satisfaction. Invisible parts of the process can be autonomously managed by the firm as long as they do not negatively influence the value of the result to the stakeholder. As the example described in the International Spotlight shows, pager production is neither visible nor can it be influenced by the customers. The development of a code of communication, however, strongly integrated Chinese customers in a process needed to create the expected customer value of the pager, that is, to allow its use as a kind of telephone.

INTERNATIONAL SPOTLIGHT

INTEGRATIVE VALUE CREATION IN CHINA

At the end of 1995, there were some 14 million paging subscribers in China. Resourceful Chinese people used the pager not as an accessory to the phone, but as a sort of primitive substitute for it. The conventional phone system had a penetration rate of some three to four lines for every 100 Chinese, meaning that even if you found a phone, the other party might not have been in a position to receive your call. Only the well-heeled business people were able to overcome this annoyance with a costly mobile phone. So native genius stepped into the breach. Chinese paging subscribers spontaneously devised a method of carrying code books, allowing them to interpret numeric messages flashed on their pagers: 75416, for example, might mean sell gravel at 6500 yuan a ton or bring home a cabbage for dinner. Pagers in the second half of the 1990s had alphanumeric displays that read out short bursts of Chinese characters, eliminating the need for number codes.*

* ("The Pager Race", *Fortune*, May 27, 1996, 120.)

It is important to note that management can strongly influence the integrativeness of their company's value-creation processes as well as the level of intangiblity of exchange results. Customers of Bentley cars, for example, are not simply offered a ready-to-drive vehicle. Volkswagen AG, the owner of Bentley, offers its customers a highly individualized and intangible status symbol. For that purpose, potential customers are invited to choose many features of their car, to stay in a luxury hotel close to the car factory to watch the production of their car, and to join the club of Bentley owners.

Competition

Survival and success of complex value-creation systems depend on the attractiveness of values provided to their stakeholders. Management must continually monitor the value perception of stakeholders, try to raise their perceived value, and scan the potential for creating new value. The problem is that there is not only one business organization that works on establishing, improving, and maintaining its value-creation systems. Many organizations try to do the same. They compete for the necessary skills and resources.[7]

Competition for suppliers

As a result of competition, the owners of skills and resources have the opportunity to choose the partner they want to deal with. For example, graduates from MBA programs in the UK may choose the companies they want to work for, and Danish consumers can choose from which marketer they want to buy their yoghurt. Because potential stakeholders tend to behave in their perceived own best interests, they will participate in those value-creation systems which offer them the most attractive value in exchange.[8] A Dutch group of investors, for example, will have a close look at the financial performance and the future potential of a firm before they decide to take a share in its capital. Therefore, to be and to stay successful over time, a company must be able to establish and maintain a value-creation system that provides more attractive value to its stakeholders than competitors do. In the best case scenario, the values appear positively unique to the exchange partners.

To offer unique value to their company's stakeholders management must continually look for ways to make exchange offers attractively different to what stakeholders consider as normal (Figure 1.7).

For example, by reconsidering the traditional basis of appeal of its competitors, the Body Shop, headquartered in the UK, discovered a unique way of creating value to its customers. By avoiding high-tech cosmetic science, extensive packaging, and mass advertising to establish a glamorous image, the Body Shop made substantial cost savings which the company passed on to their customers via significantly lower prices. In addition, they placed great emphasis on natural ingredients, healthy living, and environmental protection activities – all elements new to competition in the field of cosmetics.

Competition may exist in exchange relationships with customers but also in exchanges with other stakeholders, such as intermediaries, suppliers, subcontractors, or consultants as long as those agents feel they have a choice between various offers which provide substitutable value. For example, when Procter & Gamble wants French Carrefour to offer its products to consumers, it is in competition with other firms which Carrefour feels provide similar value to them, such as Colgate Palmolive, Unilever, or Bloch.

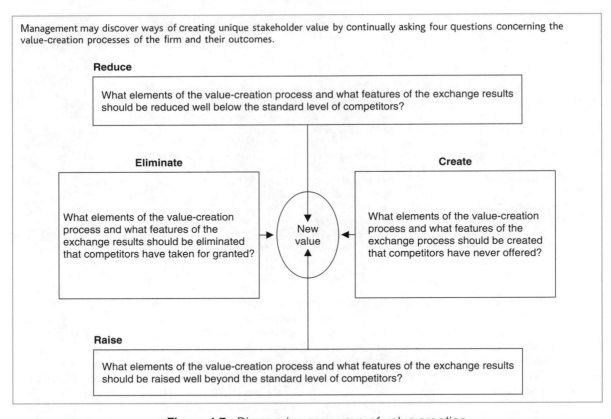

Management may discover ways of creating unique stakeholder value by continually asking four questions concerning the value-creation processes of the firm and their outcomes.

Reduce

What elements of the value-creation process and what features of the exchange results should be reduced well below the standard level of competitors?

Eliminate

What elements of the value-creation process and what features of the exchange results should be eliminated that competitors have taken for granted?

New value

Create

What elements of the value-creation process and what features of the exchange process should be created that competitors have never offered?

Raise

What elements of the value-creation process and what features of the exchange results should be raised well beyond the standard level of competitors?

Figure 1.7 Discovering new ways of value creation
Source: Adapted from Kim, W.Ch. and R. Mauborgne (1999), "Creating New Market Space", *Harvard Business Review*, January–February, 85.

Competition among suppliers

There is not only competition among companies in need of skills and resources. There may also be competition among the suppliers of those skills and resources. For example, when Paris-based L'Oréal has some assistant product manager positions to fill in Portugal, there will be more than one candidate for each position. The company can organize assessment centres to select the best-suited people. Companies may also select their suppliers of raw materials, components, energy, and many kinds of services, such as communication, logistics, or consulting. They may also choose the kind of customers they want to have. For example, Patek Philippe, the Geneva-based manufacturer of high prestige watches, has selected a small group of high-income customers all over the world who can afford to buy its products. That is, management has to assess all potential voluntary exchange relationships to select the best-suited stakeholders for their value-creation system(s).

Competition among value-creation systems

It is important to note, however, that competition not only takes place among individual firms striving to have more attractive exchange partners than their competitors. To offer attractive value to Carrefour, Procter & Gamble needs partners in the value-creation process, such as reliable suppliers of raw or packaging materials, transportation and product handling firms which ensure just-in-time delivery, or communication agencies helping to attract consumers' interest and increase their desire to purchase. Competition takes place among entire value-creation systems, even if those systems may overlap because partners participate in a variety of value-creation systems. Company management, therefore, have to strive for the most effective and efficient functioning of their company's value-creation system. They must determine what parts of the value-creation processes need how much direct control by their company in order to be executed most attractively for the stakeholders. Processes that are central to the creation of unique values for important stakeholders should be executed by the company itself. Others may be left to close cooperation partners or even independent suppliers.[9]

Interests and power

In their attempt to provide unique value to selected as well as imposed stakeholders management encounters the problem that the owners of the skills and resources needed to fulfil the aim of the company may have largely different interests, aspirations, and expectations.[10] To completely satisfy the interests of one stakeholder group could be in the interest of another, be insignificant for a third, but may also be conflicting with expectations of a fourth group. For example, if Nike, the US sports shoes manufacturer, attempts to fulfil its shareholders' profit expectations by keeping costs of production in less industrially developed countries as low as possible, the firm may simultaneously fulfil the expectations of their

overseas customers in offering shoes at affordable prices, but may hurt the interests of young black potential customers in the USA who lose job opportunities. Suppliers of leather may not feel concerned at all, whereas human rights activists may find the working conditions in Nike's Southeast Asian manufacturing plants intolerable. Therefore, a major challenge for the management of a value-creation system is to find the right balance among values offered to the various stakeholders.

The challenge of offering attractive values to stakeholders with divergent interests is further complicated by the fact that – at a given point in time – the various stakeholders have more or less power to carry their interests through.[11] Management, therefore, must not only consider those interests but also the power of stakeholders, their capabilities, and potential actions. Toolbox 1.4 describes an analytical technique which helps to identify the most influential players and their interrelationships.

TOOLBOX 1.4

VALUE-CREATION SYSTEM ANALYSIS

The systems analysis technique presented here conceives the power of an agent as its influence on the behaviour of another. Because actors do not necessarily use all their potential influence, their power is not well measured by their actual influence on the behaviour of others. Therefore, the technique presented here is based on estimates of the potential influence of the agents in a social system.

As a first step, the value-creation system has to be defined exactly in order to determine its limits. Then, the stakeholders belonging to the defined value-creation system are listed. Together with the firm, all stakeholders

Potential of influence on ➔ of	A	B	C	D	E	Sum A (Influence)
A						
B						
C						
D						
E						
Sum B (Influenceability)						

Exhibit A Matrix of interrelationships between actors in a value-creation system

are entered into a matrix (see Exhibit A). Next, the extent to which each of these (groups of) agents is able to influence actively the behaviour of other agents in the value-creation system or the extent to which they may be influenced by those other agents is estimated.

The influence of each agent (group of agents) on every other agent (group of agents) is estimated on a scale reaching from 0 (for no potential influence at all) to 3 (for very strong potential influence). When the lines of the matrix are summed up, each sum expresses the potential of influence of the respective (group of) agent(s) on all the other agents in the value-creation system. The sums of the columns stand for the potential of the rest of the agents in the system to influence the respective (group of) agent(s).

The results of this analysis may be visualized by the use of a diagram such as the one shown in Exhibit B. Autonomous agents are elements of the value-creation system who have a strong influence on the exchange processes in the system but themselves may be hardly influenced by other agents (see media and public administration in Exhibit B). The other extreme are reactive agents who may be strongly influenced by the other agents in the system, but have only very little potential influence on the exchange processes in the system (see suppliers and banks in Exhibit B). Critical agents (see intermediaries, the competitor, and the firm itself in the example of Exhibit B) have a potential above-average influence on the rest of the value-creation system and are subject to being influenced potentially

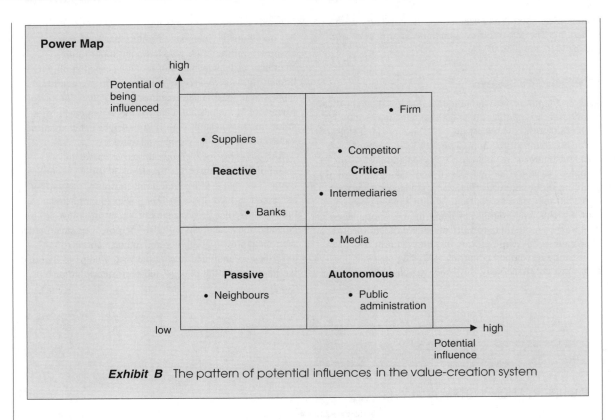

Power Map

Exhibit B   The pattern of potential influences in the value-creation system

more than average by the other members of the system. Passive agents neither have particular potential influence on the value-creation system nor they are potentially influenced above average (see the neighbours in Exhibit B). Such a diagram offers fruitful insights to which agents in a value-creation system – critical and autonomous agents – are to be given more attention than others.

Each stakeholder (group) has a minimum aspiration level, that is, the level of fulfilment of its expectations for the given value-creation system which this system cannot fall short without significantly dissatisfying the stakeholder (see Figure 1.8). A voluntary stakeholder who feels it is receiving value below its minimum aspiration level tends to leave the exchange system. Imposed stakeholders who feel value below their minimum aspiration level will tend to use their influence on other members of the value-creation system to get their supposed right. Because both consequences may create conflicts and, ultimately, may put the entire value-creation system into question, management will give increased attention to the interests and expectations of more powerful stakeholders. That is, more resources will be spent researching their specific expectations and offering them unique value. However, company resources are limited.[12] Time and capital are as scarce as attention capacity and information processing capability.[13] Any attention given to one stakeholder group consumes resources that cannot be employed in attending to another stakeholder group.

Therefore, management will try to satisfy less powerful stakeholders with value that reaches or just goes beyond their minimum aspiration level.

Stakeholders' interests and expectations develop over time. The development may be driven by improving offers of business organizations competing for skills and resources. For example, when Zumtobel-Staff AG, one of the leading suppliers of light systems in the world, was the first to offer a computer simulation of the physical and economic effects of their systems to their potential customers in industry and public administrations, the value of the offer was considered so highly attractive that customers were ready to pay for the additional service. Only two years later, when all the major suppliers of light systems were able to simulate the effects of their systems, customers were no longer ready to pay extra for the service. Again two years later, customers considered the results of simulation runs as part of the normal product. Companies not able to provide them were no longer considered as relevant suppliers.

Management will try to offer unique value to the most powerful agents in the firm's value-creation system. Less powerful agents will be satisfied with just above their minimum aspiration level.

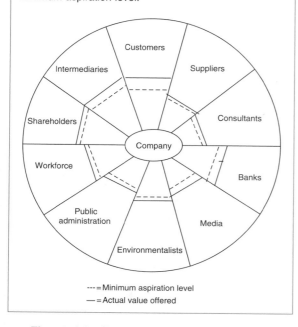

Figure 1.8 Stakeholder value management
Source: Adapted from Doyle P. (1992) "What are the Excellent Companies?", *Journal of Marketing Management*, 8, 101–116.

Changes in interests and expectations may also be driven by changes in the socio-cultural, economic-technological, as well as political-legal environments of a firm. For example, before gene-technology developed special genes for corn plants to make them resistant to insects or for tomatoes to make them look fresh even after considerable time in storage, environmentalists did not ask for any indication of origin on packaged food. Today, food retailers in the German-speaking areas of Europe are confronted with consumer protection agencies who insist on obvious labelling on food as to whether the food contains gene-manipulated ingredients or not. To be on top of development, therefore, management has to continually monitor weak signals of changes in the firm's environment. For that purpose, it must determine what elements of the general environment are relevant to the firm and how those elements interact.

Layers of system environments

Figure 1.9 shows a general nested model of a firm's environments. It demonstrates that the decision makers of a company live in their firm's internal environment, which is embedded in the market environment of the company, which, in turn, is surrounded by the macro environment. All of these environments may influence each other, and management has to consider the various relationships in governing their organization.[14]

Market environment

Market

Any system of complex exchange in which tangible as well as intangible products are exchanged to create value for voluntary or imposed exchange partners can be conceived as a market. This definition of a market clearly departs from traditional definitions which conceive a market as a group of products (goods and services) that a group of customers consider as substitutes in a certain usage situation, which in turn is important to the customers.[15]

Traditional definitions of a market are based on a linear and sequential conception of customer value-creation processes, the so-called value chain. In this concept, a supplier provides a product to a customer who transforms that product into another one by adding value and selling it to his customer who, in turn, adds to the value chain (see Figure 1.10 for an example). The value chain concept does not take into account, however, that customer value in many instances is created not only directly in the exchange between a supplier and a customer but also indirectly through complex exchanges among interrelated agents. For example, when Denmark-based Borealis, one of the world's leading producers of plastics, decided to introduce polypropylene as a new basic material in the European window market, they found out that the traditional value chain from the plastics manufacturer to window producers, to construction retailers, to final customers would not create enough customer value to change customer preferences from buying PVC windows to the new material. The attractiveness of polypropylene windows compared to traditional solutions strongly depends on the importance customers place on environmental protection. Borealis, therefore, considered environmentalists, norm setters in public administration, window-testing institutes, and home and construction magazines as essential partners in their value-creation system.

In addition, there is also a market when customers are not significantly involved with a usage situation. In a great number of consumption situations, customers are neither highly involved with the situation nor with the goods and services used. Nevertheless, in order to enable that consumption, a system of complex exchange must be in place.

A company's decision makers live in their firm's internal environment which is embedded in the market environment of the company, which in turn is surrounded by the macro environment.

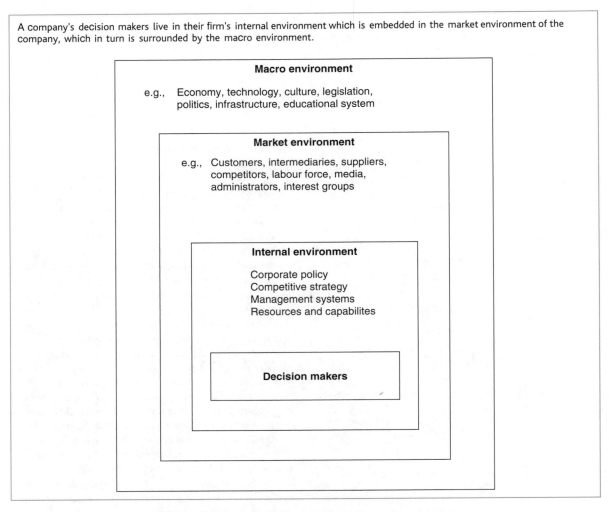

Figure 1.9   A nested model of a firm's environment

Market boundaries

A market is not a predetermined fact a company must accept and adapt to. Market boundaries and structures are largely defined by the perceptions and resulting actions of the most important agents. Customers, for example, define market boundaries by perceiving substitutability of offered values, by determining the totality of needs that can be satisfied by an offer, or by defining situations in which various offers can be used. For example, couples living in suburbs may consider driving, taking the train or a bus, and calling a taxi as substitutes when they want to go into town for a show. Customers may perceive substitutability of values on different levels. On the product level, for example, French consumers may consider Evian,

Contrexeville, and Volvic as three substitutable brands of mineral water. On the level of product categories, mineral water may be seen as substitutable with tap water or fruit juices. And on a needs level, all these may be perceived as substitutable by any potable liquids.

Intermediaries strongly influence market structures, by deciding what offers appear similar to them and how to group them. If a retailer, such as British Tesco, considers cat, dog, rabbit, and bird food as belonging to the category of animal food, it may place them together on the shelves of its shops and contribute to a certain structure of the market. If Marks & Spencer, in contrast, considers dog food, toys, brushes, and cushions for dogs as constituting a category, it structures the market in a significantly different manner.

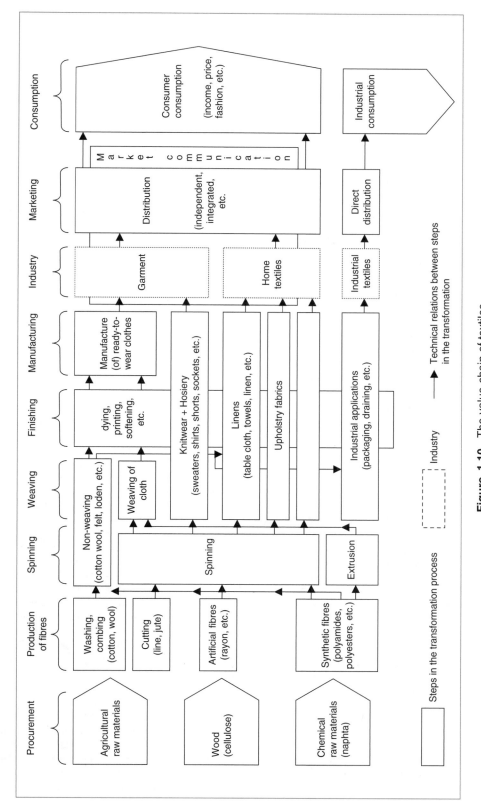

Figure 1.10 The value-chain of textiles

Source: Manzoni (1983), "Le textile", in *L'industrie en France*, edited by B. Bellon and J.M. Chevalier, Paris Flammarion

Suppliers of similar products, who normally are considered to belong to the same industry, may not automatically participate in the same market. Japan's Casio and Swiss Rado, for example, both belong to the watch industry. However, neither customers nor intermediaries consider them as belonging to the same market. A supplier can strongly influence those perceptions by shaping the value it is offering to potential customers or intermediaries and by specifically communicating about the offer.

Strategic groups

Companies relying on the same basic value-creation processes, that is, on similar combinations of capabilities available in their value-creation systems, are called strategic groups. In Germany, for example, Mercedes, BMW, and Audi tend to select partners for their value-creation systems in a way which assures high quality combined with differentiation. They form one strategic group compared to the car makers from South Korea, Kia, Hyundai, and Daiwoo, which form another strategic group relying mainly on value-creation systems which provide low cost to offer low consumer prices. Both strategic groups have created their own markets. Customers consider their offered values as clearly different. But inside strategic groups, values offered by their members may be perceived as largely substitutable. Imitation of capabilities available in competitors' value-creation systems, therefore, leads to increased competition and decreased attractiveness of provided values.

Selection of market partners

By carefully selecting target customers and partners for the firm's value-creation system, management can significantly influence the kind of market their company is in. For example, Bloomberg, one of the largest and most profitable business-information providers in the world, have chosen traders and analysts as their customers, compared to other firms in the online financial-information industry, such as Reuters, which provide their services to the IT managers of brokerage and investment firms. By shifting their focus upstream from purchasers to users, Bloomberg laid the basis for an entirely new value-creation system. They not only offered easy-to-use terminals with two flat-panel monitors and a built-in analytic capability to run "what if" scenarios and perform longitudinal analyses, they also added information and purchasing services, such as travel arrangements, real estate listings, or information about wines, aimed at enhancing traders' personal lives.[16]

While in consumer markets companies tend to choose specific groups of potential customers as their targets, in business-to-business markets it may be useful to develop and keep continual contacts with all potential customers, because of their lower number and resulting higher transparency. For example, when TSB, a large British bank, planned to merge with Lloyds Bank, another British bank, to create the UK's largest retail bank in terms of branches and customers, it used US-based specialist JP Morgan to handle its negotiations with Lloyds. The decision to go with JP Morgan was not only based on the firm's reputation in the merger and acquisition business, it was also due to the fact that TSB's chief executive, Peter Ellwood, had known the US bank's financial institutions M&A specialist, Terry Eccles, for two years before any talk of a merger with Lloyds bank arose.[17]

As the Bloomberg example shows, the decision to serve particular target customers requires a careful selection of partners for the firm's value-creation system. They should add to the firm's capabilities of providing attractive value to those customers. For example, when considering the establishment of a value-creation system in Japan, where it is highly unusual to transfer business from one intermediary to another, management of Lego, the Danish toy manufacturer, will need to assess very closely potential intermediaries. Information about their organization, their capital equipment, the kind and number of customers they serve, their approach to doing business, their information system, and the product range they cover provides some insight into their capabilities. Experiences of Western companies in Japan suggest that marketers should pay special attention to existing networks among producers and intermediaries. It may be very difficult to establish a successful value-creation system, even with a superior product, if the intermediaries necessary to reach the ultimate customer are linked to domestic firms or other international suppliers.

When selecting potential suppliers of services, parts, or systems, management should consider the size and number of such firms, their ability to fulfil the company's quality standards, their creativity in developing new solutions to customer problems, their readiness to specifically invest in the potential relationship, potentially available substitutions, the importance of the supplied service or good to the firm's product, the importance of the firm as a customer of the suppliers, and the threat of potential forward integration (when the supplier gains control of the next level of distribution, toward the customer) by the supplier. Suppliers may be linked to certain customers. Companies such as Ford, Honda, and Volkswagen commonly sign long-range contracts with (or even hold equity shares in) their suppliers such as producers of metal sheets (e.g. Thyssen, the largest supplier of this product category in Europe), electrical systems (e.g., Germany's Bosch), climatization equipment (e.g., worldwide operating Webasto headquartered near Munich). The suppliers conform strictly to the larger company's product specifications, exchange technical know-how, cooperate in product development, and may profit from their customers' financial assistance.

As we have seen, not all members of a firm's value-creation systems may be freely selected. Management can only try to avoid the establishment of value-creation systems containing stakeholders with interests that run against their firm's objectives. For example, a Swiss engineering firm having developed a highly effective plant for the burning of industrial toxic waste may have identified chemical and pharmaceutical plants in Germany as their potential customers. Those customers may be strongly interested in the offer of the firm and willing to pay a good price. German subcontractors to the Swiss company may be as interested in the firm entering the market as shareholders and workforce expecting the company's success to grow. Nevertheless, the attractiveness of this value-creation system may be very much diminished by green activists together with the media (via public administration), who have adverse interests and the power to keep customers from buying.

To help achieve the firm's objectives, management will need to take care of relationships with imposed but important stakeholders, such as public administrators, trade unions, legislators, or consultants of potential customers. External decision influencers such as the clients of potential customers have to be determined. For example, what plastic raw material a manufacturer of car bumpers will buy is strongly influenced by the specifications of the carmakers. Those specifications will be a co-production of procurement, quality assurance, and marketing personnel of the manufacturer's clients. In public administration markets, the information search and supplier evaluation step often contains formal bidding requirements. Public agencies may be forced by law to accept the lowest bid that meets the particular set of specifications. Firms who wish to establish value-creation systems in these markets must develop excellent relationships with agents or consultants setting those specifications to be able to influence specification-setting beforehand.

Macro environment

A company's macro environment is generally defined as the political, legal, economic, ecological, social, cultural, and technological dimensions of the universe in which the market environment of the firm is embedded. Whereas the macro environment of a company strongly influences the structure and state of its market environment, individual members of the market environment are restricted in their influence on the development of the macro environment.

Management have to be aware of current, and potential future, developments in the relevant dimensions of their firm's macro environment. For example, when Zuegg, the Verona-based leading Italian manufacturer of fruit juice and second largest marketer of jam in the country, planned its expansion to other European markets, it had to analyse the foreseeable and potential developments in a number of dimensions of the macro environment relevant to its business. Legislation concerning food preparation, product declaration, packaging, and recycling had to be studied. The potential impact of culture, in terms of consumption patterns, country-of-origin prejudices, or ecological awareness was considered. Trends in economic and demographic development, such as unemployment rate, distribution of purchasing power, or aging of population were analysed, and the effects of changes in the technological environment concerning transportation, warehousing infrastructure, and media had to be considered.

The practical problem for managers analysing the macro-environment of their value-creation system is its complexity and the difficulty to foresee developments in the future. Toolbox 1.5 describes a method called scenario technique that helps reduce the environmental complexity and that can also establish potential pictures of the relevant macro environment on a chosen time horizon.

TOOLBOX 1.5

SCENARIO TECHNIQUE

The scenario technique is a strategic planning technique. First, the essential dimensions of the macro environment that influence the company and its operating environment are determined by a brainstorming of the decision-making group. For a US manufacturer of electric power plants, for example, important dimensions of the British macro environment may be the political situation, the technological development, legislation, the existing infrastructure, or the development of the economy. Each of these dimensions must be specified by relevant factors of influence on the company's value-creation system. Relevant factors of technological development concerning the market of electrical power plants may be, for example, the development of anti-pollution equipment, the security technology for atomic power stations, and the further development of photovoltaic technology.

Then, systems analysis, as described in Toolbox 1.4, is used to identify the interrelationships between those dimensions and their relative importance for the future development of the firm's macro environment. When a time horizon is fixed for the analysis (one possibility would be, for example, to take the time needed to enter the market plus five years), potential future developments with respect to each influencing factor on each dimension of the macro environment can be formulated. They describe the potential extreme states of development of the factors at the time horizon. For example, the development of photo voltaic technology may have completely stopped because of a lack of marketable results or, at the other extreme, may have reached a point where every household can produce the energy they need during daytime.

After having analysed the logical fit of all pairs of potential states of development of the influencing factors at the time horizon (on a scale from "the two states are highly probable to occur simultaneously = 2" to "the two states may occur together, but are independent of each other =

0" to "the two states are strongly contradictory = −2"), the consistency of all potential combinations of factor states, can be calculated. The two most highly consistent scenarios, having the highest summed scores, with the greatest discrepancy between their assumed factor states, can be selected as scenarios. They describe the two most different potential pictures of the macro environment at the time horizon. The scenarios can be compared to the current situation. Management can assess the impact of each scenario on the company's market environment and its value-creation system.

The scenario approach helps to avoid focusing too much on markets which are only attractive in the short run. The firm becomes alert to potential developments – such as changes in customers' basic values, countries' financial stability, or the development of new technologies – that may have a strong impact on the attractiveness of a market.

Market and macro environments of a company are not separated from each other by objective and clear-cut boundaries. Depending on the value-creation system of a company and its capabilities, varying parts belong to its market and macro environments. American Motorola Corp. and Finland's Nokia Mobira Oy, the two leading marketers of cellular phone equipment in the world, for example, have reached a level of importance in their market so that regulators will not easily pass them by without consulting them when new norms and regulations have to be set. For them, parts of the regulatory environment can be personalized. The regulators with whom they have relationships belong to their market environment. A very small, but internationally active firm such as Omicron Electronics, the leader in the global market niche of test sets for protective relays, transducers, and energy meters of electrical utilities and industry, can hardly directly influence parts of the regulatory environment by building personal or organizational relationships. For them, legislation is part of the given macro environment.

Internal environment

The decision makers of companies play their role as part of an organization which has an implicit, if not explicitly stated, corporate policy that lays out the ground rules of why and how it wants to function. It follows a corporate strategy – a basic indication of where to do business and how; based on management systems – such as the organization structure or the controlling system; as well as specific capabilities – a combination of resources such as personnel, capital, or know-how, and skills – which results

in specific actions. These elements make up the internal environment of the firm.

The firm's internal environment defines the boundaries of its macro and market environments. For example, when Coca-Cola decided to serve the soft drink markets of the world, it defined its relevant market environment to be all customers, organizations, and institutions concerned with or interested in the production, distribution, and consumption of soft drinks worldwide. The macro environment was defined as all factors that influence the market environment, such as drinking habits, commercial legislation, retailing infrastructure, or the climate in different parts of the world. When Coca-Cola went a step further to enter the market of alcoholic beverages it substantially widened the boundaries of its market environment. This also increased the range of factors from the macro environment that had to be considered, for example social campaigns against drinking and driving. Coke's withdrawal from the alcoholic beverages market may well have been hastened by its having to play a "different game" in that market from its traditional market where it was much more familiar with the rules, norms, and expectations of stakeholders.

The internal environment also limits the firm's potential to influence the development of its market environment, and its set of alternative responses to trends in the macro environment. If a big globally operating corporation, such as Novartis, which resulted from the merger of Ciba Geigy and Sandoz in 1996, develops a new pharmaceutical substance, many smaller manufacturers of drugs will be forced to purchase that substance in order to stay competitive with their final products. If the same firm decides to concentrate its production of basic substances for antibiotics in one country, factories in other countries will go out of operation. Some stakeholders, such as trade unions or politicians, supported by the local media, may try to use their power to force the firm into developing "social plans" to decrease the impact of those shutdowns on the former workforce and the local economy. A small drug manufacturer will not be able to spend enough money in research and development to influence the worldwide use of pharmaceutical substances. But, on the other hand, it will also have fewer problems with the general public when management decides to change the location of the factory.

The internal environment of a firm has no clear-cut boundaries with its market environment. Increasing numbers of cooperative agreements and deepening relationships between companies to fight mutual competitors in globalizing industries have contributed to management increasingly often having to consider (parts of) internal environments of partner firms when taking decisions.[18] For example, when Mercedes Benz, the Stuttgart (Germany)-based manufacturer of high quality vehicles decided to develop, produce, and market a small Swatch-car together with SMH, the Swiss holding of watch-producing companies, they established a joint task force. Task force members interacted intensively. The two companies had formed an interface that partly abolished the formal boundaries between their internal environments. Mercedes managers could no longer take decisions concerning the Swatch-car project without considering the strategy, resources, and capabilities of their Swiss partner. When SMH drew back from the partnership, Mercedes managers were able to free themselves from that obligation. But when they decided to outsource the responsibility for the production of essential parts of the car to Magna International, the Canada-based supplier of automotive parts, Mercedes managers formed a new intensive interface with a cooperation partner.

Marketing

The complexity and dynamics of the environments just described make management depend on techniques, methods, and approaches that enable them to master that challenge. Marketing thought and technology can make significant contributions to the establishment and maintenance of highly attractive value-creation systems in complex and dynamic environments.

Definition

Marketing may be defined as the processes established by an organization to understand, develop, and influence exchanges with individuals, groups, or organizations in a way to reach the company's objectives.

Exchange processes are at the heart of marketing thought and action. There is no restriction on the nature of the exchange or its form. Simple spontaneous transactions are considered as well as long-lasting exchange relationships. Exchanges of an organization are relevant to marketing whether they are commercial or non-commercial. Therefore, marketing may be practised by all kinds of organizations, independent of their purpose and their profit or non-profit objectives.

Scientists as well as marketing practitioners focus on processes encompassing intelligence, decision-making, and action related to exchange processes of an organization. They use bundles of techniques and methods united by a specific approach.

Marketing approach

The marketing approach is characterized by a view of the world that considers exchanges to be based on value creation for all exchange partners in a system of complex exchange. Marketing thinking questions some aspects of the functioning of markets in modern societies, which are otherwise thought to be implicitly understood, such as the rationality of decision-making or the duality of production and consumption. Marketing thinking should consider exchanges under conditions of hyper-reality, fragmentation, reversibility of production and consumption, the juxtaposition of opposites and the non-differentiation between subject and object.

Marketing processes

Marketing techniques and methods may be grouped into four bundles, which form specific processes.

Marketing intelligence

First, marketing processes are concerned with the conditions of (potential) exchanges. That is, they focus on gathering, processing, and disseminating information concerning the objectives, interests, expectations, and the functioning of potential and current exchange partners of the organization. Exchange conditions to be researched are not restricted to the traditional aspects of transaction, such as the product, price, and distribution or communication efforts. Exchange conditions encompass all elements that may have an influence on the establishment and maintenance of exchange relationships, such as specific interests, power, dependencies, investments, the situational context, usage and consumption processes, cognitions, or affects.

Selection and management of value-creation systems

Marketing processes focus on using the gathered information for the selection of exchange partners best suited to establish a value-creation system that provides unique value to its members. Marketing processes do not focus on (potential) customers and competitors only. They consider all (potential) stakeholders directly or indirectly involved in an (potential) exchange. Those stakeholders' specific interests and power are considered in managing the level of resources attributed to each of them and the level of value provided.

Value creation

Marketing processes are concerned with creating exchange offers of highly attractive and potentially unique value to the selected exchange partners as well as to important stakeholders imposed on an organization's value-creation system. In creating valuable offers, marketing people combine internally and externally available skills and resources with information from the selected value-creation system to continually provide new exchange offers or improve existing offers to exchange partners.

Value generation

Finally marketing processes focus on all elements needed for the generation of exchange partner value. The success and long-term survival of companies depend on their capability to offer unique and attractive values to their stakeholders in a manner that provides for the stakeholders' different interests and power as well as for developments in the company's macro environment. Value generation in general demands acquisition of skills and resources as well as their coordination in a value-creation system (see Special focus). New skills and additional resources need to be continually developed for the future.

The problem is that most skills and resources are available to more than one firm. Therefore, a major achievement of a company's management is to combine skills and resources in such a unique way that distinctive capabilities result. For example Benetton, based in Treviso, Italy, combines its flexible dye works helping to achieve high quality final products with barcode-reading cash registers at all points of sale that provide real

Special focus

DELIVERING SUPERIOR VALUE BASED ON STRONG MARKET RELATING CAPABILITY

In the middle of the 1990s, Canadian Pacific Hotels, which owned 27 high quality hotels across Canada, was proficient in conventions, corporate meetings, and group travel but wanted to excel with business travellers. This is a notoriously difficult customer group to serve. But it is also very lucrative and, therefore, much coveted by many other hotel chains.

The first step was to start intensive information gathering and learning about what would create the highest value for those potential guests. Frequent guest programmes seemed to have little appeal. Beyond-the-call-of-duty efforts to rectify problems when they happened were highly appreciated. But what business travellers mostly wanted was recognition of their individual preferences and great flexibility on arrival and check-out time. Canadian Pacific Hotels responded by committing to customers in their frequent guest club that they would make extraordinary efforts to satisfy their preferences for type of bed, location in the hotel, and other amenities.

However, creating the organizational capabilities to deliver on this promise proved remarkably difficult. Management first had to map each step of the total service process from check-in to checkout. Standard performances for each sub-process were set. Then, management went on to find out what changes had to be made to the services, the delivery process, and the knowledge and skills of staff to deliver on the commitment to personalized service. The biggest hurdle was the organization's traditional bias towards handling large tour groups. Skills, mind-sets, and processes at hand were not the ones needed to satisfy individual executives, who did not want to be asked about their needs every time they checked in. Even small enhancements such as free local calls or gift shop discounts required significant changes in information systems. The management structure needed to be changed. Each hotel was given a champion with broad, cross-functional authority to ensure the hotel lived up to the ambitious commitment. Finally incentive systems were installed to make sure every property was in compliance and performance was meeting or exceeding the standards.

The market rewarded the efforts. In 1996, Canadian Pacific Hotel's share of Canadian business travel increased by 16 per cent, although the total market was up just 3 per cent, and Canadian Pacific Hotels added no new properties.

Source: Adapted from Day, G.S. (2000), "Managing Market Relationships", Journal of the Academy of Marketing Science, 28(1), 26–27.

time information about sales. By centralizing detailed sales information from all points of sale in the world, Benetton can instantly react by adapting the colours of its products to the current demand.

Capabilities are distinctive if they cannot be procured from a supplier, are difficult to imitate, and are non-substitutable. Such capabilities may extend from highly specialized to more general. Sharp Corporation, the Japanese consumer-electronics company, for example, has specialized technological expertise in optoelectronics. Its most successful technology has been liquid crystal displays which are critical components in nearly all of Sharp's products. Relying on the distinctive capability of being able to develop optoelectronical applications for consumer products, Sharp has successfully extended its scope into many new businesses where the value of the firm's offer to its customers largely depends on that core technology. Tyco International, is an example of a company with more general capabilities but which, nevertheless, are distinctive compared with its competitors. It is a USD 12 billion conglomerate that creates value for its stakeholders mainly through a set of highly developed management systems.[19]

An organization will reach its objectives and be successful in the long run only if it possesses (can develop or acquire) and sustains distinctive capabilities to generate values for its customers that are more attractive than those that customers have experienced before. Additionally, other important stakeholders must be offered benefits which make them promote or at least accept the organization's objectives and activities. The challenge for managers of all business and non-profit organizations, therefore, is to develop and implement such a unique position.

SUMMARY

To be able to fulfil their purpose companies need specific skills and resources. Those skills and resources are owned by various individuals, organizations, and institutions that will only lend or give them away in exchange for appropriate compensations. Compensations are considered appropriate if they represent an attractive value for the potential exchange partners. Compensations may result from direct or indirect relationships which can be voluntary or imposed on the exchange partners. In any case, the owners of skills and resources needed to fulfil the company's purpose have differing interests and power. Therefore, in order to ensure the timely inflow of skills and resources in the quality and quantity needed to fulfil their purpose, companies must selectively establish and carefully maintain systems of complex exchange that can be regarded as value-creation systems.

Because there is not merely a single business organization in need of skills and resources, their owners have the opportunity to select their exchange partners. Competition among suppliers of value forces them to continually work on enhancing the attractiveness of their offer in order to make it unique. Uniqueness of offered value can be achieved best if a company selects the members of its value-creation system and combines the skills and resources available from internal and external sources into distinctive capabilities.

Stakeholder selection and development of distinctive capabilities are major challenges for a company's strategic management. Because the decisions and actions needed to strategically manage both value-creation system selection and distinctive capability development are strongly interrelated, they must be carried out in an integrated way. This can be best achieved by the formation and implementation of consistent strategies on all hierarchical levels of decision-making. As the following chapters will show, marketing thinking and technology make valuable contributions to any kind of strategy formation.

Discussion questions

1. Why can a company be considered as a resource transformation system?
2. Find an example of a system of complex exchange. Explain how and why this system functions.
3. Select a company with which you are fairly familiar. Establish a list of its stakeholders. Estimate their potential mutual influence and draw a power map. What conclusions can you draw for the management of exchange processes in that system?
4. Find an example of a product you use every day and establish a means–end hierarchy. What is the supplier offering to you?

5. Find an example of a consumer product or a service, form a group of colleagues who are ready to participate, and discuss the benefits as well as the sacrifices they perceive in accepting the supplier's offer. What conclusions can you draw as to how to improve the total product?

6. Select an example of a product or a service and describe it as a bundle of value-creation processes and as a bundle of resulting consequences. How could the supplier of this total product creatively change the product's level of integrativeness and intangibility?

7. Select a product category with which you are fairly familiar and establish a list of "standard" elements of the value-creation process and "standard" features of the exchange results for the existing products in that category. Try to develop an attractively unique offer by eliminating, reducing, or increasing existing elements and features as well as creating new ones.

8. Find examples of a consumer and an industrial product manufacturer and try to establish a list of the major dimensions of their macro environments. What influence do those dimensions exert on the value-creation systems of the selected firms?

9. Why is marketing most valuable as a management perspective and as a source of techniques for managers of value-creation systems?

Notes and references

1. Pfeffer, J. and G.R. Salancik (1978), *The External Control of Organizations: A Resource Dependence Perspective*, New York: Harper & Row.
2. Freeman, R. (1984), *Strategic Management: A Stakeholder Approach*, Boston: Pitman.
3. March, J.G. and H.A. Simon (1958), *Organizations*, New York: Wiley.
4. Emerson, R.M. (1972), "Exchange Theory, Part I: Exchange Relations and Network Structures", in *Sociological Theories in Progress*, 2, M. Zelditch and B. Anderson, eds, Boston: Houghton Mifflin, 58–87.
5. Reynolds, T.J. and J. Gutman (1988), Laddering Theory, Methods, Analysis, and Interpretation, *Journal of Advertising Research*, 28, S. 11–31.
6. Loyer, M. (1996), "Luxury Companies Focus on Services", *International Herald Tribune*, March 16–17, 20.
7. Williamson, O.E. (1985), *The Economic Institutions of Capitalism*, New York: Free Press.
8. Thibaut, J.W. and H.H. Kelley (1959), *The Social Psychology of Groups*, New York: Wiley.
9. Williamson, O.E. (1975), *Markets and Hierarchies: Analysis and Antitrust Implications*, New York: Free Press.
10. Harrison, J.S. and C.H. St John (1994), *Strategic Management of Organizations and Stakeholders*, St Paul, MN: West.
11. Granovetter, M. (1985), "Economic Action and Social Structure: The Problem of Embeddedness", *American Journal of Sociology*, 91, 481–510.
12. Barney, J.B. (1991), "Firm Resources and Sustained Competitive Advantage", *Journal of Management*, 17, 99–120.
13. Senge, P. (1990), *The Fifth Discipline*, New York: Doubleday/Currency.
14. Gummesson, E. (1997), *Relationship-Marketing: Von 4P zu 30R*, Landsberg/Lech: Moderne Industrie.
15. Day, G., A.D. Shocker, and R.K. Srivastava (1979), "Customer oriented Approaches to Identifying Product-Markets", *Journal of Marketing*, 43, 4, 8–19.
16. Kim, W.Ch. and R. Mauborgne (1999), "Creating New Market Space", *Harvard Business Review*, January–February, 83–93.
17. Eade, Ph. (1995), "The ins and outs of target practice", *Euromoney*, November, 51–56.
18. Williamson, O.E. (1975), op.cit.
19. Collis, D.J. and C.A. Montgomery (1998), "Creating Corporate Advantage", *Harvard Business Review*, May–June, 71–83.

Further reading

Doyle, P. (1992), "What are the Excellent Companies?", *Journal of Marketing Management*, 8, 101–116.
Kim, W.Ch. and R. Mauborgne (1999), "Creating New Market Space", *Harvard Business Review*, January–February, 83–93.
Botschen, G. and A. Hemetsberger (1998), "Diagnosing Means-End Structures to determine the Degree of Potential Marketing-Program Standardization", *Journal of Business Research*, 42, 2, June 1998, 151–159.

Strategic management and marketing

2

Learning objectives

After studying this chapter you will be able to

1 Describe the fundamental decisions of strategic management
2 Discuss the impact of a market-based versus a resource-based view on strategic management
3 Explain the purpose and the minimum content of a strategy
4 Discuss the paradoxes of strategy formation processes
5 Understand the need for strategic processes in all levels of management
6 Explain the impact of the marketing approach on the various hierarchical levels of strategy formation.

SPOTLIGHT

Getzner Werkstoffe, a small company located at Bürs in the Austrian Alps, is the European market leader in polyurethane-elastomere production for construction and industrial purposes. In 2000, the company looked back at a year in which 115 people, only 33 of which were production workers, had managed to grow the company's total sales by 100 per cent. This sales was unevenly split across global and product-markets: about 40 per cent came from Germany, 13 per cent from the Austrian home market, 37 per cent was made in the rest of Europe, and only 9 per cent in the rest of the world. Two-thirds of total sales resulted from business with railway companies, about 15 per cent was made in the construction business, and the rest came from industrial business. Getzner Werkstoffe had two protected trademarks, Sylomer and Sylodyn. They spent 15 per cent of their turnover on R&D purposes.

The company's top management believed the following capabilities to be the major foundations for the tremendous success of the firm:

■ material specific know-how in analysis and measurement techniques,
■ the ability to chemically formulate user/application-specific materials,
■ flexible production through continuous casting,
■ the casting of preformed parts, and

■ the efficient management of complex international projects.

Management had formulated the business domain of their firm based on these capabilities. They considered the reduction of vibrations as the central benefit offered to their customers. This benefit was provided to organizations constructing railways as well as buildings, and to those having to resolve vibration problems in their industrial businesses, such as the suspending of machines, stabilizing the interiors of yachts, or suspending the floors of transportation devices. The technology by which the benefit was provided was defined in a twofold manner — on the one hand, as foamed polyurethane in mats, strips, or sheets as well as casted preformed parts and on the other hand, in the engineering of system solutions and the recycling of polyurethane.

The biggest question Getzner Werkstoffe was facing in the year 2000 was how to keep the company growing at a sustainable speed. Strategic project groups were created who focused on further globalization, intensification of market coverage, product innovation for as yet uncovered markets, enlargement and re-enforcement of core capabilities, cooperation with potential business partners, and cost management. Marketing was considered a driving force in all of these project groups.

Strategic management

Marketing processes are established and maintained to reach the objectives of a business organization. These objectives legitimize decisions and provide sense to action. However, the objectives of organizations are neither given nor fixed forever. They need to be continually developed in a process that leads from wishful thinking to reason-based decisions. Objectives may be reformulated in the course of exchange processes, due to unforeseen developments in the macro, market, or internal environments. Similarly, once established, value-creation systems are not automatically available to an organization over time. Expectations of stakeholders are continually changing. Competitors do their best to excel. And changes in the legal, technological, cultural, or economic environments may demand new capabilities of the organization. To cope successfully with these challenges, the leaders of an organization need to manage strategically its value-creation system(s) and its distinctive capabilities. Such capabilities are to be proactively developed. Management has to ensure that they are sustained and continually adapted over time. Furthermore, it is one of top management's most important obligations to allocate appropriate resources to all of the mentioned processes. These processes constitute the core of strategic management.

Strategic management is a continuous and consciously managed cooperation process by a business organization's leading managers. Based on their general view of how business may be successfully managed, those leaders search for, determine, and disseminate the objectives of the organizational unit, define the value-creation system(s) to be established, developed, and sustained by that unit, and lay the foundations for coherently developing or acquiring distinctive capabilities to provide the stakeholders with unique values. They allocate scarce resources of their organization in a coordinated way, and control the outcomes of the above mentioned activities (Figure 2.1).

As Chapter 1 has shown, marketing provides a specific approach to business. Therefore, this chapter will focus on the contribution of the marketing approach to strategic management of business organizations (Figure 2.2). First, it describes the fundamental decisions to be taken in strategically managing an organization, relating them to their drivers, that is, to internal and external stimuli, the motives of decision makers, and the objectives on which the decision-makers have agreed . The need for integrating various individual views to manage a business organization consistently becomes evident. Such integration can only be achieved by the cooperative and continual formation of guiding frameworks and their implementation on various hierarchical levels of an organization. This chapter will discuss the purpose as well as the minimum content of such guiding frameworks – also called strategies. Various ways of conceiving strategy

Strategic management is a continuous and consciously managed cooperation process by a business organization's leading managers. Based on their general view of how business may be successfully managed, they search for, determine, and disseminate the objectives of the organizational unit. They define the value-creation system(s) to be established, developed, and sustained by that unit, lay the foundations for coherently developing or acquiring distinctive capabilities to provide the company's stakeholders with unique values, allocate scarce resources of their organization in a coordinated way, and control the outcomes of these activities.

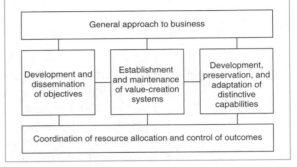

Figure 2.1   Core processes of strategic management

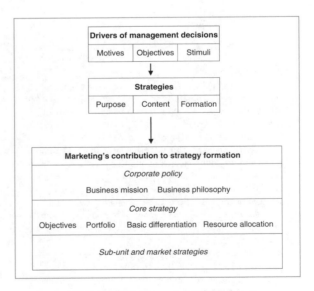

Figure 2.2   Layout of Chapter 2

formation will be described. Finally, this chapter will show how the marketing approach may significantly influence the flow and outcome of strategy formation as well as implementation processes.

Drivers of management decisions

Basic decisions

The resources of a business organization, even the world's largest, are not unlimited. As there are always a greater number of attractive market opportunities around the world than can be pursued, and there are always more potential distinctive capabilities than can be developed or acquired, management has to make selective resource allocation decisions. In many companies those decisions are based on experience or intuition. Sometimes they are based on partial analysis – for example, on the sales volume of product lines during recent years. But also resource allocation mechanisms such as "first come, first served" or even "those who shout the loudest get the most" can be found. With increasing international competition even companies operating only locally will encounter major problems with such approaches. Intuition allows the managers to recognize "typical" situations, based on past experience, and – in a stable environment – to draw the right conclusions in an extremely short time. If the business environment changes in a way not fully understood or not recognized by managers, however, the value of their experience is sharply diminished. A decision based on domestic experiences or on experiences gained in another country-market may lead to satisfactory results in the short run, but if managers ignore changes in seemingly familiar environments, the quality of the decision over the long term can become questionable.

To be able to take reasoned decisions on how much of available resources to allocate to various actions of capability and value-creation system development, in strategically leading their organizations, entrepreneurs or top management have to first answer four fundamental questions:

1. What objectives should our organization reach?
2. What value-creation system(s) should our organization establish or participate in?
3. What distinctive capabilities does the organization need to stay successful over time?
4. How do we proactively develop and sustain those distinctive capabilities?

It is important to note, however, that all of the answers to these questions are interrelated. The determination of realistic objectives by the dominant management group of the firm depends on the value-creation system(s) the firm is able to establish due to its distinctive capabilities. The selection of value-creation systems depends on the objectives set as well as the capabilities currently available to the firm or those that could potentially be developed in the future. The distinctive capabilities needed depend on which value-creation systems are the most attractive and will, therefore, be selected. Distinctive capabilities cannot be proactively developed and sustained without guidance from corporate objectives and envisioned value-creation systems. Finally, resource allocation does not make much sense without the other four decisions. But allocation of adequate resources is an essential condition for any selection of value-creation systems as well as the development of distinctive capabilities (Figure 2.3).

Motives

Figure 2.3 shows that managers' decisions concerning the objectives of their organization, the selection of the kind and number of value-creation systems, the distinctive capabilities that need to be developed or acquired, the processes to develop and sustain those distinctive capabilities and the allocation of resources largely depend on their motives. These motives may be classified as either defensive or offensive.

Defensive motives

Defensive motives may be, for example, to protect positions now reached or to keep risks at a low "acceptable" level. When defensive motives dominate, management will tend to set rather modest objectives, such as protecting domestic market share from a foreign competitor or to ascertain a satisfactory level of sales or profit. For example, US-based Emerson Electric, operating in an industry where new ideas are rare, emphasizes finding incremental improvements in sales and margins.

Management dominated by defensive motives will be hesitant to become involved in new business. Some managers will even react negatively to the idea of entering new product or country markets. They may be generally reluctant to change, taking a position of "wait and see". They may follow traditional lines of business, relying on capabilities that have proven successful in the past and being satisfied with their local business success. With their lack of specific knowledge, they may fear the additional stress of entering new businesses or developing new capabilities.

Offensive motives

Instead of passively reacting to stimuli from external or internal environments, managers with offensive motives proactively consider business opportunities. They set rather challenging objectives. For example, from the beginnings of his company, Hermann Hirsch, the main owner of Austria-based Hirsch Armbänder GmbH the leading watchstrap company in the world, wanted it to become the world market leader in leather watchstraps. He actively and systematically located and responded to business opportunities, such as the acquisition of Spidel, his biggest US-based competitor. Innovative managers are

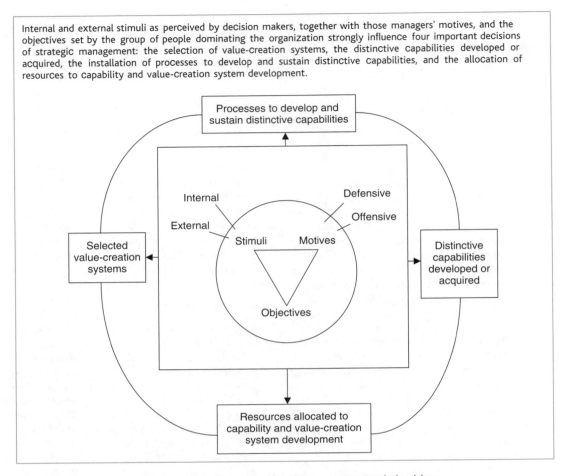

Internal and external stimuli as perceived by decision makers, together with those managers' motives, and the objectives set by the group of people dominating the organization strongly influence four important decisions of strategic management: the selection of value-creation systems, the distinctive capabilities developed or acquired, the installation of processes to develop and sustain distinctive capabilities, and the allocation of resources to capability and value-creation system development.

Figure 2.3 Drivers of basic management decisions

ready to engage their company in more dissimilar ("riskier") value-creation systems, such as in Hirsch's case the establishment of a joint venture with a partner from Hong Kong or the investment in a production and sales unit in India.

Managers governed by offensive motives tend to be concerned with the long-term growth potential resulting from a value-creation system or a distinctive capability. Offensive motives make managers look for opportunities to either apply existing capabilities (technologies, expertise, experience) in a greater number of markets or to develop new distinctive capabilities that will be needed to be successful in emerging markets. For example, in what the Japanese called "Compaq shokku", in 1992, the Houston personal-computer maker brought US-style competition to Japan: It started selling desktop PCs for less than half of what Japanese manufacturers had been asking. Other US PC marketers, such as Apple, caught on, and within three years, American companies drove PC prices down by 37 per cent in the Japanese market, and

seized one-third of the USD 12.3 billion market.[1] This turned out to be shortsighted, however. When Japanese PC makers retaliated, the price structure of the market was so badly hit that the Japanese PC market lost most of its attractiveness to US firms.

Objectives

If the dominant management group of an organization is able to integrate the motives of its individual members they may agree upon the organization's major objectives. Formulated in writing and communicated to the other members of the organization, these objectives reach an "official" status. They drive the sensitivity of organization members for external and internal stimuli and become an important influencing factor in fundamental management decisions. For example, if a company seeks a high return on investment, management will tend to select value-creation systems where the company can achieve a leadership position without high investments in the development of new capabilities. Companies that give a high priority to market share may invest in the acquisition of additional distinctive capabilities to offer a broader range of values to potential customers.

Depending on the objectives agreed upon, management will be more or less willing to cooperate with stakeholders or even competitors in the development of their distinctive capabilities. A company dominated by the objective of defending market and technological leadership, such as Gore Associates, the manufacturer and marketer of Gore fibres (such as Goretex) for industrial and consumer products, may tend to rely exclusively on internal learning and R&D processes. Nobody else is allowed to participate in existing know-how and its further development. Whereas managers striving for technological leadership in their industry, such as French Matra, may actively search for cooperation with suppliers and customers who are able to contribute significantly to the development of the firm's distinctive capabilities. As the example of IBM and Apple cooperating in the development of a new operating system for PCs has shown, such managers may even cooperate with a competitor in their attempt to outperform or pre-empt suppliers of substitutive technologies.

Stimuli

The answers of decision makers to the fundamental questions of strategic management not only depend on the personal motives of the decision makers and their resulting objectives. Basic strategic decisions are strongly based on the interpretation of external and internal stimuli facing the decision makers.

External stimuli

External stimuli may include unsolicited orders from foreign customers, perceived market opportunities, competitive pressures in a saturated home market, or technological developments. Honda, for example, today the leading manufacturer of motorcycles, once found competition from Yamaha so strong in its Japanese home market that it decided to enter the less competitive markets of Europe and the US in order to grow.

Internal stimuli

Internal stimuli may include superior technology, strong marketing skills, or excess capacity in the areas of production, finance, marketing, or management. The design of Louis Vuitton luggage, its high quality/high prestige image, and the attractive shape of their stores in France, for example, resulted in so many Japanese tourists buying their products that the firm decided to open their own stores in Japan. In 1996, sales to Japanese customers

accounted for about 30 per cent of the company's total sales. When Apple Computers, as another example, first marketed its PC, the product had such superior graphic facilities that customers in the communication business around the world wanted to use them. Together with the company's capability of developing a superior user-friendly surface, these distinctive capabilities allowed Apple's entry in the global business market.

Interpretation of stimuli

An organization's top managers become aware of such internal or external stimuli. But each manager is likely to have different knowledge and skills, varying experiences, and differing personal motives, which make them sensitive to the stimuli in variying degrees and so lead to different reactions. Human decision-making is never based directly on objective criteria but on subjective interpretation of the experiences stored in memory and information gathered from the environment. Decision makers have to decide what information is needed and what information can be ignored. What managers consider relevant in a given decision situation is determined by their cognitive frameworks, that is, their "theories in use"[2] and assumptions about their environments, the methods they use to observe and analyse those environments, and their personal involvement with the decision which needs to be taken.

Consequently, management's reactions to business opportunities are not always governed by rational analysis, profit-and-loss evaluations, or capital budgeting schemes. Often they are based on psychic distance, that is, the perception of varying familiarity with new markets or capabilities compared with customary ones. Entering new markets or developing new distinctive capabilities exposes managers to unknown environments and conditions, such as different buyer behaviour or innovative technologies, which increases their perceived risk. In international business, for example, management may have heard of important differences, such as different symbolic meanings of colour. White is a symbol of death in Japan. There, products packaged in white boxes do not sell as well as they do in the US, where white symbolizes purity. Knowing little about such differences makes managers anxious about doing business in "foreign lands". They experience psychic distance.

In order to reduce this tension of dealing with the "unknown", managers often choose to expand into markets or to develop capabilities which they perceive as being more similar to what they have experienced so far. However, such similarity judgements may be entirely wrong. For example, the management of a manufacturer of industrial thermostats may be misled when considering the market of household thermostats as a natural extension of the company's current business. The company may possess all the capabilities needed to satisfy their industrial business customers, such as strong R&D,

made-to-order production, exact technical quality assurance, and a technically sophisticated sales force. But those capabilities may not be of any great relevance in serving the household market, where expertise in product design, branding, mass production and distribution are needed for success. The similarity of distinctive capabilities needed to successfully build a new value-creation system for the firm should be considered.

Motives and objectives will influence managers' sensitivity for internal and external stimuli as well as the interpretation of data. Even managers who try to be as objective as possible in their analyses and evaluation of results, will tend to find potential value-creation systems more attractive when they fit their basic orientation, and they will more easily find distinctive capabilities to be sustained or developed in their preferred areas of activity. Therefore, to reach decisions top management can agree on, the different views of managers need to be integrated at least to a certain extent.

Integration of perspectives

Strategic management integrates two basic views of how to successfully manage a company: market-based management and resource-based management.[3]

Market-based management

The market-based view primarily focuses on market opportunities. Understanding the expectations and aspirations of potential customers, determining and selecting the most attractive markets, and providing them with more attractive offers than those of competitors, managers with a market-based view try to adapt their organization's specific capabilities so as to develop and maintain a defendable market position. For example, when US-based Home Depot's management found out that the company could revolutionize the do-it-yourself business in North America by offering home owners the expertise of professional home contractors with markedly lower prices for merchandise than hardware stores, they started recruiting sales assistants with significant trade experience, often former carpenters or painters. These assistants were trained to consult and assist customers for any project from installing kitchens to building a deck. Home Depot started sponsoring in-store clinics that teach customers such skills as electrical wiring, plumbing, or carpentry. Simultaneously, Home Depot created a self-service warehouse format that lowered overhead and maintenance costs, generated cost savings in purchasing, and minimized stock-outs. In 20 years, the company has become a USD 24 billion business that in 1999 expected to have more than 1100 stores in the Americas by the end of the year 2000.[4]

Adopting a market-based view, however, does not mean, "hear the voice of the customer and adapt your offerings". Such an approach may be successful in the short run. But it inevitably leads to a perpetuation of the status quo. A market-based view of management is most often characterized by an attempt to **drive the market**, that is, changing the composition and/or the roles of players in the market as well as the behaviour of stakeholders.[5] Calyx and Corolla, a US company active in the home delivery of flowers, for example, deconstructed the value-creation systems generally existing in their kind of business by eliminating wholesalers, distributors, and retailers from their distribution system. Calyx and Corolla trained the growers in arranging flowers, used Federal Express to directly ship the flowers from the growers to the customers, and made consumers accept this direct way of buying flowers.[6]

A business organization could make customers consider attributes of their offer which they previously have not evaluated. It may build or remove customer and competitor constraints, and create new or reverse existing preferences. IKEA, the Swedish globally active furniture retailer, for example, forces customers visiting their shops to pass the entire set of displays following a clearly marked route to the central exit which is never visible until the customer reaches it. An in-store child care, a Swedish buffet restaurant and extended opening hours make the long time consumers stay in the shop more enjoyable.

Adapting to existing needs, creating new expectations, and changing the rules and players in the market game are complementary, simultaneously happening over time. For example, Barnes & Noble, the US bookstore company, distributes books following the conventional channel from writers, to book publishers, manufacturers, and retail outlets. Simultaneously, the company pursues book distribution via the Internet. Together with other Internet suppliers such as Amazon.com, they have the potential to both change the behaviour of book consumers and alter the typical value-creation system of the industry.[7]

Resource-based management

The resource-based view assumes that sustainable competitive advantage of an organization will result in superior financial performance.[8] Competitive advantage is based on bundles of tangible and intangible resources and skills;[9] in other words, on distinctive capabilities that add value for stakeholders, are difficult to duplicate (imitate, replace by substitutive processes),[10] and cannot be appropriated (except through cooperation, merger, or acquisition).[11] For example, Wolford, the luxury hosiery and clothes maker based in Austria, has machinery that is difficult to duplicate because each machine is specifically adapted by company technicians to their highly sophisticated production needs. In addition, the tights are sewn by people trained on sewing machines for half a year until they are capable of sewing the specifically fitting Wolford products. A globally renowned brand such as French Hermès, as another example, is a valuable intangible resource which cannot be appropriated except through acquisition.

Starting from a vision of a competitively superior combination of skills and resources, managers with a resource-based view try to develop value-creation systems which more completely satisfy the stakeholders' expectations than those of competitors. For example, in 1966, when Daniel Ferguson became CEO of Newell, an old-line manufacturer of brass curtain rods with annual revenues of USD14 million, he began to develop a "build on what we do best" philosophy for Newell: manufacturing high-volume, low-cost products, and selling them to large-scale mass retailers. In July 1967, Ferguson defined the company's focus as manufacturing volume merchandise lines and distributing combinations of those lines to the volume merchandisers. Steadily pursuing this focus, Newell had sales of nearly USD3 billion by 1997. Today, the products Newell makes range from propane torches to hair accessories to office products. The line across this bizarre-looking collection of items comes from the common capabilities they draw on: relationship building and management with discount retailers, efficient high-volume manufacturing, and superior service, including on-time delivery and programme merchandising. These corporate capabilities enhance the competitiveness of every business Newell owns. The company will never compete in high-tech, seasonal, or fashion markets because they require capabilities Newell does not have. Nor will it enter businesses whose dominant channel of distribution is outside discount retailing.[12]

Integration of approaches

The problem with these seemingly antagonistic approaches to strategic management – the market-based versus the resource-based view – is that they cannot reasonably exist without each other. In the case of resource-based management, in order to determine what are currently their organization's distinctive capabilities and also what capabilities the firm needs to develop or acquire for future success, managers need to know the purpose of those capabilities. They must have an idea of some (potential) stakeholders' problems, expectations, or aspirations which could be resolved or satisfied by those capabilities. Market-based management, on the other hand, cannot successfully select attractive value-creation systems without considering the company's existing or potential distinctive capabilities and how they may be sustained in a competitive environment. Therefore, strategic management combines both approaches in a circular way of reasoning, not allowing one to dominate the other. Strategic management simultaneously strives for adapting capabilities to offer attractive values to selected stakeholders and for selecting value-creation systems

fitting the existing or potential distinctive capabilities of the organization. To reach both objectives simultaneously, strategic management provides for continual strategy formation and implementation processes on various hierarchical levels.

Strategies

Complex exchange processes may develop successfully either by chance, or based on deliberate decisions and actions following careful analyses, or a combination of both. Many managers try to formulate what they call a strategy to come to grips with the problem of developing and sustaining distinctive capabilities needed to offer attractive values to all stakeholders selected by or imposed on their organization.

Purpose

A basic objective of most organizations is to ensure their long-term survival. As we have seen so far, management can make their organization a long-term success by establishing a complex and organic value-creation system. The problem is that such a system is embedded in a dynamic environment. An analogy from the ecological sciences shows that the survival of populations strongly depends on their potential to adapt effectively to changes in their environment. Populations with genes that provide a highly specialized reaction repertoire may be extremely successful at a given point in time. They may be able to specifically adapt to the given environment. Dinosaurs, for example, dominated the world during an age when the climate was warmer and more humid than today. Changes in the environment, however, may leave such populations increasingly un-adapted, and subject to extinction. When the climate of the world cooled down, dinosaurs disappeared. In comparison, populations with a less specialized potential of reactions, that is, populations with a greater variety of potential adaptations, may not be as successful in a given environment. But such populations will have a much better chance of surviving when environmental conditions change. Some mammals, for example, already existed during the age dominated by the dinosaurs. Because of their greater potential for adaptation, some of them survived the climatic changes of the world.

Diversity

In a business environment where trade liberalization, deregulation, globalization, and socio-cultural development are continually changing the rules of the business game, and where new competitors and new technologies present decision makers with challenges to master in increasingly shortened spans of time, the analogy from ecology may have some interesting implications. In accordance with results from social psychological group decision-making research, we may conclude that a greater diversity of managers' views and evaluations of business matters may increase an organization's chances for long-term success.[13] Diverse beliefs and preferences of managers on all hierarchical levels may increase the organization's sensitivity to weak signals of change coming from the environments. The organization will have more time and a broader range of potential reactions to select an adequate way of response. A greater diversity of beliefs and preferences and a greater variety of potential reactions will contribute to a more successful selection of stakeholders, to satisfactory exchanges with those partners, and to increased sensitivity for adaptation to changing environments.

Coordination

However, a great diversity of managers' views and evaluations and a broad variety of considered reactions to changes in the environments of an organization may mean conflict or even chaos. Diversity may imply disagreement over strongly held preferences and beliefs that will not be open for discussion. High levels of conflict, which compromise the resolution of important issues, are not acceptable to managers who feel responsible for their organization's fulfilment of its stakeholders' expectations. To achieve its objectives, therefore, any organization needs some coordination. Coordination requires at least a minimum level of mutual understanding. That is, members of an organization should to a substantial degree share interpretations and evaluations, which are central to the establishment and maintenance of present and future value-creation systems.

Dynamic stability

In general, socialization in a group, an organization, or a culture leads to a minimum level of shared reality among the members of this social unit. In a business organization the question is, how can a balance be achieved between the two seemingly conflicting goals of cultivating an optimal diversity of views and potential (re)actions and of ensuring the necessary amount of coordination.

An analogy from physics may be helpful in seeking an answer to this question: A person who wants to ride a bike will continually pedal to move the wheels. In fact, as soon as the wheels stop turning the bike falls over. In physics, this phenomenon is called "dynamic stability": The bike is moving forward in a stable manner only because its wheels do not stand still.

Transferring the idea of dynamic stability to an organization means that a value-creation system cannot be successfully maintained by following a rationally planned linear sequence of actions. Continual changes in environments require flexible reactions and pro-actions, that is, deviations from the straight path to set objectives. To keep the entire organization on its intended general path, situation-specific reactions or pro-actions to demands of the value-creation system and its environments must be allowed and must take place in an organization, even if they – momentarily – lead away from the intended direction.

Guiding framework

To achieve dynamic stability, any organization needs a guiding framework which clearly indicates the general direction in which the most influential people want the organization to go[14] and simultaneously defines a leeway for adaptations to situational needs (see Figure 2.4). Like the guard rails along a motorway, the framework marks out the limits of the amount of space for the members of the organization to react adequately to demands from daily business. As long as their decisions and actions remain inside the guard rails, the organization as a whole will move in the intended direction.

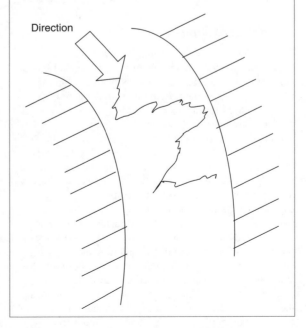

A strategy may be conceived as a guiding framework. Not unlike the guard rails along a motorway, it indicates the general direction an organizational unit is to take, but leaves enough room for the members of the organization to take operative decisions and actions that fit the current state of environments.

Direction

Figure 2.4   Strategy as a guiding framework

Such a guiding framework may be called a strategy. A strategy of an organizational unit provides direction to its members without inappropriately restricting the room of organizational sub-units as well as individual members to move. A strategy helps to develop some shared reality among members of an organization. They are provided with a direction that gives sense to their joint activities. A defined field of action and general rules of behaviour based on shared values differentiate their organizational unit from others. Both direction and differentiation contribute to the development of a sense of community, the perception of identity.

Content

To be able to fulfil its purpose of giving direction and sense without over-restricting situational flexibility of action, any strategy has to contain a certain minimum level of information (Figure 2.5). That is, as a guiding framework, a strategy must provide a mission statement containing the leading idea, a definition of the business domain, and the objectives to be achieved. In addition, a strategy must define a philosophy, that is, the general rules of behaviour to be followed.

Leading idea

The leading idea states the general purpose of the organizational unit for which the strategy has been formulated. The leading idea of a company, expresses the rationale for the existence of the organization – the vision of its founders or top managers.

To fulfil its purpose of giving direction and sense without over-restricting situational flexibility of action, any strategy has to contain statements of mission and of philosophy. The mission defines the leading idea, the business domain, and the objectives (including their priorities) of the organizational unit. The philosophy states the rules of behaviour to be followed by its members.

Strategy

Mission	Philosophy
Leading idea	Rules of behaviour
Business domain	
Objectives and priorities	

Figure 2.5 Minimum contents of a strategy

It is the answer to the question: "What does this organization want to bring about?" For example, Webasto AG, the Germany-based supplier of air conditioning systems for automotive vehicles, has formulated its general purpose as: "We provide comfort in driving". A project group formed at British Rover to decrease the overheads of their company, as another example, could formulate the leading idea of significantly contributing to an increase in competitiveness of their company. Toolbox 2.1 shows how a leading idea may be developed.

TOOLBOX 2.1

DEVELOPING A LEADING IDEA

A leading idea of an organization is to be formulated in a way so as to provide orientation to the perceptions, thoughts, and actions of organization members. It should have leadership quality by giving sense to the membership of the organization. In order to do this, the leading idea must be highly interesting to potential collaborators, expressing desirable values to be generated by the activities of the organization. But it must also be formulated in a way that makes it credible, understandable, and realistic.

In developing a leading idea for an organization managers have to consider

- the specific capabilities available to their organization,
- the basic values dominating its culture,
- existing and future problems of potential customers that may be resolved by the available capabilities,

- respecting the interests and expectations of other important stakeholders, and
- their personal preferences and preoccupations.

The process of developing a leading idea may be started by confronting the members of the development team with various stimuli relating to changes to be expected in the environments of the organization. This can be done, for example, by impulse presentations from all kinds of creative people, by sending team members "out in the street" to observe what is going on "out there", by running scenario workshops, or by making them listen to the exchange of experiences among customers at work shops, symposia, and other meetings. Having received a number of external impulses enriching their view of what impact the organization could have on its environment, the leaders of the organizational unit may then develop a first outline of a potential leading idea. During the discussion process it is very important to make all leaders specify their preferences and preoccupations. A leading idea that does not take these preferences into account will never be able to serve its purpose. It cannot fulfill its leading character for organizational members, if the leaders of the organization do not support and disseminate the vision based on their everyday model.

By presenting the outline of a leading idea to a selected group of other managers, the leaders not only enhance their commitment to the idea. The presentation of the outline may also serve as a kick-off meeting for a small group discussion process on how to further develop the leading idea, and what consequences the implementation of the vision would have on the organization. Then, in a plenary meeting of the various working groups, their views will be exchanged, and a shared vision can be formulated. Again, this process serves the purpose of clarifying basic values underlying all judgements, exchanging basic views on what is important, and creating some shared reality.

Business domain

The leading idea becomes more precise when followed by a definition of the domain to be covered by the activities of the organizational unit (Figure 2.6). Decision-makers have to determine which benefits the organizational unit wants to provide to whom, using which technologies (or ways to provide those benefits) for that purpose. For example, Liechtenstein-based HILTI AG, one of the world's largest suppliers of all kinds of industrial fastenings, defined its business as follows: "We satisfy market needs in the field of fastening technology for customers involved in small and industrial construction and for all other industrial purposes by offering tools, equipment, and elements in combination with pre- and after-sales service from the detection of the customers' needs to their satisfaction."

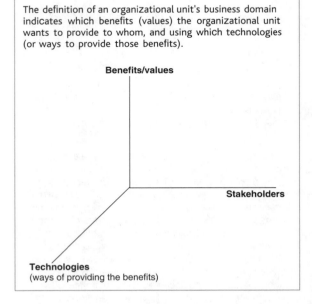

Figure 2.6 Defining the business domain of an organizational unit

Objectives and priorities

Then, any strategy must indicate the objectives to be reached by the organizational unit. They give an answer to the question: "What do we want to achieve (for ourselves) with our business?" A project group concerned with decreasing overheads, for example, may set the objective of cutting indirect costs by 25 per cent without decreasing the current level of customer service.

Because objectives are not always consistent – for example, a high growth rate goal may conflict with a goal restricting the use of foreign capital – and opportunities to reach simultaneously all objectives may be lacking, the strategy indicates which priorities should be pursued. The strategy of a business concern with a number of subsidiaries, such as Swisslog, a Swiss supplier of integrated logistics systems to various industries, may, for example, allow interim financing by foreign capital when growth cannot be exclusively financed by the firm's cash flow.

Rules of behaviour

Finally, a strategy must express the rules of behaviour to be followed by the members of the organizational unit in dealing with their colleagues as well as with external stakeholders. Internally, for example, rules may be formulated on how to handle conflicts or how to treat ideas that diverge from generally accepted views. Internal rules will also indicate how scarce resources are to be allocated to the projects, products, or organizational sub-units competing for them. For the external relations of a company, rules such as how to deal with customers, suppliers, public administrators, or the media will be part of the strategy (see Special focus for an example).

Strategy formation

According to the extent literature, there are various perspectives on strategy formation.[15] These perspectives range from viewing strategies as the result of a deliberate, rationally driven, proactive, analytical, and linear decision process to strategies which emerge out of unintentional

Special focus

"ACTING WITH INTEGRITY"

NORTEL's Core Values

"As an operating principle, we will conduct our business honestly and ethically wherever we operate in the world. Acting with integrity builds credibility – that fragile, intangible asset that's so hard to gain, so easy to lose, and so difficult to regain. Ethical conduct is the way we protect our credibility as a company, establish respect for the dignity of every individual, earn the trust of our partners and customers, and define the character of our business."

Core Values: A guide to ethical business practice

New ways of organizing people and work within the corporation are giving each of us more decision-making responsibility. Given the complexity and constantly changing nature of our work and our world, no book of hard-and-fast rules – however long and detailed – could ever adequately cover all the dilemmas people face. In this context, every Nortel employee is asked to take leadership in ethical decision making.

We create superior value for our customers.
We work to provide shareholder value.
Our people are our strength.
We share one vision. We are one team.
We have only one standard – excellence.
We embrace change and reward innovation.
We fulfill our commitments and act with integrity.

Personal values and corporate integrity

In most situations, our personal values and honesty will guide us to the right decision. But in our capacity as employees and representatives of Nortel, we must also always consider how our actions affect the integrity and credibility of the corporation as a whole. Our business ethics must reflect the standard of conduct outlined in this document – a standard grounded in the corporation's values, and governing Nortel's relationships with all stakeholders.

Our decisions as to what is ethical business practice in a Nortel context must be guided by the seven Core Values that form the fundamental basis of our conduct as a business. From these statements stem a series of commitments that we as Nortel employees make to each other, to shareholders, customers, suppliers, and the communities in which we do business.

A shared responsibility

The final core value emphasizes our intention to fulfill our commitments and to do so with integrity. Integrity means "wholeness" – it means that all the parts are aligned and work together. It means, for example, that each individual within the corporation is doing his or her best to live by the standard of business conduct outlined in this Code.

"Acting with integrity" also means that while we may not always be sure of every answer, we will not say one thing and then do another. We will not make promises that we have no intention of keeping or cannot be reasonably sure we will be able to keep. We will strive to the best of our ability to support all the commitments that the corporation has made to conducting business in an honest and ethical manner.

Putting the values to work: Ethical commitments

The following pages take a more in-depth look at what it means to put these values to work in our business. The section entitled *"Living the Commitments: Guidelines for Ethical Decision-Making"* outlines your role in enabling the corporation to meet its commitments to stakeholders and maintain its ethical standards. When individuals choose to disregard the Code, we all could suffer from damage to the corporate reputation and the ensuing loss of customers community and employee goodwill, and profitability. Serious violations of the standards may result in termination of employment. Actions that are against the law may be subject to criminal prosecution.

You have a personal responsibility to make sure that all your words and actions live up to these statements. You have a responsibility to ask questions when you have doubts about the ethical implications of any given situation or proposed course of action. You have a responsibility to report any concerns about business practices within the corporation that may violate this *Code of Business Conduct*.

Source: NORTEL Northern Telecom, Code of Business Conduct.

patterns of incremental reactions to highly unpredictable situational demands.[16]

Rational perspective

The rational perspective considers strategy formation as a predominantly explicit and logical activity.[17] It relies on the capacity of managers to analyse rationally the phenomena present in the internal and external environments of their company, to forecast the future development of those phenomena, and to derive the analytically appropriate path of action based on those forecasts. Even if the boundedness of rationality and the influence of emotions on the decision-making processes are not denied,[18] a basically linear sequence of steps of rational analyses and decisions is postulated in which all-important factors are considered and objectively evaluated.[19]

According to this view strategists recognize opportunities and threats. They analyse the internal and external reasons for these opportunities and threats, formulate objectives, determine potential alternative courses of action, evaluate them, select the best alternative, and implement their decisions.[20] According to this view, managers adopt individually different ways of analysing phenomena in the external and internal environments of their organizations because of their varying perceptions of the importance and relevance of those phenomena. Based on the results of their analyses, strategists make deliberate choices and calculated attempts of influence.[21] The strategic pattern of decisions which are finally taken is then executed as planned by the decision makers. Organizations, therefore, can be managed proactively, and managers are rationally accountable to the stakeholders of their organizations.

Intuition, that is, unconscious and uncodified decision rules largely derived from experience, may play a certain role in such processes. They are not necessarily illogical. As a kind of intellectual routine and habit, based on cognitive pattern recognition, intuition represents heuristic abbreviations which decision makers will undertake in their processes of analysis and decision-making. Such short cuts seem to be inevitable. But because pattern recognition may lead to serious biases when environmental facts deviate from the previous experience of managers, intuitive short cuts are to be viewed with some suspicion.[22]

Subjective perspective

According to this view of strategy formation, strategic problems are wicked.[23] They are not easily and not objectively defined because they are open to the managers' interpretation.[24] Problem solutions cannot be analytically identified in an objective manner. Cognitive maps shared by the decision makers strongly influence what is considered best.[25] Solutions to strategic problems need to be found creatively, in a process of making sense of events and cues from external and internal environments,[26] reflecting their relationships and meaning, envisioning their potential consequences as well as the consequences of related organizational actions, and acting accordingly.[27] This process is not thought to be linear and sequential. The various steps take place in any potential sequence or even in parallel and at any time. Flow and outcomes of strategy formation processes are strongly influenced by the dominant logic of management.[28] Effective evaluations will be ultimately decisive.

Incremental perspective

The incremental perspective of strategy formation focuses on the building of knowledge, resources, or capabilities within the firm as a reaction to external events that have already taken place or that are foreseen by decision makers. To illustrate, Repsol, a Spanish manufacturer of granules for the production of plastic wrapping materials which has been concentrating on compound technology for special applications in the food industry, may find that growing environmental concerns of consumers will force governments to raise recycling standards in the coming years. To prepare for new specifications of customers and to pre-empt competitive entry in its markets the company may broaden its focus to include the recycling potential of its material, in time.

The incremental perspective on strategy formation highlights the adaptive evolution of organizations. As any action changes the nature of the problem which has led to that action, a difference between pro-action and reaction is difficult to maintain and no meaningful split can be made between formulation and implementation of strategy. Thinking and acting are intertwined. Managers tend to learn as they go along.[29]

Deterministic perspective

The deterministic view of strategy formation is based on the idea that environments have a strong selective influence on individuals as well as organizations.[30] According to this perspective, current events are determined by preceding events. Changes in the external environment of an organization have a deterministic impact on the organization's internal environment. Following this perspective, the capabilities of an organization have been built up through past activities and learning, but depend exclusively on the development of the external environments (whether those capabilities are adequate or not).

For managers adopting a deterministic perspective of strategy formation, environments are a given. Managers only take a passive role. They cannot freely define or choose the market environment they prefer for their organization. Management's major concern is to assure proper adaptation of the organization. Maximizing the fit with external demands should result in the successful survival of their organization. While this view of strategy formation clearly addresses the strong influence of changes in the external environments on the fit of capabilities and the values offered by an organization, it tends to underestimate the role of proactive development potentially brought about by managers.

Probabilistic perspective

The probabilistic approach to strategy formation emphasizes the dynamic and interactive nature of competitive value-creation systems.[31] It addresses the interdependencies and interactions among various stakeholders and the business organization as well as among competitors in a market. Managers adopting the probabilistic view of strategy formation are convinced that they, as well as their counterparts managing competing organizations, can influence the dynamics of their organizations' external environments. Based on the assumption that the particular actions of one player lead to predictable reactions of others, such managers try to be pro-active. They are mainly concerned with obtaining an adequate share of external skills and resources for their organization by setting "the rules of the game". Similarly, implementation activities are driven by a focus on pro-active internal micro-politics.

To illustrate, in developing a market strategy for their product, Fiat Punto managers, for example, may consider that their car forms an exchange between consumers and Fiat dealers. The exchange takes place only if the customers as well as the dealers believe that they will gain something at least as valuable as the value of what they bring to the exchange. Some of those benefits on both sides cannot be achieved from the simple dyadic exchange relationship between customers and car dealers. Others, such as family members enjoying the car, friends interested in its performance, journalists reporting their experience when testing the car, or reliable service personnel working for the dealer, have to play their role in the exchange to fulfil some of the expectations (such as social acceptance or good reputation). In addition, competitors, such as VW, Audi, Ford, or Opel, will make their offers to the potential customers through the

value-creation systems they have established. From a probabilistic perspective, the Fiat Punto market strategy will have to be formed considering potential influences and interactions among stakeholders and value-creation systems. Actions need to be planned and set in time considering the probable reactions of other stakeholders as well as competition. While such a perspective contributes to the understanding of the dynamics inherent in complex exchanges and competition, it does not account for unpredictable reactions.

Chaos perspective

The chaos school of thought considers external environments as highly complex and unpredictable. Insignificant events may lead to major consequences. The stability of a market system is reached through its continual instability. Possibilities for accurate prediction, planning, and control are very limited at best. As a consequence, the chaos perspective emphasizes the need for creativity in reaction to external and internal events. It highlights the importance of speed and spontaneity in strategy formation and implementation processes based on technological leadership. Rational planning of linear sequences of action and their straight implementation to achieve predetermined objectives are considered impossible.[32] In its consequences for management rationale and action, the chaos perspective comes close to the Chinese way of strategic thinking outlined in the International Spotlight.

INTERNATIONAL SPOTLIGHT

ESSENTIAL DIFFERENCES BETWEEN WESTERN AND CHINESE STRATEGIC THINKING

When comparing the strategic approaches of managers who have socialized in Western cultures to managers who have socialized in the Chinese culture, major differences can be detected. Those differences have a significant impact on strategic decision-making and implementation.

Western thinking	Chinese thinking
Conception of Time	
Time is sequential: a sequence of events, of singular actions; it is masterable and at the same time chaotic.	Time is revolving, it is part of a strategy: it keeps transformation processes in balance and coherent without decreasing their innovative force.

Western thinking	Chinese thinking
Logic of development	
Plans allow actions to be modelled in advance; they give direction to future developments. Actions can be "normed".	Effects come into existence by themselves but strategists should do everything to keep processes already started pointing in the intended direction and to take advantage of favourable situations.
Projection vs anticipation	
The strategist constructs a model of reality and projects it into the future; she/he tries to understand and to diminish the divergence between the model predictions and what really happens.	The strategist detects: by observing present events she/he places herself/himself at the source of processes where reality is still emerging. Permanent monitoring of processes allows the detection of weak signals, of traces of the future.
Philosophy of action vs process	
A strategist seizes opportunities, takes decisions, and implements them forcefully; the sequence is objectives – decision – action.	A strategist is part of her/his environment; she/he monitors it, influences others, adapts to situations, lets things develop.
Analytical vs holistic logic	
Contraries exclude each other, a third does not exist.	Contraries determine each other, they are interdependent: the strategist knows how to make the difference and to use it for her/his purposes.
Effectiveness	
Effectiveness is the direct result of costly and risky action.	Effectiveness inversely depends on transformation: the more subtle the transformation the greater the effectiveness.
Role of the strategist	
A strategist is a leader: every action is reversible at any instant; leaders must continually renew their efforts; they must persuade. The successful strategist starts by fighting her/his adversary.	The strategist is a wise person: she/he stays unseen: to make things irreversible she/he makes others proceed in her/his place; strategists enlighten, but do not shine themselves; they influence. Successful strategists first attack the strategies of their adversaries, then the adversaries alliances, then their troops, and only finally the adversaries themselves.

Source: Adapted from Julien, F. (1996), *Traité de l'éfficacité*, Paris Dumont.

Integration of perspectives?

The preceding discussion has shown that there are seemingly contradictory, or even mutually exclusive, approaches to strategy formation. Paradoxically, however, rationality versus creativity in strategic thinking, the conviction that strategies are formed deliberately versus that they emerge from coherent actions, the view that environments are given and organizations are forced to adapt versus the conviction that organizations can select an attractive market environment that fits their available capabilities all appear to make some sense at the same time.

There is no logical solution to such paradoxes. Even if all those approaches bear some truth in them, the opposites cannot be logically integrated.[33] Managers need to find ways to accommodate each perspective and its contrary simultaneously. They talk about the "laws" of existing markets and try to adapt the capabilities of their organizations to environmental restrictions they perceive as a given. At the same time they are constantly searching for possibilities to create markets by developing new offers for as yet non-existent value-creation systems. Managers to varying degrees use analytical tools and structured processes in an attempt to take rationally based decisions. They deliberately work on the development of capabilities they consider important for future success, but they simultaneously react in spontaneous and highly affective ways to perceived changes in the environment of their organizations. In formulating strategies, managers try to understand and proactively influence interactions among constituencies important to the value-creation system of their organization. But they are also aware of the impossibility to forecast exactly all significant interactions in complex environments.[34]

Therefore, any strategy formation is characterized by conscious analyses, decisions, and actions as well as by incremental processes, which result from more or less spontaneous and emotionally driven reactions to situational stimuli. For the long-term success of an organization, however, it seems to be important that those incremental processes and their consequences be monitored in the light of a more rationally derived strategy. Strategic management must be able to cover both deliberate and incremental processes, rational and affective decisions, compliance and choice, and control and chaos. How marketing can be of help in that endeavour will be discussed in the following sections.

Marketing's contribution to strategy formation

Strategic marketing

Strategic marketing is the contribution of the marketing approach and marketing technology to the continual processes of strategy formation and implementation on various hierarchical levels of an organization. Both the marketing approach to business and the application of marketing technology have a significant impact on the determination of meaningful objectives to pursue. They influence the definition of relevant markets and the selection of markets to serve. Marketing approach and technology help in determining what distinctive capabilities to acquire, to (further) develop, and to sustain. They strongly influence the selection of differentiating values to be offered to the stakeholders in the value-creation systems in which the organization participates; and finally, marketing approach and technology have an impact on the resource allocation decisions of management.

In general, marketing managers do not have the formal authority needed to direct individually those strategic processes in their organizations or individually to take strategic decisions. Nor has it turned out to be reasonable in cases where marketing managers have had such authority. But marketing managers may play an important role as process initiators and coordinators. They provide know-how concerning advanced analytical methods, and promote an integrative strategic perspective which stresses a view dominated by systems of complex exchange, mutual benefits, and processes based on distinctive competencies to create and to generate unique value.

If an organization consists only of a small group of people who continually have personal contact and do not need any hierarchical differentiation to do their jobs, a single strategy will be sufficient to guide actions. As soon as different organizational sub-units, such as business units or subsidiaries, divisions, functional departments, and process or project teams, are established, the organization needs guiding frameworks on various levels of its decision-making hierarchy (Figure 2.7). In the following Sections, we will discuss the impact of the marketing approach and technology on those potential hierarchical levels of strategy formation.

Corporate policy

The most general strategy of an organization is its corporate policy. Contributing to the formation of corporate policy, marketing people mainly bring in their basic convictions concerning the establishment of successful value-creation systems. That is, marketing people influence the process of policy formation by their approach to business: their systemic perspective, their exchange orientation, and their benefit orientation (Table 2.1).

Business mission

The business mission statement is the basic framework guiding the decisions and actions of all members of the organization. It begins with the leading idea of the organization, defines the organization's business domain, and states the major objectives to be reached according to priorities (see Figure 2.8 for an example).

The **leading idea** of an organization – also called the corporate vision– states the impact the organization wants to make through creating values. The leading idea is meant to lead all of the decisions and actions of an organization. When asked to formulate the leading idea of their organization, managers tend to emphasize the functional perspective with which they are most concerned. Production managers tend to express their company's vision in terms of production. For example, the leading idea of a company selling rails and switches to international railway and tram customers may be formulated as to be the world leader in the production of rails and switches. Sales and R&D managers who primarily think in product terms would tend to formulate that company's leading idea as "producing and offering the best rails and switches on the market". Finance or controlling managers tend to formulate the company's vision in terms of financial success. For example, "The leading idea of our company is to provide our

An organization consisting of various organizational sub-units consciously or unconsciously forms guiding frameworks on the different levels of its decision-making hierarchy. The most general strategy of an organization is its corporate policy. The core strategy defines the intended strategic position of the organization. On lower levels of strategy formation, organizational sub-units form their strategies. Ideally, all strategies on lower levels of the decision-making hierarchy are coherent with higher-level frameworks.

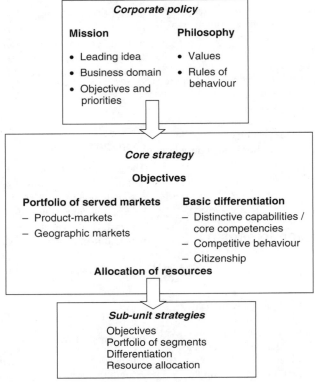

Figure 2.7   Hierarchical levels of strategy formation

Table 2.1   The impact of the marketing approach on corporate policy

With its systemic perspective, exchange and benefit orientations, the marketing approach to business influences the formation of corporate policy.

Orientation	Corporate policy
Benefit	Leading idea, business domain, major objectives and priorities, values, rules of behaviour
Systems	Business domain, major objectives and priorities, rules of behaviour
Exchange	Business domain, major objectives and priorities, values, rules of behaviour

SAFCOL, the South African forestry company, has defined the following mission statement:

SAFCOL, a company charged with the management and imaginative development of the State's investment in forestry, is dedicated to growing its business in the forestry and forestry products industry through technical business excellence and sensitive customer service, thereby achieving recognition as a leader and top performer in the forestry industry. The company will be proactive in growing with the nation through its policies of equal opportunities and providing rewarding and challenging careers for all its employees. In its activities SAFCOL will ensure compatibility with the protection of the environment and hence a green heritage for South Africa.

Figure 2.8   The business mission of SAFCOL

shareholders with returns on capital employed significantly above industry average."

However, in formulating the leading idea of their organization top management should be aware of the effect the vision tends to have on the focus of all other people working in that business organization. A production- or product-oriented formulation would put mainly internal problems and decisions in the focus of interest. A leading idea concentrating on financial success would over-emphasize the financial results to be achieved, not saying anything about how to reach these results, that is, about the impact the organization wants to make.

To avoid such shortcomings, managers adhering to the marketing approach tend to focus their formulation of a leading idea on the benefits or values to be offered by

their organization. For example, Salomon, the French marketer of sports equipment and world leader in ski sports, has formulated its corporate vision as follows: "At Salomon everybody is passionate about sports. It is our goal to develop products for all people in the world doing sports and to provide an additional service level which together allow sports-people to make progress and discover great new experiences."

In a second step, the mission statement defines the **business domain** the organization intends to cover. The business domain delimits the relevant market(s) of the organization in general terms. In theory, an organization can choose among alternatives ranging from focusing on one specific benefit for one customer group applying a single technology, to providing a broad range of benefits to all potential customers through applying all available technologies. A restrictive business definition might be, for example, to "enhance convenience of young urban professionals through an office delivery network of whole-food lunch". An extensive business definition would be to "satisfy all kinds of drinking needs for all consumers, offering all varieties of available drinks." In practice, the definition of the business domain will depend on the distinctive capabilities available to the organization, as much as on available market opportunities.

Managers with a marketing approach to business will make sure that the definition of their organization's business domain is not too product focused. For example, they will argue against definitions such as "our business is to produce and market steel coils". Marketing oriented decision-makers will define the business domain in a way that clearly demonstrates their understanding that products are no more than specific ways of providing certain benefits. Toolbox 2.2 shows how a rather simple way of hierarchical analysis may help to broaden the view of managers on what benefits their organization is providing.

TOOLBOX 2.2

THE PROBLEM SOLUTION HIERARCHY

Developing a problem solution hierarchy may help to open up the view of managers from a narrow product-oriented to a broader value-oriented perspective. The tool is based on the assumption that products are not used, applied, or consumed for their own sake, but in order to resolve a customer problem or to gain a customer benefit.

Starting with the product the organization is currently providing to the customers and listing the products in direct competition with this product, the question is asked: "Why would anybody buy this product?" The most simple answer to this question is, because the person wants to possess this kind of product. Accordingly, as the example in the exhibit shows, customers of an electric drill from Black & Decker, Bosch, or HILTI would buy that product because they want to possess an electric drill.

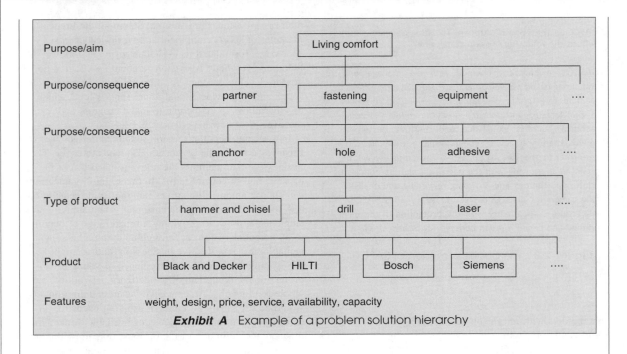

Exhibit A Example of a problem solution hierarchy

Asking the question, "Why would anybody want to possess such a product?" leads one step further in the problem solution hierarchy. In the given example, the answer may be, because the customer needs a hole. Such an answer would lead the manufacturer of electric drills to consider itself as being in the hole-making business. Defining the business as hole-making, first, means no longer thinking in terms of products but of its consequences; and second, opens up the perspective for competitors offering other technical solutions to produce similar consequences. In the case of the example, competing technical solutions would be a chisel, but also a laser. Depending on the expectations of the customers, both offer value to their users, and need to be considered when a company generates its own offer.

The problem solution hierarchy does not stop at that level, however. Taking a closer look at the first consequence of a product (or its application/use) leads to the question, "What would a customer need that consequence for?" In the case of the example shown in Exhibit A, a customer might want to have a hole because of various reasons: for example, she may want to look through something, need to fasten something on a wall, or plan to decorate her home in a way deviating from the norm. Depending on the answer, the supplier of electric drills finds itself to be in the observation, fastening, or decoration business, with competitors offering value in greatly different ways, but all of them serving a similar benefit. At the same time, the ways of offering their own product through distribution and communication as well as the space for creative product innovation ideas become multifaceted.

Managers with a marketing oriented approach to business will also be aware that the long-term success of their organization does not only depend on the offer and delivery of attractive value to customers. Such managers are convinced that the well-being of their organization depends on relationships with a variety of interrelated stakeholders. In these relationships a certain minimum level of expectation must be fulfilled in a way to minimize interference with each other. Marketing oriented managers, therefore, will try to influence the process of defining their organization's business domain in a way that avoids any dominant position of a stakeholder group in the minds of

people working in the organization. According to the marketing approach they will advocate a formulation of the business domain that fosters a dynamic balance among benefits provided to all-important stakeholders.

Relevant market(s) of an organization defined in such a manner will usually exist in a number of geographic areas. The geographic delimitation of relevant market(s) will depend on the major objectives top management wants the organization to achieve and on their priorities. The third part of a business mission consists of these **major objectives** as well as their **priorities**. Objectives often include the intended rate of growth, the return on investment, on sales or on capital employed, the market share or relative size of total sales to be reached (e.g., be one of the three major players), the acceptable level of risk, the approach to technology, innovation, and cooperation, the intended image and goodwill, the establishment of a specific working climate within the organization, and intended levels of stakeholder satisfaction. But management are free to emphasize any other objectives they consider important for the long-term success of their company.

For example, the Austrian company Doppelmayr, the world-leading producer of ski lifts, chair lifts, and cable cars, has formulated objectives demanding the application of latest technology in the products and production processes of the firm, a cost structure which allows lower production costs than the major competitors, a consolidated corporate real growth rate of an average 10 per cent a year, the exceptional use of foreign capital for the purpose of interim financing only, and capital flows from subsidiaries to the headquarters. Dupont, the US chemicals giant, has stated an objective of zero accidents where injuries to personnel keep them from working.

In the process of defining the major objectives of their organization, managers with a marketing approach to business will watch carefully for a balance among these objectives and among the benefits to be gained by the various members of the value-creation system.[35] Considerations of total quality will predominate in a double sense. On the one hand, the organic development of distinctive capabilities needed to serve attractively the stakeholders in the selected markets will be considered more important than growth combined with ambitious short-term financial objectives. Marketing oriented managers, for example, are aware of the fact that the return on capital employed (RCE) of a manufacturing firm can only very exceptionally reach the RCE-level of a mutual fund. They know that sheer size of an organization gained by the acquisition of others provides dominance in stakeholder relationships, but simultaneously creates ample space for competitors to exploit an increasing number of opportunities arising from stakeholders who are dissatisfied with the exchanges taking place. On the other hand, marketing oriented managers understand that customer delight is an important objective, but it should not be reached to the detriment of other important constituencies of the value-creation system. Reaching high standards in security, health, and environmental protection, for example, is substantial for the long-term success of a business organization. Marketing oriented managers look out for the provision of highly attractive value to all important stakeholders in their value-creation system.

Business philosophy

The second constituent part of corporate policy, the business philosophy, formulates the basic values and rules of behaviour the leaders of an organization want to be respected inside the organization as well as in contacts with stakeholders from outside. If such a complex system of values and rules of behaviour (social norms) is shared by the members of an organization and shapes organizational processes and behaviour, it constitutes the culture of the organization. The **culture of an organization** represents general frames of reference that its members use to interpret events and facts in the organization's environments.[36] Organizational culture results in observable behaviour among personnel, traditions, rituals, stories told about past events, and specialized language.[37] For example, high-tech firms such as Intel, the US producer of processors for PCs, use a different vocabulary in their everyday work than do financial firms, such as Coopers and Leybrant.

Business philosophy is supposed to be the basic statement defining organizational culture. It should guide the manner in which relationships with business partners and other groups of individuals affected by the activities of the organization are managed. For example, 93 per cent of all Fortune 1000 firms have formulated corporate ethics codes, which in many cases are part of their business philosophy. Managers who have adopted a marketing approach to business will consider value/benefit orientation, a (value-creation) systems perspective, and exchange orientation as the fundamentals of any business philosophy. Following this conviction, making the related values and resulting rules of behaviour part of an organization's culture results in a major capability difficult to imitate and impossible to procure.[38]

In a stakeholder value-creation oriented culture, thinking and action to provide attractive value to the important stakeholders of the organization is pre-eminent to the members of the firm, and behavioural norms that promote value-creating activities are positively reinforced. However, stating business philosophy in writing will not be sufficient for its effective implementation. Through communication and coordination, as well as by shaping the management systems of their organization, leading managers continually send signals to their collaborators regarding their priorities. Some companies, such as Gore Associates, the US-based creator of Goretex, for example, have replaced their functional departments by process and project oriented teams. They make all of their people continually aware that the focus of their activities is on the creation and generation of value to stakeholders. Austria-based Voest Alpine GmbH treats every customer order as a project, handled by a project group of people from sales, manufacturing, and logistics. None of the project team members receives any premium if the order is not fulfilled as per the conditions specified in the sales contract. Only if members of an organization perceive the signals from communication and coordination activities of top management as well as from management systems as being consistent can a marketing oriented organizational culture develop that positively contributes to strategic management.

Business philosophy also contributes to a certain **organizational identity**. Identity develops from the perceptions of organizational behaviour by the members of the organization and its stakeholders. Every organization has a unique identity, which is more or less formally or consciously managed. For example, through their spectacular actions to prevent hunters from killing whales or companies from dumping highly toxic waste into the sea, Greenpeace has developed a unique identity. It is significantly different from the identity of Amnesty International, trying to make politicians and public administrations do their jobs without violating basic human rights. The specific identity of an organization influences its reputation. It makes it easier or more difficult to establish and to maintain satisfactory exchange relationships with selected and imposed members of a value-creation system. Marketing oriented managers, therefore, try to establish a framework of rules of behaviour and mechanisms of reinforcement that sustain an organizational identity which is attractive to all-important stakeholders.

Core strategy

Based on corporate policy, which mainly builds on capabilities available to the organization as well as the personal preferences of the people leading the organization, management assesses the alternatives as to how to successfully position their organization in the chosen environment. That is, the rather general statements of corporate mission and philosophy are at first considered strictly as the expression of top management's wishes and need to be checked for their feasibility and, consequently, to be reformulated in a more precise manner. For that purpose, the distinctive capabilities directly or indirectly available to the firm must be related with benefits that are highly attractive to selected and imposed stakeholders. Management must check the distinctiveness of the capabilities available to their organization and the uniqueness (compared to competitive offers) of values the organization can provide by establishing and sustaining one or a number of value-creation systems. Challenges arising from developments in the macro-environment have to be analysed for their potential to represent opportunities for or threats to the future development of the organization. Chapters 3 and 4 will show in detail that marketing has a significant impact on the entire process. The marketing approach provides a distinct perspective of what elements are particularly important. Marketing technology contributes a great number of tools for analyses and decision-making.

The resulting core strategy defines the **intended strategic position** of the organization. Following the minimum content of a strategy needed to serve the purpose of a guiding framework, the core strategy must at the very least state the objectives of the organization, its portfolio of served markets including the applied technologies, and the basic way in which the organization intends to differentiate itself from its competitors. Most core strategies also contain a statement of how to allocate the resources of the organization.

Objectives

First, the core strategy restates the objectives generally defined in corporate policy in a more precise way. Based on extended analyses of the macro, market, and internal environments of the organization, management is now able to specify precisely what their organization is to achieve. Chapters 3 and 4 will focus on the role of marketing in the various steps of analyses.

Portfolio of served markets

Second, the core strategy defines the portfolio of the organization. The portfolio contains the product-market(s) and the geographic markets to be served. **Product-markets** define what selected benefits (values) are to be provided to which customers and related stakeholders by the use of what technologies. **Geographic markets** define the areas of the world a business organization intends to serve. Alcan, the world's second largest manufacturer of aluminium and aluminium products based in Montreal, for example, has defined a portfolio containing product-markets with customer groups reaching from the transportation, construction, and tobacco industries, to can manufacturers, food and beverage producers, pharmaceutical companies, and retailing organizations. For all of these customer groups, foil, sheet, and coated products, such as yoghurt lids, cable wrap, can, and body or fin stock are manufactured in a way to satisfy their very specific needs. The firm is active in more than 50 countries all over the world and has at its disposal all technologies from bauxite mining to the production and delivery of finished products.[39]

In determining their organization's portfolio, top management, which has adopted a global business perspective, will primarily think in product-market terms. That is, the focus will be on cross-national customer segments in particular value categories, whereas specific characteristics of geographic sub-markets will only influence the degree of adaptation and resource allocation decisions. For example, firms such as Boeing, Compaq, or Whirlpool serve certain segments of a global product-market. They use information about different technical standards for product adaptation in country-markets. Information on local customer activities or on legal restrictions of financial transfers may affect decisions on how many resources to deploy in what geographic area. In each case, characteristics of the specific product-market relevant to business success have to be assessed across country-markets in order to allow a comparison of the attractiveness of geographic sub-markets.

If the mission of the organization contains the objective of keeping the business local, management has no need to consider other geographic markets. It must continually screen the global business environment, however, to make sure that their organization's local competitive advantage can be sustained. Developments in other local parts of the same product-market have to be followed in order to prevent unpleasant surprises from competitors intruding on the local home market. A Spanish producer of modern kitchen furniture serving young and affluent consumers in Catalonia, for example, has to watch for developments in similar product-markets in Europe. From there, competitors who try to enter the home market of the Spanish firm could emerge.

If the mission of an organization contains the objective of internationalizing business from a local market base, geographic markets in terms of country-markets may be prominent in the managers' minds. They will try to determine characteristics relevant to the attractiveness of geographically limited product-markets. An organization wishing to grow quickly, for example, will choose country-markets in which its product-market is large enough and has sufficient purchasing power to support a high growth rate. Management that prefers a more stable development, or a slower growth, may look for country-markets where its product-market is in later stages of development.

Because management's decision concerning the portfolio of their organization will bind resources for a substantial amount of time, the risk involved is high. To take a reasoned decision, management need to undertake a market assessment procedure that allows them to evaluate carefully the attractiveness of different product- and geographic markets. Toolbox 2.3 describes one particular way of comparing the attractiveness of a number of markets.

TOOLBOX 2.3

PORTFOLIO ANALYSIS

The literature suggests various ways of comparing the attractiveness of markets or products by the use of a portfolio technique.[i] Here only one of these, the Market Attractiveness/Competitive Position-Portfolio technique, first developed by McKinsey, is presented.

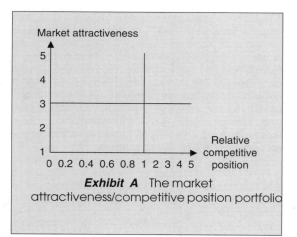

Exhibit A The market attractiveness/competitive position portfolio

In contrast to the portfolio technique suggested by the Boston Consulting Group which only uses two factors – market growth and relative market share – for the explanation of (potential) success (that is measured by cash flow), the portfolio technique suggested by McKinsey is based on two dimensions – market attractiveness and relative competitive position – which are composed of various factors of influence (see Exhibit A) that are used to explain success in terms of return (on investment, capital employed, or other).

In a first step, the factors of influence to be used on each of the dimensions have to be determined. For the assessment of market attractiveness, management may select the factors of influence best fitting the business of their organization from lists such as the one shown in the Exhibit B. If the factors are chosen in a way to allow an assessment of market attractiveness independent of the organization's actual situation, the resulting ranking of markets will "objectively" reveal how well selected are the markets currently served by the organization compared to potential markets. Following a rule of thumb, the number of selected factors should not be less than four and not be more than eight. Those factors should be (as) independent of each other (as possible).

Exhibit B List of potential factors of influence on market attractiveness

Market factors
Potential
Volume
Number of customers
Growth

Price sensitivity
Negotiation power of customers/suppliers
Seasonality of demand
Diversity of expectations

Competitive factors
Type of competitor
Intensity of competition
Danger of substitution

Degree of concentration
Speed of competitors entering/leaving the market
Dynamics of change in market shares

Economic/financial factors
Achievable margins
Market entry/exit barriers
Intensity of needed investments

Access to resources
Experience/scale effects
Usage capacity

Technological factors
Technological level
Differentiation potential
Access to know-how

Specificity of needed investments
Technical complexity
Speed of technological change

Environmental factors
Social acceptance
Taxation

Legal regulations/technical norms
Influence of interest/pressure groups

The relative competitive position of the organization is determined best by comparing the scores of the major competitors to the scores of the organization in question for each of the specific success factors in each of the markets under consideration. Because success factors vary according to markets, they need to be specifically determined. No meaningful general list of factors of influence can be presented here. One way of determining success factors would be to make experienced managers write stories of success and failure that have happened in a specific business; and derive the common factors leading to success or failure from those stories by content analysis. Chapter 4 will discusses the process of determining market-specific success factors in more detail.

In a second step, measurement scales for each of the factors to be applied in the process need to be defined. The scales should have at least three and a maximum of nine measurement points. It can be tricky to define nine clearly different measurement points on factors which are difficult to quantify, such as negotiation power of customers or social acceptance, so often five-point scales with defined extremes and means are best suited for practical purposes.

Then, weights for each of the factors of influence may be determined. Weighing the factors according to their importance seems highly reasonable to most managers. However, care has to be given to some practical considerations. First, from where should the weights be derived? Corporate policy seems to be a possible source. A fight over weights according to personal preferences and functional interests should be avoided. Second, weights should be kept simple, for example from 1 to 3. Managers

may be able to judge if a factor of influence is twice as important than another. But they are rarely able to make a difference between, for example, an importance of 15 and 35 on a 100-point scale. Third, factor weights must be agreed on before the scores of measurement objects on each of the factors are determined. If not, these scores will influence the discussion of factor weights in a way to bias the results according to individually preferred outcomes of the portfolio-analysis.

Steps one to three of the portfolio technique described here are best conducted in teams of cross-functional membership. The teams should be set up of people having to bear the potential consequences of the outcomes of their analysis. If they jointly select the factors to be used for the assessment of market attractiveness and relative competitive position and if they work to agree on the appropriate measurement scales for each of the factors, a great amount of information is exchanged and some shared reality is created. This is highly important for the general acceptance of analysis process results.

Then, market attractiveness and relative competitive position have to be assessed. For both, it seems preferable to let the team members first make their evaluations individually and then compare the individual evaluations in a plenary discussion of the team. This, again, leads to an intensive exchange of information if evaluations on various factors appear to be different (despite the use of the same scales). It is important to make sure that evaluations of measurement objects (markets, own company, and competitors) are made independently (according to the scales) and not relative to each other because the scores agreed upon are then added up for a measure of market attractiveness and a measure of competitive position.

Dividing each market's sum of attractiveness scores by the number of evaluation factors used for assessment provides management with market attractiveness scores to be entered in the portfolio (Exhibit A). To determine the relative competitive position of the organization in the various markets first, a score for the competitive position of the company in question as well as for each major competitor in each market is determined. This is achieved by dividing the sum of scores across the success factors by the number of success factors used for the analysis. (If importance weights have been determined for the success factors, the sum of scores is to be divided by the sum of weights.) The resulting scores for the organization's competitive positions in the assessed markets have to be compared to those of the major competitors. This comparison can be done in various ways. One potential way is to divide the score of the organization in question by the average summed score of competition. A relative competitive position of 1 would express that the organization is as well competitively situated as the average major competitor. This way of comparison makes sense if there are no significant differences among the major competitors. If competitors have largely different competitive positions, another way of calculating the relative competitive position needs to be found, for example, the comparison with the strongest competitor in each market only.

[i] Wind, Y., V. Mahajan, and D.J. Swire (1983), "An Empirical Comparison of Standardized Portfolio Methods", *Journal of Marketing*, 47, 89–99; Haspeslagh, P. (1982), "Portfolio Planning: Uses and Limits", *Harvard Business Review*, January/February, 58–73.

According to the two basic approaches to strategic management, the resource-based and the market-based view, the assessment of potential markets may start either from the distinctive capabilities available to the organization or from an "objective" analysis of market attractiveness. In the first case, potential markets are assessed to check the ability of the organization to provide superior value through its distinctive capabilities. The risk of this approach is of being rather static. By basing market assessments on the fit between existing capabilities and market needs, there is a tendency to find those markets that are currently served to be the most attractive. Potentially more attractive markets which need other capabilities to be successfully served are being overlooked.

Therefore, an analysis of market attractiveness independent of current organizational capabilities seems to be advisable, at least in addition to the first approach. When markets have been evaluated based on criteria independent of the organization's current strengths, in a second step the ability of the organization to provide superior value in the most attractive markets can be checked. In both cases, the relevant dimensions of those markets' economic, cultural, political, and legal environments, and the specific operating environments of product- and geographic markets have also to be carefully analysed to determine the most attractive markets. Chapter 3 will provide more details on the contribution of marketing to that assessment procedure.

Basic differentiation

Before management can decide what markets should be served, how, and in what sequence, it has to consider the **competitive position** of the organization in each of the attractive markets. Only if the organization is able to satisfy the existing and potential expectations of customers and other important stakeholders in the pre-selected markets to a level which makes it more attractive than its competitors, can long-term success be ensured. That is, management has to select the most promising way of differentiation – the way the organization intends to provide more attractive values than its competitors in the selected markets.

To be able to differentiate effectively the values offered to stakeholders in a market, the organizational capabilities determining the value perception of those stakeholders, that is, the market-specific **success factors**, have to be determined for each of the pre-selected markets. For example, an Italian manufacturer of furniture may find the Scandinavian living room furniture market to be among the most attractive options. To be a successful contender there, a marketer needs to rise to Scandinavian expectations for design and weight, as well as do-it-yourself potential. Through an assessment of its own skills and resources, the Italian firm may discover that it can easily meet the design and weight factors, but has no experience in the production and marketing of do-it-yourself furniture.

A comparison with the most important competitors will help the organization identify whether it can excel in any of the success factors – that is, if the organization will be able to profit from **distinctive competencies**, which – hopefully – can be transformed into **competitive advantages**. A competitive advantage exists only if a distinctive competency can be used to provide superior stakeholder benefit(s). Further, through such a comparison the organization can identify which, if any, major capability it is missing that prevents the organization from successfully serving a market. In the case of the Italian furniture manufacturer, the company may find out that the most important Danish and Swedish competitors have an advantage in the do-it-yourself area, whereas the Italian firm has a competitive edge in creative design. Chapter 4 will describe marketing's impact on the process of finding effective differentiation possibilities and will suggest some tools to be applied.

Based on the preceding analyses the core strategy defines the ground rules of the organization's **competitive behaviour**. Table 2.2 provides an overview of what kind of rules top management may define in dynamically developing market environments.

Because the choice in differentiation largely depends on the capabilities available to the firm, the core strategy first states the capabilities management considers distinctive, also called the **core competencies** of the organization. Choices of competitive action range from a frontal attack on any competitor, to cooperative agreements that allow not only peaceful coexistence but also the exploitation of mutual strengths, achieving synergy. Microsoft, for example, frontally attacks any rival in its major product-markets, but cooperates with the most powerful marketers of PCs, such as Dell or Compaq, to increase the value provided to its customers and other important stakeholders.

The rules of competitive behaviour also comprise decisions concerning the **innovation behaviour** of the organization. The core strategy states whether the organization intends to pioneer markets with new technologies and products, to be an innovator (a quick follower), or to be an imitator. Based on available capabilities, a ground rule may be to develop new technologies and products in the organization, to outsource parts of product development, or to stay

on top of innovative developments by acquiring licenses or even pioneering organizations. For example, car producers tend to let suppliers develop major parts of new car models, such as the engine, breaks, gearbox, the electronic equipment, or the interior design. Schering-Plough, an 8 billion USD marketer of pharmaceuticals for allergies, infections, and tumours as well as for lung, heart and skin diseases, with headquarters in Kenilworth, New Jersey, as another example, has acquired the distribution rights (for Europe and some other parts of the world) for an innovative drug called Remicade which was developed by Dutch Centoor B.V., a small biotechnology lab based in Leiden. AT&T, the US telecommunications giant, has successfully acquired smaller organizations pioneering communication technology.

The rules of competitive behaviour may also define the speed and means of **growth** and the way the organization intends to manage it. The span of potential decisions ranges from (slow) exclusively self-financed growth based on the existing business, to rapid expansion through externally financed mergers or acquisitions.

Finally, as part of the statement of basic differentiation and because competition takes place in the entire value-creation system of the organization, the core strategy should contain some rules of behaviour concerning the organization's role in society. Rules already defined in business philosophy may be refined or reinstated. They determine the organization's intended **citizenship**.

Table 2.2 Rules of competitive behaviour

In dynamically developing market environments, business organizations need to combine great flexibility with effective coordination of their activities in order to be able to seize opportunities fast and at limited risk. Clearly defined and communicated rules concerning competitive behaviour may strongly contribute to coordinated action without overriding control mechanisms.

Type of rule	Purpose
How-to rules	Spell out key features of how central processes are executed. "What makes our process unique?"
Boundary rules	Indicate which opportunities can be pursued and which do not fit the intended strategic position. "What is our kind of business; and what do we leave to others?"
Priority rules	Help managers find and rank acceptable opportunities. "What makes an opportunity particularly attractive to us?"
Timing rules	Synchronize the pace of decision-making and action-taking in various parts of the organization. "How long do we take for that kind of process and how do we coordinate it with others?"
Exit rules	Tell managers when to pull out of an "opportunity". "What makes us stop a process or a project?"

Adapted from Eisenhardt, K.M. and D.N. Sull (2001), "Strategy as Simple Rules", *Harvard Business Review*, January, 107–116.

Resource allocation

In making resource allocation decisions, management has to find a balance between trying to serve too many markets or to develop too many distinctive capabilities, and selecting too small a number of markets or distinctive capabilities. Firms such as Japan's Matsushita, one of the world's leading marketers of consumer electronics, Stockholm and Zurich-based ABB, the giant electrical products and engineering company, or Kodak, the US-based world leader in photographic material, have sufficient resources to master a full range of capabilities necessary to serve globally an extended range of product-markets. Matsushita, for example, is able to serve different groups of consumers looking for various kinds of visual-acoustic home entertainment. ABB can provide different problem solutions for various customer groups in the field of electrical installations, efficiently serving all geographic markets in need of their products and services. Such companies strive to dominate global markets.

For smaller business organizations, spreading available resources across many markets and capabilities inevitably leads to a lack of sufficient resources in some or each of them, keeping the business from efficiently exploiting its opportunities. To avoid such a mistake, the Jefferson Smurfit Group, an international paper and packaging concern based in Ireland, for example, has decided that its Asian expansion plans should proceed in a "phased approach". In 1995, the company made its first direct investment in Asia with privately owned Singapore-based New Toyo to form Smurfit Toyo, which makes folding cartons. Additionally, Smurfit formed a joint venture in China, where it bought a linerboard mill near Shanghai. The goal was to become familiar with these markets before making any major financial commitments.[40]

In the other extreme, a highly specialized organization with limited resources but strong distinctive capabilities in its business domain may decide to serve a regional or global market niche. Austrian RSB-Roundtech, for example, specializing in formwork for round constructions such as egg-shaped digesters, water towers, telecom towers, or funnels, with a personnel capacity of less than 100, is active in the most highly industrialized countries including Japan and the USA, but also in countries such as Camaroun, Korea, Indonesia, Malaysia, and Zaire. The company's management also focuses their resource allocation on the further development of round construction formwork, global logistics, and personnel development to stay ahead of competitors.

Sub-unit and market strategies

Objectives, portfolio, basic differentiation, and resource allocation decisions stated in the core strategy define the **intended strategic position** of a company that should ensure its long-term success. In a next step, management on lower hierarchical levels of the organization must take similar but more detailed decisions. If the core strategy states that the company contains more than one organizational sub-unit, such as strategic business units, divisions, subsidiaries, product lines, or project groups, the intended strategic position for each of those units has to be determined.

If the portfolio of the organization contains more than one product- or geographic market, management has to position the firm in every selected market. That is, management must specifically determine market segments to serve (that is, the value-creation systems to be established and sustained), the way it wants to attractively differentiate the sub-units' exchange offers from the most important competitors, and how much of available resources should be committed to what segment activities.

Project teams may be formed for specific purposes. For example, if a retailer such as Germany's Rewe, one of the largest retailing organizations in Europe, thinks that the future success of the firm will depend on its closeness to the customers via Internet sales and home delivery, the company will have to develop new distinctive capabilities. Because some of the needed skills may not be available and some of the necessary resources may take too long to be built up inside the company, Rewe may need to procure them from outside sources. Before starting project activities, project management will develop a strategy as a guiding framework for all the people involved in such a project.

Despite the fact that sub-unit strategies have to be formed in the light of existing stakeholders and competition, the strategies of organizational sub-units must fit the core strategy of the firm. HILTI's global strategic position, for example, involves offering high-quality, high-priced fastening solutions employing the latest technology, to all construction businesses throughout the world. It would not be acceptable, for the Asia regional management to decide to expand market share by competing on low prices while the core strategy of the company states that HILTI is to be the price leader wherever the firm is active.

Sub-unit strategies are also interrelated. They must be checked for their logical fit. For example, if new international markets are to be entered, a project team may be established to develop market entry strategies. Those strategies will be strongly influenced by the intended strategic position of the total organization as well as the intended positions in the served markets. If international markets are served only to reach operational goals, such as boosting the total sales volume or for taking up excess capacity, and if control over local marketing activities is considered less important, low-risk market entry modes will be favoured. Indirect exporting or exporting via importers in each country-market, for example, requires the lowest level of resources. If internationalization of business is a core strategic objective and the company wants to keep its local positions under close control, it will take bolder steps, such as direct investment. Swatch, for example, after unsuccessfully trying to enter the US and some major European markets through exclusive distributorships decided to invest directly abroad to maximize control over marketing activities linked to its name.

SUMMARY

Strategic management is a continuous and consciously managed cooperation process by the managers leading a business organization. They search for, determine, and disseminate the objectives of the organizational unit. They define the value-creation system(s) to be established, developed, and sustained by the organization and lay the foundations for coherently developing or acquiring distinctive capabilities to provide the stakeholders in this system with unique values. Finally, leading managers allocate scarce resources of their organizational unit in a coordinated way and control the outcomes of the above-mentioned activities.

Strategic management is first based on the leading managers' individual perception of internal and external stimuli, and the motives of decision makers as well as their objectives. To consistently manage a business organization, those individual views need to be integrated. Integration can be achieved by cooperative and continual strategy formation and implementation processes on various hierarchical levels of an organization.

Strategic management integrates two basic views of how to manage a company successfully. Market-based management primarily focuses on market opportunities. By understanding the expectations and aspirations of potential customers, determining and selecting the most attractive markets, and providing them with more attractive offers than those of the competitors, managers with a market-based view try to adapt the specific capabilities of their organization in a way which develops and maintains a defendable market position. Resource-based management assumes that a sustainable competitive advantage of an organization will result in superior financial performance. Starting from a vision of a competitively superior combination of skills and resources, managers with a resource-based view try to develop value-creation systems which more attractively satisfy the stakeholders' expectations than those of their competitors. Strategic management combines both approaches. It simultaneously strives to adapt capabilities in order to offer attractive values to selected stakeholders and to select value-creation systems fitting the existing or potential distinctive capabilities of the organization. To reach both objectives, strategic management provides for continual strategy formation and implementation processes on various hierarchical levels.

A strategy may be conceived as a guiding framework which clearly indicates the general direction in which the most influential people want their organization to go and simultaneously defines a leeway for adaptations to situational needs. A strategy provides direction to the members of an organizational unit without inappropriately restricting their room to move. It helps to develop some shared reality among the members of an organization, providing sense to their joint activities through a leading idea, a defined field of action, objectives and their priorities, and general rules of behaviour. A strategy differentiates an organizational unit from others.

There are various perspectives on how strategies are (to be) formed. They vary from viewing strategies as the result of a deliberate, rationally driven, proactive, analytical, and linear decision process to strategies emerging from unintentional patterns of incremental reactions to highly unpredictable situational demands. In organizational life, any strategy formation is characterized by conscious analyses, decisions, and actions as well as by incremental processes, which result from more or less spontaneous and emotionally driven reactions to situational stimuli. Strategic management must be able to cover all deliberate and incremental processes, rational and affective decisions, compliance and choice, and control and chaos.

Strategic marketing can be of great help. It is the contribution of the marketing approach and marketing technology to the continual processes of strategy formation and implementation on various hierarchical levels of an organization. Both the marketing approach to business and the application of marketing technology have a significant impact on the determination of meaningful objectives to pursue. They influence the definition of relevant markets and the selection of markets to serve. Marketing approach and technology help in determining what distinctive capabilities to acquire, develop, and sustain. They strongly influence the selection of differentiating values to be offered to the stakeholders in the value-creation systems in which the organization participates; and finally, marketing approach and technology have an impact on the resource allocation decisions of management. Chapters 3 and 4 will elaborate on those strategic marketing processes.

Discussion questions

1. Explain the difference between strategic management and operative management of an organization.
2. Select an example of a business organization and show how internal and external stimuli, motives of decision-makers, and objectives may have an impact on the answers to the four basic questions of strategic management.
3. Summarize the basic convictions underlying market-based versus resource-based management. What is your point of view and why?
4. Do organizations need a strategy? Prepare a well-founded statement for a panel discussion in class.
5. Contact a higher-level manager and report his/her perspective on strategy formation to your class. What are the consequences of this perspective for how the organization or one of its sub-units is managed?
6. Discuss the paradoxes of strategy formation processes. What consequences can you draw for managing an organization?
7. Select the example of an organization as an example and describe how marketing approach and marketing technology may influence the content as well as the formation of corporate policy.
8. What parts of a core strategy are most influenced by marketing? What could happen if the influence of marketing was missing? Prepare for class discussion.
9. Take a product of your choice and develop a problem solution hierarchy. How does the definition of business domain of the organization producing the product change from one level in the hierarchy to the next? What competitors do you find?
10. What questions must marketing be able to answer in order to make a significant contribution to strategically managing a business organization?

Notes and references

1. Brull, S.V. and G. McWilliams (1996), " 'Fujitsu Shokku' Is Jolting American PC Makers", *Business Week*, February, 19, 50.
2. Argyris, C. and D. Schön (1974), *Theory in Practice: Increasing Professional Effectiveness*, London.
3. Porter, M. (1996), What is Strategy?, *Harvard Business Review*, 74(6), 61–78.
4. Kim, W. C. and R. Mauborgne (1999), op. cit.
5. Jaworski, B., A.K. Kohli, and A. Sahay (2000), "Market-Driven Versus Driving Markets", *Journal of the Academy of Marketing Science*, 28(1), 45–54.
6. Ibid., 48.
7. Ibid., 47.
8. Wernerfelt, B. (1984), "From Critical Resources to Corporate Strategy", *Strategic Management Journal*, 5(2), 171–180.
9. Stalk, G., P. Evans, and L.E. Shulman (1992), "Competing on Capabilities: The New Rules of Corporate Strategy", *Harvard Business Review*, 70(2), 57–69.
10. Bharadwaj, S.P., P. Varadarajan, and J. Fahy (1993), "Sustainable Competitive Advantage in Service Industries: A Conceptual Model and Research Propositions", *Journal of Marketing*, 57(4), 83–99.
11. Grant, R.M. (1991), "The Resource-Based Theory of Competitive Advantage – Implications for Strategy Formulation", *California Management Review*, 33(3), 114–135.
12. Collis, D.J. and C.A. Montgomery (1998), op. cit.
13. Miller, C.C., L.M. Burke, and W.H. Glick (1998),"Cognitive Diversity Among Upper-Echelon Executives: Implications for Strategic Decision Processes," *Strategic Management Journal*, 19, 39–58.
14. Hamel, G. and C.K. Prahalad (1989), "Strategic Intent", *Harvard Business Review*, May/June, 63–77.
15. Combe, I.A. (1999), Multiple Strategy Paradigms: An Integrational Framework, *Journal of Marketing Management*, 15, 341–359.
16. Mintzberg, H. and J.A. Waters (1985), "Of Strategies: Deliberate and Emergent", *Strategic Management Journal*, July/September, 257–72.
17. Andrews, K. (1987), *The Concept of Corporate Strategy*, Homewood, IL: Irwin.
18. Simon, H.A. (1987), "Making Management Decisions: The Role of Intuition and Emotion", *Academy of Management Executive*, 1, 57–64.
19. Huff, A.S. and R.K. Reger (1987), "A Review of Strategic Process Research", *Journal of Management*, 13, 211–236.
20. Simon, H.A. (1957), *Models of Man*, New York: Wiley.
21. Teck, H.H. and K. Weigelt (1997), "Game Theory and Strategic Thinking", in Day, G. and D.J. Reibstein (eds), *Wharton on Dynamic Competitive Strategy*, New York: Wiley.
22. Argyris, C. (1990), *Overcoming Organizational Defenses: Facilitating Organizational Learning*, Allyn & Bacon, Needham, MA.
23. Mason, R.O. and I.I. Mitroff (1981), *Challenging Strategic Planning Assumptions*, New York: Wiley.

24. Smircich, L. and C. Stubbart (1985), "Strategic Management in an Enacted World", *Academy of Management Review*, 10, 724–736.
25. Weick, K.E. and M.G. Bougnon (1986), "Organizations as Cognitive Maps", in Sims, H.P. Jr and D.A. Gioia (eds), *The Thinking Organization*, San Francisco: Jossey-Bass, 102–135.
26. Weick, K.E. (1979), *The Social Psychology of Organizing*, New York: Random House.
27. Starbuck, W.H. and F.J. Milliken (1988), "Executives' Perceptual Filters: What They Notice and How They Make Sense", in D.C. Hambrick (ed.), *The Executive Effect: Concepts and Methods for Studying Top Managers*, Vol. 2, JAI Press, Greenwich, CT, 35–65.
28. Prahalad, C.K. and R.A. Bettis (1986), The Dominant Logic: A New Linkage Between Diversity and Performance", *Strategic Management Journal*, November/December, 485–601.
29. Quinn, J.B. (1978), "Strategic Change: 'Logical Incrementalism' ", *Sloan Management Review*, Fall, 7–21.
30. Bourgeois, L.J.(1984), "Strategic Management and Determinism", *Academy of Management Review*, 9, 586–596.
31. Dickson, P.R., P.W. Farris, and W.J.M.I. Verbeke (2001), "Dynamic Strategic Thinking", *Journal of the Academy of Marketing Science*, 29(3), 216–237.
32. Stacey, R. (1993), "Strategy as Order Emerging from Chaos", *Long Range Planning*, 26(1), 10–17.
33. Quinn, R.E. (1988), *Beyond Rational Management: Mastering the Paradoxes and Competing Demands of High Performance*, San Francisco: Jossey-Bass.
34. Bhide, A. (1994), "How Entrepreneurs Craft Strategies That Work", *Harvard Business Review*, March–April, 150–161.
35. Greenly, G.E. and G.R. Foxall (1996), "Consumer and Non-Consumer Stakeholder Orientations in UK Companies", *Journal of Business Research*, 32, 105–116.
36. Smircich, L. (1983), "Concepts of Culture and Organizational Analysis", *Administrative Science Quarterly*, 28, 339–358.
37. Pettigrew, A.M. (1979), "On Studying Organizational Cultures", *Administrative Science Quarterly*, 24, 570–581.
38. Hunt, S.D. and R.M. Morgan (1995), "The Competitive Advantage Theory of Competition", *Journal of Marketing*, 59(2), 1–15.
39. "Alu-Hochzeit wird rasch vollzogen", *Der Standard*, August 12, 1999, 25.
40. Marks, D. (1996), "Smurfit Issues Cautious Outlook Despite a 32 per cent Jump in Profit in '95", *The Wall Street Journal Europe*, April 11, 3.

Further reading

Collis, D.J. and C.A. Montgomery (1998), "Creating Corporate Advantage", *Harvard Business Review*, May–June, 71–83.
De Wit, B. and R. Meyer (1998), *Strategy: Process, Content, Context*, International Thomson Business Press: London.
Eisenhardt, K.M. and D.N. Sull (2001), "Strategy as Simple Rules", *Harvard Business Review*, January, 107–116.
Homburg, Ch., H. Krohmer, and J.P. Workman, Jr (1999), "Strategic Consensus and Performance: The Role of Strategy Type and Market-Related Dynamism", *Strategic Management Journal*, 20, 339–357.
Lowendahl, B. and O. Revang (1998),"Challenges to Existing Strategy Theory in a Postindustrial Society," *Strategic Management Journal*, 19, 755–773.
Sidhu, J.S., E.J. Nijssen, and H.R. Commandeur (2000), "Business Domain Definition Practice: Does it Affect Organizational Performance?", *Long Range Planning*, 33, 376–401.
Varadarajan, P.R. and S. Jayachandran (1999), "Marketing Strategy: An Assessment of the State of the Field and Outlook", *Journal of the Academy of Marketing Science*, 27(2), 120–143.

Strategic positioning step 1: Determining relevant markets

3

Learning objectives

After studying this chapter you will be able to

1 Describe the structure of a rational market assessment process
2 Discuss the ways of delimiting relevant markets
3 Differentiate among various approaches to market segmentation
4 Make a reasoned choice among potential segmentation criteria.

SPOTLIGHT

In 1998, Sulzer Metco was the second largest player in the thermal spray industry, with offices in 17 countries of Europe, Asia, and the Americas. The company conducted business mainly in the aerospace and automotive industries, with additional activities in land-based gas turbines, paper and pulp, printing, medical equipment, textiles, and steel. In 1998, the worldwide thermal spray industry was estimated at USD 2.6 billion. It contained four parts: coating services, materials, equipment, and engineered systems. Profit margins for coating services were higher than for manufacturing equipment or materials.

Thermal spray was a process which applied coating material to the surface of an object in order to improve resistance and performance. Many industries required thermal coating, and applications ranged from household products to medical implants. Therefore, suppliers of equipment, materials, or services needed to understand many products and manufacturing processes. Customers usually experienced predictable wear, corrosion, or safety problems under certain operating conditions, and thermal coating was one of many possible solutions. The customers chose a process based on cost, quality, and performance of the coating.

The aerospace industry was the most important customer segment in 1998. Sales went to some 240 customers worldwide, including engine builders, such as Pratt & Whitney or Rolls Royce; airframe manufacturers, such as Boeing; airlines, like Lufthansa and Swissair; subcontractors that provided coated parts, such as Alfa Romeo; and specialist repair shops, like

Interturbine. Aerospace customers demanded high level engineering support, global after-sales service from equipment suppliers, competitive pricing for materials, just-in-time delivery, ability to meet stringent specifications, knowledge of new materials, and one-stop-shopping for outside coating services.

Because of highly different specific applications, varying levels of experience with thermal coating, and different market environments, the expectations of other customer segments were strongly varying.

The leading management team of Sulzer Metco had to develop a strategy that would guide the company for the coming years. Bruno Walser, President of Sulzer Metco, described the process:

If you imagine a complex matrix, each box of the matrix is a business in and of itself. There are hundreds of little markets, all with different life cycles. We have to decide what we are going to do in each box. For example, we must determine what is the life cycle of the product, what technology is used, who are the competitors, who are the customers, what is the innovation rate, should we deliver materials only or add coating to it. It is not a neat little package. It is a very complex process.

Source: Adapted from Sulzer Metco (D): Global Strategy for the 21st Century, Babson College, William F. Glavin Center for Global Entrepreneurial Leadership, 1999.

Determining relevant markets

Based on the mission and philosophy of the organization stated in the corporate policy, managers need to define more precisely the value-creation system(s) to be established and maintained by their organizations. The first step in this process is to delimit the relevant market. Marketing-oriented managers will base their delimitation of the relevant market on customer problems to be resolved or on benefits to be provided to customers instead of products to be delivered. They will preliminarily define the geographic extension of their market and its extension in time (see Figure 3.1).

Then decision makers will use some market characteristics which are important to them to make a basic check of the general attractiveness of the relevant market. The current state of the macro environment will be considered. An analysis of potential future developments may result in scenarios which provide the framework for a closer inspection of the market environment in the business domain.

By analysing the various stakeholders (including potential customers), the competitors, and their inter-relatedness, information is gained on the current structure of the relevant market and its potential future development. In order to detect which stakeholders are driving the value-creation system, the decision-making processes and the various relationships among stakeholders in the market need to be closely inspected. When the drivers of the market, that is, the real customers, have been identified, their purchase decision-making processes will be analysed. This is of particular importance when the customers' purchase decision-making processes involve more than one person.

An analysis of potential purchase decision-makers' and purchase influencers' problems and activities leads to a deeper understanding of their expectations. Significant differences in customer expectations and capabilities may reveal the need to group the potential customers into more homogenous segments. In turn, each of these segments may be characterized by different kinds of stakeholders (including competitors) leading to different power relations from one segment to another. Combining the segment-specific data on potential customers and related stakeholders results in profiles of different sub-markets that constitute the relevant total market of the organization.

This chapter will discuss the various steps outlined above leading to an in-depth knowledge of the organization's relevant market.

Delimiting the total market

Markets are not predetermined. The decision makers in any business organization or its sub-units determine what they consider their relevant market, that is, the general value-creation system they want or of which they perceive their organization to be a part. As has been discussed in Chapter 1, to define the limits of a relevant market is rather delicate. On the one hand, the process and its outcome are greatly subjective, depending on the perception of the decision makers. At the same time, the definition of the relevant market is decisive for the rest of the strategic positioning process because it delimits the organization's field of potential action.

Product category

Some managers define the relevant market of their organization in product terms. They consider all stakeholders (including competitors) interested in the development, production, and distribution of a certain product category as constituting a market. Managers of AXA, the French insurance giant, for example, may consider organizations as well as individuals in need of insurance contracts, public regulators, intermediaries, such as insurance brokers, the media as well as competitors offering similar products as their relevant market. What belongs to a product category is defined in terms of technical substitutability, as well as physical or functional comparability.

This definition is not evident, however. Should Wolford, the manufacturer of high quality fashion tights consider all kinds of tights as belonging to their relevant product category, or only tights coming close to their level of quality? In the first case, the relevant market would be enormous – representing billions of pairs of tights a year – and Wolford's market share would be very small. In the second case, Wolford would be one of the market share leaders in a relevant market that only represents about three per cent of sales of the total product category.

The problem is that by defining the relevant market in product category terms managers may consider potential customers as members of their relevant market who do not even think about the supplier's offering. At the same time and more importantly, potential customers may consider product offerings that are not considered as competitors by the organizational decision-makers as substitutes. Some potential insurance customers may, for example, consider well-trained dogs and guns as substitutes to an insurance policy.

Customer problems/benefits

In delimiting the relevant market, marketing-oriented managers focus on the resolved customer problems or the provided customer benefits. That is, they are not so much interested in physical comparability, technical substitutability, similarity of manufacturing processes, or common distribution channels of products. They try to find out what offerings customers consider substitutable. This can be most easily achieved by introspection. The

Based on the mission and philosophy of the organization stated in corporate policy, managers need to define more precisely the value-creation system(s) to be established and maintained by their organizations. An analysis of the relevant macro environment and its potential future developments results in various scenarios. They provide the framework for a closer inspection of the market environment in the business domain. The relevant market of the organization may be determined by analysing the various stakeholders (including potential customers), the competitors, and their inter-relatedness. An analysis of potential customers' problems and activities/applications leads to a deeper understanding of their expectations. Significant differences in customer expectations and capabilities may reveal the need for grouping the potential customers into more homogenous segments. In turn, each of the segments may be characterized by different kinds of stakeholders (including competitors) leading to different power relations from one segment to another. Combining the segment-specific data on potential customers and related stakeholders results in profiles of different sub-markets.

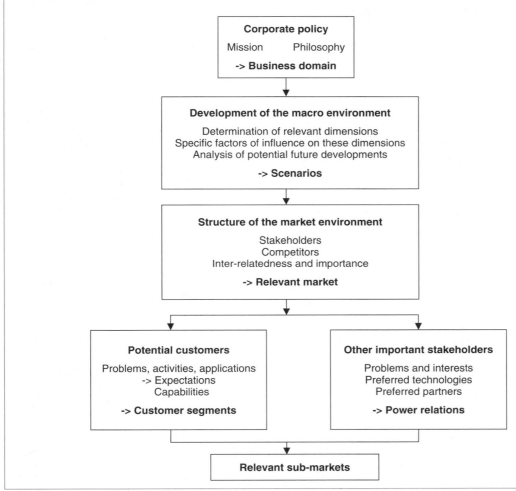

Figure 3.1 The strategic positioning process step 1: Determining relevant markets

problem with this approach is that perceptions of managers may be quite different from the view of potential customers. For example, managers of a Finnish manufacturer of cross-country skiing equipment might consider the relevant market as consisting of all potential customers interested in high quality equipment for cross-country skiing plus all competitors and stakeholders related to that business. For the potential customers, cross-country skiing, however, may only be one way to enjoy leisure time in winter outside of their homes. They might consider driving snowmobiles, ice fishing, or deer watching as alternative activities providing other but basically similar benefits. This would mean that the relevant market is much bigger than what company decision-makers imagine. There would be many more competitors, potential customers, and other important stakeholders belonging to the relevant market. Potentially dangerous threats could be overlooked and interesting opportunities may stay unnoticed.

Thus, observing customer behaviour, measuring cross elasticities of demand, or applying interview techniques such as the elicitation of the evoked sets of customers and other important stakeholders is highly important to a benefit-oriented determination of relevant markets (see Toolbox 3.1).

TOOLBOX 3.1

DETERMINING CUSTOMERS' PERCEIVED MARKET BOUNDARIES

Exhibit A lists some ways of defining market boundaries based on customer behaviour or perceptions.

> **Exhibit A** Customer-based approaches to the definition of market boundaries
>
> | | |
> | --- | --- |
> | Analysis of purchase or usage behaviour | Cross-elasticity of demand |
> | Decision sequence analysis | Brand switching |
> | Customer identification of product groups | Evoked set |

The approaches listed in the first column of Exhibit A indicate which offers customers consider for solving the same problem. The approaches in the second column of Exhibit A provide indications of the degree of substitutability between offers as perceived by (potential) customers.

By analysing **purchase or usage behaviour**, the marketer wants to find out similarities in buying or usage of product variants for specific purposes. From these similarities, market boundaries are derived. The more often two products are bought and used for the same purpose the more they are considered belonging to the same market. If a product is mainly purchased and used for a purpose for which other products are not considered relevant, it represents a distinct class. The problem with this approach is that it requires too much data on customer purchasing or usage behaviour to be easily applicable at the level of individual product offerings.

Decision sequence analysis utilizes verbal records of customer choice processes, which indicate the sequence in which various criteria are employed to reach the final choice. Those records are gathered during the customers' choice process by making them think out loud. Crude measures of the extent of substitutability between offers can be obtained from the verbal records by noting what alternatives are actually considered and at what point they are eliminated from further considerations. Offers eliminated at later stages of the process are more substitutable than those eliminated earlier. This approach can give

valuable insights into the hierarchy of product types and variants within a generic product class. The problem is that customers may be unwilling to talk about their decision-making sequence, the registration of their thoughts may evoke significant biases in decision-making, and purchase decision-making in some product categories may take place over a prolonged period of time, making data collection practically impossible.

Customers may be asked directly to **identify product groups**. They may be given a set of products and asked to enumerate as many uses for them as possible. Then, respondents are asked to suggest additional products appropriate to these uses. The lists of substitutable products for specific uses generated this way are then presented to an independent sample of potential customers who are asked to judge the suitability of each product for each use. The analysis of the gathered product-by-uses data results in establishing an index of the frequency of association of an offer with a given usage situation. This index might be used to establish a measure of substitutability to be used for the determination of market boundaries.

Economists consider **cross-elasticity of demand** as the standard for measuring substitutability of various offers. For example, the European Commission uses this measure in particular to analyse the potential abuse of dominant market positions by big companies. The cross-elasticity of demand between two offers is defined by the percentage change in the extent of demand of one divided by the percentage change in the price of the second, when everything else affecting demand for either offer remains the same:

$$\text{Elasticity } q_1, p_2 = \frac{dq_1/q_1}{dp_2/p_2} \qquad \begin{aligned} q_1 &= \text{quantity sold of product 1} \\ p_2 &= \text{price of product 2} \end{aligned}$$

A cross-elasticity of zero indicates no relation between the offers. An increasing positive measure indicates increasing substitutability. Increasing complementarity is indicated by an increasingly negative measure. Despite the theoretical elegancy of this measure, cross-elasticity of demand is rarely used to determine market boundaries because of a theoretical problem: if simultaneous estimation of all potentially relevant cross-elasticitis were to be attempted, some a priori determination of the relevant market would be needed in order to include price change for all competing offers.

Brand switching is usually measured by the probability of purchasing offer A, given that offer B was purchased on the last occasion. Such measures are estimated from panel data where the purchasing behaviour of a representative number of customers is registered. The premise is that brand-switching probabilities provide an estimate of substitutability. As with cross-elasticity of demand, the estimation of brand switching rates is based on some previous decision of which brands to include in the sequence of purchases to be observed.

In **evoked set** research the marketer tries to find out what specific product offers or suppliers are preferred by (potential) customers in a certain consumption or usage situation. For that purpose (potential) customers are confronted with a consumption or usage situation and are asked what specific product offer or preferred supplier spontaneously comes to their mind. After having been asked another question for distraction, the (potential) customer is asked what would be the second preferred product offer or supplier if the first one was not available or unable to deliver. This procedure is repeated until the respondent stops it by answering that there is no further product/brand or supplier he or she would select. The members of a customer's evoked set can be considered substitutable; the first mentioned having the highest probability to be selected.

On balance, those empirical methods which explicitly recognize the variety of usage situations have the widest applicability and yield the maximum insights. Regardless of method, however, the lack of defensible criteria for recognizing market boundaries leads to the conclusion that all boundaries are ultimately arbitrary.

Source: Adapted from Day, G.S., A.D. Shocker and R.K. Srivastava (1979), "Customer-Oriented Approaches to Identifying Product-Markets", *Journal of Marketing*, 43 (October), 8–19.

Geographic extension

In addition to delimiting the relevant market by customer benefits, market boundaries need to be set in geographic terms, such as the national market, the EU, or all highly industrialized countries. Again, there is no objective way to geographically delimit the relevant total market of an organization. As discussed in Chapter 2, the decision strongly depends upon the major objectives top management wants the organization to achieve and their priorities. But the decision is also strongly influenced by the personal preferences of the decision makers, such as having many international contacts or being the leader of a globally operating firm versus having a peaceful life as a local dignitary only.

Time

Some organizations additionally delimit their relevant market in terms of time; for example, when a tourism organization specializing in guided mountain climbing sees its market as restricted to the local area and to the summer and fall seasons. As the example of Austrian Alpinschule Innsbruck shows, this need not be the case. Offering guided tours all over the globe, the company has developed continual business on a global level.

Important market characteristics

To avoid spending time and personal resources on a closer analysis of a relevant market that ultimately turns out to be of very limited general attractiveness, the considered total market needs to be assessed. On this very basic level of analysis, market attractiveness mainly depends on the substantiality of the market, its contribution to the fulfilment of the organizational mission, and the position the organization has achieved, can sustain or reach in the market.

Substantiality

The substantiality of a market is determined mainly by its size, that is the number of customers, their purchasing power or investment expenses, and their creditworthiness. The size of a market may be expressed in terms of total sales volume, measured by some standard unit such as tons or number of customers serviced, or in terms of value (currency unit volume); the latter is referred to as market volume.

To take into account potential changes in a market's substantiality, managers should also determine its rate of growth. The growth rate of a market is an indicator of market potential, that is, the market volume potentially reached by the activities of all suppliers. The rate of growth can also be considered an indicator of the market's stage in its life cycle. Early stages are associated with greater potential, growing market volume, and an increasing return on investment. Later stages are characterized by stagnant or declining sales accompanied by low potential return on investment for new entrants to the market. For example, compact disk sales grew rapidly in Europe in the early 1990s. Many marketers entered the market, their sales rose rapidly, and their profits increased. But when market growth slows, as in the CD markets in the end of the 1990s, marketers will be faced with not only lower profits as they increase their promotion costs, but lower prices in an attempt to keep sales active.

Contribution to the organizational mission

If a market is substantial, its attractiveness additionally depends on the degree to which serving the market may contribute to fulfil the organizational mission. Non-profit organizations, such as the Red Cross or Greenpeace, for example, will find value-creation systems more attractive that allow them to fulfil their purpose more effectively. Profit-oriented firms will assess the potential profitability of markets taking into account their fit with values defined as essential to the company's business.

Profitability, to a certain extent, depends on the intensity of competition in a market. Therefore, the major current and potentially emerging competitors, and their market position, competitive strategy, and expected reactions to the market activities of the organization have to be determined. Competitors' reactions will depend on how they perceive the threat resulting from the strengths, weaknesses, strategy, and market behaviour of the organization. The impact of competitive reactions on the potential success of the organization will depend on their intensity and speed. Management, therefore, needs to assess the potential reactions of competitors to determine the level of attractiveness of the relevant market.

If the intensity of competition seems acceptable, the potential return on investments in the relevant market will be estimated. Organizations looking for profit will do a quantitative comparison of necessary investments with potential cash flows. Non-profit organizations will compare the resources they need to invest with the impact they can have on the part of society they have tentatively selected as their relevant market. A market should not be considered attractive before this analysis has revealed a positive outcome. Market dynamics have to be considered. Italy-based Generali, one of Europe's biggest international insurance companies, for example, accepted substantial losses in Hungary from 1990 to 1994. But as one of very few insurance companies to invest in this newly opened market, they achieved a comfortable market share position which allowed the transferral of their first earnings to headquarters in 1995.

Difficulties

In conducting a general assessment of attractiveness of a relevant market, management may encounter three major difficulties: a lack of reliable or available data, the impossibility of reliably forecasting future developments and returns, and the potential meaninglessness of results.

Most data for analytical purposes are either product-oriented, not reliable, or simply not available. Product-oriented statistics are useless for relevant markets creatively defined in terms of solved customer problems or benefits sought. If the relevant market has been defined in product terms, in the best of all cases reliable official statistics are available informing about total sales and market volume. But existing data are often not useable because classifications are made in very different ways from one country to another. Industry statistics based on the US SIC code, for example, group products and companies in ways not directly comparable with EU statistics.

Additionally, available data may be unreliable, because they are outdated or were not gathered in an appropriate way. Sometimes data are even purposefully biased for political reasons. When the two Germanys were united in the early 1990s, for example, it turned out that the former East German administration had published industry statistics which were more made up to show fulfilment of economic plans than giving a picture of the real state of the various industries. In the domain of electronic business, as another example, data concerning future market developments such as forecasts of market potential have turned out to be subject to wishful thinking.

Even more often market data are not available because the relevant market is highly specific, defined in a way not known to others. Or there are only very few suppliers preventing statistical institutions from publishing the data for competitive reasons. In such cases, if some market data are available, indicators can be used for an estimation of market size. The volume of the market for disposable nappies, for example, can be estimated from the number of babies born per year, minus deaths, weighted by average household income. Although such a simple indicator does not account for consumption behaviour or the activities of competitors, it will give management a good estimate of the approximate size of the market. Toolbox 3.2 gives examples of what management can do when data are scarce in international business.

Secondly, the substantiality of a relevant market and its potential contribution to the mission of the organization not only depend on the market itself but also on the development of the macro environment. That is, defining a relevant market based on current data and assessing its attractiveness only for the given point in time may be misleading.

Depending on management's expectations concerning the evolution of the macro environment, for example, a rather small market currently demanding high investments without yielding any returns may look either very promising or deterring. The example of the auction of UMTS licences in Germany in the summer of the year 2000 has shown impressively how much managers rely on forecast developments of their businesses' macro environments. At the moment of the auction no hard facts based on current data justified the investment of a total of DM 100 billion.

As another example, in 1993 France's Peugeot had considerable ambitions in China. The automaker announced it would invest USD 1 billion by the turn of the century to boost output at its joint-venture plant in

TOOLBOX 3.2

ESTIMATING MARKET SUBSTANTIALITY IN EMERGING MARKETS

If, in international business, neither the number of consumers nor their purchasing power can be reliably determined, total exports of similar products from the most important industrialized countries to the geographic areas of interest may provide a simple estimate of market volume. However, such an estimate does not account for exports from the country in question or for the activity of domestic suppliers. Management can compare the size of industries already existing in served country-markets with the approximate size of the same industries in a potential market. Relating those figures to the market share attained in served markets (that is, the organization's own sales volume in units or value compared to the total sales or market volume) and expressing market share in terms of total sales leads to a rough estimate of the market volume in the potential market.

Take the example of a Belgium-based producer of small electrical engines which is active in most EU markets

and wants to estimate the market volume for its products in Brazil. There are no reliable national statistics for this special market. Nevertheless, management can proceed in the following way:

Decision makers may take Portugal as a basis for comparison – because it is the least industrially developed of its served EU markets. First, they list the industries which are the potential clients of their products, such as manufacturers of do-it-yourself tools, pumps, food, and chemical products. Then they evaluate the size of those industries and the competitive position of their company in the respective market segments. The firm's market shares in the different parts of the Portuguese market are then expressed as shares of total sales of small electrical engines in Portugal. Multiplying the result of a comparison of the size of relevant industries in Portugal and Brazil with those sales figures leads to an estimate of the probable size of the market in Brazil.

Exhibit A Estimation of market volume based on sales and market share in other markets

Industry	Industry size and firm's competitive position in served market	Market share[i] in %	Total sales[i]	Industry size in potential market	Estimate of product-market volume
DIY-tools	small, strong position	40		3× bigger?	
Pumps	small, weak position	15		no estimate	
Food	big, strong position	60		7× bigger?	
Chemical	small, strong position	35		5× bigger?	
Comments					

[i] in market related to served industry

Guangzhou from 20,000 units to 150,000. But the meddling of government created major problems. In the early 1990s, when China regarded cars as a "pillar industry" of the future, policymakers pushed to set up huge plants. But when the economy overheated, Beijing imposed tight-money policies that suppressed car demand. The result: In 1996, passenger-car sales rose by 19 per cent, to 382,000. Capacity, however, reached 700,000 and continued to grow dramatically. Compounding the problem was that passenger-car prices were fixed by the government at between USD 15,600 and USD 26,000. At those levels, few manufacturers could realize profits because of their low production volume.

Peugeot turned out only 2674 vehicles.[1] In 2001 they had stopped their entire car manufacturing activities in China.

To get away with pure speculation in assessing the attractiveness of a relevant market, managers tend to ask specialized consultants for their forecasts instead of relying exclusively on their own (positive or negative) expectations. However, the consultants may have substantial self-interests. Managers would be better advised to establish at least two scenarios with greatly differing potential developments of the relevant dimensions of the market's macro environments (see Chapter 1) and analyse their impact on the attractiveness of the relevant market. If the analysis shows that interesting returns could be expected at an acceptable level of risk, the relevant market may be considered attractive.

The remaining problem, however, is that the results of a general assessment of the attractiveness of a total relevant market may be meaningless. This is the case, if the relevant market consists of various sub-markets or segments with varying volume, growth rates, cycles of demand, regional concentrations of customers, varying competitors, size of potential orders, or customers with different expectations. For example, total markets with stagnant sales volumes very often contain niches with highly attractive growth rates. Averages across differing sub-markets or market segments may lead to wrong conclusions. Therefore, even a relevant market that is (superficially) looking attractive needs to be analysed in more detail.

Decision-making processes

The most important question to be answered in further analysing an attractive-looking relevant market is, who is driving the market? Who are the real decision-makers significantly influencing what is exchanged, how, when, and under what conditions? Is it the direct exchange partners the organization is serving with its product, or the exchange partners' customers, those who buy, or those who use the product? For example, are the mothers buying new satchels for their kids driving the market? Is it their children asking their mothers to buy a specific model, for example with the picture of a Teletubby or a Pokemon? Or is it the media together with the retailers continually pushing new fads into the market? The most influential members of a market may be determined by a systems analysis as described in Toolbox 1.4.

When the drivers of a market are determined, their purchase decision-making processes may be researched, finally leading to a closer look at individual problems to resolve, at expectations concerning potential problem solutions, and aspirations concerning future benefits.

The "customers"

The real market-drivers of a value-creation system are members of the value-generation chain (including those who contribute to the generation of value by ultimately consuming a product), and these are the "customers". All the other members of the value-creation system, even if they include those who are directly served by the organization, are more or less important stakeholders.

Independent of the customers' position in the chain of value-generation, further analysis of a relevant market first focuses on these most important players. For example, if a pharmaceutical company, such as Swiss Novartis, plans to launch a new slimming agent, they have to determine who

their customers are. A quick and superficial response would be – the consumers of the new drug. But if the agent needs to be prescribed by medical doctors and is to be sold through distributors delivering to pharmacies, the real decision maker could be one of those. Presumably doctors have a significant influence on drug consumption and in particular the brand choice of their patients, even if the consumers of the new slimming agent pay and consume it. Pharmacists can stock and – at least informally – promote the new drug. But they can also boycott it. Therefore, the marketer of pharmaceuticals needs to analyse carefully the decision processes surrounding the offer, before deciding on whom to focus as "the customer".

Such an analysis of decision processes and power of influence in a market can be conducted in a cross-sectional or a longitudinal way. A cross-sectional analysis focuses on a certain point in time. Management could decide, for example, to focus their interest on the configuration of the value-creation system at the time when the direct exchange partner of their organization takes his or her purchasing decision. In contrast, a longitudinal analysis looks at an emerging process over time. That is, management may analyse a purchasing process as a series of episodes with potentially varying players with changing roles and influence over time. To allow in-depth understanding of how the value-creation system works, such a longitudinal approach to customer decision-making should include post-purchase episodes in which the customers co-create value by product consumption or usage as well as communication about the product. Such a longitudinal approach is by far more complex and resource-consuming than a simple cross-sectional analysis. However, if a market is relatively new and highly important to an organization, the information gained about the functioning of the system very much compensates for the resources spent.

Purchase decision-making

Once the group of exchange partners, who are thought to be the real customers of the organization in the market, has been determined, their buying decision processes need to be analysed in some detail. The decision processes may be significantly different if the customers are consumers rather than organizations or institutions.

Depending on the product and the cultural norms of society or a group, buying processes of consumers can involve an individual person or a group of persons. Individual consumers may be influenced by prescription-makers, opinion leaders, role models, or members of a reference group. **Prescription makers** consult or advise decision makers, or even prescribe a product to them. A typical example would be a medical doctor prescribing a pharmaceutical product to a patient. But even children may act as prescription makers, such as the so-called little emperors – the single children of Chinese families – who see their parents and grandparents spending up to 60 per cent of their disposable income in pampering them. In a similar manner, children strongly influence their mothers in Western societies in what brands of cereals, desserts or dresses to buy for them. **Opinion leaders** influence the purchase decision-making process of consumers by their social role. They may be family members, friends, or other people who are felt to be especially experienced or knowledgeable in the buying decision to be made. Their opinion is directly sought by the decision makers or may be transmitted by the media. **Role models** function in a similar manner because of their special status. They may, for example, be movie stars or sports champions, such as Air Jordan who was a role model for an entire generation of basketball-shoe wearers. **Reference persons** influence the buying decision maker because of their importance in the social group to which the decision-makers belong or to which they want to be related.

In a study of family purchasing roles in Saudi Arabia, for example, the researchers found that in general, the husband continues to play a more dominant role in deciding what to purchase, and, as in most nations, the roles vary by decision stages, and by product category. Husbands, for example, are a more dominant influence on "how much to spend". But husband and wives are together involved in "when to buy". Husbands exert more influence on the purchase of a car, while wives dominate decisions in women's clothing.[2]

International marketers should be careful not to project their gender prejudices or individual cultural experiences on other cultures. For example, more than half of all ties purchased in Germany and Austria are bought by women. And a significant amount of women's underwear is bought by men. A careful analysis of the target consumers' buying behaviour seems to be advisable. Chapter 8 will further elaborate on consumer behaviour.

Organizational customers are frequently grouped into multifunctional teams called "buying centres" (Figure 3.2). For example, Spanish Seat, when purchasing automatic transfer equipment for the production of a new car model, would use a team approach in making the purchase decision. The team might include representatives from various functional areas, such as production, finance, engineering, maintenance and purchasing as well as a member of top management. Together they would weigh organizational objectives and the potential contributions of competing suppliers to achieve those objectives against the cost of the competing offers.

How each individual member of the buying centre acts in the purchase decision process will depend on the stage of the process, the role he or she perceive themselves to play inside the group and the formal as well as informal influence of that person. The possible roles involved in a buying centre include initiator, consultant, gatekeeper, decision maker, purchaser, and user.[3] In a smaller company these roles may be played by a single person or, at most, by a few people. As the size of the organization and the price, complexity, or importance of

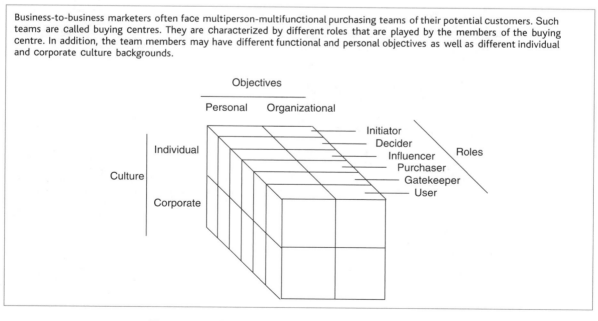

Business-to-business marketers often face multiperson-multifunctional purchasing teams of their potential customers. Such teams are called buying centres. They are characterized by different roles that are played by the members of the buying centre. In addition, the team members may have different functional and personal objectives as well as different individual and corporate culture backgrounds.

Figure 3.2 Buying centres of organizational customers

the buying decision are increasing, these roles are likely to be played by different individuals. Chapter 7 will further elaborate on this.

In addition to the organizational objectives and objectives related to the role each member of the buying centre plays, personal problems, expectations, and aspirations of the various members of the purchasing team are likely to affect the final decision. For example, the team member representing production might prefer offers that have a short delivery time and fit the maintenance know-how of the firm's service crew. The procurement manager might prefer the least expensive offer because performance appraisals of her organization highly value any reductions of capital employed, and the member of top management might focus on references provided by competing suppliers because he wants to take a safe decision. There might also be a power struggle among some members of the buying centre because of personal reasons.

When serving globally active organizational customers, the problem of multiple roles and objectives may be complicated still further. In addition to having potentially different personal and corporate objectives, role players may come from different cultures or be located in different companies belonging to the firm. A marketer selling to Procter & Gamble's European headquarters, based in Geneva, Switzerland, may face a buying centre whose members are American, French, Irish, and Taiwanese. Although the negotiations would be conducted in English, the cultural background of each member and specific career experiences in different parts of the firm would result in a complex matrix of roles, objectives, and cultures which is very difficult to handle for the international marketer.

Individual problems, expectations and aspirations

To be able to serve potential customers in a focused way to make the organization a highly attractive supplier to those customers, the relevant problems, expectations, and aspirations of buying decision-makers and decision-influencers have to be assessed. Customer problems, expectations, and aspirations are relevant to an organization if they concern the defined business domain of that organization – in other words, if they can be (at least partly) satisfied by the capabilities (potentially) available to the organization.

At this point management should keep in mind that when asked potential customers are only able to identify expectations related to objects and problems with which they are familiar. For example, somebody who knows something about potato chips may develop expectations of getting those chips with mayonnaise or tomato ketchup. But somebody who does not know what a computer chip is cannot have or develop any expectations concerning that product. Really innovative solutions to customer problems are rarely found by asking customers to describe their needs.

Therefore, when searching for potential customer expectations, the researcher should focus on problems customers perceive and want to be solved and on customer aspirations concerning potential problem solutions. For example, management of a Spanish subsidiary of Sara Lee Corporation made focus groups of consumers talk about their experiences with medical soaps for people with allergy problems and with beauty products having various scents (see Toolbox 3.3 for a description of the focus group interview technique). The discussions

TOOLBOX 3.3

FOCUS GROUP INTERVIEWS

Interviews with more than one respondent at a time are called group interviews. Focus group interviews are characterized by an interviewer launching a discussion among the participating group members and keeping the discussion going on along a predetermined line where contents (focus) are relevant to the interview purpose. The discussion is tape-recorded or video-recorded, transcribed and content analysed. If the focus group is virtual, that is, participants are chatting via electronic media, the discussion can be electronically registered and analysed without transcription.

Focus groups for interview purposes generally have 8 to 12 participants. If groups are smaller, extrovert individuals tend to dominate the discussion. Bigger groups allow less participation by each individual, and result in boredom and frustration, which may diminish the richness of data to be gathered from the interview. Participants for each focus group are selected in a way to make the exchange of ideas, experiences, and opinions flow as freely and intensively as possible. For that purpose, "experts" are avoided. They tend to dominate and potentially intimidate all other group members by their specific knowledge. Focus groups should also not contain relatives and friends. Personal ties have a tendency to bias group discussions by specific focuses or avoidance of sensitive issues. Participants are selected in a way to form relatively homogeneous focus groups. People with similar levels of education, hierarchical status in their organizations, from similar social backgrounds, neighbourhoods, or functional areas in their organizations are more inclined to communicate freely with each other. They have a similar level of expression capability and there are less potential conflicts among participants. The disadvantage is that there is less diversity in points of view. For that reason, a number of focus group interviews with relatively homogeneous groups may need to be conducted.

Focus group interviews have a minimum duration of about 30 minutes. But they may last several days, depending on the importance of the discussed subjects for the group members and the extension of the field of interest. The kind of participants, the duration, and the contents of focus group interviews have an influence on the location where the interviews take place. Focus group interviews may be conducted in shopping malls (where consumers are asked to participate), in the premises of the market research firm conducting the interviews (when specific equipment such as one-way mirrors is needed), in premises of organizational interview partners (when in-house focus groups are selected), in seminar and resort hotels (when personal interaction is needed and the interviews take a longer time), or on the Internet (e.g., when participants should not meet personally to avoid negative effects of social desirability).

The biggest advantage of focus group interviews compared to individual interviews is the greater stimulation of participants through the contributions of the other group members. Groups are more creative in generating information than individuals. One comment stimulates another, leading to a snowball effect. In addition, in contrast to individual interviews, participants of focus group interviews do not feel a "need to answer". Their participation is more spontaneous, and there is probably less information made up by the respondents in the interview situation. The group provides them with shelter against "aggressive" questions from an interviewer. The speed of information gathering and cost efficiency are higher.

Major disadvantages of focus group interviews are potential biases by group effects and non-representativeness. If the content of the interview is subject to social desirability or touches areas of intimacy, outcomes will be unreliable. Additionally, focus group interviews do not fulfil the conditions (size of sample, selection of respondents) that make their results statistically representative. That is, the research method should only be used when group dynamics lead to greater richness of gathered information than individual questioning and when statistical representativeness of results is of minor importance.

Source: Adapted from Morgan, D.L. (1998), *The Focus Group Guidebook*, Thousand Oaks, Cal. et al.: Sage.

showed that consumers were disappointed about the high price of medical soaps to be bought in pharmacies and at the same time, struggled with the negative effects of regular beauty products on their skin. Based on that knowledge, the people from Sara Lee developed a product called Sanex that exactly fulfilled the aspirations of the consumers concerning a potential problem solution: an affordable liquid soap to be bought in supermarkets with no negative side effects on sensitive skins.

Because the problem recognition of potential customers is dynamically changing, organizations have a certain influence on what problems potential customers are aware of and on what aspirations they have concerning potential solutions. Learning, understanding, and responding to customer problems and expectations, therefore is only part of a marketing-oriented manager's job. They also need to be creative in finding out what problems potential customers could be made aware of, and how basic aspirations could be transformed into new specific expectations. For that purpose, intimate knowledge of customer behaviour as consumers, users, or appliers of products in situations that are relevant to the business of the organization, based on close relationships and sensitive observation are more important than most questioning techniques typical of common market research.

Customer segmentation

When analysing the relevant market of their organization in the way described above, management may become aware of the heterogeneity of this market. They may find various customers with different problems searching for benefits only to be provided by varying technologies. That is, the relevant market may be constituted of several sub-markets or segments. How such segments may be detected, analysed, and profiled will be discussed below.

Similarities versus differences

What managers find in analysing the relevant market of their organization depends on what they are looking for. If they start from the point of view that every potential customer is different, managers will find unique features for every customer. If they think that differences in customer problems, expectations, and behaviour are of minor importance, managers will find their market to be rather homogeneous. A highly fragmented market demands specific adaptations, may be even individualization of an organization's exchange offers. In contrast, a rather homogeneous market may be served with a largely standardized product. The differences in capabilities needed for marketing intelligence, value creation, and value generation are tremendous. Sophisticated managers, therefore, will apply both perspectives. Finding out and weighing up their consequences will help them to take reasonable decisions in terms of the mission of their organization.

Standardization

When the purchase decision process as well as product consumption, usage, or application processes of potential customers have been studied and a list of current as well as potential customer expectations has been drawn up, as a first step management may focus on expectations that are common to all decision makers. Similarities in expectations and in the levels of these expectations are of most interest.

Because customers perceive a considerable amount of product categories as being of minor importance to their life or their business they may not have developed specific expectations concerning these product categories. Thus, they may consider products of a certain category as largely similar, may be rather easily influenced concerning expectations "to have", or may be ready to trade off the fulfilment of existing expectations against a lower price. In such cases an organization can standardize its exchange offer across its customers, and economies of scale in production and marketing can bring down the price of mass-produced products. A low price is an additional incentive for many customers to forgo their individuality and settle for standardized products. Thus, Japan's Honda was able to market a small motorcycle to a worldwide market, including the Americas, the EU, and the fast developing economies of East Asia, that appealed to customers as a necessary means of transport at a much lower price than local competitors. The Special focus describes two basic ways of how organizations can standardize their total product.

Special focus

BASIC WAYS OF TOTAL PRODUCT STANDARDIZATION VS INDIVIDUALIZATION

Standardization

Basically, organizations have two ways to standardize their total products: the premium prototype and the common denominator approach. When choosing the *premium prototype approach* of standardization, management identifies the most demanding customers and conditions of product use and develops an appropriate standard product to meet these conditions. For example, in its effort to cut costs by producing vehicles and parts for markets worldwide instead of making an array of vehicles that are different for each continent, Detroit-based General Motors, which in 1995 had 12 different types of four-cylinder engines alone, decided to adopt a global engine policy. GM invested USD 1.3 billion to develop a generation of four-cylinder engines for use around the world. Engineering costs were dramatically reduced driving a hard line on parts costs, as GM was able to deal with a smaller number of suppliers.

The major problem with the premium prototype approach is that many customers may not need the product features of their most demanding peers and may be happy enough with lower quality and performance standards. They may be unwilling to pay for a level of performance that seems exaggerated to them. As a consequence the cost savings from standardization may be eaten up by the lower margins.

A *common denominator approach* is possible where functional benefits dominate the customers' perceptions, or the product is similarly used across different environments.

Examples for product categories where functional benefits dominate for most customers are PCs, software, camcorders, calculators, or suitcases. Walldorf, Germany-based SAP, for example, which has a growing market share of about one-third of all business administration computer programs sold worldwide, sells standard software packages. Their implementation necessitates an adaptation of the customer firms to the features of the product. Customers are willing to undergo such adaptations to participate in the "standard" of information technology (which also eases e-business with exchange partners).

Finally, for some products such as pop music, ethnic food, or fashion clothes, adaptation to individual expectations would be counterproductive. Their major benefit stems from the product not being adapted. Decision makers should not overlook, however, that even for these products some adaptation might be well accepted by local customers. Mexican restaurants in the US or in Europe, for example, are better off serving their food not exactly the way it would be served in the home country. That is, having determined (potentially) shared expectations across all customers and the potential managerial consequences of focusing on those expectations, the decision makers of an organization, in a second step, should determine in what respect and why the levels of the remaining expectations are different.

Individualization

Individualization can be achieved in adaptive, cosmetic, autonomous, or collaborative ways.[i] When customers want a product to perform in different ways on different occasions, suppliers may choose *adaptive individualization*. That is, they may offer a standard product that is designed in a way so as to allow users to alter it themselves. For example, most software applications have the built-in technical potential to be adapted to the needs of individual customers by their users. Car seats, fashion watches, or home shopping services may accommodate users having different needs at different times. Customers can derive independently their own individual value from the standard product because it allows multiple permutations changing the product's functionality, its emotional value or both. For example, America Online, the US online provider that entered a joint venture with Germany's Bertelsmann to set up a Europeanized version of their service, gives its global subscribers the ability to create their own stock portfolios that list only the particular equities and funds they wish to track. In addition, it automatically delivers information from financial publications on the investments in the customers' portfolio, saving them considerable time in information search.

When customers use a product the same way but differ in the benefits they expect – as for example the worldwide users of Swatch products – suppliers may opt for *cosmetic individualization*. That is, the organization offers a standard core-product with a certain number of expected features which delivers the functional (basic) benefit – such as indicating the time or offering the ability to phone. In addition, symbolic product features and the processes creating them are individualized to provide emotional value. For example, Hertz Corp., the world-leading rental car company based in the US, still uses standard rental cars in its #1 Club Gold Program. But customers belonging to the programme bypass the queue at the counter. They get shuttle service to the car park, find their name displayed on a screen that directs them to the location of their car, and find the back of the car open for their luggage, and the heater or air conditioning turned on when the weather demands it.

Efforts to individualize products cosmetically with large shares of tangible features and autonomous value-creation processes will be focussed near or at the end of the value-generation chain. For example, the name of the client may be added to a clock face or a strap chosen by the customer may be mounted to give the watch a personal note. When a product is highly integrative and most of its features are immaterial, it is the processes which involve customers and can make a positive difference from the customers' point of view which will be individualized. For example, an internationally operating bank, such as The Netherlands-based Rabobank International which focuses on corporate, investment, and private banking in more than 30 countries in Europe, the Americas, and Asia/Australia, will have largely standardized back office procedures but may design its offices and train its customer contact personnel in a way that treats its customers according to their individual expectations.

When the needs of the customers are well known to or at least identifiable for a supplier and when the customers do not want to bother with the product because it does not seem important enough to them, management may decide to apply *autonomous individualization*. Companies such as the Franco-British Sema Group or US-based Electronic Data Systems, both specialists in computer services, for example, take over all hardware and software installation, integration, and maintenance activities of their industrial customers. The customers – in the case of Sema these are mainly cellular operators in Europe and Asia – source their computer systems activities out because they do not consider them as being part of their core competence. The suppliers take over the responsibility of keeping the systems running at a specified level of availability.

The supplier observes customer behaviour over time without direct information-gathering interactions. The product is individualized according to the determined preference structure and usage behaviour of each customer within a standard package. The customer may not even be aware of the individualization. For example, customers of Ritz-Carlton hotels are observed in relation to their consumption behaviour during each stay. The information is stored in a database, and service is tailored to each customer on their next visit.

When customers have to take one-off decisions based on difficult trade-offs between product features, such as comfort for elegance or flexibility for functionality, and when the decisions seem important enough to the customers to exert some effort, management may choose *collaborative individualization*. In this case, supplier and customer together determine the features of the total product. The supplier helps the customers to articulate their expectations with regard to the product and their problems with known offers. Together they identify the precise offering that fulfils the customers needs. For example, Chicago-based International Components Corporation (ICC), the world-leading manufacturer of (battery) chargers, collaborates with its customers in 13 countries in all parts of the globe. In most cases customers approach the company with their product and ask ICC for advice on how to charge it. The company then designs and produces the charger for that product, with a prototype typically available for testing within a few weeks.

Such collaborative individualization has been the rule in most international contractual businesses such as mechanical or software engineering, legal services, or business consulting. A special example is employment-services of temp agencies. International agencies, such as Netherlands-based Randstad, are able to offer international clients an exclusive contract to provide them with the number of suitably qualified personnel they need in all their operating units.

In consumer product marketing, collaborative individualization has not found many supporters so far. Most mass marketers have tried to increase the value provided to their customers by adding new features or improving existing processes. As a consequence and because of the great variability of individual needs, product port-folios have become more and more complex, therefore more difficult and expensive to manage. In addition, large assortments of unsold products have piled up in stock or expensive, largely unused service capacity has been built up because of erroneous forecasts of exactly which products will be needed at what time.

By collaboratively individualizing its products, an organ-ization replaces back end adaptations to customer needs and circumstances with front-end specifications on how the most attractive product for the individual customer should be designed. No inventories of finished products are waiting to find their customers. Raw materials or component parts are stocked to be able to react quickly to individual customer demand. Customer contact personnel are trained to interact sensitively with clients who have strongly differing demands. For example, Paris Miki, a Japanese eyewear retailer that owns the largest number of eyewear stores in the world, has developed the Mikissimes Design System. The system first takes a digital picture of each customer's face and analyses its characteristics as well as a set of customer statements concerning the kind of look he or she desires. Then it recommends a distinctive lens size and shape and displays the lenses on the digital image of the consumer's face. The consumer and the optician next jointly adjust the shape and size of the lenses until the customer is pleased with the look. In a similar way, consumers select the nose bridge, hinges, and arms. Then they receive a photo-quality picture of themselves with the proposed glasses. Finally, the glasses are produced in one hour.

Collaborative individualization can also take place in the production and delivery stages of a product, for example, when, customers specify where, when, and how the ordered products should be delivered. This is the case in Just-in-Time contracts between carmakers such as Italy's Fiat and its suppliers, but also in grocery home delivery services where customers not only order the products they need but also indicate when they want them to be delivered.

Sources: Adapted from AP-Dow Jones News Service (1996), "Rabobank Aims to Double International Activities", *The Wall Street Journal Europe*, July 9, 8. Blumenstein, R. (1996), "GM to Develop Engine Family For Models Around the World", *The Wall Street Journal Europe*, May 15, 5; Fisher, L. (1997), "Charged Up and Ready to Roll", *Accountancy – International Edition*, February, 30–31; Gilmore, J. and B.J. Pine II (1997), "The Four Faces of Mass Customization", *Harvard Business Review*, January–February, 91–101; Haas, P. (1996), "SAP: réussite allemande dans le logiciel", *Le Figaro économie*, 11 mars, 8; Walters, P.G.P. and B. Toyne (1989), "Product Modification and Standardization in International Markets: Strategic Options and Facilitating Policies", *Columbia Journal of World Business*, Winter, 37–44.

Individualization

When the involvement of customers with a product category is more than minimal, their expectations are more profiled and pronounced. Not meeting those expectations by an undifferentiated offer may not provide enough value to the customers to make the offer seem attractive, even when the price is very low. Even if the product has been accepted because of its low price, a lack of fulfilment of expectations may lead to customer dissatisfaction.

Moreover, increasing competition has made it difficult for most profit as well as non-profit organizations located in highly industrialized countries to offer successfully any standardized products to their customers. Despite ongoing cost reduction programmes, most organizations need to continually raise the value their products offer to the customers in order to stay internationally competitive. The most attractive value for private as well as organizational customers comes from direct or indirect personal benefits derived from a product. Because of the diversity of customer expectations and aspirations, serving each customer individually may maximize the offered value.

When taking an individualized approach to business, an organization needs to treat every single customer as a particular segment of the relevant market with specific requirements that must be fulfilled. To do this, management will first have to determine the points of common uniqueness, that is, to find out where the potential customers generally differ in their problems in need of resolution, expected benefits, application, usage, or consumption behaviour. To get a complete picture, product features and processes creating customer value have to be considered. From this analysis, management can conclude what features and processes to individualize and at what stage in the value-generation process – during product design, production, delivery, or use – to provide the greatest customer value at the lowest possible cost. The Special focus describes four basic ways of individualizing the total product of an organization.

However, there are some essential problems related to individualization. First, when being confronted with a group purchase decision, such as in the case of an organizational buying centre or a family buying decision, the customer needs to be split into the constituent members of the group, with each potentially having different expectations. Going one step further, the search for differences in expectations in order to maximize adaptation of organizational offers may result in a situational split of individuals themselves. Individual customers may have quite different expectation profiles depending on (the subjective interpretation of) the situation they are in. Thus the struggle for maximum adaptation requires highly customer-specific information.

Customers need to be individually profiled by their key preferences and characteristics and ranked according to their attractiveness to the organization. Because expectations and preferences develop dynamically, customer behaviour must be continually observed and individual offers adapted. As a result, the complexity of marketing intelligence, value creation, and value generation strongly increases. Even when relying on sophisticated systems of electronic data gathering, storage, and analysis, costs tend to go up. For managers trying to find a way out of this dilemma, the answer may be customer segmentation.

Segmentation

When perceived problems, sought benefits, expectations, or behaviour are very similar among certain customers but significantly different compared with others, organizations tend to segment their relevant market. Segmenting refers to the division of a rather heterogeneous unit into more homogeneous sub-units based on certain criteria (see Toolbox 3.4). The general objective of any customer segmentation conducted by business organizations is to improve the chances of making exchange offers that provide unique value to selected partners, thereby gaining the best value in exchange themselves. Fulfilling the specific expectations of different groups of customers leads to a rather high level of customer satisfaction at relatively lower levels of value generation complexity compared to individualization.

Customer segmentation must be clearly differentiated from product segmentation. Product segmentation consists of splitting an organization's various offers into more homogeneous groups of products in order to structure the business of the organization. Whereas product segmentation focuses on physical or process similarities of products, customer segmentation is based on similarities and differences in expectations and behaviour of (potential) customers.

Customer segmentation may take place on all the various levels of the decision-making hierarchy of organizations. Whatever the level, however, potential exchange partners are grouped in a way to allow the organization specifically to use, adapt, develop, or procure the necessary capabilities for providing highly attractive benefits to a selected group(s) of exchange partners. The major difference between segmentation attempts on higher levels (e.g. corporate, division, business unit) and lower levels (e.g. product line, product) of decision-making is to be found in the aggregation level of data. The further down in the hierarchy segmentation decisions are taken, the more specific the data used.

For example, a marketer of hair-styling products, such as French L'Oréal, may segment that business (which is only part of their total range of activities) into a consumer and a business-to-business division. Each of them needs clearly different capabilities, as for example in logistics and customer relationship management, to provide attractive benefits to the major stakeholders in the market.

TOOLBOX 3.4

TYPOLOGICAL ANALYSIS

Typological analysis consists of specific methods applied in a series of steps to split a universe of potential customers into groups – called customer types – with significantly different lifestyles (expressed through activities, interests, and opinions), and to characterize these types of customers by their socio-demographic characteristics as well as media usage and purchasing behaviour.

Typological analysis usually starts with the development of an item battery, that is, a number of statements, for the measurement of consumers' activities, interests, and opinions (AIO). Via a subsequent exploratory factor analysis the data gathered from the application of this item battery to a large sample of consumers (because of methodological reasons there need to be at least 5000 interviewees in the sample) are reduced to their underlying principal traits. That is, factor analysis reduces the consumers' responses to all individual statements to the general reasons why the interviewees have responded to the items in the way they did. By calculating factor scores for each respondent, a profile can be developed for

each individual, indicating the importance of each factor for the respective person's behaviour. Subsequent cluster analysis of the factor scores leads to a grouping (i.e., clustering) of the respondents according to their similarity in factor scores. The clusters of consumers detected in this manner can each be described by the characteristics of an average cluster member as well as by their media and purchasing behaviour.

Development of an AIO item battery

The development of an AIO item battery is usually based on focus group interviews, individual in-depth interviews, sequence-oriented problem identification, and/or expert knowledge about activities, interests, and opinions of consumers that characterize their specific way of life. Based on the findings of such qualitative studies and on extent knowledge from former research, a great number of statements are formulated that try to express the detected ways of customers' thinking, acting, and evaluating. Each statement is reviewed so that its wording is as precise as possible and it does not evoke an obvious "socially acceptable" response. Some statements will be positively stated and others in a negative manner to reduce potential biases from response tendencies such as "yea-saying".

This considerable number of statements must be reduced to a smaller number that is acceptable in a survey research without losing the respondents' willingness to participate. But at the same time the selected statements (called items) must be representative of the entire spectrum of potential types of activities, interests, and opinions that exist in the population under study. How the reduction is achieved depends on the researchers' theoretical knowledge about general dimensions underlying the consumers' responses to the various items. If researchers have no theoretical concept on which they have based the development of their item pool, the reduction of items may be achieved by exploratory factor analysis. If the item pool has been developed on the basis of a theoretical concept about what lifestyles (dimensions) underlie the consumers' responses to the statements, confirmatory factor analysis is the appropriate method to be chosen.

Exploratory factor analysis

Exploratory factor analysis starts from a matrix showing the correlation coefficients among the interviewees' standardized responses to the individual items. Through this standardization of data, biases which have come about through varying response styles are eliminated. Then the correlation matrix is tested for its suitability to be factor analysed. That is, a sufficient number of the correlation coefficients must be significant to allow factor analysing the data. If Bartlett's test of sphericity shows significance and the Kaiser–Meyer–Olkin measure of sampling adequacy is above 0.70, factor analysis may be applied.

But before the procedure can be started, the researchers need to take a number of decisions. They must decide how to estimate commonalities, how to limit the number of extracted factors, and how to rotate them. For all three questions there are no clear-cut rules, but there is some theoretical reasoning and some statistical criteria on which to base the decisions.

Basically factor analysis tries to reduce a number of variables to a smaller number of factors which are causally responsible for the empirically measured correlations among those variables. But depending on what values are placed in the diagonal of the correlation matrix (that is, whether commonalities are estimated either by setting them equal to 1 or by using the squared multiple correlation of each variable as an estimate) there are two basic approaches: principal components analysis and principal factors analysis. When opting for the first alternative, in interpreting the resulting factors researchers have to answer the question of how the variables highly loading on a factor may be expressed by a common denominator. On the other hand, when researchers select the second alternative, the question to answer is, what is the reason for the high loadings of certain variables on each individual factor? In most cases of typological analysis the principal

components version is considered adequate because the main reason for factor analysing the data is to reduce the amount of variables to be handled in the subsequent steps of the process.

The next decision to be taken concerns the number of factors to be extracted. Too many factors will result in factor splitting. Having too few factors in the solution will distort the meaning of the results. There is no fixed rule on how to proceed. But two tools have proven to be helpful: Kaiser's roots criteria and Cattell's scree test. Following the roots criteria, all factors with a root greater than 1 are kept for further analysis. A root of >1 means that the factor explains more variance than each of the variables alone. Using the roots criteria only makes sense when a principal components analysis has been conducted and the number of variables does not exceed 40. It indicates the minimum of factors to be extracted. In a scree test the roots of factors are plotted in a diagram according to their decreasing value. A large break in the plot of the roots is taken to indicate the point where the extraction of factors should stop. This point indicates the maximum of factors to be extracted.

To improve the ease of interpreting the factors resulting from the analysis, generally a rotation of factors is conducted to come as close as possible to a simple structure. A simple structure is a factor solution where each variable is clearly related to only one factor. That is, simply speaking, it has a high loading on one factor (>0.50) and low loadings on all the other factors.

There are various ways of rotating the factors. The most common rotation procedure, called *Varimax*, should not be used if the existence of a general factor may be theoretically expected. In this case a *Quartimax* rotation is better suited. In typological analysis there is always more than one factor representing different lifestyles. But it may be useful to perform an orthogonal and an oblique rotation of factors. An orthogonal rotation relies on the assumption that the extracted factors are independent of each other. This may not be the case in typological analysis. Therefore, an oblique rotation allowing for correlated factors may lead to a simpler structure and improved interpretation potential of factors.

For each individual participating in the survey, a score on each factor may be calculated. These factor scores indicate the relevance of each factor to the respective person. They result in individual factor score profiles, which may be used as input into cluster analysis.

Cluster analysis

Cluster analysis is a way of sorting items into a small number of homogeneous groups. Through its use, customer segments are formed, which are internally homogeneous and externally heterogeneous in terms of the factor scores determined in the previous step. Because cluster analysis is quite capable of producing a segmentation solution, even if natural clusters do not exist, it is worth visually examining the data. Factor scores may be visualized, for example, by a star plot or three-dimensional plots, to see if any patterns are evident. If no clusters can be envisioned, it is likely that no natural clusters exist. Even if clusters seem to exist, plotting factor scores may show that there is great variability within clusters. Cluster averages are statistical artefacts. They do not represent the actual profile of any set of observations.

Before starting cluster analysis, the total sample of observations may be randomly split into two sub-samples, one for the formation of clusters, the other for the validation of results. Available data are split into the factor scores used for cluster formation and descriptive variables, such as socio-economic variables, data on buying behaviour, and data concerning the use of products and media, that are used for the profiling of clusters in a later stage of typological analysis. Once the data has been prepared, cluster analysis is just a matter of grouping together those observations which are alike. The problem is how to determine likeness and how to group the observations.

In general, if the measurement level of data is metric (interval or ratio scaled) a distance measure may be employed. Distance measures seek out observations which are close together on all dimensions. If data are non-metric (nominal or ordinal scaled) another similarity measure, such as matching, is needed. Because factor scores are metric, a distance measure is adequate for establishing a customer typology. In most cases, a multidimensional version of Euclidean distance, the Mahalanobi distance, is used.

The most widely used form of grouping observations into clusters is hierarchical. This starts with all the observations being separate. That is, each customer in the sample is first considered a segment on its own. Then, the two segments (customers) that are most alike are joined to form a cluster. Step by step, similar customers are integrated. If two other customers are more similar to each other than to the formed cluster, a new segment is formed and similar customers are joined. From one step to the next the number of clusters continually decreases but their internal heterogeneity increases. The process continues until there is only one single segment left.

Because customers once attributed to a segment stay there throughout the following clustering steps, the critical question in hierarchical clustering is, how to measure the distance between two customers who have been joined and any other customer? The algorithm selected for that decision has far more influence on the final results than does the measure of likeness. The most widely recognized approach uses minimum variance within clusters as the rule for segment formation. This approach tends to produce robust, dense, spherical clusters with distinct characteristics.

Another way of forming clusters is called non-hierarchical partitioning. Here the number of clusters is decided at the start. For each segment, a starting partition is defined. For example, when k segments are to be formed, the first k customers may be selected as preliminary cluster centres and all other members of the sample may be evenly and randomly assigned to the k clusters. Then, in iterative steps, customers are shuttled from cluster to cluster in an attempt to minimize heterogeneity inside clusters and to maximize their difference. Segments are reformed until no further improvement of the homogeneity criterion can be achieved or a pre-specified number of iterations have been performed.

The best practice may be to take advantage of the strengths of both approaches, using hierarchical clustering first to form a reasonable number of clusters, then applying partitioning to re-allocate observations and clusters to find a best fit. Then hierarchical clustering may be reused to reduce the number of clusters and partitioning to find once again the best re-allocation solution. But both partitioning and hierarchical clustering approaches require the user to decide the number of segments in the final solution. The most common approach to do this is to observe the clustering process and note when the stress of bringing two clusters together becomes particularly large. A scree plot provides a graphical way of presenting the change in stress. It shows the change in error sum of squares when the solution goes from a higher to a lower level of the number of clusters. In addition, for practical purposes the usefulness of a segmentation solution is important for its choice.

When the number of segments is fixed their validity needs to be tested. A first step is to test the variability of observations concerning customer communication and buying behaviour as well as expectations (not used for clustering purposes) across clusters. A second step is to use a hold-out sample to do another cluster analysis and test the stability of the cluster results.

Description of typical cluster members

When clusters of consumers are formed on the basis of preferred activities, interests, and opinions, their typical members must be described in terms of buying, consumption, and media usage behaviour. This may be done through cross tabulation of cluster membership with buying, consumption and media usage data.

Source: Adapted from Churchill, G.A., Jr (1979), "A Paradigm for Developing Better Measures of Marketing Constructs", *Journal of Marketing Research*, February, 64–73; Saunders, J. (1994), "Cluster Analysis", *Journal of Marketing Management*, 10, 13–28; Stewart, D.W. (1981), "The Application and Misapplication of Factor Analysis in Marketing Research", *Journal of Marketing Research*, February, 51–62.

The business-to-business division, however, serving hairdressers, will not be confronted with potential customers having expectations that are homogeneous enough to be satisfied with a single bundle of value-generating activities. Further segmentation will be needed that may result in various groups of hairdressers, such as chain stores, discount stores, high fashion, and traditional stores. For that purpose, more precise data concerning hairdresser expectations and behaviour is needed. This is even more the case if the group of chain stores is to be further segmented according to the members' strategic positioning and resulting demands.

Objectives of customer segmentation

The general objective of customer segmentation is to improve the potential of an organization to make exchange offers that provide unique value to selected partners, thereby gaining the best value in exchange for the own organization. Based on this general objective, some more specific objectives can be derived.

Homogeneity

The first objective is segment homogeneity. Customer segments are to be determined in a way that maximizes their homogeneity in terms of internal similarity of customer expectations and relevant behaviour, yet simultaneously maximizes the difference in expectations and behaviour among segments. That is, homogeneity is not measured in terms of similarity of customer characteristics, such as age, income, membership of a certain industry, or function of the purchase decision makers inside their organization. Such characteristics are only used to describe the typical members of segments determined in a way that maximizes similarity of benefits sought and relevant behaviour of the customers.

The smaller the number of customers belonging to a segment the higher segment homogeneity tends to be. Segments of size one – as in the case of individualization – theoretically should be most homogeneous. Because of group decision-making phenomena and individual expectations as well as behaviour varying by situations, however, even segments of size one are not totally homogeneous over time. The problem is that decreasing sizes of segments very often go in parallel with lowered potential of contribution to the mission of the organization. That is, in determining customer segments, management must find a balance between the pursuit of greatest homogeneity and the potential contribution of segments to the success of their organization.

Contribution to the organization's mission

Having a customer segment that is homogeneous alone will not suffice. Serving the segment should also contribute to the fulfilment of the organizational mission. Non-profit organizations, such as street-worker associations or Amnesty International, will form customer segments in a way that contributes towards fulfilling their purpose more effectively. Profit-oriented firms will try to ensure that customer segments are substantial, attractive margins are provided, and that serving them is not in conflict with the organization's code of ethics.

Accessibility

Accessibility refers to the ability of an organization to reach effectively the potential customers in a segment. To be successful, the organization must be able to communicate with potential customers and to distribute its products to them. For that purpose, potential customers must be identified. But individual members of a segment may be more or less anonymous to the marketer. Many consumer markets, such as food products, consumer durables, or entertainment, are mass markets. Therefore, customers tend to be rather anonymous compared to business-to-business markets and government markets, unless the production or the delivery of the consumer product needs participation by identified consumers, such as in tourism, financial services, direct mail business, or in e-commerce, where a consumer database can be built up. The objective is to segment customers in a way that at least allows profiling of the "typical" members of each segment in terms of their communication and buying behaviour.

Responsiveness

Responsiveness refers to whether potential customers in a segment will react favourably to the offer of the organization. First estimates may be wrong in this respect. Shredded Wheat cereal has never become well established in the French market, for example, because it is too "British", yet the very "American" McDonald's, despite early conjecture that such a style of eating – alien to French habits – would never be accepted by local customers, has become a big success in France.

To avoid the risk of guessing, it seems reasonable to determine the most important factors influencing the responsiveness of a customer segment. However, such an analysis may require primary research that is too expensive for many smaller firms at that stage of marketing decision-making. To get a cheap but reliable estimate of how responsive potential customers in a segment might be to the offer of their organization, managers may evaluate existing direct or indirect contacts with customers from that segment. Fasti, an Austria-based small firm manufacturing special machines to dehydrate plastic granulates, for example, when assessing the attractiveness of East Asian customer segments, analysed some business deals which had been solicited by customers from those markets. The firm also analysed how much business it did already in that part of the world through indirect customer contacts, that is, by supplying to manufacturers of plastic extrusion machines located in Europe and the USA.

In international business an indicator of the responsiveness of a customer segment could be cultural or political prejudices which strongly influence the image of a potential supplier. For example, in many European countries, products manufactured in Germany, such as passenger cars or machinery, profit from a cultural prejudice that attributes particular technical skills and superior reliability to Germans. The level and kind of predominant international commercial relations of a country can also be a good indicator of the responsiveness of geographically defined segments. If potential customers in a country are used to daily business with suppliers from the home country of the business organization, it will be easier to approach those customers.

Stability

To be managerially useful, customer segments need a certain amount of stability. That is, the expectation profiles and relevant customer behaviour should be stable over a long enough period of time that setting up segment-specific systems of value creation and value generation makes economic sense to the supplier.

Note that stability is not defined in terms of segment members. What expectations customers have, what benefits they are seeking, and how they behave as customers may individually vary according to situations and over time. Some consumers in France, for example, may drop in at a local coffee shop in the morning to have a cup of coffee and a croissant, may then go out for lunch with a business partner to a first-class restaurant, and finally have a family dinner in the evening. In each situation they belong to a different customer segment in terms of expectations, benefits, and consumer behaviour. At any point in time, however, there will be a certain number of customers searching a specific bundle of benefits. They represent a segment, which is stable in managerial terms. That is, the coffee shop and the first-class restaurant will have clients all day long. These customers will be different persons but they will be very similar in terms of the benefits they are seeking. Thus, management of both organizations will be able to develop highly focused value offers for their customer segments.

The segmentation process

Figure 3.3 outlines the general sequence of steps to be followed in segmenting all the customers in a relevant market. Customer segmentation starts with management's choice of a basic segmentation approach. In the next step, the segmentation criteria best suited for the relevant market must be determined. Applying those criteria, the (potential) customers are grouped into segments that are highly different and internally homogeneous in relation both to their expectations and their behaviour. These segments then need to be profiled either by their specific expectations or benefits sought or by their typical characteristics and/or relevant behaviour.

Basic segmentation approaches

The choice of a basic segmentation approach is crucial for the homogeneity of resulting segments in terms of similarity of customer expectations and behaviour. It is also potentially related to the accessibility and stability of

defined customer segments. The degree of homogeneity, accessibility, and stability of segments in turn strongly influences the quality of marketing decision-making.

Organizations may segment their (potential) customers based on attributes that are either causally related to those customers' behaviour or based on the customers' current and potential future expectations, that is, the benefits they are seeking (Figure 3.4).

When choosing the first approach, management must determine what customer attributes have a significant influence on the behaviour of those customers in the relevant market. Based on the selected characteristics, attribute-homogeneous customer segments are determined. To check for homogeneity in terms of expectations and to gain a better idea of why the defined segments behave in different ways, profiles of typical customer expectations have to be established for each segment. In most cases, knowledge of typical customer attributes in the various segments eases the communicative as well as distributive access to those segments. However, the stability of segment-specific expectation profiles over time may turn out to be questionable.

Segmentation based on (potential) customers' current and potential future expectations starts with the

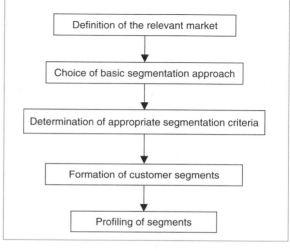

Based on the definition of the relevant market, customer segmentation starts with the choice of a basic segment-ation approach. Irrespective of whether character-istics/behaviour of the customers or their expectations are selected, in the next step the segmentation criteria best suited for the relevant market must be determined. Applying those criteria, the (potential) customers are grouped into segments that are highly different and internally homogeneous with regard to their expectations as well as customer behaviour. These segments are then finally profiled either by their specific expectations or benefits sought or by their typical characteristics and/or relevant behaviour.

Figure 3.3 The customer segmentation process

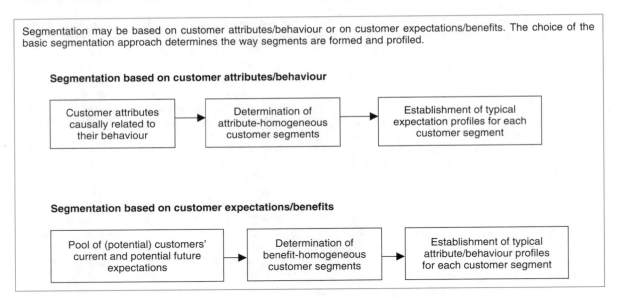

Segmentation may be based on customer attributes/behaviour or on customer expectations/benefits. The choice of the basic segmentation approach determines the way segments are formed and profiled.

Segmentation based on customer attributes/behaviour

Customer attributes causally related to their behaviour → Determination of attribute-homogeneous customer segments → Establishment of typical expectation profiles for each customer segment

Segmentation based on customer expectations/benefits

Pool of (potential) customers' current and potential future expectations → Determination of benefit-homogeneous customer segments → Establishment of typical attribute/behaviour profiles for each customer segment

Figure 3.4 Basic approaches to customer segmentation

establishment of an exhaustive pool of expectations. This pool is split into bundles of expectations which tend to occur together and, in addition, are as different as possible from other bundles of expectations. Each bundle of typically jointly occurring expectations stands for a benefit-homogeneous customer segment. The problem is that management does not know who those customers are. Therefore, to make the defined segments accessible in a focused and low cost manner, each customer segment needs to be profiled by the typical attributes/behaviour of the customers belonging to the segment. This may turn out to be very difficult because benefit-homogeneous segments tend to have varying members over time. On the other hand, they are rather stable in terms of benefits sought by those varying customers.

Depending on the chosen basic approach to segmentation, the following steps in the segmentation process will look different and may demand the application of different methods. These variations will be described in the following sections.

Choice of segmentation criteria

Whether attributes/behaviour of the customers or their expectations/benefits sought are selected as the basis of segmentation, in the next step the segmentation criteria best suited for the relevant market must be determined.

The choice of segmentation criteria determines the meaningfulness of any segmentation attempt. Selected

criteria should be easily measurable. That is, they should be directly observable or should be gathered fast and at a low cost. More importantly, segmentation criteria must have a significant impact on the customers' value perceptions. That is, they must causally influence the expectations as well as the buying, consumption, or usage behaviour of the customers. If the selected segmentation criteria are only easy to measure but not causally related to customer expectations and behaviour, even the most sophisticated segmentation techniques will not result in a managerially useful split of the market. For practical purposes, the selection of segmentation criteria very often is a compromise between behavioural relevancy and ease of data gathering.

Customer attributes

Most organizations prefer using customer attributes or behaviour for segmentation purposes. For example, characteristics of hairdressers, such as being located in cities versus in villages, the occupational structure of their clients, the turnover of the shop, or the competitive differentiation of the firm (traditional vs highly fashionable, cheap vs sophisticated), may significantly contribute to an explanation of the behaviour of those hairdressers in their business relationships with suppliers of hairstyling products. In the following section potential attributes to be used in consumer versus organizational customer segmentation will be discussed.

Potential attributes for segmenting consumers

Figure 3.5 contains a list of potential attributes to be used in consumer segmentation. In general, data concerning (socio-) **demographic characteristics** and purchasing behaviour are easiest to get hold of. Public administrations and private research firms, such as GfK or Nielsen, systematically gather such data. The problem with demographics is that they may not be the real causes for differences in consumer expectations and behaviour. Take for example 14- to 18-year-old females involved in higher education and having a high-income family background. Despite this relatively complex and restrictive definition of a consumer segment, suppliers of fashionable dresses, evening bars, museums, producers of CDs and many others will not find much homogeneity in expectations and consumer behaviour concerning their offerings.

Behavioural attributes, that is, data on consumer purchasing and consumption patterns such as recency, frequency, and monetary value of purchase, at least provide the opportunity to form homogeneous segments in terms of relevant behaviour. But in most cases it remains unclear why the members of segments formed with such data behave as they do. For example, if research data shows that 17 per cent of the US population consume about 80 per cent of the country's total beer production, this group may be described with characteristics such as age, level of education, income, or occupation. But there is no indication why those people drink that much beer. To make the segment accessible in terms of focused communication, additional information is needed about consumers' expectations and benefits sought. It may even turn out that the reasons why those people drink so much beer are significantly different and demand additional segmentation efforts.

Psychological attributes, such as motives, attitudes, or values, are more closely related to consumer expectations. But they are more difficult to measure, and their forecasting power concerning consumer behaviour has been shown to be rather limited. Measurement of **psychographic characteristics** is most complex and expensive. If standardized, data on consumer lifestyles, that is, specific combinations of activities, interests, and opinions, may be used for explaining expectations and relevant behaviour concerning consumer goods and services across national boarders (see Toolbox 3.4). This is particularly interesting for organizations serving several European markets where available socio-demographic data are still not entirely comparable.

Potential attributes for segmenting organizational customers

Figure 3.6 lists potential criteria for the segmentation of organizational customers. As in consumer segmentation, segmenting organizational customers based on one single customer attribute may be of limited success. **Demographic characteristics**, such as industry or location, as well as the technological level of customers may be useful to divide customers roughly into groups with significantly different expectations and behaviour. For example, customers in highly industrialized countries with a Latin culture will probably expect to be handled in a way that is clearly different from the expectations of customers in less industrialized countries with an Islamic culture. But such a rough segmentation most often does not provide information on how specifically to serve those customers. The differences in expectations and behaviour within each of such preliminary segments are still too great.

Segmenting organizational customers according to their specific **kind of value-generation processes**, for example attributing them either to process production (pulp and paper), series production (car manufacturing), or customized production (engineering), may provide better indications on how to serve customers in such segments. However, even selecting this characteristic will often lead to rather heterogeneous segments because other factors strongly influencing purchasing decision and product usage behaviour may not have been considered.

A list of examples of personal attributes which may be used as segmentation criteria in consumer marketing is as follows.

- **Demographic**: Age, gender, educational level, income/purchasing power, profession, location of residence (area, size of agglomeration, region, country), ethnicity, religion
- **Socio-demographic**: Social status/class, stage in family life cycle, role in family
- **Behavioural**: User status, intensity of use, urgency/reason/cycles of demand, usage situation, preferred points of purchase, frequency of purchase, purchase volume (value, sizes), brand/store loyalty
- **Psychological**: Motives, attitudes, involvement, preferences, values
- **Psychographic**: Personality, lifestyle (activities, interests, opinions)

Figure 3.5 Potential criteria for consumer segmentation

Because organizational procurement decisions may be taken both by individuals and by buying centres, potential segmentation criteria may be not only characteristics of the purchasing organization or the individual procurement manager but also attributes of the buying centre. Attributes are either directly observable or have to be derived from customer behaviour.

Directly observable attributes

- **of the organization**
  Demographic characteristics (location, size, industry, ownership, back market), organizational structure, applied technology, technological level (know-how, equipment, infrastructure), product application (kind of value-generation process), financial status, market share, financial or supply relationships with other organizations; user status, order size, purchasing frequency, kind of purchase, urgency of demand
- **of the buying centre**
  Size, structure, socio-economic profiles of decision makers (age, qualification, function, hierarchical level)

Indirectly observable attributes

- **of the organization**
  Objectives, philosophy, degree of centralization, purchasing rules (supplier selection criteria, purchasing process), purchasing behaviour (loyalty, sourcing, cooperativeness)
- **of the buying centre**
  Information behaviour, decision style, level of risk-taking, innovativeness, cooperativeness, roles of members, power structure;
  Importance of decision to individuals, personal motives, attitudes, personal risk-taking.

Figure 3.6 Potential criteria for segmenting organizational customers

Therefore, literature suggests that organizations wanting to serve organizational customers in a way that maximizes perceived customer value combine a number of customer characteristics in their segmentation effort.[4] In most cases, the use of a hierarchy of segmentation criteria will be appropriate. For example, the European customers of a steel maker such as Luxembourg-based Arbed might be segmented using the industry they belong to (automotive, durable consumer goods, machinery, construction), their annual consumption of steel, the quality standards they impose, and the intensity of customer service they require, in that order.

Selection of segmentation criteria

The selection of segmentation criteria from a list of customer attributes should be based on theoretical considerations as well as empirical evidence. There exists a substantial amount of knowledge about the drivers of consumer and organizational customer behaviour. Chapter 7 will elaborate on them. This knowledge helps to decide what kind of criteria basically to select. To make a reasoned selection inside the chosen category of criteria, however, management needs intimate knowledge of exchange processes in their relevant market. Toolbox 3.5 describes some tools available to support this step of the customer segmentation process. Because there is no single best way of segmenting a universe of potential customers and no way of finding "the right solution", alternative sets of segmentation criteria should be considered.

Customer expectations

In contrast to customer attributes, benefits customers expect to be generated by a certain product before, during, and after its consumption, use, or application are directly relevant to customer behaviour. They determine the meaning of the total product to the customer, defining its subjective value. Knowing the benefits sought by a customer group allows organizations developing, communicating, and distributing their product in a way to create the highest possible customer value.

Managers opting for benefit- or expectation-based segmentation of customers may either use product attributes, benefits derived from those product attributes, personal goals[5] that can be reached via those benefits, or cognitive structures relating two or all of those elements as criteria for defining customer segments.

Most of the expectation-based segmentation studies published in the literature have applied concrete or abstract **product attributes** indicated by potential

TOOLBOX 3.5

DETERMINATION OF APPROPRIATE SEGMENTATION CRITERIA

Multiple regression analysis and automatic interaction detection analysis are potential methods to help select customer characteristics that are suitable for segmentation purposes. They can help identify the attributes most strongly influencing the reaction of customers to an organization's offerings.

Multiple regression analysis

Multiple linear regression analysis is a statistical technique that provides management with information about the size and direction of linear and additive relationships of a number of potentially explanatory variables with another variable that is to be explained:

$$Y' = a + b_1 X_1 + b_2 X_2 + \ldots + b_n X_n$$

In this function, Y' is the estimate for the real value Y of the variable to be explained; a is a constant, and X_1 to X_n represent the explanatory variables. The values b_1 to b_n are called partial regression coefficients. They indicate the average change of Y as an effect of a unit change of the related X_i, holding off all effects from changes of other explanatory variables. The regression function is considered reliable if the regression error, that is, the difference between Y' and the empirically determined value of Y, is a minimum across all potential combinations of sizes of X_1 to X_n. The quality of the determined function is measured by the squared correlation coefficient between Y' and Y, which is called coefficient of multiple determination (R^2). This coefficient indicates the share of variance of the dependent variable explained by the regression function.

The size and direction of standardized partial regression coefficients indicate the importance of the explanatory variables for changes in the value of the dependent variable. Partial correlation coefficients may be calculated for each explanatory variable. Their square indicates the contribution of the explanatory variable to explaining the variance of the dependent variable that has not already been explained by other explanatory variables in the function. Therefore, multiple regression results can tell managers what customer attributes have what impact on the customers' relevant behaviour (for example, their frequency or volume of purchases of a certain product).

Proper application of multiple linear regression demands data at least measured on an interval level. But specific variations of multiple regression analysis that allow the use of data measured on ordinal or nominal levels have been developed. In addition, multiple regression is based on several assumptions concerning the explanatory variables as well as the regression error. Explanatory variables are assumed to have a stable influence on the dependent variable over time. They are assumed to be on the same level of causality concerning their explanatory power for the dependent variable. They have to be independent of each other and must not be influenced by the dependent variable. They are assumed not to interact, that is, their total effect on the dependent variable is equal to the sum of individual effects of all explanatory variables. And in linear regression, a linear relationship between each of the explanatory variables and the dependent variable is taken for granted.

The measurement error is the difference between the value of the dependent variable estimated by the regression function and the empirically determined value of the dependent variable. In multiple regressions it is assumed that the error is normally distributed (with a mean of zero) and its variance is the same for all value combinations of the explanatory variables in the statistical universe.

Automatic interaction detection analysis

Automatic Interaction Detection provides management with a means to explore interactions in a data set in a systematic manner. First, a dependent variable, such as sales volume or the response rate to direct mailings, has to be determined. The dependent variable should be of high importance to customer behaviour relevant for the organization. It must be measurable at intervals, although for practical purposes it is often converted to a dichotomous variable, such as using or not using a certain product. Explanatory variables, which are to be potentially used for segmentation, must have a theoretically based potential to provide an explanation why customers behave in a certain way. These predictor variables can only be split in a dichotomous fashion. This presents no problem for dichotomous characteristics, such as gender. But premature collapsing of other variables, such as age or industry membership, into a dichotomous split could obscure real differences in customer behaviour. For that reason, Chi-square Automatic Interaction Detection (CHAID) has been developed.

This method allows management to produce a tree diagram showing the most important predictor variables and interactions associated with the dependent variable. A chi-square significance test is used to identify the most significant predictors. Because the procedure relies on few assumptions about the data, it can be used in most situations. As a disadvantage, the significance of a chi-square test for independence is affected by the number of degrees of freedom. When the number of degrees of freedom for the chi-square test becomes too small, identification of significant predictors could be based on spurious effects. Therefore, in CHAID, a (Bonferroni) correction to the p-value is used to provide for that problem.

As a first step, CHAID forms full 2-way tables with the dependent variable for each potential segmentation characteristic. All eligible pairs of categories of a predictor variable are compared and similar pairs merged into a single category. Eligibility of category pairs depends on the type of customer attribute. For variables measured at a nominal level, any combination of categories is possible. For characteristics measured at ordinal level or higher, only adjacent categories can be merged. Pairs of the new categories are compared and adjusted p-values calculated. The sample is split using the predictor that has the lowest adjusted p-value. The new categories of the predictor are used to subdivide the sample into segments (see Exhibit A). The process is then repeated on the segments until no additional significant split is possible or until the segment size falls below a given level.

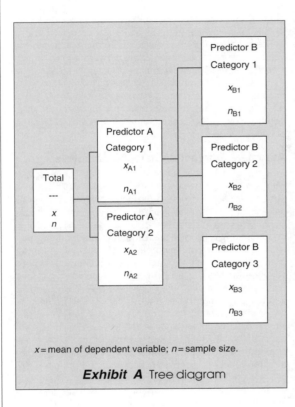

x = mean of dependent variable; n = sample size.

Exhibit A Tree diagram

Expectations × attributes – matrix

A major disadvantage of the above statistical techniques for determining appropriate customer attributes for segmentation purposes is the need for adequate databases. Despite the development of statistical methods allowing data to be used on lower measurement levels and relaxing most of the described assumptions, many small-sized profit and most non-profit organizations possess the necessary resources neither for gathering such data nor for purchasing them. But management has a lot of practical experience with customers that may be crosschecked in a non-representative qualitative fashion. Managers may use this intimate knowledge of their business to find appropriate segmentation criteria in a less technical but systematic way of reasoning. The tool to be used is called Expectations × Attributes – Matrix (see Exhibit B for an example).

To establish the matrix, all the customer expectations found in earlier stages of the market assessment process are listed. Expectations held by all customers at very similar observation levels are dropped from that list. The remaining expectations are listed in the lines of the matrix. Then management use their experience to find customer attributes having explanatory potential for differences in the remaining expectations across customers. These characteristics are noted in the columns of the matrix. For each attribute and each expectation the following question is asked: Does a difference in observation levels of this attribute lead to a difference in expectation levels? If yes, a cross is put in the respective case of the matrix, if no there is a blank left in the case. Finally, the crosses in each of the columns are added. The attributes reaching the highest sums of crosses are the best criteria for segmentation, because they explain most of the differences in customer expectations. If a combination of attributes is able to explain most of the variations in expectations, they may be used together for forming homogeneous segments.

Source: Adapted from Backhaus, K., B. Erichson, W. Plinke and R. Weiber (2000), *Multivariate Analysemethoden*, Berlin et al.: Springer; Mühlbacher, H. (1998), Différenciation stratégique, *Décisions Marketing*, 14, 23–30; Perreault, W.D. and H.C. Barksdale (1980), "A Model-Free Approach for Analysis of Complex Contingency Data in Survey Research", *Journal of Marketing Research*, 17, 503–515.

Exhibit B The Expectations× Attributes – Matrix

Attributes / Expectations	A_1	A_2	A_3	A_4	A_5	...	A_n
E_1: Effect	–	x	–	–	x	...	–
E_2: Price	x	–	x	–	–	...	x
E_3: Documentation	–	–	x	–	x	...	x
E_k: Personal relationship	–	–	x	x	–	...	x
Sum	1	1	3	1	2	...	3

A_1: Profession; A_2: Office size; A_3: Innovativeness; A_4: Age; A_5: Specialization: ...

customers as being the determinant of their choice.[6] The reason for this choice may be twofold. On the one hand, means–end chain theory[7] proposes that product attributes lead to consequences that may cause benefit perceptions of customers, which in turn are related to aspired values. Following this theory, product attributes stand for the meaning of a total product to a customer. On the other hand, using determinant product category attributes for segmentation purposes is rather easy. It demands less research effort than segmenting customers based on their perceived or expected benefits, personal goals, or even the structure of cognitive relations among preferred product attributes, benefits, and personal goals.

The problem with using product attributes for expectation-based customer segmentation is that attributes may only represent the functional part of customer benefits provided by a product. Additionally, a singular product attribute may result in more than one benefit perception. For example, the look of a dress may lead to the perceived benefits of individuality, comfort, and the fact that it goes along readily with other clothes. Vice versa, a number of product attributes may only provoke one single benefit perception of customers. For example, the tastiness, authenticity, freshness, and perceived quality of a dish may all lead to the perceived benefit of good taste. Therefore, using the **consequences** customers perceive as resulting from product attributes as segmentation criteria is more advisable. To stay with the example of the dish, such consequences could be variation (based on the attribute "broad assortment"), time saving (based on the attributes "convenience", "easy", and "quick preparation"), or healthiness (based on "tastiness" and "authenticity").

Personal goals, or what a person wishes to achieve,[8] may be better suited for benefit-oriented segmentation purposes than values, that is, what a person feels they do because of social norms. Because of their predominantly cognitive basis, personal goals are easier to research than values or motivations.

Finally, **cognitive structures** of customers towards the organization's product category may also serve as segmentation criteria. Customers may be grouped according to their similarity in cognitive relations among product attributes and perceived consequences and/or the similarity of relations among consequences and personal goals. Greatest homogeneity of customer segments results when segments are formed based on the similarities of total cognitive structures. However, the feasibility of such an approach is limited by the current lack of appropriate statistical procedures and the low probability of detecting highly similar individual cognitive structures.

Forming segments

Applying the selected segmentation criteria, the (potential) customers are grouped into segments that are highly different but internally homogeneous with regard to their expectations and behaviour.

Consumer segmentation

Consumer segments are formed in different ways depending on the basic approach to segmentation adopted by management. How consumer segments may be formed based on psychographic characteristics is described in the Toolbox 3.4. The International Spotlight provides an example of potential results from such a procedure.

The formation of segments based on consumer expectations is described in Toolbox 3.6.

INTERNATIONAL SPOTLIGHT

CONSUMER SEGMENTATION IN CHINA

A national survey of Chinese consumers conducted by Gallup Research Co. Ltd in 1997 included a minimum of 400 interviews and was conducted in major cities such as Beijing, Shanghai, Guangzhou, and Chongqing. Additional interviews in other areas classified as urban brought the total of urban sector interviews to 2609. The interviews lasted for about one hour and were conducted in seven primary languages. Each interview comprised more than 400 questions from a structured questionnaire. The results are shown in the following Exhibit A and Exhibits B–D.

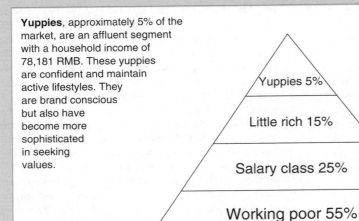

Yuppies, approximately 5% of the market, are an affluent segment with a household income of 78,181 RMB. These yuppies are confident and maintain active lifestyles. They are brand conscious but also have become more sophisticated in seeking values.

Little rich families constitute 15% of urban China. With a household income of 29,266 RMB, they are better off than most Chinese. They are socially active and brand conscious. However, they feel insecure and concerned about the future.

Salary class households consist of 25% of the urban population, have an annual income of 15,166 RMB, and are the largest group employed in the state sector. They are conservative and satisfied with the status quo, yet they are more established in social status and sometimes seek out foreign brands.

Working poor families represent 55% of urban China and have an annual income of 6917 RMB. They are largely impoverished, immobile, and the least satisfied. Most of their income goes on the necessities, leaving them little for other things. They buy mostly domestic brands.

Exhibit A The pyramid of China's urban consumer market

Exhibit B Urban consumer segments in China: Demographics

Segment/demographics	Working poor	Salary class	Little rich	Yuppies
Household income (RMB)	0–10,000	10,001–20,000	20,001–40,000	>40,000
Sample Percentage of total	886 (55)	406 (25)	241 (15)	78 (5)
Household income*	6,917	15,166	29,266	78,181
Family size	3.42	3.55	4.16	4.04
Age**	41.26	41.49	40.13	36.04
Sex (male) (%)**	54.7	46.2	46.7	64.1
Marital status (%)*				
Single	9.9	10.4	18.7	20.5
Married	84.7	88.6	78.0	78.2
Divorced/widowed	5.4	1.0	3.3	1.3
Education (%)*				
Elementary or less	28.6	9.9	11.2	2.8
Middle/high school	58.1	65.2	70.1	67.5
College plus	13.2	14.8	18.7	29.8

Occupation (%)*			
Business owners	5.2	6.2	15.2	29.1
Government employees	7.8	19.1	6.6	17.7
Professionals	14.2	17.1	20.5	17.7
Factory workers	24.4	22.8	19.8	13.9

Notes: Chi-square procedures were used for categorical variables such as marital status, education, and occupation.
* ANOVA F-value is significant at $p < 0.001$
** ANOVA F-value is significant at $p < 0.05$

Exhibit C Urban consumer segments in China: Psychographics, lifestyles, and media use

Segment/Dimension	Working poor	Salary class	Little rich	Yuppies
Consumer attitudes (%)				
Work hard and get rich*	45.7	26.8	43.3	32.0
Satisfaction with life*	68.0	83.7	72.5	79.8
Live one's own life*	33.1	40.4	36.7	48.0
Live a pure and honest life*	8.3	16.0	10.4	5.3
Willing to pay for brands*	43.5	53.0	43.4	67.6
Prefer foreign goods*	21.8	24.1	27.6	47.8
Lifestyle activities (%)				
Reading*	68.1	81.0	88.4	79.5
Going to movies*	29.3	39.8	48.1	51.3
Going to parks*	32.7	37.8	44.6	60.3
Domestic travel*	29.6	45.2	53.3	67.9
Karaoke bar*	25.0	33.3	47.7	50.0
Media use (minutes)				
Television time (insignificant)	136	139	143	146
Radio time***	57	40	41	42
Newspaper time***	44	43	52	60
Magazine time***	46	52	67	61

Notes: Based on media used the previous day and the amount of time spent using each medium.
* ANOVA F-value is significant at $p < 0.001$
** ANOVA F-value is significant at $p < 0.01$
*** ANOVA F-value is significant at $p < 0.05$

Exhibit D Urban consumer segments in China: Consumption patterns in selected products

Segment/Product	Working poor (%)	Salary class (%)	Little rich (%)	Yuppies (%)
Colour television*	73.4	89.9	93.9	100
Foreign brand	(62.5)	(63.5)	(62.2)	(50.0)
Microwave oven*	2.5	16.3	11.7	21.8
Foreign brand	(1.6)	(14.6)	(8.8)	(15.4)

Exhibit D (Continued)

Segment/Product	Working poor (%)	Salary class (%)	Little rich (%)	Yuppies (%)
Air conditioner*	6.4	12.1	19.1	46.2
Foreign brand	(5.2)	(8.4)	(14.9)	(30.8)
Compact disc player *	7.3	12.6	32	55.1
Foreign brand	(5.9)	(6.7)	(15.8)	(24.4)
Mobile telephone*	2.8	10.1	11.7	32.9
Foreign brand	(1.7)	(5.2)	(4.6)	(17.7)
Computer*	2.6	3.5	5.4	14.1
Foreign brand	(1.5)	(2.2)	(4.2)	(9.0)
Private car*	1.9	0.7	5.0	11.5
Foreign brand	(1.1)	(0.7)	(2.9)	(7.7)
Tea*	90.2	97.0	92.3	92.0
Ice cream*	16.6	35.4	34.2	37.2
Soft drink*	19.5	47.8	46.5	60.3
Beer*	46.8	67.7	50.2	71.8
Credit card*	4.1	10.6	10.8	40.0
Life insurance*	24.7	29.6	43.6	42.3
Foreign brand	(22.8)	(28.1)	(41.9)	(41.0)

Notes: Purchase of foreign brands is listed in parentheses.
*ANOVA F-value is significant at $p < 0.001$

Source: Adapted from Geng, C. and L. Qiming (2001), "Emerging Market Segments in a Transitional Economy: A Study of Urban Consumers in China", *Journal of International Marketing*, 9, (1), 84–106.

TOOLBOX 3.6

BENEFIT SEGMENTATION

Benefit segmentation was introduced in the literature by Haley[i] in the late 1960s. Since then it has gained some attention, but has not managed to become a widespread approach in consumer or organizational customer segmentation.

Benefit segmentation starts with the determination of product attributes that customers consider relevant.[ii] For this purpose data gathering techniques such as in-depth interviews, free association, triadic sorting, free sorting, or attribute selection are applied. In a *free association* task, respondents are asked to freely enumerate all relevant attributes of a given product category that come to their minds. They are not aided in that task by any lists. In a *triadic sorting* task respondents are confronted with

groups of three different products of the same product category. They are asked to indicate all-important attributes that are shared by the three products versus important attributes that are unique to individual products. In *free sorting* a great number of products from the same product category are presented to the respondents. Respondents are asked to group the products according to their similarity, and consequently, to indicate the product attributes that they used for grouping.

In a second step, the importance of each relevant product attribute to the customers has to be determined. Several techniques can be applied for that purpose. When using an *attribute selection* task, the previously determined list of product attributes is shown to the respondents.

Respondents are asked to select those attributes from the list that they consider important for the buying decision at hand. When applying a *constant sum technique*, respondents are asked to distribute a certain number of points across the attributes presented in a list according to their importance to them. The advantage of this technique is that it results in interval-scaled importance weights for the presented attributes. In a *dual questioning approach* respondents are asked to indicate the importance of the product attributes presented on the list (on a scale from "very important" to "totally unimportant") and how different those attributes are across offerings known to the respondent[iii] (on a scale from "very different" to "very similar"). By adding or multiplying the responses of each individual, this approach allows the researcher to find out what attributes are determinant for the customers' choice.

The selection of a data-gathering task will depend on the relevant market and the research objectives. The number of attributes considered important will vary depending on the importance of the product category and the importance of the purchase decision as perceived by the customers. In general, however, consumers use a rather restricted number of (3–5) product attributes for the evaluation of potential choices.[iv] In any case, the researcher must consider situation-specific changes in product attribute importance. For example, potential customers of tour operators will perceive varying attributes of winter vacation packages as important depending on whether they are thinking of a family vacation, a vacation with their spouse, or with their boy friend or girl friend.

Based on the results of importance measurement by a constant sum scale or dual questioning, the importance of product attributes in providing the benefits customers want can be further analysed by conjoint analysis. Conjoint analysis is based on experimental choice analysis.[v] In a choice-based conjoint task, respondents are confronted with choice sets of combinations offering systematically varied levels of product attributes deemed important. The respondents are asked to select the offerings they prefer. It is assumed that the choices of customers are based on the level of benefits (the utility) they can gain from the specific combination of product attribute levels of each choice set. Based on the choices made by the respondents, that is, their reactions to combinations of varied attribute levels, individual utility functions can be determined (Toolbox 5.2 describes conjoint analysis in more detail). These functions serve as a database for segmenting the potential customers by a clustering method.

Take the example of benefit segmenting potential customers of apartments in Germany. The researcher may present the description of a specific decision situation together with pairs or triples of systematically varied offers of apartments to a sample of potential customers. The offers contain information concerning attributes of apartments found to be considered important in the given situation by potential customers in a preceding study. Those attributes may be the size of the bathroom, the existence of a terrace or balcony, the number of apartments in the building, the type of street where the apartment is located, the thermal and phonic insulation, and the rent

to be paid per square metre. Each of the attributes may have three selected levels that cover the range of realistic possibilities.

The number of presented attributes is limited by their perceived importance and by the limitations of human information processing capacity. When the number of presented attributes exceeds a level of about 5, respondents will focus their attention on those attributes that seem more important to them. To avoid biases in data gathering due to tiredness, boredom, or learning effects, respondents can only be asked for a limited number of choices. Therefore, information about individual utilities is limited. Reliable individual utility functions on which segmentation should be based can hardly be determined. Aggregation of individual data, to raise the amount of information available for the statistical estimation procedure, on the other hand, is only feasible when individual utility functions are highly homogeneous. Because such a situation would make segmentation meaningless, for practical purposes, a two-step or multi-step approach is used.

As a first step, a preliminary analysis of individual conjoint data provides the input for cluster analysis. Segments of potential customers are formed based on a rough estimate of their utility function, that is, their specific profile of how much various product attributes contribute to the total perceived utility of an offer. In the example of the apartment market, there may be a group of customers who strongly value a low rent per square metre combined with superior thermal and phonic insulation of the apartment. Another group of customers may value more highly the size of the bathroom and the existence of a terrace or balcony, whereas a third group may derive most benefit from a low number of apartments in the building and the type of street where the apartment is located.

When applying a latent class approach, which has proven to be particularly efficient, respondents are not precisely assigned to one single segment.[vi] On the contrary, for each respondent, the probabilities of belonging to each of the individual segments, called latent classes, are calculated. Thus, the individual data of each respondent contribute to the determination of the utility functions of each latent class (segment).

The latent-class method is based on the assumption that the observed choices of respondents are based on a fixed number of "real" utility functions, each being typical for one segment of customers.[vii] Therefore, the number of latent classes is to be fixed beforehand. Typically, however, researchers do not have a clear notion of how many segments exist in the relevant market. Thus, they need to run the estimation procedure several times with varying numbers of potential segments. Then, statistical procedures such as the Consistent Akaike Information Criterion (CAIC) can be combined with pragmatic reasons to decide how many benefit segments should ultimately be considered.[viii] Such pragmatic reasons for preferring a certain number of segments may be the extent to which the formed segments seem sizable and accessible enough to be successfully served.

Product attributes are not the benefits customers seek. They only represent the means for reaching those benefits.

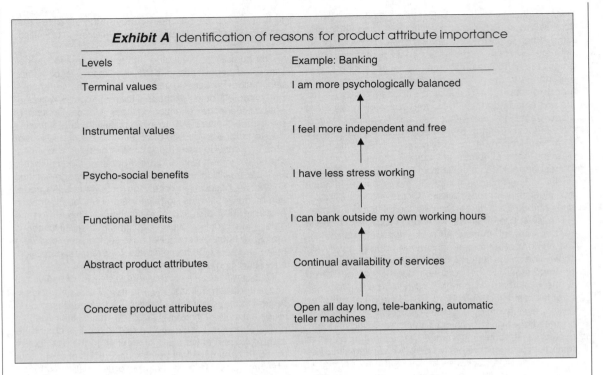

Exhibit A Identification of reasons for product attribute importance

Levels	Example: Banking
Terminal values	I am more psychologically balanced
Instrumental values	I feel more independent and free
Psycho-social benefits	I have less stress working
Functional benefits	I can bank outside my own working hours
Abstract product attributes	Continual availability of services
Concrete product attributes	Open all day long, tele-banking, automatic teller machines

In their attempt to form benefit segments, therefore, researchers may want to determine the reasons why potential customers regard the identified product attributes as important before they do any clustering. Despite various biases of which managers should be aware, the laddering procedure described in Toolbox 1.2 has been proposed in the literature as being applicable for that purpose.[ix] For each respondent, it results into a sequence leading potentially from concrete product attributes to terminal values (see Exhibit A). Individual ladders are considered measures of the respondents' real but non-observable means–end structures with respect to the product category in question.

The means–end chains of all respondents are statistically put into one multidimensional perceptual space. In this perceptual space, the distance between attributes, consequences, and values is a representation of their "closeness" defined by the probability that two items appear in the same ladder.

As a subsequent step, attributes, consequences, and values are clustered according to their coordinates in the multidimensional space. Each resulting cluster represents a "topic", that is, attributes, consequences, and values that were frequently mentioned together during the laddering task. Then, the ladders of individual respondents can be assigned to the "topic" best representing that ladder. The respondents clustered around a topic represent a specific benefit segment. Since this procedure allocates individual ladders to identified topics with only some probability, each individual can belong to more than one segment.

i.   Haley, R.J. (1968), "Benefit Segmentation: A Decision Oriented Research Tool", *Journal of Marketing*, July, 30–35.

ii. Mühlbacher, H. and G. Botschen (1990), "Benefit-Segmentierung von Dienstleistungsmärkten", *Marketing ZFP*, 3, 159–168.

iii. Vernette, E. (1987), "Identifier les attributs determinants: une comparaison de six methodes", *Recherche et Application en Marketing*, 2(4), 1–21.

iv. Hansen, F. (1976), "Psychological Theories of Consumer Choice", *Journal of Consumer Research*, 3, 117–142.

v.   Louviere, J.J. (1991), "Experimental Choice Analysis: Introduction and Review", *Journal of Business Research*, 23, 291–297.

vi. Kamakura, W. and G. Russel (1989), "A Probabilistic Choice Model for Market Segmentation and Elasticity Structure", *Journal of Marketing Research*, 26, 379–390.

vii. Teichert, T. (2000), "Das Latent-Class Verfahren zur Segmentierung von wahlbasierten Conjoint-Daten – Befunde einer empirischen Anwendung", *Marketing ZFP*, 3, 227–239.

viii. Kamakura, W., M. Wedel, and J. Agrawal (1994), "Concomitant Latent Class Models for Conjoint Analysis", *International Journal of Research in Marketing*, 11, 451–464.

ix. Botschen, G. and A. Hemetsberger (1998), "Diagnosing Means-End Structures to determine the Degree of Potential Marketing-Program Standardization", *Journal of Business Research*, 42(2), June 1998, 151–159.

Segmentation of organizational customers

The sequence of analytical procedures presented in Toolbox 3.5 may also be used in benefit segmentation of organizational customers.

For segmenting organizational customers based on their attributes, a multi-step segmentation approach seems to be most adequate. A suggestion in the literature was first to do a macro-segmentation of all potential customers on the basis of attributes of the customer organizations, followed by micro segmentation of resulting segments based on characteristics of the buying centres and their members.[9] There is only one step needed if the results of macro-segmentation fulfil the segmentation objectives. But may also be reached in three steps, starting with organizational attributes, followed by characteristics of the buying centre, and finally attributes of the members of the buying centres.

The problem with this approach is at least twofold: Data about the characteristics of buying centres and of people participating in a procurement decision process are more difficult to gather than data concerning organizations. It may be highly resource consuming if not impossible to find out who the members are of the buying centres in all potential customer organizations, what role they play at what time, and what their individual attributes are. In addition, the structure and the participants of buying centres may change from one purchasing decision to another, undermining the stability of available data for segmentation as well as segmentation results.

As a consequence, a nested approach to segmenting organizational customers has been suggested.[10] Following this approach, segmentation is started with easily recognizable attributes of organizational customers that are relevant for purchase decision-making, such as industry, size, location, technological level, or kind of purchase. If this first step leads to segments that allow the focused creation and generation of customer value, the segmentation process is stopped (Toolbox 3.7). If customer expectations and behaviour in the segments formed are still too heterogeneous, in a second step, more refined segments are formed using data that are more difficult to gather, such as the urgency or continuity of demand or the specific application of the product. In most cases, the segmentation process can be stopped at that level. If it has not yet led to segments coming up to segmentation objectives, data on expectations of buying centre members, such as the expected price level or the level of technical service, may need to be used for further segmentation.

TOOLBOX 3.7

A NESTED APPROACH TO SEGMENTING ORGANIZATIONAL CUSTOMERS

According to this approach, segmentation is started with easily recognizable attributes of organizational customers that are relevant for purchase decision-making, such as industry, size, location, technological level, or kind of purchase (see Exhibit A). If this first step leads to segments that allow the focused creation and generation of customer value, the segmentation process is stopped. For example, a metallurgical engineering firm, such as Austrian VA Siemens Industrial Engineering, would be able to clearly focus some of its marketing activities if it is able to define a segment of continuous-casting customers in the steel industry in highly industrialized countries who need to revamp their production line, and another segment of potential customers in newly industrialized countries planning to install new steel-making capacities.

If customer expectations and behaviour in the segments formed are still too heterogeneous, as a second step, more refined segments are formed using data that are more difficult to gather, such as the purchasing approach, the

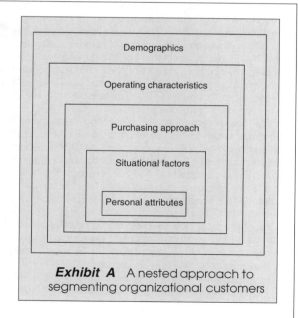

Exhibit A A nested approach to segmenting organizational customers

urgency or continuity of demand, or the specific application of the product. A manufacturer of yoghurt lids, such as Alu Swiss, for example, may find that there is a significant difference in expectations and buying behaviour between dairy companies in which the purchasing processes is led by a single procurement manager versus the entrepreneur or a production manager responsible for product quality.

In most cases, the segmentation process can be stopped at that level. If it has not yet led to managerially meaningful results, data on expectations of buying centre members, such as the expected price level, the level of technical service, user friendliness, or relationship building, may need to be gathered. A benefit segmentation approach may turn out to be fruitful.

Even if the sequence of characteristics suggested in Exhibit A may need to be changed depending on the relevant market to be segmented, this approach has proven to be managerially useful. Nevertheless, its resource-saving execution demands the establishment of a customer information system for effectively gathering, storing, and updating data on customer's decision-making processes.

Source: Adapted from Bonoma, T.V. and B.P. Shapiro (1984), *Segmenting the Industrial Market*, Lexington: Lexington Books.

Profiling customer segments

Finally, the customer segments formed through one of the processes described need to be profiled. Segments based on customer attributes are described by the expectations of their "typical member" or the benefits they are seeking (see International Spotlight). Resulting profiles must be significantly different to make managerial sense. If they are not different enough, the selected segmentation criteria have to be reconsidered. Toolbox 3.8 describes the potential statistical procedures to be applied in profiling segments.

TOOLBOX 3.8

PROFILING CUSTOMER SEGMENTS

When customer segments have been formed, each customer has a certain probability of belonging to a certain segment. For an organization to be able to reach the members of a segment by means of communication and distribution, the "typical" member of each segment must be described by data concerning their attributes, communication, buying and usage/consumption behaviour, and expectations. The question is which variables to select for a managerially useful description.

The best-suited variables for profiling segments will be those which contribute most to the explanation of differences in behaviour among segments. Management must search for the variables which best explain segment membership of customers. For that purpose, multivariate statistical techniques may be applied. The technique to select depends on the measurement level of available data and their level of accordance with the specific assumptions of the technique. In profiling customer segments, the dependent variable is segment membership, which in most cases is of a categorical nature. Some customer characteristics such as the age or disposable income of consumers, or the size of customer organizations as well as their urgency of need or the potential size of their orders may be ratio or interval-scaled. In such cases, discriminant analysis may be used for the selection of profiling variables.

Discriminant analysis is a regression-type treatment of data. It is applied for the explanation of the value of a nominally scaled variable with two or more categories when the available explanatory (independent) variables are metric, that is, when they are scaled on an interval or ratio level. The basic assumptions of discriminant analysis which need to be fulfilled by the data are that

- the relevant market consists of at least two segments with at least two members each;
- there are at least two variables used for profiling the segments, and not more profiling variables than the population of the smallest segment minus two;
- none of the variables used for profiling the segments may be expressed by a linear combination of the other descriptor variables (that is, variable A is not a combination of variables B + C + D + . . .);
- the covariance matrices are approximately similar among the segments (that is, the relationships among profiling variables are very similar across segments); and
- each segment represents a sample from a multivariate normally distributed population of descriptor variables (that is, for each segment the variables used for profiling this segment are normally distributed).

To avoid violating the assumptions of discriminant analysis, from the very beginning the number of customer segments should not be very large whereas the population of each segment should be substantial and approximately equal in size. The procedure starts with determining a linear combination of the profiling (i.e., descriptor) variables that best discriminates among the pre-specified segments. This linear combination is called a discriminant function. Additional discriminant functions may be determined which explain parts of the variance in the data not explained by previously formed functions. The standardized discriminant coefficients for each descriptor variable in each function indicate the variable's usefulness in profiling the segments.

Based on the discriminant functions and the individual value levels on each descriptor variable a discriminant value can be calculated for each customer in the sample. This discriminant value determines individual segment membership. It can be used to test the value of the discriminant functions for explaining segment membership. Actual segment membership is compared with estimated membership on the basis of discriminant values. In a classification matrix, the number of cases correctly attributed to segments compared to the number of misplaced cases is shown. The hit rate may be compared with a random result, with the probability of belonging to the largest segment, or with chance proportional to segment sizes. To avoid estimation bias caused by the use of the same sample for determining discriminant values and hit rate, the total sample may be randomly split in a calibration sample for the determination of the discriminant functions and a validation sample.

The nature of many variables to be potentially used for profiling segments precludes the use of interval, ratio or even ordinal measures. Some variables may by their very nature be categorical, for example the gender or socio-economic class of consumers, or industry membership as well as the technological level of organizational customers. In such cases, **Multinomial Logit Model Analysis** can be used to determine the best variables for explaining segment behaviour.

Logit models are a special class of log-linear models, which can be used to examine the relationship between a categorical dependent variable (segment membership), and one or more non-metric independent variables (for example, location). In a logit model, the value of the dependent variable is based upon the "log odds". It is the variation of this measure, which is to be explained by a (non-) linear function of the independent variables. Odds are the ratio between an individual's (customer) frequency of being in one category (segment) and the frequency of not being in that category. For example, if 20 per cent of potential customers belong to a segment and 80 per cent belong to other segments, then odds that a customer belongs to the segment are $20/80 = 0.25$. Statistical analysis is performed on the log of the ratio (the "logit") and the effects of the explanatory variables.

Source: Adapted from Agresti, A. (1990), *Categorical Data Analysis*, New York: Willey; Backhaus, K., B. Erichson, W. Plinke, and R. Weiber (2000), *Multivariate Analysemethoden*, 9.Aufl., Berlin et al.: Springer.

Customer segments formed on the basis of expectations or expected benefits are to be described by attributes and relevant communication, purchasing, and usage/consumption behaviour of their "typical member", by the product attributes such a typical member specifically prefers, and the values that are of high importance to such a model person. If no clear profile of attributes can be established, the benefit segments must be reconsidered, because the marketer will have difficulties reaching selected segments with the necessary focused communication and distribution activities.

Market segments

Customer segmentation will result in a number of groups that may not be equally attractive to serve. A comparison of segment attractiveness is needed to establish a rank order indicating which segments should be considered more closely. However, segment attractiveness does not only depend on the customers constituting the segment. Each segment is embedded in a market environment with a number of stakeholders more or less interested in or concerned with the (potential) exchange relationship of the

organization and its (potential) customers. Therefore, to be able to determine meaningfully the attractiveness of serving customer segments, the most important stakeholders in each of the segments have to be identified and analysed. Market segments or sub-markets are formed.

Important stakeholders may vary from one segment to another. They may have supportive or averse interests and more or less power to carry them through. Therefore, the attractiveness of customer segments will be raised or diminished by the existence of such stakeholders. For example, a British engineering firm which has developed a highly effective plant for the burning of industrial toxic waste may have identified the attractive-looking segment of chemical and pharmaceutical plants in Switzerland. The attractiveness of this segment is very much diminished, however, if green activists together with the media (via public administration) have the power to keep decision makers in the segment from buying.

External decision influencers such as consultants or the clients of the potential customers have to be determined. What plastic raw material a manufacturer of car bumpers will buy, for example, is strongly influenced by the specifications of the car makers. Those specifications will be a co-production of procurement, quality assurance, and marketing personnel of the manufacturer's clients. In institutional markets, the information search and supplier evaluation step often contains formal bidding requirements. Public agencies may be forced by law to accept the lowest bid that meets the particular set of specifications. International marketers who wish to compete in these markets must develop excellent relationships with the agents or consultants setting those specifications to be able to influence specification-setting beforehand.

To identify the most influential stakeholders for each segment, an exhaustive list of organizations, institutions, and people who actively participate in the value-creation system or have a vested interest in it, such as public administrators, legislators, environmentalists, or unions, is created. Then, their power to influence the value-creation system is analysed. For example, in a country such as France, unions may play a much greater role in the textile market than in Portugal or Greece, and a much lesser role than in Indonesia. The most important players and their specific interests are identified. The total information gathered up to that point is used for determining sub-market or market segment attractiveness.

SUMMARY

The first step in any strategic positioning process is to determine the relevant total market. The decision makers will use market characteristics important to them to check the general attractiveness of the relevant market. Then, the current state of the macro environment and its potential future developments are considered, before the present structure of the relevant market and its potential future shape are analysed more closely. To detect the stakeholders driving the value-creation system, the decision-making processes and the various relationships among stakeholders as well as potential customer purchase decision-making processes are analysed.

When scrutinizing their relevant market in such a careful way, management may become aware of the heterogeneity of this market. They may find various customers with different problems searching for benefits only to be provided by varying technologies. That is, the relevant market may comprise several sub-markets or segments. To allow economically meaningful allocation of scarce resources, these sub-markets need some closer inspection.

Customer segmentation may be based on attributes causally related to customer behaviour or on customer expectations. Therefore, the segmentation criteria best suited for the relevant market must be determined. Then the (potential) customers are split into segments that are highly different and internally homogeneous with regard to their expectations as well as behaviour. These segments are finally profiled either by their specific expectations or benefits sought or by their typical characteristics and/or relevant behaviour.

Customer segmentation will result in a number of segments that may not be equally attractive to serve. However, segment attractiveness does not only depend on the customers constituting the segment. Each segment is embedded in a market environment with a number of stakeholders more or less interested in or concerned with the (potential) exchange relationship of the organization and its (potential) customers. Therefore, the most important stakeholders related to each of the segments need to be identified. Market segments or sub-markets are formed. In the next step, the sub-markets will be assessed for their attractiveness and a rank order established indicating which segments should be considered serving. This process will be discussed in the following chapter.

Discussion questions

1. Why is it difficult to define exactly the boundaries of the relevant market of an organization? Discuss.
2. How can the substantiality of a relevant market be estimated? Select an example, gather the information you need, and come up with an estimate.
3. Contact a company selling to organizational customers. Try to find out who are the drivers of (one of) their value-creation system(s), and what the purchase decision-making processes look like inside the organization of these "real customers".
4. What methods of exploring customer problems and related expectations do you know? Take one of them and prepare a presentation of its practical application for your class.

5. Discuss the basic differences between segmenting customers by their attributes versus their expected benefits. What are the pros and cons of each alternative?
6. Contact an organization of your choice and ask the managers if they segment their customers and how. Try to find out the reasons for their approach and prepare a discussion for class.
7. How would you suggest determining the best-suited customer segmentation criteria for a market of your choice? Explain your reasons why.

8. Explain why a nested approach to segmenting organizational customers may be useful.
9. Search for an example of a typological analysis in the library or the Internet and explore the applied methodology. Are there any differences to what has been explained in Toolbox 3.4?
10. How can adding information about additional stakeholders and competitors to a customer segment change the view about the attractiveness of that segment? Explain by using a positive and a negative example.

Notes and references

1. Roberts, D. (1997), "Where's that Pot of Gold", *Business Week*, February 3, 54–59.
2. Yavas, U., E. Babakus, and N. Delener, "Family Purchasing Roles in Saudi Arabia", working paper 1991.
3. Woodside, A. and N. Vyas (1987), *Industrial Purchasing Strategies*, New York: Lexington Books.
4. Wind, Y. and R. Cardozo (1974), "Industrial Market Segmentation", *Industrial Marketing Management*, 3, 153–164.
5. Jolibert, A. and G. Baumgartner (1997), "Values, Motivations, and Personal Goals: Revisited", *Psychology & Marketing*, 14(7), 675–688.
6. Moriarty, R.T. and D.J. Reibstein (1986), "Benefit Segmentation in Industrial Markets", *Journal of Business Research*, 14, 463–486.
7. Reynolds, T.J. and J. Gutman (1988), "Laddering Theory, Method, Analysis, and Interpretation", *Journal of Advertising Research*, 28 (February/March), 11–31.
8. Emmons, R.A. (1989), "The Personal Striving Approach to Personality", in L.A. Pervin (ed.), *Goal Concept in Personality and Social Psychology*, Hillsdale, NJ: Lawrence Erlbaum, pp. 87–125.
9. Wind, Y. and R. Cardozo (1974), op. cit.
10. Bonoma, T.V. and B.P. Shapiro (1984), *Segmenting the Industrial Market*, Lexington: Lexington Books.

Further reading

Firat, A.F. and C.J. Shultz II (1997), "From Segmentation to Fragmentation, Markets and Marketing Strategy in the Post-modern Era", *European Journal of Marketing*, 31, (3/4), 183–207.

Wedel, M. and W.A. Kamakura (1998), *Market Segmentation. Conceptual and Methodological Foundations*, Dordrecht: Kluwer.

4 Strategic positioning step 2: Assessing the attractiveness of markets and the relative competitive position

Learning objectives

After studying this chapter you will be able to

1 Assess comparatively the attractiveness of markets
2 Derive success factors for each market
3 Derive success factors from challenges of the macro environment
4 Determine the most important competitors in each market
5 Assess the relative competitive position of an organization

SPOTLIGHT

Papierfabrik Wattens AG, a member of the privately held Trierenberg Holding AG, is one of the world-leading producers of cigarette paper, and is committed to becoming the number one supplier of the cigarette industry. With 330 personnel the company has a share of about 14 per cent of the cigarette paper and plug wrap paper world markets. To achieve its objective of becoming the number one supplier in the world, management of the relatively small Papierfabrik Wattens has to assess carefully the attractiveness of the various sub-markets of its relevant market and determine the firm's competitive position in those markets in order to spend available resources in the most effective way.

At the beginning of the 21st century, the top cigarette-producing countries in the world are China (30.5 per cent of total production), the USA (12.4 per cent), Indonesia (4 per cent), and Japan (3.4 per cent). Four customers dominate the world market. Global trends to be turned into opportunities are: increasing regulations and restrictions concerning cigarettes, the marketing of cigarettes and places where people can smoke; as well as changes in smoking behaviour and in the structure of customer markets. The increasing number of women choosing to smoke and the growing number of younger smokers both increase the demand for newly designed cigarettes. This trend is reinforced by the fact that in economically developing countries the smoking of cigarettes is a sign of status.

Mega-mergers in the cigarette industry lead to increasing volumes of cigarette paper supplies, standardization on a global level, negotiation with central procurement units, and increasing demands on supply chain management.

Success factors in supplying to world-leading cigarette producers seem to be: a company philosophy that is strongly committed to tobacco, a high and profitable market share, substantial production capacity, a full range of products, quality assurance at the latest level, continuous technical improvement, strong R&D capabilities, environmental commitment, and assurance of the supply chain to customers. Only if Papierfabrik Wattens is able to excel on these success factors compared with its major competitors it will be able to reach the set objective.

Market attractiveness and competitive position

The previous chapter has shown that often the relevant market of an organization consists of a number of sub-markets or segments with differing customer expectations, competitors, and other important stakeholders. To allow a selection of sub-markets to be served and for economically meaningful resource allocation decisions to be made, the attractiveness of the detected sub-markets needs to be assessed. In this process, first of all, evaluation criteria have to be selected that are relevant to the business domain of the organization. Objectives and priorities of the organization as stated in the core strategy may serve as a guideline to assessment criteria selection (Figure 4.1).

Based on the selected criteria the sub-markets can be evaluated. To make evaluations more reliable, comparable among evaluators, and open for informed discussion, for each of the selected assessment criteria a measurement scale has to be defined that can be applied across all market segments that are to be assessed. The assessment procedure results in a rank order of sub-markets by their attractiveness. Focusing any further analysis on the most attractive sub-markets reduces the amount of data gathering and treatment in the following steps of the process.

The selection of markets to serve cannot only be based on their attractiveness, because this has been assessed independently of the organization's available capabilities. Management must now determine if their organization possesses the capabilities necessary for successfully serving those sub-markets. To that end, first of all, the most important stakeholders in each of the attractive sub-markets are screened for their specific expectations. These are added to the list of current and potential future customer expectations to be satisfied. Starting from this list of expectations, the capabilities an organization needs in order to fulfil them attractively are determined for each sub-market. That is, market-segment-specific lists of success factors are created.

These lists of success factors are used for a comparison of the main competitors' strengths and weaknesses with those of their own organization, resulting in a picture of positively as well as negatively differentiating capabilities.

The relative competitive position of the organization can be determined for each of the attractive sub-markets. The attractiveness of the sub-markets together with the relative competitive position of the organization in each of those sub-markets will serve as essential bases for the final selection of markets to serve.

This chapter discusses each of the steps outlined in the strategic positioning process which have to be gone through: from the assessment of potential sub-markets to the determination of the relative competitive positions in each of the most attractive sub-markets.

Assessing sub-market attractiveness

To determine and compare sub-market attractiveness, management can select assessment criteria, develop measurement scales on each of the criteria, evaluate the attractiveness of each sub-market or market segment, and, finally, compare the results among sub-markets/segments.

Assessment criteria

Figure 4.2 shows a list of potential factors of influence on sub-market attractiveness as they are cited in the literature.

Each of the criteria may be partly useful for preliminary screening. But to be valuable for strategic positioning purposes, the assessment of potential new sub-markets must be based on criteria which are relevant to the business domain of the organization. Political risk may be a relevant characteristic, for example, if the business of the organization demands investment in various international markets. It may be totally irrelevant, however, if the organization intends to sell products to customers who do not need any after-sales service. Which criteria are the most relevant will vary from one business to another.

To select strategically and operationally meaningful assessment criteria, managers need a guideline. Most often, decision makers select assessment criteria based on perceived current strengths and weaknesses of their own organization. However, such a selection guideline masks the "real" attractiveness of segments. It inhibits decision-makers from finding sub-markets attractive

To allow economically meaningful resource allocation decisions, the attractiveness of the relevant sub-markets needs to be assessed. First, evaluation criteria are selected. Then, the sub-markets are evaluated, resulting in a rank order by attractiveness, which reduces the amount of data gathering and analysis in the following steps of the process. In order to select the markets to be served, management must determine if their organization possesses the capabilities needed to serve successfully the most attractive sub-markets. First, the most important stakeholders in each of the attractive sub-markets are analysed for their specific expectations, which are added to the list of customer expectations to be satisfied. Starting from this list of expectations the capabilities an organization needs to attractively fulfil them, that is the success factors, are determined for each sub-market. The lists of success factors are used for a comparison of the main competitors' strengths and weaknesses with those of the own organization, resulting in a picture of positively as well as negatively differentiating capabilities. The relative competitive position of the organization can be determined for each of the attractive sub-markets.

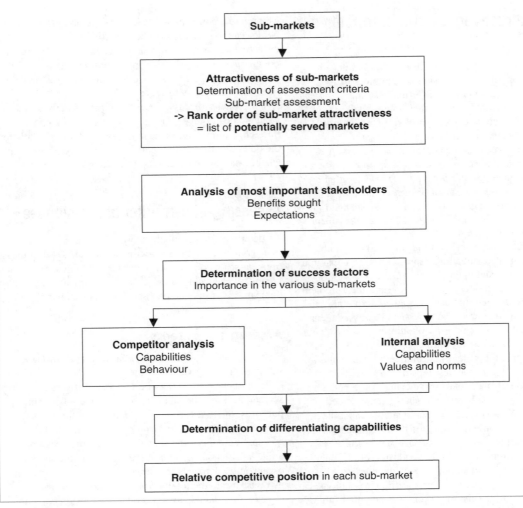

Figure 4.1 The strategic positioning process Part 2: Assessing the attractiveness of markets and the relative competitive position

Mainly based on their mission statement, organizations must develop their individual list of assessment criteria for sub-market attractiveness. An overview of potential criteria may help in this respect.

Market factors

Potential	Price sensitivity
Volume	Negotiation power of customers/suppliers
Number of customers	Constancy of demand
Growth	Diversity of expectations

Competitive factors

Type of competitors	Degree of concentration
Intensity of competition	Speed of competitors entering/leaving the market
Danger of substitution	Dynamics of change in market shares

Economic/financial factors

Achievable margins	Access to resources
Market entry/exit barriers	Experience/scale effects
Intensity of needed investments	Usage capacity

Technological factors

Technological level	Specificity of needed investments
Differentiation potential	Technical complexity
Access to know-how	Speed of technological change

Environmental factors

Social acceptance	Legal regulations/technical norms
Taxation	Influence of interest/pressure groups

Figure 4.2   List of potential factors of influence on sub-market attractiveness

where the organization currently does not possess the capabilities needed to serve them successfully. The result is a simple reproduction of market segment choices the organization has made more or less consciously so far.

In contrast, objectives and priorities of the organization as stated in the core strategy may well serve the purpose of giving a guideline to assessment criteria selection. For example, if a company seeks a high return on investment, it must select markets in which it can achieve a leadership position, in which demand is high in relation to supply, and in which customers have sufficient purchasing power. Therefore, the size of competitors present in the market, the ratio of market potential to market volume, and the economic wealth of potential customers may be relevant criteria for assessing sub-market attractiveness.

Measurement scales

When the decision makers have selected the assessment criteria they want to use, they could start evaluating the sub-markets they have formed by comparing them on each of the criteria. In most cases such rank ordering is a rather simple procedure which can quickly be accomplished. Its disadvantages are that individual evaluators may apply different logical bases of assessment, which stay

unmentioned, and that assessments will result into a mainly emotional rank order of market segments on each of the criteria. In addition, there is a formal reason why rank ordering of sub-markets on various evaluation criteria is not advisable. Ranks cannot be added or averaged, and therefore, no total attractiveness score for each of the sub-markets can be determined.

To make evaluations more reliable, comparable among evaluators, and open for informed discussion, for each of the selected assessment criteria, a measurement scale has to be defined that can be applied across all sub-markets to be assessed. Decision makers will have few problems in defining quantitative scales for criteria such as market volume, attainable average margins, or necessary continual investments into research and development. Difficulties may arise for rather more qualitative criteria such as intensity of competition, technical complexity, or social acceptance. For such criteria, managers need to agree first on an operative definition of the criteria relevant for their kind of business and then find indicators allowing measurement of the defined phenomena. As an illustration of the difficulties management may encounter during such a process, Appendix 4.1 discusses various views on what determines the intensity of competition. Based on a shared view of what is driving competition in the relevant market of their organization emerging from such a discussion, management may decide, for example, to measure intensity of competition by the reaction time of competitors to the launch of an innovative product, or competitor reactions to a price cut.

When the decision makers have agreed on the measurement scales to be used, the attractiveness of all sub-markets may be assessed.

Assessment procedure

For the comparative evaluation of sub-market attractiveness, profit-oriented organizations may estimate the net present values of investments in building and maintaining successful business relationships with the customers in each segment. Alternatively applied scoring models in many cases provide more reliable results.

The attractiveness of sub-markets may be assessed according to the substantiality of the segments, their ease of access, their responsiveness to activities of the organization, and their potential contribution to the fulfilment of the organization's mission. Each of these super-criteria needs to be expressed by specific criteria depending on the business of the organization. For each of the criteria, a measurement scale must be determined to allow inter-subjective comparison of evaluations. The following table gives an example.

Assessment criteria	Weight	Evaluation			Measurement scale
		Seg 1	Seg 2	Seg 3	
Substantiality Volume (in units per year) Growth (in % of volume)					<50 = 1, 260–450 = 3, >660 = 5 <0 = 1, 4–6 = 3, >10 = 5
Accessibility Intensity of competition					Competitors react to organizational activities: with aggressive frontal attack = 1 avoiding frontal attacks = 3 cooperatively = 5
Danger of substitution					Customers: search for other technical solution s 3 = 1 are satisfied with current technical solution = 3 no other technical solutions seem feasible = 5
Responsiveness Urgency of need					Average lead time: <3 weeks and > 14 weeks = 1 6–7 weeks and 13–14 weeks = 3 10 weeks = 5
Innovativeness					Segment members tend to be: laggards = 1 followers = 3 innovators = 5
Contribution to mission Attainable margins (in %) Price sensitivity					<10 = 1, 18–22 = 3, >30 = 5 Loss of market share to major competitor at a price difference of 10% ≥ 10 = 1, 4–6 = 3, 0 = 5
Fit with code of ethics					Serving the segment: conflicts with ethical standards = 1 is in line with ethical standards = 3 reinforces ethical standards = 5
Sum	100				

Scale: 1 = very unattractive
          3 = average
          5 = very attractive

Market segment attractiveness = $\dfrac{\text{Sum of scores}}{100}$

Figure 4.3 A scoring model for assessing sub-market attractiveness

Instead of exclusively relying on estimates of future streams of income, scoring models use a broader range of information, including exchange relationships with other important stakeholders (Figure 4.3). Scoring models based on adapted assessment criteria may also be used by non-profit organizations.

The scoring procedure may be based on the assessment of sub-market:

- substantiality (e.g., volume and growth),
- accessibility (e.g., intensity of competition and danger of substitution),

- responsiveness (e.g., urgency of need and innovativeness), and
- contribution to the mission (e.g., attainable margins, price sensitivity, and fit with code of ethics).

In international marketing, the market assessment procedure is more complex. As illustrated by the International Spotlight it consists of at least two steps. The first step is to reduce the great number of potential geographically/politically defined markets to a preliminarily attractive looking short list that is assessed more closely in a second step, which may be similar to the one described above.

INTERNATIONAL SPOTLIGHT

ASSESSING GEOGRAPHIC SUB-MARKETS

In assessing the attractiveness of geographically or politically delineated sub-markets, such as countries or economically cooperating regions, managers first select evaluation criteria from the macro and operating environments of those markets based on the corporate policy of their organization (see Exhibit A). With regard to the macro environment, for example, legal measures such as restrictions on advertising can be effective barriers to entry in a sub-market that otherwise would seem attractive to an organization. Take the example of the Chinese smoking market. Because of its enormous population and entrenched smoking habits, the Chinese market looks very attractive to every tobacco products marketer. Legal ban on tobacco advertising, however, reduces this attractiveness: China has adopted total bans on all forms of tobacco promotion, including posters and magazine ads.

Companies that give a high priority to technological innovation tend to favour sub-markets characterized by high levels of technological sophistication where customers seek technical solutions that require significant research and development. Other companies prefer sub-markets in which their level of applied technology fits the needs of the targeted customers. Thus, a Portuguese producer of hand scythes may not consider Danish homeowners as attractive customers, but may be very interested in potential markets in sub-Saharan Africa. Relevant market assessment criteria in those cases might be the level of technological sophistication reached, the quality of available infrastructure, or the availability and quality of higher education institutions.

Companies that rely on their global identity and the goodwill of intermediaries, customers, and suppliers will look for sub-markets in areas where their home country or company name has already earned a positive reputation. A Danish marketer of food products such as yoghurt, cheese, pork meat, or bacon, for example, will focus on sub-markets where Denmark is known as a country

that manufactures high-quality food. It will not consider markets in which Danish products are avoided for ideological, political, or religious reasons. In such cases, managers will find criteria, such as volume of imports, amount of political influence on individual firms, legal restrictions concerning their market, or influence of religion on purchase decisions, as relevant for the assessment of sub-market attractiveness.

In a second step, the sub-markets are classified by selected criteria to narrow their number to the markets of greatest attractiveness. The exclusion procedure consists of (1) a stepwise application of knock-out criteria or (2) a grouping of sub-markets into homogeneous clusters and a subsequent rank ordering of the remaining markets through a scoring model.

1. Stepwise market exclusion
    In the first case, management applies evaluation criteria, which allow the exclusion of sub-markets if they do not reach a given standard. For example, a producer of cellular communication equipment such as Sweden-based Ericsson may exclude markets from further investigation if they lack the needed infrastructure. From the remaining markets some may have technical norms (they use a specific communication technology) the company is not able to or does not want to fulfil. In the case of Ericsson this could be, for example, Japan using a standard that is different to the European norm. The reduced number of markets is further diminished when all country-markets are deleted where legal restrictions, such as state monopolies or required import licenses, make market entry extremely difficult. Finally, the list of potential markets may become even shorter, if Ericsson's top management has set ethical standards which do not allow for serving markets where dictatorships exist.

The major advantage of this market exclusion procedure is its simplicity and speed. The use of assessment criteria that lead directly to the elimination of a number of country-markets is appropriate, if the criteria are directly related to the corporate policy of the firm, such as ethical standards, or represent constitutive features of the chosen product-market, such as the level of electrical supply infrastructure for a marketer of refrigerators.

There are several disadvantages to be considered, however. First, the application of KO criteria tends to support market assessment dependent on the firm's existing strengths and weaknesses. Even very promising markets will not be further considered if, currently, the firm does not possess the necessary skills and resources to serve them successfully. For example, when a Belgian firm assesses the attractiveness of international markets in the field of sewage disposal, they may use "existing customer relations" and "available language skills" as part of the assessment criteria. The result may be a restricted choice of markets: the attractive US market will not be considered further, because the company does not have any relations with potential customers there, and all Spanish-speaking countries are ruled out because of a lack of language skills. Such a procedure deprives a company of any perspective of strategic international development.

Second, the stepwise use of assessment criteria does not consider trade-offs between different market characteristics. For example, the quality of available telecommunication and transportation infrastructure in the Czech Republic might not be up to the level of neighbouring Germany, but labour costs are only about 10 percent. If both factors are of importance for a firm, such as a Japanese producer of textiles or a Korean manufacturer of cars considering implantation in Europe, it is important to use them simultaneously when comparing the attractiveness of the markets. Market clustering based on a set of assessment criteria is an appropriate solution.

2. Market clustering

The procedure used in sub-market clustering consists of the following steps:

– Splitting the global market into groups of geographic sub-markets so that the resulting clusters are more homogeneous than the global market as a whole.
– Describing the "typical" member in each cluster.
– Evaluating the attractiveness of each cluster.
– Selecting the most attractive cluster or clusters for further analysis.

Geographic markets will be most effectively clustered with criteria that consider the specifics of the relevant

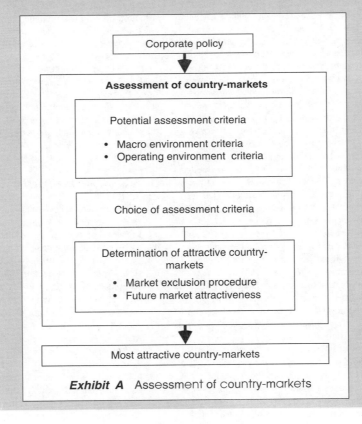

Exhibit A Assessment of country-markets

market. Characteristics often used include the product related purchasing power of potential customers, the growth rate of the relevant market, profit-generation potential, transferability of funds, number and size of competitors (intensity of competition), availability of intermediaries, or local subsidies readily available to the internationally operating organization. For example, US companies, such as Dell Computers, entered the markets of the European Community via Ireland. They did so because total labour cost is relatively low and the Irish government offers attractive incentives for new industrial plants. Assessment and market selection in such a case depends on strategic considerations, not just on easily accessible, general data about the macro environment of potential markets, such as GNP, number of inhabitants, or average household income.

Geographic markets belonging to the cluster(s) of attractive sub-markets are further investigated. If the number of these markets is still too big to allow a quick and cost-efficient analysis of details, a scoring procedure can be used to rank order the sub-markets according to their relative attractiveness. Only for the best-ranked sub-markets will future opportunities and threats be estimated.

The sub-markets achieving the highest scores are the most attractive. They will be primarily considered in the following steps of the strategic positioning process. But in many instances the decision to serve a sub-market or a market segment commits the resources of an organization for a considerable amount of time. Therefore, the decision should not be based on the current attractiveness of a market alone. It should also consider potential changes in market attractiveness that may arise from future developments in environmental conditions or from the activities of the organization.

Future changes in attractiveness

To get an estimate of the impact of a sub-market on the attractiveness of potential future developments in the macro and operating environments, the scenario technique described in Toolbox 1.2 can be applied. In addition, gap analysis as shown in Figure 4.4 is a tool to grasp potential changes of sub-market attractiveness caused by activities of the organization. The potential of total sales in a sub-market is never fully exhausted. The current market volume may be increased through a stimulation of use

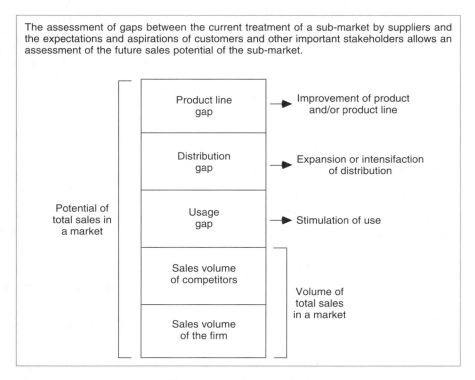

Figure 4.4 Gap analysis

(usage gap), an expansion or intensification of distribution (distribution gap), or an improvement in the total product (product gap).

By analysing what gaps exist in a sub-market and to what extent, management can determine the potential of their organization to expand the current total sales volume in this segment. The final result of the described analysis will be a rank order of attractiveness of the sub-markets constituting the relevant market of the organization.

Determining the relative competitive position

The relative competitive position of an organization in a market depends on its differentiating capabilities, that is, on the strengths and weaknesses of the organization compared to its major competitors (Figure 4.1). Many managers tend to determine the strengths and weaknesses of their organization by answering two questions: "What are we good in?" and "What are competitors able to do better?" In general, answers to these questions can be found quite quickly. But these answers might simply reflect the preferences and prejudices of the respondents combined with their response styles and micro-politics.[1] If, for example, a manager who is responsible for market communication tends to have a critical view of things and considers the resources allocated to communication purposes to be insufficient, he or she will state that market communication is a weakness of the organization. If, on the other hand, the person is rather more optimistic and wants to defend what she or he has done so far, this manager may state that market communication is a strength of the organization.

This approach to determining an organization's strengths and weaknesses is not only highly subjective but may also lead to disagreement among managers. There is also the problem that the selection of criteria for comparison with competitors is totally arbitrary. A comparative analysis between the organization and its major competitors may be done over a great number of criteria. To be efficient and effective, however, such a comparison of strengths and weaknesses should only focus on capabilities, that is bundles of resources and related skills needed by an organization to serve successfully a given market at present and in the future.[2] For example, to serve successfully customers such as Nokia, Intel, Siemens, or Alcatel with die-bonding machines (fixing microchips on substrates) a supplier will need high innovation capacity, flexible process organization, close relationships with customers leading the technological development, and effective recruiting of highly skilled personnel. These capabilities are called success factors. Success factors can be determined in various ways.[3] It is essential, however, that success in business and therefore factors leading to success are always related to the creation and generation of superior stakeholder value (compared to competitors) under certain conditions of the macro environment.

In the following, the logical steps in a process of determining an organization's relative competitive position as presented in Figure 4.1 will be discussed in detail.

Success factors

When searching for the success factors in a sub-market, an organization has to make a clear distinction between core factors and success factors (Figure 4.5).

Core factors

Core factors are the capabilities an organization needs to be considered as a relevant exchange partner by the (potential) customers and other important stakeholders in this sub-market, and to be able to master present and future challenges from the macro environment.

A Brazilian producer of pharmaceuticals not able to provide the medical test information required by French medical administrators will not be able to participate in that market, for example. Thus, the competitors in the pharmaceutical market in France will not be different from one another, as far as the capabilities necessary for providing test information are concerned. To attract Scandinavian and British summer tourists, as another example, a vacation area must be able to guarantee sunshine. Italy, Greece, and Spain, competing for those tourists, can satisfy the demand, but they are not different from each other regarding that core factor. The decision by Scandinavian customers of what country to choose for their summer vacation will depend on other criteria, such as the quality of services, the opportunity to relax or to socialize, or the price level, depending on the customer segment. The bundles of skills and resources needed to be evaluated as being more attractive than competitors on those criteria are the so-called success factors.

Success factors

Success factors are the capabilities an organization needs in a sub-market to distinguish itself attractively from its competitors – seen from the potential customers' and other most important stakeholders' point of view – and to be able to profit from present and future challenges from the macro environment of this sub-market. Business success will depend on how the organization scores on these factors compared to its major competitors.

Determination of success factors in the market environment

Management need to determine the capabilities necessary in a sub-market in order to distinguish their organization

Total capabilities of an organization can be distinguished into core factors, success factors, and slack. Core factors are the bundles of skills and resources an organization needs to be considered as a relevant supplier by the customers and other important stakeholders in a market, and to survive present and future challenges from the macro environment. Success factors are the capabilities an organization needs to be considered as an attractive supplier by the customers and other important stakeholders in the market, and to profit from present and future challenges from the macro environment. All other capabilities can be regarded as slack. That is, they may be "nice to have" but have no positive impact on the success of the organization.

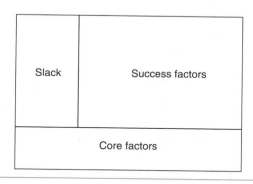

Figure 4.5 The core and success factors of an organization

Source: Grunert, K.G. and C. Ellegaard (1993), "The Concept of Key Success Factors: Theory and Method", in M.J. Baker (ed.), *Perspectives on Marketing Management*, Vol. 3, pp. 245–274, Chichester: John Wiley & Sons Ltd.

attractively from competitors; this can be based either on their own experience or on advise from consultants or by deriving the success factors from customer and stakeholder expectations.

Experience of managers

When determining the success factors in attractive potential sub-markets, management can rely on past experience. To find agreement among the experiences of a group of managers, a tool called Stories of Success and Failure may be used (see Toolbox 4.1).

From writing such stories and analysing their content regarding reasons for success and failure, hints may be derived about what capabilities are decisive for the success of an organization in a specific sub-market. In a similar way, the stories of success and failure of competitors in the relevant market may be compared. In both cases, in order to avoid conflicts among managers participating in the analysis there is a need for a clear and shared definition of what is to be considered a success. But even then, there might be dispute about what to compare and how to interpret available data.

To overcome the problem of potential dispute, top management may invite a consultant to conduct in-depth interviews with members of the organization who come from various hierarchical levels and functional areas and have different amounts of experience within the organization. From these interviews the consultant

TOOLBOX 4.1

STORIES OF SUCCESS AND FAILURE

Stories of success and failure are used to detect core and success factors in a market based on the experience of managers belonging to the organization. For that purpose, selected managers with different functional backgrounds, hierarchical levels and varying length of experience are presented with a list of items to be kept in mind when answering a list of questions. The list of items may look like Exhibit A.

Exhibit A Items to be considered during the assessment process

Leadership	Products
Information system/processes	Pricing
Organizational structure/processes	Market communication
Personnel skills/commitment	Distribution
Financial resources/engineering	Logistics
Production	Research and development

The questions managers are asked to answer are the following:

1. Our organization has been successful in the past. Please think of three occasions you consider as excellent examples: Please describe the occasions in detail and indicate what the reasons were for the success of our organization?

2. Sometimes things have also gone wrong in our organization. Please think of three occasions you consider being typical examples of failure: Please describe the occasions in detail and indicate what the reasons were for that failure?

3. What do we have to consider with particular emphasis in the future, what skills and resources do we need to develop carefully, to acquire or to sustain, to be successful in the future? Please explain why.

When the managers have answered the questions in writing, they are either invited to present their answers in a plenary meeting where conclusions are drawn from the detected similarities; or the answers are content analysed first and only the summary findings are presented and discussed in the meeting. When the first procedure is chosen, every participant in the strategy development team gets the opportunity to defend their view. Therefore, the approach is much more time-consuming, but it is also more involving than the alternative way of proceeding.

may detect patterns of behaviour based on specific resources that have proven successful in the past. These patterns may be validated with controlling data of the organization and presented to strategic decision makers.

But even when choosing this less controversial way of data gathering and analysis, the biggest danger in relying on past experience of managers is their potential use of **heuristics**. Heuristics are unconscious cognitive processes managers use to help them cope with their environment. To act quickly, managers tend to structure their knowledge so that it can be acted upon, choosing the most likely explanation and ignoring alternatives. In their need for validity to confirm their beliefs, managers will tend to select the options that fit the ideas and prejudices that they have already formed. Three kinds of heuristics – anchoring, availability and representativeness – may strongly influence managers' judgement of success factors in their business.

The **anchoring** heuristics refers to a person's inability to change their views in the light of new information. Instead, the person interprets any information in such a way so as to be able to think and carry on as before, as if nothing has happened to change the situation. Since managers have committed themselves to the development of certain capabilities, anchoring bias can prevent the original stance from being re-evaluated thoroughly.[4]

The **availability** heuristics is based on a person's tendency to consider events more probable if they can be imagined vividly. That is, when searching for success factors managers relying on their experience will tend to find them more easily and more convincingly for themselves in the areas of their daily operations. Finally, **representativeness** heuristics makes managers ignore relevant information from the environment because of personal prejudices. They select certain stimuli and consider them as being representative of a situation they have experienced several times before. For example, managers may have been operating in an industry where new product launches of competitors "represent" the familiar situation and the almost automatic response is to follow quickly to avoid being left behind. In such a case, managers will tend to perceive the capability of quickly developing and launching new products as being a success factor independent of whatever other market they are analysing for success factors.[5]

In addition, when deriving success factors from past experience oftentimes managers will have worked in teams for a substantial amount of time. In such cases **groupthink** may strongly bias the results.[6] In particular when they get along well with each other, groups of managers can start to assume that everyone in the team thinks the same way. This perceived unanimity puts pressure on potentially deviant group members to conform to the majority view (even if the others are not present during an interview). The result is the team considering only a limited number of potential success factors. The more uncertain the development of the environment, the more individual managers will tend to conform.

Finally, in the ever-changing environment of markets, past experience is likely to be quickly outdated and in addition it is dangerous to generalize from one sub-market to another. French Gervais-Danone, for example, knows from its US experience that a big budget for national consumer advertising is very important for getting enough shelf space in supermarkets all over the country. But will that experience also be true in Japan? It may be much more important there to use networking skills, that is to build up personal and maybe financial relationships with wholesalers, to obtain the desired shelf space.

Advice of consultants

Experienced consultants may have extensive knowledge based on work with numerous and diverse organizations. Their large database seems to enable individuals or organizations to discover what distinguishes winning companies from losers. That is, they seem to be in a good position to determine general success factors for an industry. However, because existing and potential expectations of customers and other important stakeholders vary among different sub-markets and sub-market segments, attempts to define general success factors across markets have achieved high levels of attention but not much enduring success.[7]

Large-scale empirical studies, such as the **PIMS Program**[8] (Profit Impact of Market Strategies) launched by the US-based Strategic Planning Institute, have attempted to determine factors which significantly influence success in various markets on an international level and across these markets. The companies participating in this project have to fill out a questionnaire regularly for each of their businesses describing that business in terms of served market as well as technology, indicating the achieved results and competition, giving information concerning the industry, and forecasts concerning the development of prices and costs.

Participating firms are provided with information about the relationship of factors such as market growth, market share, degree of vertical integration, or relative product quality on business performance (in terms of return on investment and cash flow). By the use of so-called PAR reports, management of participating firms may compare their business units' results to the average return on investment (ROI) and cash flow in a market, relative to a certain market share, a certain level of investment (e.g., in new product development), and for a given basic strategy (such as cost or technological leadership). Those comparisons may help to understand the influence of such general factors on a firm's potential for success in a given market. The limitations of the approach are manifold. Besides the important amount of data to be regularly gathered and transmitted, management should be aware that the analysis is backward oriented. It can only describe what happened in the past. Second, it is based on statistical measures of association among variables and not on causality. And most important of all, it does not tell managers what specific capabilities determine success or failure in the individual sub-markets of their business domain.

Benchmarking studies conducted by consulting firms across industries have tried to resolve that weakness (see Toolbox 4.2). They first determine the most successful organization in an industry and then compare its strategy, structure, resources, skills, processes, and activities with less successful competitors. The difference in success is related to detected differences in the observed variables.

TOOLBOX 4.2

BENCHMARKING

Benchmarking is a comparison process involving more than two organizations. In conducting a benchmarking study, first of all the object of comparison must be determined. The object may be the strategy of the participating organizations, one or more of their operative activities, or (parts of) their management system.

Then the object of comparison must be operationalized, that is exactly specified and defined in exact terms, to make it measurable. For example, if the logistics systems of a number of fashion goods companies is to be benchmarked, the participants or the organization conducting the study must determine exactly what to compare. They could agree to look specifically at the warehousing information system or the transportation system. Having agreed on the transportation system, for example, the analysts will again have to specify exactly what to compare. This may be the selected transportation partners, the selected transportation devices, the time needed for delivery, or the frequency of delivery. Based on these definitions, measurement methods and measures have to be fixed.

Having established the tools of comparison, the performance of the participating organizations may be assessed. This can be done either by comparing each of the organizations with the artefact of the average participant, or by comparing with the "best of class". Using the best of class as the point of comparison may make it possible to understand why this organization performs better than the others, if the name of the leader is known. Based on the results of comparison, possibilities for improvement can be discussed and implemented.

To make benchmarking a worthwhile excercise, some points should be noted of: First, the entire process should be conducted in a team comprising all managers responsible for potentially necessary improvements. How well such improvements are implemented and the set goals achieved should be controlled by the same team. Furthermore, benchmarking makes sense only if it is performed as an ongoing process leading to continuos improvements.

A major problem may be finding participants for the benchmarking group. Only very few managers are convinced that revealing to competitors the organization's strategy, how operations are conducted or how management systems work, is not dangerous because the usefulness of that information very much depends on the skills of people in competitor organizations and their way of cooperation. Some managers would not hesitate to exchange at least some partial information with competitors in order to get some fresh ideas about the way forward.

If comparisons with the average are conducted, participants may be more easily acquired because they stay anonymous. But the value of comparisons is limited because they are restricted to measurement results. Why those results occur has to be guessed or is subject to statistical association analyses which are limited in managerial reliability. In addition, anonymity may not be assured if a business domain or an industry contains a rather small number of competitors.

A third way would be to compare with an organization not belonging to the same business domain. That is, an organization is selected which is famous for managing a certain process, such as new product development, distribution logistics, or customer maintenance services. If this organization is willing to cooperate, benchmarking participants may get in-depth information how things are managed and executed in the selected benchmark organization. In most cases, they will not be able to directly implement in their own organizations what they have seen. But they might get valuable impulses for developing their own solutions.

This approach seems particularly interesting for the operative purposes of continual improvement. However, from a strategy development-point of view it is rather laden with problems. First, depending on the definition of success different organizations may be leaders in their industry. Second, from a value creation and generation perspective it may be either difficult to define clear-cut industries or industry membership may not be stable. Thirdly, benchmarking looks to the past. The success factors found have no innovative nature and depend on perceptual biases of the consultants. Depending on their focus and experience they will favour particular factors, such as cost or organizational structure, knowledge management, or productivity. Finally, benchmarking results induce a tendency in their buyers to imitate the leader of the industry. By trying to reinforce capabilities, which are the bases of competitors' success, however, managers may neglect some potentially unique capabilities of their own organization. Valuable opportunities for effective differentiation based on available skills and resources that are related to (potential) customer and stakeholder expectations will stay unnoticed.[9]

Customer and stakeholder expectations

From a marketing point of view, the best way to determine the success factors in a sub-market seems to start from the list of current and potential future expectations of (potential) customers as well as other important stakeholders in each of the sub-markets. From that list the capabilities an organization needs to fulfil those expectations in such a way as to be considered an attractive exchange partner, can be derived. The resulting capabilities allowing successful differentiation from competitors may be called the success factors in the sub-market.

Profiles of customer as well as other stakeholder expectations vary from one attractive sub-market to another. Because capabilities needed to fulfil those expectations may, therefore, be different across sub-markets, core and success factors have to be determined for each individual sub-market. Figure 4.6 contains a form, which helps managers to go through a formal process of deriving core and success factors for each sub-market. It also contains simplified examples for the various kinds of potential expectations and how they may be transformed into core and success factors.

In the first column of the form are listed the most important stakeholders in the given sub-market. They have specific expectations concerning organizations being potential (or imposed) exchange partners in the market. Potential customers of Yves St Laurent in China, for example, expect their products to be easily distinguishable from ordinary clothes, to help express wealth and success, but also to be affordable (for them) and to have a certain level of fabric quality. Employees in shops selling Yves St Laurent products in China expect to be much better paid than sales personnel in shops selling Chinese products. They expect to receive free housing and have secure jobs.

Not only such expectations are listed in the second column of the form shown in Figure 4.6, they are also distinguished into three categories: basic, critical, and may-be expectations.[10] The category of **basic expectations** contains all expectations, that have to be fulfilled at a level pre-specified by the customers or stakeholders in order for an organization to be considered

Success factors may be derived from critical as well as high potential may-be expectations of important stakeholders in a market (sub-market, segment). For that purpose, the expectations of all important stakeholders are listed and categorized into basic versus critical/may-be categories. The importance stakeholders' attribute to the fulfilment of these expectations is noted. Then the capabilities (= bundles of skills and resources) needed by an organization to fulfil the various expectations are determined. Success factors are the capabilities an organization needs to fulfil critical and high potential "may-be" expectations.

Stakeholders	Expectations		Importance	Core factors	Success factors
	Basic	Critical/Maybe			
Customers	ISO 9001		5	Certificate	
		Simultaneous engineering	4		Technical team, Know-how, EDI
	Just-in-time		5	PPS PDR	
	Stock at premises		4	Warehouse at customer	
		Amount of stock Structure of stock	2		Lean cost structure, warehousing system, transportation system
		Personal treatment	3		Staff commitment to customer relations
Consultants	Specified quality		5	R&D capacity Quality control	
		Latest level of information	4		Consultant communication system
Public administration	Respect of legislation on pollution		5	Quality control R&D capacity	

Figure 4.6 Deriving success factors from expectations of customers and other important stakeholders

a relevant exchange partner. Nippon Cable, a Japanese manufacturer of lifts, for example, must guarantee the security of users and the availability of spare parts for twenty years after the end of construction, to be considered a relevant supplier in Malaysia.

Fulfilling a basic expectation does not lead to exchange partner satisfaction or delight. Because the stakeholders have exact ideas of what to expect from an exchange partner, there is no potential for attractive differentiation to competitors. Either it is impossible to do better than the pre-specified aspiration level, or it does not make sense because stakeholders are not willing to honour such positive deviation (e.g., through paying higher prices, staying loyal, or exchanging know-how). For example, Magna International, a Canada-based supplier of automotive parts and systems, has to deliver its products "just-in-time" to French car factories, that is at exactly pre-specified times, not earlier and not later, if they want to continue to do business with their customers. There is

no way to do better than to be just in time. But if delivery just in time cannot be guaranteed the customer will be strongly dissatisfied and cease the supply contract.

Expectations belonging to the "critical" and "may-be" categories offer a theoretical differentiation potential to the organization. The category of **critical expectations** contains expectations for which important stakeholders have a pre-specified minimum aspiration level. But they are willing and able to recognize positively an exchange partner doing better than this level. If the minimum aspiration level is not fulfilled, the exchange partner is not considered relevant or customers and other stakeholders are strongly dissatisfied with what they get. If the organization is able to do better than the minimum aspired and better than competitors, customers or stakeholders will be delighted.

For example, when Swedish customers buy a car they expect the distributor to provide a customer service level they consider "normal". But when introducing their Lexus model, Toyota had the opportunity to differentiate their offer from competitors by providing the customers with rental cars for free until delivery of the new car, bringing the new car to the customer's home, and programming the position of the driver's seat, mirrors and steering wheel to fit all individual family members holding a driver's licence.

May-be expectations are characterized by stakeholders not having a pre-specified aspiration level. The expectation is either not important enough to provoke customers or stakeholders to think about it, or customers and stakeholders may not be aware of the expectation. They may have related problems, needs, or interests, but they do not know about the potential solution. Such a situation occurs when an organization plans to market a product or service, which is an innovation to the market or contains innovative features. Until a few years ago, European consumers, for example, did not know about home delivery of meals, except for serving handicapped people. For Domino's Pizza, the US-based home delivery specialist, when analysing

success factors in Western Europe, this expectation belonged to the "may-be" category. The company needed to make customers aware of this need satisfaction potential.

If an expectation of which stakeholders are aware is not considered important enough to develop a minimum aspiration level, an organization does not have much opportunity to differentiate positively from competitors by fulfilling that expectation, even if it clearly performs better. But it does not do much harm either if the organization is weaker than its competitors in fulfilling that expectation. The expectation may be classified as strategically **neutral**.

On the other hand, if customers or stakeholders have not been aware of a potential expectation thus far, but then an exchange partner is able to convince them of its importance, and in addition, is able to fulfil the expectation better than its competitors, this may result in exchange partners' delight. Such expectation may be classified as strategically **high potential**.

TOOLBOX 4.3

CATEGORIZING STAKEHOLDER EXPECTATIONS

Stakeholder expectations may be categorized based on insights of management or based on empirical analyses.

Experience of managers

A simple way to categorize stakeholder expectations into the categories of basic, critical, and may-be expectations is to follow the process outlined in Exhibit A. The total list of stakeholder expectations is first split according to the existence of a minimum aspiration level that must be reached. If such a minimum level exists, the expectation is classified either as basic or critical. If such a minimum aspiration is missing, the expectation is a may-be.

Then the expectations grouped into critical/basic are analysed for their potential of going beyond the minimum aspiration level. If it is possible to do better than that level and if stakeholders are able to recognize and willing to value positively the fact that a supplier goes beyond their minimum aspiration level, the expectation is classified as being "critical". If not, it is a basic expectation.

May-be expectations can be split into "neutral" or "high potential" depending on the ability of suppliers to make stakeholders aware of the importance of an expectation to them. Because the described procedure is based on the experience of managers with stakeholders in day-to-day contact, it might be rather difficult to determine reliably if an expectation that so far has not been of importance to stakeholders may be turned into a more important expectation. An empirical analysis may become unavoidable.

Dual questioning

One way of empirically determining the categorization of expectations may be dual questioning. For dual questioning, first of all, an exhaustive list of expectations has to be created. It is important to note that managers should refrain from presenting a list of expectations that has been prefabricated based on their own views. If – in the frame of a qualitative pre-study – stakeholders are allowed to respond freely to the question of what they expect, expectations may occur that managers so far have not even thought of. The interviews may even become more fruitful if respondents are not directly asked about their expectations but are invited to talk about problems they encounter which are relevant to the total product the organization is offering (see the SOPI technique or focus groups). The resulting list of expectations will be more extensive and more precise. For example, instead of good service respondents may talk about response time, delivery time, or repair capability.

Expectations of which customers and other stakeholders, are not aware but which may be fulfilled by the organization in an attractive manner will be added to the list. Then, the list of expectations is presented to a representative sample of respondents. This may be done in personal interviews but also by mail or by the Internet.

First, respondents are asked to rate each of the expectations on a scale from extremely important to totally unimportant. Then, the respondents are asked to go through the list again, rating each expectation according to the

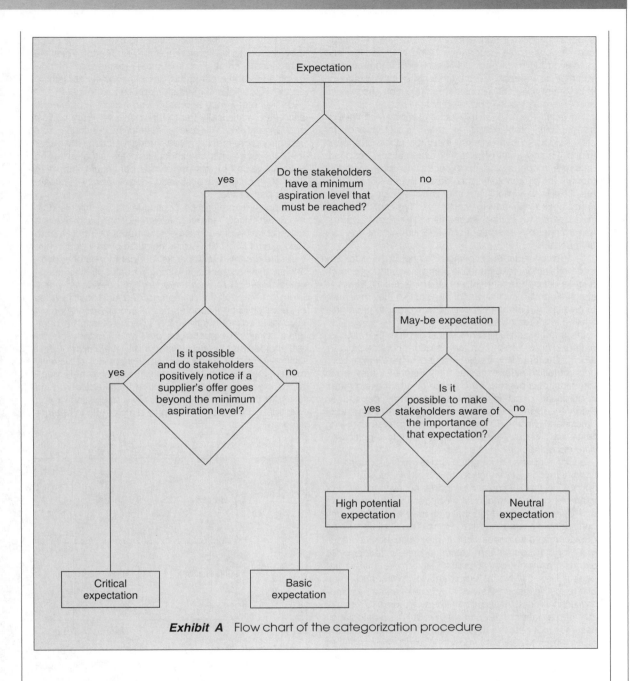

Exhibit A   Flow chart of the categorization procedure

perceived difference of suppliers (known to the respondents) in potentially fulfilling each of the expectations. The scale may range from "suppliers are very different in their potential to fulfil this expectation" to "suppliers are very similar in their potential to fulfil this expectation".

By multiplying the importance score of each expectation with the respective score for the perceived difference in supplier fulfilment potential, managers receive information allowing a tentative classification of expectations. Expectations that are rated highly important but relevant suppliers are not considered different in fulfilment potential may be considered "the basic" expectations. Whereas expectations that are rated at least important and there is a difference in perceived supplier fulfilment potential may be classified as "critical" expectations. If the importance rating is rather low and perceived fulfilment potential is very similar the expectation may be "neutral". On the other hand, if the difference in fulfilment potential is considered quite high, the expectation may be classified as "high potential".

However, the use of this rather simple technique is fraught with problems.[i] First, there is a tendency for stakeholders to overestimate the importance of expectations. Facing a list of potential expectations, respondents are made aware of expectations they have not thought of or seriously considered before. But if they are listed, why not say that they are of a certain importance (yeah-saying tendency)? Typically the result is a rating where no expectation is below average importance on a scale from very important to very unimportant.

In addition, dual questioning does not provide for any trade-offs among expectations. Each evaluation of importance is given independently of others. In reality, however, stakeholders are well aware of the fact that they may have to give up part of their expectations in order to get others fulfilled to a greater extent.

Importance and fulfilment weights given by the respondents may also depend on the situation the stakeholders are in. Customers have been found to rate the importance of fulfilment of expectations differently if they are in the midst of a purchasing process or after having made a purchase decision. The responses may depend on the interviewees' interpretation of what is the meaning of "important". Whether importance is interpreted as being "essential" or as "desirable" may lead to significantly different ratings of expectations.

Lastly, response styles, social desirability, or strategic considerations of respondents may have a significant impact on the outcome of importance evaluations. For example, in an international study researchers may find that Spanish respondents have more expectations they consider very important than Finns. This finding may be due to real differences. But it may also be the result of European southerners having a greater tendency to express extreme positions than the more introverted people from the North. When known beforehand, such differences in response styles may be eliminated by standardizing the data, that is by transforming them to a mean of zero and a standard deviation of one. But this manipulation assumes that data are at least interval scaled (that is, the difference between "very important" and "important" is as great as between "unimportant" and "very unimportant") and the difference in response profile is not due to real differences in preferences.

Factor analysis of correspondence

A more sophisticated way of categorizing stakeholder expectations is using Factor Analysis of Correspondence. First, various current and (may be) potential offers are presented to a random sample representing all major stakeholders in the market under consideration.

Researchers ask the interviewees to express how much they like or dislike (preference for) each offer. Then the respondents are asked about their perception of how much each of the offers they think they know something about fulfils a list of expectations presented to them.

Overall preference and perceived fulfilment of expectations are statistically treated in a way to figure on just one factorial axis. This axis represents the continuum from very strong preference to very strong rejection. The closer the fulfilment levels of expectations are situated to the extreme values of this preference continuum, the more they contribute in a positive or negative way to stakeholder preference.

Folding the preference continuum in the middle (into a positive "liking" and negative "rejection" part) allows a representation of each expectation as a point on a map (see Exhibit B). The coordinates of the overall preference measure are used to separate four categories of expectations. If an expectation strongly contributes to stakeholder rejection of an offer when it is considered unfulfilled, the expectation is categorized as "basic". If an expectation strongly contributes to overall preference if it is considered highly fulfilled it is a "high potential" expectation. "Critical" expectations play an important role for stakeholder preference, whatever the evaluation of their fulfilment level is. If they consider them not sufficiently fulfilled, stakeholders tend to reject the offer. If the expectations are considered highly fulfilled, stakeholders tend to prefer the offer. Whether perceived as fulfilled or not, "neutral" expectations never play a major role in determining preference.

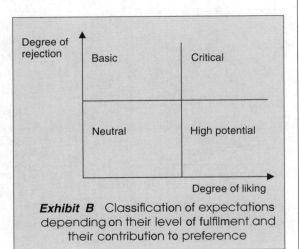

Exhibit B Classification of expectations depending on their level of fulfilment and their contribution to preference

[i] Oliver, R.L. (1997), *Satisfaction: A Behavioral Perspective on the Customer*, New York: McGraw Hill, pp. 55ff.

Source: Adapted from Llosa, S. (1997), L'Analyse de la Contribution des Eléments du Service à la Satisfaction: Un modèle tétraclasse; *Décisions Marketing*, Nr. 10, Janv.–Avr.

Toolbox 4.3 describes two tools of how to split stakeholder expectations into the given categories. It is important to note that category membership of expectations may change over time. Current may-be expectations with high strategic potential may become critical expectations with stakeholders developing minimum expectation levels. Remember the example of Zumtobel AG, one of Europe's leading light system providers, who first offered a light system simulation possibility, and customers were delighted and willing to pay extra money for it. After two years, their competitors had followed suit, and major customers expected light system simulation as part of any offer. Zumtobel had to provide a more powerful system at no extra cost to the customers to differentiate attractively.

Following this logic, one-time critical expectations can convert into basic expectations because intensive competition has driven the fulfilment level to an extent where stakeholders automatically expect it and suppliers are not able to do better in an economically meaningful way. In the case of Zumtobel AG, for example, after two more years, providing the results of light system simulation had become a must to all suppliers participating in a tender.

Having split the expectations of customers and other important stakeholders into different categories, managers must attribute an importance weight (seen from the stakeholder perspective) to each expectation. Higher weights point to greater importance for the organization to possess the capabilities needed to satisfy the respective expectations.

Importance weights of expectations can be determined through informed guessing by managers based on experience gained in relationships with stakeholders. Or they may be empirically measured through interviews with (potential) exchange partners if the market under consideration is new to the organization, new stakeholders have occurred, or managers' experiences do not seem to be reliable enough because the importance of fulfilling certain expectations may change over time. Toolbox 4.4 describes some ways of empirically determining the importance of expectations.

TOOLBOX 4.4

DETERMINING THE IMPORTANCE OF EXPECTATIONS

There are various ways of determining the importance of stakeholder expectations. Each of them has its advantages and disadvantages. Management has to be aware of the respective trade-offs when selecting one of the procedures.

Asking managers

The most simple looking and fastest way to determine the importance of stakeholder expectations is to ask experienced managers who deal with those stakeholders in daily operations. It can be supposed that such managers have quite a good idea of what their partners expect and how important it is to them. In practice, the result very often is a short list of rather generally stated expectations, such as good quality, fast delivery, competitive price, and good service with different importance rankings depending on the responding manager. Even if such lists are longer and more precise and importance rankings tend to converge, they should be checked with stakeholders. As has been discussed in the text, managers are subject to heuristics, which may heavily distort what stakeholders are really looking for and with what preferences.

Direct questioning

The easiest way to proceed is first to automatically attribute high importance scores (e.g., 5 on an importance scale of 1 = unimportant to 5 = very important) to all basic expectations. They must be fulfilled if the organization wants to be considered a relevant supplier to the market. Then, the importance of stakeholder expectations which have been found to belong to the critical and may-be categories and which are presented on a list is empirically determined by asking potential customers and other stakeholders to indicate the importance of their fulfilment. When applying this technique the researcher must be aware of the same problems as mentioned for the Dual Questioning approach described in Toolbox 4.3.

Constant-sum scale

Applying a constant-sum scale helps to avoid some of these problems. Stakeholders are presented with a list of potential expectations and asked to allocate a given sum of points (e.g., 100) to these expectations according to their importance of being fulfilled. The number of points attributed to the each of the expectations expresses their importance on an interval scale. To be able to distribute meaningfully the limited number of given points, respondents have to compare their expectations. Trade-offs are considered. Response styles do not have any influence on the results.

However, the meaning of "importance" still needs to be unambiguously clarified. And the current situation of the respondents (e.g. whether before or after a purchase) may still influence their evaluations. An additional disadvantage of the constant-sum technique is the potentially substantial number of expectations to be compared to each other. The longer the list of expectations, the more difficult the task becomes for respondents to allocate the points in a meaningful way. This difficulty may be overcome by asking the respondents to proceed by pair-wise comparison. That is, first to establish a rank order of expectations according to their importance by comparing them two by two, and then to allocate a certain number of points to each of the expectations to express the differences in importance. The greater ease of this procedure for the respondents is counteracted by the substantially greater amount of time needed for the task.

Regression to total preference

Another way of gathering information about the importance of fulfilling expectations of stakeholders is to present various existing offers and perhaps a potential offer to a sample of respondents, asking them for their preference. Subsequently, the respondents are presented with a list of expectations and asked how much each of the potential choices fulfils each of the expectations. By regressing the expectation fulfilment ratings against the overall preference judgment for each presented offer, a regression function may be estimated. The regression weights derived for each of the expectations then serve as proxies for importance.

This seemingly elegant method suffers from a number of assumptions, which may not be realistic. The first assumption is that the respondents know all of the potential choices, or at least are able to imagine them with all their consequences. Second, in order to allow the use of a regression technique, the expectations must be independent of each other. If they are not, the regression weights will be biased. Third, the importance of expectations is assumed to be independent of the customers' perception of the fulfilment level of expectations. This may not hold for may-be expectations. This problem could be resolved by using dummy variables. But lastly, regression also assumes invariance of the parameters over time. That is, the importance of each of the expectations is assumed to stay constant over time.

Taking into account the various problems related to each of the described measurement techniques, marketing managers must be aware that there is no one best approach. They need to decide what level of accuracy they want for doing their analysis and what disadvantages (of the selected technique) they are ready to accept.

In the next step, capabilities are derived which an organization needs in order to fulfil the listed expectations. Capabilities needed to satisfy "basic" expectations are classified as "core factors". The organization must possess those core factors to be considered a relevant exchange partner. Magna International, for example, must have a production planning and control system as well as a distribution logistics system, which allows them exact delivery to their clients in the automotive industry. The state of each component control panel, for example, in the process from its order to the end of production and its position in the logistics chain to the customer must be traceable.

Capabilities needed to satisfy "critical" and "may-be" expectations with high strategic potential are success factors. They allow the organization to be more or less attractive to the stakeholders in the market and to differentiate itself from major competitors. For example, success factors in the case of Domino's Pizza may have been the logistics system, the location of pizza production sites, and the motivation of personnel. Because operative solutions may wear out rather quickly (stakeholders become acquainted with them and tend to consider the solution as a minimum level), it is important to define success factors in more general terms. To stay with the example cited above, one of the success factors for Domino's Pizza has not been to possess a fleet of transportation vehicles, but a superior logistics capability compared with competitors. The specific combination of skills and resources will change over time.

Because managers tend to interpret reality according to their previous decisions and actions, there is a danger of relating certain capabilities mistakenly with the fulfilment of expectations. For example, managers who have worked with buffer stock during most of their career tend to consider a well-functioning warehousing system as being a must for an excellent delivery service level expected by customers. Thinking of innovative solutions to this expectation, leaving well-established paths may need innovation-oriented leadership or external coaching by consultants.

In addition, the intensity with which a capability contributes to the fulfilment of an expectation may be overestimated by managers having contributed to the development of that capability inside their organization. To keep such misinterpretations to a minimum, discussions should be conducted in multi-functional teams, perhaps with the help of outside coaches, and results should be empirically cross-checked.

Deriving success factors from challenges of the macro environment

Core factors as well as success factors not only depend on the expectations of customers and important stakeholders in a sub-market. An organization must be able to master challenges from the current state and future development of the macro environment of its relevant market. Capabilities that the organization needs in order to keep those challenges from becoming a threat belong to the list of core factors. Capabilities needed to turn challenges from the macro environment into opportunities are added to the list of success factors. How the challenges may be determined and how core and success factors are derived from those challenges will be described in the following.

The management team responsible for strategically positioning their organizational unit may proceed as described in Toolbox 1.5 introducing the scenario technique. First, the dimensions of the macro environment that are relevant to the business of the organization are determined. For a supplier to the food and beverage industry, such as Austria-based Teich AG, a specialist in aluminium packaging solutions, relevant dimensions may be, for example, legal regulations, technology, consumer behaviour, and the economy. For each of the relevant dimensions, the most important factors influencing the business of the organization are determined. In the example cited above, legal regulations concerning the quality of food and beverages, international trade, and transportation, as well as labour regulations may be of

importance to the business of Teich. On the technology dimension, the development of packaging materials and machinery may be important together with printing and food treatment technology. For each of the most important factors of influence, their current state of development is described and the two most different potential future states of development on a specified time horizon are estimated. Combinations of these future states according to their logical fit will result in a number of more or less coherent scenarios from which the two internally most coherent, externally most different scenarios (compared with each other) will be selected for further analysis.

Each of the scenarios contains the description of a future potential macro environment that represents certain challenges to all organizations trying to be successful under the given conditions. Depending on the capabilities available to master those challenges, they may represent opportunities or threats to any organization. Table 4.1 contains a form that may be used in analysing what capabilities an organization must possess to overcome those challenges and what capabilities are needed to make them become opportunities for increased success.

The list of core factors in a sub-market is completed by capabilities the organization needs in order to master (potential) challenges from the macro environment. That is, bundles of skills and resources needed to keep challenges from becoming a threat to the organization. For example, if the political and economic situation in a country is not stable, as in many Latin American countries, an organization interested in serving a market there will need specific skills (such as establishing informal relationships with influential people) combined with resources (such as local management without much capital investment) to stay in business over time.

Table 4.1 Determining success factors from challenges from the macro environment

Management can derive core and success factors starting from foreseeable challenges from the development of the macro environment of their organization. Core factors are capabilities needed to avoid challenges turning into threats for the organization. They must exist, be developed, or be acquired for the sake of the organization's survival in the market. Success factors are capabilities needed to turn challenges into opportunities for the organization. They should exist, be developed, or be acquired to ensure future competitive advantages in the market.

Dimension	Foreseeable challenge	Importance	Core-factors	Success factors
Economy	Increasing intensity of competition	5		Relative cost position. Level of awareness. Reputation. Level of distribution
Technology	Development of new material	2	Technology information system. New material supplies	Joint material development with supplier
Legislation	Tightening of environmental standards	3	Access to new technologies	Influence on norm setters. Flexibility of production
Politics	Instability of governments	1		Informal contacts with influential people

Success factors are capabilities helping an organization to turn current as well as potential future challenges from the macro environment into opportunities. Take the example of India, where population density is high and increasing and the per capita income is steadily growing. To grasp the opportunity of reaching young and educated people living in urban areas a consumer products manufacturer such as Wilkinson, the British globally established shaving products firm, will need a distribution system which tightly covers all those areas. For producers of telecommunication equipment such as Sweden's Ericsson, the development of technical standards is of great importance. For them a success factor in a market such as India may be their ability to influence norm-setting bodies.

Competitor analysis

To assess their organization's potential for success in the most attractive sub-markets, management has to determine first, if the organization possesses the necessary core factors. If it does not, but the sub-market is highly attractive, management may look for ways of acquiring the necessary capabilities. Building them from internal bases may be time consuming as well as capital intensive. Sourcing the capabilities by cooperating with potential partners in an extended value-creation system may be difficult if competition is intense. Acquiring another organization possessing the necessary capabilities is often the fastest way. But very often this solution does not take into account the difficulties of integrating two organizations. Therefore, most organizations will rather focus on markets for which they already possess the necessary core factors.

Take the example of Daimler based in Stuttgart, Germany, wanting to enter the seemingly attractive North American market of customers not able to afford a Mercedes. They could have started to develop a second brand and build their own distribution and service network; an extremely demanding endeavour. They could have collaborated with another car manufacturer to source the necessary capabilities. But this would have only partly resolved the problem. Thus, they decided to merge with Chrysler. A seemingly quick fix to the missing core factors, but as it turned out, a very expensive and resource consuming one. Integrating the two organizations to realize the theoretically existing synergies proved to be a major task.

If the basic capabilities are available to the organization, its strengths and weaknesses with regard to the success factors in each attractive sub-market should be analysed. The result of this analysis must be compared to the strengths and weaknesses of major competitors. For practical purposes, the assessment starts with competitor analysis to avoid too much of a biased perspective towards factors where the organization has its strengths.

In analysing its major competitors, an organization seeks to find out how well their capabilities fit the success factors in a sub-market. To be able to complete such an evaluation, management first has to determine the structure of its competitive environment, that is the relevant competitors, their membership in strategic groups, as well as barriers to market exit (see Appendix 4.1). Then management has to gather information about the relevant capabilities of the most important competitors (Figure 4.7).

Structure of the competitive environment

In analysing competition, management first has to decide who are the relevant competitors.

Relevant competitors

Every company in an industry may define its market differently. For example, a Norwegian marketer of cross-country skis may consider its business to be restricted to the Scandinavian countries, while a global competitor like France-based Rossignol defines its market as all country-markets where you can possibly do any cross-country skiing. In that case, the Norwegian marketer would have a significantly different view of the relevant operating environment and therefore, of (potentially) relevant competitors. In addition, market definitions may be based on the products offered or on the benefits provided.

The most important competitors will be organizations which supply similar goods. Besides existing competitors there may be a threat to new upcoming competitors. Major business organizations which have not served the market so far, might consider doing so in the future. Therefore, management must have a closer look at potential candidates and existing barriers to market entry.

But relevant competitors may include not only domestic or international suppliers of similar goods. Marketers of substitutive goods, that is, any organization supplying products or services providing the same customer benefit, must be considered potential competitors. From this broader perspective, for example, Red Bull, an activating soft drink made in Austria for young people who want to be "cool" not only competes with Dutch Grolsch beer but it may also compete with French Chevignon shirts.

New competitors may arise from the development of a new technology. A marketer of fuel, such as Royal Dutch Shell, might see important competitors emerge when the production of electrical energy through photovoltaic is sufficiently developed to be highly efficient. It may feel the need to follow closely the development of this technology and to consider companies working in that field as potential important competitors. But such competitors might also emerge from a change in customer behaviour. If an increasing number of people tend to avoid heating their homes during the coldest part of the

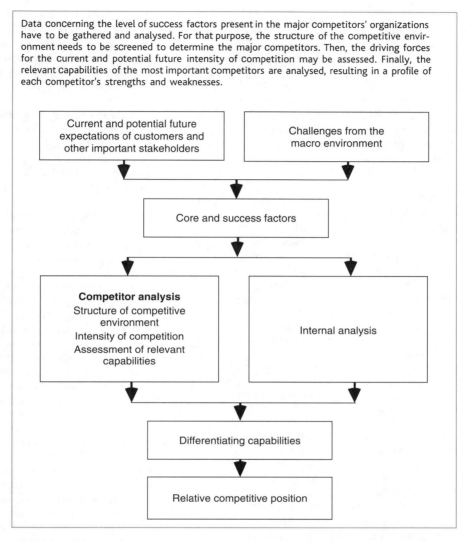

Data concerning the level of success factors present in the major competitors' organizations have to be gathered and analysed. For that purpose, the structure of the competitive environment needs to be screened to determine the major competitors. Then, the driving forces for the current and potential future intensity of competition may be assessed. Finally, the relevant capabilities of the most important competitors are analysed, resulting in a profile of each competitor's strengths and weaknesses.

Figure 4.7 Determining the relative competitive position: Competitor analysis

year by spending extended vacations in warmer regions of the world, Shell will be confronted with major competitors from the vacation services industry. Therefore, the determination of major competitors is not only a task that demands thorough analysis of the industry to which an organization belongs to but also a screening of the environment in search of potential substitutive problem solutions that might result in new competitors in a significantly changed market environment.

In addition, creating attractive value to potential customers and other important stakeholders has increasingly become a task that cannot be fulfilled by single organizations. Complex and continually renewed capabilities are required that only networks of

organizations cooperating with each other are able to provide economically. In such cases entire value-creation systems are competing against each other. Therefore, meaningful competitor analysis needs to compare those value-creation systems instead of single organizations. Their ability to offer distinctive value to exchange partners needs to be understood in a dynamic way. That is, not only the current state of the network in terms of total capabilities is to be analysed, but also the potential development of current as well as new value-creation processes.

For example, the motorcycle division of Germany's BMW not only competes with the respective divisions of Honda and Yamaha, but with their value-creation systems consisting of network partners such as suppliers (for example delivering suspension systems or tyres), logistics partners (ensuring fast and reliable delivery of motor cycles and spare parts around the world), retailers (being responsible for most customer services), or motor cycle racers (contributing to the reputation of the brand). For BMW management to assess their relative competitive position, they must understand how at present and in the future interaction among the parts of such competitive networks may be able to create and generate superior value compared with its own system.

Strategic groups

Not all the existing suppliers of similar products or services in a market are automatically potential competitors of an organization. There may exist strategic groups with differing relevance to its competitive position. Strategic groups may be defined in terms either of the behaviour or of cognitions of their members. That is, a strategic group either consists of a group of organizations serving a given market by following a similar core strategy[11] or of a group of organizations in which the dominant decision makers have similar mental models of the market environment.[12]

The similarity of core strategies is observable by the **scope** – that is what the organizations do (based on what capabilities) in terms of their business domain, the served market segments, their differentiation, and geographic extension; and by their resource deployment – that is, how they do it. For example, Mercedes, BMW, and Audi tend to base their competitive strategies on high quality combined with differentiation. They form one strategic group compared to the carmakers from South Korea, Kia, Hyundai, and Daewoo, which form another strategic group relying mainly on cost/price leadership. The first group defends its position through intensive R&D, technological pioneering, and an exclusive image; whereas the second group optimizes its cost position through high production volumes, rationalization, low wages, and lean management.

Senior executives of organizations that present similar products or benefits to the stakeholders in a particular market to a varying extent share views about the boundaries of the market, that is, the competitive domain. In addition, they agree to a greater or lesser extent about the legitimate competitive process inside that domain. For example, some top executives in the air travel industry implicitly agree that their market is global, low cost is essential for price competition to fill airplane capacities, and growth by acquisition and strategic alliances is the way to attractive profitability. Some others believe that there are regional markets in which superior service, punctuality, and attractive connecting flights with major carriers allow asking for significantly higher prices. These mental models of senior executives about the relevant market environment strongly influence their strategic

decisions and the behaviour of their organizations through the way those decisions are implemented. In turn, organizational performance resulting from that behaviour strongly influences the executives' mental models.[13] In the air travel example, both mental models may lead to business success and may, therefore, be continually reinforced.

The similarity of mental models of key decision makers may be measured by analysing their cognitive maps. For example, content analysis of company publications, such as presidents' letters to stockholders published in annual reports, interviews in trade magazines, or homepages in the Internet may provide the data for analysis.

Detecting cognitive maps may turn out to be a burdensome task. Determining strategic groups from a behavioural or a cognitive perspective tends to produce similar results.[14] Therefore, managers, knowing that mental models, strategic decision-making, resource allocation, and organizational performance influence each other, tend to define strategic groups in terms of criteria driving competition in the analysed market. The criteria will depend on the business domain. However, it is important that they are strategically decisive and represent mobility barriers for the members of any strategic group, that is, they do not allow an easy and fast switch from one group to another. Such criteria may be, for example, the segments of the market the organization is focusing on, the extent of integration of various steps of the value chain, the intensity of cooperation with partners, expenditures in R&D, or the level of integration of the distribution system.

Then, competitors are described by the selected criteria. The descriptions are used as data for defining the strategic groups. There are basically two ways of forming the groups: a graphic analysis using two essential criteria or the construction of clusters through cluster analysis or factor analysis based on a larger number of criteria. Figure 4.8 shows an example of a two-dimensional graphical analysis. Factor analysis may be executed as described in Toolbox 4.6

Competitive structure

Having determined the current strategic groups in the markets under consideration, management can focus their further analysis on those groups which seem most relevant for assessing the relative competitive position of their own organization. Because the boundaries of strategic groups may not be as clear cut, and the core strategy of the organization not as fixed by available capabilities as theoretical concepts demand, it may be necessary to look at more than one strategic group per (sub-) market. To determine the most important competitors in those strategic groups their competitive structure has to be analysed.

The Figure shows a sample group map of the luxury industry serving a global market. The map is based on two criteria: directly operated stores as a percentage of total sales, and the share of watches, jewellery, and accessories as a percentage of total sales.

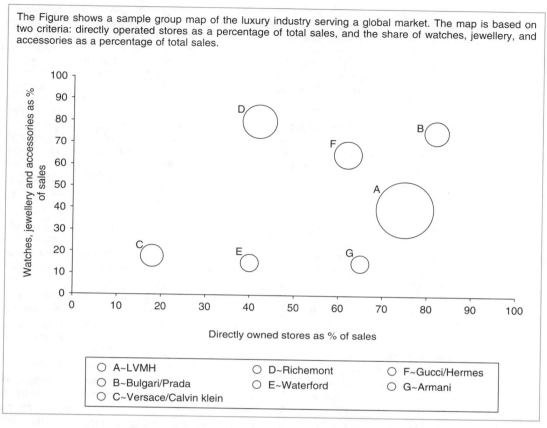

Figure 4.8   A two-dimensional analysis of strategic group membership

Source: O'Higgins, E. and Duggan, S. (2001), "A Note on the Global Luxury Goods Industry in 2000", *Teaching Note*, University College Dublin, p. 9.

TOOLBOX 4.5

EXPECTATIONS-RELATED TOP-OF-MIND ANALYSIS

Expectations-related top-of-mind analysis (TOMA) is an interview technique, which can be used in personal, telephone, and computer contacts with respondents. The results of TOMA explain purchase decisions of customers or preference of other important stakeholders by the spontaneous activation of knowledge and effects. It is based on the research finding that automatic cognitive processes together with closely associated emotions dominate a great deal of purchase decision-making processes. Therefore, spontaneous associations of brands, retail outlets, or supplier names to expectations or benefits sought are

better predictors of recurring purchase decision-making than multi-attribute models such as semantic profiles often used in image analysis.

During a TOMA interview, the interviewer (a person or a PC) presents a list of important critical expectations and some may-be expectations of high strategic potential – one by one – to a sample of respondents representing (potential) customers or other important stakeholders. For each expectation customers or other stakeholders are asked to indicate the name of the supplier, provider, or outlet that best fulfils the expectation and first comes to their mind.

Because meanings of expectations may vary depending on the specific usage or consumption situation, it is necessary to start the interview with a description of the situation respondents should imagine when giving their answers. For example, the expectations of enjoyable social contact and free-time activities may mean different things depending on if respondents are thinking of a family vacation with their little children or a vacation alone with their spouse.

To make sure that results are exclusively relying on automatic cognitive processing, only answers given in less than three seconds time are used for data analysis. To gather additional data on competitors after a first run, the list of expectations may be gone through a second time asking for the name of the supplier, provider, or outlet thought of as worst in fulfilling the expectation.

Spontaneously indicated names of organizations best or worst fulfilling an expectation constitute the list of competitors from the customer/stakeholder perspective in respect to this expectation. Names most often recalled in a positive sense across expectations are the major competitors. Because data analysis will provide perceptual profiles of best and worst fulfilled expectations by competitor, very useful additional information for determining the relative competitive position of the host organization may be gained.

The competitive structure of a strategic group may be defined in terms of the number, and size, similarity of positioning, relative market share, rate of growth, or technical sophistication of organizations belonging to that group. Management has grouped competitors according to criteria chosen on the basis of its own interpretation of what is driving competition in the market or what the cognitive maps of top executives are in the market. Therefore, the **number** of competitors that management considers belong to a strategic group may be less important than the number of (potential) suppliers' customers consider relevant. To check for potential differences in perception, management may analyse the customers' evoked sets for the specific good or the benefit to be provided, that is, they may try to find out the top-ranked suppliers in the minds of potential customers. Another approach would be to apply expectations-related Top-of-Mind Analysis as described in Toolbox 4.5.

The **size** of the most important competitors can be estimated from such data as number of employees or annual sales volume. These numbers should be evaluated carefully, because they are influenced by the nature of the product or service and the production technology used. The number of people working for a shoe manufacturer in Brazil, for example, may be similar to the number working for a competitor in Italy. But this does not mean that the companies are of the same size, because the two firms may employ different production technologies. In many cases, therefore, it will be necessary to estimate competitors' production capacities.

Members of a strategic group are not totally uniform. Despite their similar strategic orientation, they try to establish individually different positions in the minds of (potential) exchange partners. Thus, management may be interested in what **position** the members of the relevant strategic group effectively have achieved in the minds of customers and important stakeholders. Among others, Multidimensional Scaling, Correspondence Analysis, and Policy Capturing as described in Toolbox 4.6 are potential tools to be used for that purpose.

TOOLBOX 4.6

DETERMINING THE POSITION OF COMPETITORS IN THE MINDS OF EXCHANGE PARTNERS

Members of a strategic group are supposed to have a certain position in the perceptual space, that is, the minds of actual and potential exchange partners. This perceptual space, in general, is multidimensional. That is, exchange partners make up their minds about (potential) suppliers or their offers along various assessment criteria, which are related to each other and may interact.

There are a number of methods to determine the position of competing members of a strategic group in the perceptual space of exchange partners. These methods can only be applied to organizations or their offers with which stakeholders are familiar. This knowledge either is based on own experience or has developed indirectly through media, personal communication or through observation. The available methods use data on the perceived potential of suppliers or their offers to fulfil stakeholder expectations or data on their perceived similarity. In the following, the basic approaches of exploratory factor analysis, multidimensional scaling, factor analysis of correspondence, and policy capturing will be outlined.

Exploratory factor analysis

When using factor analysis for determining the position of competitors in the minds of stakeholders, first their relevant critical and strategically high potential expectations need to be determined. Then, a random sample of respondents is asked to evaluate (for example, using a rating scale) each competitor they think they know, in terms of how much it is able to fulfil each of the expectations. Exploratory factor analysis (see Toolbox 3.4) of the data is used to determine the factors underlying the evaluations expressed by the respondents. Those factors can be used to graphically represent the position of each member of the strategic group in a space spanned out by the factors which represent the dimensions of the space. For that purpose, factor scores are calculated for each member on each dimension, and the evaluated organizations or their offers are each represented by a point in the multidimensional space. The closer the points are to each other, the more similar is their perceived position in the minds of the stakeholders.

Multidimensional scaling

In the case of multidimensional scaling (MDS), respondents only have to indicate their perception of similarity or dissimilarity of the members of the strategic group or their offers. The obtained similarity data can be used to determine the configuration of the competitors in the perceptual space of the stakeholders. The method follows a certain sequence of steps:

1. Measuring similarity perceptions
    Similarity measurement is based on the assumption that stakeholders compare (potential) suppliers according to implicit dimensions, which are to be detected without asking directly. Similarity perceptions can be measured by **rank ordering**, applying the anchor point method, or by rating. In rank ordering, respondents are presented pairs of competitors, which they are asked to rank order according to their similarity. With K competitors, there are $K(K-1)/2$ potential pairs to be evaluated. Thus, the number of pairs increases very fast with the number of competitors to be evaluated. To ease the task of respondents and to avoid rejection, respondents may be asked to establish first two categories of pairs: those that seem to be similar versus those seeming dissimilar. These categories are then split again into even more similar versus less similar and dissimilar versus less dissimilar, and so forth, until a full rank order is established. The ranks of pairs are used as input data for MDS, starting with the most similar having rank 1.

    The **anchor point method** uses each competitor once as an anchor point for a comparison with all other competitors, to rank order those according to their similarity with the anchor point. The most similar competitor gets rank 1. For K competitors there are $K(K-1)$ dual comparisons to be made, which is twice as much as with rank ordering or rating. Because the rank orders given by a respondent may depend on the anchor point, the data matrix resulting from that method of comparison is more realistic, but asymmetric. A transformation into a triangular (=symmetric) matrix needs to be conducted by applying methods specifically developed for that purpose.

    In **rating**, pairs of competitors are individually rated with regard to their similarity on a usually 7–9 point scale ranging from "totally similar" to "totally dissimilar". The resulting values from $K(K-1)/2$ ratings are the input for MDS. This task is the quickest for respondents. But it delivers the least precise data because various pairs will get the same similarity ratings. These ties lead to increased instability of the MDS solution. For MDS based on individual data, rank ordering is preferable. However, if data aggregated across respondents, using medians or averages, are used as input to MDS, rating is advantageous because of the greater ease of data gathering.

2. Selection of a distance measure
    The similarities of competitors perceived by the respondents have to be transformed into distances. The greater the dissimilarities the greater the distance. Thus, a distance measure has to be selected from a number of potential choices.

    The **Euclidian metric** measures the shortest distance between two points, that is a straight line. The theoretical assumption behind this measure is that respondents evaluate the similarity between two competitors by simultaneously considering all evaluation criteria at once.

    The **City-block metric** measures the distance between two points as the sum of absolute distances on all dimensions used for comparison. The theoretical assumption underlying this measure is that respondents, when evaluating the similarity of two competitors, compare dimension by dimension.

    The **Minkowski metric** is a generalization of the above measures. It is statistically most elegant, but the basic psychological assumption concerning the comparison process of respondents is less clear.

3. Determination of the graphical configuration
    In a space of minimum dimensionality, MDS tries to find a configuration of points which represents the dissimilarity of competitors as closely as possible. That is, the rank order of distances among the competitors in the space should reflect their rank order of dissimilarities. Statistically speaking, ordinal data from similarity judgements of respondents are transferred into metric multidimensional distances.

    To find this configuration, the algorithm starts with a first arbitrary solution and tries to improve it in a stepwise manner, until the so-called stress criterion is minimized. The stress criterion indicates how badly a configuration fulfils the condition of reproducing the original rank order.

4. Determining the number of dimensions and their interpretation

The number of dimensions used for the graphical configuration should represent the number of dimensions used by stakeholders in the comparison of competitors. In most cases researchers may have some hypothesis about how many dimensions stakeholders use in making comparisons, but they do not really know. Statistically, to find a perfect fit between the rank order of graphical distances and the rank order of dissimilarities perceived by respondents, a space of maximum $K-1$ dimensions may be needed. But to make the configuration interpretable the number of dimensions should be kept quite low.

Some criteria to resolve that problem are the measures of stress and of data compression, as well as the ease of interpretation of the outcome. The improvement of **stress** by adding another dimension is exponentially decreasing. If the achieved improvement in stress becomes marginal, the researcher should refrain from adding another dimension (a very low stress may be an indicator for a degenerated solution where the objects are clustered in the middle of the system of coordinates).

The compression of data, indicated by the **data compression coefficient** Q, which expresses the ratio of the amount of input data to output data, improves with a decreasing number of dimensions used for the graphical description of distances among a certain number of objects to compare. Coefficient Q should be greater or equal to 2. That is, for a two-dimensional configuration to be meaningful, an input of comparison data covering at least nine competitors is needed. For a three-dimensional solution the minimum is 13 competitors.

Interpretation of dimensions can be made easier by statistically rotating the dimensions according to, for example, the Varimax criterion, and by projecting expectations respondents have used for comparison into the perceptual space. For that purpose, respondents are first asked for their similarity evaluations of competitors and then, in a second step, to evaluate the competitors with regard to their fulfilment potential for a number of critical and strategically high potential expectations which have been determined in a previous study. Each expectation can be statistically represented as a vector in the perceptual space of the respondents. By turning the vectors step by step around the centre of the coordinates, the correlations between vectors and similarity evaluations are maximized. The closer a vector is located to a dimension the better it is suited for the interpretation of the dimension. Compared to exploratory factor analysis, MDS has the advantage of researchers not needing to know the relevant evaluation criteria of stakeholders beforehand, avoiding the assumption that evaluations are made on a metric level of data, and results not being influenced by the selection of evaluation criteria and their verbalization. Disadvantages to be considered are the large number of competitors to be compared in order to derive meaningful results, the greater extent of data to be gathered, and the greater difficulty of interpreting the meaning of the dimensions of the perceptual space. A particular problem may be the assumption that all competitors are being compared along the same criteria. Part of successful competition is to try to impose exactly the contrary. But uniqueness of values offered to the stakeholders would mean that there is no common perceptual space.

Analysis of correspondence

Like MDS, correspondence analysis may be used to analyse the similarity of organizations or their offers as perceived by customers and other important stakeholders.[i] The objects compared in the study are also depicted as points in a space. And their graphical distance is a measure of closeness in the perception of respondents.

In contrast to MDS, however, the number of competitors to be compared has no lower limit. Competitors or their offers are not directly compared with each other. Each of the competing organizations is evaluated individually with regard to their potential for fulfilling a list of expectations, determined in a preceding study. There is also no limit to the measurement level of data. That is, nominal data can be used as input to correspondence analysis. For example, reactions to items like "the organization is located in my home country" or "we have a delivery contract with this organization" are as well suited as ordinal data from evaluations of how much a (potential) supplier is able to fulfil an expectation, such as "commitment to punctual delivery".

The graphical results produced by correspondence analysis not only provide the positions of the competing organizations in the perceptual space of respondents, but also depict the position of the fulfilment levels of each expectation in the same space. Therefore, interpretation of results is much easier than with MDS.

Data are gathered by first presenting a list of competing organizations or products to the respondents asking if they know any of them. Then, respondents are asked to evaluate the potential of organizations/products with which they are familiar for fulfilling the expectations given on another list. The answers result in evaluation tables for each expectation containing the evaluations of all competing organizations/products known to the respondents.

As an example, Exhibit A shows such a table for the expectation "positive effect on personal status" giving the fulfilment levels of six brands of passenger cars as perceived by 250 respondents.

Each cell value in the table is transferred into a chi-square value, which indicates the ratio of the empirically detected frequency in a cell of the table to the statistically expected frequency. The expected frequency can be calculated based on the total frequency of a value level across all competitors. In the example of Exhibit A, the value level "increased" has a total frequency of 390. The expected frequency for each of the brands, therefore, can be calculated by dividing 390 by 6 (no. of brands) = 65.

Exhibit A	Expectation: positive effect on personal status					
Personal status is	Smart	VW	Chrysler	Toyota	Saab	Porsche
increased	20	20	50	0	100	200
not affected	30	210	150	150	50	40
decreased	200	20	50	100	100	10

As a result, the chi-square values for Saab and Porsche are highly positive, whereas for the other brands the chi-square values are negative. Saab and Porsche "correspond" better with "increased personal status" than the other brands in the study. In the graphical representation of the perceptual space, the two brands should be located closer to "increased personal status" than the other brands.

In the next step, the chi-square values are treated in a similar way to exploratory factor analysis, producing dimensions in relation to which competitors/brands as well as levels of expectation fulfilment are located. The more dimensions are extracted from the data the more precise the graphical representation will reproduce the data. But at the same time, the managerial interpretation of the graphical result becomes more difficult.

The graphical analysis of the data indicates

- what expectations are perceived as closely related to each other (those expectations have similar frequency profiles of fulfilment across competitors),
- what competitors are perceived as belonging to the same group,
- what groups of competitors are characterized by which bundles of expectation fulfilment?

Similar to principal components analysis, the total variance in the data – called total inertia – is explained by several components (dimensions). The amount of variance explained by each component is expressed as a percentage of total variance. The maximum number of components is equal to the smaller number of rows or columns minus one. This maximum number would allow a graphical representation of raw data without any loss of information. But the higher the number of dimensions the more difficult the interpretation of results becomes. The number of dimensions to be used for the graphical representation of relationships in the data depends on the percentage of total variance explained by each of the dimensions and their chi-square values. The number of dimensions finally used should allow an explanation of a minimum of 80 per cent of total variance.

Exhibit B shows the perceptual space detected in the example from the passenger car industry. Brands located close to each other have been evaluated similarly with regard to their potential to fulfil the expectations presented to the respondents. Thus, Porsche and Toyota are perceived as quite different in terms of the expectations of design, sportiness, resell-value, and effect on personal status. In contrast, Saab has turned out to be perceived being a relevant competitor, at least as far as the expectations presented to the respondents in the study.

This result reveals a major weakness of correspondence analysis compared to MDS. Its results can only be reliable to the extent that the list of expectations presented to the respondents contains all relevant expectations and their respective levels.

To be meaningfully applied, analysis of correspondence should be based on

- a large data matrix which does not allow a direct estimate of the relations among variables,
- a homogeneous data matrix allowing calculation of the statistical distances among rows and columns as well as their interpretation, and
- an amorphous data matrix, that is, the structure of data is unknown to the researcher or only partly perceivable.

Policy capturing

When analysing business decision makers in particular, the method of policy capturing[ii] may be applied. Based on the analysis of actual decisions, policy capturing provides a way of identifying actual judgement policies. Decisions and supplier assessment criteria are analysed in a way to provide a model depicting the assessment criteria and their weights.

Policy capturing starts from the assumption that individuals, when making a decision, are governed by an underlying judgement "policy", that is, a cognitive model, which allows them to integrate the various pertinent items of information into a single judgement. The objective of the method is to uncover that cognitive model.

The first step of the procedure involves personal interviews with customers. They are asked to think of their purchasing objectives and then to identify as many supplier criteria as they can that might in any way reflect effectiveness or ineffectiveness in achieving the objectives. The purpose of this step is to generate a fairly exhaustive list of all potential assessment criteria that might be used by any purchasing decision maker to evaluate potential suppliers and their offers.

The next step involves the isolation of those criteria that are actually used by purchasing decision makers in their assessment of suppliers and their offers, and the relative weightings of those criteria. This can be accomplished by having respondents make evaluations regarding various

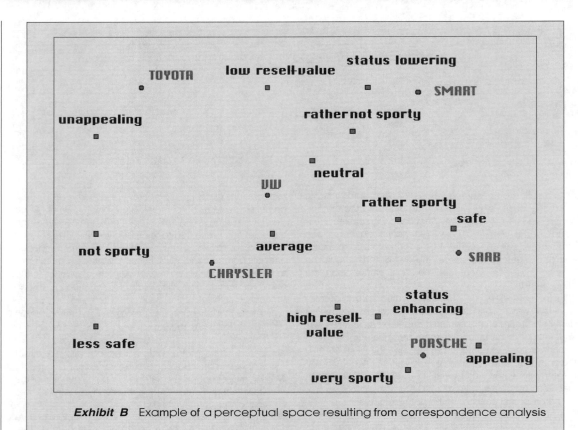

Exhibit B   Example of a perceptual space resulting from correspondence analysis

potential suppliers. With the ratings of those suppliers as dependent variables and the measures of the assessment criteria as the independent variables, multiple (stepwise) regressions can be used to determine which criteria have been used in the ratings, as well as the weighting factors of those criteria.

Because assessment criteria and their levels may be interrelated in the cognitive models of purchasers, an intercorrelation matrix needs to be constructed to test criteria (linear) independence. In addition, before

starting regression analysis, raw data need to be standardized to avoid biases by response styles of interviewees.

---

[i] Benzécri, J.P. (1973), *L'Analyse des Données, Part II, L'Analyse des Correspondances*, Paris: Dunod.

[ii] Hitt, M.A. and R.D. Middlemist (1979), "A Methodology to Develop the Criteria and Criteria Weightings for Assessing Subunit Effectiveness in Organizations", *Academy of Management Journal*, 22, (2), 356–374.

The **market shares** of competing organizations are a measure of their competitive strength (in the past). They indicate what portion of total sales volume or share of voice (for non-profit organizations) in the market has been captured by each competitor. They may also be viewed as indicators of competitors' strategies. A large market share points towards cost leadership in profit-oriented markets, whereas smaller shares may be a result of niche strategies, that is the organizations' focus on a selected part of the market. Such conclusions can be misleading, however, without knowledge of how stable the competitive situation

is. Thus, growth or decline in competitors' market shares must be monitored.

Competitor information sources

When the most important competitors are determined for each of the most attractive sub-markets, their skills and resources related to the success factors in those sub-markets may be assessed. The means for how to obtain the necessary information range from the illegal activity of industrial espionage to the acceptable, and universal, practice of using salespeople to monitor public actions of competitors in the field (see Special focus). Management has to find the most efficient way of gathering the information needed for evaluating the strengths and weaknesses of major competitors in a market, without leaving the ethical path of research.

Some firms disassemble the products of their competitors, like for example Xerox with Canon copiers. Others, such as GM and Toyota, enter into joint ventures to obtain information on the manufacturing techniques of their competitors or set up an office in their major competitor's home country, like IBM did in Japan, to have current information on what competitors are doing. In most cases it will be easier and less expensive to use information sources such as personal contacts with suppliers (including banks and communication agencies), producers of complementary products, consultants or mutual customers, trade fares, trade magazines, data banks, or publications of competitors. Companies that have instituted formal intelligence programs such as Digital Equipment, Eastman Kodak, or Gillette have an advantage over others which do competitor research on an ad hoc basis.

Internal analysis

When competitor analysis is completed, the next step is to add internal analysis data to allow a comparison of the extent to which the organization and its competitors possess the success factors needed in the most attractive sub-markets. To reduce workload and avoid any waste of time, only data related to the success factors in each of the attractive sub-markets are to be gathered. Data sources may be internal documents, experience of members of the organization, reports of consultants, customer complaints, or market research.

Determining differentiating capabilities

Having gathered the data needed for assessing the fulfilment potential of their organization compared with its most important competitors, management can summarize that data in terms of a profile of strengths and weaknesses for each competitor and for their own organization for each sub-market (Figure 4.9). The profiles for each sub-market are then compared and the relative competitive position of the organization determined.

Profiles of strengths and weaknesses

Having finished the assessment of skills and resources related to the success factors in the most attractive potential sub-markets, management can establish profiles of strengths and weaknesses of their organization and its major competitors.

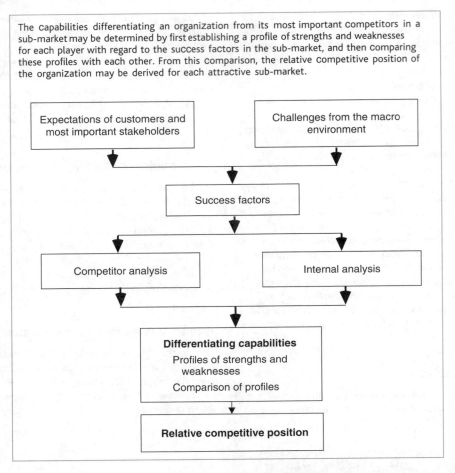

The capabilities differentiating an organization from its most important competitors in a sub-market may be determined by first establishing a profile of strengths and weaknesses for each player with regard to the success factors in the sub-market, and then comparing these profiles with each other. From this comparison, the relative competitive position of the organization may be derived for each attractive sub-market.

Figure 4.9   Determining the relative competitive position: Differentiating capabilities

A profile of strengths and weaknesses lists the success factors in a market and indicates how well the existing skills and resources of an organization fit them. Table 4.2 gives an example of a strengths and weaknesses profile of a competitor in the metallurgical engineering business in an LDC market. This profile reveals that the competitor can provide a number of references, has easy access to cheap loans, and enjoys high mobility of personnel. On the other hand, counter purchase capabilities, which are important for market success, as well as government relations, are less well developed.

Importance weights for the various success factors may be derived from the importance of fulfilment of the related expectations to customers and other stakeholders and from the importance of related (future) challenges from the macro environment (see Figure 4.6 and Table 4.1). They provide additional information about the appropriateness of capabilities available to competitors and the organization.

As Figure 4.10 shows, ideally the capabilities of an organization and the success factors in a market fit perfectly (Case 1). For example, the Nigerian government may be interested in attracting communications-equipment industries – which would bring in new technologies, utilize local materials, and allow Nigerians to move quickly into upper-level positions. At the same time a Finnish supplier, who is able to provide those benefits, seeks to market its know-how in the construction of turnkey plants for communications equipment in developing countries.

At times, however, the capabilities of an organization are not relevant to a particular sub-market. For example, the sophisticated distribution know-how of a producer of frozen foods such as Eskimo-Iglo, a daughter firm of Unilever, may not be relevant in a market that lacks a sophisticated transportation and storage infrastructure, such as the Ukraine (Case 2). On the other hand, even if the Brazilian market for atomic power-generation plants

Table 4.2 Profile of a major competitor's strengths and weaknesses

Management must evaluate to what extent each of the most important competitors as well as their own organization possesses the success factors in a sub-market. For that purpose they may list the success factors and compare the available skills and resources to those success factors on a scale from 1, "no relevant capabilities available", to 9, "excellent fit of available capabilities".

Competitor: Lurgi   Evaluation   Market: Angola

Success factors	Weakness								Strength
References	1	2	3	4	5	6	7	**8**	9
Counter purchase capability	1	2	**3**	4	5	6	7	8	9
Access to cheap loans	1	2	3	4	5	6	7	8	**9**
Relations to government	1	2	3	**4**	5	6	7	8	9
Training facilities	1	2	3	4	**5**	6	7	8	9
Project management experience	1	2	3	4	5	**6**	7	8	9
Mobility of personnel	1	2	3	4	5	6	7	**8**	9

appears to present a major opportunity for EDF (*Electricité de France*), the firm will not be able to respond to this opportunity if it lacks technical personnel speaking Portuguese and understanding the local culture which is a success factor in this market (Case 3). In short, a market opportunity cannot be translated into a specific business opportunity unless the organization's capabilities match the most important success factors in the market. Where the match is strong, the organization possesses a strength, where it is weak the organization has a weakness or its capabilities are not relevant to the market.

Comparison of profiles

To possess certain strengths is not enough to be successful in a market. If major competitors are able to match equally the same success factors, a distinction in the market becomes more difficult. Therefore, the profile of an organization's strengths and weaknesses has to be compared with the profiles of its major competitors (Table 4.3). This may lead to a list of success factors which the firm matches better than its competitors. The related capabilities are called **differentiating capabilities**. Management can rely on them in the development of a strategy. Apple Computer, for example, is well known for its superior know-how in the development of user-friendly computer interfaces. User-friendliness is a success factor in all markets where the personal computer is mainly used for visualization purposes. Apple has built its globally successful strategy on this distinctive competency.

Before management can take a final decision on what sub-markets to serve, they will need to check the capability of their organization to offer unique value to the customers and other important stakeholders in those sub-markets. That is, they need to check if their organization possesses any **competitive advantage.** By going through the list of differentiating capabilities for the sub-markets under consideration, management can identify the specific sources of competitive advantage of their organization. For example, it may be critical for a French producer of steel construction parts who wants to start a joint venture in Russia to be able to establish firm relationships with members of the supply system, such as steel mills and transportation companies, in order to ensure timely distribution. If the firm has long-term experience in building such relationships because of the company's actual involvement in Romania it may possess a differentiating capability that can be transformed into a competitive advantage.

However, differentiating capabilities may become competitive advantages only if the organization can successfully transform them into benefits for potential customers or other important stakeholders. Being capable of highly flexible low cost production, for example, can only become a competitive advantage when it can be transformed into low-priced customized products. Customers and stakeholders will have a high propensity to develop preferences and long-term relationships with the provider of such benefits if they are highly attractive to them.

Competitive advantages are strongest when they are unique to the organization, that is, when they cannot be easily duplicated. The family ties of owners and managers of Taiwanese and Hong Kong-based companies with business people from The People's Republic of China, for example, give them a competitive advantage over US companies in obtaining joint-venture contracts with Chinese firms. Management should not overlook, however, that competitors might develop capabilities quite fast through acquisitions, mergers, or cooperation. Finally,

Before an organization decides to pursue a market opportunity, it needs to determine whether it has the necessary
strengths to turn that opportunity into a viable business.
The line that runs from the lower left to the upper right
corners represents a match between capabilities available
to the organization and success factors in the market.

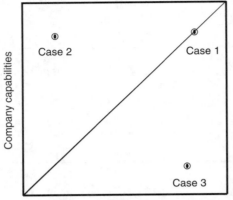

Case 1 – a Finnish turnkey plant supplier for communication equipment and the Nigerian government,
which is interested in improving the country's
communication infrastructure with locally manufactured equipment.
Case 2 – a European producer of frozen foods with
sophisticated distribution know-how, and the
Ukrainian market, which lacks a sufficiently reliable transportation and storage system.
Case 3 – the Brazilian market for atomic power-
generation equipment and a French manufacturer that lacks technical personnel who speak
Portuguese.

Figure 4.10 The fit among capabilities of an
organization and the success factors in a sub-market

a competitive advantage only exists if the customers and
stakeholders are ready to value the offered benefits by
adequate exchange reactions, such as paying a good price
or providing good will.

Sometimes organizations do not have any actual
particular differentiating capabilities in a market. In such
cases, they may either avoid serving the market or they
must develop differences from their competitors. Such
differentiation may take the form of providing creative
solutions to previously unsolved problems, applying new
technologies, making customers desire benefits that are
not currently offered, or simply promoting or distributing
in a new way.

The relative competitive position

The competitive position of an organization compared to
its most important rivals in a market may be analysed in a
number of ways, starting from a comparison of indicators
to an analysis of the position in the value chain to a
comparison of strengths and weaknesses and of portfolio
analysis. **Portfolio analysis** has been introduced in
Toolbox 2.3. It is able to provide a complex picture of
how various businesses of an organization or its products
are located in terms of their lifecycle compared with
competitors.

A **comparison of indicators**, such as the number of
customers per square metre of sales surface (in retailing),
the share of voice in major electronic media (for lobbying
organizations), the ROCE (return on capital employed) for
manufacturing firms, or EVA (economic value added) for
companies listed on the stock exchange, can be conducted
based on internal and available data from consultants or
statistical agencies. Toolbox 4.2 on benchmarking
discussed a potential technique for gathering the data
needed for a more detailed comparison.

A comparison of the **position in the value chain**
between the organization and its most important
competitors is discussed in Appendix 4.1. It shows how
the organization is embedded among its suppliers and
customers, what share it contributes to the total value of
the final product, how far it is able to influence the
processes of value creation and generation to the final
customers, and what are the effects of this position on
profitability compared with competitors.

The **comparison of profiles of strengths and
weaknesses** – as described above – provides a picture of
the organization's relative position in each success factor
of a sub-market. However, to simplify the comparison
with competitors across sub-markets for the purpose of
sub-market selection an overall measure of the **relative
competitive position** in each single sub-market is needed.
This measure can be calculated by first summing the
weighed scores each player in a sub-market attains across
all success factors and then dividing the score by the sum
of the weights (Table 4.4). How the total scores attained
by each of the players are compared with each other
depends on the model of competition managers have in
mind. If they want to be the number one in each served
market they have to beat the strongest competitor. That is,
they will compare their total score with that of the
strongest competitor.

If management wants their organizational unit to be
one of the top three in each sub-market they serve, they
will compare the total score of their organization with the
average total score of the three most important
competitors. Finally, if management considers that they
have to compete with all the major competitors at once,
they may tend to compare their organization's total
score to the sum of total scores of the major
competitors.

Table 4.3 Comparison of profiles of strengths and weaknesses

Strengths and weaknesses profiles of major competitors and the organization may be visually compared by introducing them into one single form. The distances between points in various colours representing each other player indicate the differences in evaluation. The more positively distant a point representing the evaluation of the organization from points representing competitors, the stronger is the position of the organization concerning that success factor. The column "Comments" is used for explanations why the depicted differences exist.

Success factors	Impor-tance	Evaluation	Comments
		very weak very strong	
		1 2 3 4 5 6 7 8 9	
		1 2 3 4 5 6 7 8 9	
		1 2 3 4 5 6 7 8 9	
		1 2 3 4 5 6 7 8 9	
		1 2 3 4 5 6 7 8 9	
		1 2 3 4 5 6 7 8 9	

Table 4.4 Determining the relative competitive position

Success factors	Sub-market 1 evaluations					Sub-market 2 evaluations				
	W	O	C_1	C_2	C_3	W	O	C_1	C_2	C_3
Sum of scores										
Total score = $\sum$/Number of success factors										
Rel. Comp. position										

W = importance weight   O = organization   C = competitor

Relative competitive position in the sub-market = $\dfrac{\text{Total score of the organization}}{\text{Total score of strongest competitor}}$

or: $\dfrac{\text{Total score of the organization}}{\text{Average total score of competitors}}$

or: $\dfrac{\text{Total score of the organization}}{\text{Sum of total scores of competitors}}$

None of these ways to determine the relative competitive position is objectively better or worse. But managers selecting a specific way of calculation should be aware of the model of competition they are assuming. The relative competitive positions they have determined for their organization in the most attractive sub-markets will be used for finally selecting the markets to serve. How this can be done will be described in the following chapter.

SUMMARY

To provide the bases for selecting the sub-markets to serve and to determine the way to differentiate their organization from competitors, management needs to assess the attractiveness of potential sub-markets as well as the differentiating capabilities available to their organization.

The assessment of sub-market attractiveness starts with determining criteria of market attractiveness. Corporate policy as well as core strategy of the organization provide valuable sources for the selection of appropriate criteria. For each of the selected criteria, measurement scales need to be developed. Agreement on the scales should allow an assessment procedure to be followed, which is transparent and acceptable to every member of the management team responsible. The resulting measures of sub-market attractiveness may need some correction according to potential future changes before they can be used for market selection purposes.

The assessment of the relative competitive position of an organization in the various potential sub-markets to serve may be based on the determination of core and success factors for each sub-market. A success factor, that is, capabilities needed to provide attractive offers to the stakeholders in a market, may be derived from various information sources. Market-oriented managers will base their search for success factors on current as well as potential future expectations of customers and other important stakeholders and, additionally, on current and foreseeable challenges from the macro environment.

Competitor analysis starts with determining relevant competitors in each potential sub-market to be served. Because competitors follow various basic strategic orientations, they may be clustered into strategic groups. Management will analyse more closely those competitors that belong to the same strategic group as their organization. In addition, the competitive structure of each of the sub-markets will need some attention before an internal analysis is conducted. To allow direct comparison, the internal analysis focuses on the same success factors as competitor analysis.

Finally, the data gathered by the analytical steps above can be used for determining differentiating capabilities of the organization. For that purpose, the profiles of strengths and weaknesses of competitors and the organization are compared with each other. If the organization is able to excel on an important success factor because of superior available capabilities, these capabilities can be used for differentiation purposes in the market.

The comparison of profiles of strengths and weaknesses also provides a basis for determining the relative competitive position of the organization in each potential sub-market. Together with the evaluation of market attractiveness, this relative competitive position will be used for market selection and differentiation decisions to be discussed in the following chapter.

Appendix 4.1

FACTORS INFLUENCING THE INTENSITY OF COMPETITION

The intensity of competition in a market depends on a great variety of factors. Depending on the perspective of the observer certain factors tend to become the focus of interest. For example, from the structural perspective of an industrial economist,[15] intensity of competition may be seen as depending on characteristics of some pre-specified important stakeholders in a market and the resulting relations between those stakeholders and the focal organization.

Also, from this perspective, the intensity of competition in a market depends on structural factors. These factors are to be found in direct competition among organizations currently serving the customers with similar products, in the threat of new direct competitors and substitutive problem solutions entering the market, as well as the negotiation power of suppliers and customers.

Following this theoretical model, direct competition, that is, rivalry among current suppliers of similar products, is reinforced by market exit barriers, technically fixed quantum leaps in production capacity, missing product differentiation, limited market growth, and a growing number of competitors.

Market exit barriers may result in an intensification of competitive action, because they prevent competitors from going out of business. Such barriers can be economic, technical, legal, social, or emotional. If a government is interested in a firm, then a national airline such as Italy's Alitalia, for example, may not be able to go out of business because the government finds ways to subsidize its heavy losses. Those subsidies allow the company to stay in fierce price competition with foreign competitors. Exit barriers such as this result in biased competition. Legal barriers to market exit may be, for example, high litigation such as in France when agency agreements may have to be terminated. Economic barriers to leave a market may be high fixed costs. An example of a combination of economic, technical, and emotional barriers can be cited from the US market. It takes a substantial time for US industrial customers to trust foreign suppliers in their willingness to stay in the market and to ensure spare parts delivery. Foreign suppliers must be aware that they cannot go in and out of the market as the level of demand in their home market may change. They may need to invest substantially in their US distribution and customer service system. It will be extremely hard for them to make a comeback in the US market if they once leave it for some time. In the assessment of intensity of competition, therefore, management must include such barriers.

Product differentiation may be missing because the targeted customers are not willing to recognize and pay for differences among various offers. In such a case, competition by suppliers of similar products will be intense. How intense the competition through **substitute offers** may become will depend on the subjective exchange value that substitutes are able to present. Technologically new solutions to customer problems may endanger well-established market relationships. If purchase, consumption, or usage situations of customers are so similar that competitors have great difficulty in presenting new attractive benefits, price competition by substitutive offers may impose a maximum price thereby limiting attainable margins.

The **business configuration** of organizations will make them more or less vulnerable to competitors. Business configuration is the level of concentration of activities of an organization in specific places or regions versus their spread across the world. A competitor may have concentrated the production of a part of its products in one place, such as BMW producing its diesel engines in Steyr, Austria. A concentrated approach may profit from experience curve effects and cost advantages independent of output size, for example because of the special skills of the available workforce, lower wages, or lower taxes. It often demands high basic investments, which reduces the probability of new competitors entering the market. But it increases the risk of political instability, strikes, or delivery problems.

Other competitors may have located production and sales of their products at different places across the world, such as British-Dutch Unilever, one of the world's leading firms in grocery products, which has production and sales units in the Americas as well as in Europe and Asia. They may have strongly increased the level of local competition by profiting from their closeness to the customers and the local content of their products, avoiding high transportation costs, closed distribution channels, and governmental policies hostile to foreign-located companies.

The **length of the value chain** covered by competitors, that is, how much of the entire production and marketing process from the procurement of raw materials to after-sales customer services is handled by an organization, is another potential factor of influence on the intensity of competition. European and US companies have traditionally relied on the integration of more steps of the value chain than big Japanese companies, such as Mitsubishi. Japan's strategically leading firms tend to restrict the part of the value chain that they cover themselves to the core of their business: that is, customer contact and core technology. All other parts of the total product value are generated by subcontractors, which either focus on small parts of the entire process such as just-in-time delivery of parts or provide system solutions like the development and production of the entire pollution equipment for a truck. Toyota, for example, only manufactures about 30 per cent of the value of their cars themselves. European imitators of this business model have managed to decrease the intensity of competition they are facing. Selva, a Bolzano (Italy) based company in the high-style furniture business, for example, have found that their strengths resided mainly in marketing activities, that is, defining international customer segments, designing attractive style furniture, and promoting and distributing it. Production was outsourced to firms specializing in certain processes.

Competitors covering a shorter part of the value chain can develop an enhanced innovation potential by focusing on their specialities. They need fewer assets and less profit from a smaller and more stable number of personnel, which not only is easier to manage but also represents a lower amount of relative fixed costs. But, intensity of competition may also be reduced by organizations covering a larger part of the value creation and generation. Zegna, another Italian firm marketing top-end menswear, is successful in managing most parts of the value chain. Not only do they put together their own clothes – at plants in Italy, Spain, and Switzerland – but they also spin the yarn and weave the cotton, cashmere, and wool fabrics that go into garments. Zegna has established more than thirty of its own shops in top locations around the world, along with more than 120 closely managed in-store boutiques. Zegna's success lies in its ability to manage the complexity of the value chain in such a way as to satisfy the expectations of an exclusive customer segment.[16]

The length of the value chain covered by an organization will to a certain degree depend on the **negotiation power of suppliers and customers** or intermediaries. Their negotiation power is reflected in the ability to change the balance of exchange to their favour. A high degree of concentration of suppliers increases the intensity of competition for resources. A high concentration of customers or intermediaries will intensify competition for their preference. If transaction costs, such as specific investment needs, technological dependency, or transportation is low, customers will easily be able to switch suppliers. In terms of their capacity to integrate vertically, customers as well as suppliers may even emerge as direct competitors.

In addition, the degree of **diversification**, that is, the number of markets competitors are serving based on a certain number of technologies, will influence intensity of competition. Diversified competitors – such as the big Korean conglomerate Daewoo, which produce everything from steel, or semiconductors, to cars and consumer electronics – can strategically transfer resources among their businesses. They are able to invest in a market to counter the activities of a competitor even when the short-term economic situation does not allow more specialized competitors to spend their funds.

If competitors spread available resources over too many markets, they will suffer from "under-spending" in at least some of those markets. Competition will be less intensive. And the competitors may be easily attacked through a concentrated effort. That is one of the reported reasons why Allied Domecq, the British producer of such well-known alcoholic beverage brands as Beefeater gin or Kahlua liquor after having bought the Spanish and Mexican spirits group Pedro Domecq and then suffering a subsequent 15 per cent drop of sales in 1995, decided to reshape their business to focus on fewer brands and markets.[17] On the other hand, if the resources of competitors are focused on a small number of markets "overspending" may take place. Competitors may be involved in very intensive competition because they are able to spend slack resources in defence of their positions.

The impact of **market growth** and the **number of competitors** on intensity of competition remains less clear. Business in many high-tech markets, for example, has shown that competition is not necessarily less intensive if a market is growing fast. On the other hand, stagnating markets may be characterized by rather inactive competitors if they have come to the conclusion that the market is rather unattractive. And merger mania in a number of markets such as air travel has shown that a decreasing number of competitors is no guarantee that competition will become less fierce.

Thus, factors other than structural seem to influence intensity of competition. From a behavioural perspective, they seem to be related to the mental models of business adopted by the top decision-making players in a market. Those mental models find their expression in business mission, business philosophy, and the core strategy of organizations.

For example, depending on a more or less focused **mission** restricting the size of their business domain competitors will react differently to competitive action. If a competitor defines its business domain as sweatbands for European women who ski, the size of the market is different than if it is defined as sweatbands for European women involved in sports. Depending on this definition the competitor either will not respond to the market entry of a new company with sweatbands for summer sports or will take actions to limit the success of the new entrant. On the other hand, a competitor having defined a narrow business domain will defend its market niche more fervently than competitors with business domains containing many markets to which they allocate their limited resources.

Competitive behaviour is strongly influenced by the values shared by the dominant group in the organization. **Business philosophy** may prompt some competitors to seek confrontation; others may be ready to cooperate where both parties can win. Microsoft, for example, attacks any competitor trying to do business in what they consider to be an attractive market. Germany's chemical giant BASF and US-based DuPont, on the other hand, decided to cooperate in an equal share joint venture to produce and market materials for nylon manufacturing in Asia. Although they are competitors in other markets they decided to invest about USD 750 million in what they intend to be a "long-term engagement in the Asian nylon markets".[18]

Core strategy decisions strongly influence the behaviour of competitors. For example, a competitor such as Korea's Samsung in consumer electronics may have decided to become a cost leader. Other competitors have decided to be specialists in one or more market niches, such as Gucci, the Italian marketer of fashionable women accessories. Others strive to be technological leaders, such as Fuchs, a small German engineering firm in the field of electrical arch furnaces for steel production, or are content with being a "me too" follower, such as Acer, the PC producer, from Taiwan. Each of these organizations will consider other organizations serving their market with a similar basic strategic orientation as direct competitors. Thus, they will compete against them more intensively than against others which are more strategically differentiated.

Another core strategy decision potentially influencing the intensity of competition concerns the degree of internationalization. More internationally active competitors might have the potential to react to a firm entering their "home" market by expanding their coverage of the entrant's home market. Such "cross subsidization" took place, for example, when Riva, the biggest Italian producer of high quality metal sheets, tried to increase its market share in the French and German automotive industries. German Thyssen and France's Sacilor (now Arcelor) fervently counter-attacked by saturating the Italian market with very low prices. Local competitors may apply what is called their "local charm", a better knowledge of the local culture, and strong personal ties in a closely knit network of mixed business and social relationships. Competition may be as intensive, but it is based on other capabilities.

Discussion questions

1. Choose an organization and develop a list of assessment criteria for potential markets. Explain the reasons for your selection of criteria.
2. How would you try to assess the future attractiveness of a potential market? Discuss the reasons for your choice of approach.
3. Compare the ways of determining success factors in a potential market. What pros and cons do you see for each of the alternatives?
4. Discuss the impact of various categories of expectations on the determination of differentiating capabilities.
5. How would you suggest determining the importance of stakeholder expectations? Explain the reasons for your choice.
6. Explain how success factors may be derived from challenges in an organization's macro environment.
7. Choose an organization and try to determine its most important competitors. What factors do you consider and why?
8. Compare some marketing research tools for determining an organization's relevant competitors from the customers' point of view.
9. Contact an organization of your choice and ask some managers what information sources about competitors they use. What additional information sources would you suggest using and why?
10. Explain and compare the ways an organization can determine its differentiating capabilities.

Notes and references

1. Stevenson, H.H. (1976), "Defining Strengths and Weaknesses", *Sloan Management Review*, 17 (Spring), 51–68.
2. Amit, R. and P.J.H. Shoemaker (1993), "Strategic Assets and Organizational Rent", *Strategic Management Journal*, 14, 33–46.
3. Day, G.S. and R. Wensley (1988), "Assessing Advantage: A Framework for Diagnosing Competitive Superiority", *Journal of Marketing*, 52, April, 1–20.
4. Tversky, A. and D. Kahnemann (1974), "Judgement Under Uncertainty: Heuristics and Biases", *Science*, 185, 1124–1131.
5. Arnold, J., C.L. Cooper, and I.T. Robertson (1998), *Work Psychology: Understanding Human Behaviour in the Workplace*, London: Finacial Times Pitman.
6. Janis, I.L. (1972), *Victims of Groupthink*, Boston, MA: Houghton Mifflin.
7. Peters, T.J. and R.H. Waterman Jr (1982), *In Search of Excellence*, New York: Harper & Row.
8. The PIMS Program (1980), Cambridge, Mass.: Strategic Planning Institute.
9. Campbell, A. (1999), "Taylored, not Benchmarked", *Harvard Business Review*, March/April, 41–50.
10. Llosa, S. (1996), *Contribution à l'étude de la satisfaction dans les services*, Doctoral Thesis, University of Aix–Marseille, Institut d'Administration des Entreprises.
11. Hunt, M.S. (1972), *Competition in the Major Home Appliance Industry*, *1960–1970*, Doctoral dissertation, Harvard University.
12. Smircich, L. and C. Stubbart (1985), "Strategic Management in an Enacted World", *Academy of Management Review*, 10, 724–736.
13. Hodgkinson, G.P. (1997), "The Cognitive Analysis of Competitive Structures: A Review and Critique", *Human Relations*, 50 (6), 625–654.
14. Osborne, J.D., C.I. Stubbart, and A. Ramaprasad (2001), "Strategic Groups and Competitive Enactment: A Study of Dynamic Relationships between Mental Models and Performance", *Strategic Management Journal*, 22, 435–454.
15. Porter, M.E. (1980), *Competitive Strategy*, Free Press: New York.
16. Rossant, J. (1996), "Is That a Zegna You're Wearing ?", *Business Week*, March 4, pp. 84f.
17. AP-Dow Jones News Service (1996), "Allied Domecq Posts Fall in Profit on Lower Sales", *The Wall Street Journal Europe*, May 15.
18. "BASF, DuPont Plan Joint Venture in Asia To Manufacture Nylon", *The Wall Street Journal Europe*, 11 April 1996.

Further reading

Hooley, G., J. Saunders and N. Piercy (2003), *Marketing Strategy and Competitive Positioning*, 3rd Ed., Prentice Hall: London.

5 Strategic positioning step 3: Selecting and implementing the intended market position

Learning objectives

After studying this chapter you will be able to

1 Compare the basic methods of market selection
2 Discuss the usefulness of portfolio analysis for market selection
3 Explain how cooperation increases the potential for success
4 Compare the basic methods of differentiation
5 Select the benefits to be emphasized specifically in a sub-market
6 Discuss methods of increasing the potential for differentiation
7 Assess the potential success of a selected method of differentiation
8 Explain the factors influencing marketing strategy implementation

---

SPOTLIGHT

Hilti Corporation, headquartered in Schaan, Liechten-stein, develops, manufactures, and markets high quality power tools and fastening systems to professional customers in the construction and building industries. By the end of the 20th century, Hilti had between 11,000 and 12,000 employees in 100 countries. With its premium product and quality service, Hilti places great emphasis on understanding and responding to the expectations of its customers. Its value proposition is to sell not only innovative products but also superior application expertise through "system solutions": tools and consumables (e.g. screws, fasteners, and drill bits) supported by services (e.g. application training, technical

literature, comprehensive repair service, and environ-mentally sound product disposal).

Hilti's major competitors are Black & Decker, the largest power tool marketer worldwide, which is also known for its sales of easy-to-use equipment to consumers through DIY channels; Germany's Bosch, which maintains a strong position in automotive and electromotor products sold exclusively through dealers; Japan-based Makita, which is well known for its electronic equipment; and Würth, the German retailer of construction supplies, which employs a direct sales force.

In 1996, Hilti launched a new strategy: "Champion 3C". The strategy focused on the customer through competence and concentration. The customer was seen as the most important stakeholder of the organization. Hilti's competence relied on the technological and marketing/direct sales capabilities of the firm, while concentration stood for the focus on those markets and product offers that had the greatest potential for sustainable leadership positions and long-term profit.

Hilti divided its customer base into three segments. One of the segments consisted of large construction companies, such as French Bouygues or Suez Lyonnaise, which focused on large projects, worked on an international scale, and specialized in project management. Because those customers had highly complex applications, Hilti decided to provide them with advanced technical advice to differentiate from competitors. In addition,

Hilti offered professional purchasing managers a single sourcing opportunity to help them decrease the number of suppliers and reduce costs through decreased working capital, tailored delivery, invoicing, and payment terms.

The new strategy was presented to the company's market organizations and business units as a broad direction. Hilti's top management viewed local implementation as critical. Implementation efforts were governed by five fundamental values: tolerance of differing opinions, acceptance of change, self-responsibility, freedom of choice, and learning.

Source: Adapted from Shaner, J. (2000), *Hilti France: Strategy Implementation (A)*, IMD: Lausanne, Switzerland.

Selecting and implementing the intended market position

Most organizations have to take on new challenges and continually develop their portfolio of markets served if they want to survive in their competitive environment. Basic guidelines of what business to pursue and what to leave for others, as formulated by the defined business domain, delimit the field of action. However, in most cases, the number of potential markets to be served remains greater than the financial or personal resources available to the organization to serve them properly. A selection has to be made.

A management training organization, for example, is confronted with a large number of sub-markets, such as top executives and entrepreneurs, as well as people from middle and lower management levels. Within each of those sub-markets, there may be various segments of potential customers such as functional specialists to be upgraded or kept on the latest level of development, general managers to be reinforced in their social skills, highly experienced people to be updated, or high potentials to be prepared for higher level responsibilities. Because of resource and capability restrictions, no management training organization may be able to serve all those segments simultaneously in a way which provides highly attractive value. A selection needs to be made. Because this selection has a significant impact on the potential success of the organization, it has to be made with great care.

As described so far, the strategic positioning process provides management with the data needed for market (sub-market or segment) selection. To select the sub-markets to be served, management can combine information about the distinctive capabilities of their organization in each of the potential sub-markets with the

levels of attractiveness of those markets. The goal is to decide whether to stay with the current portfolio, to expand or reduce the field of action, or to replace the focus on some particular markets with others. At least a rank order may be established, which indicates the intensity of serving the markets. (Figure 5.1)

Before a final decision can be taken on which markets are to be served with what intensity, however, the way the organization wants to differentiate its exchange offers from competitors in those markets needs to be decided. Potential ways of differentiation can be determined by comparing the organization's differentiating capabilities with the customers' and other stakeholders' perceived importance of expectations within each of the sub-markets. Only the sub-markets for which the organization possesses or for which it can acquire relevant capabilities for attractive differentiation can be selected as targets. In the example of the management training organization, the availability of trainers with superior experience in coaching and social system analysis may lead to a differentiation from competitors through more socially competent reflection, advice, or training in leading their organizations. Senior executives and high potentials may, therefore, be selected as target markets.

Having developed unique value propositions for the selected markets, management can analyse the potential economic as well as psychological results of implementing those propositions. If the potential results appear to contribute to the fulfilment of the organization's mission satisfactorily, the intended market position of the organization (or the respective organizational sub-unit) is fixed. Rules of behaviour, structural consequences, processes, and measures of success in striving to achieve the intended position can be established, further developed, or simply reinforced.

By combining information about the relative competitive position of their organization in the various sub-markets with the levels of attractiveness of those markets, management may select the sub-markets to be served and determine the intensity of serving them. Before a final decision can be made, however, the way the organization wants to attractively differentiate its exchange offers from competitors within the sub-markets to be served needs to be determined. Having developed a unique value proposition, management may analyse the potential economic as well as psychological results of implementing that proposition. If the potential results appear to contribute to the fulfilment of the organization's mission, the intended market position of the organization or the organizational sub-unit is fixed.

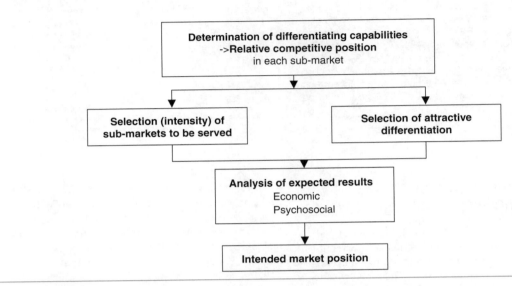

Figure 5.1 The strategic positioning process Part 3: Selecting the intended market position

However, as the discussion in Chapter 2 has shown, strategy is not a tightly linked activity system. It is a framework containing guidelines that

- open up a space in which opportunities may be sought and exploited,
- simultaneously delimit the field in which to operate,
- indicate the general direction to be taken (objectives), and
- prescribe rules of behaviour to be followed in the search for opportunities and their exploitation.[1]

Following the waterfall principle, the precision of those guidelines is increasing from general objectives, priorities, and principles in corporate policy to more closely specified market boundaries, objectives, and rules of behaviour in core strategy, business unit strategies, and strategies for product lines or projects. Consequently, the implementation of any strategy does not consist of management prescribing what has to be done and controlling its execution while the staff of the organization

is preoccupied with busily executing what others have decided. Management's role in implementation is more to continually search for the "right" objectives, to formulate principles, to be a living example of rules of behaviour, and to establish structures and processes which help members of the organization reach the objectives and follow the rules.

That is, strategy formulation process, content, and implementation are not distinct. In a continuous feedback system, strategy formulation and implementation occur simultaneously. Actions are taken not only based on an analytically developed, continually communicated, and consciously shared strategic framework, but also simply as spontaneous reactions to stimuli from the market and macro environment. These actions drive the organization in a certain direction. Actions and resulting outcomes are interpreted by management and, in turn, influence their formulation of the strategic framework.

This chapter concentrates first on the selection of an intended market position and then discusses various issues concerning the implementation of the selected position from the described perspective.

Selecting the markets to serve

Basic options

In selecting the number and kind of markets to serve, as well as the intensity of serving them, an organization can choose from four basic options: market penetration, geographic expansion, market development, and diversification (see Figure 5.2).

Market penetration

The highest degree of resource concentration occurs when an organization decides to penetrate a market in a limited geographic area that it already serves. This leads to production and marketing experience curve effects, which allow the organization to lower prices and improve quality at the same time. The result is increasingly loyal customers.

Markets that are in an early stage of development require a greater investment of resources. For example, when Netherlands-based Philips first introduced compact disks, a large budget was necessary to train sales personnel, both within the company and in stores that would sell the new product, and to communicate the benefits of the new technology to customers through advertising and promotion campaigns. If the market has high growth potential, such an investment is justified because it will establish a strong competitive position before other firms enter the market.

Market penetration involves the use of several different tactics, such as product-line stretching, product proliferation, and product improvement.

1. *Product-line stretching*. To stretch its product line, an organization that has successfully served a small segment of its relevant market in the past gradually adds new items to the existing product line in order to reach a broader market. Japanese car producers, for example, began their market penetration in Europe with inexpensive, middle-sized cars. From there, they stretched their product line to small cars, then started offering larger and stronger cars. Their latest move has been to challenge European competitors with luxury and sports car models.

2. *Product proliferation*. When an organization chooses to penetrate the market through product proliferation, it introduces as many different models or types of their total product as possible at each point in the product line. For example, Casio, the Japanese calculator and watch manufacturer, introduced a variety of hand calculators, with different functions, features, and designs, to meet the expectations of most customer segments in the market, from low-price calculators for everyday purposes to highly sophisticated devices for special applications. The company has been using the same tactic with watches in the lower price ranges of the market.

3. *Product improvement*. When an organization continually augments the capabilities and reliability of its products, extends warranties and services, and applies improved technologies quickly, it has chosen the tactic of product improvement. An example of a company which uses such a tactic is Japan-based Komatsu, the most important competitor to Caterpillar in the market of earth-moving and construction equipment. They have taken a significant share of the market by continually improving the quality of their products, including an extension of their warranties and an extension of the range of their products' application through enhanced technologies.

Market penetration involves a trade-off: the more an organization limits the number of markets it serves, the more opportunities it leaves for competitors to increase their presence in other markets. Japanese companies, for instance, strengthened their competitive positions in Southeast Asia and Latin America before entering the US market. They were not challenged in these markets by US competitors, who at that time focused their activities on European markets.

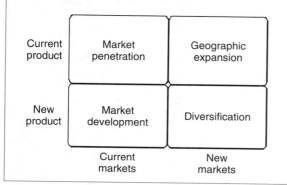

Basically, an organization can choose between serving current markets more intensively and entering new markets, either with products that are currently available or with products that are new to potential customers.

Figure 5.2 Basic portfolio options
Source: Adapted from H.I. Ansoff (1957), "Strategies for Diversification", *Harvard Business Review*, September–October, 113–124.

Geographic expansion

Expanding operations to new geographic areas is most appropriate when the organization is relatively small and has developed an innovative product for which patents offer little protection, or when the advantage of an organization's new product can be matched by competition in a fairly short time. For example, Austria-based Omicron, a small firm specializing in electronic testing equipment, had developed an innovative test set for protective relays, transducers, and energy meters of electric utilities and industry. It expanded globally in three years' time by cooperating with Germany's Siemens AG, which let them use their distribution network. Geographic expansion is especially appropriate if the life cycles of the organization's products in different markets are similar, as is often the case for industrial goods and consumer durables in developed economies, including the newly industrialized countries.

Even when at the limit, an organization is not obliged to sell its innovative products in its home market before entering another one. If other markets are better suited to the new product, the organization may launch it there. For example, Matsushita, the Japanese consumer electronics giant, exported its colour TV sets to the United States five years before it introduced them at home. Its managers did not believe that the Japanese market was ready for the new product.

Geographic expansion is also appropriate when important competitors are opening up new markets, or when opportunities in new markets will be available for only a short time. These occasions often arise within high-tech industries like computer technology and advanced circuit technology. The speed with which new computer chips, for example, can be matched by competitors means that they are marketed globally as quickly as possible to take advantage of product superiority as long as possible.

Additionally, geographic expansion becomes necessary when intense price competition in slow-growing markets leads to diminishing profit margins. To achieve higher sales volume, the organization introduces its products in markets where few product modifications are required. For example, faced with strong competition from Japan's Fuji and Germany's Agfa-Gevaert in US, European, and Japanese markets, which were growing at very low speeds, Eastman Kodak Co. turned to China. There, the 35 mm film sales have quintupled since the early 1980s to roughly 120 million rolls in 1995. Only one of the country's seven domestic makers, Lucky Film Corporation, had a truly national brand in 1996. Though just 12 per cent of China's population of 1.3 billion people owned a camera, photography quickly became as popular in China as in Japan. By the end of the century, China overtook Japan, becoming the world's second largest film market after the United States.[2]

Market development

In following the basic strategy of market development, an organization focuses its operations on offering a stream of new products to the markets it currently serves. This approach is appropriate if the organization is well established in its geographic markets and lacks the motivation, ability, or knowledge to adapt to a new environment. Market development is the most suitable option when current products have matured, and new products have the potential to grow quickly.

For example, in the past, Japanese Hirata Technical only produced car body parts for Honda. Capitalizing on this business relationship and their specific local marketing expertise, the company has now branched out into making parts for dry batteries.[3]

Diversification

Diversification may be an attractive alternative when served markets stagnate, and new markets in new geographic areas are generating a high return on investment and have high growth potential. Körber/Hauni, the German world's top manufacturer of cigarette machines, for example, was confronted with a stagnating market in the late 1980s, when smoking became less popular and cigarette machines more efficient. While Körber/Hauni clearly defended its leadership in this market, it also entered into a quick and active diversification programme. The company founded Hauni Elektronik, which launched a breakthrough innovation in the field of oxygen production from normal air. E.C.H. Will, another spin-off of the company's diversification programme, established a world market share of 90 per cent for cut-size sheeters (machines that cut small papers for items such as passports and cheque books).[4]

However, there are two dangers associated with diversification. First, entering a new market in a new geographic area is risky, especially when it involves a technology (type of customer problem solution) that is new to the organization. The new business may have only a few aspects in common with existing operations, so the organization may benefit very little from synergy. Second, even if the organization is able to overcome this problem, competitors may have chosen a more focused portfolio strategy and may dominate the markets in which the organization does not have enough experience to develop strong competitive advantages.

For example, it may seem attractive to Cathay Pacific, the Hong Kong-based airline, to invest in a hotel chain in Australia because tourism from the United States, Japan, and Europe is increasing there and customers can be flown in on the company's jets. However, Cathay Pacific may find itself confronted with US or European competitors specializing in global hotel management and possessing long-established relations with international tour operators and travel agencies. It may also be faced with Australian competitors with more knowledge of the intricacies of Australian regulations and a stronger lobbying position when it comes to construction and operating permissions.

Selection of markets

To decide what markets should be served, management must examine simultaneously the attractiveness of potential markets, sub-markets, or market segments and the competitive position of their organization in those markets. On the one hand, management will try to focus the activities of their organization on the most attractive markets. On the other hand, it has to consider the differentiating capabilities currently available and those that will be available in the near future to serve those markets. Additionally, the decision makers have to ensure that the market portfolio of the organization is well balanced in terms of current and future contributions to the business mission. The priority of Swiss-based Zurich Insurance Co., for example, is to increase earnings power by maintaining a consistent policy of focusing on selective growth. They are active in non-life and life insurance,

reinsurance, and asset management, and benefit from having one of the industry's most global networks, an expanded position in the US market through acquisitions, a sharply focused approach to customers, and product innovation.[5]

Market portfolio

A possible method of simultaneously analysing the attractiveness of markets (sub-markets or market segments) and the competitive position of an organization (a business unit, a product line, or a product) in those markets is portfolio analysis, as described in Toolbox 2.3. The resulting portfolio positions may be used for the comparison of potential sub-markets (Figure 5.3).

Aside from the disadvantages of the portfolio method already discussed, such as the selection and weighing of assessment criteria and the determination of the relative competitive position, there are others management should be aware of when interpreting the results. First, portfolio analysis does not provide for interdependencies among the compared sub-markets. Depending on how the

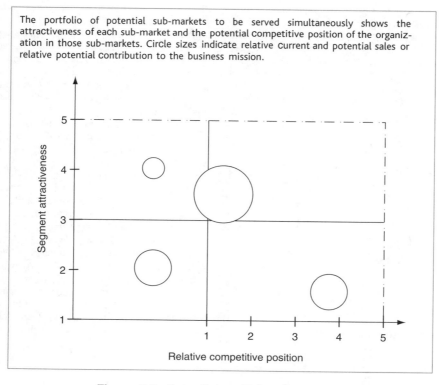

The portfolio of potential sub-markets to be served simultaneously shows the attractiveness of each sub-market and the potential competitive position of the organization in those sub-markets. Circle sizes indicate relative current and potential sales or relative potential contribution to the business mission.

Figure 5.3   Potential portfolio of sub-markets

sub-markets have been defined, they may contain the same customers, may need the same technological basis, and may have shared sources of costs of value-creation or value generation. For example, if customer segments have been formed based on benefits sought or application, the same customers may be present in various segments. They may expect an organization serving them in one situation to also do so in another. Therefore, if management decides to eliminate one sub-market, it may lose another or at least have a much worse competitive position there.

Second, portfolio analysis tends to be applied in a backward-looking manner. Often, only the sub-markets already being served by the organization are taken into account. To avoid that problem, in defining the

sub-markets to compare, management has to consciously include new potential markets. If these potential markets already exist, their attractiveness can be determined. The potential relative competitive position must be estimated. However, this does not present a real problem, if the strengths and weaknesses comparison has been done as described in Chapter 4, based on success factors in the sub-market. For new sub-markets to be created, only estimates of attractiveness and competitive position can be used.

Third, internationally operating organizations are faced with more complex decisions. The International Spotlight describes approaches to handle this increased complexity and gives some examples for the potential application of portfolio analysis.

INTERNATIONAL SPOTLIGHT

INTERNATIONAL PORTFOLIO ANALYSIS

Portfolio analysis provides an overview of how an organization has allocated its resources to date, what range of attractive markets exist, and what the competitive position of the organization is in those markets. For internationally operating organizations, portfolio analysis is more complex than for a domestic business because it must provide for additional units of analysis. It starts at the corporate level, where geographically defined markets and markets defined by benefits provided to a number of stakeholders, as well as the available technologies, must be compared. It proceeds to the business unit level, where customer segments and product lines can be analysed for each of the units on the superior level

of analysis. Then, it covers the product-line level, where, for each product line and customer segment, the related portfolio of products can be assessed (see Exhibit A).

For example, a firm such as Nike, the US marketer of sports footwear, may start a global portfolio analysis on the corporate level. There, not only it will compare different product-markets, like low-price sports fashion for young consumers, footwear for fashion-conscious sports amateurs, or expensive high-tech solutions for sports professionals, but the company must also consider the attractiveness of the geographic markets it currently serves and compare its competitive position there to other potential markets.

Exhibit B shows a portfolio comparing geographically defined sub-markets of low-price sports fashion for young consumers, along with market attractiveness and the relative competitive position of the analysing company. Such a portfolio can be used to determine where the company has acted successfully to seize opportunities in attractive areas, and where it has allowed competitors to establish strong positions before it began to build forces. By comparing the firm's current portfolio of country-markets to opportunities, management can determine if the company is over-committed in less attractive markets, leaving highly attractive markets untapped. In Exhibit B, Belgium and Denmark represent attractive markets that need more attention, when compared to Canada. In addition, the company can analyse different levels of technology (such as complete automation vs. hand assembly) used to produce its shoes.

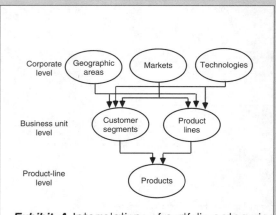

Exhibit A Interrelations of portfolio categories

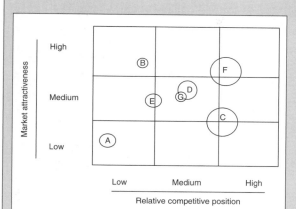

Exhibit B Portfolio of country-markets

Note: Circle sizes are proportional to market share in a country-market. Letters represent country markets:
A = Austria, B = Belgium, C = Canada, D = Denmark,
E = Spain, F = France,
G = Greece.

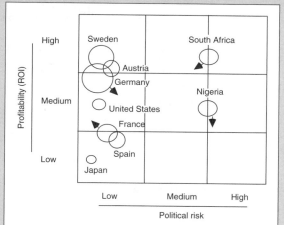

Exhibit C Political risk/profitability portfolio of country-markets

Note: Circle sizes are proportional to potential country-market sales. Arrows indicate the expected direction of change in country-market positions in the coming three years.

At the business unit level, customer segments – such as rebellious high-school kids, young, single professionals who work out on weekends, or middle-aged women who break up their time at home with their small children by going to a spa to exercise – may be compared in terms of their attractiveness and the firm's competitive position in each geographic market. The portfolio position of product lines, like sporty leisure shoes or health care shoes for children, can also be analysed per country, market, or in relation to a certain production technology. Of course, Nike may assess the product mix of every product line, such as running, walking, or tennis shoes, as well as the product mix for each customer segment.

In addition to the higher number of units of analysis to compare when conducting portfolio analysis, internationally operating organizations have to consider even more factors to determine the positions of their potential markets in a portfolio. Factors such as political and financial risk, transferability of funds, taxes and subsidies, and/or the potential for standardization could influence the portfolio structure. Such factors have to be included in the comparison to increase the information level of the analysis for decision purposes. For example, trade between Ireland and Bolivia, although profitable, may be less attractive due to insecurities with regard to Bolivia's government and administrative barriers in the form of import restrictions. Such factors can be taken into account in the development of the scale which is used to measure attractiveness, but they can also be considered explicitly in the way the

portfolio is designed. Exhibit C shows an example of how portfolio analysis can compare profitability to political risk in various country-markets.

Having a balanced portfolio is of no help to the organization if the funds generated in one market cannot be freely transferred to another. For example, if an agricultural products company such as Charoen Pokphand, based in Bangkok, has cash cows in the Philippines, Indonesia, and China, but is not allowed to transfer funds from there to its newly started business units in Eastern Europe, the international business strategy will be handicapped. To check this situation, the transferability of funds earned in different regions of the world can be introduced in the assessment (see Exhibit D).

Management decisions will be guided by the rules regarding the extent of internationalization stated in the organization's corporate policy. If major competitors are all active on a global scale, as is the case in the commercial aircraft, computer, and watch industries, geographic market restriction could turn out to be fatal. On the other hand, in cases such as the furniture industry, where most business is carried out locally, the example of Sweden-based IKEA demonstrates that an above-average extent of internationalization can be very successful. IKEA started internationalizing their business through supply agreements with factories in Eastern Europe, and has opened stores in Western Europe and later in the USA and Asia at a time when their competitors concentrated on local business opportunities.

Market attractiveness/ Competitive position	International transferiability of funds		Region
	High	Low	
High attractiveness/ Strong competitive position			Pacific Rim
			EU
			NAFTA
High attractiveness/ Weak competitive position			Pacific Rim
			EU
			NAFTA
Low attractiveness/ Strong competitive position			Pacific Rim
			EU
			NAFTA
Low attractiveness/ Weak competitive position			Pacific Rim
			EU
			NAFTA

Note: Circle sizes are proportional to share of total sales.

Exhibit D Portfolio combining market attractiveness/competitive position analysis with international transferability of funds

Technology portfolio

Markets are characterized not only by specific benefits provided to certain customer groups, but also by the technologies applied to generate the intended benefits. Management, therefore, must decide what technologies to hold in its portfolio to adequately contribute to the solution of the problems of their customers and other important stakeholders. To make informed decisions, management can assess the attractiveness of each available technology for the sub-markets under consideration and compare it to the relative strengths of the organization within those technological fields. The technology portfolio has to be considered in all market selection decisions, as it reveals the sustainability of distinctive capabilities for the delivery of superior total products.

Figure 5.4 shows that the attractiveness of a technology is defined by its potential for customer problem solution and diffusion. A technology's problem-solving potential depends on its scientific and technical potential for further development, as well as on the amount of time and development risks until the technology is available. Micro mechanics, for example, is a field of technology which has enormous potential for future application not only in toys but also in medicine, such as the treatment of high cholesterol. Japanese researchers have worked on its development for 20 years. They have made significant progress, but as yet, no application with a strong economic impact has resulted.

The diffusion potential of a technology is determined by its general customer and stakeholder acceptance, and

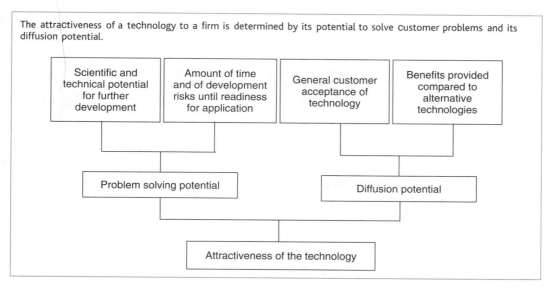

Figure 5.4 Factors influencing the attractiveness of a technology to a firm

Source: Adapted from Specht, G. (1994), "Portfolioansätze als Instrument zur Unterstüzung strategischer Programmentscheidungen", in Corsten, H. (ed.), *Handbuch Produktionsmanagement*, Gabler: Wiebaden, p. 105.

by the benefits provided by the technology compared to alternatives. For example, microbiological cloning is a technology with great potential for further development. A company, such as UK-based pharmaceutical manufacturer Glaxo, that holds this technology in its portfolio, however, must be aware of the risks it takes with regard to legal regulations or resistance from environmentalists in certain countries such as Germany.

The relative strength of an organization in a field of technology depends on the potential for differentiation from competitors and for implementation of the technology in the organization (see Figure 5.5). The potential of an organization to differentiate itself from competitors in a field of technology is determined by the (technology specific) know-how available to the organization relative to its competitors and the opportunity to become a technological leader in the field.

The potential for implementation depends on how well a technology fits into the competitive strategy of the organization and the availability of complementary technologies in the organization. For example, if a laser technology for cutting purposes fits the competitive strategy of being a technological leader in cutting problem solutions, and the company possesses the engineering expertise to construct the relevant machinery, the potential for successful implementation of this technology in the company is very good.

Market selection

Based on potential market and technology portfolios, management can take decisions on what benefits to provide to which stakeholders based on what technologies (Table 5.1). An additional portfolio of currently served and potential geographic markets (see International Spotlight) may help to determine the geographic focus of the organization. When using the described portfolios for strategic marketing decisions, managers should keep in mind that these tools are useful to achieve some structured insights in a field of complex interdependencies, but they do not provide a formula-based decision model on which they can blindly rely. Some tentative conclusions to be drawn from the established portfolios will be discussed in the following.

Where the organization possesses strong competitive positions in attractive sub-markets or technologies, the portfolio should build on those strengths. Focusing on the strengths of their organization compared to competitors, managers strive to make their organizations even more different by enhancing the difference in capabilities detected in competitor analysis. Their organizations develop and sustain unique profiles of bundles of skills and resources, which give them the opportunity to offer unique value to their stakeholders. Only those weaknesses that represent an existential threat to the success of the organization are diminished (Figure 5.6).

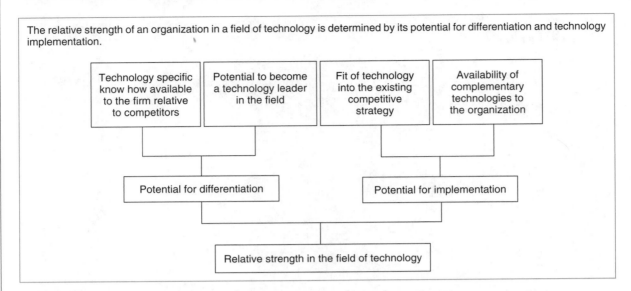

The relative strength of an organization in a field of technology is determined by its potential for differentiation and technology implementation.

Figure 5.5 Factors influencing the relative strength of an organization in a field of technology

Source: Adapted from Specht, G. (1994), "Portfolioansätze als Instrument zur Unterstützung strategischer Programmentscheidungen", in Corsten, H. (ed.), *Handbuch Produktionsmanagement*, Gabler: Wiebaden, 105.

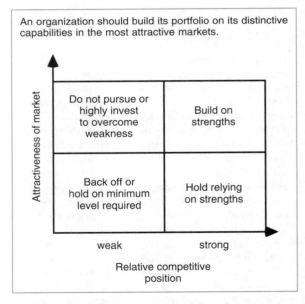

An organization should build its portfolio on its distinctive capabilities in the most attractive markets.

Figure 5.6 Matching distinctive capabilities with market attractiveness

Where attractive opportunities exist but the organization is in a relatively weak competitive position, management should either not further pursue those opportunities or invest a substantial part of its resources to overcome the weaknesses. Such investment may, for example, not only take the form of intensive research and development, the search for a cooperation partner in distribution and logistics, but may also result in a takeover of a firm that possesses the missing competencies. The North American market for ski-lift equipment, for example, may look promising to an Italian producer such as Leitner. However, the firm should refrain from investing in this market if it finds out that competitors are in a better cost position because they have production facilities in place, or the firm should undertake an intensive search to find a North American partner for a strategic alliance.

Managers who focus on reducing the weaknesses of their organization compared to their competitors run a risk. As they strive to match their rivals by building up or acquiring missing capabilities, competing organizations tend to converge. Where managers share a set of beliefs about how to compete in their industry or strategic group, organizations become increasingly similar in their available capabilities. Competitors end up not knowing how to differentiate from each other. Creating and generating unique customer value seems impossible to managers. They tend to consider their products commodities, which can only be sold via the lowest price or the strongest share of voice. In the end, formerly attractive sub-markets become unattractive.

When an organization has distinctive strengths in a comparatively unattractive sub-market, management should first find out what evaluation criteria contributes to labelling the market as unattractive. Market attractiveness is not necessarily a given. For example, the growth rate of a market, its level of profitability, or intensity of competition may at least partly depend on the actions set by the organization. That is, first, ways of improving market attractiveness are to be checked for their feasibility.

If the attractiveness of the sub-market cannot be increased by means available to the organization, management may decide to hold the attained position, by investing as much of its resources as needed. For example, if a Finnish chemical engineering company, such as Jacob Poeri, has long-lasting relationships with customers in Eastern European countries with economic difficulties, such as Romania, Ukraine, or Bulgaria, it might decide to maintain those relationships to be positioned for potential future orders. But it will not do more than is necessary to hold its position. Similarly, if an organization has a weakness in serving a comparatively unattractive sub-market, it will not pursue that market.

Management has to decide if they want their organization to focus on one sub-market, a number of selected sub-markets, or to serve all potential sub-markets. As shown by Table 5.1, technologies currently used or new to the organization may be applied to provide currently served or new stakeholders with customary or new benefits. Decision criteria, in addition to market attractiveness and competitive position, may be the spread of limited resources, the fit of needed capabilities, and the fit of expectation profiles of customers and other important stakeholders. Serving all attractive potential sub-markets will lead to success only if it can be based on shared technologies, and if the organization possesses sufficient financial and personal resources. St Paul- and Austin-based 3M, for example, expands to all potential markets for which it can offer attractive value by applying one or more of 12 basic technologies. Organizations with rather limited resources will tend to focus on a limited number of sub-markets in order to be able to concentrate a substantial amount of these resources on each of the targets. Such penetration decisions are only viable, however, if the selected sub-markets have substantial volume and the organization can build a defendable competitive position.

If the capabilities needed for successfully serving the selected sub-markets converge, the organization can develop and more easily sustain core competencies that allow differentiation from competitors over an extended period of time. A close fit of customer and stakeholder expectation profiles in the selected sub-markets is important for smaller organizations to develop and sustain an unambiguous identity. If, for example, a hotel on the Italian Riviera tries to simultaneously accommodate families, retired people, bus travellers, sales representatives, and management training groups, it will have substantial problems in offering value to all of them.

An organization will be most successful if it has a balanced mix of sub-markets, those with different cash-flow positions and resource requirements; and when it serves an attractive mix of customer segments, those at different stages of product adoption with product lines that contain products at different stages of maturity. That is, the situation of the organization is at its best when some parts of the market portfolio provide the resources needed by others for their positive development, and when the choice of market and technology portfolios provides for a balance of business cycles in industries as well as regions of the world.

For example, Japan's Sony Corp. cannot count on its TV sets always selling well and being highly profitable. A portfolio of product lines would spread the market risk. If profits decline as its TVs move through the product lifecycle, Sony will need new products to help maintain sales and cash flow. Thus, over time, Sony developed

---

Table 5.1 Options for market selection

In selecting the sub-markets or segments to serve, management must combine stakeholders, benefits, and technologies. In each category, management can rely on current stakeholder relations and capabilities, but may also choose to enter new fields of activity.

	Technologies			
	Currently used		New to the organization	
Benefits	Customary	New	Customary	New
Current	Market penetration	Benefit extension	Technological extension	Total extension
Stakeholders				
New	Geographic expansion	Benefit/customer diversification	Technology/customer diversification	Total diversification

high-fi towers, the Walkman, the Watchman, compact discs, and video cameras, investing in them in the expectation that future sales and profits of these products would be strong. Because the investment that is needed to be at the forefront of technological development is substantial, Sony decided to serve only one broad market: consumer electronics. But again, in order to spread the risk of this decision and to profit from given opportunities, the firm developed a global portfolio of country-markets in which it serves different customer segments. These include teens buying their first stereo equipment to play pop music, or lovers of classical music who are ready to spend substantial amounts of money to own the best recordings and to enjoy perfect sound reproduction.

Differentiation

Before a final decision about the market portfolio of the organization can be taken, a way to attractively differentiate the exchange offers of the organization from competitors in the potential markets needs to be found. Differentiation may relate to the product of an organization, that is, the result of its value generation processes or these processes themselves. Sophisticated differentiation allows the creation of "new" markets. For example, in the mid-1990s, competition in the US PC market became increasingly fierce. There were signs that demand for home PCs was levelling off. In 1996, only 8 per cent of US households were on the Internet. During this year, Japanese Bandai Digital Entertainment, instead of seeking head-on confrontation with PC manufacturers, unveiled Pippin, a stripped down Macintosh developed with Apple that looked like a video game machine, offered Internet access and a CD-ROM, and plugged into a TV set. Bandai sold parents on Pippin's educational benefits accessible through the Net, while pitching kids on games. Its price was closer to that of a VCR than a PC. The company created its "own new market".[6]

Direct confrontation will also be successfully avoided by changing some of the rules of the "game". US-based PC makers Dell Computer and Gateway 2000, for example, have discovered that experienced business clients and knowledgeable consumers looking for the most cutting-edge PC models know what they want, and therefore are ready to order hardware by phone. Both companies decided to build to order, rather than run up big inventories of various finished systems like most PC firms (35 for Dell versus 110 days for Compaq Computer). They created a mail-order market, which represents about 20 per cent of total PC sales in the United States and around 30 per cent of total PC sales in the UK.[7]

Having developed a unique value proposition, management can analyse the potential economic as well as psychological results of implementing that proposition. If the potential results appear to lead to the fulfilment of the organizational mission, the intended market position of the organization or the respective organizational sub-unit is fixed. In the following, potential approaches to differentiation will be discussed and methods will be introduced for evaluating their potential success in a market.

Foundations of successful competition

To be able to successfully implement their intended sub-market portfolio, organizations must find and develop a way of attractively differentiating themselves (or their products) from competitors. Successful differentiation should be based on distinctive capabilities that are currently available or can be built up or acquired and sustained for some time.

For example, Hong Kong's very successful apparel makers Toppy, Esprit, and Theme all share something that Japanese apparel makers lack: cost competitiveness. Most of the clothes are made in China, and each of the three firms designs, produces, and markets its wares itself. In Japan, they are displayed near fashions from DKNY, Max Mara, and Calvin Klein, but sell for half the price of the New York brands. They possess another plus that Europeans and Americans cannot match: a grasp of the fashion sense of Oriental women. Their colours are not overly bold, and the widespread use of materials like silk appeals to Asian customers.[8]

Although specific to each organization and market, distinctive capabilities are the bases of four broad categories of differentiation – cost leadership, generation of superior value, time leadership, and reliable relationships. Successful differentiation can be based on one or a combination of these categories. The best performers are likely to be driven by capabilities that combine efficiency and stakeholder orientation.[9]

Cost leadership

A business organization striving for cost leadership does everything necessary to have the lowest costs per unit marketed and to pass this advantage on to their customers through low prices. Japan's three biggest semiconductor manufacturers, Hitachi, Mitsubishi Electric, and NEC, for example, have poured billions of dollars into new factories in 1996 despite signs that the chip market was headed for a downturn. In earlier downturns, Japanese chip manufacturers had cut back on investments to protect profits. The result was a steady loss of market share to more aggressive Korean rivals such as Samsung Electronics. By 1993, Samsung had taken the leading market share in memory chips from the Japanese largely by investing heavily while the Japanese hesitated.

The costs an organization is facing largely depend on its production volume and the number of products (product lines) in its programme. Figure 5.7 shows that

When discussing how size affects total costs, managers must be aware of the countervailing effects of production volume and programme size. Increasing production volumes and decreasing programme size lead to reduced cost per unit. If production volume and programme size increase simultaneously, total costs may first decrease because of a thinner spread of fixed costs and learning effects. However, with increasing programme size, complexity rises and total costs might increase because costs of complexity are growing faster than learning and fixed cost digression effects.

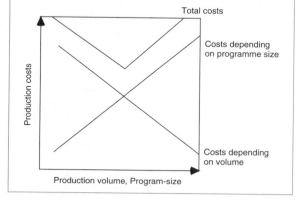

Figure 5.7 Cost curves depending on production volume and programme size

due to economies of scale an increase of production volume of a single product leads to a decrease of costs per unit (doubling the volume may lead to cost decreases of 15–25 per cent). At the same time, any increase in the number of products produced and marketed increases the costs of inventory, storage, transportation, and overheads. Experience shows that cutting the number of products by half increases productivity up to 30 per cent and decreases costs by around 17 per cent. This leads to a cost curve of the shape shown in Figure 5.7.

From there, we can conclude that large, mass producing firms such as IBM, Matsushita, Philips, Siemens, or Alcatel can make maximum use of economies of scale and accumulate experience in all functional areas. Because of their broad range of products, however, they run the risk of lower productivity than smaller, more focused competitors. To achieve reductions of programme costs, the firms have to reduce the variety of their own production. They seek partnerships with more focused suppliers and cooperative ventures. In the automotive industry, for example, Japanese car producers buy 70 per cent of their products from suppliers with which they have close relations. Partnerships with suppliers and competitors permit an organization to maintain a large product programme at lower costs and provide access to technology and management expertise that would otherwise not be available.

Non-dominant organizations, whether large or small, may cater to special market needs, concentrating their resources in a narrow field where they have a distinct competitive advantage. They can dominate the competition in the chosen market niche. Focusing on a small range of products allows them to market higher volumes and to produce at lower costs per unit. For example, NutraSweet – a low-calorie sweetener used in soft drinks such as Diet Coke and Diet Pepsi, and a business unit of US-based Monsanto – was protected by patents in Europe until 1987 and in the United States until 1992. It used that time to explore the processes for making Aspartame, the chemical name for the substance, giving it a significant cost advantage that could not be matched by any competitor when legal protection came to an end. Just prior to US patent expiration, both Coke and Pepsi signed new long-term contracts with Monsanto.

An example of a smaller company successfully focusing on a special market to gain economies of scale is Portugal's Corticeira Amorim, which controls around a third of the country's cork manufacturing. Amorim makes 70 per cent of the world's cork floorings, about 15 per cent of the world's wine corks (the world uses about 25 billion corks a year), and almost 95 per cent of the cork-based gaskets Portugal produces to seal engine joints. To further improve its cost position, the company has been buying up cork distributors in almost 30 countries and has begun to distribute for smaller Portuguese producers.[10]

Superior value

Differentiation by superior customer value is based on the capability of an organization to differentiate from competitors through higher attractiveness of its total product. Organizations possessing in-depth knowledge of current and potential aspirations of their potential customers and other important stakeholders may offer highly valued product characteristics or additional services targeted to special needs. Customer preference is not achieved through lower prices but through higher perceived value of the product.

Wolford, the Austrian producer of high quality tights, has concentrated its innovation on high fashion and the production technology for seamless tights. Wolford cannot compete with prices of tights marketed by Sarah Lee which are targeted to the mass market. The company focuses its activities on the upscale sub-market, which is estimated to represent only 3 per cent of the total market. In doing so, Wolford has gained a reputation as a European fashion leader and is growing faster than the industry average.

The perceived value of a product may be continually increased or at least sustained by innovation. Product innovation involves developing new solutions to customer problems (e.g. a new technology to produce irrigation water from sea water), making existing products more useful (such as developing portable VCRs which can assist in industrial selling), adding new services (e.g. introducing banking by phone or on-line), or challenging the total product portfolio. Dornier, a German manufacturer of weaving machines, found that its products were too sophisticated and expensive for most Latin American customers. It started a second-hand machinery market for those customers, adapting used machines which the company had had to take back from customers who had bought new equipment in highly technologically developed markets.

Time leadership

Time leadership – also called chrono-competition – is a way of differentiating by being faster than competitors in value-creation and value-generation processes. Management must decide what role their organization should play concerning innovation processes in its served markets – should it be an innovation leader or a follower. Related to this decision, a general rule must be formulated concerning the intended rate of innovation, that is, how fast product and process innovations should follow each other and be transferred into value generation to the exchange partners.

(1) Time leadership in value-creation

Product innovation leadership is not necessarily the same as pioneering. **Pioneering** organizations are the first to introduce a new solution to a customer problem in the market. They have the opportunity to develop market know-how earlier than their competitors, enjoy customer loyalty, influence the direction of technological development, set industry standards, and experience high rates of market share growth leading to effective performance. However, they also experience all the difficulties of introducing an innovation such as high development costs, quality problems, legal constraints, misperceptions of customers and reluctance of intermediaries concerning new products.

Product **innovation leadership** is not so much characterized by being the first to market as by managerial factors which help an organization profit from the opportunities of a pioneer and reduce its disadvantages: a vision of the mass market, managerial persistence, financial commitment, and relentless innovation. To be or to become an early leader in a new product category, an organization must have managers who are able to envision the full potential of the new product. They need to develop the vision of a substantial market. Only the volume of such a market can provide the economies of scale and experience needed to overcome start-up problems such as high costs, limited features, or missing distribution.

For example, Ampex pioneered the video recorder market in 1956 and was the leading supplier for several years. At USD 50,000 each, initial recorder sales were limited. RCA and Toshiba, the only competitors, were way behind. So Ampex had almost a monopoly in sales and R&D. However, the company's managers did little to improve quality or lower costs. Instead, they sought to reduce Ampex's dependence on video recorder sales and pursued diversification into audio products and computer peripherals. In contrast, at JVC, Yuma Shiraishi, manager of video recorder development, asked his engineers to develop a machine that could sell for USD 500, while using little tape and retaining high picture quality. It took JVC engineers 20 years to realize the goal. But when their efforts were successful in the mid-1970s, JVC's video sales went from USD 2 million to almost 2 billion in the following 15 years.[11]

When deciding what product innovation behaviour guidelines to formulate for their organization, management should be aware that most successful products are not the immediate result of technological breakthroughs but the fruit of small, incremental innovations in design, engineering, manufacturing, and marketing over extended periods of time. Currently successful products have only survived because management maintained their commitment to the product over a long period of slow but continual progress. For example, it took Siemens VAI, one of the top three metallurgical engineering firms of the world, more than 12 years to develop COREX, a direct reduction technology for iron production, which largely reduces the costs and environmental stress of the process, from the first technical solution to the point where customers around the world started to accept the new technology as a feasible alternative. In 1995, contracts were signed in Australia, India, Korea, and South Africa, finally rewarding management for their persistence.

As the examples show, it can take significant time to overcome R&D as well as marketing odds of product innovations. Therefore, the management of an organization wanting to be an innovation leader must be able and willing to commit substantial financial resources to last through this struggle. Also, it must be aware that innovation is an ongoing process of continual product and process improvement which will not take place in a large bureaucracy when people are satisfied with their first success, or when management fears to undermine current market success through the cannibalization of established products. IBM, for example, stymied its development of minicomputers and workstations to protect mainframe sales, even though competitors kept making inroads into the mainframe market. When they finally decided to put more energy into the development of this product category, they were slow to bring out new products because of their bureaucratic approval process.[12]

To maintain an innovation leadership position an organization must continually develop and implement new technologies or acquire them through licensing, strategic partnerships, or acquisitions. Japanese companies historically have bought the rights to use technologies that have been developed by companies in other advanced economies. They then improved the basic technology until they reached a level of experience and expertise that allowed them to take the lead in technology development.

If an organization cannot be among the innovation leaders in a market, it does not necessarily lack the potential for success, but it faces greater difficulty and must choose its target markets with more care. An **innovation follower** or late entrant may be able to avoid the mistakes made by the pioneer. Research and development costs may also be lower. Therefore, the innovation follower may be able to match the costs of the pioneer. However, to be in a position to become market leader and to set standards and influence the development of a market, the organization must hold a dominant position in a product category related to the new product. Such a position allows leveraging assets such as name recognition, an existing distribution network, production facilities, and managerial expertise.

Royal Crown achieved great success when it expanded diet cola from the niche of people with special dietary needs and introduced it to the mass market in the 1960s. However, it was virtually powerless to prevent Coca-Cola from capturing market leadership within one year of its late market entry in 1982.[13] Merck, a producer of pharmaceutical products, also successfully pursues such a follower strategy. Operating in many different markets where it faces primarily local competition, it can use its global distribution network to quickly introduce the products, services, or ideas of its more innovative, but localized, competitors in the markets where they are not present.

(2) Time leadership in value generation
A series of examples of successful companies such as Benetton or Motorola seems to indicate that in the most economically developed regions of the world, time leadership in value generation has been an important distinctive capability in the 1990s.

The fashion division of Benetton, for example, has on-line connections between its shops and a central logistics unit in Italy. This central unit is informed about stock movements and developments in demand wherever they occur. Because their knitwear is only produced and stocked without colours, greatest variety and quick response are ensured without uncontrollable risk. The products are dyed in the colours and numbers needed, and are sent out by overnight delivery to the shops.

Motorola's US production plant for cellular phones takes orders by computer connections with sales outlets and delivers the products in the following 48 hours. Such speed and flexibility was achieved by expanding just-in-time principles to the entire value-generation process. Tasks which are not needed to supply the intended customer benefits were eliminated. System response time was further reduced by parallel instead of sequential processing. Work is done in small batches, eliminating idle or dead time wherever it existed.

To be faster than competitors in any respect requires highly flexible production facilities with semi-autonomous groups of workers, just-in- time delivery, short production runs, total quality management, and fast and continuous product and process innovation, often in close cooperation with suppliers and customers, in small steps and through multifunctional teams. Under such conditions, a high diversity of products can be delivered quickly and reliably at a low cost compared to competitive offers.

(3) Rate of innovation
Finally, for both value creation and value generation, the rate of innovation of the organization compared to the average rate for the market is of major concern. The rate of innovation in a market is heavily influenced by the traditions and basic values of customers. The innovation rate of an organization strongly depends on the speed of innovation processes inside the organization. German car manufacturers, for example, preferred not to change their models too often, not only in order to communicate an image of reliable quality and craftsmanship, but also to let their products develop a strong visual image in the minds of their relatively conservative customers in the home market. This kind of innovation behaviour was of advantage in European markets. By contrast, in the United States, customers are interested in rapid product changes, and in East Asia they expect continual product improvement. There, the quality of a company's products is judged partly on the basis of the firm's rate of product innovation.

Faster innovation processes allow an organization to flood its served markets with new products or product features. Such continual product innovation in small steps can lead to significant advantages over competitors. Japanese manufacturers of air conditioners, for example, after a few years of small but continual steps of product innovation were seven to ten years ahead in product technology compared to their US competitors. However, this can also lead to economic trouble as experienced by Mazda. The company had 6 models 20 years ago, selling about one million cars. In 1996, when Ford took over a majority stake in its shares, Mazda was offering 29 models but selling the same number of cars. The increased complexity of their assortment had dramatically decreased Mazda's profits.

Competing by reliable relationships

The general market behaviour of an organization can be more or less aggressive. It may emphasize confrontation in competing for scarce resources or cooperation with partners in complex exchange relationships. At first sight, confrontation seems to be the rule. However, exchanges in most cases are a no zero-sum game. An organization cannot win only what it takes away from its exchange partners. The importance of time leadership should not lead management to neglect the fourth basic method of successful differentiation: reliable relationships, or a network of positive personal and institutional relations with important stakeholders in the value-creation systems of which the organization is a part.

For example, after improving their cost position by restructuring organizational processes which also led to substantial gains in speed of new product development, Swiss-based Basler, one of the largest insurance companies in Europe, discovered that the most important factor for long-term success in their markets is the establishment and maintenance of close relationships with customers.

As another example, IBM has followed a policy of good local citizenship for a long time now. On the French Riviera, where they have established their European research and development centre, the company sponsored the kindergarten, schools on all other levels, local festivals, concerts, and even the restoration of historical buildings. Such behaviour was attractive not only to IBM's highly trained international workforce, who were then ensured a culturally pleasant environment in which to live, where their children could obtain an excellent education, but also to local administrators who, in reaction, largely facilitated the firm's business in the region.

Small organizations may manage close relationships on a local basis, taking advantage of distinctive capabilities.

Dainichi Kiko, a Japanese robot manufacturer, concentrates on close relationships with small customers who lack in-house, automated production system development capabilities. Such organizations may also rely on close contacts with administrative stakeholders leading to government preferences for purchasing from specific suppliers. Additionally, they may build on trustful personal relationships with key local personalities, such as "market mammies" in West Africa or "bazaari" in Iran, who have strong influence on business deals in developing economies.

Selecting the benefits to be emphasized

Although the specific way an organization selects to differentiate from others may be sorted into one of the categories discussed above, those categories are much too broad to be useful for practical decision-making. Management needs to determine the particular benefits to be emphasized in each of the served sub-markets or segments to differentiate from competitors successfully. Based on the data gathered during the described process of strategic positioning, management may use tools such as the Value Curve or Congruency Analysis described in Toolbox 5.1.

With the results of these specific analyses for each sub-market at hand, management can decide what benefits are to be emphasized in order to differentiate attractively from competitors. Because any organization only possesses a limited number of distinctive capabilities or core competencies which it can build and sustain, it is highly important that management selects sub-markets and differentiating benefits which may be successfully served/provided by that limited number of capabilities.

TOOLBOX 5.1

SELECTING THE BENEFITS TO BE EMPHASIZED

To select the benefits to be emphasized specifically in each of the sub-markets served, management can apply some of the tools presented in the following.

Value curve

The value curve is a graphic depiction of the way an organization configures its offering to customers. It gives a comparison of the relative level of potential fulfilment of critical and may-be expectations highly important to customers and other relevant stakeholders. As Exhibit A shows, the Value Curve is drawn by plotting the performance of the total product relative to important competitors,

along with the critical and may-be expectations considered most important by the customers and relevant stakeholders in a sub-market. Expectations where the relative potential performance level of the organization's offering is significantly higher than the level of competition can be used for differentiation purposes. The organization may emphasize its superior capability to create the related benefit(s).

Congruency analysis

Congruency analysis combines the results of the strengths and weaknesses analysis for a sub-market with the

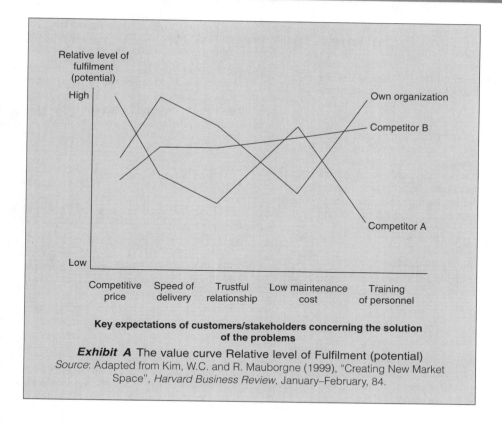

Exhibit A The value curve Relative level of Fulfilment (potential)
Source: Adapted from Kim, W.C. and R. Mauborgne (1999), "Creating New Market Space", *Harvard Business Review*, January–February, 84.

important critical and may-be expectations of customers and important stakeholders in this sub-market. Congruency analysis takes into account the substantiality of the benefit offered to customers and stakeholders, as well as its level of uniqueness. Because the success factors used for comparison in strengths and weaknesses analysis have been deducted from the expectations of customers and stakeholders, the scores the organization and its major competitors have received on those success factors can now be related back to the expectations. They are a measure for the competing organizations' fulfilment potential of important (scale value of 3 and above) current and future potential expectations. A form as shown in Exhibit B can be used to facilitate the comparison.

Exhibit B Congruency analysis

This exhibit contains a simplified example from an industrial engineering market segment. The analysing organization possesses the differentiating capability to be a cost leader. However, low price is a very important expectation only in sub-market 1. There, the low price and the excellent references of the organization can be selected for differentiation. In sub-market 2, the potential customers are particularly interested in the technologies available to a supplier and in the capability to train the workforce. The company can fulfil the first expectation very well, but it cannot differentiate itself in that respect from competitors 2 and 4. Because, both of these competitors are as weak as the company in terms of training capabilities, there is a certain possibility of attractive differentiation through the number and quality of references (importance level = 4). In sub-market 3, where short delivery time (until starting up the plant) and personal contacts dominate the expectations of customers, the firm could also count on its superior references. However, to have a chance of success, the company would have to diminish its significant weaknesses in personal contacts and delivery time.

Expectations of customers and other important stakeholders	Importance of expectations in sub-markets			Fulfilment potential				
	1	2	3	Own organization	Comp etitor 1	Comp etitor 2	Comp etitor 3	Comp etitor 4
References	5	4	4	4	3	2	2	3
Technologies	3	5	3	5	3	5	2	4
Low price	5	3	2	5	2	3	1	3
Short delivery time	3	3	5	2	5	3	4	5
Training of workforce	2	5	4	1	4	2	4	1
Personal contacts	3	4	5	1	4	3	5	1

Scales: 1 = unimportant/very weak
3 = important/average
5 = very important/very strong

A very similar kind of analysis may be conducted graphically by comparing the perceived importance of customers' and stakeholders' critical and may-be expectations with the relative potential of the organization to fulfil them (Exhibit C). The relative fulfilment potential of the organization is determined based on the results from the comparative analysis of strengths and weaknesses. It is the ratio between the fulfilment potential of the organization and the fulfilment potential of the strongest competitor by expectation.

If an organization's relative fulfilment potential for an expectation, which is at least important to the customers or stakeholders in the sub-market (scale value of 3 or more), reaches a value of 1 or more, the organization should do its best to keep or enhance that position. To differentiate attractively from competitors, management can emphasize the benefits resulting from the fulfilment of the expectation. If the organization has a superior fulfilment potential for an expectation that is considered less important by customers or stakeholders,

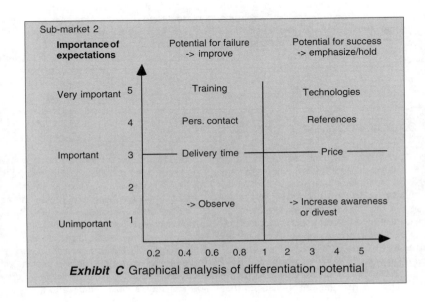

Exhibit C Graphical analysis of differentiation potential

$$\text{Relative fulfilment potential} = \frac{\text{Fulfilment potential of organization}}{\text{Fulfilment potential of strongest competitor}}$$

management can either try to increase the perceived importance of that expectation or should diminish its fulfilment potential by divesting the specific capability. A relative fulfilment potential below a value of 1 for an important expectation represents a potential for failure. The organization must strive to improve its position or avoid serving the sub-market. For currently unimportant expectations which can be better fulfilled by competitors, management should carefully observe the competitors' actions. If they succeed in making customers and stakeholders aware of the importance of these expectations, the organization may have a disadvantage with regard to its differentiation.

Increasing the potential for differentiation

Sometimes an organization does not have any particular distinctive capability for serving an attractive market. In such cases, it must develop or acquire differences between itself and its competitors, or develop a new market. Such differentiation may take the form of providing creative solutions to previously unsolved problems, applying new technologies, developing customer benefits that are not currently offered, or simply promoting or distributing in a new way; for example, as previously seen, Bandai Digital Entertainment created its "own new market".

Creating new markets

To create unique value propositions, managers may look systematically across the self-defined borders of the industry or of the strategic group they consider their organization belonging to, or they may systematically rethink the limits of their total product starting from a customer benefit perspective.[14]

For example, US-based Intuit changed the way individuals and small businesses manage their finances. Before they launched the product Quicken, few people used financial software for personal purposes. Intuit's management looked across industry borders and found the pencil to be a major competitor. It had two decisive advantages over computerized solutions – extremely low cost and simplicity of use. The resulting value-creation process focused on combining the major advantages of the computer – speed and accuracy – with the advantages of the pencil – simplicity of use and low price. The resulting product was a tremendous success.[15]

Cooperation

Many small- and medium-sized organizations that wish to serve particular markets may possess the required technical know-how to be able to offer attractive products and services, but lack experience or financial and personnel resources. Through a form of cooperation, such as business clusters, supply agreements, original equipment manufacturing (OEM), licensing agreements, joint ventures, and/or the use of strategic alliances (even with competitors), such organizations can supplement their strengths with those of partners.

Aprilia, a motorbike company based in Noale near Venice, and nearby Nordica, a world leader in ski boots, are examples of European firms using "network" manufacturing in business clusters. This type of cooperation allows even very small supplier firms to profit from internationalization. Neither Aprilia, which rivals large companies like Italy's Piaggio, France's Peugeot, and Japan's Honda Motor, nor Nordica manufactures a single component. Instead, they work closely with hundreds of suppliers specializing in the production of parts, whereby they can reach economies of scale and profit from experience. Aprilia's and Nordica's own resources go into design, assembly, and international marketing.

Energia, a Russian aerospace firm based in Kaliningrad, has established a joint venture with middle-sized German Kayser-Threde GmbH to secure access to sources of capital. The advanced technological equipment and industrial expertise of the Russian partner helped the German firm become a major provider of remote sensing services to customers in Asia, Western Europe, and North America.[16]

Large companies can also profit from cooperation. More than 25 major car and truck companies worldwide have joined together in over 300 strategic partnerships. The Ford Probe and the Mazda MX-6, for example, are made in the same plant. Peugeot and Fiat as well as Ford and Volkswagen have joint ventures through which minivans are produced and sold under the brand names of each of the partners. Renault, Europe's fourth largest producer of heavy trucks, cooperates with MAN, Germany's second largest heavy truck maker, and, in another business, with General Motors to develop and market light commercial vehicles called panel vans.[17] Cooperation allows companies to enter more markets faster, cheaper, and with a broader product line than if they tried it alone.

As with any management decision, there are risks associated with strategic partnerships. Often, failure to foresee differences in corporate cultures can place the partnership at risk. Other problems occur when the partnership pushes one, if not both, of the new partners into areas in which they have no previous experience. Yet another problem with establishing a strategic partnership is the cost of a one-way flow of technology. If guarantees are not established and strictly enforced, an organization might share technology only to find that it faces additional competition later from its supposed partner.

Success in a strategic partnership occurs when each partner brings to the alliance capabilities that the other partner lacks. The best partners might be those which do not have a dominant share of the market or do not even belong to the same industry. In the last decade, US-based Corning Glass has cooperated with more than 14 different alliance partners in Europe, Asia, and Latin America in order to learn about potential improvements in designing and manufacturing different glass and ceramic-based products, to penetrate new markets, and to share the risks of technical development. With Novartis of Switzerland, it focused on medical diagnostics. The partnership with Siemens concentrated on fibre optics. The partnership with NGK Insulators of Japan produced ceramics for catalytic converters and pollution control equipment.[18]

Acquisition and mergers

During the process of assessing potential markets, management may find very attractive sub-markets which their organization cannot serve adequately because of missing capabilities. If management considers those markets of great importance to the organization, and speed is key in order to attain an attractive competitive position, management may decide to acquire another organization to build a presence instantly. The first company to offer anti-lock braking systems (ABS) for cars, Robert Bosch GmbH of Stuttgart, Germany, was confronted with the demands from its major car manufacturing clients to deliver entire product systems instead of only electronic parts to improve braking systems. Therefore, it acquired 24 brake-producing factories in Europe, Latin America, and the US, as well as shares of joint ventures in China, India, and Korea through US-based Allied Signal Inc.[19]

The pressure to match global standards of efficiency and financial resources available to market and product development also contributes to an increasing number of mergers, particularly in Europe, where many firms in industries such as airlines, autos, banking, or media traditionally had avoided international mergers and contented themselves instead with local markets. For example, Infogrames Entertainment, a French multimedia company, and Ocean International Ltd, a similar privately held British company whose catalogue of simulation, adventure, and arcade software games was complementary to that of the French company, merged in a move that created Europe's biggest entity in the quickly growing multimedia industry.

To be successful in acquiring other businesses, an organization must constantly survey its market environment for potential acquisition candidates, and then assess the attractiveness of the targets, the appropriate approach to initiating the acquisition, and the steps necessary to integrate the business effectively into their own organization.

Japanese-owned ICL has a special planning group called Acquisition Group, which studies and evaluates targets on a global basis. How difficult integration processes can be is illustrated by the acquisition of a controlling interest of Ford Motor Co. in Mazda Motor Corp.[20] and by the merger of Daimler Benz and Chrysler.

Assessing the potential for success

In order to make a final decision on what sub-markets to select and how to differentiate from competitors in those markets, an assessment of the success potential of such a decision is required. Different managers will define success differently. However, there are two broad categories, economic success and psychosocial success, which need to be achieved. How they are defined and measured will vary to a great extent depending on the mission of the organization and the acting people.

Psychosocial success

The selection of sub-markets to be served, as well as the selection of benefits to be emphasized, has an impact on the reputation of an organization. For example, a trade union may have built its name by fighting for the rights of blue-collar workers. However, this segment of the market is decreasing in size. The trade union, therefore, may start offering its services to employees because that market is bigger and growing. In order to provide attractive benefits to the new potential customers, tax advice and higher qualification training programmes for managers may be offered. Consequently, the reputation of the trade union may change dramatically. The risk is that it may become less attractive to workers and not attractive enough to employees. Therefore, the impact of the intended market position on the standing of the organization has to be checked before starting implementation programmes.

Actions taken to attain the intended market position not only potentially influence the perception of external partners, but also have an impact on the identity of the organization as perceived by its personnel, and on their consequent commitment to participating in value-creation and value-generation processes. If, for example, a local hospital in the Black Forest of Germany, which has always catered solely to the people living in that area, is turned into a private clinic for wealthy patients from all over Europe, some personnel may be neither willing nor able to follow that move. Others will be eager to take part in the change of market position. Management must at least try to foresee such reactions and their impact on the potential for realizing the intended market position.

A great deal depends on management's ability to communicate the intended position inside their organization, and on the resulting capability of the organization to communicate the attractiveness and uniqueness of the value provided to customers and stakeholders. Multidimensional Scaling and Factor Analysis of Correspondence (see Toolbox 4.6) are tools to test the potential of reaching the intended position in the perception of market partners as well as to what extent the position has been reached.

Customer and stakeholder perceptions not only depend on the communication capabilities of an organization. Their satisfaction with the values provided by the organization during value-creation and value generation processes will also have a strong impact on further preference and word-of-mouth. Chapter 6 will discuss some techniques to test potential customer satisfaction. Satisfied customers and stakeholders have a tendency to stay loyal to the value provider. Increased retention of customers has a positive impact on the economic success of a selected market position.

Economic success

Reaching the intended market position must be financially feasible to the organization and must contribute to fulfilling its mission. The financial feasibility depends on the financial resources available to the organization, the expenses to be covered for reaching the intended market position, and management's willingness to spend the needed amount of resources.

Management will tend to accept the cost of attaining the intended market position if the contribution to fulfilling the business mission seems attractive enough. In a non-profit organization this contribution may be, for example, to reinforce a social idea, to enhance the awareness for a public issue, or to improve the standard of living of a disadvantaged part of society. In most profit-oriented organizations success criteria are measures such as forecast contribution to gross-profit, return on investment or capital employed, net present value of future cash flows, or economic value added. Toolbox 5.2 describes examples of tools to be potentially applied in an analysis of economic success.

A major difficulty in assessing the potential future economic success of an intended market position is to reliably evaluate the sustainability of differentiating capabilities. Management has to estimate the probability of competitors being able to develop, procure, or acquire the same capability, to imitate the unique benefits provided to customers and stakeholders, or to find an

TOOLBOX 5.2

ASSESSMENT OF POTENTIAL ECONOMIC SUCCESS

Potential economic success of an intended market position may be assessed in a variety of ways. If management is mainly interested in contributions to gross profit or return-on-assets, they may apply Focus Group Interviews or an Analysis of Contribution Potential.

If estimates of potential market shares are of particular interest, Conjoint Analysis may be applied.

Focus group analysis

Toolbox 3.3 outlined the basics of Focus Group Interviews. This technique can be applied in determining the economic value potential customers attribute to a new exchange offer.

Focus group participants are first introduced to the new total product and the benefits it intends to provide.

Then, they are asked individually to indicate (e.g., in writing) the price they would be ready to pay for this product. The group interviewer starts a discussion among the focus group participants about the pros and cons they perceive when considering the offer and comparing it to current alternatives and when considering the consequences of its acceptance or rejection. At the end of the discussion, again, participants are asked individually to indicate the economic value they attribute to the discussed offer. Depending on the direction of changes from the first evaluation to the second, researchers get an idea of how much the supplying organization may charge for the new product. A comparison of this price to the planned cost of the product per customer helps to estimate the potential financial success of its intended market position.

Analysis of a sub-market's contribution potential

If the potential contribution of the selected differentiation of the organization in a sub-market to financial success is to be estimated, a procedure as suggested by Bonoma and Shapiro (1989) can be applied.

If it has not been done previously, the estimation procedure starts by assessing the realistic size of the sub-market, or the probable number of effective customers (Exhibit A). Starting from an estimate of the total number of potential customers in the sub-market, first, the often smaller number of customers who can be reached with the available resources is estimated. Then, out of those, the number of qualified customers is determined. That is, the customers the organization does not want to serve, because, for example, of economic, ethical, or reputation reasons, are deducted. From that reduced number of potential customers, the number of first trials (see Conjoint Analysis following this) and of probable repeat buyers may be estimated. The resulting figure is a realistic estimate of the size of the sub-market at current resources.

Having estimated the realistic size of the sub-market, its potential contribution to the organization's financial success can be assessed (Exhibit B). Starting with an average individual customer, the average order size for that customer can be estimated. Based on order size and average content of order, the direct cost of obtaining and processing an order can be assessed. Comparing average sales per customer order with direct cost per order results in the contribution margin per average customer order, which can be expressed as a percentage of sales. The ratio of that percentage of sales to the assets needed for generating total estimated sales is an indicator of the potential profitability of the sub-market.

Conjoint analysis

Conjoint Analysis is a scaling technique which helps marketing researchers find out what leads stakeholders to prefer one exchange offer over another. It is also able to assess the market share a specific offer may reach in a defined market. Conjoint Analysis is also called Trade-off Analysis because it models the mutual dependencies of characteristics of exchange offers as well as

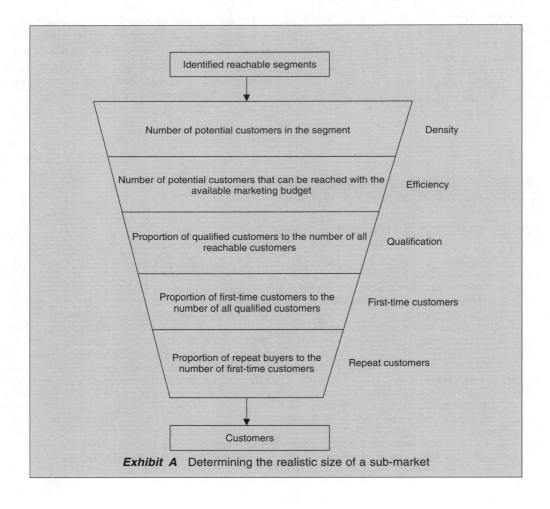

Exhibit A Determining the realistic size of a sub-market

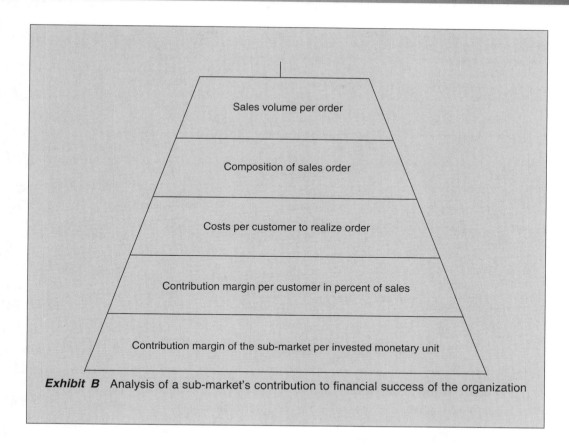

Exhibit B   Analysis of a sub-market's contribution to financial success of the organization

acceptable trade-offs between them. It is applicable in situations where the stakeholders go through a conscious decision-making process of comparing potential choices.

When the sub-market to be served and the intended method of differentiation have been selected, researchers present a verbal and/or visual description of the exchange offer, together with various current and potential competitive offers, to a random sample of customers or important stakeholders. The respondents are asked to rank-order the offers according to their preference, or to rate each of the offers individually on a scale of preference from "like very much" to "dislike very much". The descriptions of the offers might be presented on paper or on a computer screen. They may be presented all together, in triples, or in pairs, or individually, depending on the specific Conjoint Analysis technique selected by the researcher.

To give a simplified example, to test the potential success of the intended market position of a winter tourism destination, four characteristics (destination, kind of accommodation, length of stay, and total cost per day) could be exposed to respondents in the way shown in Exhibit C.

Each of the nine offers in Exhibit C consists of four characteristics with three attribute levels each. Their combination is composed in such a way as to avoid any correlation of characteristics in the presentation format. Such an orthogonal design allows one to determine the rank order of the presented stimuli and of all 81 potential combinations of characteristics and attribute levels.

Data may be treated with various algorithms. However, each of them provides the researcher with information about the importance of each characteristic for preference (or rating) judgements (Exhibit D) and about the relative utility of each attribute level (Exhibit E) on an individual basis.

The market share to be reached with the intended offer may be assessed in various ways. The "First-Choice-Model", for example, assumes that customers will take the offer producing the highest total utility. Therefore, the total utility (the sum of utilities across all characteristics) is calculated for the intended offer and compared with the total utilities of competing offers. The percentage of respondents receiving the highest total utility from the intended offer is equal to the expected market share. Second choices, which may have a certain impact on market share, are not considered.

The "Share of Preference Model", as another example, uses a logit transformation of utilities into shares of preference to determine the share of total preference of a respondent reached by the intended offer:

$$ShP_{ik} = \frac{E^{bU_{ik}}}{\sum E^{bU_{iKJ}}}$$

ShP_{ik} = Share of total preference of product k for respondent i

b = individual constant

U_{ik} = Total utility of product k for respondent i

J = all competitive product offers

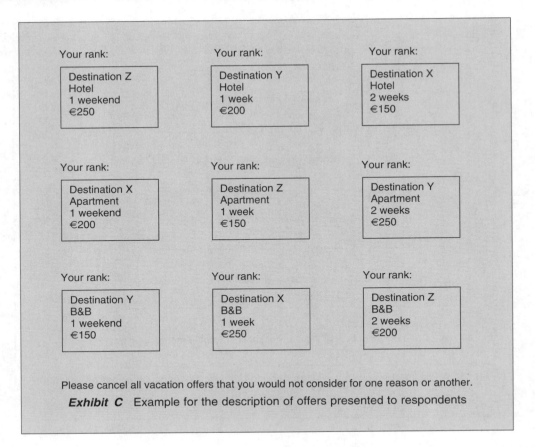

Your rank:

Destination Z
Hotel
1 weekend
€250

Your rank:

Destination Y
Hotel
1 week
€200

Your rank:

Destination X
Hotel
2 weeks
€150

Your rank:

Destination X
Apartment
1 weekend
€200

Your rank:

Destination Z
Apartment
1 week
€150

Your rank:

Destination Y
Apartment
2 weeks
€250

Your rank:

Destination Y
B&B
1 weekend
€150

Your rank:

Destination X
B&B
1 week
€250

Your rank:

Destination Z
B&B
2 weeks
€200

Please cancel all vacation offers that you would not consider for one reason or another.

Exhibit C Example for the description of offers presented to respondents

Exhibit D Importance of each characteristic for an individual respondent

Characteristics	Relative importance (%)
Destination	46
Total cost per day	4
Accommodation	14
Length of stay	36
Total	100

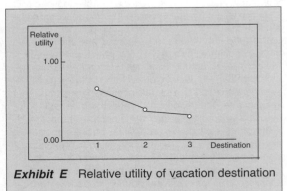

Exhibit E Relative utility of vacation destination

The "Purchase Likelihood Model" correlates the total utilities determined for each respondent with purchasing intentions indicated by the respondents. This alternative is mainly used when the other two approaches are not feasible because the intended offer is unique.

When applying Conjoint Analysis, there are a number of limitations of which one must be aware. These include its sensitivity to multi-colinearity between characteristics; the influence of the number of attribute levels used on the measured relative importance of characteristics; the assumed non-hierarchical structure of the customer decision-making process (all characteristics are used on the same level of decision making); and the limited number of characteristics to be used in a choice task compared to the limited closeness to reality of a rating task with a high number of characteristics. Despite those limitations, the technique has a great number of practical applications in designing and testing new product offers as well as in assessing potential market share.

alternative solution with greater attractiveness. For that purpose, management needs a well-established marketing intelligence system as will be discussed in the following chapters.

The intended market position

At this point in the strategic marketing process, the intended market position of the organization or one of its sub-units can be formulated. This should include statements on what goals to achieve, what markets to serve based on what technology, how to compete in the selected markets, and the amount of resources to employ for each purpose. The intended market position expresses the core strategy of the total organization, the business unit strategy for organizational sub-units, and the positioning strategy for a product or project group. Because of their knowledge of potential customers, intermediaries, and competitors in attractive markets, as well as their skills in the comparative analysis of market conditions, marketing people should have a significant impact on the formation and content of their organization's intended market position.

The statement of intended market position serves as a guideline for the following operative decisions of the organization. It needs to be transformed into activities concerning marketing intelligence, value-creation and value-generation processes. These processes will be discussed in the remaining parts of the book.

Implementing the intended market position

Implementation starts in the mind of people. To make and keep an organization successful, top management must develop and continually refine a shared understanding of their organization's intended market position (Figure 5.8). Transformation of the intended market position into adequate actions needs consensus of management and staff concerning

- the relevant market and its future development,
- the specific position the organization intends to occupy in the minds of exchange partners, and
- the distinctive capabilities, which allow reaching that position (including the processes for creating and delivering superior value to the stakeholders).

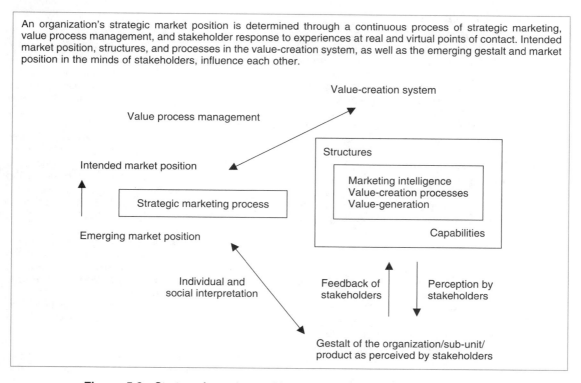

An organization's strategic market position is determined through a continuous process of strategic marketing, value process management, and stakeholder response to experiences at real and virtual points of contact. Intended market position, structures, and processes in the value-creation system, as well as the emerging gestalt and market position in the minds of stakeholders, influence each other.

Figure 5.8 Strategy formation and implementation as a continuous process

Consensus is facilitated by leadership and coordination. Basic coordination may be achieved by establishing a framework of values and general rules of behaviour for the value processes needed to reach the intended market position. This framework contains organizational structures, that is, formal organization, communication and decision-making structures, and organizational processes.[21]

Organizational structures help all members of an organization to reduce the complexity of their environment. They are most visibly expressed by the management systems of an organization. Determining what stimuli from the environment are relevant and which may be neglected, management systems enable organizations to formally prepare, implement, and evaluate their decisions. They strongly contribute to the development of frames of reference or mental maps[22] shared by managers and the staff of the organization favouring a set of choice alternatives by simultaneously excluding many others. For example, if the organizational structure and the reporting system of an organization do not provide for key accounts, they will tend not to exist in the minds of personnel. Relationships with customers will be managed without acknowledging differences, and no specific information concerning major accounts will be gathered.

As well as establishing formal structures, value process management comprises managing all processes of an organization which take place in direct relation with stakeholders or which have an impact on stakeholder relations. Management must be concerned about current and future availability of the skills needed to conduct those processes, and coordinate them in a way that, as an entity, they provide unique value to the stakeholders, are as efficient as possible, and make sense to the members of the organization (Special focus).

The stakeholders of an organization encounter the results of value-creation, value-generation, and marketing intelligence processes, or even participate in parts of these processes at various contact points, such as watching TV advertisements, talking to sales people, contacting the homepage, being interviewed as member of a focus group, or using the organization's product. At each contact point, the stakeholders receive cues they attribute to the organization and/or its product. The various pieces of information concerning an organization are related to each other. Over time, they form a total perception – a gestalt – of the organization (Figure 5.7). When a stakeholder comes across one of the cues, which is a part of the total perception, the entire gestalt is brought into awareness.

Special focus

SENSE MAKING IN ORGANIZATIONS

Sense making is a reciprocal psychological process of information seeking, ascription of meaning, and action (or non-action) under standards and rules given in a cultural setting. It involves placing perceived stimuli into some type of cognitive framework, that is, into a certain network of interrelated cognitions which directs interpretations of stimuli. As Frost and Morgan suggest, when people make sense of things, they "read into the meanings they wish to see; they vest objects, utterances, actions, and so forth with subjective meaning which helps make their world intelligible to themselves"[i] (p. 207).

Sense making is a process that continually takes place in organizations. All managers and staff have the need to understand their working environment. According to Weik, sense making in organizations has seven properties. Sense making is

■ grounded in identity construction
The sense-making person relate their search for and interpretation of stimuli, as well as their choice of actions, to their own identity. In organizations, this identity consists of two entities: the individual and the person as a representative of their organization. The sense maker's identity is undergoing continual redefinition while presenting some of its self to others and trying to decide which self is appropriate.

■ retrospective
The ascription of meaning is an intentional process and focuses on what has already occurred. Because there are too many potential meanings to everything in an organization, its members need values, priorities, and clarity about preferences in order to make up their minds about what matters.

■ enactive of sensible environments
Organizational, market, and macro environments contain cues for the sense-making person. However, the parts of those environments that are considered relevant and how they are perceived, being related to each other, are based on individual and social construction. That is, members of an organization produce part of the environment they face.

■ social
Thoughts, feelings, and actions of individuals are influenced by the actual, imagined, or implied presence of others. Decisions in organizations are made in the presence of others, or are made with the knowledge that they will have to be implemented, understood, or approved by others. In an organization, symbolic interaction is as important to sense making as the shared experience of collective action.

■ ongoing
Sense making is a continuous process dominating awareness. Emotions have a significant impact on that

process because recall and retrospect tend to be mood-congruent.

■ focused on and by extracted cues
What is not noticed cannot be used for sense making. What is noticed – or is extracted from a multitude of possible cues – are simple, familiar structures that are the bases for individuals' development of a larger sense of what may be occurring. What appears familiar depends on personal dispositions and on the context in an organization. As a consequence, small changes in organizational context can have large effects on the sense people make.

■ driven by plausibility rather than accuracy
Sense making is not an accurate process. Right or wrong have no absolute measures. People are looking for accounts that are credible and socially acceptable.

Managers striving to implement an intended market position may be more successful if they are aware of the omnipresent existence of sense making. They can develop structures to reinforce these processes in such a way as to reach defined objectives without much pressure or control.

Source: Based on Weik, K.E. (1995), *Sensemaking in Organizations*, Thousand Oaks, CAL: Sage Publications.
[i] Frost, P.J. and G. Morgan (1983), "Symbols and Sensemaking: The Realization of a Framework", in L.R. Pondy, P.J. Frost, G. Morgan, and T.C. Dandridge (eds), Organizational Symbolism, Greenwich, CT: Jai, pp. 207–236.

For example, consumers may combine the experience of the modern architecture of the outlets of a retail chain, the freshness of its fruits and vegetables, the speed of being served at the cash register, the ease with which they found the parking lot, and the splendid taste of the food prepared by following the retailer's recipes offered on their homepage, to form the gestalt of a retailer caring for its customers' quality of life.

When the gestalt is interpreted and emotionally evaluated based on individual and social processes, the organization attains a specific position in the minds of customers, a more or less valued identity. That is, stakeholders develop an emotionally laden, relatively stable holistic representation of what the organization is all about.

The market position emerging through the stakeholders' experiences during direct and indirect, real and virtual contacts with an organization may more or less fit the position intended by top management. As Figure 5.7 shows, strategic marketing processes, the continual formation of value-creation systems through value process management, and the gestalt of an organization emerging in the stakeholders' minds are interrelated in an ongoing process. It is the role of management to concurrently analyse and evaluate the fit among the various elements. Managers lead their organizations by doing their best to foresee potential changes of stakeholder perceptions due to developments in the market and macro environments, by initiating the development or acquisition of new capabilities, by continually auditing current structures and processes for their appropriateness, and by giving impulses as well as drawing conclusions in an ongoing strategic marketing process.

Leadership

Top management commitment

The most important factor determining an organization's potential for success is top management's ability and willingness to lead the organization in its efforts. A study of small- and medium-sized companies in Finland, Germany, Japan, South Korea, and South Africa, for example, found that companies are significantly more successful in foreign markets (i.e., they have much higher proportions of non-domestic sales) when their top managers have a global perspective[23] which they effectively communicate. These companies are even more successful than competitors that enjoy advantages in such areas as products, distribution systems, and capital.

For an organization to be competitive, top management must be committed to achieving and maintaining the intended market position. Adequate resources need to be persistently allocated. The development or acquisition of appropriate skills must be supported. And, because it may take some time before financial success can be achieved, top management must have some patience instead of a short-term view of financial matters.

Stimulating shared mental maps

Implementation is strongly dependent on management sending clear, consistent signals regarding values, rules, and priorities through verbal communication, visible actions, and shaping management systems. By these means, the members of the organization are stimulated to develop shared mental maps and agreement about rules of market behaviour.

The top management of Lego, the Danish company famous for their toy bricks, aimed to make Lego the strongest brand among families with children by 2005. Imagination, invention, togetherness, learning, and fun were central contents of the intended market position. To launch the renewed vision of Lego's market position, Kjeld Kirk Kristiansen, company owner and president, held company-wide seminars in an attempt to inspire his people. More than 7000 managers and employees from all over the world were invited to participate in workshops called "pit stops". At these workshops, individuals shared their dreams for the company and themselves. In addition, Lego organized "dream-outs", where employees worked on solving problems such as finding ways to improve the distribution channels in the United States. By allowing the members of the organization to personally experience the central values of the brand[24] through these activities, the company stimulated the development of a shared frame of reference. Leaders may strongly contribute to implementation efforts among employees by serving as role models. People learn much of their behaviour through imitation. If leaders consistently demonstrate behaviour that can be related to business and personal success, many of their staff will start imitating them. For example, if a top manager such as Lou Gerstner, the CEO of IBM, regularly visits customers to stay in close contact with the market, the firm's product and R&D managers will also have to go to the field regularly.

Team moderation

As the example shows, in implementation processes, leaders become team moderators. They coordinate the various objectives, interests, and motives of process participants by providing a context (or frame of reference) that leads to shared mental maps and shared sense making of actions[25] (see Special focus). To make the members of their organizations personally involved in implementing the intended market position, leaders let them participate in the decision-making process or in developing action plans. That is, the strategic marketing process, on whatever level of the decision-making hierarchy it occurs, is neither a task for a "lonely hero", nor that for marketing or strategy departments. Ownership of the strategy will only develop in teams of managers from all functions of the organization needed to implement the strategy. Those managers will be personally involved with realizing what they have thought out.

Team involvement also provides a basis for continual strategy formation. Feedback and measurement of success in all parts of the organization participating in the creation and generation of value to the stakeholders allow for corrective implementation. The intended market position

as well as action plans can be adapted according to what the organization and its members learn during implementation. Team processes may be continually improved.

Conflict management

Leaders of an organization must be able to cope with all kinds of potential conflicts. Table 5.2 contains various approaches to conflict management. Some managers aggravate conflicts by denying their existence. Others try to resolve conflicts by replacing employees or managers who resist direction. Managers who perceive such replacements as losses of important management know-how or experience may seek to resolve or even avoid conflicts by improving the level of information and greater participation of the people concerned.

But there is no universal formula for conflict resolution. For example, managers trying to avoid conflicts by increasing participation should be aware that collective decisions tend to unfold in an incremental manner from processes of negotiation and compromise among participants living in different social realities and holding various self-interests. They often depend more on the partisan values and power of the interest groups involved in the process than on rational analysis. Thus, such decisions are easier to implement, but they will not be of highest potential quality. Successful managers apply the most appropriate conflict management technique specific to the situation in order to safeguard the implementation of the intended market position.

Organizational structures

There may exist a breach between the rhetoric of top management expressing their intended market position and the behaviour of managers and staff. Such discrepancy is often due to management systems promoting other values and rules of behaviour than what top management espouses. For example, many business leaders have put forward the importance of strong relationships with

---

Table 5.2 Approaches to conflict management

There are several ways to approach avoidance or the resolution of conflicts within structural, process, and mixed approaches. Successful conflict management requires the selection of an appropriate approach depending on the specific situation.

Structural approaches	Process approaches	Mixed approaches
Common goals	De-escalation	Rules
Reward system	Confrontation	Liaison roles
Regrouping	Collaboration	Task forces/teams
Rotation		Integrator roles
Separation		

current customers and of a substantial share of total sales due to new products. At the same time, reward systems of their organizations still provide sales people with higher income for greater sales volumes, pushing growth instead of profitable relationships and product innovation.

To make their organization implement the intended market position, management may need to align the frame of reference of their collaborators with what they want the organization to achieve. Organizational structures, internalized policies, and rules of behaviour may have to be changed. Such change constantly occurs in a marginal way because management systems are subject to external influences such as the development of values in society and sub-cultures, as well as internal social processes. The structures of an organization continually adapt to environmental developments in small steps. Such ongoing changes, however, do not automatically lead to the implementation of an intended market position. If a poor fit exists between the impact of current management systems on decisions and actions of staff and the intended market position of the organization, management intervention may become necessary.

Management must install a monitoring process which systematically compares current organizational structures to the basic values and rules of behaviour appropriate for reaching the intended market position. To keep the mental maps of managers and staff dynamically adapting to ongoing changes in the environment without losing track of the intended market position, management may also want to instil a combination of knowledge and change management which ensures their organization's learning capability.

Knowledge management is a conscious way of gathering, treating, and disseminating information which is essential for sustaining current and building future differentiating capabilities of an organization. Because the formulation–implementation dichotomy of strategic marketing has been shown to be ineffective, it is also counter-productive if certain hierarchical levels or functional units monopolize control of knowledge. On the other hand, providing knowledge access opportunities to all who might need that knowledge for fulfilling their specific role in the organization's value processes helps compress time needed for implementing the intended market position.

Opportunities for knowledge gathering and dissemination can be given in formal and informal ways. A formal way, for example, is writing, distributing, and training people with manuals or establishing open access to an Intranet. Informal opportunities for knowledge exchange, such as a cafeteria for breaks where people from different areas of the organization can meet or simply observing more experienced colleagues at work, often are more efficient. Such informal knowledge transfer opportunities not only help to transfer tacit knowledge, that is, know-how, which cannot be given through formal sources. They are also more involving personally. Leaders, therefore, must continually work on combinations of formal and informal opportunities for knowledge acquisition and exchange to keep their organizations learning.

Organizational processes

Organizational processes are sequences of interrelated actions, which are coordinated by the actors pursuing specific, and possibly conflicting, interests and are intended to lead to certain results. In contrast to structures, which are excluding, processes are open to impulses from the environment. They focus more on sequences of events and on sustainable success potentials in the market than on internal power. For example, if an organization has established value process management, market communication, sales, production, and logistics, then customer service personnel will cooperate to reach and keep a pre-specified level of customer satisfaction instead of independently focusing on the perfection of their own functions and on rivalries over reasons for success or failure. Toolbox 5.3 describes some techniques supporting the implementation of value process management.

TOOLBOX 5.3

BASIC TECHNIQUES SUPPORTING IMPLEMENTATION OF VALUE PROCESS MANAGEMENT

There are five techniques supporting successful implementation of value process management, which may be applied individually or in combination with each other.

1. Clearly determine and communicate the value-creation system on which to focus

Before any value process design can be meaningfully discussed, implemented, or improved, all stakeholders constituting the value-creation system, the organization, or one of its sub-units is supposed to focus on need to be described. The stakeholders' specific interests, their interrelations, and the kind of interactions occurring between them need to be clearly determined and communicated: Who are the stakeholders to be considered intensively? Who may be dealt with less intensively without any harm to the organization? How will the value-creation system change over time? (see Toolboxes 1.4, Value-creation system analysis, and 1.5, Scenario technique). Sharing the perception of how the value-creation system of the organizational unit is structured, and who is playing what role in that system, provides a solid basis for successful value process management.

2. Fluctuate between internal and external perspectives

In order to manage value processes of an organization successfully, management needs to understand and apply the perspectives of internal and external players equally well. The internal perspective consists of the mental maps dominating the various functional areas and hierarchical levels of the organization. The external perspective reflects the sometimes contradictory multitude of interests and expectations of the various stakeholders in the value-creation system.

Value process management has the general objective of providing unique attractive value to important stakeholders. However, this does not imply a disproportionate, increasing focus on external stimuli. Instead, it is based on a sensitive selection of such stimuli. The selection focuses on the potential of the organization to fulfil its mission in a sustainable way, based on currently available and potential capabilities. Demands and challenges from market and macro environments are interpreted from internal and external points of view. Conclusions on value process design and actions to take are drawn from both perspectives.

To represent both perspectives in analysis and decision making, management may hire consultants to provide the external view, may invite representatives of important stakeholders to express their views, or may establish two teams of organizational members – one to represent the internal and the other to represent the external view of market reality. The two teams are invited to present their analyses and conclusions to top management who can then compare the results and make informed decisions.

3. Fluctuate between exclusion and inclusion

Depending on the dynamics of the served sub-markets and segments, an organization may rely more or less on currently available differentiating capabilities. In rather unstable environments, organizations must be highly sensitive to weak signals of change in value-creation systems. These signals announce the need to develop or acquire new capabilities for fulfilling new expectations and turning arising challenges into opportunities. Like a modern passenger car which is equipped with electronic sensors that monitor all sorts of environmental conditions and adapt the characteristics of the car to these conditions before a dangerous situation might occur, an organization must develop and carefully maintain its specific sensors. Inclusion and sensitive treatment of many signals is needed to detect changes at the outset.

As Chapter 6 will show, marketing intelligence processes may be installed formally for that purpose. However, reinforcing informal processes of signal detection and interpretation is as important. Therefore, organizational leaders may favour and actively support a basic attitude towards inclusion that increases the awareness of all members of the organization to external signals.

However, too much inclusion carries the risk of resulting in hectic actions taken at very high cost. Sheer speed in reaction to whatever is emerging in the market and macro environments can be detrimental. Neither the members of the organization nor its stakeholders are able to develop a clear gestalt of an organization that is changing its intentions and modes of action too quickly. In addition, to avoid information overload under such conditions, managers tend to exclude environmental cues individually, resulting in diverse views of what is happening and what needs to be done.

For any organization, systematic exclusion is a must. It defines what the organization is not willing to do and what developments are not of relevance to management decision-making. Exclusion helps in stabilizing organizational processes, reassuring the members of the organization, and developing shared mental maps. It is strongly based on the continual communication of the organization's corporate policy and core strategy by its leading managers.

4. Manage interfaces as close cooperative relationships instead of competitive zero-sum games

Organizational members have diverse functional preoccupations, different educational training, and have to achieve specific objectives. These influences make them more or less sensitive to external stimuli of different kinds and from different sources. Sales people will be preoccupied with their customers' reaction to new competitive products or with potential new market entrants, whereas finance managers tend to closely follow the development of interest and currency rates or changes in tax regulations. Those different preoccupations lead people from functionally diverse sub-units to live in varying subjective realities.

However, to a certain extent, every member of an organization takes part in marketing intelligence, value-creation, or value-generation processes. Management has to be sure that all part-time marketers from various functions needed for a sub-process are coordinated in their decisions and actions. This is more difficult to accomplish when the functional groups which participate in a process, and which are supposed to produce a predefined end result jointly, consider each other as competitors for scarce resources or rewards. Organizing the procurement, sales, and customer service units as profit centres and the production, logistics, and finance units as cost centres may not only increase the differences in their perception of reality, it will lead to unit egoism and disturb process cohesion. In the short run, the efficiency of each of the units may be enhanced, but the total value provided to stakeholders will be diminished.

Therefore, the associations between functional areas need to be managed like long-term cooperative relationships. That is, managers of the affected sub-units coached by managers from superior levels have to first determine their shared process objectives. Then, they can design the optimal sequence of actions necessary to reach those objectives in the most efficient manner. Based on that process design, they can negotiate their way of cooperation, resulting in a "contract" that should guarantee the fulfilment of process objectives as well as functional necessities.

5. Align process and structure

The value processes of an organization may be supported or impeded by organizational structure. Values and rules of behaviour expressed in the shape of management systems, such as formal organization and information, incentives and controlling system, strongly influence what is important to the members of an organization and what is not. Therefore, to effectively implement value processes that help reach the intended market position, structural changes may be required.

To get a coherent picture of what adaptations need to be made to management systems, management has to install regular management system audits. Starting from the intended market position and the value processes

needed to reach that position, management systems are screened to determine their fit. Again, because functional units have too much of a function-related bias influencing their perceptions, multifunctional teams, which may be assisted by people external to the organization, are better suited to do the job. They can observe and illustrate what effects current structures have on mental maps and on the behaviour of managers and staff. Consequently, they are able to suggest certain changes and how to achieve them.

Source: Adapted from Sutrich, O. (1993), Prozessmarketing oder: Das Ende des Marketing-Mix?, in Gester, P.-W., B. Heitger and C. Schmitz (Hrsg.), *Managerie – Systemisches Denken und Handeln im Management*, Heidelberg: Auer, 218–241.

Multifunctional cooperation

As Chapter 1 has discussed, value is created and generated in social-technical systems to which all players contribute in various ways. Those value-creation systems are imagined, established, and maintained by the players. Each player participates in the life of the system, co-determines the quality of interaction, and the value of participating in the system.[26] Many value-creation and value-generation processes are so complex that they can only be conducted in close cooperation with stakeholders.

This is particularly the case for parts of value-creation and value-generation processes which are conducted inside business organizations. They need multifunctional cooperation. For such cooperation to be effective, it requires all members of an organization to be aware that they share responsibility for relations with exchange partners, and that they all influence stakeholder relationships during at least part of their working time. The responsibility for customer relationships, for example, includes all other functions in an organization. People from logistics, procurement, production, finance, software-engineering, installation, and maintenance of a supplier of paint systems such as German Dürr will need to closely cooperate in generating unique value. They are all part-time marketers.[27] Full-time and part-time marketers together constitute the marketing function of an organization.

By acknowledging the participation of a great number of people from various functional areas of an organization in the core marketing processes, functional departments lose their importance. Value process management means breaking down functional boundaries as they currently exist in most organizations. Business functions become integrated, or at least closely coupled, when organizations shift from hierarchy to managing core processes.

Process coordination

Because all functions of an organization and a substantial number of members of an organization participate in the implementation of the intended market position,

coordination of all activities is a major challenge. Full-time marketers specializing in fields such as marketing intelligence, market communication, product, brand, or distribution management, as well as sales, slip into the roles of process champions. They serve as coaches, educators, team leaders, and initiators. By building and maintaining well-functioning relationships among all staff members participating in the marketing processes, and by making and keeping those people constantly aware of their important role in developing and sustaining mutually beneficial exchange relationships with stakeholders, full-time marketers keep the marketing processes of their organization vigorously alive.[28]

Due to their complexity, value-creation as well as value-generation processes may need to be broken up into units that operate independently, but function as a whole through close cooperation at jointly defined interfaces.[29] To avoid major conflicts during the negotiation of interface relationships by process participants, higher management levels must clearly spell out the objectives to be achieved by the total process and the general rules to be followed, while providing each module flexibility in performing its task.

Performance measurement

Measuring performance is important in providing players with feedback concerning their contribution to the successful achievement of the intended market position. Most business organizations use financial performance measures. Financial outcome measures such as profit, cash flow, EBIT, or return on assets hold managers accountable for a limited number of seemingly objective measures. They are rather abstract and difficult for many members of an organization to relate to in their work, but easy to install, placing few demands on leaders' social competencies. Managers as well as staff members are held accountable for outcomes and given strong incentives to meet their targets. In dynamically developing market and macro environments, however, all sorts of events outside the influence of managers may affect their performance.

For example, after an unexpected economic downturn because of speculation at the stock exchange, financial control would punish managers because profit was below budget. If, however, they anticipated the downturn and cut inventories and developed new products to invigorate the market, they should instead be rewarded for having increased the potential for future success. Financial control is measuring the impact of past activities on current results, giving information neither on reasons for success or failure nor on future success potentials.

Thus, rather than measuring outputs, managers concerned with value processes tend to favour process control, which focuses on evaluating decisions and actions of managers.[30] Process control requires familiarity with the logical sequence of activities and events in a process leading to a desired result. Based on that knowledge, both quantitative and qualitative assessments can be made that capture the nuances of a particular process. Through intensive interaction with managers participating in a process, leaders may act as coaches and sounding boards.

Process-oriented performance measurement has to answer questions concerning effectiveness and efficiency of processes. Effectiveness focuses on the potential rearranging of internal and external marketing intelligence and value processes: What value-creation, value-generation, and intelligence processes exist? What are they needed for? Could they be avoided or at least composed in a different manner to reach even better results? Figure 5.9 shows how IKEA, the Swedish furniture-retailing giant, has increased the value provided to its stakeholders and itself by rearranging core processes in its value-creation system. Process efficiency is assessed by monitoring the functioning of the process in terms of quality, quantity, and intensity, by auditing

the logical and time-wise coordination of sub-processes, and by examining their continual improvement in terms of increasing speed and decreasing costs.

Finally, financial control limits performance to the satisfaction of one single stakeholder group, that is, the capital owners. Therefore, a number of organizations are attempting to measure performance with a broader horizon. A potential measurement tool which reinforces the implementation of an intended market position because of its broader perspective and potential process orientation is the Balanced Scorecard (described in Toolbox 5.4).[31]

Total quality management

The Balanced Scorecard reaches its total value for strategy implementation purposes only when it is used together with Total Quality Management (TQM).[32] TQM combines the external orientation of quality management, that is, "fitness for use", with the internal orientation of "conformance to requirements". TQM strives for the most attractive fulfilment of customer and other stakeholder expectations by creating and generating value exactly to predefined standards.[33] For TQM, an organization has to approach quality in a systematic, process-oriented manner, instead of a departmentalized ad hoc approach. Every member of the organization has to understand their role and grasp the importance of that role in providing unique value to exchange partners together with other members of the organization. To reach that goal, top management has to make sure that quality planning, assurance, and control are supported effectively by regular training sessions. Continuous quality improvement has to become the standard, traced with measurable indicators (see Toolbox 5.4) of return on quality.[34]

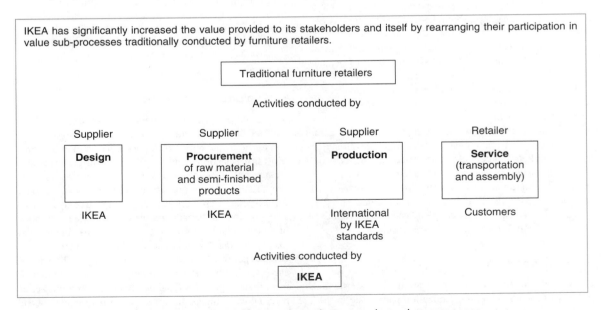

Figure 5.9 Increasing value through rearranging value processes

TOOLBOX 5.4

THE BALANCED SCORECARD

The Balanced Scorecard measures the performance of an organization in terms of strategic objectives that need to be operationalized, such as "closeness to stakeholders", "market leadership", or "fast reaction capability". Operationalization means transformation into quantifiable measures such as "level of customer satisfaction", "number of new products launched in the last year compared to the strongest competitor", or "delivery in one week from customer order".

In addition to financial objectives, the Balanced Scorecard, as proposed by Kaplan and Norton[i], measures performance with regard to customers and internal value processes, as well as product improvement and the organization's learning capability. It covers a substantial number of factors heavily influencing strategy formation and implementation. However, each case of implementing an intended market position has both general and specific properties, which combine in a unique way. Therefore, the contents of the Balanced Scorecard can be broadened, for example, to include all relations with important stakeholders; and can be adapted to the specific business domain of the organization, for example, measuring the flexibility of organizational structures. A special application called Brand Report Card has been suggested by Keller, who showed how to apply the basic idea of the Balanced Scorecard to the strategic management of a brand.[ii]

The operationalization of strategic objectives into quantitative measures depends on the intended market position. For example, depending on the way the organization wants to differentiate itself from its competition, the level of customer satisfaction or retention may be more important than the number of new customers gained in a business period. Managers need to reach an agreement on which measures are the most suitable for their organization's specific situation.

The Balanced Scorecard does not only provide multiple indicators of how well an organization is doing in its attempt to reach the intended market position. The method also requires managers from all organizational sub-units to derive specific objectives for each of the areas covered by the scorecard, which must be fulfilled if the intended market position is to be attained. Managers need to think in detail about their organizational sub-unit's specific contribution to implementing the intended position.

Additionally, managers are forced to develop action plans on how to achieve the objectives fixed in the scorecard. Thus, the scorecard is a driver of implementation which helps managers evaluate their progress towards reaching the intended market position.

Once transformed into quantitative measures which become the focus of regular feedback, strategic objectives receive increased attention by all affected members of the organization. However, there is a danger that all other issues will tend to be neglected, and decisions and activities may be biased to fulfil the set goals. Therefore, the defined measures need to be regularly reconsidered for their fit with the evolving market position.

[i] Kaplan, R.S. and D.P. Norton (1996), "Using the Balanced Scorecard as a Strategic Management System", *Harvard Business Review*, January–February, 75–85.
[ii] Keller, K.L. (2000), "The Brand Report Card", *Harvard Business Review*, January–February, 147–157.

SUMMARY

The selection of markets to serve and of benefits to emphasize in attractively differentiating from competitors are the bases for defining the intended market position of an organization or one of its organizational sub-units. Market selection is based on the relative competitive position of the organization in the most attractive markets and concerns the technologies needed to serve those markets.

The way of effective differentiation is best selected by comparing the expectation fulfilment potentials of the organization and its most important competitors. Because differentiating capabilities may not be sufficient to provide unique value in a sustainable manner, organizations may need either to create new markets, cooperate with partners adding to their capabilities, or acquire other organizations.

Before a final decision can be taken, the potential success of the selected combination of markets and differentiation must be assessed. Aside from economic success, the potential to reach psychological and social objectives needs to be considered. If the potential for success seems to be satisfactory, the intended market position of the organization is formulated.

Leadership, organizational structures, and organizational processes are essential for implementing strategic marketing decisions, and simultaneously they influence the decisions made. Strategic decision-making and implementation are concurrent processes. Therefore, it is as important to focus on how and why actions are initiated in an organization as what actions are initiated.

Discussion questions

1. Search for and present examples of organizations having selected one of the basic options of expanding their business. What are the probable reasons for their selection?

2. Why is it important for any organization to decide on their technology portfolio in parallel to their market portfolio?

3. Is it possible to combine all four basic ways of successful competition? Give a detailed response and find some practical examples for the points you make.

4. What tools would you employ for selecting the benefits to emphasize to the stakeholders of an organization of your choice? Explain the reasons why.

5. Find some practical examples of organizations which have created new markets. What exactly did they do? How did they proceed and why?

6. Find an example of successful cooperation and an example where cooperation failed to increase the differentiation potential of partnering organizations. What may have been the underlying reasons for success and failure?

7. Do a literature search: What are the reported reasons why more than 80 per cent of all mergers fail to reach the objectives announced in pre-merger communication campaigns?

8. Why is it not sufficient to estimate the potential economic success of an intended market position?

9. In your opinion, what are the most important factors making the difference between successful and less successful implementation of an intended market position?

10. What is different about an organization that focuses on marketing processes, instead of marketing as a business function among others?

Notes and references

1. Eisenhardt, K.M. and D.N. Sull (2001), "Strategy as Simple Rules", *Harvard Business Review*, January, 107–116.
2. Smith, C.S. (1996), "Kodak, Fuji Face Off in Neutral Territory: China's Vast Market, *The Wall Street Journal*, May 24, A1, A6.
3. "Fabulous and Fabless", *The Economist*, March 29, 1997, 69.
4. Simon, H. (1992), "Lessons from Germany's Midsize Giants", *Harvard Business Review*, March–April, 115–123.
5. Studer M. (1996), "Swiss Insurer Sees Extension of Profit Surge", *The Wall Street Journal Europe*, May 30, 13.
6. Johnson B. (1996), "Will the Web Win Appeal World Wide?", *Advertising Age*, March 25, 36.
7. Burrows, P. (1995), "The Computer is in the Mail (Really)", *Business Week*, January 23, 44–45.
8. Sakamaki, S. (1996), "Asian Invasion", *Far Eastern Economic Review*, May 2, 69.
9. Wright, P., M. Kroll, P. Chan, and K. Hamel (1991), "Strategic Profiles and Performance: An Empirical Test of Selected Key Propositions", *Journal of the Academy of Marketing Science*, 19, (Summer), 245–254.
10. "It grows on trees", *The Economist*, May 4, 1996, 64.
11. Tellis, G.J. and P.N. Golder (1996), "First to Market, First to Fail? Real Causes of Enduring Market Leadership", *Sloan Management Review*, Winter, 65–75.
12. Ibid.
13. Ibid.
14. Kim, W.C. and R. Mauborgne (1999), "Creating New Market Space", *Harvard Business Review*, January–February, 83–92.
15. Ibid., 86.
16. Elenkov, D.S. (1995), "Executive Insights: The Russian Aerospace Industry – Survey with Implications for American Firms in the Global Marketplace", *Journal of International Marketing*, 3, 2, 71–81.
17. Mitchener, B. (1996), "Renault May Seek Tie-Ups, But It Rules Out a Merger", *The Wall Street Journal Europe*, July 5–6, 3.
18. Lei, D. and J.W. Slocum, Jr (1992), "Global Strategy, Competence-Building and Strategic Alliances", *California Management Review*, Fall, 81–97.
19. "Bosch schließt zu den größten Bremsern auf", *Der Standard*, 2–3 March, 1996, 27.
20. Reitman, V. (1996), "Japan Is Aghast as Foreigner Takes the Wheel at Mazda", *The Wall Street Journal*, April 15, A11.
21. Cravens, D.W., G. Greenley, N.F. Piercy, and St Slater (1997), "Integrating Contemporary Strategic Perspectives", *Long Range Planning*, August, 493–506.
22. Senge, P. (1990), *The Fifth Discipline*, New York, NY: Currency/Doubleday.
23. Müller St. (1991), "Die Psyche des Managers als Determinante des Exporterfolges: Eine kulturvergleichende Studie zur Auslandsorientierung von Managern aus 6 Ländern", Stuttgart: M&P Verlag.
24. Hatch, M.J. and M. Schultz (2001), "Are the Strategic Stars Aligned for Your Corporate Brand?", *Harvard Business Review*, February, 134.
25. Weik, K.E. (1995), *Sensemaking in Organizations*, Thousand Oaks, CAL: Sage Publications.

26. Hedberg, B.G., J. Dahlgren, J. Hansson, and N.-G.Olve (1997), *Virtual Organizations and Beyond: Discover Imaginary Systems*, London: Wiley.

27. Gummesson, E. (1991), "Marketing-Orientation Revisited: The Crucial Role of the Part-Time Marketer", *European Journal of Marketing*, 25(22), 60–75.

28. Gummesson, E. (1998), "Implementation Requires a Relationship Marketing Paradigm", *Journal of the Academy of Marketing Science*, 26(3), 242–249.

29. Baldwin, C.Y. and K.B. Clark (1997), "Managing in an Age of Modularity", *Harvard Business Review*, September–October, 84–93.

30. Collis, D.J. and C.A. Montgomery (1998), "Creating Corporate Advantage", *Harvard Business Review*, May–June, 71–83.

31. Kaplan, R.S. and D.P. Norton (1996), *Balanced Scorecard*, Boston, MA: Harvard Business School Press.

32. Hackman, J.R. and R. Wageman (1995), "Total Quality Management: Empirical, Conceptual, and Practical Issues", *Administrative Science Quarterly*, 40, 309–342.

33. Malcolm Baldrige National Quality Award (1997), *Criteria for Performance Excellence*, Gaithersburg, MD: US Department of Commerce.

34. Rust, R.T., A.J. Zahorik, and T.L. Keiningham (1994), *Return on Quality*, Chicago, IL: Probus.

Further reading

Hackman, J.R. and R. Wageman (1995), "Total Quality Management: Empirical, Conceptual, and Practical Issues", *Administrative Science Quarterly*, 40, 309–342.

Hatch, M.J. and M. Schultz (2001), "Are the Strategic Stars aligned for Your Corporate Brand?", *Harvard Business Review*, February, 129–134.

Kaplan, R.S. and D.P. Norton (1996), "Using the Balanced Scorecard as a Strategic Management System", *Harvard Business Review*, January–February, 75–85.

Keller, K.L. (2000), "The Brand Report Card", *Harvard Business Review*, January–February, 147–157.

Kim, W.C. and R. Mauborgne (1999), "Creating New Market Space", *Harvard Business Review*, January–February, 83–92.

Weik, K.E. (1995), *Sensemaking in Organizations*, Thousand Oaks, CAL: Sage Publications

Part II
Marketing Intelligence

Marketing intelligence

6

Learning objectives

After studying this chapter you will be able to

1 Understand the purpose of market intelligence
2 Explain the four key components used to define a problem
3 Describe the three methods of gathering data
4 Explain the differences between primary and secondary data
5 Understand how questionnaires, observations, experiments and panels are used in marketing
6 Explain the four types of equivalence in an international context
7 Understand the sampling process
8 Select an analytical technique in a given marketing research context
9 Forecast sales
10 Explain the differences between marketing models and marketing expert systems
11 Understand the relationship between marketing intelligence and information systems

SPOTLIGHT

Over ten meetings of experts were necessary to conceive the new hypermarket covering 16,000 square meters, located in the vicinity of the Euro Disney park in the commercial centre of Val d'Europe, east of Paris. This new hypermarket concept is intended to turn Auchan hypermarkets into "a hypermarket where life is better", a place mixing pleasure, purchasing comfort, and good prices. It has taken more than two years to achieve this third-generation hypermarket based on the expectations and needs of customers. Audacious decoration and sophisticated lighting make it look like a department store. A new shopping logic has been provided, using at least a hundred focus groups, each consisting of about fifteen consumers. The store is now divided into spaces devoted to "taking better care of yourself", "taking better care of your home", "feeding yourself better" and "making the most of your free time". This example illustrates the importance of marketing intelligence to generate new product concepts.

Marketing intelligence is a key element in providing added value to the company. It generated an estimated 5961 million euros of sales in the European Union and 5922 millions euros in the USA in 2000. Marketing intelligence is intended to help decision-making. Its purpose is to obtain, analyse and interpret data, in a formal and scientific way, in order to provide the decision maker with useful information.

Marketing intelligence comprises a variety of activities, from marketing decisions of a strategic to tactical nature, from internal issues concerning the company to the business environment. It can be used for diagnosing a problem or finding a resolution. Exhibit A illustrates the range of marketing intelligence activity carried out by

Exhibit A Expenditure by type of research (2000, in %)

	France	Spain	Italy	Sweden	U.K.	Germany
Ad hoc	54	64	59	63	69	46
Panels	28	17	N.A.	7	9	N.A.
Omnibus	6	–	N.A.	4	3	N.A.
Other continuous	12	19	N.A.	26	18	N.A.

"Other continuous" comprises tracking services, retail scanning and media research (people meter)
Total continuous (panels, omnibus and other continuous) is 41 in Italy and 54 in Germany
Source: Esomar, Annual Market Study (2000)

companies. In particular, it shows that most expenditure in Western European countries, other than Germany and France, is for ad hoc or specific studies. The purchase of panel data is the second largest area of expenditure in European market research. In addition, the exhibit shows the strong variation in expenditure patterns among countries. So you can see that expenditure on panel data, in proportion to the expenditure for ad hoc market research, is much less in Italy than in Germany or France.

Marketing intelligence must provide information that reflects reality, otherwise it will lead to bad decision-making. It requires a fairly formal approach, because it is planned and follows scientific procedures. For this reason, the first section "Marketing Intelligence Processes" will describe the various steps in the process of developing a market research study.

Marketing intelligence does not only rely upon surveys. Data can be collected by various other methods as well. The various methods of data collection will be the subject of the section "Collection of information".

Data collected is transformed into useful information for marketing decision-making. This vital phase for marketing intelligence will be presented in the section "The use of information".

Marketing intelligence processes

Marketing intelligence relies on market research studies. A market research study is prepared and conducted in four stages (Figure 6.1). First, a problem or an opportunity needs to be recognized to start a market research process. A research plan is developed based on the problem or opportunity. After executing this plan, research results are gathered in a report that is presented to the people who ordered the study. These processes follow a logical sequence because each preceding step influences the one that follows. For example, insufficient precision in defining the research problem will lead to ineffective research design, which in turn will deliver unsatisfactory research results, even if the research design is perfectly executed. As a consequence, marketing managers must take equal care all four stages of market research processes.

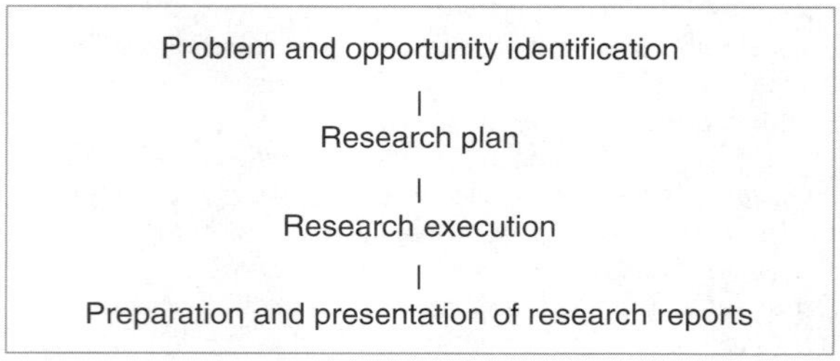

Identification of a problem or opportunity

This first phase, apparently trivial for the novice, is sometimes more difficult than it appears. It is not always easy to know the origin of an observed problem. For example, a decrease in turnover requires a thorough study of its probable origins (an obsolete product, a price that is too high compared to competition, slow economic growth). In addition, it is essential to define the problem in sufficiently broad terms. For example, it is not appropriate to study the decrease in turnover of a bicycle manufacturer by only taking into account its immediate competitors in the bicycle market. Developments in markets of substitute products such as motorcycles or motorbikes must also be considered.

This stage requires a comprehensive and systematic examination of the problem using information provided by the marketing manager and various individuals in the company familiar with the context of the problem. In order to identify the research problem properly, it may be

Problem and opportunity identification
|
Research plan
|
Research execution
|
Preparation and presentation of research reports

Figure 6.1   Sequence of market research process

necessary to do exploratory research, which helps to generate ideas and to confirm intuitive ideas. For example, it may be relevant to consider the consequences of the study for the company and its employees because the stated problem (e.g., selecting a new brand name) may hide more latent problems (e.g., the desire of a brand manager to show his dynamism or his ability).

At this stage, a list of all the information available about the opportunity or the problem is created. This makes it possible to define the aims of the study and the information that must be collected, the questions that need to be answered and the way in which the marketing manager will use the information. For example, a wrongly set price requires an investigation of competitors' prices and of the acceptable prices among target consumers, and often an experiment is used to obtain this information.

The research plan

The research plan formally describes the characteristics of the study and the procedures employed to carry it out. In general, it begins with a summary of the aims of the study and the questions that will be answered by the research.

A research plan includes the choice of the research design and the data to be collected, the methods selected to collect this data and the techniques to analyse and transform data into useful information. It is completed by a budget including not only cost estimates but also a time schedule.

Three research designs are available to study a marketing problem: exploratory, descriptive and causal.

■ Exploratory research is intended to discover ideas and insights, using literature and empirical techniques such as focus groups, case analysis or surveys among experts. For example, to get ideas on the trend in flower fashion for next year's trade exhibition, a company uses interviews with experts and focus groups.
■ Descriptive research is typically concerned with the determination of the frequency with which something occurs (e.g., the number or percentage of consumers selecting the option "tastes nice") or the relationship between two variables (e.g., the percentage of consumers saying "tastes nice" to different competing products and the percentage of brand users). It uses sample surveys or panels.
■ Causal research is used for the determination of cause and effect relationships (for example the impact on sales of two competing advertising messages). It makes use of experiments.

Once the choice of a methodological framework has been justified, the plan must present information on the variables to be considered and on the choice of when to use descriptive or causal research. It must also specify the nature of the data (longitudinal – collected at different points in time, or cross-sectional – collected at one point in time), the sources (primary, secondary), the type (causal or not) and the form (verbal or not – such as mechanical observation obtained with audiometers or scanners).

Execution of research

Conducting the research corresponds to the execution of the research plan and the implementation of the choices relating to measurement, data collection and analysis. These three aspects will be further developed in later sections because of their importance.

Preparation and presentation of the report

The report must be relevant to the reader. The visual material has an important role. Clarity, explanation, precision and exhaustiveness with respect to the research problem and its questions are essential elements of a good research report. The structure of a research report typically looks like this:

1. Title page
2. Table of contents
3. Introduction (presents the problems and objectives)
4. Summary (a mini-report which summarizes the report)
5. Methodology used (data collection and analysis)
6. Results
7. Conclusions and recommendations
8. Appendices.

Collection of information

The collection of information includes the selection of information sources, the selection of the sample from which the data is obtained, and the selection and application of methods of gathering data.

Sources of information

Information collection is carried out first using secondary sources, that is, from existing sources where the information was collected to meet objectives other than those of the current study. When information collected from secondary sources is insufficient, information is collected from sources used especially to satisfy the requirements of the study at hand. These are known as primary sources.

Before searching for primary sources of information, it is advisable to check if the necessary information has not already been collected by the company (using an internal source) or by external sources, such as survey firms, trade associations, statistical collections, books, and so on. Secondary information can be found in abundant supply. It is easy to get hold of and often costs little. The disadvantage of secondary information is its potential inadequacy for the research problem at hand. For example, a French database of businesses does not include every hospital. Therefore it is not the best source of information for businesses wanting to get information on hospitals. In addition, secondary information can prove to be out of date.

On the other hand, secondary information is sometimes invaluable in order to validate primary information, to study the way in which the variables are measured, to obtain lists of companies or quite simply to be exploited as it is. For example, the Kompass file in France provides a detailed list of information on all businesses. The ProQuest database provides an Internet service where one can find all articles published worldwide on a given topic.

Secondary sources of information can be of either internal or external origin. Internal sources are the least expensive. They come from various departments of the company (e.g., accounting, finance, marketing, customer service, purchasing, etc.). Data on customers may be provided by all kinds of employees (those who have direct or indirect contact with customers) such as the customer service department or the accounting department. The accounting, finance or production department obtain information on sales. Data on competition may be collected from reports of visits by the sales force, customer service and field engineers.

External sources are either institutional (government agencies, institutions, associations) or commercial. Government agencies, institutions and associations provide a great number of sources of information. The census bureau, ministries, universities, national scientific councils, professional associations, national and international institutions such as the World Bank or the Bank for International Settlements, and specialized journals illustrate the diversity and the richness of these sources.

Survey firms collect information in order to resell it. These companies can be classified in two categories: those that collect data by subscription and those that provide periodic data in a standard form ready to be exploited by the client companies (panel). Studies by subscription may be carried out for omnibus investigations, in which participating organizations pay for inserting the questions that interest them. Another form of study by subscription

is market and store tests. Research companies such as Nielsen and GfK offer their services to other companies; they test products in stores or in given geographical areas. Their role is to collect information for their customers. They can also provide more elaborate services such as the analysis of data collected.

Longitudinal studies or panels are carried out by companies like Nielsen, Taylor Nelson Sofres and GfK, which collect information of a comparable nature, periodically (weekly, monthly, twice yearly) and on various target groups (consumers, communities, distributors, for example). They provide this information in a standard form (Table 6.1). This information summarizes the changing nature of behaviour, purchase frequency and loyalty. Market trends (especially market shares of various brands) may be followed through time, as well as the structure of demand (scale of customer purchases, quantity purchased, prices paid) and distribution channels used by competitors.

The advantages of panels lie in the lower cost to each subscriber because the overall cost is shared by several subscribing companies, and in the considerable quantity of information that they provide – although this often creates problems of data analysis for the companies acquiring the information. The disadvantages of panels stem from the potential lack of representativeness. The phenomena of mortality (people who leave the panel) and refusal by some important companies to participate bring this about – for example, Aldi the important German discount retailing chain, does not participate in the retailer panel Nielsen. In order to counteract this, the companies running panels try to make their members loyal by rewarding them in various ways (rebates, gifts). Another possible bias of panels comes from the potentially abnormal character of the answers given when the participants feel observed and/or perceive themselves as experts.

A recent development in panels is called an access panel. Members among consumers are recruited to participate regularly in tests or studies at a European level. For example, the Ipsos access panel contains 115,000 households (roughly 250,000 individuals). An access panel is updated once a year using all available files. The advantage of an access panel is getting information about consumer characteristics in advance, so that follow-up studies can be quickly arranged, such as samples of an unusual population group or comparative tests between populations. Members of the panel can be interviewed by mail, phone or computer-assisted telephones (CATI) or the Web (CAWI). Because of its easy adaptation to the population selected by the customer firms, the access panel is most suited to surveys requiring information on the usage of a product, attitudes towards a product or the screening of new product concepts.

Table 6.1 GFK Panel data (Running-report hypermarkets distribution)

Color TV:	Feb 98–Jan 99 Distribution	% of ACV	Dec 97–Jan 98 Distribution	% of ACV	Feb 98–Mar 98 Distribution	% of ACV	Apr 98–May 98 Distribution	% of ACV	Jun 98–Jul 98 Distribution	% of ACV
Mono	90	100	91	100	88	100	91	100	88	100
Stereo	88	100	91	100	88	100	91	100	88	100
Teletext	87	100	91	100	88	100	90	100	86	100
50 Hertz	90	100	91	100	88	100	89	100	84	100
100 Hertz	69	93	66	88	60	84	70	92	71	96
Dolby Surround	63	88	79	98	67	90	64	88	69	93
4:3 Screens	90	100	91	100	88	100	91	100	88	100
16:9 Screens	73	96	82	98	70	91	77	97	78	99
Up to 1000 F	85	98	88	98	80	94	81	97	86	99
1000 to 1500 F	89	100	91	100	88	100	90	100	86	100
1501 to 2000 F	87	100	90	100	85	100	90	100	84	100
2001 to 2500 F	79	99	88	100	82	99	78	98	76	99
2501 to 3000 F	82	99	85	100	80	99	85	100	80	100
3001 to 3500 F	72	95	78	97	73	90	70	96	71	97
3501 to 4000 F	79	99	87	99	81	98	79	99	80	99
4001 to 4500 F	53	78	57	77	48	69	59	82	52	79
4501 to 5000 F	72	95	79	93	67	88	69	92	74	98
5001 to 5500 F	58	84	73	93	63	85	60	83	60	90
5501 to 6000 F	64	88	75	95	57	80	76	95	69	94
6001 to 6500 F	25	45	35	55	31	53	27	49	31	49
6501 to 7000 F	51	75	58	83	39	59	49	75	57	81
7001 to 7500 F	16	28	16	32	21	37	22	34	15	23
7501 to 8000 F	27	50	29	49	25	39	24	50	20	39
8000 F and more	46	73	49	73	35	57	45	72	60	89

Table 6.1 (Continued)

	Feb 98–Jan 99		Dec 97–Jan 98		Feb 98–Mar 98		Apr 98–May 98		Jun 98–Jul 98	
	Distribution	% of ACV	Distribution	% of ACV	Distribution	% of ACV	Distribution	% of ACV	Distribution	% of ACV
Up to 14 Inches	90	100	91	100	87	100	91	100	88	100
15	4	5	4	5	10	11	4	8	1	3
16	20	35	29	46	22	40	19	29	19	35
17	8	11	19	23	16	18	10	13	8	11
20	77	97	86	97	78	97	79	98	71	96
21 Mono	85	100	89	100	85	100	89	100	83	100
21 Stereo	84	99	90	100	83	99	85	100	81	98
24–25 Mono	48	68	45	59	54	71	64	92	55	73
24–25 St 4/3	65	91	83	97	73	95	73	94	62	89
24–25 St 16/9	25	41	35	55	21	35	32	55	29	47
27–29 Mono	57	77	76	93	71	91	68	91	60	82
27–29 St 4/3	87	100	91	100	87	100	86	100	84	100
27–29 St 16/9	69	94	79	96	67	87	74	96	76	98
+ 29 4/3	56	81	66	87	50	71	57	84	62	87
+ 29 16/9	47	76	43	64	34	54	42	72	58	87

Methods of data collection

In selecting an appropriate method of data collection, market researchers have to choose among observation, experimentation and surveys. Some forms of observation offer the advantage that they do not need the explicit agreement or co-operation of the people observed. Experimentation involves the manipulation of certain factors relating to the phenomenon under investigation, with results compared for a test group and a control group. Surveys use various methods of data collection: personal contact, mail, telephone, computer or the Internet. These various methods will be discussed in turn.

Observation

There are various forms of observation: audit, tracking, content analysis, mechanical observation and individual observation. Their use varies greatly.

Tracking past behaviour is seldom employed. It consists of collecting information on past behaviour without informing the consumer, for example studies of waste or dustbins.

An audit in market research consists of examining various documents and inventories. Sales audits are most frequently used to detect trends in the sales of a geographical area, or of a store. Store audits deliver information such as whether a product is stocked or not, what facing is granted to the product or what prices are being charged.

Content analysis is used to study the marketing communication of competitors (topics, subject, words, visuals) and to analyse their positioning.

Mechanical observation allows the recording of the behaviour of people by using certain devices. The people meter, for example, records the television channels chosen by the viewers and the time of viewing. A scanner or optical character reader built-in in checkout counters, in front of the cashier, records the products bought by consumers, based on the bar codes printed on the product packaging. This tool provides information with a wider timeframe, a better degree of accuracy and a greater speed than manual data collection in the stores.

Individual observation can be used in a controlled environment. Certain manufacturers of toys, like Fisher Price, observe their employees' children playing in the nursery at the factory. However, observation can also be carried out externally. For example, observation may consist of recording the number plates of cars on the car park of a hypermarket, in order to find out where shoppers come from. Participant observation occurs when the individual being observed is involved in the study as an "actor" while simultaneously collecting observation data. Although participant observation generates insightful data, it can be fraught with inaccuracies as a result of the dual role played by the individual. Therefore, non-participatory or unobtrusive observation is often preferred.

Experimentation

During experiments, the researcher intervenes before an observation. He manipulates certain variables, such as product, price, promotion or distribution channel, while measuring the effect of other variables, such as competition or socio-demographic characteristics of interviewees (e.g., age or sex). The experimentation is intended to evaluate the relationships between cause and effect. For example, a researcher may be interested in the influence of a new packaging on the development of sales. In addition, experiments are designed so as to establish the relative influence of the manipulated variables.

As Toolbox 6.1 shows, there are various types of experimental design, and the conditions of an experiment can be manipulated in different ways.

TOOLBOX 6.1

SOME WELL-KNOWN EXPERIMENTAL DESIGNS

One-way ANOVA is a design in which one explanatory variable (e.g., different product designs) is handled without repeated measurements on the subjects. In a one-way ANOVA the effect of the manipulated variable is tested against a target variable such as preference, or intent to purchase.

The factorial design is a design in which at least two explanatory variables (e.g., different product designs and colours) are handled without repeated measurement. The effect of the manipulated variables and their interactions are tested on a target variable. In a non-repeated design, subjects are randomly assigned to treatments (combination of variable level such as design 1 with colour 2 if there are two types of designs and colours). Repeated measurement designs are used if several measurements are made on the same respondent. Subjects are non-randomly assigned to treatments in these designs. Fractional designs (such as the Latin square) are ways to avoid presenting too many combinations of manipulated variables (or factors) and thus use a reduced selection of combinations. In a Latin square design, three manipulated variables are divided into an equal number of levels. Using a reduced selection of variable combinations, Latin square does not allow the researcher to examine interactions of manipulated variables.

The experimental method is employed to study two types of problems: concept/product and market/store tests. Concept/product tests offer the customer an idea of the product (or the product itself) and measure the customer's choice or the probability of purchase. Concept tests precede product tests and various procedures are available. If prototypes exist, one can ask the customer to choose the best one. The customer sample can be divided into groups which have to judge only one prototype (monadic procedure) or each interviewee may have to evaluate all of the prototypes (comparative procedure). If one varies the characteristics of the product to determine those that are the most important for the buyer, various designs of the product can be proposed to the consumer. If the characteristics of the product are systematically varied, the most useful procedure consists of classifying all the combinations obtained by all the respondents in order of preference. This procedure is called conjoint analysis (see Chapter 14 on pricing decision). It uses either factorial designs or fractional designs. In addition to the analysis of the components of the physical product, it allows testing of prices, packaging, brand names, and other product features (Toolbox 6.2).

TOOLBOX 6.2

ADVERTISING TEST

The techniques Selector (Burke Marketing Research) and Apex (Asi Market Research) make it possible to test the effectiveness of advertisements for product concepts. They involve the use of television channels to broadcast advertisements to one or several samples of consumers recruited by telephone. Each message is received by only one sample of consumers. Product concepts are sent to the consumers in the form of a set of photographs of commonly used products (one of which is the new product). Customers are asked, after receiving each batch (before the message, after the message), to choose the product that they would prefer to receive.

Product tests use attitudes and purchasing intentions as indicators of behaviour. Therefore they are known to be of limited use in predicting purchases. As a result, other procedures such as market tests are used.

Market tests can be broken up into standard tests (market tests in a region or city), simulated market tests (stores laboratories, purchases from catalogues) or mini-market tests, mobile store-caravans and store tests (Figure 6.4). The cost of operationalization of these methods varies. Because of the very high costs of regional market tests, other procedures have been further developed. Regional market tests cost more because manufacturers need to use their own sales force to convince traders to stock the product and also have to invest in the products and advertising.

Market tests make it possible to study the rate of purchase and repurchase and the market share based on varying marketing conditions. They can be carried out in real stores (e.g., in-store tests) or more secretly in artificial or fictitious markets (e.g., in a store laboratory) (Table 6.2). Market tests may require the use of real money (purchase from a catalogue) or may be fictitious (store laboratory).

Experimental market tests provide the opportunity to combine various methods of observation in a city. They therefore allow a better detection of the relationship between cause and effect and facilitate the management of experiments. The so-called single source concept is based on the fact that one can combine four independent data sources into one. Purchases are automatically recorded through scanners found in all super and hypermarkets in the area. Socio-demographic data is gathered from household panels recruited in a given area. Promotional actions in stores are checked weekly; and a people meter or a monitoring device set up on the TV sets of panel members monitors household television viewing behaviour. Combining these data sources produces a single base of compatible data. However, the management of a single source of data (Figure 6.2) is complicated.

Table 6.2 Classification of market tests

Market test	A test of a real product in a limited geographical area (region)
Experimental market test	Consumer purchases are analysed in the main stores of cities (Ludwigshafen in Germany and GfK or Chateau Thierry for TNS in France)
Store test	Retailer's panel uses 10–20 stores in different geographical areas to measure the purchasing level of consumers (mini tests of Nielsen)
Mobile store	Consumers do their shopping in a mobile supermarket where new products are offered amongst competitive stable products (Van tests in UK)
Catalogue purchase	Products are presented and purchased through a catalogue
Laboratory store	Consumers purchase products in a fictitious store displaying only one product category and using a coupon with a face value equal to the price of a new product or part of it (Assessor).

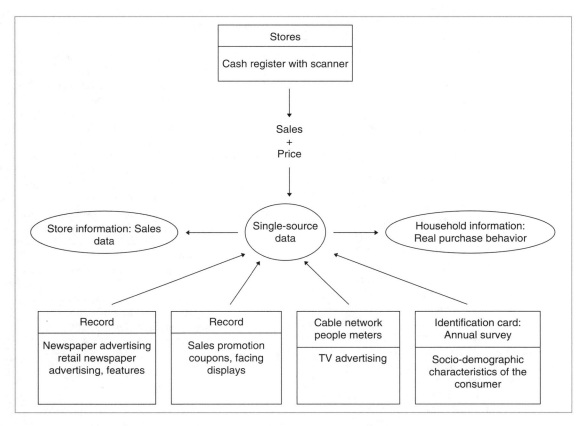

Figure 6.2 Single-source database
Source: G. Hermet and A. Jolibert (1995), *La part de marché*, Paris, Economica.

It requires important investments as well as certain prerequisites:

- a panel of retailers whose checkout counters are equipped with scanners recording sales, the consumer's panel member card as well as the price charged for each article;
- a panel of consumers equipped with an identification card, which is presented at the checkout counter at the time of purchase; an annual investigation into the demographic characteristics and the attitudes of these households which makes it possible to correlate these characteristics with purchasing behaviour;
- the recording of the promotions carried out in each store (premiums, contests, stop shelves, special displays, features, etc.), of the merchandising (facing, display arrangement, etc.) and of the advertisements (newspaper, mailing) by a network of investigators;
- the monitoring of household television viewing by means of audiometers; the Behaviourscan system in the United States, GfK with Ludwigshafen in Germany or GfK–Médiamétrie in Angers and Le Mans relies furthermore on the use of a cabled network which facilitates advertising tests on television. The network, when necessary, may be split, allowing simultaneously the exposure of alternative advertising campaigns and the evaluation of their impact on buyer behaviour.

One of the major problems raised by the operation of a single source relates to the procedure of establishing a panel. One has to choose between two possibilities, the results of which are likely to differ:

- to set up a panel in one or more closed zones in order to cover the purchases in the majority of the stores of the zone, then to aggregate the zones to ensure a national representation. This procedure is followed by the TNS in the zones of Chateau Thierry (France), by GfK in Ludwigshafen (Germany), and by or GfK–Médiamétrie in Angers (France);
- Another solution is to set up panels of consumers around certain stores spread geographically who declare themselves loyal to a certain store (option selected by Nielsen). However, store-loyal customers are special consumers since only 10 per cent of households are store loyal for a period of 12 weeks. Furthermore, their purchasing behaviour is less sensitive to sales promotion and national brands. Therefore, data obtained on those panels may not be representative of the target population.

In simulated market testing, consumers are interviewed mainly in shopping malls. During the interview, they are shown the new product and are asked to rate its characteristics. Then, the consumers are exposed to commercials for the product and its competitors. In a simulated store, the consumers then have the opportunity to buy the product using money or coupons. After a period corresponding to the duration of product usage, follow-up phone interviews are conducted with the participants to assess their evaluation of the product and their intention to re-purchase. One of the main advantages of simulated market tests is that companies are protected from competitors' knowledge. They are also cheaper than regional market tests and are a good way to detect weak products. However, as with experimental market tests, they cannot provide information about the firm's ability to secure retailers or trade support.

Interview

An interview is a data-gathering method that requires the participation of the respondent. Four data collection modes can be used:

1. direct contact by an interviewer,
2. contact by mail,
3. contact by telephone,
4. contact by computer terminal or the Web

Table 6.3 presents a breakdown of expenditure for interviews carried out according to these various modes, in France and in other major European countries. The pattern of expenditure varies considerably from country to country. In France, for example, expenditure devoted to postal studies is much less than in Sweden. On the other hand, the expenditure devoted to focus groups and in-depth interviews is greater in France than in other European countries. Such variations are explained by both physical and cultural reasons. Months of snow and impassable roads do not support face-to-face interviews in Scandinavian countries. Similarly, it takes three hours to analyse a focus group in Belgium and three days in France, which shows the difference in the approaches of analysts in these two countries.

Various interview methods can be combined in the research plan. For example, following a direct contact by interview, one can give the respondent a questionnaire to be self-completed and returned by mail. Each method has specific advantages and disadvantages. The choice of method depends on its usefulness for the purpose of a given study.

Direct personal interviews

Direct contact by interviewers is potentially the most promising collection method for the best quality and quantity of information collected. Personal interviews allow close control of the conditions under which the

Table 6.3 Expenditure for interviews through various modes in Europe in 2000 (in %)

	France	Belgium	Spain	U.K.	Italy	Sweden
Quantitative	40	37	46	55	47	54
Mail	2	2	3	6	2	13
Telephone	10	18	19	16	21	32
Face to face	21	14	18	31	24	8
In the street	6	7	18	8	7	6
At home	15	7		23	17	2
Other quantitative	7	2	6	2	6	3
Qualitative	14	17	18	14	12	9
Group discussions	7	N.A.	15	10	8	8
In-depth interviews	4	N.A.	3	4	2	1
Other qualitative	3	N.A.	–	–	2	–

Note: German data are not available for 2000.
Source: Esomar, Annual Market Study (2000).

investigation is carried out (check understanding of the interviewee, the order of questions, characteristics of the interviewer etc.). But they are the most expensive approach. In addition, the possible interaction between the interviewer and the interviewee may bias the data collected. The direct contact between interviewer and respondent can take various forms. These forms can be classified according to the number of interviews, the degree of structure of the interview and whether the interview is direct or indirect.

■ *Direct contact and the number of interviewees*
Face-to-face interviewing is best suited for confidential or embarrassing topics. The aim of the interviewer is to encourage the respondent to answer with complete freedom on a given subject. It can prove very useful in industrial marketing, for example, where it is not possible to use focus groups with managers working for competing companies.

For cost purposes and where the subject under investigation is appropriate, it is sometimes useful to employ focus groups. Focus groups bring together about 7 to 12 people around a moderator. The role of the moderator is to encourage the people to express themselves, to prevent some from speaking too much and others too little, and to stop any interviewee straying too far from the topic. The moderator avoids intervening on the topic and can make use of an interview guide. There are also other techniques that can be used during interviews (sensory tests, technical tests of expression, creativity test).

Face-to-face interviews and focus groups can be used not only to define a research problem more precisely and to improve the structure of a questionnaire, but also:

– to generate ideas,
– to pre-test advertisements and new products,
– to collect information concerning customers, decision-making and purchasing processes, concerning the benefits sought, the problems with using a product or service and the factors leading to customer satisfaction/dissatisfaction.

■ *Direct contact and the structure of interviews*
Some interviews can be *very structured*. Interviews are structured when the interviewer asks questions to the interviewee from a questionnaire formulated beforehand. Interviews may also be *less structured*. During semi-structured interviews, the interviewer introduces topics into the discussion that were decided beforehand, as with focus groups. A semi-structured individual interview begins using the same principle as an unstructured interview, but it is conducted using a rough interview guide comprising a set of topics that the interviewer wishes to discuss. The topics can be raised in an unspecified order or according to a precise protocol. For example, to find out about the usage frequency of a mail order company, one could use the following protocol:

– ask the respondents how they spend their time each week,
– then discuss their "shopping",
– then discuss store-use frequency,

- then discuss their opinion of mail order companies,
- then discuss their opinion of a particular mail order company.

Interviewees will express themselves openly on each topic, developing their ideas as they come to mind. Sometimes, especially in industrial marketing, the protocol is much more precise and clearly structured, but not as formalized as in a questionnaire.

■ *Indirect character of the interview*
This is based upon the ideas projected/provided by the interviewee. It is useful to understand consumer

purchasing motivations and barriers. Starting from a given stimulus, an interviewee projects his attitudes or opinions. Various methods are selected to collect the information obtained by the projective techniques (Toolbox 6.5). However, the results are difficult to interpret and it is not easy to generalise the results.

In group interviews, the degree of structure varies according to the type of group being used and the desired degree of creativity. The technique of the nominal group (Toolbox 6.3) is used for the identification of a product's salient attributes or dimensions of a marketing problem.

TOOLBOX 6.3

NOMINAL GROUP TECHNIQUE

The nominal group technique is a qualitative technique initially used for organizational planning. It may be used as an alternative to focus group interviewing. The essential characteristics of nominal group technique are that

- It provides a list of ideas relevant to the topic in question
- It is a group method
- It provides structured output that can be analysed at an individual level
- It results in high respondent involvement and commitment
- The process of identifying and scoring makes it possible to study both inter- and intragroup differences.

The process of conducting a nominal group study involves six rounds:

1. The session moderator provides participants with an initial statement of the topic area to be discussed. Participants are asked to reflect individually on the topic and to record personal responses on a worksheet containing a written statement of the issue being addressed.
2. The group moderator then asks a participant chosen at random to state one of the responses he has arrived at individually. This response is written in a concise yet complete manner on a large flipchart. The participant is allowed to explain his response

briefly so that its meaning is clear to other participants. This process is repeated in round-robin fashion until all participants have had a chance to give a response.
3. Participants are allowed and even encouraged to express additional ideas that have been stimulated by the remarks of others.
4. This round involves consolidation and review of the complete set of ideas. The moderator reviews the responses recorded on a flipchart to eliminate duplications and to ensure that all responses are clearly understood by the participants.
5. Participants are subsequently requested to establish the relative importance that should be accorded to each of the response ideas.
6. The final stage is the compilation of results. Rankings allocated to the various ideas of each participant are aggregated to provide a measure of overall importance

This technique contains structured phases starting with questionnaires to find out the opinions of the participants in the group. It is similar to the Delphi method (Toolbox 6.4), which is adopted for purposes such as medium- and long-term sales forecast. Both use questionnaires as an anonymous means of discussion between members of the group.

Source: Claxton, J.D. J.R. Brent Richie and J.L. Zaichkowsky (1980), "The Nominal Group Technique: Its Potential for consumer Research" *Journal of Consumer Research*, 7, 3, 308–313, 1980

TOOLBOX 6.4

THE DELPHI TECHNIQUE

The Delphi technique is a qualitative forecasting technique developed at the RAND Corporation in the 1950s and 1960s. While it was initially only used for technology forecasting, its use is now widespread. The aim of this technique is to develop forecasts by conducting what has been described as an anonymous debate by questionnaire. The essential characteristics of any Delphi study are:

- a panel of expert respondents
- anonymity of respondents and individual responses
- feedback of summarised results
- feedback on comments which support or reject summarised findings

The flow while conducting a Delphi study is as follows:
Starting from a given topic, the interviewer listens to the interviewee and reformulates his remarks without intervening (in-depth interview) in order to obtain information on various dimensions of a research problem. Unstructured individual interviews focus on a specific topic in a general way, but they are not directed according to a precise and prepared protocol. The topic is introduced in order to put the product or the service in its context. The introductory sentences can even depart from the subject; for example, for a study on tyres, one may initially ask the interviewees to talk about their travels, for a study on do-it-yourself, one may start talking about leisure activities. The role of the interviewer is a delicate one, and requires appropriate training: Interviewers must endeavour not to influence the interviewees, while still encouraging them to speak by having a friendly and interested attitude. For this purpose, certain techniques such as "reminders" may be used which consist of repeating the last words pronounced by the interviewee.

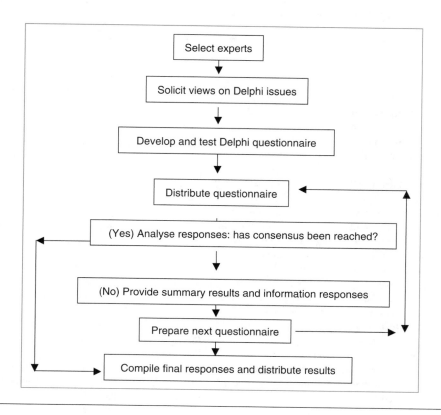

TOOLBOX 6.5

SELECTED PROJECTIVE TECHNIQUES

Projective techniques are verbal or non-verbal. Their purpose is to evoke ideas from and to clarify the ideas of the interviewee.

Drawings are particularly interesting when testing product concepts intended for children. They can also be used with adults to find out, for example, the way a product is used. Collage is also employed. It consists of cutting out images and words from different newspapers, magazines and reassembling them to express the interviewee's feelings. It makes it possible to test the perception of advertising campaigns, brands and so on.

In the Thematic Apperception Test (TAT): the subject tells a story starting from images that are put to him. Murray proposed two series of 10 images made up of drawings, photographs, pictures and paintings. The significance of all images is intentionally ambiguous, using unclear drawings. The content is analysed using five topics, starting from Murray's principle of transcription: the stories judged by the interviewee contain a hero with whom the interviewee must identify and to whom he attributes his own motivations. Other people interact with the hero, they represent the forces of the family and social network that influence the subject. The five points of analysis are motivations and feelings of the hero, other people influen-

cing the hero, the story and its outcome, and analysis of the evoked topics, interests and feelings.

In associative techniques, the interviewee associates images and words with various brands. In a word association task, a word, for example a brand name, is presented to the interviewees and they are asked to say words that come to their mind. In other tasks, words are presented on cards that the interviewee lays out in front of the brands with which he associates them. Associations are then interpreted to reveal, sometimes, unconscious judgements.

Completion techniques require the interviewee to express himself or herself, by finishing an incomplete story starting from incomplete sentences.

In construction techniques, a drawing or a photograph showing, for example, two individuals in a particular situation are presented. One of them pronounces a sentence indicated in a bubble ("speech balloon" in a comic strip). This sentence is intentionally aggressive and involves the "annoyance" of the second individual, into whose place the interviewees project themselves by filling an empty bubble. The analysis of the answers is graded along two dimensions: direction of the aggression and the type of reaction.

Mail interviews

Mail interviews involve sending a questionnaire by post. They have relatively low cost and are useful for reaching geographically dispersed populations. In addition, since the respondent is not subject to major time constraints in answering, mail interviews allow deeper reflection, in particular on past behaviour.

The low response rates, which can be as low as 2 to 20 per cent, are a major disadvantage. This problem of non-response may cause biases in the statistical properties of the sample (randomness, reliability). Some protocols make it possible to improve the response rate as well as the speed and quality of the answers. These protocols concern the envelope (including a stamped, addressed return envelope), the covering letter (patronage, personalization, previous phone call or an expiry date), the characteristics of the questionnaire (colour, anonymity, size, length), the notification (preliminary, parallel, post hoc) and the rewards offered (money, gifts).

The absence of control over the interviewee is also a weakness of mail interviews. Once the questionnaire is sent, one cannot know if it has reached the right recipient, if it has been properly completed or by whom.

In fact, the mail survey restricts the type and the form of questions. This is because of the absence of an

interviewer who could reduce ambiguity and interpret and clarify questions. Consequently, questions must be simple.

Phone interviews

Telephone interviews can be used with consumers as well as with companies and organizations. The telephone numbers necessary for the interviews can be obtained from directories or from lists of customers of specialized companies. It is also possible to use random telephone number generation techniques.

This method of investigation offers various advantages. It is less expensive per interview than the face-to-face interview, while being able to collect the same type of information. It also enables one to get hold of people difficult to reach (celebrities, professionals, leaders). Finally, it enables the researcher to control the collection of information better than with the other modes. In particular, when interviewers are centralized in the same location, they may be monitored by means of selective listening.

The telephone interview has limitations due to the restrictions on the number of questions, the potential type of questions and the length of time involved. In general, telephone interviews are shorter than face-to-face interviews. This is due, in particular, to the way that they are used. They are used primarily for the collection of information concerning advertising recall and behaviour at a given point of time. The average duration of a telephone interview is 10–15 minutes. Questions are generally open-ended. Answers can be pre-coded and are filled in by the interviewer. It is therefore advisable not to ask multiple-choice questions comprising more than five categories of answer.

Computers can be used to facilitate telephone investigations and, in particular, to augment the cost advantage and reduce the constraints imposed by the simplicity of the questions (e.g., by automatic selection of respondents, by direct input of answers by the interviewer, to the computer by automatic quota control, by selecting questions according to previous responses). The computer can also facilitate the use of smaller samples. A predetermined statistical confidence level can be set and interviewing ceases when the sample size is large enough to achieve this level (sequential sampling); so the overall sample size can often be reduced and this brings about cost savings.

This then facilitates studies in which the sequence of the questions is complex and dependent, in particular, on answers to previous questions (conjoint analysis). In this case, the telephone interviews are computer assisted and are called CATI (computer-assisted telephone interview). Other advantages associated with the use of computers are presented in the following section.

Computer and web interview

Interviews using stand-alone computer terminals are not as widespread as Web interviews. In both types, questions and a set of potential answers are displayed on the screen, and the interviewees input their answers using a keyboard. These methods of research are sometimes called CAPI (Computer-assisted personal interview) and CAWI (Computer-assisted web interview) or online interviewing. The computer terminal can be used in various ways. It can be installed in the home of the interviewee and used to replace a phone interview. It can also be used as a substitute for mail interviews when people use the Web or Internet, or when the members of a panel are equipped with terminals. A similar situation can be observed when the sales force or interviewers (e.g., in the retailing industry) are equipped with portable terminals. In addition, computers can be used during temporary exhibitions (shows, trade fairs) to question certain groups of people that could not be reached otherwise. Computer interviewing may be more frequently observed in pop-up surveying that consists of a Web-based questionnaire which appears in a new browser window when a person uses a website.

Interviewing via a computer has various advantages such as reduced costs and a definite completion date as interviews can be instantaneous. It offers other advantages such as

- control of answers and the possibility of automatic data recording,
- recording of the time taken for the interviewee to answer,
- the management of filter questions,
- the opportunity to gather data worldwide,
- dynamic sampling which makes it possible to stop the study as soon as the results obtained reach a predetermined confidence level.

As with telephone interviews, the limits of computer interviews are

- the length of the questionnaire,
- the type of question asked (generally closed and pre-coded) and
- the population reached (for Web interviews, computers are needed, therefore the population reached is limited to individuals equipped with computers and other parts of the population are under-represented in the sample).

The four methods of data collection, that is, direct contact, mail interview, telephone interview, and computer interview, have characteristics that can be disadvantages or advantages depending on the problem to solve, the sample size and the non-response rate. Table 6.4 provides a comparison of those characteristics.

The questionnaire

A questionnaire is a tool intended to measure data that will be the subject of analysis. To understand the proper use of that tool, in the following sections first the problems related to measurement in empirical research will be discussed. Subsequently, the process of questionnaire construction will be described.

Measurement

Measurement is achieved by means of open or closed questions, and using various types of scales. Open questions give the respondent great latitude in what they may say. These are questions such as, which brand of coffee do you know?

Closed questions restrict the choice of the respondent to a pre-determined number of answers, such as: what is your marital status?

1. Single
2. Married without children
3. Married with children
4. Widow(er)
5. Divorced

Table 6.4 Comparisons of the different modes of data gathering

Characteristics	Face to face	Telephone	Computer and Web	Mail
Unit cost of data collection	most expensive	moderately expensive	less expensive than phone	least expensive
Speed of data collection	moderately slow	fast	fastest	slowest
Quantity of data	most	least	medium	considerable
Control of data collection environment	very good	good	very good	none
Control of data collection process (field force)	potentially difficult	moderately good	very good	very good
Number of staff employed	large	moderate	small	small
Range of possible questions	good	limited	moderate	moderate
Geographical dispersion of study participants	limited	good	more than phone	very good
Refusal, non-response problem	least	moderate	moderate	greatest
Perceived anonymity of study participants	low	moderate	moderate	high
Diversity of questions	good	limited	moderate	moderate

Four types of measurement scale can be distinguished:

■ nominal scales, which make it possible to classify answers in categories (a question about the respondent's job is measured on a nominal scale),

■ ordinal scales, which allow, in particular, a classification by order of preference (for brands, for example),

■ interval scales and ratio scales. Interval scales differ from ratio scales by the presence of a relative (or arbitrary) origin in the first and of an absolute origin in the second. Whether the origin is fixed or relative is of interest when coding the questionnaire. An interval scale permits comparisons to be made between responses. A zero can be allocated to the middle or the end point of an interval scale without altering these comparisons. The best-known interval scales (Figure 6.3) are

– the Likert scale made up of statements about the research object. Interviewees are asked to indicate the strength of their disagreement or agreement with those assertions.

– the semantic differential scale consisting of bipolar adjectives (seven-point scale).

Examples of ratio scales (absolute origin) in a survey are the size of a company, its turnover or the age of the subject. All of these have an absolute zero.

Scales provide different amounts of information. Nominal scales provide the least because the numbers on this scale are used only to identify individuals and only allow counting; interval and ratio scales provide the most because they allow the calculation of means, standard deviations and differences between subjects; the ordinal scale is in an intermediate situation which shows the relative standing of objects. However, the difference between two ranks says nothing about the interval separating two objects.

The development of measurement scales to record the answers to questions requires various decisions to be made:

■ How many points the scale should have is difficult to be decided. While many researchers agree on the value of seven points (plus or minus two), the number of points selected depends on several factors such as the method of investigation, the ability of the respondent and the objective of the research.

■ The choice of verbal stimuli which define the contents of the scale and so are used as a point of reference for the answers is also tricky. The possibilities are the use of only one word, antonyms at the ends of the scale or words describing each level of the scale. There is no single clear-cut answer, each option having advantages and disadvantages.

■ The choice of whether the scale is presented vertically or horizontally. Horizontal scales are generally preferred because they use less space on mail questionnaires.

■ The choice of discontinuous features, squares, faces, etc. helps to identify the levels of the scale. For example, smiley faces are often used in questionnaires concerning tourism because they seem to get a better response.

Semantic differential scale
Store A is
Cheap ——— ——— ——— ——— ——— ——— ——— Expensive

Likert scale
Store A is cheap

Strongly disagree   Disagree   Undecided   Agree   Strongly Agree

Smiley faces scale
Store A is

Cheap ——————————————————————————— Expensive

Stapel scale
Store A is well described by the following word
+3 very well
+2 well
+1 quite well
cheap
−1 quite badly
−2 badly
−3 very badly

Figure 6.3 Different interval scales

Questionnaire construction

When constructing a questionnaire, several steps need to be followed (Figure 6.4).

First, the information requirements and the marketing problem need to be reviewed. Second, a list of potential research questions is prepared that will be analysed and classified by order of importance. Then the choice is made based upon cost and budgetary constraints.

The questions selected are then evaluated in a third step, according to the ability of respondents to answer them coherently. Those questions that the respondents can understand and are able and willing to answer must then be carefully constructed.

The questions asked can be open ended or closed. Open-ended questions offer greater freedom to the respondent, while closed questions restrict the choice of the respondent to the categories selected by the researcher. The type of question chosen depends on several factors, such as the method of collection, the nature of the data to be collected, the objectives of the research, the initial knowledge of the researcher and the analysis to be carried out. For example, focus groups require open-ended

questions. If the researcher wants to conduct quantitative analysis, he or she tends to use interval or ratio scales which provide richer information than ordinal or nominal scales. Exploratory research tends to use focus groups and open-ended questions, while causal research uses experiments and closed questions. At an early stage of the research (i.e., exploratory) the researcher uses more open questions than at a later stage (causal).

Question wording is really important. Questions should be short, specific, impartial and clear, that is, avoiding ambiguous words such as *you, frequently* and *much*.

The structure of the questionnaire is designed to make it easy to read and to answer, and to avoid biases. In particular, it is advisable to check for biases that certain questions create in the answers to other questions which come later in the questionnaire. It is also a good idea to group together questions on the same topic and to begin a questionnaire with the easiest questions for the interviewee.

A questionnaire can be divided into three major parts: the introduction, the body of the questionnaire and the classification section. In the first part, the purposes of the

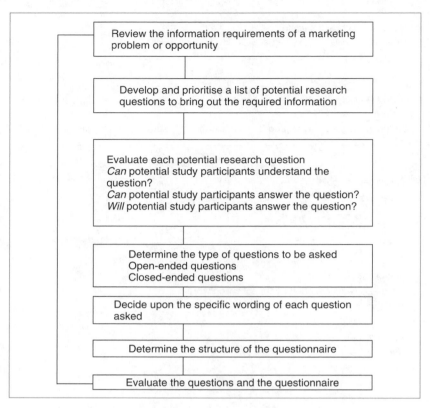

Figure 6.4   Steps in constructing a questionnaire

Source: R.A. Peterson (1982), *Marketing Research*, Plano, Business Publications.

study and background information are presented to encourage participants to answer (anonymity, request for cooperation, importance of the questionnaire, etc.). The second part includes the questions to be asked in the study. In the third part, questions describing the characteristics of the respondent/firm/organisation are asked.

Before using a questionnaire, it is a good idea to pre-test it by choosing a convenience sample so as to study the behaviour of respondents with respect to the questions. The pre-test can try out different data collection methods prior to the main study. Information collected in this phase can then be used to modify the questionnaire and its method of administration.

Sampling

For reasons of speed and cost, researchers limit themselves, in general, to questioning a part or sample of the population, and the results obtained from it will be extrapolated to the whole population. A census

of the population can only be justified if the size of the population and the costs of the study are low, which is not often the case.

To obtain a sample representative of the population and enable an assessment of population characteristics (mean, standard deviation, proportion, etc.), a certain number of preliminary decisions must be made. They concern the definition of the population to be studied, the determination of the sampling frame, the choice of a sampling method and the choice of the sample size (Figure 6.5).

The definition of the population to be studied must be chosen using characteristics that are relevant for the research problem, such as socio-demographic variables (age, social and economic strata, and geographical location) or consumption variables. The sampling frame consists of a list of the individuals or companies that make up the population under investigation. Ideally the sampling frame coincides exactly with the population. However, discrepancies between the population (i.e., households) and the sampling frame (i.e., telephone directory) generally occur. The population may be larger (when all

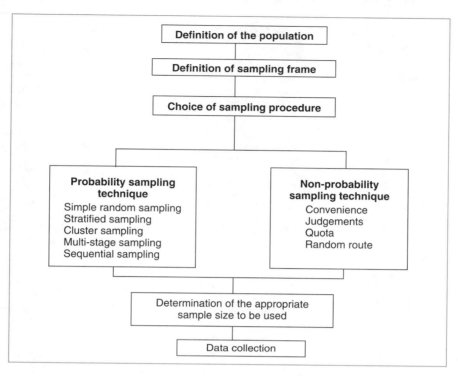

Figure 6.5 Sampling design process

households are not included in the telephone directory) or smaller (when households with multiple telephones are included in the directory) than the sampling frame.

A sample is then extracted from the population by means of a sampling procedure. Two types of method can be used: probability and non-probability sampling. The first enables one to estimate the characteristics of the population from the data found in the sample, within a certain margin of error linked to the sample size. With non-probability sampling one cannot state statistical error measurements for population characteristics, but such samples can generate interesting insights nevertheless.

Table 6.5 compares the principal characteristics of sampling procedures. To avoid certain disadvantages resulting from the direct selection of the basic units from the sampling frame (absence or difficulty in constituting the basic list, high cost because of geographical dispersion), several methods use selection on intermediate or aggregated levels of units (e.g., cities, buildings) composed of basic units (subjects).

With the exception of sequential sampling, for which the size is fixed during the process of sampling based upon the results gradually obtained, the other methods require the initial determination of the sample size. This depends on several factors. Choosing a sample requires a good balance between these various factors. For example,

the size of a simple random sample is computed according to the following formula:

$$n = (z^2/H^2)\sigma^2$$

where n is the sample size

H the required precision of the population mean ($+$ or $-$ of the true population value)

σ standard error of the population

z desired degree of confidence associated with the estimate ($z = 1.96$ for a 95 per cent confidence interval)

This formula is adapted to small samples with respect to the population size. It shows that the sample size increases with an increase in the desired degree of confidence and the required precision (a smaller H value) as well as the standard error of the population.

However, a very important decision may require a larger sample size than a less important decision because it needs more precision in parameter estimation. The type of research (in exploratory research, a small sample size is acceptable), the nature of further statistical analysis (the more sophisticated the analysis is, the larger the sample size must be) and the method of data gathering (taking account of the possible non response rate) influence the choice of the sample size. Other factors such as budget

Table 6.5 Comparison of selected sampling procedures

Sampling procedure	Advantages	Disadvantages
Simple random sampling each population member has an equal probability of being selected	1. sample is representative of the population 2. Estimate parameters of population with a known confidence interval	1. needs a sampling frame 2. More time and money needed
Stratified sampling population is segmented into strata or homogeneous subgroups. Within each stratum, a random sample is drawn	1. all strata are included 2. greater precisions of population parameters because of the homogeneity within strata or smaller size of total sample	1. Appropriate criteria of stratification have to be known in advance 2. more complex and costlier than simple random sampling
Systematic sampling each *n*th subject is selected within the sample	1. simple sample selection. 2. greater precision than simple random sampling	1. population list must be available 2. possible biases in the sample selection process if the selected variable varies in a regular way
Cluster sampling 1. Random sampling of groups of elements (cluster) 2. Random selection of elements within each selected cluster	1. population list is not available 2. lower cost than simple random sampling	1. lower precision than in simple random sampling
Multistage or area sampling 1. Random sampling of groups of elements (area), e.g., region 2. Random selection of blocks within each selected area, e.g., metropolitan area 3. Random selection of elements within each selected block, e.g., county 4. The random selection process may be continued depending upon need	1. involves population grouped by identifiable geographic areas like blocks, communities 2. saves time and costs because of the concentration of households covered in each block	1. Need for a map covering the population and divided into smaller areas (such as census) 2. lower precision than simple random sampling
Quota sampling Sample is divided into sub-groups whose quotas have the same proportions as those of the population. Subjects are selected if they possess the characteristics requested for one category	1. Lesser time and money needed than in simple random sampling	1. no confidence interval for the results 2. precision of the parameters of the population is inferior to simple random sampling 3. lack of control on the subjects selected
Random route (politz method) starting point and route are defined in advance	1. very similar to simple random sample but subjects do not have equal probability of being selected 2. more secure than quota sampling	1. same disadvantage as quota sampling 2. costlier than quota sampling

and time constraints as well as size of the population, when the potential size of the sample exceeds a substantial proportion of the population (e.g., 10 per cent of the population for a simple random sampling) or variations in the strata that constitute the population, may influence the determination of the sample size. Therefore, the determination of the size is the outcome of the judgement based on these various factors.

Gathering international information

International studies face problems particularly concerned with the competitive situation and the comparability of data obtained. Competent market research firms are hard to find in some countries or certain areas, which makes it difficult to have an exclusive contract with a research company (a company and its competitors cannot be the customers of the same research company). In addition, government authorization may be necessary when carrying out market research (China) or studies on certain types of product (e.g., tobacco in Japan). Secondary data sources may prove to be unreliable (e.g., national censuses) or non-existent because, for example, of the absence of trade associations.

A major problem with international studies is the comparability of data. Comparable data would make it possible to launch simultaneous studies in several countries, and to carry out studies on areas defined by behavioural similarities rather than national boundaries and to create homogeneous international data banks. The creation of international data banks is one of the current objectives of large panel companies. However, particularly in Europe, they face cultural differences and the absence of common European standards. The difficulties associated with international studies in obtaining comparable data (in particular primary) arise from the differences in the process of data acquisition and the cultural biases in the answers obtained. (International Spotlight).

To obtain comparable data, the following conditions should be met:

- the constructs used, the measurement of the concepts, and the samples in each country, must be equivalent
- the administration of the measurement instruments is to be closely controlled according to a given standard.

Table 6.6 provides examples of potential biases occurring in international data collection.

Research has been undertaken in Europe in order to eliminate some of these biases. ESOMAR was particularly interested in achieving sample comparability while eliminating biases resulting from socio-demographic data. Thus, standard questions were devised for the measurement of certain socio-demographic variables. These led to equivalent concepts of household, income, the individual in charge of ordinary purchases of the household, level of education, profession and economic status.

INTERNATIONAL SPOTLIGHT

FACTORS INFLUENCING THE COMPARABILITY OF DATA

When conducting comparative consumer research, a key concern is the equivalence of the data collected in different countries. Data equivalence arises in four areas of research design:

1. **Construct equivalence involves** functional equivalence (does the same product serve the same function in different countries?), conceptual equivalence (does the same concept or behaviour have the same meaning in different countries?), category equivalence (is the same object classification scheme used in different countries?)
2. **Measure equivalence involves** calibration equivalence (are measurement units comparable?), translation equivalence (where verbal stimuli are used, is their meaning exactly the same in the different languages used?), metric equivalence (the way that responses are scored on a rating scale may have different interpretations and meaning from one country to the other).
3. **Sampling equivalence involves** respondent equivalence (are similar respondents – husbands, wives or children – responsible for the same tasks in different countries?), sample equivalence (is the sample is comparable on key characteristics across different countries-education, income, age?), sampling procedure equivalence (have the same sampling procedures been used in the different countries?), sampling frame equivalence (are there differences in the availability or completeness of sampling frames such as telephone books?)
4. **Data collection equivalence involves** data gathering method equivalence (was the same method used? – mail, telephone, interviewer?), time equivalence (differences potentially arising from the time of administration of the study – are there seasonality differences between countries and were the studies conducted simultaneously?), contextual equivalence (might differences arise as a result of the context in which the research is conducted?)

Source: Douglas S.P. and C.S. Craig (1984), "Establishing Equivalence in Comparative Consumer Research", in *Comparative Marketing Systems*, edited by E. Kaynak and R. Savitt, New York: Praeger Publisher, 93–113.

Table 6.6 Examples of influencing factors in the comparability of data

Type of equivalence	Example
Functional equivalence	Bikes are used in France mainly for sport, while they are used for the purpose of transportation in the Netherlands and China.
Conceptual equivalence	To be engaged in UK is a formal engagement to marry. In Italy or Spain, it is used to indicate that two people are going out together.
Category equivalence	In France and Italy, cheese is often eaten at the end of a meal. Consumers from Netherlands and Germany prefer to eat cheese at breakfast. In Switzerland it is often eaten melted for dinner.
Calibration equivalence	Yellow in Japan is a sacred colour that nobody will touch. Purple in Brazil is related to death.
Translation equivalence	"I.P." (French firm whose business concerns information and advertising – Information Publicité) can be translated into English as "I pee"! An advertising message from the French Post office, literally, "phone is the plane of the heart" has been translated as "Fly the heart to heart line", or "Direkt flug von Herz zu Herz".
Metric equivalence	UK satisfaction scales go from 1 to 7. French scales go from 1 to 10.
Respondent equivalence	Respondents are difficult to locate when several households or generations live in the same place (for example, Hong Kong)
Sample equivalence	Occupation, income and age categories vary from one European country to other
Sampling frame equivalence	Telephone directory is not available in some countries, in others it is not useful because of a very low rate of phone penetration (Venezuela, for example, has 6 phones for 100 inhabitants)
Sampling procedure equivalence	Random sample is impossible to use without a very high replacement rate, because of a lack of fixed place of abode (Djakarta, for example) or a lack of street names and house numbering.
Data collection equivalence	Phone surveys are difficult to use where there is a low penetration rate but also where respondents are reluctant to answer the telephone (among women in non-urban areas of Latin America) Mail surveys cannot be used in some countries because of postal system deficiencies (areas with no service, no home delivery in non urban areas) or because of a high rate of illiteracy Face-to-face interviews cannot be used because of travel barriers (due to climate or slow means of travel), lack of qualified interviewers, lack of privacy during the interviewing process (presence of the spouse when the woman is interviewed), concerns of the interviewee of talking to a civil servant, a salesman, a criminal concern about interviewer bias due to race (Chinese may not wish to be interviewed by Malaysians) or sex (in Latin America, interviewers are generally males).

Respondents can also be an important source of bias impairing data comparability. Seven biases have been identified:

1. Courtesy bias – tendency to give an answer thought to be desired by the interviewer;
2. Social desirability bias – tendency to give an answer that reflects what is regarded as normal or good in a given culture. Such biases can be observed in Asia, Latin America and in Europe, especially in Turkey and Greece;
3. Topic bias can be more of an issue in one culture than in another; alcoholism is discussed more readily by respondents in the Scandinavian countries than in the Latin countries;
4. Cultural bias comes from a marked cultural feature; the Japanese, for example, tend to underestimate the amount that their goods or their properties are worth because of their greater modesty;
5. Response-style bias – tendency of respondents in some countries to give more extreme answers than those in other countries. For example, Italians over-grade systematically, while Germans tend to under-grade;
6. Respondent characteristics bias concerns the characteristics of the respondent. It arises from respondent heterogeneity. For example, a bias towards

extreme answers can be characteristic of older people in one country and of younger people in another country.

7. Non-response bias caused by different non-response rates in different countries. For example, the non-response rate in Great Britain and Ireland is higher than in other countries in Europe.

Some of these biases can be corrected (Toolbox 6.6); others can only be noted and taken into account in the analysis of the results.

The use of information

Information collected on the market is used in various ways. It can be employed in statistical analysis to feed models or expert systems, or as one of the components of a marketing information system (MIS).

Data analysis

Data collected is the subject of qualitative and/or quantitative analysis. These two types of analysis are sometimes seen as in opposition to each other. Qualitative analysis takes as a starting point a subjective approach that portrays the individual as a complex being, whose unconscious behaviour requires interpretation. The quantitative approach portrays the individual as a logical agent, whose behaviour is determined by certain variables which have to be identified by empirical studies undertaken on a large scale. These two types of analysis

are also complementary, the qualitative approach often preceding a quantitative analysis.

Qualitative analysis

Many firms use qualitative analysis and it contributes to various objectives. It can be used to explore a problem. In this case, it can precede quantitative analysis; so by using focus groups, words and expressions used by consumers can be established in order to include them in a questionnaire.

It can also be used, for example, to study unconscious consumer needs. The techniques selected may be, for example, projective tests, depth interviews and focus groups. The analysis consists of interpreting the transmitted messages, the tone of voice, the hesitations and omissions. It also aims to identify topics that matter to consumers and the links between them. Qualitative analyses can be subjective and dependent on the training and the ability of the analyst.

Qualitative studies have specific characteristics:

- they are carried out on a few individuals, claiming neither exhaustiveness nor statistical reliability;
- involving in-depth analysis of individual behaviour, they can be lengthy (a focus group discussions may last more than 2 hours);
- high skill levels are involved in their management and interpretation. A thorough scientific training (in psychology, social psychology, semiotics) and a lot of experience are needed.

TOOLBOX 6.6

RESPONSE BIASES AND THEIR CORRECTION

Response bias	Potential corrections
Courtesy bias	■ disguise the objective of the questions by careful formulation ■ cluster questions based upon their social desirability ■ Decrease the social desirability of the response by making it easier to provide a socially non-acceptable response. This can be done by prefacing questions by affirmations telling the interviewees that others feel the same
Topic bias	■ use observations and not surveys ■ improve probing techniques used by the interviewer
Cultural bias	–
Respondent characteristics bias	■ Check national samples for the distribution of socio-demographic variables used
Response-style bias	■ standardization of data
Non-response bias	■ elimination of threatening, ambiguous, monotonous questions ■ improved formulation of questioning, which helps to involve the respondent

The most widely used techniques are non-directed and semi-directed interviews, focus groups, and associative and projective techniques. However, many other techniques can be used to conduct qualitative analysis, such as role-playing, semiotics, comparative techniques, protocols and Information Display Board (Toolbox 6.7).

Analysts may use software for qualitative data analysis, which makes it possible to calculate the frequency of use of certain words, themes or topics. Software may compare various pieces of text to identify patterns or relationships. Software helps analysts do what they have always done manually. However, because of the speed at which software can perform these operations, the researcher is able to try out ideas or follow up hunches that would not have been considered when working manually.

Qualitative analysis techniques are not homogeneous. Certain experts use traditional techniques such as focus groups, while others use techniques that are closer to quantitative data analysis. An approach such as "semiometrics", for example, consists of building a semantic space: the researcher develops a body of words that represent the set of options that individuals perceive, measures the variations between words used by the survey and then establishes a chart depicting this space using multidimensional scaling techniques. Examples like semiometrics emphasise the difficulty (and perhaps pointlessness) of making a clear-cut distinction between qualitative and quantitative approaches.

Quantitative analysis

Quantitative analysis requires the creation of a database. Some databases can be very large such as those of Calyx or Consodata, which contain several thousand questionnaires. Quantitative analysis focuses on the choice of statistical analysis techniques. The decision to use one technique rather than another depends on two criteria:

1. The first is the type of information and, in particular, the scale of measurement selected.
2. The second aims to establish the likelihood of causal relations between the studied variables.

TOOLBOX 6.7

MISCELLANEOUS TECHNIQUES USED FOR QUALITATIVE DATA ANALYSIS

■ Role-playing is a form of projective technique in which the interviewee will play a role according to a scenario leaving him/her with considerable freedom to improvise. The role-playing technique may be associated with methods of creativity like synectics and give creative insights into motivation.

■ Semiotic analysis focuses on linguistic and non-linguistic signs. Semiotics aims to identify their explicit and implicit meanings. Products are signs. Therefore, semiotics is applied to products, advertising messages, brand image, and symbolic consumption.

■ The product comparisons and brand comparison make it possible to obtain perceptual or attitudinal dimensions. Different techniques can be used to make comparisons:
  – The paired comparison technique: pair-wise comparisons are made between the products and brands on the market. For each pair, one asks how two products resemble or differ from each other.
  – The anchor technique: in this case, a product is drawn randomly from among the brands existing in the market. One asks the consumer how it differs from the other brands.

■ COG techniques (consumer-oriented grid): each consumer is questioned on what he likes or dislikes about each product. Only attitudinal dimensions are obtained (not perceptual). This makes it possibleto create a grid of attitudes showing dimensions in rows, against products in columns. This grid can subsequently be used as a basis for quantitative study.

■ Kelly grid: products composing the market are randomly drawn in threes (triads), and the interviewee indicates how two products are similar (emergent pole) and how they differ from the third (implicit pole). In this way one obtains scales with one or two poles, named "constructs", which are close to those used by the consumer. For example, when the products, A, C and D are drawn, the interviewee declares that A and C resemble each other because they are expensive and differ from D which is cheap. One obtains a "construct" expensive–cheap, which shows the poles of the comparison in the words of the interviewee. Another triad is then presented to the interviewee. This process ends when the interviewee does not provide any new construct. Then another interviewee is asked.

- The nominal group technique provides a structured approach permitting the generation of a lot of ideas. The participants (8–12) privately answer a question raised by the mediator. Then the procedure proceeds to cluster ideas, to discuss and clarify ideas, followed by a phase of voting on the importance of each idea. This "rationalizing" technique makes it possible to obtain a lot of ideas in a short period and, thanks to the initial phase of private idea generation, one avoids the problems of hierarchy and domination that may exist between the participants.
- The protocol technique consists of asking an individual to think aloud about carrying out a task, for example a purchase or seeing an advertising message. The verbal record is called a protocol. The protocol data are then used by an analyst to study the consumer decision process and to develop a model of the process used in making judgements.
- The information display board technique (IDB) is a laboratory procedure, which consists of giving the subjects a certain amount of information and inviting them to use all, or part of, the information to clarify a simulated choice decision. Information contained in a table generally of product attributes or brand attributes is hidden from the consumer. The subject can open a set of boxes and must then choose a product (or brand). In this way he reveals the most important attributes in his choice, their order, and satisfactory levels for each attribute.
- The eye movement tracking technique may help to find out what actually attracts consumer attention. For example, it can be used to study the focus of attention on certain locations of a promotional brochure pages and whether key material has been read. The sequence of eye movements used by each subject is recorded using a sensing device. To enable the sensing device to give accurate measures, the subject's head must often be restrained to prevent large head movement.

Descriptive methods can consist of a simple sorting task, intended to classify the answers to the questions a priori (closed questions) or a posteriori (open questions). This type of analysis leads to the calculation of measures of central tendency (average, median, mode) and of dispersion indicators (variance, standard deviation, percentiles) of histograms and indices. Panel data analysis as described in Table 6.7 uses such indices.

Table 6.8 presents a fictitious example of results from a retail panel in which the examination of the distribution and the per cent of All Commodity Volume (ACV) of brands A and C show a greater effectiveness of the distribution policy for brand A: the number of stores offering brand A is smaller than those offering brand C, but these stores have much more significant sales.

Descriptive methods (Table 6.9) are intended to highlight the existing structure of variables or subjects (consumers). When they are used with variables, they make it possible to study perception, product positioning, and images of products, brands and companies (principal

---

Table 6.7 Examples of indices used in consumer and retail panels

Indexes	Meaning
Distribution	Distribution is the percentage of stores offering the brand, including those which are out of stock when the inventory is made
% of ACV	% of All Commodity Volume is the percentage of total sales of a product category, sold by the stores offering the brand
MAS	Monthly average sales are the monthly sales divided by the number of stores or the % of ACV
PQ	Quantity purchased by 100 households
PH	Percentage of purchasing households
PQ/PH	Quantity purchased by one household
Sales/% of ACV	Sales for one unit of ACV
Distribution/% of ACV	Index of relative quality of the stores offering the brand
Market share/ % of ACV	Market share served
ACV	Sales in local currency

Table 6.8 Example of distribution and % of ACV computation

Brands	Stores					Total
	1	2	3	4	5	
A	–	550	–	–	150	700
B	100	850	–	50	100	1100
C	Out of stock		50	50	–	100
Total product category	100	1400	50	100	250	1900

Brands	Market share	Distribution	% of ACV
A	36.84	40	96.94
B	57.89	80	97.36
C	5.26	60	13.15

Table 6.9 Descriptive methods

Focus	Ratio/interval scales	Ordinal scales	Nominal scales
Variable	Principal component factor analysis	Multidimensional scaling	Correspondence factor analysis
Subjects	Clustering		

components factor analysis, non-metric multidimensional scaling, correspondence analysis). When used to explore the existence of patterns among subjects (consumers), different classification techniques are available to carry out market segmentation (cluster analysis).

Explanatory methods are used to detect associations. Causality (nature and direction of the relationship) must be based on a theory or an idea that is grounded in reality. Causality makes it possible to distinguish one or more explanatory variables (e.g., AIO variables) likely to explain one or more response variables (e.g., various type of products consumed).

Many explanatory techniques are available. The choice between them depends on the measurement scale used and the number of variables to be linked (one, two or several), which makes it possible to discriminate between the explanatory methods available (Table 6.10). Thus, multiple regressions can be distinguished from canonical analysis by the number of response variables that are taken into account (one variable in regression, two or more in canonical analysis). Among nonparametric tests, chi-squared tests make it possible to study how two nominal variables are linked in a contingency table. For example, this may be used to investigate the relationship between occupation and sex to discover if men or women are over-represented in particular occupations.

These techniques can be used in many ways. These include sales forecasts (in particular, regression), the explanation of the behaviour of groups of companies or consumers (discriminant analysis or logit, log linear analysis), pre-tests of products or price sensitivity (analysis of variance, conjoint analysis) and market segmentation (discriminant analysis, Automatic Interaction Detector [AID]).

Models

Data collected can be used in models that are simplified representations of reality. They take into account only certain aspects of reality, particularly those that are considered the most important. They are generally used by large companies; rarely do small businesses make use of models, despite the existence of software that work on desktop computers.

The construction of a model requires three stages:

1. specification of the model
2. parameter estimation
3. Model evaluation

Specification consists of choosing the variables to be included and the relations that link these variables. Parameter estimation uses statistical methods and accumulated databases to provide values for model parameters. Model evaluation is a stage in which the accuracy of the model in explaining, describing or predicting is analysed (Toolbox 6.8).

Table 6.10 Explanatory techniques

			Dependent variables					
			Interval/ratio		Ordinal		Nominal	
			1	+1	1	+1	1	+1
Interval ratio	1		Simple regression	Canonical analysis	–	–	Discriminant analysis	–
	+1		Multiple regression	Canonical analysis	–	–	Discriminant analysis	–
Ordinal	1		–	–	Non-parametric statistics	–	–	–
	+1		–	–	–	–	–	–
Nominal	1		t test, one-way ANOVA	Multivariate analysis of variance	Non parametric statistics, conjoint measurement	–	X^2, logit, loglinear	X^2
	+1		ANOVA	Multivariate analysis of variance	Conjoint measurement	–	X^2, logit, loglinear	–

(row label: Independent variables)

TOOLBOX 6.8

MODEL CONSTRUCTION

If one wishes to model consumer brand knowledge, one may specify gross rating points (GRP; the number of exposures to a media campaign per 100 individuals belonging to the target or the population.) as the key variable likely to explain knowledge.

Model specification
The relation between the *GRP* and knowledge *(C)* can then be specified in the following way:

$$\ln \left(\frac{1 - C_t}{1 - C_{t-1}} \right) = a - bGRP_t$$

where
  C_t: knowledge at the moment T,
  a, b: parameters.
Parameter estimation
The second stage consists of estimating the parameters of the model with the available data (panels, store tests, survey, etc.). To estimate a and b, it is necessary to collect information on C_t, C_{t-1} and GRP_t. The parameter estimate uses the techniques of data analysis, especially regression analysis.
Model evaluation
Once a model is validated, it can be used. Thus, it is possible to employ the model presented in the preceding example to predict C_{t-1} and C_t using GRP_t, and

parameters a and b are evaluated during the construction of the model. The accuracy of the forecast is then evaluated.

Interviews are recorded and their content is subjected to different kinds of analysis:

■ thematic: the topics discussed are listed.
■ hierarchical: each topic is classified according to its importance. Topics and subtopics are distinguished. For example, under the topic "holidays", one will distinguish the subtopic "leisure activities", and beneath that, the subtopic "movies". Several types of classification are possible.
■ Chronological: the order in which the topics are thought of and the connections between the topics are investigated.
■ Semantics: the meaning of the words employed and the sentence construction are examined.
■ Symbolic system: symbols, comparisons and metaphors are analysed.
■ Psychological and psychoanalytical: this type of analysis requires an interpretation by specialists in this field to detect consumer motivations or what prevents them from being turned into purchases.

Results may be used either for marketing decisions or as input for questionnaire design.

Marketing models can be classified in various ways, according to the aggregation level of demand on which they focus, the elements of purchasing behaviour or their usage.

Models focus on demand at lower or higher levels of aggregation. Some models concern the sales of a sector or an entire product class. Other models study the sales of various brands or the market share of a given brand.

Models also vary in the degree of detail used to describe behaviour. Some models are used to study the influence of the marketing-mix on the market share of the company or on turnover, without taking into account the behaviour of the buyer. Others concern the relationship between the marketing-mix and some company performance indicators, moderated by certain purchasing behaviour variables.

Models can be used to describe a decision-making process or the way in which a market develops. They can also be used as normative tools, to indicate the decisions that should be taken to achieve given objectives and, in particular, in accordance with the marketing-mix. They can also be built for predictive purposes.

A particularly important use of models is for sales forecasting. Data may be gathered by means of surveys on individuals or on companies (surveys on attitudes and intentions to purchase, investment and sales forecast and inventory level changes) and by judgement. Table 6.11 describes the various modelling techniques available. Sales forecasts are particularly important for new product launches. Some forecasting models are employed at the time of market pre-tests and others at a later stage, during market tests.

Table 6.11   Sales forecasting methods

Judgemental methods	Sales force composite judgement	Each salesperson provides a judgement on the development of his/her trade area. All individual forecasts are pooled to provide an overall forecast.
	Executive opinion jury	Executives from sales, production, finance, purchasing and adminis-tration are brought together to provide an overall estimate of forecast.
	Delphi approach	Differs from the previous method on three characteristics: anonymity, information feedback and group response. Participants do not know each other. Forecasts are provided using a set of meetings in which a summary of each individual opinion of the last meeting is presented to participants.
Extrapolative methods	Trend extrapolation	Past observations are assumed to be a function of time. The identified trend is used to forecast. Common functions are in the form of straight line, exponential or S-shape curves.
	Exponential smoothing	Forecast is based upon the weighted sum of past data. Weights are a function of parameter of smoothing chosen by the researcher or stat-istical techniques. This technique can be easily adapted to take into account trend and seasonality.
	Box/Jenkins method	As for exponential smoothing, forecast is based upon the weighted sum of past data. However, the weights computation is more complex. Arima models offer a set of different models amongst which the best fitted model has to be selected.
Causal methods	Regression	Y variable is explained by a set of causes or independent variables. Relationship between Y and causal variables is identified by the exam-ination of past data.
	Simultaneous equations	The structure is similar to regression; however, there are several dependent variables. Forecasts are based upon hypotheses on func-tional form.
	Input–output analysis	Input–output models are built on the idea that to obtain a given quantity of goods (output), it requires a given quantity of products(input). Once the quantity of goods requested by consumers is known, this model provides the quantity of a product necessary to satisfy demand, see sections on models used for market pre-test and market test.
	New product models	Durable and non-durable goods models

Models used for market pre-test

These models use information provided by store laboratories (e.g., assessor model) or by consumers during product tests in their homes (e.g., Bases model). The type of information entered influences the models' output. For example, information coming from store laboratories allows comparisons between available products, while home tests only focus on the product tested and so do not provide comparative information.

Pre-test models of markets enable the company to test the degree of interest in product concepts and, in particular, the proportion of the target market likely to buy the product at least once. They also allow various marketing-mix scenarios to be tested.

Models used for market test

There are two groups of market test models. The first group focuses on products that are not repeatedly purchased (durable goods, for example). The second group focuses on frequently bought products, for which repeat purchasing is very important.

Durable goods models use sales observations of a company over a period of 12–18 months. These observations are then used to estimate the parameters of the model and a generalized logistic model is often applied. Some of these models ignore environmental factors while others allow them to be included.

The majority of non-durable goods models largely use data obtained from panels. Non-durable goods models belonging to this category have different objectives. Certain models are concerned only with sales forecasts; others also make it possible to evaluate the marketing-mix. The complexity of these models results in high implementation costs.

Non-durable goods models are based on the modelling of various stages that lead consumers to repeat their purchase of a given brand. These stages take account of consumer awareness or knowledge of the brand, first trial purchase and the repurchase of the product. Models available are not necessarily used for all of these various stages. For example, one model may focus on the first trial, while another model may take into account not only the first trial stages but also the repurchase stage and their links.

Expert systems

Expert systems are a means of capturing, codifying and making available to others specialized human expertise that is enhanced by using the storage capacity of a computer. They are an application of artificial intelligence. Expert systems are particularly helpful for problems that cannot be solved by the marketing models currently available, because of the absence of adequate algorithms or calculation procedures. They are mainly used to solve poorly structured or badly defined problems like those often raised in strategic marketing. They thus constitute an analytical tool complementary to models.

Contrasts between marketing models and expert systems are presented in Table 6.12. Taking into account the potential importance of expert systems for marketing decisions, in the following discussion we first present the components of such systems, and then explain their potential applications in marketing.

The structure of expert systems

Expert systems consist of four main parts: the knowledge base, the fact base, an inference engine and the environment of the system.

The knowledge base gathers all available expert know-how in the field without necessarily saying how the knowledge will be used. In this base, knowledge is represented by means of various rules, scenarios and scripts (sequences of events registered in the memory as a whole).

The fact base or database aims to record the description of cases previously investigated. It is fed by the user or the inference engine (for deduced facts). The answers provided to the questions raised by the expert system are stored in a database, which can be used to evaluate the various parameters of the problem to be solved.

Table 6.12 Differences between models and expert systems

	Models	Expert systems
Adaptation to problems that cannot be solved by algorithms	No	Yes
Inclusion of new information	No	Yes
Learning ability	No	Yes
Interactivity	No	Yes
Inclusion of an incomplete set of parameters	No	Yes
Self-adaptation to specific problems	No	Yes

The job of the inference engine is to solve the problems submitted to the system. It chooses suitable knowledge and uses it to build an analytical process that leads to the solution of the problem at hand.

The environment of the system includes two modules: the user interface and the explanations module. The interface is a method of acquiring knowledge that allows an expert or an individual to add data into the system. The explanation module is intended to ensure that the results of the process can be understood by non-technical users. It provides not only the knowledge components used but also the complementary components that provide a clear explanation of the reasoning used by the expert system. Therefore, it can be used as a tool for vocational training.

Potential applications of expert systems in marketing

The use of expert systems in marketing is increasing. The main expert systems available are shown in Table 6.13. Those relating to the management of market shares, such as Coverstory or Scan Expert, use retail panels. They provide explanations for the variations in the observed market share and are invaluable in the decision-making process. The other systems relate to more specific aspects of the marketing-mix such as advertising or price.

Marketing Information Systems (MIS)

Whether the information collected is of internal or external origin, collected ad hoc or on an ongoing basis, the data collected by the company must be accessible to marketing managers. The channel by which this information can be communicated before, during or after decision-making is called the marketing information system (MIS) or marketing management support systems.

The purpose of the MIS is to cope with the flow and the accumulation of data. It centralizes and organizes the systems.data collected. It analyses the data in order to transform it into standardized, usable and accessible information such as charts, plans and worksheets. This information allows the company to monitor the environment and helps the decision-making process. The marketing information system is described in Figure 6.6.

The components of a marketing information system are the following:

- databases using information collected within the company or its environment;
- statistical methods to analyse this data;
- methods of decision optimization. If those are algorithms (for well-defined and repetitive problems), they are used in models. When they are of heuristic nature (for badly defined and weakly structured problems), they are used in expert systems;
- models which allow the analysis of data but can also call upon statistical methods and methods of optimization

Progress in data-processing technology (e.g., the availability of interactive languages) enables the construction of marketing information systems. However, there are difficulties that prevent the construction of completely integrated systems. Among these difficulties are the very high cost of a completely integrated system, the diversity of needs of the potential users and the problems arising from the storage of certain types of information, in particular those that are dispersed, split up, fuzzy, or only available in verbal or image form.

Because of these difficulties, MIS are built to handle only certain types of data. They are best adapted for the exploitation of panel data. Companies like L'Oréal or Henkel can exploit panel data over long periods. The information provided by the MIS relates to, for example, data on the sales per product, per channel of distribution and per market, as well as their longitudinal trends.

Table 6.13 Main marketing expert systems	
Expert systems on market share management	Other expert systems
Coverstory (R.I.)	Adcad (advertising)
Scan expert (Nielsen)	Innovator (Financial products selection)
Panelyser (GfK)	Pricing strategy advisor
Partners (IRI)	Xgel (Sales force management)
Promotion scan (IRI)	More 12 (Direct marketing)

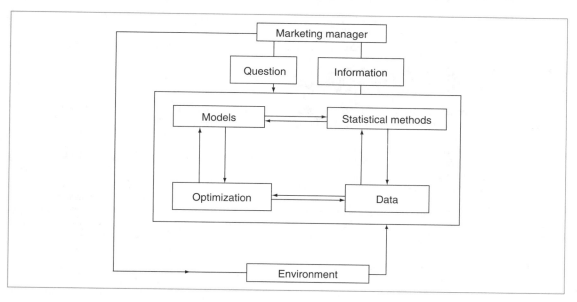

Figure 6.6 The structure of MIS

Source: Little D.C. (1979), "Decision Support Systems for Marketing Management", *Journal of Marketing*, 43, 3, 9–27.

SUMMARY

The purpose of market research is to obtain, analyse and interpret data in order to provide the decision maker with useful information.

The basic steps of planning marketing research are

1. problem and opportunity identification
2. research design development
3. research implementation
4. preparation and presentation of research report.

The three basic methods for obtaining data are

1. observation,
2. experimentation, and
3. interviews.

There are four types of interview:

1. personal,
2. telephone,
3. computer and
4. mail, where data is gathered through interviews or having respondents fill out questionnaires. Questionnaires should be unbiased and objective.

Four types of scales of measurement can be distinguished:

1. nominal,
2. ordinal, and
3. interval and ratio.

Sampling is a method of selecting statistically reliable units from a total population. Basic sampling designs for marketing research are:

1. random,
2. systematic,
3. stratified and
4. quota sampling.

The first three sampling methods are based on statistical probability, where subjects have a known or equal chance of being chosen. Quota sampling depends on judgemental decisions.

Experimentation is a procedure for organizing data to increase the validity and reliability of research findings. It focuses on controlling some variables and manipulating others to determine cause and effect relationships.

International studies face equivalence problems that threaten the comparability of data. Equivalence must be established for constructs, concept measurement, samples and administration of measuring instruments.

Data collected is analysed using qualitative or quantitative techniques that include sales forecasting. They can be used in marketing models, expert systems and marketing information systems.

Discussion questions

1. Give some examples of marketing problems that could be solved using information gained by observation
2. Why is the sales forecast important for a company?
3. Identify six types of sales forecasting methods
4. Under what conditions are market tests useful for sales forecasting? Discuss the advantages and disadvantages of market tests.
5. What is the MIS likely to include? Can it be used in organizations of all sizes?
6. For what kind of problems are expert systems best suited?
7. What are the major limitations of using secondary data to solve marketing problems?
8. Select an existing model and identify the three stages required to put it in place.
9. Why is it necessary to analyse simultaneously distribution and per cent of ACV?
10. If a survey to include all homes with listed telephone numbers is conducted, what sampling technique should be used?
11. What are the advantages and disadvantages of using executive judgement as a sales forecasting technique?
12. What are the potential sources of non-equivalence in international market studies?
13. What are the advantages and disadvantages of access panels?
14. What is a single source? For what use it is best suited?

Further reading

F.M. Bass (1969), A New Product Model for Consumer Durables, *Management Science*, 5, 215–227.

R. Batsell and Y. Wind (1980), Product Testing: Current Methods and Needed Developments, *Journal of the Market Research Society*, 22, 2, 115–137.

R. Burke (1994), Artificial Intelligence for Designing Marketing Decision Making Tools, in *Marketing Information Revolution*, edited by R.C. Blattberg, R. Glazer and J.D.C. Little, Boston: Harvard Business School Press, 204-229.

G.A. Churchill Jr (1999), *Marketing Research: Methodological Foundations*, Seventh Edition, Orlando, Florida: Dryden Press.

J.D. Claxton, R. Brent Jr and J.L. Zaichkowsky (1980), The Nominal Group Technique: It's Potential for Consumer Research, *Journal of Consumer Research*, 7, 3, 308–313.

M. de Souza (1984), For a Better Understanding of Individuals: Non-Verbal Approaches, *Methodological Advances in Marketing Research in Theory and Practice*, Amsterdam, Netherlands Esomar, 163–176.

S.P. Douglas and C.S. Craig (1984), Establishing Equivalence in Comparative Consumer Research, in *Comparative Marketing Systems*, edited by E. Kaynak and R. Savit, New York: Praeger, 93–113.

ESOMAR (1990), Getting Ready for Single European Sample Survey: Amsterdam, Esomar.

F.J. Fowler (1993), *Survey Research Methods*, Second Edition, London: Sage.

M.H. Hansen, W.N. Hurwitz, and G. Madow (1993), *Sample Survey Methods and Theory*, Vol. 1, New York: Wiley.

J.F. Hair, R.E. Anderson, R.L. Tatham, and W.C. Black (1998), *Multivariate Data Analysis*, Fifth Edition, Upper Saddle River, New Jersey: Prentice Hall.

R.A. Krueger (1988), *Focus Group, A Practical Guide for Applied Research*, Newbury Park, California, Sage.

J.M. Kushner (1982), Market Research in non Western Context: The Asian Example, *Journal of the Marketing Research Society*, 24, 2, 116–122.

P.S.H. Leeflang and D.R. Wittink (2000) Building Models for Marketing Decisions: Past, Present, Future, *International Journal of Research in Marketing*, 17, 2 and 3, 105–126.

G. Lilien Ph. Kotler, and K.S. Moorthy (1992), *Marketing Models*, Englewood Cliffs, New Jersey, Prentice Hall.

G. Lilien and A. Rangaswamy (1998), *Marketing Engineering*, Reading, Massachussetts, Addison Wesley.

S. Madridakis and S.C. Wheelwright (1985), *Forecasting: Methods and Applications*, Second Edition, Wiley.

V. Mahajan and E. Müller (1979), Innovation Diffusion and New Product Growth Models in Marketing, *Journal of Marketing*, 43, 4, 55–68.

P. Naert and P. Leeflang (1978), *Building Implementable Marketing Models*, Boston: Martinius Nijhoff Social Sciences Division.

J. Schmitz (1994), Expert Systems for Scanner Data in Practice, in *Marketing Information Revolution*, edited by R.C. Blattberg, R. Glazer and J.D.C. Little, Boston: Harvard Business School Press, 102–119.

Wierenga, B. and Van Bruggen G.H. (1997), The Integration of Marketing Problem-solving Modes and Marketing Management Support Systems, *Journal of Marketing*, 61, 3, 21–37.

B.J. Winer (1971), *Statistical Principles in Experimental Design*, New York: McGraw Hill.

Part III

Value-Creation Process

Consumer behaviour

7

Learning objectives

After studying this chapter you will be able to

1 Become familiar with the needs and motivations that may affect the consumer's buying decision process
2 Examine how psychological factors influence the consumer's buying decision process
3 Explore how socio-cultural factors may affect the consumer's buying decision process
4 Examine the purchasing roles in the family's decision-making process
5 Become familiar with situational variables
6 Understand the types of decision consumers make when purchasing
7 Become familiar with the elements of a buying centre
8 Explore the stages of the organisational buying decision process and examine the influencers affecting the process
9 Become familiar with the criteria used according to this process
10 Examine the marketing relationship
11 Understand post-purchasing behaviour

SPOTLIGHT

Vietnamese consumers differ from Western consumers in their attitudes towards products. The pressure to conform to group norms is stronger in Vietnam. Therefore, the Vietnamese value the social image created by products such us luxury goods, which emphasize affiliation to a particular social group. Products may be fashionable because they are associated with social status, rather than because they have, for example, a flavour that consumers prefer. Due to the importance Vietnamese consumers give to interpersonal relationship, they care little about personal products, such as pets they own. Cultural stereotypes affect their perception and evaluation of products. French products are associated with aestheticism, refined taste, sensual pleasure, elegance and fine judgement, while German products are associated with high quality. When dissatisfied, Vietnamese consumers are reluctant to complain because of the value they place on social harmony and saving face. Complaining may generate a loss of face because showing anger suggests low social status. People of high status should not express their anger publicly according to the reciprocation principle, which states that if you are rude to someone, then he is entitled to be rude to you.

Customers make choices based on their perception of the value that products and services deliver to them. Customer value is the difference between the value that the customer gains from owning and using the product, and the costs of obtaining that product.

Customers often fail to evaluate a product's value and its costs accurately or objectively and act on the basis of perceived value. Gains are not only based upon utilitarian product performance, which depends on concrete product or brand characteristics. They may also be obtained by social benefits, which provide the customer with status; by hedonic benefits, which refer to a product's capacity to provide pleasure and fun; and by experiential or emotional response benefits (see Spotlight). Costs not only include the price paid, but they also involve the time spent and the psychological efforts involved. It follows that numerous factors may contribute to the perceived value of a product or service.

Four groups of factors are likely to influence the perceived value during the buying process (Figure 7.1): the marketing-mix used by manufacturers and distributors, psychological factors, socio-cultural factors and situational factors. For pedagogical purposes, only the last three groups of factors will be examined in this chapter. Factors that directly relate to the marketing-mix are analysed in Chapters 12–16. The industrial buyer will be examined in the later sections of this chapter.

The importance attached to consumer satisfaction is the consequence of the central place that this idea occupies in the marketing concept. Consumer behaviour analysis is vital for the company because of the consequences which it involves for all marketing decisions: brand positioning, market segmentation, new product development, advertising strategies, and choice of the distribution channels.

Psychological factors

Several influencing factors affect the consumer during the decision-making process. Independent of marketing-mix variables such as advertising, which is used to influence the consumer, differences observed in behaviour can arise from psychological, socio-cultural and situational factors. Psychological factors include needs and motivations, personality, perception, beliefs and attitudes, and lifstyles. The separation of psychological, socio-cultural and situational factors, although debatable (personality, for example, is a psychological factor but its formation is not independent of socio-cultural factors), is conveniently used for presentation purposes.

Needs, drives, desires and motivations

A need becomes apparent when an individual feels a variation between his actual situation and an ideal

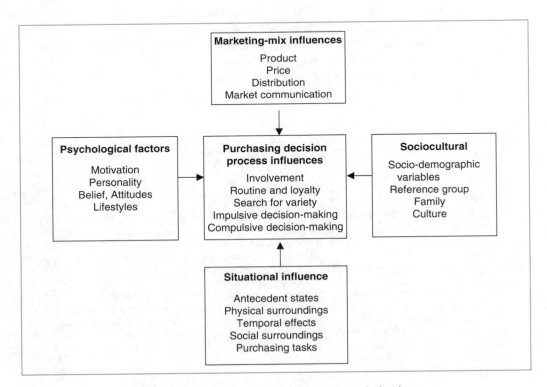

Figure 7.1 Factors influencing consumer behaviour

situation. As a result, the consumer feels that something is missing, which creates a state of tension. This feeling pushes the consumer to act or it justifies the want. Various forms of needs exist, some of them arising from instincts. Sometimes innate needs, originating from instincts, are distinguished from needs that are learned. Drives, which are the dynamic translation of this state of tension, are transformed into desires or wants when they are directed towards an object. The motivation is then the psychic force which pushes the individual to act in order to reduce the state of tension and thus to appease his needs, by directing them towards an object.

In spite of the crucial part played by needs in marketing, there is no single theory relating uniquely to needs. The variety of theories used to explain needs comes from their origin (learning, psychoanalytical, personality, cognitive, values, involvement theory) and from their focus (origin of the need starting with an instinct, an arousal, existence of a hierarchy, or conflicts of needs). These various theories, which in the current state of knowledge are not integrated, will be presented in the following paragraphs.

Freud's theory underlines the role played by instincts – innate or unconscious patterns of behaviour. Much human behaviour stems from a fundamental conflict between a person's desire to gratify physiological needs and the necessity to be a member of the society. A struggle for equilibrium occurs between these forces and a person's development hinges on the way this struggle occurs during childhood. Although aspects of Freudian theory have been controversial and have led to the neo-Freudian reaction, this theory emphasizes that needs are in the unconscious, and as a result consumers cannot necessarily tell us their true motivations for choosing products, and that symbolism in products may reflect a compromise of this fundamental conflict. Using the product channels unacceptable desires. Freudian ideas relate especially to the sexual associations of products. Motivational research applies these ideas to products and advertising. This form of research relies on in-depth interviews with individual consumers.

Neo-Freudians added a variety of other needs to the importance of sexual instincts. Adler insists on the fight for superiority which makes it possible to overcome the feeling of inferiority acquired during childhood, Fromm and Sullivan write about the aversion to loneliness, Horney is concerned with anxiety and the need for safety.

Need arousal theory is founded on the postulate that a consumer seeks to be stimulated, or has a need for stimulation, until it reaches an optimum threshold which provides both pleasure and comfort. Too much or not enough stimulation proves to be unpleasant and uncomfortable. Excessive stimulation results in efforts to reduce stimulation by, for example, avoiding new and unfamiliar brands. Insufficient stimulation leads the consumer to seek stimulation, that is, to express a need for variety or innovation (to seek information on other products, to buy unfamiliar products, to change brand, or to change store). This search for variety then provides pleasure or comfort, which makes it possible for consumers to reach the optimum level of stimulation.

Maslow's theory postulates the existence of a universal hierarchical system of needs. A consumer must have satisfied needs at one level, before satisfying needs at a higher level. In addition, a need of a lower nature that has been satisfied still remains in the set of needs. The hierarchy suggested by Maslow is as follows:

1. Physiological needs: hunger, thirst and related products (medicines, staple items, etc.)
2. Safety needs: security, protection, and related products (insurance, alarm systems, etc.)
3. Social needs: love and friendship, and related products (clothing, clubs, etc.)
4. Personal needs: self-esteem, prestige, status and related products (cars, furniture, etc.)
5. Self-actualization needs: self-development, personal fulfilment and related products (hobbies, education, etc.)

This hierarchy provides a complete categorization of needs that form the origin of motivations. It shows their diversity, from the primary needs (physiological) to the learned or secondary needs. It offers an explanation of needs that cannot be satisfied, because of the hierarchy.

The pre-eminent position given to self-actualization in the hierarchy corresponds to the hierarchy of needs of the US consumer. This hierarchy is disputed because it cannot be adapted to other cultures with less materialistic tendencies. Bollinger and Hofstede observe that in contrast to the United States and Great Britain, for which the dominating need of the hierarchy is the need for self-actualization, France, Spain, Portugal and former Yugoslavia have dominating safety and social needs.

The theory of self-concept postulates that an individual acts according to the idea that the individual has of themselves. This concept starts with the contacts that one has with one's environment and includes

- actual self: what the individual thinks they are
- Self image: what the individual believes they are
- ideal self: what the individual aspires to be,
- social self: How others see the individual.
- extended self: There are as many selves as there are social roles within society (family, community, group). For example, what we (family, couple) are (the real we) or what we aspire to be (the ideal we).

Self-concept influences the way in which needs are translated into purchasing motivation concerning products and brands. Consumers prefer products and brands that are congruent with their self-concept.

Field's theory provides an explanatory framework for motivation conflicts. The degree to which the product or service satisfies a motivation will determine its attraction (positive force) or its rejection (negative force). The individual will decide in accordance with the strongest force. However, when motivations are of roughly equal forces, the consumer perceives a conflict which can have three different origins:

1. a conflict between two favourable solutions (travel in Ireland or travel in Thailand),
2. a conflict between two solutions of which one is perceived to be favourable and the other unfavourable (the purchase of a TV set can be perceived as favourable for its enjoyment and unfavourable for children's school work),
3. a conflict between two solutions, both perceived as being unfavourable (If a car has important mechanical problems, is it necessary to buy another one or to carry out an expensive repair?)

Conflict resolution can be carried out by the consumers themselves or through the actions of the marketer. The consumer can eliminate the conflict, by modifying their initial objectives, by treating them differently on a hierarchical basis. The European consumer may hesitate between a holiday in Ireland and a holiday in Thailand. If the consumer finally decides to attach greater importance to proximity than exoticism, he will choose Ireland. Of course, the actions of sales representatives can also influence the consumer in his choices.

Value theory provides another explanation for needs and motivations. Values are motivations. They are cognitive representations of needs. They consist of concepts or beliefs in how one should behave, or the purpose of existence, which transcend particular situations, guiding the selection or the evaluation of behaviour. The relative importance of different values is unique to each individual. Values concern universal needs such as biological needs (pleasure, love, intimacy), needs for social interaction (honesty, equality), humanistic needs relating to well-being and survival of the group (peace in the world, national safety) and needs for professional success (need for achievement, financial ease, autonomy). They particularly affect a consumer's attitude towards products through the importance granted to various product attributes.

Two main methods can be used to identify individual values. The macro methods aim to identify values with inventories while the micro methods aim to identify the bonds that exist between product attributes and their underlying values.

Various inventories allow the quantification and aggregation of individual values: Rokeach inventory, List of Values (LOV), Schwartz and Bilsky inventory, whose major dimensions are presented in Figure 7.2, and the inventory of European values (European Values Survey or EVS). The first three inventories are related and based on the Rokeach inventory. LOV is a simplification of Rokeach, focusing on individual values. Schwartz and Blisky supplements Rokeach for cross-cultural studies. The EVS is quite different because it focuses on ethics, through nine social topics: leisure, work, individual, life direction, morality, religion, family, other people, and policy.

Micro methods are based on means–ends chains (product attributes–consequences–values). These are ladders which

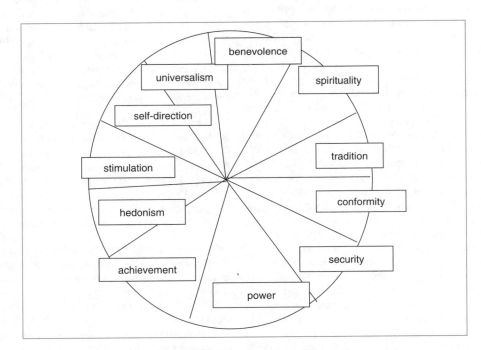

Figure 7.2 Values' motivational domains

focus on the linkages between product attributes, personal consequences (outcomes) and personal values (Table 7.1).

Figure 7.3 shows an application of the analysis of a means–ends chain. The identification of the chains by an expert is very useful since it provides information necessary for marketing communication or for market segmentation.

Toolbox 7.1 presents different methods for the identification of means–ends chains.

Table 7.1 Means–ends chain model

Abstraction level	Example	Comments
Terminal values ↑	Self-esteem	Preferred final state
Instrumental values ↑	To be perceived by others	Preferred behavioural mode of conduct
Sociopsychological consequences ↑	Others consider me as very peculiar	Social (how others feel) and psychological (how I feel) consequences of product usage
Functional consequences ↑	Easy to handle	Is the product performing as it is supposed to? Is it doing what it is supposed to?
Abstract attributes ↑	Good quality	Abstract representation of several concrete attributes, subjective, cannot be directly perceived by senses
Concrete attributes	Price	Cognitive representation of physical product attributes can be directly perceived

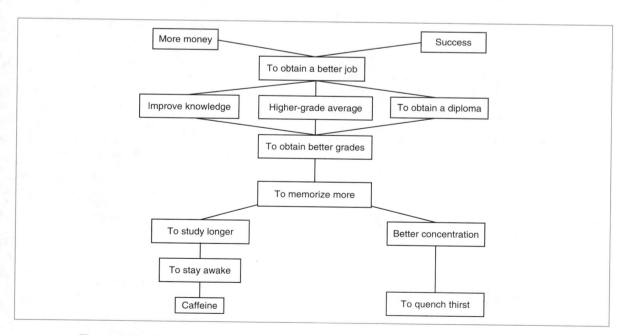

Figure 7.3 Means–ends chain for beverage consumption while preparing for an exam

TOOLBOX 7.1

LINKING CONSUMERS' VALUES TO PRODUCTS

There are four methods for assessing the links between consumer values and products.

The first three methods use a standard universal value inventory (e.g., Rokeach inventory, with 18 items as terminal or end-state values and 18 items as instrumental values) the LOV inventory (a collapsed nine-item version of the Rokeach inventory) or the Schwartz and Bilsky inventory (an extended 56-item version of the Rokeach inventory). The Rokeach inventory suffers from two weaknesses.

1. This inventory has been intuitively derived and therefore lacks scientific ground.
2. It is also a cultural conceptualization. The assumption that the same values are manifest across different consumption contexts has an intuitive appeal. However, conventional value researchers do recognize that subgroups within a nation (a proxy for culture) exhibit different value hierarchies. Such subgroups are identified by socio-economic variables. The cultural variations of values are treated as variations around a central tendency. They neglect the intercultural differences related to the context in which values arise.

Method 1 Product-oriented method

This method is usually called laddering. Its central principle is that the meaning of a brand depends upon higher-order, more-personnel elements brand attributes are linked to. Consumers are asked to describe their feelings about products in such a way that ultimate values come out. Laddering begins by finding out the attributes the customers use in their choice, then by asking a consumer about the benefits offered by a specific product attribute or product and then probing further through a series of why-type questions to trace out the perceptual linkages among lower-order functional benefits (functional, psychosocial consequences) and finally instrumental and terminal values.

Three broadly defined levels are as follows:

Product Attributes (e.g., an overnight delivery service category: Drop box)

↓

Consequences which are reasons why the attribute is important to the consumer (e.g., for an overnight delivery service category: saves time, convenient)

↓

Values which are the end states governing drives of the individual (e.g., for an overnight delivery service category: self-esteem, Accomplishment)

The laddering technique suffers from the following weaknesses:

- Probing further through a series of why-type queries to trace out the perceptual linkages among lower-order functional benefits, psychosocial consequences and finally instrumental and terminal values (Rokeach Values) does not leave any opportunity to the respondent to freely interpret focal attributes' meaning according to actual usage experience.
- The identified linkages between attributes–consequences–values are largely abstracted out of resulting means–end.
- The means–end approach is product-centric rather than consumer-centric, the elicited attribute linkages can be quite questionable because the approach does not refer to a real consumption situation and therefore may generate artificial linkages.
- The terms labelling the connection between terminal features and terminal values will be shaped by micro-cultural beliefs and meanings the consumer uses to understand the attributes in question (most critical information in a means–end model lies not in the primary boxes (identified consequences and values) but rather in their connections. Linking cultural meanings and narrative structure are abstracted away in the analysis because the consumer focuses on the link that comes to his mind without referring to a real consumption situation.
- Cultural content of the identified values is also abstracted away by means–end analysis. The same delimited set of universal values are elicited by laddering interviews and hence can be directly compared across consumers. As a result, this approach elides the meaning-based distinctions among consumer values that emerge across different micro-cultural and subcultural contexts of meanings.
- The means–end process relies upon associations between values and products which may or may not be causal. For example, if a set of respondents value achievement and tend to drive Mercedes Benz automobiles, we are tempted to infer that Mercedes is a reward for high achievement. If we control for socio-economic status, the relationship may disappear. It may be that socio-economic status (not need for achievement) explains Mercedes ownership and need for achievement simultaneously.

Method 2 Consumer-oriented method

This method starts from the consumer and not from the product. Consumers are asked about core values and then asked to describe these values in terms of selected products. This process involves three steps:

1. Providing a list of values:
   Which five of these values are the most important in your life? (e.g., self expression)

   ↓

2. Providing a list of products: for each of the five values indicate which five of these items makes this value possible? (sports car, skis, hair colouring, running shoes, tennis racquet)

   ↓

3. How-type questions: how does this product facilitate or enable this feeling (go fast, look cool, have time to think, use in many different ways)

Step 3 helps to discover the missing links between values and products. Values used are borrowed from the LOV or Rokeach value systems.

This method suffers from the same weaknesses as Method 1. However, as consumers are buying values, feelings and benefits, not technologies and attributes, it appears to be more logical and therefore should generate less artificial links.

Method 3   Segmentation based on values

This method segments the market according to a selected-value Rokeach-based inventory. Its purpose is to identify associations between segments based on values and usage frequency of products. Segments have different value systems and therefore identify consumption subcultures.

However, it has been found that terminal values exert little direct influence on actual consumer attitudes and behaviour. Only between 1 and 6 per cent of product usage is explained by values.

Method 4   Interpretive method

This method uses depth interviews to identify values in consumption practices. It relies upon interpretation of verbatim interview texts. This process allows to freely interpret focal attributes' meaning according to goals or values in any actual usage experience.

It focuses on what a consumer likes about an attribute, its likely benefits, situational uses, drawbacks, and anticipated problems.

This method suffers from two weaknesses: the importance of the interpretative workload and the difficulty of the sample selection.

1. The workload of any interpretive method is very important due to the time spent for each interview, its transcription and its analysis.
2. The sample is not a random sample. Respondents are selected for their variance according to the consumption context. They have to vary according to the newness of the context, their social class, working status and so forth.

Involvement theory provides another explanation of the origin of motivations. Involvement is a motivation characterized by the intensity of importance, interest, and attraction of the consumer towards a product or a class of products. It varies according to consumer types, products and purchase situations. Involvement can be moderated by the perceived risk associated with the purchase of a product or the destination of the product, for example a gift.

Involvement has cognitive and emotional components. Cognitive components result from the utility motivations which focus on functional characteristics of the product, while emotional components are related to emotional needs that a product can satisfy.

Various scales are available to measure involvement. The oldest scale used is that of Kapferer and Laurent, which focuses mostly on involvement antecedents, which are

- personal interest in the product's category (its importance),
- sign value allotted by a consumer to a product category (the self-image which one wishes to portray),
- pleasure value (hedonic value of a product category),
- importance of negative consequences (negative consequences of a poor purchase decision),
- subjective probability of poor purchase decision.

Table 7.2 shows the average involvement profile of various product categories. For example, dresses and perfumes have higher involvement scores on interest and pleasure dimensions than pasta products and batteries.

Other scales prefer to measure the concept itself and for this reason tend to be unidimensional, which makes them shorter and easier to use. For example, the Strazzieri scale includes three components, personal relevance, interest and attraction, which generate a single global dimension.

Personality

The influence of personality on a consumer's purchasing behaviour has interested many market researchers, in particular its relationship with attention, perception, and innovation diffusion. Personality is defined as "the single configuration of characteristics, beliefs, behaviours and practices specific to each individual". Part of this configuration is innate, the other results from social training, and therefore is due to the specific experiences and history of each individual.

Personality psychology has long been plagued by a plethora of personality constructs that sometimes differ in name but measure practically the same thing.

Table 7.2   Average involvement scores for some product categories

Product category	Interest	Pleasure/emotion	Sign	Risk importance	Error probability
Woman's dress	123	147	166	129	99
Perfume	120	154	164	116	97
Noodles	69	73	74	56	80
Battery	36	39	59	65	98
Champagne	75	128	123	123	119
Vacuum cleaner	108	94	78	130	111

Note: Scores had been standardized, for each scale the mean is 100, and the standard deviation is 50.
Source: J.N. Kapferer and G. Laurent, Consumer involvement Profiles: A New Practical Approach to Consumer Involvement, *Journal of Advertising Research*, 25, December 1985–January 1986, 51.

Psychoanalytical theories propose various types of personality characteristics, which are sometimes used in the interpretation of consumer behaviour, sales force activity and in studies of negotiation between buyers and sellers. These distinctions include those made by Jung between "extroversion" and "introversion", by Horney between "compliant", "aggressive" and "detached", and by Fromm between "receptive", "exploitative", "accumulative", "commercial" and "productive" orientations. They are used as a basis for the interpretation of many motivation studies. Some of these theories gave birth to various tests (e.g., Myers-Briggs Indicator or the CAD scale (compliance, aggression, detachment)).

These theories are useful for motivation studies of individuals but are more difficult to use when working with groups of individuals (the aggregation problem).

The traits theory has had more success with market researchers. The trait concept suggests the idea of very stable personal characteristics, with personality defined as a structure of traits. The Edwards Personality Preference Schedule (as shown in Toolbox 7.2) includes such traits as achievement, deference, order, exhibition, autonomy, affiliation, introspection, dependence, dominance, abasement or inferiority, nurturance or benevolence, change, endurance, heterosexuality, and aggressiveness,

TOOLBOX 7.2

The Edward Personality Preference Schedule includes 15 traits:

1. Achievement
2. Deference
3. Order
4. Exhibition
5. Autonomy
6. Affiliation
7. Introception
8. Succorance or dependence
9. Dominance
10. Abasement or inferiority
11. Nurturance or benevolence
12. Change
13. Endurance
14. Heterosexuality
15. Aggressiveness

The Thurstone Temperament Schedule measures seven characteristics:

1. Active
2. Vigorous
3. Impulsive
4. Dominant
5. Stable
6. Sociable
7. Reflective

Cattell identified sixteen traits:

1. Reserved–Outgoing
2. Dull–Bright
3. Affected by feelings–Emotionally stable
4. Humble–Assertive
5. Sober–Happy go lucky
6. Expedient–Conscientous
7. Shy–Venturesome
8. Tough-minded–Tender-minded
9. Trusting–Suspicious
10. Practical–Imaginative
11. Forthright–Astute
12. Self-assured–Apprehensive
13. Conservative–Experimenting
14. Group dependant–Self-sufficient
15. Undisciplined self-conflict–Controlled
16. Relaxed–Tense

where each individual possesses all of these traits but with different degrees of intensity. Traits make it possible to develop typologies of individuals. The more standardized character of trait theory explains its success among market researchers. Several other scales or tests have been used, such as Cattel Personality Factor Inventory (1957), Gordon Personality Profiles (1963) and Thurstone temperament schedule (1953).

More recently, five main personality traits have been identified and are correlated with many other personality traits:

1. Openness to experience
2. Conscientiousness,
3. Extraversion or a tendency to be sociable,
4. Agreeableness
5. Neuroticism or emotional stability.

Another theory, which is very similar to traits theory, is the cognitive theory of personality. Using this theory, scales are developed according to diverse aspects of the personality, such as dogmatism, authority and social attitudes. Self-concept theory considers several aspects of the personality:

■ self-image: what we believe we are, with the comparison of what we think we are compared to other individuals and their environment;
■ ideal self: what we aspire to be.

These latter theories were used as a basis for measuring lifestyles, which refer simultaneously to self-concept, personality, values and attitudes. However, lifestyles gave birth to studies whose range seems more to belong to the field of sociology than to individual psychology. It is perhaps for this reason that the lifestyles approach has been successful in the field of marketing, whereas the personality approaches that were based on in-depth analysis of individuals sometimes proved to be quite unwieldy.

Perception

Perception corresponds to various activities concerned with the processing of information. Three psychological concepts play an important role: senses, attention and interpretation.

1. sensory activity corresponds to the arousal of the senses (sight, hearing, touch, smell, and taste) caused by the acquired information or by needs;
2. attention is the process which makes it possible to select information that will be processed once the senses have been activated;
3. interpretation of marketing and environmental stimuli (any physical, visual or verbal communication) is based on information processing and memory activation.

Perception was first defined as an arousal process using one's senses. So perception is based on sensory activity. Sensations have been studied in particular in psychology. A minimal sensory threshold is necessary to cause a stimulation of the brain. Stimuli are not perceived below certain thresholds (e.g., subliminal stimuli). Similarly, sensory inputs must reach certain differential thresholds (or minimal variations) to enable us to experience differences between stimuli. The law of Bouguer-Weber shows that detection is a function of not only the variation of intensity of the stimulus, but also the level of intensity reached by the stimulus before the variation. For example, if a consumer has his senses aroused by a variation of price, this change will be more important the higher the price.

Attention is needed to notice a TV ad or a new product on the shelf. Attention is the concentration of a consumer's cognitive capacity on a specific stimulus, and is selective because consumers have a limited capacity. Selectivity is based on a consumer's belief about the relevance of information either to their needs or to protect themselves from threatening or contradictory stimuli. In advertising, marketers should use ambiguous messages when the product is important but its benefits are not clear-cut. On the other hand, messages should be unambiguous if the product's benefits are clear-cut and if the product is targeted to a well-defined market segment.

Each person stores incoming information in their memory, where it generates cognitive responses or thoughts. These thoughts are explored in advertising, where arguments, counterarguments or the evaluation of the message source cancel out the effect of the advertising message. Selective distortion, or perceptual bias, is the tendency of consumers to interpret stimuli in a way that supports what they already believe. To interpret marketing information, consumers categorize it and make inferences. Marketers should understand the evoked set (limited set of brands evoked or known) and the consideration set (brands fitting to consumer expectations in a given purchasing situation) and how this will affect brand positioning. Inferences about brands, prices and stores are beliefs that consumers form from past experience and associations. Consumers associate brands with symbols, resulting in the formation of brand image, store image, and brand positioning. The result is that perception is subjective, and therefore each individual can perceive things differently even though affected by the same stimuli as many others.

Consumers perceive risks in everything they do because each action can produce unforeseeable consequences. Perceived risk theory attempts to specify the way that a risk is created and how the consumer faces it. Perceived risk varies directly with purchase importance, consumer personality and situation.

Consumers may face different types of risk in making purchasing decisions. Four types of risks are generally identified:

1. financial risk, related to the loss of money,
2. risk of waste of time, related to the time spent in case of product failure,
3. physical risk or risk of bodily harm which is caused by products whose consumption or use is dangerous for one's health,
4. psychosocial risk, which means that a purchase may not meet the standard of an important reference group. Visible items are particularly subject to social risk.

To reduce risk, consumers use various strategies. These strategies aim to increase the certainty of the purchase outcome or reduce the consequence of failure.

1. Choosing a brand approved by the experts.
2. Remaining loyal to a brand.
3. Buying the most popular brand or a product benefiting from a very good company image.
4. Using private testing.
5. Relying upon reputation or image of point of sale.
6. Using a free sample before purchase.
7. Obtaining a warranty or a guarantee.
8. Buying brands approved by government tests.
9. Visiting various points of sale for comparison before purchase and thus obtaining additional information.
10. Purchasing the most expensive brand.
11. Relying on the opinion of family members (word of mouth).

Marketers should attempt to reduce risks by reducing the consequences from a product failing and increasing the likelihood of success. In order to reduce the consequences of product failure various strategies can be pursued, such as warranties, money-back guarantees, liberal returns policies, reduced price offers and reduced packaging. In order to increase the likelihood of a successful purchase, marketers can use endorsements by experts, free samples and detailed information on the product.

Attitude

There are many definitions of attitude. A thorough definition is provided by Eagly and Chaiken: "an attitude is a psychological tendency that is expressed by evaluating a particular entity with some degree of favour or disfavour". Other characteristics of atitude are as follows:

■ Attitude is a tendency. Attitudes are durable and stable, at least for a certain period. Changing attitudes is an important topic for marketing managers. It is usually better to ensure that a product fits with existing attitudes rather than to try to change attitudes.

■ Attitude is related to an entity or object of evaluation. An attitude may concern a person, an object or a real situation. For the marketing manager, the distinction between an attitude with respect to a product and an attitude with respect to the purchase of a product is essential. One can be positive about a model of car but unfavourable to the purchase for reasons which do not concern the product itself (e.g., the financial situation).

■ Attitude leads to preference. The evaluative dimension of attitudes and its connection with the choice decision is based upon the structure of attitudes organized systematically. The marketing manager, when seeking to understand a product universe, is interested in the structure of attitudes. Concepts such as differentiation and market structure, often studied in marketing research, provide information on attitude structure.

Attitudes are the outcome of several factors, such as

■ culture
■ family
■ oneself
■ personal experience
■ information acquired by word of mouth, mass media, influencers or leaders of opinion.

Pleasant experiences with respect to a product are of course likely to create favourable attitudes, while unpleasant experiences have the opposite effect. However, the formation of attitude can also be indirect, based on associative transfers or more elaborate mental constructions. Attitude with regard to various alternatives results from the processing of received or memorized information.

Consumers use various evaluative rules. Three main rules have been identified, namely compensatory and non-compensatory processes and heuristics.

A compensatory process is a linear addition and thus assumes that a positive score obtained on one attribute can compensate any deficit in another attribute or characteristic of a product. The compensatory process makes use of determinant beliefs about product attributes and their importance for the consumer. It is thus important to distinguish between beliefs and characteristics.

Product characteristics, such as the size or the maximum speed of a car, are objective data. Beliefs, on the other hand, are more subjective than characteristics. In the 1970s, research showed that consumers perceived the Austin 850 (a make of car) to be fast even though its maximum speed was quite low. This objective characteristic was meaningless for the purchasers who "believed" it was a fast car. The role of beliefs is even more important when one is interested in "psychological characteristics"; These exist as beliefs only. To say that a car makes one feel young or distinguished only makes sense within the relationship created between a person and a product. It is the consumer who allocates this psychological characteristic to a product because of physical characteristics of form, or of colour. This attribution process involves an interpretation which defines a belief.

However, the complete set of beliefs attributed to products and brands is not useful to explain the purchasing decision: only beliefs connected directly to a decision are of interest to marketers. These are the determinant beliefs. A determinant belief must meet three criteria:

- The first criterion, importance, means that the attributes concerned are considered to be important in a consumer's brand choice.
- The second criterion, distinctiveness, refers to the perceived differences between brands. For a consumer, safety can be an important dimension in choosing a car, but if they consider all the cars belonging to his evoked set as being secure, they will not choose cars on this dimension since it does not enable them to distinguish between models.
- The third criterion is salience. A salient belief comes to mind at the time of the consumption decision, and so is psychologically related to the choice decision.

There may well be other beliefs which, even though important and distinctive, do not play a role in the decision process – they are not salient.

In marketing, an attitude with respect to the purchase (behaviour) of a brand is a function of

- the belief strength that a brand possesses an attribute (subjective probability: that Peugeot car (205) has a given speed);
- the importance of the belief for the consumer (importance of speed for the consumers' choice).

A global attitude score is obtained by multiplying the belief score by the importance score of a given attribute and summing across all determinant attributes. Toolbox 7.3 gives an example of belief and importance scores for toothpastes of brands W, X, Y and Z. By using a compensatory model, the preferred brand will be brand X (score of attitude 80) followed by brand Z (69), brand Y (63) and brand W (55).

TOOLBOX 7.3

RESEARCHING ATTITUDE FORMATION

Toothpaste attributes	Brand beliefs				Importance
	Brand W	Brand X	Brand Y	Brand Z	
Prevents tooth decay	2	7	7	4	7
Taste	6	6	4	6	5
Whitens teeth	7	5	2	7	1

7 = very strong belief or importance, 1 = very weak belief or importance

An individual has evaluated four toothpaste brands W, X, Y, Z on three attributes. Belief scores of each brand are provided in the above table (from 1 to 7). The individual has also provided an importance score for each attribute (from 1 to 7).

If the individual is using a compensatory process, the preferred brand will be brand X (score of attitude 84) followed by brand Y (71), brand Z (65) and brand W (51).

Brand X's score is equal to: $(7 \times 7) + (6 \times 5) + (5 \times 1)$.

If the individual is using a conjunctive process and has set up minimum threshold scores for each, then the following can be inferred:

- Preventing tooth decay: 5 – brands X and Y are selected

- Taste: 4 – all brands are selected
- Whiten teeth: 5 – brands W, X, Z are selected

As brand X reaches the minimum threshold requested on all attributes, it will be preferred to other brands.

If the individual is using a disjunctive process and supposing that the consumer values the prevention of decay most highly, two brands, X and Y will be preferred because they both reach the maximum score of 7 for this attribute.

If the individual is using a lexicographical process, on the most important attribute (decay prevention), brand X and Y are equal (they both score 7 on this attribute)

On the second most important attribute (taste), X (5) overrides Y (2) and therefore will be the preferred brand.

A non-compensatory process does not assume the compensation between attributes. The deficit in one attribute cannot be compensated by the good evaluation of another attribute of a brand. Three strictly non-compensatory processes have been identified:

1. In the disjunctive process, the object of the attitude is evaluated on its most important attributes, regardless of its value for others. For example, a very fast car might be preferred by a driver with a taste for speed, even though the car is not secure/safe, or comfortable, or economical, or reliable and so on. This process applies especially where a particular product attribute elicits high involvement, which is not very common. The process uses a maximum threshold since the consumer seeks to obtain the product possessing the maximum score on the determinant attributes. Going back to the example of Toolbox 7.3, and supposing that the consumer values decay prevention most highly, two brands X and Y will be preferred because both reach the maximum score of 7 on that attribute.
2. The conjunctive process uses a minimum threshold. The object selected will achieve greater than a minimum score for each attribute. This type of model does not make it possible to decide between brands or products when several of them exceed the acceptable thresholds. It should then be combined with other models. If we consider the example presented in Toolbox 7.2 and if we suppose that the consumer sets a minimum threshold of 3 before a brand can be considered, only brands X and Z can be part of the brands set where the choice will be carried out since they exceed the necessary threshold on all three attributes.
3. The lexicographical process uses a sequential approach: a consumer initially classifies the attributes in order of importance. If he cannot distinguish between two brands sufficiently on the first attribute, he then examines the second attribute in order of importance, and so on until a distinction is possible. In the example presented in Toolbox 7.3, brand X will be preferred. Although X and Y are equal on the most important attribute, X beats Y for the attribute taste, the second in order of importance.

The heuristic process is a cognitive short cut. For example, there should not be rational differences in preference between beef with 75 per cent meat and beef with 25 per cent fat. However, it was observed that when consumers were asked whether they preferred one or the other, a large majority expressed a strong preference for the beef with 75 per cent meat. The heuristic process does not show that the consumer is irrational but simply that his rationality can be impaired by selective representation of information.

Three heuristics are used in the formation of attitudes:

1. heuristics of representativeness, where an object is allocated to a category on the basis of its resemblance to a typical object in the product category
2. heuristics of availability, where judgements support the most widely available objects or events, or the most frequently evoked
3. heuristics of anchoring and adjustment, where the evaluation is influenced by the value used as an anchor or projecting point. If the anchor is modified, the consumer adjusts their standard.

Since attitudes are internal to the consumer, they cannot be observed directly. Three components are generally used to reveal attitudes:

1. The cognitive component: the structured system representing the set of knowledge of the consumer about the object of the attitude (the attributes and benefits of products and brands).
2. The affective component: concerning feelings and emotional reactions. This represents a consumer's overall evaluation of the brand, and is central to the study of attitudes because it shows favourable or unfavourable predispositions to the brand.
3. The conative component: This indicates the intention or a consumer's tendency to buy. Marketers regard the alternative producing the highest buying intention to be the best choice. Therefore, they use it as the closest substitute to determine the effectiveness of the marketing-mix components in marketing planning.

The relationship between the three components is known as the hierarchy of effects. The order of these three components is affected by the purchase situation. The following sequence corresponds to a high involvement decision.

Beliefs ⟶ Evaluation ⟶ Behaviour

Consumers search for information and then base their brand beliefs on the brand they perceive to buy. Then they evaluate the brand and make a purchase decision accordingly.

Other sequences have been built according to their respective buying situations, based on experience or low involvement. The three components, cognitive, evaluative or affective, and conative, occur in different orders. In low-involvement situations, where the consumer is passive, this hierarchy is modified as follows:

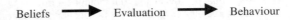

Beliefs ⟶ Behaviour ⟶ Evaluation

With low involvement, attitude is not as important as with high involvement. Therefore, attitude does not predict behaviour as well in conditions of low involvement as in conditions of high involvement.

Experiential hierarchy occurs for hedonic products and is based primarily on consumers' emotional response to a brand. Consumers first evaluate a brand on a global basis, relying on their feelings and emotions:

Evaluation ➡ Behaviour ➡ Beliefs

In experiential hierarchy, consumers are more likely to be aware of stimuli such as symbols and imagery. As a result, marketers can directly refer to brand evaluation without influencing beliefs.

An attitude can be changed. Brand beliefs are easier to change than the desired benefits and attitude towards a product. However, for hedonic products (bought on emotion) attitude is the relevant factor for change. Attitudes towards low-involvement products and brands are easier to change because the consumer is not committed to the brand. For low-involvement products, marketers attempt to increase the attractiveness (through a spokesperson) and the credibility of the message source

(through testimonials or an expert spokesperson) to accelerate attitude change.

Lifestyle

A lifestyle is a system of actions by which the individual communicates their preferences and their standards to their environment. Lifestyle aroused the interest of researchers because they hoped that it would provide a better prediction of purchasing behaviour than personality.

Lifestyle is measured using different factors. Consumption modes are measured on the basis of products and services purchased. The CREDOC (research centre for the study and the observation of the living conditions) uses consumption modes as the basis of its investigation.

The lifestyle concept is more generally understood upstream of the purchasing act and is hypothesized to influence it. Thus gathering information according to activities (work, hobbies, entertainment, social events, shopping), interests (family, work, home, community, food), and opinions (about themselves, social issues, politics, business) is the basis of the AIO approach, which is dominant in the United States. The AIO inventory, is characterized by a relative absence of theoretical structure.

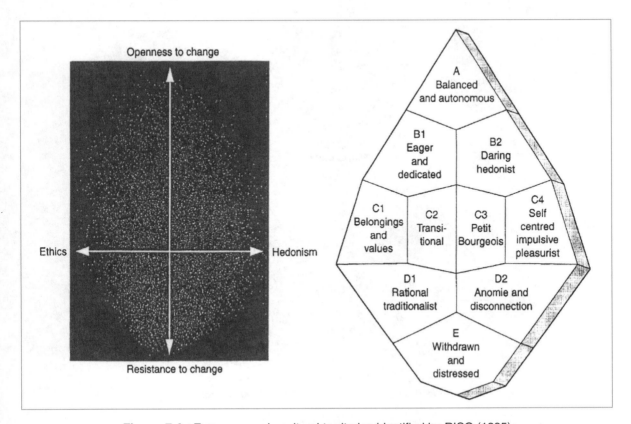

Figure 7.4 European socio-cultural territories identified by RISC (1995)

Source: RISC C. Hasson (1995), Monitoring Social Change, *Journal of the Marketing Research Society*, 37, 1, 69–80.

Exploratory methods of statistical analysis (factor analysis, cluster analysis) are used to identify lifestyles. Such inventories are global and consist of many questions (300–400). Shorter inventories focus only on one product and the benefits sought by consumers.

Methods used in Europe by companies such as RISC and CCA (Centre for Advanced Communication) are structured and are centered on values. Since 1980, RISC (International Research Institute on Social Change) has developed lifestyle surveys which detect socio-cultural trends in various European states. Common dimensions are identified using correspondence factor analyses of questions focusing on 34 Eurotrends (e.g., ethnocentrism, involvement in society). These trends are distributed along two axes (see Figure 7.4): openness to change or resistance to change and ethics or hedonism.

RISC divides the European population into ten segments. For example, on the first axis, starting from the centre of the population of each country, one can distinguish "balanced and autonomous" and "withdrawn and distressed" segments, while on the second axis other segments such as "Belonging and Values" and "Self-centred impulsive hedonist" appear.

Figure 7.5 shows the density of the first brand choice of BMW for the ten segments in different European countries. The highest-density segments for France, Germany and Italy are located on the hedonist pole. In Spain, BMW attracts the segments most open to change and hedonism. In Great Britain, while BMW attracts the hedonist segment, it also sustains the interest of the most conservative segment of the population.

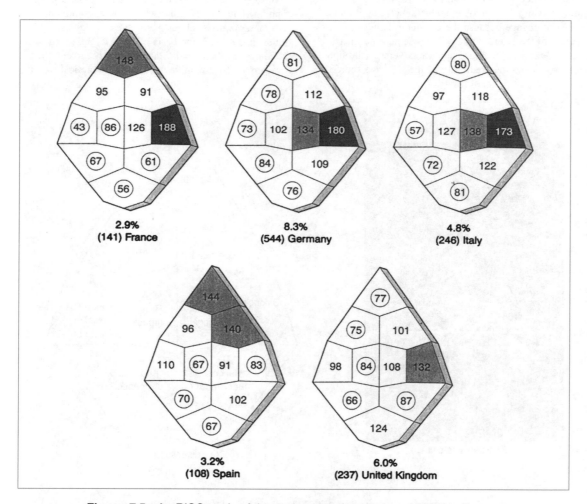

Figure 7.5　An RISC study of the socio-cultural territories of BMW in Europe

Source: C. Hasson (1995), Monitoring Social Change, *Journal of the Marketing Research Society*, 37, 1, 79.

The CCA aims at detecting cultural or macro-sociological trends which influence consumers' values and consequently their behaviour towards products. Two axes structure consumer values:

1. valuables pole–values pole and,
2. movement pole–settlement pole.

Six great European mindsets can be identified: socio-ambitious, socio-militants, socio-competitive, socio-notables, socio-withdrawn and socio-dreamers. These mindsets are subdivided into sixteen euro-styles or lifestyles (e.g., scout and citizen for the "socio-militants" mentality) (Figure 7.6). Each socio-style is characterized by a set of values, socio-demographics, motivations and different consumption preferences. Thus "dandy" (a socio-ambitious euro-style) represents modest youth, who are ambitious for hedonic success, afraid of the future, who seek reassuring structures, who are above average in leisure electronics ownership (HIFI video photo) and so on.

Methods and inventories used by CCA and RISC are proprietary and therefore are not available for detailed scrutiny. They can be the subject of disputes because of the secrecy which surrounds the methods used to obtain such results, and their ability to explain purchasing behaviour is controversial.

Socio-cultural factors

Four socio-cultural factors influencing consumer behaviour will be discussed:

1. socio-demographic factors
2. reference groups
3. family
4. culture

Socio-demographic factors

Socio-demographic variables reflect the structures of the population and the processes which affect it. Socio-demographic variables predict purchasing behaviour better than lifestyles.

They can be classified according to three criteria:

1. demographic factors: birth rate, life expectancy, mortality, immigration–emigration, and so on;
2. size and geographical distribution of the population;
3. profile of the population: age, sex, dwelling, occupational status, marital status, size and structure of the family, education, income and so on. Age has been investigated in particular detail. The teen or adolescent

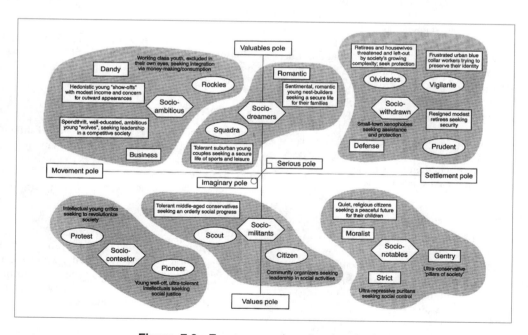

Figure 7.6 European socio-cultural territories
Source: Based on Cathelat (1990) and Voller and Winkler (1991).

market is characterized by a search for identity, partly because of a conflict between the need to rebel, to be independent of the family and society, and the need to be socially accepted.

The predictive capacity of the socio-demographic variables seems to be more problematic when they are used to describe individual behaviour with respect to brands, rather than collective or group behaviour.

They are used for market planning as well as market segmentation.

Some socio-demographic variables can be combined to give rise to indicators such as the family life cycle or social class. Other socio-demographic variables are used as a basis for more subjective variables such as cognitive or felt age, which is a better consumption predictor than chronological age for older people.

Family life cycle

Buying is shaped by the family life cycle, that is, the family members naturally pass through a certain number of stages which can be characterized by marital status, household size, age of the head of household, presence of more or fewer children and so on. There are many ideas related to the family life cycle. The most well known in marketing is that of Wells and Gubar, which identifies 9 stages. Each stage of the life cycle corresponds to different consumption patterns, needs, and resources. Young couples without children will spend more on travel and movies than would young couples that have children younger than six.

The family life cycle must be used with caution. It does not work for all products. For transportation behaviour, the age when someone can get a driving licence is more important than marital status. Non-traditional stages such as unmarried couples, couples marrying later in life, childless couples, single parents and so on are of keen interest to marketers. More recently, life-cycle concepts have explicitly taken into account late marriages and births, the absence of children, re-marriages, cohabitation, single-parent families and single people.

Social class

Social class can be identified using macro criteria such as profession, education, family income, and forms of property. Each social class is associated with a social status which produces a rank order between classes.

The criteria used and their respective weightings vary according to the systems used. In North America, the criteria used include profession, education, income, dwelling area and house type.

In Europe, the ESOMAR association proposed a standard to harmonize the various national systems used based upon occupation and the number of years of education of the principal contributor to the household income. This standard differentiates between seven social classes.

In France, social classes are primarily identified starting from the socio-professional categories of INSEE. Four classes are emphasised:

1. the higher or dominant class, which creates categories that have either a line authority (top professionals), a cultural authority (professors), or an economic capacity (corporate managers);
2. the middle class or lower middle-class, which involves intermediate professions in the company and in public service and also craftsmen, and commercial employees;
3. the popular class, which is made up of farmers and general workers;
4. the lower-income class comprising, unskilled workers, farm labourers, people receiving social welfare and the economically inactive (unemployed, small pensioners).

Each social class tends to share values, which are reflected in life style, and exhibit similar buying behaviour. Bourdieu shows that the French dominant class is characterized by the purchase of pianos, playing golf, concert attendance and playing bridge, while the popular class is interested in card games, football, rugby, and public festivities.

Social class shows a predictive power, greater than that of income alone, for purchases of products that are of symbolic significance.

Growth in income, education and the influence of the mass media have not reduced the influence of social class. Munson and Spivey show that the differences observed between social classes remain, in spite of these changes.

Reference groups

A person's behaviour is influenced by many different groups. A reference group is a membership group or aspirational group which influences (positively or negatively) the evaluation, aspiration and behaviour of an individual. The influence exerted by such a group comes from the

- credibility of the information provided by the group;
- conformity to the group norms, reinforced by the rewards which are granted to those who respect them;
- need that individuals have to express their own values – the reference group being used then as a means of expression and attachment.

Various factors support reference group influence. Some are more product or brand orientated, while others relate to a consumer's characteristics. The visibility of consumption and ownership of a scarce product increases the importance of reference groups. Thus brand choice and the consumption of luxury products, which can be observed by others (e.g., golf club membership, skis, sailing boats), are influenced by these groups. The importance of perceived risk associated with a purchase reinforces the influence of the group. The symbolism of the consumption of certain categories of product such as cars, clothes, beer and cigarettes supports the influence of the group since consumers obtain an image of others from the products they consume. Individual characteristics support the influence of reference groups. An individual's desire for social approval increases the importance which the individual attaches to reference groups, while individual self-confidence exerts the opposite effect. Self-concept is also closely associated with reference groups.

Within groups, some consumers enjoy a power or an influence greater than others because of their knowledge of a particular subject. They are opinion leaders. Their influence is reinforced by the greater credibility that a consumer attaches to what they say.

Opinion leadership varies according to the product category. Opinion leaders cannot be identified by means of personality characteristics or socio-demographic variables, but rather by their field of influence. Opinion leaders can be identified by their knowledge, interest and their participation in the exchange of information concerning the product categories that interests them.

The influence of opinion leaders varies for different products. The conditions under which influence is exerted are similar to those which one observes for reference groups. It is stronger for complex, involving products, where consumption can be observed by others. Opinion leaders are more influential when they possess characteristics similar to other people belonging to the group (e.g., socio-demographics).

Opinion leaders transmit both positive and negative information about products, which originate from their own experience, the degree of satisfaction or dissatisfaction obtained with the product, or the standards of the groups to which opinion leaders belong. Negative information carries more weight than positive information in the decision-making process of consumers.

Opinion leaders play a central part in the diffusion of products. Their ability to generate imitation is one of the parameters of the models of innovation diffusion. Their influence increases the closer the consumer gets to making a purchase decision.

Innovators also have an important role in groups. Like opinion leaders, they facilitate the diffusion of products by influencing those who follow their example and encouraging them to consume by the information they provide, and by the demonstrations that they carry out. Innovating can be a personal tendency, which is characterized by the attractiveness of the innovation, the autonomy in the innovative decision, and the preference for risk-taking by testing the innovation. Other behaviour indicators, such as the time of adoption of the new products or the possession of new products, are also used to detect innovators.

As with opinion leaders, the characteristics of innovators vary according to product category because there are no generalized innovators. However, some general characteristics of innovators can be highlighted. They concern the desire for stimulation, a favourable attitude towards risk, frequent use of similar products, a high degree of opinion leadership, the importance attached to the mass media and external sources of information for the social system of the innovator.

The family

The family is used as a reference group by the consumer. A purchasing decision is not always made by one family member. Many products require the participation of several members of the family. The roles played are extremely varied. Thus, it is possible to identify, for example,

- the initiator, who identifies the idea or need;
- the influencer, who seeks to influence the other family members;
- the information gatherer, who collects information;
- the decision maker, who makes the purchasing decision;
- the purchasing agent, who proceeds to make the purchase;
- the consumer, who uses or consumes the product.

Roles are generated by the domestic organization or by the allocation of functions and can be played by the parents or by the children. Children play an important role for products in which they are involved (e.g., breakfast, toys) and also in domains involving the whole family (restaurant, holidays). Four decision types have been identified:

1. the husband dominates;
2. the wife dominates;
3. decisions are made in an autonomous way by one or more of the family members;
4. decisions are syncretic, or taken jointly by the whole family.

Because of the existence of these roles, the influence of each family member is likely to vary according to the stages of the decision-making process. Other factors intervene in the distribution of the roles. There is, for example, the degree of involvement or risk assessed by each member of the household. The more important the product or the buying decision is, or the more risky it is for one of the members, the more the member will want to take part in that decision.

These roles are dependent upon the cultural and social norms of household members. Thus Todd distinguishes four main family systems in Europe which are characterized by parent–children relationships (liberal or authoritative) and by sibling relationships (equal or uneven). These are as follows (see Figure 7.7):

- the absolute nuclear family in which the relations between parents and children are liberal and the relations between siblings are non-egalitarian. The term "nuclear" indicates that the family does not extend beyond the parent–children relationship;

- the egalitarian nuclear family in which the relations between parents and children are liberal and the relations between siblings are egalitarian;
- the community family where the relations between parents and children are authoritarian and the relations between siblings egalitarian;
- the founder family where the relations between parents and children are authoritarian and the relations between siblings non-egalitarian.

The most traditional types (community, non-egalitarian, authoritarian families) are especially characteristic of older, rural societies. Modern times have pushed them towards a more nuclear, more liberal and egalitarian type.

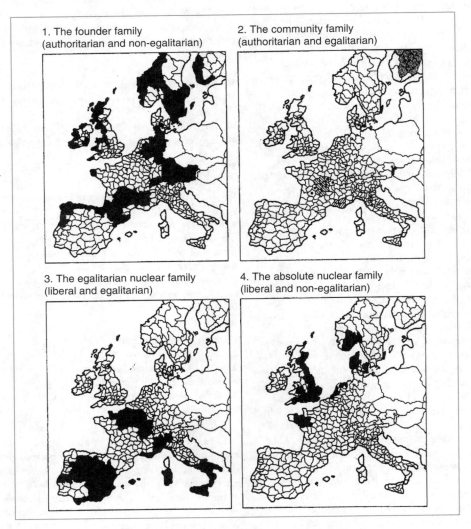

1. The founder family (authoritarian and non-egalitarian)

2. The community family (authoritarian and egalitarian)

3. The egalitarian nuclear family (liberal and egalitarian)

4. The absolute nuclear family (liberal and non-egalitarian)

Figure 7.7 Old family structure in Europe

Source: E. Todd (1990), *L' invention de l'Europe*, Sevil, Paris.

The resources (economic, temporal, psychological, intellectual and physical) which are available to the household members also influence role allocation. Individual power within the household is proportional to resources. When a husband's income contribution to the household is low, information search and purchase decisions are more often joint. This is less so when the income contribution of the husband is high.

Social class also plays a role in domestic organization. Glaude and Singly observe that in the working class, women play a dominant role, whereas the men in the higher classes play a more active role, with women confined to the role of a "domestic person". They observe in addition that when the woman is active, the roles tend to become much more equal.

Domestic organization changes with the duration of marriage. Couples married for longer tend to have more specialist roles. This change also depends on the changes in society.

The detection of roles can prove to be delicate because of the problems that arise when measuring the relative influence of different parties and the difficulties in gathering information. This explains why the two members of a couple often provide contradictory information.

Household members use the following strategies to solve their conflicts and to express their point of view:

- each prevails in their field of influence,
- each prevails based on their expertise,
- bargaining (taking it in turns to buy their preferred choice),
- criticism of the preferences of the other,
- use of blackmail.

These strategies vary according to demographic variables and attitudes of the couple with respect to traditional or non-traditional households.

Culture

The importance of behaviour and thought is frequently referred to in definitions of culture. Therefore culture can be described as "the structured manner in which a human group thinks, feels and reacts, which is especially acquired and transmitted by symbols and which represents its specific identity". It results in decision-making processes, the acquisition of information and different modes of consumption.

However, the knowledge of common characteristics or differences between cultures is insufficient, and a deeper understanding of certain basic factors is needed. These factors depend upon the level of analysis selected (Figure 7.8).

At the individual level, cultural influences can be characterized along four dimensions:

1. The relation of the individual with authority concerns the existence of hierarchical relations in the family, social classes, reference groups and so on. For example, in China, filial devotion is the most important relation of the three fundamental human relations: parent–child, husband–wife, brother–sister. Consequently, Chinese consumer behaviour often cannot be regarded as a reflection of an individual's own preferences and will.

2. The relationship with one's own ego concerns self-control, and in particular the control of impulsive tendencies. The principle of ego control is very important for the Chinese consumer. The Chinese consumer shall not be excessively negligent or complacent with respect to important aspects of life. So extravagant or frivolous products may not be appreciated in a Chinese cultural context.

3. The relationship to risk concerns the tendency to avoid uncertainty and thus relates to the development of attitudes or behaviours (risk avoidance). So in China, where culture emphasizes tradition, risk-taking is unwise, and changes in attitudes and behaviour towards products and brands are considered to take longer than in Western Europe.

4. Propensity to accept change or the receptivity of a culture to changes in its modes of consumption. In China, where risk-taking is uncommon, new products are treated sceptically and are accepted only after lengthy resistance.

These four dimensions must be analysed through cultural components:

- material culture (technologies, economic structure),
- social institutions (social organizations, educational systems, political structures),
- systems of values (on human nature, our relationships to nature, meaning of time, social relations, etc.),
- aesthetic systems (visual and graphic arts, folklore, music, theatre, dance),
- language.

Culture, through various manifestations, influences purchasing behaviour and spending patterns. For example, norms and values are attributed to products by various means such as advertising and fashion. In addition, behaviour, such as buying and exchanging (e.g., gift), makes it possible to transfer ideas and values to people.

Culture is the product of the environment, which results from the interaction of large-scale factors (ecological, economic, genetic, historical). Taking, for example, the market for baths in Japan, one can consider it as being very specific to the Japanese culture, and more particularly one can consider individual behaviours as being strongly influenced by the interaction of a social factor (social significance of the bath) with an ecological factor (the relative water shortage). The bath is not

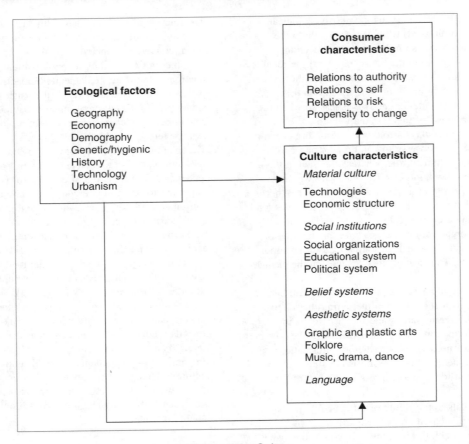

Figure 7.8 Culture

Source: T. Clark (1990), International Marketing and National Character: A Review and Proposal for and Integrative Theory, *Journal of Marketing*, 54, 4, 66–79.

intended to be used for washing, it is more for serving a social behaviour intended to support interpersonal communications. Before using the bath must be preceded by a shower so that the bathers are clean. For this reason, bath water can be considered, after the bath has been taken, to be reusable (shortage of water reinforcing this behaviour). The same water can thus be used for several baths and as a last resort can be used to wash linen. This behaviour gave rise to an unusual market of reheating baths and of pumps that allow the transfer of water from the bathtub into the washing machine.

In addition, it is interesting to note that the influence of a culture can extend to several countries or areas, but it can also prove to be specific to an individual country if it is strong and cohesive. Culture perpetuation depends on the extent to which a country either resists or is able to selectively borrow or incorporate newer cultural traits. China provides a striking example. The conqueror who established himself over this huge culturally united civilized population inevitably found himself swamped, acculturated and ultimately absorbed.

Improvements in transportation and communications, the existence of common existing needs, decreases in trade barriers, and the Americanization of consumption values tend to decrease cultural differences and therefore justify the use of global strategies. However, whether to sell on a local, global or global/local basis is an important decision which international marketers must make. Such a decision depends upon cultural differences. Because of substantial differences between countries, international marketers may have to adjust for cultural differences and therefore adopt different marketing-mixes.

Sub-culture

A culture can be divided into subcultures on the basis of ethnicity, geography and lifestyles. Within subcultures there are greater similarities in people's attitudes, values and action. For example, stronger preferences for certain types of clothing, furniture, food and restaurant, musical tastes and fashion may be observed.

In many countries sub cultures on the basis of ethnic background are found. In the United States, white, African, Hispanic and Asian subcultures differ according to their values, norms, tastes and purchases. In Europe, Germany itself has a Turkish subculture, with France having a Maghrebian subculture and England having an Indian subculture. In Latin America, Bolivia has Quechua-Aymaras and Metis subcultures, while Italian and German subcultures exist in Southern Brazil.

Subcultures can also be defined by lifestyles. Personal freedom and closeness to nature are values shared by Harley motorbike owners in the US, and beach and snow surfers in the US and Europe. These subcultures possess specific symbols (brands), leaders and clothing norms.

Marketers should recognize that subculture differences may dictate considerable variation. To deal effectively with theses differences, marketers may have to alter their product promotion and distribution systems or price to satisfy members of particular subcultures.

Situational effects

Situational effects include all the factors that are particular to a place or time, not related to factors specific to a consumer or to the attributes of the products, and thus having a systematic and observable effect on consumer behaviour.

Circumstances regarding product usage, and the purchase or exposure to a media are of particular interest to the marketing manager. It is clear that marketers should take into account the needs and preferences of particular situations. Product-usage matrices are, for example, very useful to analyse market segmentation, brand positioning or to detect opportunities for new products (Table 7.3)

Situations can be analysed according to five objectives or perceived characteristics.

1. Antecedent states of a consumer
   Antecedent states include a consumer's mood (state of anxiety, degree of excitation) and their tangible conditions (tiredness, disease, amount of cash in hand).

For example, being in a good mood makes it easier to have a change of attitude.

2. Physical surroundings
   Physical surroundings relate to the apparent characteristics of a situation, geographical location, decor, sound, smell, lighting, temperature, shelf layout or any material surrounding the brand under investigation (discussed in Chapter 13 on merchandising).

   For example, the musical environment of an individual, his familiarity with the music or its structure, affects the process of decision-making. Thus, music with a slow tempo slows down in-store traffic, and increases the volume of store sales.

3. Temporal effects
   Temporal perspective is a dimension which can be specified in various ways, either in a unit of time (time of the day, season) or in relative terms compared to a previous or future event (time passed since the last purchase). Thus, the time available to carry out purchases influences buying behaviour. Shortage of time influences the consumer to change brands more frequently and to make more unplanned purchases than when pressure of time is not felt.

4. Social surroundings
   Social surroundings relate to the absence or presence of other people, their characteristics (parents, friends, etc.), their apparent role (salesmen or not) and the interaction between the people present. Social surroundings influence purchase decision-making. This is underlined in the decision-making process in the family and in reference groups.

5. Purchasing tasks
   The reason for making a purchase can radically reduce the purchasing decision-making process and its result (e.g., a product purchased for personal use, for another person of the family or to be given as a gift). Shopping for gifts increases consumer involvement, and the number of information sources consulted within the store (in addition to external sources of information).

Table 7.3 Product usage matrix

Product form	Family dog (dog is a member of the family)	Work dog (guarding, hunting)	Reluctant owner (does not really want the dog)
Canned, all meat	X		
Canned, mixed grain and meat			X
Dry		X	
Semi-moist	X		

Source: G.L. Urban and J. Hauser (1993), Design and Marketing of New Products, Eaglewood Cliffs, Prentice Hall, 2nd edition.

Types of buying decision

The decision-making process of the consumer varies according to the influence exerted by various individual variables, socio-cultural factors, the circumstances of the purchase and its consumption, and the marketing-mix. Thus, one could characterize various types of decisions depending specifically on the involvement of the consumer:

- the high-involvement purchase
- the habitual and loyalty purchase
- the low-involvement purchase
- the impulse purchase
- the compulsive purchase
- the variety-seeking buying decision

High involvement buying decisions

Decisions taken in a state of high involvement are complex decisions. The decision-making process generally corresponds to a sequence of stages in the following order:

- recognition of the need
- active research of information
- data processing
- evaluation of alternatives: (i.e., attitude formation)
- intention to purchase
- purchase decision

Recognition of the need or the occurrence of a problem due to an unfulfilled need is characterized by the consumer's acknowledgement of the existence of a need or problem to be solved. The understanding of this phase is based on the analysis of needs. It is exploited, for example, in advertising or by the sales force, whose role involves directing needs towards a company's products, emphasizing product benefits and therefore arousing wants.

Search for information can be carried out by seeking internal information held in memory or external information from various personal sources (e.g., friends, family) or public sources (consumer association journals, the company through its marketing actions, various media, the sales force, or retailers). Therefore, consumers can implement the choice criteria, selecting the brands that can be considered for purchase and which constitute the evoked set of the consumer. This phase involves the use of perception.

Evaluation of alternatives or the formation of attitudes follows the information-search phase. At this stage, a consumer forms an attitude towards the various brands that may be bought while basing their beliefs on their perceptions of the characteristics associated with each brand and the importance they have for the consumer. Consumers use in particular the rules of combinations

(discussed in the section "Attitudes") to lead to an evaluation of the solutions.

Intention to purchase focuses on brands that obtain the highest evaluation in terms of expected satisfaction. Intention to purchase is an intermediate phase between the stages of evaluation and purchase and corresponds to a period during which various actions are undertaken by the buyer towards the seller (e.g., negotiating better conditions of delivery, payment, etc.), to raise the necessary finance for the purchase or to gain the agreement of other people (other members of the household). Various actions or certain events occurring in the store (brand out of stock, price change) or before entering the store (new information modifying the evaluation) can still modify the intention to purchase.

The purchase is the transformation of an intention into behaviour. It is naturally sensitive to the influence of the purchasing situation but also to marketing actions such as sales force at the store, brands and merchandising.

Habitual buying behaviour

The majority of the purchasing decisions are not characterized by high involvement. Routine decision-making, or habitual buying behaviour, is often involved. Habitual buying behaviour is the result of a learning process based on repeated experience, and characterized by a limited problem-solving process. In this process, the quantity of necessary information decreases, the range of stimuli narrows, the number of evaluative criteria declines, and the buying decision time is shorter and supports the use of heuristics, while the probability of purchase increases. If this process is not altered by other variables (the appearance of new competitors, unavailability of the brand, decline in quality, new marketing messages, and cognitive dissonance), it can lead to an automatic purchase or habitual buying. In this case, the decision made is instantaneous; the only stimuli used are those which start the automatic mechanism of response, because there is no real period of thought. As a result, some researchers concluded that the majority of purchases are "impulsive", particularly in the context of purchasing in a supermarket. In fact, this is not impulsive buying but habitual buying behaviour.

In habitual buying behaviour, the consumer tends to buy the most popular brand. The reasons for this include risk reduction (product failure, financial loss), saving time and facilitating the decision-making process.

Loyalty buying behaviour

There is a close link between habitual and loyalty buying behaviour. Brand loyalty is the result of a favourable attitude towards a brand, inducing a consistent purchase of the brand over time. However, brand loyalty is related to satisfaction or positive reinforcement. The more satisfied a customer is, the greater is the brand loyalty. Loyalty is the result of a psychological process involving a preference and the expression of a particular behaviour towards a brand according to this preference. Therefore, the measurement of brand loyalty relies upon several indicators:

- last purchase behaviour: percentage of purchase of the brand most frequently bought, sequences or series of purchases which investigate the brands (e.g., stochastic models), and so on;
- attitude, which expresses the predisposition of the individual towards a given brand;
- composite measurements which use these two sets of indicators (behaviour and attitude) simultaneously.

Brand loyalty is important because of its role in marketing strategies. Retaining customers in a strongly competitive market is less costly than attracting new ones. Only the development of brand loyalty makes it possible to reach and exceed the profitability threshold of a new product launch. Marketing managers are therefore investigating various types of loyalty, such as brand loyalty, product loyalty, channel of distribution loyalty, and sales promotion tools. In supermarkets, for example, there are consumer segments that are loyal to promotion, independent of the channel of distribution, retail brand name (Auchan, Walmart, Carrefour), store or product brand.

Low involvement buying behaviour

When purchasing goods in supermarkets, it is obvious that many customers hesitate between brands that they know little about because they do not have a high involvement with the product purchased. Lack of real arguments for such brands and lack of importance attached to the choice mean that a brand has more chance of being chosen if it is recognized, that is, simply because of familiarity.

In the low involvement process, first there is information in the consumer's memory, then behaviour and, little by little, an attitude is formed. This hierarchy, where cognitive elements precede conative elements, followed by the emotional elements, generally appears when there is no difference between alternatives and/or when low involvement means that the target audience really don't care. In the low involvement process, information is passively received by watching TV, which is the most effective medium. Repeated Advertising creates familiarity.

Involvement, in addition to its impact on attitude formation, has many other consequences. Low involvement also results in weak cognitive reactions, and weak research effort and data processing, which involves weaker perceived differences between brands, and a greater tolerance towards each attribute of the product.

In low involvement situations, marketers use price and sales promotion to stimulate product trial. Advertisements should focus only on a few key points which are easily remembered and associated with brands. Visual symbols and imagery are important. High repetition and short-duration messages are preferred.

Marketers try to convert low involvement products into higher involvement ones because involvement leads to commitment, and involved consumers are more likely to be brand loyal. Marketers use different strategies to involve consumers, such as linking the product to an involving issue, to an involving personal situation, to an involving advertisement or through the introduction of an important characteristic of the product.

Impulse buying behaviour

An impulse purchase has long been defined as an unplanned purchase; it is a spontaneous purchase, without concern for the consequences that are involved. Impulse purchases are caused by many individual factors such as the absence of planning, intention, impatience, distraction, the will to avoid complexity and/or caused by the stimuli surrounding a person.

Impulse purchasing can be a pure impulse purchase, or it can be

- a purchase which is not planned because it was forgotten but which is needed by the consumer, and suddenly recalled;
- an impulse purchase caused by the stimuli present in the store (location on the shelves, attractiveness of the packaging, sales promotion).
- a planned impulse purchase, generated by a planned purchase but without being clearly specified.

Compulsive buying behaviour

A compulsive purchase corresponds to an inappropriate, repetitive, excessive consumption behaviour and is a source of problems for the individual who has a compulsion to consume. The compulsive buyer does not buy to obtain a certain utility or service from the product, but instead, simply to obtain a gratification from the act of buying itself. The effect of buying on the consumer is similar to that of a drug.

Compulsive purchase is intended to avoid a tension, anxiety or discomfort caused by an obsession. The purchase is carried out against the conscious will of a person and under the effect of an urgent need. It corresponds to a chronic personal loss of control and an incoherent desire for the product or brand caused by a buying desire in general.

Variety seeking buying behaviour

This type of decision-making in buying behaviour is the opposite of loyalty, since it induces changes of product or brand. Searching for variety is influenced by several factors:

- Random or unexplainable factors,
- factors directly at the origin of a change of brand,
- factors which are an indirect cause of the change of brand.

Factors arise from either the existence of multiple needs or changes in the preference structure.

The existence of multiple needs can originate from different preferences of the various members of a household. This heterogeneity of the preferences leads to the choice of multiple brands where each member uses only one of them (for example, brand X of chocolate for the parents, brand Y for the children). The multiple needs can also be caused by the differences in the consumption situation which generate behaviours particular to each situation (e.g., snacks that are consumed when alone are different from those that one will consume with close relations).

The existence of multiple needs can be related to different usage conditions. The consumer may decide to buy round grain for use with one type of sauce, and to buy long-grain rice for another sauce.

Finally, the consumer can be caused to change brands when this preference structure is substantially altered, perhaps because of a change in brand availability (e.g., removal of a brand, launching of a new brand) or because of change of taste due to advertising or to personal influences such as developing maturity. Changes in the preference structure can also be caused by changes in choice constraints. A change of occupation, with a pay increase, can also explain changes in brand. Direct factors can be of a personal or interpersonal origin. Personal factors can arise from the attraction of unfamiliar brands

or a change among the consumer's familiar brands (to avoid risk) or deliberately seeking information (to refresh the memory). Interpersonal factors can be a result of a need for group membership which induces consumers to imitate changes of behaviour by other people, or the need to portray a certain image of oneself by the adoption of a particular lifestyle. For example, a consumer wishing to be perceived as innovative will have a strong propensity to buy new products.

When facing variety-seeking behaviour, marketing strategy of the market leader may differ from that of minor brands. The market leader will try to encourage habitual buying behaviour by dominating shelf space and by keeping shelves fully stocked. Minor brands will encourage variety seeking by offering lower prices, special deals, coupons and free samples.

Industrial buying behaviour

Industrial buying behaviour differs from individual buying behaviour along four dimensions:

1. the decision-making process,
2. the participants in the decision-making process,
3. the factors which motivate participants,
4. interactions between organizations.

These are important for salesmen and marketing managers to understand.

The decision-making process

Although there is no single process for all organizations, the buying process can be conceptualized as a succession of stages. Table 7.4 presents 9 stages. They make it possible to include/understand the part played by the buyer as well as the constraints to which the buyer is subjected while playing that part.

Problem or need recognition (stage 1) happens when a member of the organization perceives a problem which

Table 7.4 Buy grid or stages of the buying process			
Decision-making process	**Types of buying situations**		
	New task	Modified rebuy	Straight rebuy
1. Need recognition			
2. Definition of the characteristics and quantity of items needed			
3. Development of the specifications to guide the procurement			
4. Search for and qualification of potential sources			
5. Acquisition and analysis of proposals			
6. Evaluation of proposals and selection of suppliers			
7. Negotiation with selected suppliers			
8. Final choice of supplier(s)			
9. Performance feedback and evaluation			

can be satisfied by the acquisition of a good available in a market.

Determination of product specifications and quantities of the product to buy (stage 3) is often preceded by a stage where these various elements are formulated in a rather vague way (stage 2).

Supplier selection is carried out in several stages: supplier pre-selection (stage 4), proposal solicitation and analysis (stage 5), short-listing (stage 6) followed by negotiation (stage 7), which leads to a final choice (stage 8). The final stage focuses on performance evaluation and control (stage 9). These phases show that the relations between industrial buyers and salesmen are not identical to those relations involved the sale of mass consumption goods, where the buyer often exercises little power. Power relations are important in industrial marketing. They make it possible through negotiating changes to product specifications, modes of control, price, penalties, and so on. This is why negotiation is important. Part of Chapter 11 will be devoted to this. The complexity of the purchase decision-making process depends on the newness and the importance of the purchase. Three buying situations have been identified:

1. the new task
2. the modified rebuy
3. the straight rebuy.

The most complex situations are located in the left side of Table 7.4, and the simplest in the right part. Complex situations involve the greatest number of participants and influences in the decision-making process, and the most information search. In addition, with a new task all stages of the decision-making process are involved, while a straight rebuy does not require all the stages.

Participants in the decision-making process

A buyer seldom acts in isolation (except for an unimportant repeat purchase). The group of people taking part formally or informally in the whole or a part of the process is called the buying center.

In this center, participants play standard roles corresponding to the functions that they perform in the company. Thus the buyer will represent the buying function, the initiator represents the sales function or the research or design office for example, while the user represents the manufacturing function, and so on. The principal roles are

- initiators
- influencers
- deciders
- gatekeepers controlling the flow of information to others
- buyers
- users

Each has an influence which varies according to the stage of the decision-making process (Table 7.5).

Moreover, the choice criteria used vary between participants because they depend on the specific objectives of each function.

Motivations of the buying centre

The motivations of the buying centre influence the decision criteria used. Table 7.6 provides an example of the criteria used in the textile sector.

These criteria are largely influenced by each member's role and the member's part in the buying process.

Table 7.5 Influence type according to purchasing stages

Purchasing stages	Buying center participants					
	Users	Initiators	Advisors	Buyers	Deciders	Gatekeepers
1. Problem recognition	+++		+			
2. Determination of characteristics and quantity of needed items	+++	++	+			
3. Determination of specifications (quality, size) and quantity of needed items	++	+++	+			
4. Search and qualification of potential suppliers			+	+++		
5. Obtaining and analysing proposals	+	++	+	++	+++	+
6. Selection of a shortlist			+	++	+++	
7. Negotiation with selected suppliers (delivery requirements, after-sales services, price)			+	+++	+	
8. Final choice of supplier			+	++	+++	
9. Control and evaluation				++		

+++ Major role played at this stage
++ Important role played at this stage
+ Minor role played at this stage

Table 7.6 Supplier's choice criteria in the textile sector

Criterion	Often used (%)	Seldom used (%)	Not used (%)
Supplier's reputation	85	5.2	1
Supplier's flexibility	78	8.6	1.4
Financial information on supplier	19	26	42
Product's technology	75	5	0.5
Product's age	71	9	4
Standardization level	66	4	0.5
Differentiation opportunity	58	6	3
Services offered	56	7.4	
Delivery requirement regularly met	54	3	
Price/quality ratio	51	3.8	
Payment conditions	50	3.5	

Technical and economic factors prevail in the motivations of industrial buyers. This does not exclude the influence of personality factors because it is people who buy and not the organization itself. The importance of the techno-economic factors does not necessarily mean that industrial purchases are more rational than individual purchases, because the rationality of individual industrial buyers faces the same limits of individual cognitive capacity as that of the individual consumer.

Buyer–seller interaction and relationship marketing

A sales contract in industrial marketing cannot be regarded as a single act. It is the demonstration of the interaction process between the selling organization and the buying organization. This conceptualization of the sale has various consequences:

- The seller and the buyer are active in preparing and deciding upon an order.
- Organizational buying decisions take time. Placing an order depends on the type of relationship already established with the supplier.
- The establishment of long-term relations tends to institutionalize relations between the two organizations. Multiple connections can then be established between departments (e.g., the commercial department of the seller with the purchasing department of the customer, the manufacturing department of the seller with the manufacturing department of the customer).

Interaction can be improved or worsened by various factors in the environment, such as the market (dynamism, competition intensity), the organization (organization culture, degree of centralization) or by the customer (importance of its needs, quantity, frequency, the customer's satisfaction in the past, the customer's expertise).

The behavioural consequences of relational involvement result in customer loyalty, a decline in opportunistic behaviour, and investment in relationship-specific assets. The concepts of trust with regard to the partner and satisfaction related to the relationship have been the topic of many studies in relational marketing.

Let us note finally that relationship marketing, originally developed in the field of industrial marketing, is as important in the field of the mass consumption marketing as in industrial marketing. The marketer alone cannot deliver superior customer value and satisfaction. Relationship marketing requires that marketers must work closely with other company departments (and customer's or distributor's departments) in order to form a value chain that serves the customer. For example, the marketers of a hotel chain have to design services that create value to its actual and potential customers, but other departments must also perform well in order to make it a reality. Housekeeping and maintenance staff have to deliver the standards customers want, the human resources department has to hire the right employees, the information systems department has to maintain an extensive customer database and so on.

Post-purchase evaluation

Consumer behaviour does not end with the purchase of a product. When the consumer uses the product, he is sometimes concerned with subsequent payments (when he borrowed to buy it) or decides to buy complementary options (a new lens for a camera). He can also use his increasing experience with the product as a preliminary phase for his future purchasing process.

Post-purchase evaluation occurs once a purchase has taken place. Satisfaction is at the heart of the post-purchase evaluation. It results from a comparison between a consumer's expectations about the product value and a consumer's perception of the actual performance of the product bought. If the product falls short of these expectations, the customer will be dissatisfied. But, if it matches or exceeds these expectations, then, the consumer is satisfied.

Satisfaction reinforces consumer behaviour, leading the consumer to be loyal to a brand. Dissatisfaction will modify their prior evaluation of the brand, will decrease their intention to purchase, and will engage them in negative behaviours with respect to the brand (negative word of mouth, complaints).

When a consumer is highly involved with a product and does not perceive strong differences between brands, he may feel a tension or anxiety called cognitive dissonance on hearing about brands he has not tried, or noticing certain disadvantages of the brand already bought. Faced with this dissonance, consumers will alleviate dissonance by:

■ countering the dissonance and changing the product evaluation. This is achieved by increasing the value of

the attributes of the selected product and by devaluing those which are not present in the bought product,

■ searching for information that confirms their choice, and avoiding information which tends to accentuate the dissonance.

■ changing their attitude towards the product to make it coherent with their behaviour. For example, a sales promotion can generate an unfavourable attitude with regard to the product. However, once the product has been bought, to reduce dissonance between attitude and behaviour, attitude towards the product will be modified in a more favourable direction.

Therefore, post-sales communication (advertisements or follow-up calls) should provide evidence and support to convince the consumer that they have made the right decision.

SUMMARY

Four groups of factors influence customers during their decision-making processes: the marketing mix used by manufacturers and distributors, psychological factors, socio-cultural factors and situational factors.

Psychological factors include needs and motivations, personality, perception, beliefs, attitudes and lifestyles.

Socio-cultural factors include socio-demographic variables, reference groups, family, subculture and culture.

Situational factors can be classified according to five characteristics: antecedent states, physical surroundings, temporal effects, social surroundings and purchasing tasks.

The decision-making process of the consumer varies according to the influence exerted by various individual

variables, socio-cultural factors, the circumstances of the purchase and its consumption and the marketing-mix. Thus, one could characterize various types of decisions depending specifically on the involvement of the consumer: high involvement purchase, habitual and loyal purchase, low involvement purchase, impulsive purchase, compulsive purchase, variety-seeking buying decisions.

Industrial buying behaviour differs from individual buying behaviour in four dimensions: decision-making process, participants in the decision-making process of purchase, factors motivating participants and interactions between organizations.

Discussion questions

1. What types of purchasing decision do consumers take?
2. What stages are involved in a complex purchasing decision, and are all the stages used in every purchase decision?
3. How does perception influence buyer behaviour?
4. How do needs and motives influence a person's buying decision?
5. Why are attitudes important for marketers?
6. What is culture? How does it affect a person's behaviour?
7. What is a subculture?
8. What are the roles in family decision-making?
9. Why do reference groups concern marketers?
10. What is a lifestyle?
11. How is it possible to change an attitude?

12. What is post-purchase behaviour?
13. What are the buying criteria used by organizations in making purchases? What are the three types of organizational buying situations?
14. What is an evoked set?
15. What is relationship marketing? Why is it important for marketers?
16. What are the major components of a buying centre?
17. What are the stages of the organizational buying decision process?
18. List several characteristics that differentiate organizational buying process from the consumer's buying process.
19. Why do buyers in a straight rebuy require a lot less information than those involved in a new task purchase?

Further reading

W.O. Bearden and M.J. Etzel (1982), Reference Group Influence on Product and Brand Purchase Decisions, *Journal of Consumer Research*, 9, 2, 183–194.

R.W. Belk (1975), Situational Variables and Consumer Behaviour, *Journal of Consumer Research*, 11, 2, 156–163.

J.R. Bettman (1979), *An Information Processing Theory of Consumer Choice*, Addison Wesley.

B. Cathelat (1990), *Socio-Style Système: les styles de de vie, Théories, Méthodes, Applications*, Paris, Les éditionsd'organisation.

R. Chestnut and J. Jacoby (1978), *Brand Loyalty, Measurement and Management*, New York, Wiley.

Chung Fang Yang (1989), Une conception du consommateur chinois, *Recherche et applications en marketing*, 4, 1, 17–36.

A.H. Eagly and S. Chaiken (1993), *The Psychology of Attitudes*, New York, Harcourt Brace College Publishers.

A. Furnham and P. Heaven (1999), *Personality and Social Behaviour*, London, Arnold.

C. Hasson (1995), Monitoring Social Change, *Journal of the Market Research Society*, 37, 1, 69–80.

P. Filiatrault and B. Ritchie (1980), Joint Purchasing Decisions: A Comparison of Influence, Structure in Family and Couple Decision Making Units, *Journal of Consumer Research*, 7, 2, 131–140.

D. Gerbing, S. Ahadi and J. Patton (1987) Toward a Conceptualization of Impulsivity: Components Across the Behavioural and Self-Report Domains, *Multivariate Behavioural Research*, 22, July, 357–379.

G. Laurent and J.N. Kapferer (1985), Measuring the Involvement Construct, *Journal of Consumer Research*, 22, 1, 41–53.

D. Leonard Barton (1985), Experts as Negative Opinion Leaders on the Diffusion of Technological Innovation, *Journal of Consumer Research*, 11, 4, 914–926.

R. Linton (1958), *The Tree of Culture*, New York: Random House.

L. McAlister and E. Pessemier (1982), Variety Seeking Behaviour: An Interdisciplinary Review, *Journal of Consumer Research*, 9, 3, 311–322.

R.R. McCrae and P.T. Costa (1999), A Five-Factor Theory of Personality, in *Handbook of Personality: Theory and Research*, edited by L.A. Pervin and O.P. John, New York, Guilford, 2nd edition, 139–153.

T.C. O'Guinn and R.I. Faber (1989), Compulsive Buying: A Phenomenological Exploration, *Journal of Consumer Research*, 16, 2, 147–157.

R. Oliver (1997), *Satisfaction: A Behavioural Perspective on the Consumer*, New York; Irwin/McGraw Hill.

R. Oliver (1999), Whence Consumer Loyalty, *Journal of Marketing*, 63, Special issue, 33–44.

C. Pinson and A. Jolibert (1998), The Development of Consumer Research in Europe, in *European Perspectives on Consumer Behavior*, edited by M. Lambkin, G. Foxall, F. Van Raaij and B. Heilbrunn, Prentice Hall, London, 3–59.

L. Schiffman and L. Kanuk (2004), *Consumer Behavior*, Upper Saddle River, New Jersey, Pearson, 8th edition.

R.J. Sternberg (1995), *In Search of the Human Mind*, Fort Worth, Texas, Harcourt Brace.

E. Todd (1990), *L'invention de l'Europe*, Seuil, Paris.

B. Voller and A.R. Winkler (1991), European Consumers and Environmental Behaviour, Seminar of the Growing Individualism of Consumer Lifestyles and Demand, How is Marketing Coping with it? Amsterdam: ESOMAR.

J.L. Zaichkowsky (1985), Measuring the Involvement Construct, *Journal of Consumer Research*, 12, 3, 341–352.

Product management 8

Learning objectives

After studying this chapter you will be able to

1 Define products from a marketer's point of view
2 Understand how product mix and product line policies are developed
3 Identify the attributes of a successful brand name
4 Explain the rationale for alternative brand name strategies employed by companies
5 Understand the benefits of norms and packaging in the marketing of a product
6 Explain the concept of product life cycle and relate a marketing strategy to each stage
7 Explain the concept of product positioning
8 Understand how marketing managers position products in the market place
9 Gain insight into how businesses develop an idea for a product into a commercial product
10 Grasp the importance and role of product development in the marketing-mix
11 Understand how current products can be modified
12 Explain how product deletion can be used to improve product mixes

SPOTLIGHT

Breitling is a one-hundred-year-old Swiss brand. During the Second World War, it was the official supplier of chronographs for pilots in the Royal Air Force. After the Second World War, in 1952, the Navitimer model became the official watch of pilots worldwide. Later, a more modern version, Chronomat, was launched and Breitling's two product lines (Navitimer and Chronomat) are now exported all over the world.

France had been a market where brand penetration was low. Fashion was oriented towards slender watches and Breitling watches were the opposite. Breitling was almost unknown compared with leading international brands.

The management of the French subsidiary decided to differentiate their brand by positioning it as a luxury jewelled chronograph. For that purpose they used various marketing-mix tools such as advertising, sponsorship, distribution and public relations. The advertising campaign showed a watch and a woman simultaneously, as well as a humorous testimonial from the Second World War. They also sponsored sports which appealed to young men, such as sailing, amateur golfing and boxing. Breitling invested in relationships with jeweller channels and in maintaining the longstanding links it held with the air force. Brand positioning is the basis for any successful product offering.

Positioning decisions are the basis of all product management decisions (see Chapters 3, 4 and 5). Product features and processes that are part of the product have to be selected in a way that ensures that the differentiating features of a product are recognized by customers.

To position a product, first, the features of the competing brands used by the consumer must be identified. Various elements of differentiation can then be selected:

- Positioning through distinctive attributes such as price, quality and performance of a product is most commonly used.
- Positioning through highlighting the benefit of a product, or how it satisfies a perceived need, is also often used. This strategy can be more effective than simply highlighting attributes (consider VW (small is beautiful) or the health ideals promoted by Danone and Evian).
- Positioning by usage offers another opportunity. Neutralia shampoo by Garnier is presented as a shampoo for frequent use, for normal or dry hair.
- Positioning by user type is another alternative, for example Pepsi Cola and the Pepsi generation.
- Competitor comparison is used by retailers comparing the average price point in their supermarkets.
- The discontinuous innovation of a product category can be used for product positioning. For example, the tubeless tyre is positioned against tyres requiring an inner tube, or unleaded petrol against leaded. The opportunity to use this strategy is rare but it can be effective when a product is genuinely different from others.
- A mixture of these various elements can generate differentiation and thus be employed to position the product.

A product can be a material good such as a car, an idea such as family planning, a service such as a holiday resort, or any combination of these three elements, such as heart transplantation. In most cases the total product will be a combination of various tangible and intangible elements. Therefore, components directly related to the physical parts of the product such as packaging, the brand name, or pre- and after-sales services have to be considered in product development. In creating a product, any organization has to take into account simultaneously all kinds of expectations from customers and other important stakeholders, its own technological capabilities and know-how, and its commercial and financial resources. However, product management does not only manage the development of new products. It is also responsible for reshaping products currently offered on the market and for the elimination of outdated or unsuccessful products from the offer of the organization. The general objective is to possess the most attractive offer to potential customers, supported or at least accepted by other stakeholders.

To fulfil this purpose, other tools of the marketing-mix such as price, market communication and distribution must fit with product management decisions, as the decisions made about these tools have a direct impact on the positioning of the product in the minds of customers. A toothpaste distributed in chemists, for example, may not be perceived in the same way as the same toothpaste distributed in a supermarket. The value associated with it by the customer may differ significantly.

Thus, the product management decisions and actions of a business organization have to be integrated within the broader framework of the marketing strategy of the firm. In this chapter, we will focus more specifically on basic elements of the product and on major decisions of product management such as whether to innovate, adapt, imitate, reposition or drop a product in order to build and maintain an attractive total offer.

First, the main strands of product management will be described and defined. Then, a fundamental concept of product management will be discussed: the product life cycle. The third part of the chapter will focus on new product development. And finally, product line management will be discussed.

The product concept: A total product

A product can be a good, a service, an idea, an organization, a person, or a combination of those, depending on what is marketed to potential customers. A product is always more than what the customer can touch or see. For example, in China the mobile phone has been a great market success. At the end of 2003, there were more mobile phone users in China than in any other country of the world. As described in the International Spotlight in Chapter 1, the resourceful Chinese had always used pagers, not as an accessory to a phone, but as a sort of primitive substitute for it since the conventional phone system had such a limited penetration. Consequently Chinese paging subscribers spontaneously devised a method of carrying code books, allowing them to interpret numeric messages flashed on their pagers, and China subsequently became the natural home for the mobile phone.

As this example shows, from the customer perspective, a product consists of a bundle of tangible (the pager) and intangible (ability to communicate, prestige) results created by processes that involve the customer to a greater or lesser degree. In the case of the pager, its production process was neither visible nor influenced by the customers. In the case of mobile phones, however, customers can create their individual phones from a menu of options offering colour, design and display features. Consequently, a product can be conceived as a bundle of value-generating processes and a bundle of results stemming from these processes.

Similarly a customer for a product can be either more or less involved in the value-generation process. For example, to get their hair dressed, consumers all over the world must be present during the 'production process' and must leave their hair to the skill of the hairdresser, whether the hairdresser's is a sidewalk in the streets of Xian, China, or a fine boutique in Milan, Italy, whereas the production process of a kitchen machine by French SEB does not involve future customers at all. They are only indirectly involved in the value-generation process through consumer research during the design stage and become directly involved at the very end of the marketing process, when they buy the machine from a retailer.

The product as a bundle of results stemming from value-generation processes can have either more or less tangible attributes. A vacation in a New Zealand ski resort, for example, contains elements such as the slopes, the hotel room and the food in the restaurants. All of them can be physically experienced. At the same time, the total vacation product also consists of intangible elements such as the friendliness of service personnel, the waiting time at the lifts or the 'kind of people around'.

Level of customer integration

The chain of activities by which a company generates value for its customers can be conceived as a series of processes that the firm conducts either more or less autonomously. From the creation of a product idea through product development, production to sales, however, there is always some minimum level of integration of the customer into this value-added process. All products, consumer and business/government goods, as well as all kinds of services, can be positioned on a continuum ranging from highly integrative to highly autonomous according to their value-added processes (see Chapter 1). Depending on the kind of interaction with the customer, where in the process customers are integrated, how often, and to what level of intensity, product management decisions will differ.

The integration of the customer can take the form of personnel involvement, for example, when a specialist at Ochsner Hospital in New Orleans, Louisiana, transplants a kidney into a Brazilian recipient. But customer integration can also take place by the contribution of an object, such as a PC in the case of Otten, an Austrian producer of printed textiles, when using the hotline of its international production software provider. In other instances, customers provide information for the value-creation process. For example, when the Boston Consulting Group gets an order to develop a new organizational structure for Basler Versicherungen, one of the biggest internationally operating Swiss insurance companies, the outcome of their work depends very much on the information provided by the company's personnel.

If the supplier and customer of a product need to have direct contact in order to produce customer value, the product is bound to a certain location. Such products cannot be traded and therefore cannot be exported. Internationalization of business in such cases can only be achieved through the international multiplication of self-operated or foreign-operated production sites. On the other hand, if the contact between marketer and customer can be de-coupled in both time and space and made to go via some intermediary (for example, a retailer) or medium (such as a computer), the product can be traded and exported. Banking services, for example, which for most of their history were bound to the location of a bank and its outlets, could only be internationalized by opening up subsidiaries or cooperating closely with local banks. Nowadays, electronic banking has made banking services independent of specific locations, and therefore exportable.

For some products, direct customer contact is limited to the initial phase of product development and production or to the last phase of the customer value-generation process. However, customer integration may occur in any phase. For instance, when Danish customers of sailing yachts provide the engineers of a Norwegian shipyard with specific information about their expected use of the ships – for example, winning an international race versus entertaining customers on a cruise – those customers take part in the development process of their product. The procurement manager of a food production company, such as US-based Kraft Foods, who specifies the material to be used in the production of plastic trays, participates in the purchasing process of the supplier. A French customer of Sweden's furniture giant IKEA is integrated in the company's marketing process when she describes the family's living room, the family size, structure and living habits to the salesperson, picks up the bought furniture, transports it to her home and sets it up there. Even for consumer products produced and marketed to a global mass market, such as Sensodyne toothpaste or Pampers nappies, for which autonomous processes dominate customer value generation, at least some communication has to take place in the final phase between the customer and sales personnel or a computer.

The parts of the value-generation process which take place in the presence of the customers are above their line of visibility. They strongly influence the customers' perceptions of product quality and their satisfaction with the product. The invisible remainder of the process is locally independent. It can be performed wherever is best for the supplier, if the parts or elements of the total product produced in a distant location can be physically or virtually transferred to the place of consumption or use. For example, for the user of a pizza delivery service, the order-taking process via the phone and the end of the delivery process are above the line of visibility. Where the pizza is made and how it is transported to the customer is up to the producer as long as the delivery time is short enough and the pizza looks nice and tastes good.

Products need to be managed differently depending on the intensity of interaction between customer and supplier.

The higher the intensity of interaction, the more both customer satisfaction with the product and ultimately customer retention depend on how such interactions take place. It becomes increasingly important for the firm to manage its customer interaction processes; but it also becomes increasingly difficult because social relations are hard to control. In international marketing the firm may try socialization – that is, constant training in and compliance with strong company rules of behaviour overriding personal rules of behaviour. Companies such as Kentucky Fried Chicken (KFC) or McDonald's have successfully trained their personnel to ensure a certain standard of customer interaction independent of the location of the store. But even these companies, with rather strong internal rules of behaviour, have to leave some room for customizing those rules to the requirements of local cultures. KFC in Japan, for example, adapts how customers are greeted to Japanese customs, including bowing to the customer after the sale to show the company's appreciation for the purchase.

Tangible and intangible results

The result of a firm's value-generation process is a product. Such a product can be either more or less tangible (Figure 8.1). Even a physical product, such as a Compaq computer, has intangible features, for example its ease of use or its brand name, which stands for a certain reliability. Services, such as transpacific air travel offered by Korean Air, have a much higher degree of intangibility. In this example, they also have some tangible features associated with them, for example the size of the seats, the number of rows and the quality of food served during the flight. But there need not be any tangible results of a company's value-generation process. Telephone service provided by a company such as France Telecom, for example, or a show by the US-based Harlem Globetrotters basketball team does not have any tangible features provided to customers.

For product management, it is critical to remember that customers may be attracted to a product by both tangible and intangible features. Customers do not evaluate and choose just a good (a physical product) or a service. They buy a bundle of benefits, which they expect to enjoy through the consumption or use of the total product, that is, the combination of tangible and intangible features offered by a provider. Coca-Cola, for example, is more than just a soft drink. In several languages, 'Coke is It'. This slogan recognizes that coke is not only a physical good but also offers refreshment, enjoyment, entertainment and represents the 'American Way of Life', all of which are intangible features but are part of the total product.

Customers of an international advertising agency such as US-based Grey Advertising expect the agency to do more than produce international and local campaigns which reach their objectives. They also value personal contacts with a known partner in different parts of the world and the standard application of tools with which they have experience. In addition, the name of the agency and its country of origin as well as special references may create positive associations in the managers who are to decide which partner to choose for market communication purposes.

Products conceived as combinations of material and immaterial results of a firm's customer value-creation process are not limited to goods or services. Ideas (which are immaterial only), people and organizations can also be marketed internationally. For example, social issues such as population control can be marketed in an attempt to

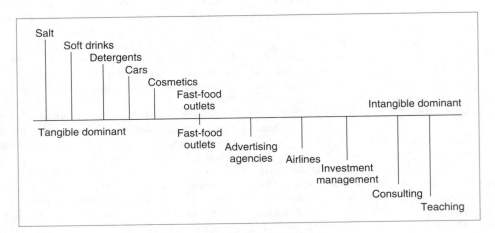

Figure 8.1 Scale of goods and services

Source: G.L. Shostack (1977), Breaking Free from Product Marketing, *Journal of Marketing*, 41, 2, 73–80.

change people's ideas about family-planning practices. To increase the attractiveness of population-control measures, for example, in many cases material incentives were added to the idea, such as portable radios for people willing to accept surgery. Politicians can be marketed too. In 1996 several candidates for the position of General Secretary of the United Nations, all from African countries, were internationally marketed not only by their governments, but also by interested foreign governments. When social organizations such as UNICEF or the Red Cross use marketing techniques for international fund-raising, the organizations themselves often are the products 'sold'. But in every case, seen from the perspective of the customer, the product offered consists of a bundle of benefits, which can be gained from the product's material and immaterial features.

The product system

Products are bundles of more or less integrative customer value-creation processes and bundles of more or less immaterial results of such processes. Both processes and results interactively influence the benefits customers derive from the total product. The total product can therefore be conceived as a system which contains elements as described in Figure 8.2.

The core-product is the starting point of a potential market transaction. In certain cases it might be sufficient to provide only the core product. For example, when a well-informed person searches for an overview of potential forms of capital investment offered by an international

bank, he or she may be satisfied with the information provided by the bank's homepage on the Internet. In most cases, however, the potential customers expect more than the core product in order to regard an offer as relevant. The investor might, for example, very much expect to be informed individually about the choices available.

Potential customers tend to have different expectations depending on their knowledge of and experience with existing offers. Consequently, in international marketing the features expected by potential customers from different country-markets vary in composition and importance. Internorm, Europe's second-largest manufacturer of doors and windows based in Austria, for example, found the expectations of Spanish customers regarding technical features such as cold and noise resistance, as well as workmanship, to be very different from those of its German and Austrian customers. The reasons for those differences in expectations are not only the climates of the countries and the contrasting lifestyles, but also the existing product offers with which consumers are familiar in their own markets.

The international marketer must decide how important it is to adapt the firm's product to the existing expectations in the served markets. The need for adaptation will depend on the customers' willingness to trade off some expected features for unexpected 'added' features (see Figure 8.2). When introducing its Lexus model in the USA, Toyota, for example, offered its potential customers a car looking very much like a Mercedes but without the same prestige. Toyota not only counteracted this perceived lack of prestige with a lower price, they also offered two weeks of trials, and offered to deliver the ordered car to the home of the customers and to program the electronically adaptable driver's seat for various family members in advance. All those were added features not expected by the American customers but were nonetheless very welcome. On the other hand, when Internorm, the Austrian window producer, tried to convince its potential Spanish customers that higher technical standards and resulting energy savings – also not expected by the customers – would justify a higher price for windows and doors, they failed.

International marketers increasingly offer additional product features over and above the features expected by customers in a local market to differentiate their products attractively from existing competitors. Ermenildo Zegna, the Italian menswear maker, for example, offers clients who buy a Zegna suit an 'idea card' that entitles them to all sorts of privileges: once a year for a two-year period, the suit will be cleaned and, if needed, repaired; should the suit be stolen or lost, the company will replace it at 50 per cent off and the client is entitled to a 50 per cent discount on his son's first Zegna suit.

When potential customers are fairly affluent relative to the price of a product or when they perceive the offered products as being largely similar, emotional attraction becomes more important in their buying decision. The symbolic features of a product can be decisive. Car buyers

A total product consists of the core-product, additional features expected by the potential customers, added features and symbolic features the supplier can provide to increase the total product's attractiveness, and the processes leading to those features.

The concept of "total product"

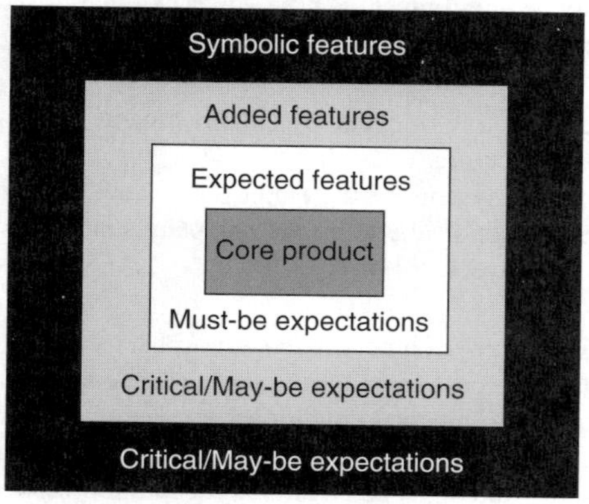

Symbolic features

Added features

Expected features

Core product

Must-be expectations

Critical/May-be expectations

Critical/May-be expectations

Figure 8.2 The total product system

all over the world, for example, will always watch the price categories and will expect certain additional services. But when the decision regarding a price category has been taken, very often symbolic features such as the brand, country of origin, status symbol, or the signal of belonging to a specific social group become important. Why would anybody buy a Ferrari bearing in mind its high price if it were not for the emotional benefit of the product?

Products may be classified according to their destination (raw materials, industrial goods, consumption goods), their duration (durable, non-durable), the type of purchase (convenience products [frequently purchased with little effort], shopping products [purchased with considerable time and effort in selection], specialty products [which possess unique features important to the consumer]), their complexity and their characteristics for the retailer such as shelf space, readability of packaging and so on.

The importance and distinctive qualities of product features in relation to those of competitors are the most important factors in customer choice. Therefore, product managers are especially interested in the relationship between product features and perceptions, attitudes and behaviour of the customers. Multi-attribute models, for example, aim to identify important beliefs, linking brands to product features (see Chapter 7). Due to belief identification, it is possible to define key features which will play a major part in the perception and attitudes of the customers.

Specific elements of the product concept

Quality management

Standards lay down common rules for manufacturing and presenting products. The ISO 9000 Standard of the International Standard Organization, for example guarantees that the product permanently conforms to certain standards. It reassures the customer that the system of quality (structure of organization, responsibilities, processes and resources to manage quality) conforms to these standards but it does not guarantee the product quality itself.

Standards can play an essential part by facilitating or prohibiting access to a market, that is, in the distribution of a product differentiation. Compatibility among products and product systems is also affected by standards. As a result, standards may become a source of power and competitiveness. The interest of firms in standards largely exceeds the simple technical framework. Standards can be

- a barrier to market entry, for competitors but also for potential new entrants
- a stimulation for the reaction of a product
- an opportunity for innovation

- a threat of exclusion from a market
- an objective instrument to express product value
- a benchmark of customers' requirements
- a tool for quality promotion/development
- a tool for developing consumer loyalty
- a tool for implementing market.

Standards may influence the value a user obtains from a product. The value of some products depends on the number of other product users. For example, the value of TV cable, Audiovideotex or fax machine depends upon the number of others using compatible products. Standards help to eliminate some incompatible systems that appear at the beginning of the product life cycle or to ensure the compatibility of systems (TV systems, tapes, data-processing systems, mobile telephone systems) and therefore induce an increase of users and product value.

Customer satisfaction is an important factor of influence in the long-term success of a company. Because customer satisfaction is strongly related to the perception of a product's quality, quality management is a central process of product management. Customer satisfaction is based on an interaction between customers' expectations concerning the product and their experience with the product. Expectations are influenced by personal experiment, beliefs and the individual capacity to use various external types of information (promises) or internal factors of the individual (desire).

In the end, product experience depends on the degree of fulfilment of customer expectation or the product's quality.

Service quality itself depends on three elements: its conceptualization, its environment and its delivery. As services are totally or partially immaterial and cannot be usually tested before purchase, customers seek tangible proofs as to what they may expect to obtain during the utilization of the service. They will make use of information coming from the environment of the service, which will allow them to infer the service quality. The environment will thus have a high importance for services. The service environment can be either external or internal. The internal environment relates to

- the marketing orientation of the company
- the service organization
- a reward system for the employees
- the interactions between the company's customers and its employees.

The external environment is the atmosphere which surrounds the customers during the service encounter. It includes environmental conditions (temperature, music, odour, etc.), space organization and its functionality (furniture), and signs and symbols (decoration, floor coverings, photographs on the walls, personal effects, office size).

The production of services requires the following six elements:

1. customers
2. physical support (instruments necessary for service, the material environment in which the service proceeds)
3. service encounter (employees interacting with the customer and the service provider)
4. the service itself
5. the system of internal organization (management but also purchasing, cleaning, maintenance of the material, handling functions)
6. other customers who use the firm at the same time and whose relations will influence the satisfaction and the perceived service quality

Service delivery is largely related to the quality of the service encountered or the interaction between the customer and the employees or the customer and the physical support of the service. Expectations of the customer with respect to the service, based upon its nature and the sequence of events which permits its delivery, influence the perceived quality of the service.

Naturally, as with material goods, the service depends on its key benefits, the major difficulty being the identification of the benefits which will sway the purchaser's choice. Qualitative methods and the method of conjoint measurements can be used for this purpose.

The customer's experience of the service provided is crucial for future patronage, so information on service quality is gathered in a variety of ways. For example, ski lift companies may use mystery shoppers to check on service and report back to them. Some firms may use former customers to find out any reasons which put them off a service. Critical incident technique is also used to measure service quality. It is based on consumer complaints.

Regular surveys may also be used where customers are asked to evaluate different service attributes such as:

- basic attributes, which when evaluated in a favourable way, contribute slightly to the satisfaction of the customer; but when evaluated negatively, they contribute strongly towards a feeling of dissatisfaction (e.g., cleanliness and cooking in a restaurant)
- added attributes which when evaluated in a positive way contribute strongly to satisfaction and which when evaluated in an unfavourable way contribute slightly to customer dissatisfaction (in a restaurant – waiting time, light, choice of beverage, originality, temperature, location)
- key attributes which have a strong influence on total satisfaction no matter what their evaluation by the customer is (in a restaurant – price, meal choice, taste, welcome)
- secondary attributes which do not play an important role in the satisfaction of the customer (in a restaurant – music, noise, reservation, bill).

Product line

Business organizations may avoid risk by focusing on more than one product. Therefore, product management must think in terms of their entire portfolio of products. Those products can form a product line, that is, a set of interdependent products: because they satisfy the same category of needs, because they are used together, focus on the same customers, are distributed in the same points of sale or are in the same price range.

Each product within a product line is allotted a unique position in the segment the company is targeting (Smart from Mercedes, for example, is intended for active urban couples without children). In general, products with the lowest price (bottom-of-the-line) aim to attract the consumers in an effort to make them discover the other products of the line. They are in general loss leader products (e.g., the C1 for Citroën). The top-of-the-line is composed of the most sophisticated products, at the highest prices. Other products in the line are product leaders or stars which generate a large percentage of sales figures and benefit for the company, others are new products intended eventually to replace the product leaders (e.g., the Peugeot 306 was designed to replace the 309) or to compete with other products (Peugeot launched the 806 to compete with the Renault Espace).

Manufacturers and retailers also manage sets of product lines or product mixes. A product line is characterized by its length and its width. The length is measured by the number of different products in a product line. The width is measured by the number of marketed lines. Table 8.1 illustrates the product line of Renault.

The composition of a product line is one of the central problems in marketing. The main difficulty is to manage a line which should be neither too long nor too short. If a product line is too long it tends to be expensive, have decreasing brand loyalties and potential cannibalization effects, and upsets relations with retailers. Cannibalization occurs when sales of an existing product are eaten up by a new product from the same firm. If the product line is too short, potential profits may be missed.

Branding

A brand is a name, a term, a symbol, a logo or a combination of these elements which make it possible to identify the products proposed by a manufacturer or a retailer and to differentiate them from competing products.

Table 8.1		Renault product line	
length of the line	6	Twingo, Clio, Megane, Laguna, Safrane, Espace	
width of the Megane line	10	Standard	Sport
		RN 1.4 RN 1.9 RT 1.4 RT 1.9 D	1.6
		RT 1.8 RXE 1.6 RXE 2.0	2.0
			2.016v

Branding is a key element of product policy. Depending on their strategy, certain companies use the same brand name for all the product lines in the company. For a long time, Peugeot has been using this strategy. Others use their brand for only a part of the product line (Mercedes is using Smart for the base model). In the first instance, differentiation is carried out by number references (307 with 207); in the second instance the brand itself contributes more to distinguish the products. Each one of these situations implies a different image of the brand. It is thus important, for each company, to define a brand policy, according to product lines and brand identity.

Brands fulfil different functions, such as indicating practicality, a guarantee, personalization, pleasure, specificity and distinctiveness:

- *Practicality* refers to the usefulness of the brand. For example, a logo makes it possible to remember easily previous choices. Faced with a choice, consumers will not try to evaluate all the offers. They will search for and buy again the product with the logo (and associated brand) which they consider satisfactory.
- *Guarantee* refers to the fact that, for certain customers and certain products, a known brand is an insurance of a certain quality level.
- *Personalization* means that the choice of certain brands can allow consumers to affirm their originality and personality.
- Via brands consumers can also obtain *pleasure* from their purchases: the variety and the profusion of offers provide a hedonic satisfaction which perhaps may disappear in a store where favourite brands are not available.
- *Specificity* occurs when a brand possesses a unique configuration of attributes. Brands cannot be separated from the product (one could speak about "branduct"). For example, the French alcohol Suze is a very specific brand, which is a product in the form of a bottle of alcohol. Bottle, alcohol and brand are closely associated.

- *Distinctiveness* occurs when the brand is the only anchor available to the consumer for product differentiation. This function is crucial when products are not well differentiated by their attributes or consumers are not involved enough with the product to appreciate a difference. An example of such a product category would be detergents.

The choice of a brand name and the elements which accompany it (logo, sign, colour) are a means of both differentiating and personalizing the product.

Before selecting a brand name, it is advisable to check it for the following:

- readability
- ease of pronunciation, memorizing
- capacity for evocation (Head and Shoulders, Fiji)
- potential for the name to be abbreviated and familiarized (Danone, Danette, Dany)
- potential for being used without modification abroad, (see Table 8.2),
- availability at the national or European patent office in Munich.

In order to survive or to become strong, a brand must be loyal to its identity over time, and must be coherent. Brand identity corresponds to the brand characteristics that brand managers are wishing to communicate to consumers. Identity may be represented by means of six facets:

1. A physical or objective characteristic
   (Laughing cow (a French cheese) = cheese spread; President = butter or Camembert cheese)
2. A personality or character (see Figure 8.3)
   (Laughing Cow = benevolent, cheerful; Peugeot = tradition)
3. A culture or value system, a source of inspiration
   (Apple = California; Citroën = engineering; Mercedes = order, Germany; Coca-Cola = America)
4. A relation (with other people)
   (Yves Saint Laurent = seduction)
5. A reflection (external image that the brand gives to the target market concerned).
   The chewing gum (Hollywood) gives the impression of focusing on a target market composed of teenagers (15–18 years) whereas in fact it reaches a much broader target market
6. A projection (image which the purchasers of the brand have of themselves)
   (customers of Lacoste perceive themselves as members of a sports club, often without reference to any kind of race or age).

Brand image is the result of the perception by consumers of the brand. It is built by communication and product

Table 8.2 Brand adaptations in China

Chinese product brands (preference for flower or bird's name)		Meaning
Feige	bike	Flying pigeon
Feng Huang	bike	Phoenix
Yong Jiu	bike	Eternal
Mudan	TV	Peony
Imported brand		
Translated according to brand pronunciation		
JVC	JVC	No chance
Benz	Benchi	Speed-gallop
Carrefour	Jia Le Fu	All the family is happy, has luck
Pierre Cardin	Pi Er Ka Dan	No meaning
Translated according to brand meaning		
Citroën	Xue Tie Long	Dragon made of steel on snow
Volkswagen	Da Zhong	People
Translated according to both criteria		
Coca Cola	Ke Kou Ke Le	Delightful, satisfactory
Viagra	Weige	Big man

Pictograms are used for writing in China. Each pictogram has a meaning which fits to a monosyllable. For a brand made of several syllables, a global meaning emerges from the juxtaposition of the pictograms.

experience. The analysis of differences between brand identity and brand image makes it possible to diagnose the strengths and weaknesses of brands.

The architecture of a brand

Various options are open to manufacturers and retailers. For manufacturers, they vary from the multiproduct brand (Danone, Gervais, Nestlé), to multibranding (Procter and Gamble, which uses several brands, e.g., Ariel, Vizir, Dash, Bonux, Zest, Camay, Monsavon). However, other options can be derived from these two main options.

A brand line uses a unique brand name for a set of homogeneous products (Renault, Dim, Lancôme). A brand umbrella uses a unique brand name for a set of heterogeneous products (Thomson, Panzani, Seb). Retailers may use different options:

- generic product, product presented without brand or distinctive sign (certain agricultural products)
- lowest price brand, intended to offer to the consumer a low price alternative to the most popular brand (lowest price with retailer's brand),

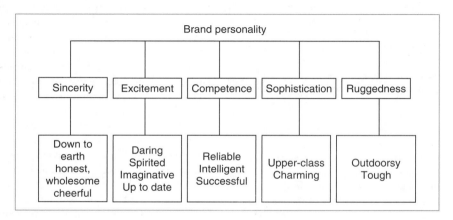

Figure 8.3 Components of brand personality

- private label brands from the retailer to compete with the leaders of the market (Tex for the textile at Carrefour)
- retailer's brand, for which the brand engages the image of the retailer.

Manufacturers may use other alternatives:

- The choice of a single brand name for the company quickly ensures a strong recollection of the product but in the event of failure, risks harming the entire product line.
- The policy of brand differentiation increases the costs of advertising but allows for more accurate segmentation.
- When a firm has very distinct product lines, its aim is to differentiate its lines, by having one brand name per line, to avoid negative opinion spoiling the name of all the company's product and to better allocate products within the product portfolio. For example: Johnson, specialist in cleaning products, created other brands for its cosmetic line (Villanova, Tahiti-Bath), just as Henkel (detergents) did for its cosmetic line FA.
- The choice of a new brand makes it possible to make a product more strongly differentiated. The Pelforth Breweries preferred to name their red beer "George Killian's" rather than "red Pelforth", therefore partly sacrificing the benefit of the Pelforth image in special beers in order to develop the new and original concept of Irish beer.
- One of the essential dangers is the cannibalism between brands – the last brand launched gaining market share at the expense of another brand from the same firm. This error is often due to insufficient positioning or of a lack of clarity.

Brand extension

Brand extension consists of using an existing brand or mother brand to launch a new product. Using a brand's equity as leverage, extension avoids an expensive campaign of familiarizing consumers with the product. Obviously, it is risky if the new product fails but also if the image of the new product is far from the brand image of the mother brand, as this causes a certain dilution of beliefs with regard to the mother brand.

For this reason, there are several conditions for brand extension:

- a "fit" effect: the consumer needs to perceive the attributes of the new product as being coherent with those of the mother brand, or very representative or typical of the mother brand;
- a leverage effect: the consumers, using only their knowledge of the brand, will think that the new brand extension is better on important attributes than the other products in the same category;

- the extension will be more successful as the perceived quality of the mother brand will be important. Thus, the chocolate brand "Noir" (black) sold by Nestlé, has been extended to a top-of-the-line brand of instant coffee, launched by Nestlé to counter the progression of Carte Noire Instinct, the top-of-the-line instant coffee from Kraft Jacobs Suchard.

Brand extension can be achieved in various ways:

- lateral extension is the extension of a brand onto related products within the same consumption universe, for example from natural yoghurts to fruit yoghurts.
- Vertical extension is the extension of a brand to products belonging to different categories, where their nature and function differ from those products currently marketed under the mother brand. Take the extension of the Kodak brand to photocopiers and of the Andros jam brand to fruit juices.

Considering the prerequisites to the success of brand extension, lateral extension appears the least risky although the dilution of beliefs is not stronger in the case of vertical extension. Benetton for example has some 30 licences throughout the world: shoes, socks, paper mills, glasses, watches, and so on.

Co-branding is a strategic alliance between two brands in order to extend existing product lines and to launch new products (Häagen Dazs and Bailey launched a cobrand of Irish ice cream). Brand association offers a certain number of advantages and disadvantages, which are presented in Table 8.3.

In order to facilitate transfers between two brands and their extensions, the associated brands need to have similar values, or 'fit', in the consumer's mind. They should also be complementary from the point of view of their critical attributes as well as in their performance of these attributes. Thus Côte d'or (a Belgian brand of chocolate) and Yoplait launched a co-branded chocolate mousse in order to help Yoplait increase its market share against the leader Nestlé. Co-branding benefits both partners by combining their various attributes.

One of the dominant concerns for managers in the new millennium is the concept of brand equity. It is the value added by the brand name and rewarded by the market in the form of increased profits or higher market shares. It can be viewed by customers and members of a channel as a financial credit, a set of associations and favourable behaviours.

The value of a brand refers to much more than simply the perceptions of the consumer. In financial terms, it could be the capitalized value of the expected profits.

Table 8.3 Advantages and disadvantages of co-branding

Advantages	Disadvantages
Operationalization of original marketing strategies	Time taken to operationalize the co-branding agreement
Speed of entering into a new market	Risk of cannibalization on one product of the two associates
Smaller penetration time of a new product	Multiplication of alliances is limited
Encircling competitor	Sharing the benefits between the two brands is not easy to fix a priori and is not always fair a posteriori
Alliance with a leader increases the recall of the other brand	
Smaller cost to explain a new product	
Communication and distribution cost shared	

However, brand value does not entirely explain the large amounts paid to buy brands; a part of the explanation lies in the prohibitive price of entry into product categories. Nowadays, in the majority of mature markets, a firm wishing to enter has in fact only two alternatives: acquisition in the product category or brand extension. Therefore brand equity is the additional (incremental) value of a business above the value of its physical features due to the position of its brand in the market and to the potential for the extension of this brand.

Packaging

The choice of packaging is one of the major decisions of product policy. The amount of attention paid to product shape and packaging has increased in the last few years. Different functions are assigned to packaging:

- to protect the product: from moisture and cold, due to fragility, and so on;
- to facilitate its transportation: weight, handling, safety;
- to facilitate its actual sale (merchandising)
  For example, product presentation in supermarkets requires certain shapes, certain qualities in appearance (yoghurt packs located on top shelves allow advertising on the side of the pot, making it possible for the consumer to see and identify the product immediately).
- to satisfy certain psychological functions (through its shape, its communication of ideas which will recall elements in its advertising, e.g., the bear cub of Cajoline) and certain practical functions (brand recognition, data transmission of the European Article Numbering code (EAN code)/Universal Product Code (UPC) in the USA, which is a set of bars printed on the packaging of most items sold in mass merchandising outlets;

- to facilitate consumption through correct use of the product, in particular because of it being an adequate size, an easy measure and so on.

It is easy to understand why packaging has become the most important source of innovation in the last 25 years (e.g., toothpaste in a measuring cap, chewing-gum in a tube, liquid detergent). The packaging of a product is consequently the focus of many handling tests: by the consumer, by the retailer at the place of storage, on the shelf and so on. Such tests include

- durability tests
- visual impact tests
- tests to measure comprehension of brand information
- tests of perception of the transmitted message.

For many goods, product shape and packaging are merged. Bottles of water, soda and wine are at the same time a product shape and a packaging.

Product life cycle

The product life cycle concept is based on an analogy with biology, according to which products live through a series of phases leading them from birth (launch) to death (elimination). In its most traditional form, the product life cycle is represented by an "S" curve comprising four phases: introduction, growth, maturity and decline (Figure 8.4).

Other theories take into account five or six phases, but the four-phase model is more common and is used by most researchers and marketing managers.

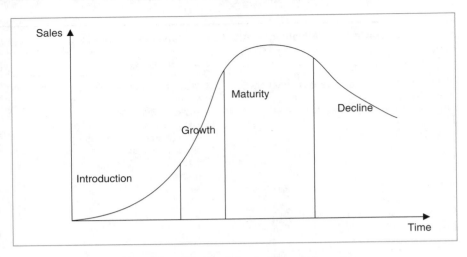

Figure 8.4   Classical product life cycle curve

This "ideal" shape of product life cycle is not in reality observed in many cases. Various shapes have been found in experimental studies. They vary according to

■ product type (industrial, durable, non-durable, mass consumption goods)
■ level of aggregation (product class [car], brand).

Life cycle curves differ as well in the length of each phase and also in their slope. Product class seems to be the most satisfactory unit of analysis in observing the traditional life cycle curve. It reflects the aggregate effect of competition between brands, and extensions generated by the emergence of new products. Despite its limitations, the concept of product life cycle is generally not questioned and deeply influences product managers in their decisions for the following two reasons:

First, the concepts of product life and death underline a fundamental principle of management: it is vital to avoid defining the objective of the company and its role according to a product, but to refer to that product as a benefit. For example, a company producing bags made of hemp found itself in a narrowing market because its traditional outlets, packaging coal, wool and cotton, were reduced when modes of packaging changed in favour of plastic bags. The company could have been very prosperous today if it had defined its activity by the benefits it provided (transport, storage) and if it had evolved while adopting new ways of achieving those benefits. One essential consequence of this principle is the need for product innovation. This type of analysis is implicit in strategic evaluation methods such as "product portfolio" analysis (see Chapter 5). The company must ensure the permanent renewal of its products, each new product being financed by the benefits generated by products belonging to the three last stages of the life cycle curve.

Second, the concept of product life cycle also makes it possible to locate management problems that arise at each phase. The influence of various elements (quality, advertising, services) varies according to the product life stages. Demand is more or less sensitive, at each stage, to each one of these factors, and thus results in a greater or lesser elasticity. The marketing-mix varies according to each stage the product is in. In the introductory stage, the marketing-mix is a major factor since it is a question of launching a new product. At the growth stage of the life cycle, there is very strong imitation by competitors. As imitations develop, marketing managers seek to differentiate their products and, at the end of the growth stage, the market is generally saturated: now it is necessary to establish products in strong and well-defined positions, corresponding to a particular demand. The search for original positioning ideas characterizing all stages is clear in the maturity stage. Then, when decline begins, the number of positions in the market place shrinks and these are held on to by only the best-established products until the sales deteriorate to such an extent that their withdrawal from the market is justified.

The concept of product life cycle, in spite of its usefulness, has some important limitations.

1. It takes very little account of the competitive environment, in particular of the differences in size between competing firms and their mode of entry into the market, which can affect the application of the recommendations through each stage of the curve.

2. Apart from the role of pioneer companies, it does not recognize the existence of strategic windows or appropriate time of entry into the market.

3. It does not have the capacity to indicate when, why, or which environmental conditions lead to drastic upheavals in the market which are due to the arrival of too many competitors into a fast growing market.

4. The effects on the shape of the curve of the strategies chosen are in general ignored in spite of the lesson brought by distribution models, which show that strategies can accelerate or slow down growth.

5. The determinism birth → life → death leads to the acceptance of the inevitable decline of the product. This analogy with biology can be contradicted by the existence of strategies which make it possible to renovate or to prolong the life cycle.

6. The environmental context of a product is neglected in spite of the fact that it influences the life cycle. An embryonic distribution and service infrastructure, for example, may slow down the penetration of the market.

7. Uncertainty concerning customers' acceptance of the product, the size and structure of the market, and the actions of competitors are not taken into account. The concept of the product life cycle supposes the absence of uncertainty because no attention is devoted to the various conditions and sources of uncertainty. In reality, at least in the early stages of the life cycle, the future shape of the curve cannot always be forecast with sufficient accuracy.

For these reasons, strategic suggestions derived from a generalization of the life cycle to include all products have been widely criticized. Indeed, taking into account the limits outlined above, the assumption that the life cycle curve of a product is the only determining factor of strategy, structure and performance can lead to incorrect assumptions when in fact, for example, product success in the maturity phase can be strongly related to the creativity of product managers. It can depend on the individual strengths of those product managers (experience, education, knowledge of marketing), their attitudes (towards planning, risk taking) and some situational factors (formalization of the process of planning, interaction with others, time pressure).

However, the idea of product life cycle is there to draw the attention of the decision maker to the subjacent forces which slow down or facilitate growth, and those that create opportunities or threats. It can also be used as a reference framework for the role played by each product in its line and the product mix.

The life cycle concept can also be applied in an international context. It can be used to explain the introduction, growth, maturity and decline of a product in developed and developing countries. The International Box details international life cycle theory.

INTERNATIONAL SPOTLIGHT

THE INTERNATIONAL PRODUCT LIFE CYCLE

The theory of the international product life cycle supposes the existence of four basic stages. In the first stage, exports of an industrially developed country dominate the world market. In the second, producers of other developed countries gradually compete with these exports in their own markets. In the third, they compete with the first country in export markets. In the last stage, they move to compete in the market of the country which was the first to launch the product. Such a life curve is repeated against competition coming from countries which are economically less developed.

Various explanations are provided for these four stages:

1. The first stage proceeds in a leading country which has a vast consumer market with a high income, and in which heavy investment in research and development takes place. This market has a potential demand for the creation of new industrial products or consumer goods. Their production is carried out in the home country, not for cost reasons (because cost is high) but rather because, during the launch of a new product, those in charge of manufacturing and development within the company need to communicate with their purchasers and their suppliers in order to adjust and to adapt the design and the performance of the product. So the first manufacturers have a world monopoly of the new product. Consumers from foreign countries then receive the products via progressive exports originating from the country of origin. This stage corresponds to the launch and the beginning of the product growth stage.

2. At the time of the second stage, the importing foreign markets have a fast growth rate. Competing companies or manufacturing subsidiaries from the home-country companies are established to benefit from these markets and the advantages which result from them (cost, other factors of production). The product then becomes quickly standardized through the increase in number of manufacturers. The foreign manufacturers compete with the products imported into their own markets; this stage corresponds to the end of the growth stage and the beginning of the maturity stage of the product.

3. The foreign manufacturers increase production for their own market. In the maturity stage, these productivity increments are sufficient to enable them to export and compete with the producers from the country of origin in third markets.

4. The last stage takes place when the foreign manufacturers have established mass production in their own market as well as in export and they then compete with the first producers in their own home market. At this stage, the market of origin becomes an importer of the very products which it originally launched.

This curve repeats itself from economically developed countries to developing countries in order to improve on costs, especially on wages.

The international life cycle theory of the product is supposed to allow the planning of a dynamic and totally sequential strategy of production, export and investment abroad. It is meant to provide a decision-making framework for the product launch in various markets. Empirical data have made it possible to check its fit against reality in the case of the electronics industry or on the database PIMS.

Various limitations of international life theory curve can be noted:

■ The particular features of a company and its experience in its own market and the foreign markets are not taken into account. The theory relates to the dynamics of the product rather than that of the multinational corporation.

■ It relies upon a certain number of assumptions which do not appear essential to the production and the international distribution of the product.

■ It presupposes the absence of differences in tastes, and the need therefore for adaptation.

■ It requires a vast market and a great effort in the research and initial development of the product. However, for many products, in particular in the food sector, a big effort in research and initial development is not necessary. Moreover, a focus on narrow but lucrative markets can counterbalance any disadvantage which may come about through an inability to access another important market.

■ For this reason, the competition of a third country can come earlier than the theory is forecasting and therefore change the product distribution rate.

■ It presupposes that tastes do not change over the duration of the life cycle or in the market of origin so that the same products can still be imported.

■ The leading country still launching a product is an enormous source of information for the competition which can watch the first company and launch equivalent products ('me-too products'), in the target countries where the original company is not yet present, thus establishing entry barriers likely to thwart the penetration of new product from the one leading company. This can take the form of the adoption of different standards, or they could modify the marketing-mix of the existing products to make the access of suppliers from other countries more difficult.

Product innovation

True innovations are rare. The majority of new products launched into a market are actually new versions of an existing product. Booz, Allen and Hamilton, in a study among 700 companies and 13,000 new industrial products and consumer goods, obtained the following statistics:

	(in %)
Genuinely new products	10
New lines of products for firms	20
Extension to an existing product line	26
Reformulated products	26
Repositioned products	7
Cost Reduction (process innovation)	11

The majority of available studies show that 60–80 per cent of companies' sales are through products under ten years old. In fact, the majority of these products are imitations or new versions of existing products (adaptation, imitation, new positioning). True innovations or discontinuous innovations, corresponding to a new market, are rare. They differ from the existing products through new features so that they are perceived as belonging to no existing set of brands (Table 8.4).

Innovation is a risky strategy, and rare, but one that may be very profitable. Several statistics illustrate the risk in innovation:

■ Nielsen (1971): 47 per cent success on 204 products studied (cosmetics, maintenance, groceries),

■ Urban and Hauser (1980): 19 per cent success for consumer goods, 27 per cent for industrial products,

■ Booz, Allen and Hamilton (1982): 57 per cent success in comparison to 37 per cent success in the same study carried out in 1968.

Few products are actually marketed compared with the great number of concepts researched or the still significant number of products developed up to the testing phase. And yet in spite of this rigorous selection process, there are many failures.

The counterpart of such risk is of course the chance to benefit, should one product succeed, from a temporary

Table 8.4 Innovations by differentiation and discontinuous innovations

Innovation by differentiation	Discontinuous innovations
A difference that relates to a latent dissatisfaction with actual product	A set of differentiations leading to a new business and a new resource combination
A market segment that is very receptive to the innovation	Induces a new way of living with the product
Interesting product advantage but easy to imitate	Durable advantage and high profit through important productivity improvement
Very efficient in sectors where products have a short life cycle	Very efficient in old sectors where products are mature
For the firms belonging to the sector, this strategy strengthens their practice	For the firms belonging to the sector, discontinuous innovations are very difficult to detect, very often impossible to create, resulting a totally new business

monopoly, with the obvious advantages this brings: the absence of direct competition, high margin and so on. Note, however, that this "monopoly revenue" is increasingly limited because of the reaction capacity of competitors quickly developing imitation products.

The development of new products requires a process including four stages:

1. idea generation
2. screening, evaluation and selection
3. product development and testing
4. launch and distribution.

Idea generation

Many methods exist to gather new ideas for products. Many industrial innovations come from customers who, starting from their own experience, modify products available on the market and adapt them to their specific needs. This encourages companies to create panels of customers or users who are interested and able to provide new ideas. Empiricism in the birth of new ideas is not negligible. Visits, the observation of competition, show rooms and fairs, and idea boxes for employees are the source of many ideas which, adapted to the constraints of another environment, give birth to new concepts or formulae. For example, the majority of European innovations in retailing, restaurants and services are based on ideas from the United States. This is why some firms organize themselves so as not to lose information likely to provide new ideas. They do so by creating files on competition, by systematically processing data given by competitors, by having a careful policy of visits to showrooms, or even, following the example of Japanese firms, by creating truly specialized services where all information on a product is checked and synthesized. The Internet is an interesting medium to interact with consumer communities. It may be used to gather ideas among opinion leaders or lead users. In addition to these empirical approaches, other more systematic methods exist to gather new product ideas.

Creative methods

Their objective is to create a number of new ideas by breaking down the structures of logical reasoning or while making use of them in an unusual way. For example, the brainstorming method is a technique that consists of bringing together six to eight people under the control of a mediator and asking participants for any ideas and associations which come to mind when presented with a stimulus. At this first stage, participants should not discuss ideas or contradict each other. Everything that comes to the mind is welcome, whatever the degree of interest. Criticism is not allowed whilst the plundering of ideas is encouraged. At the second stage, the group rigorously and logically analyses all the ideas put forward by combining them in order to find new product ideas.

Discovery matrices cross various product categories (in columns) with their characteristics (in rows) (Table 8.5). At the intersections of each product with the characteristics of the other products, new ideas may be thrown up. These "bissociations" can be renewed by changing the products panel.

Quality Function Deployment or the QFD method, developed by Mitsubishi in 1972, aims to allow marketing specialists and engineers in charge of design and production to work together closely in the design of a new product. It begins with investigations among potential customers, using in-depth interviews or focus groups, to obtain a list of attributes characterizing the existing products Those are then screened in order to keep attributes independent from each other. These are then weighted according to the importance given to them by further consumer surveys. A comparison between these characteristics and those of the competition carried out on

Table 8.5 Example of discovery matrix

	Product universe			
	underwear	socks	pants	bra
Transparent				
Coloured				
Refreshing				
Deodorant	+			
Anti-perspirant		+		

Existing products: transparent underwear, coloured bra
New products (+): anti-perspirant socks, deodorant underwear

the basis of a positioning analysis makes it possible to identify opportunities to improve. Opportunities are then investigated by engineers, which leads to the development of a new product.

Technological forecasting methods

These methods are used by very large firms or organizations. They are grounded on very different principles:

- extrapolation of past tendencies
- problem decomposition in a logical and systematic way

Starting with detailed problem decomposition, it is possible to find improvements or the bases of new products. The method "Pattern" of Honeywell is a good example (Figure 8.5).

- Expertise of people knowing the product or certain technical, social or economic aspects relating to it
  The Delphi method uses expert judgement on the likelihood of potential technological developments (new techniques, new performances and new product). In the Delphi method each expert in the group anonymously judges such a likelihood. Then, opinion feedback and other data are reported to the group before new judgements are made. This sequential

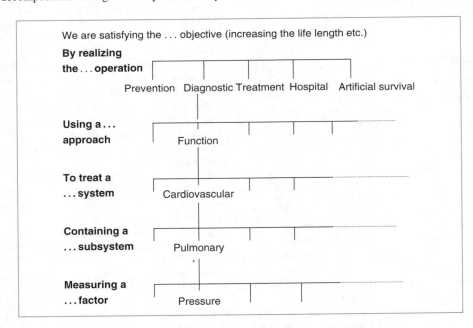

Figure 8.5 Pattern method: An example in the medical sector

process is repeated until a group agreement is reached. The results of the Delphi method can be used as a basis for construction of "scenarios" (see Chapter 1), where an imagined environment is considered (e.g., the retail environment in 2015). On the basis of this new environment, experts seek to generate new products (e.g., new selling formulae in retailing).

■ The reduction in constraints
This consists of analysing "all that restricts" (limits, embarrassment, prevention) the satisfaction of a need. Of course, it should be based on an existing need. For example, Table 8.6 illustrates new product concepts corresponding to reductions in constraint.

Screening, evaluation and selection

Often a company will hesitate between many new product ideas. Only those ideas with the greatest potential are selected for further development. Those that do not match the firm's objectives or have a limited potential are discarded. Different screening methods are available using checklists or portfolios. However, as no screening method is perfect, product testing is necessary.

Product development and testing

At this stage, the principal problem is the realization of the product concept. This requires a series of tests carried out at various phases of product development. These tests focus on the product and its elements, such as packaging or services. Here is a non-exhaustive list of tests:

■ Concept tests
Concept tests rely upon a verbal description or a model of the product that is presented to potential consumers

■ Taste or smelling tests
Generally, they are "blind" tests. Each product is tasted or smelt and then evaluated by difference. Products are presented in neutral packaging so as not to be recognized.

■ Name tests
These study the associations created by the name selected, its connotations, the adequacy of the name and whether the image desired for the product comes through.

■ Packaging tests
They examine qualities of readability, association, use and convenience of packaging for consumers. These tests are carried out among consumers, in a laboratory or during in-store testing.

■ Product tests
They aim at determining the quality of the product or the required level of its characteristics such as weight, reliability, solidity, colour and so on.

■ Placement tests
Here the product is left in consumers' hands for a sufficient length of time so that consumers can evaluate the product's qualities and defects and are able to answer a questionnaire on these.

■ Point-of-sale tests
Their aim is to analyse the reactions of consumers with respect to the purchase of the product and the results obtained by this method in a sales situation.

■ Market-tests
These are a preliminary stage to launching. The product is launched on a modest scale. All the marketing-mix variables can then be tested together.

Each of these tests requires different techniques. However, time and cost constraints do not allow for their systematic use. Moreover, their reliability is not absolute and they are not without their disadvantages.

To avoid these disadvantages companies may prefer to use pre-test experimental methodologies. The "Bases" pre-test experimental methodology was used for over 10 years in more than 8000 tests with remarkable precision. Bases is a "monadic" model of simulated market tests which above all has the advantage of making it possible to forecast the sales volume of a new product, without requiring comparison with its competing products.

Table 8.6 Example of constraint reductions

Needs	Constraints	Constraint reduction
sex	pregnancy	birth control, birth control pills for men or women
lighting	tires the eyes	more natural light, lighting which creates an ambiance
diet	food preparation obesity	precooked dishes controlled dietary food
clothing	washing	laundromat

Launch and distribution of the new product

After the various tests, the decision to launch has to be taken. It requires a decision on and the implementation of all the various components of the marketing-mix. The product launch depends on assumptions made concerning the distribution of the new product. Methodologies or models are also offered to estimate new product sales according to various combinations of the marketing-mix and, once the new product is launched, to control its distribution in order to adjust the various "parameters" of the launch operation.

Many assumptions are made on the distribution of new products. To some extent, life cycle curve theories rely upon distribution assumptions. Since 1962, Rogers has studied new product adoption and has defined several categories of consumers according to their speed of product adoption after its launch date. These are

	(in %)
innovators	(2.5)
early adopters	(13.5)
early majority	(34)
late majority	(34)
laggards	(16)

Each adopter category has definite characteristics of personality and social behaviour, for example tendency to leadership, or social influence. However, this curve is theoretical (Figure 8.6). It can be asymmetrical, and can include more or less than the five categories of adopters. It is interesting to note that distribution is very sensitive to marketing actions (e.g., promotion supports the distribution).

The mode of innovation distribution may take two forms: an S form or an exponential curve. They can be observed when certain conditions are given. Thus, the S form is frequent when

- interpersonal influence is large
- adoption of the innovation requires a certain preliminary training
- costs of adoption of the product (e.g., changing one product for another) are high
- beliefs with regard to an innovation are distributed in a unimodal way
- innovation involves a certain risk.

The exponential form of the distribution of an innovation can be observed in the contrary case.

The launch of a product requires, in addition to research, precise organization of the many tasks which it brings with it, from the launch itself, to the consistent availability of the product at the point of sale. For example, if the product is placed on supermarket shelves

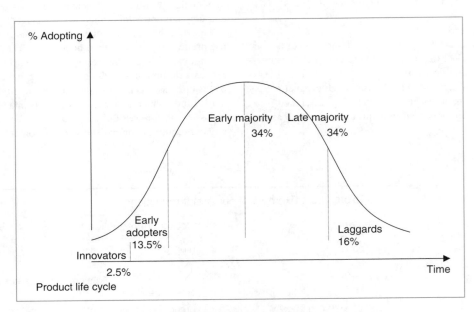

Figure 8.6 New product buyers

too early or too late, it can cause severe difficulties. If placed too early, before the start of an advertising campaign for the new product, shelf managers find that a product has low turnover and tend not to re-order it. If placed too late, the manufacturer loses sales, which is serious during the launch period.

Product line management

There are several product strategies. One is specific to a new market (the innovation); others are specific to existing markets (imitation, differentiation by adaptation or modification of the product). The aims of these three last strategies are to maintain or increase the market share for the product by the firm or to penetrate into an existing market.

These strategies will be described in the first four sub-sections of this section. A fifth sub-section will relate to one of the aspects complementary to the preceding developments, brands and the abandoning of a product. The latter is generally done step by step, without specific analysis when in fact there is much to gain by organizing it with a more methodical approach.

Innovation

Innovation makes it possible to escape cluttered markets, but it is not the only alternative available because it is rare, expensive and risky.

Various experimental studies, carried out with simulated market tests in the field of consumer goods, show that the company arriving first in a market (the pioneer) has long-term advantages over its competitors. The second company to penetrate a market cannot expect to acquire more than 71 per cent of the results of the pioneer; the third firm cannot reach more than 58 per cent. In terms of market share for industrial goods, the second

cannot expect more than 76 per cent of the pioneer's share, the late entrants barely more than 51 per cent.

These first-entrant advantages come from entry barriers which the pioneers set up and build by:

- choosing the most profitable segments of the market
- positioning their product in an optimal way
- having access to the most powerful channels of distribution
- acquiring greater experience, and if possible
- establishing the standards for the market (Table 8.7).

Pioneer advantages are stronger and more durable if the company has financial and non-financial (marketing, distribution, etc.) resources, strong entry barriers, the capacity to maintain a gap compared with its followers as regards experience, a good understanding of the important attributes of the product as seen by the consumers, and an enduring commitment towards the new product. These advantages need to be weighed against several disadvantages such as the risk of failure, the high costs of research and development, and premature technological choices related to very slow technological developments.

In addition, some factors moderate the impact of being a pioneer on the market share:

- Economic factors
  Pioneer advantages are all the more threatened when

  - demand is uncertain
  - advertising intensity is low
  - the time period before the competition enters the market is short
  - the value of experience and that of economies of scale are low, and
  - the volume for which the cost is low is small.

Table 8.7 Advantages and disadvantages of being the first mover	
Advantages	Disadvantages
Deeper consciousness	Most new products fail
Better reputation	Higher cost of R&D
Best trial rate	Premature technology risk
Higher potential brand loyalty	Technically below optimal product
Selection of the most profitable segments	Higher development cost in the market
Reaction of the leading users	Possible offerings from a substitution market
Choice of the most efficient channel of distribution	
Cost reduction due to experience or scale effect	
Price leadership	
Opportunity to establish standards	

■ Characteristics of the product
The more complex the product is, the more it innovates in a new product category, the more the advantages will be long lasting.
■ Technology
The durability of pioneer advantage is supported by:

– the possibility of protecting patents
– innovation in the process or the organization rather than in the product itself
– slow technology evolution
– the existence of transfer costs in consumer goods markets (preferably to industrial goods)
Transfer costs (costs related to changing the purchased brand) can delay new product adoption if the process of decision-making by the customers is slow.
– slow trends in the market

Product innovators have to decide if they want

■ to announce the new launch in advance
■ to innovate punctually or permanently
■ to occupy the entire new market or only a segment.

Occupying the entire market allows a more intense penetration of the market and leaves little room for competitors. It requires many products with differentiated positioning and sometimes a multitude of brands. As a consequence, this strategy is costly. It is complex and may generate cannibalism among products. Because of limits to resources, time and competency, certain large companies seek alliances to accelerate market penetration. For example, Glaxo had an alliance with Roche to penetrate the US market with their Zantac product.

A preliminary announcement of a new product launch must be made at a date which corresponds with the consumer's decision-making process, and must discourage competitors from getting started in the market.

This effect is stronger when

■ competitors hold only a weak market share
■ the sector has a low competitive reactivity
■ the protection of the patent is good.

The announcement of the launch to customers is important if

■ the company wants to develop its company image and its reputation
■ there is a significant learning process required among customers.

Pre-announcement is important if there are complementary products on the market and also to induce retailers to place the product on the shelves.

Demand and competition are evolving constantly. Thus a company which does not innovate all the time risks losing its innovator advantages. Relentless innovation is most desirable if a company wishes to widen its market by reaching new segments of customers. For consumer industrial goods, such permanent innovation relies mainly on improvements of currently marketed products and consists of minor modifications.

Imitation

Imitation is profitable when it makes its impact at the beginning of the product life cycle. It is generally ineffective when the "me too" company invests in the market later. Not taking a risk on innovation would condemn any company to an ageing of its products. To avoid both the risk of innovation failure and the risk of having outdated products, many firms seek to renew their outdated products by imitating new products launched by other firms when they are successful. The launch of Bio yoghurt by Danone, for example, was an imitation of the successful Bifidus yoghurt from B.A. In addition, imitation saves investing in research and development and is particularly well adapted to companies which have limited resources.

To be an innovative follower can be very successful or a disaster depending on the capabilities of the firm. An imitator must be guided by three ideas.

1. It must renew relentlessly its line of products.
For this purpose, it needs to focus on a business, a function or a customer benefit and not on a product, which would condemn it to undergo the "law of the life cycle", and therefore sooner or later to decline.
2. It must be innovative in its imitation
It is not a question of simply copying the innovator. The follower must be able to learn quickly and improve the product. For example, the follower could group together a set of advantages, already present in various competing products but not jointly possessed by any of them. In this respect, a particular transfer of competencies can also be carried out from one product to another similar product. For example, Bic decided to enter the disposable razor market by using its competence acquired in marketing its ballpoint pen.
3. It must be fast in entering the market
The speed of entry into the market is the most decisive criterion for a follower. Using the now famous image of the "crunched apple", Levitt compared the market with this fruit. The innovator has the first bite. The second can still find an interesting side to bite whereas the fifth or sixth! The speed of market entry initially demands great flexibility within the company that cannot be achieved without a continual evolution of the organization's structures, its information gathering, decision-making and production processes.

In terms of organizational structures, the creation of project teams including members of all functions involved in the development, production, and marketing of the new product or service (marketing, sales, production, purchasing, costs, logistic) is a very effective solution. It allows more freedom for creativity and an increased speed in the project's realization. "Task forces" and "commandos" are examples of structures corresponding to the flexibility principle.

The speed of imitation also depends on the quality of information gathered about the competition. The faster and the more relevant the data is on the decisions and first launches of competing products, the more the firm will be able to imitate in a speedy and innovative way. This is why certain firms, in particular Japanese firms, organize the gathering of information through a specialized service. Within this service, all the data given out by competitors (for example at press conferences or in contributions to trade magazines) and/or obtained by members of the company (visits, fairs) are processed, classified, verified and made available to the persons in charge of relevant product development projects. This practice contrasts with the frequent absence of "competition files", a systematic gathering of information, in many companies.

The need to keep production systems as flexible as possible can result in a time-delayed differentiation of products. That is, the variety of intermediate products is reduced to a minimum. The final features of the product are pushed back downstream in the production process or to the creation of the product. For example, Benetton produces its sweaters without dyeing them. They are stored and only dyed when market data indicate the demand for specific colours.

Adaptation or modification

Starting with the introduction into the market and throughout all its lifespan, a product must be adapted. This adaptation can take the form of "repositioning" or of improvements aimed at making the product evolve in order to make it conform to consumer expectations or making it more profitable for the company.

Repositioning can become necessary for various reasons:

- the arrival of a competitive concurrent brand that is positioned too close to the actual brand and damages it
- a consumer change in preference
- the detection of new segments of promising consumers
- an error made in the original positioning.

Repositioning is aimed either at current customers highlighting new uses, or at new users by presenting the product in a new way, or by repositioning it to focus on the new uses but starting from the original and still valid uses of the product. Thus Breitling, the Swiss watch, at the start positioned itself as the official stopwatch of pilots throughout the world, and was then repositioned in the mens' luxury watch sector, thus opening up a segment which is much broader than just pilots.

The adaptation of a product can result from improvements carried out in purchasing, manufacturing, marketing or logistics. Certain methods contribute particularly in determining potential adaptations, such as "ideas boxes", where consumers express their expectations concerning product attributes. The conjoint measurement method previously described is an example of an instrument well suited to measure the expectation of each product attribute.

Value analysis, created by Miles, an engineer at General Electric, is a particularly effective method for adapting or modifying products. It can be defined as a systematic and methodical search for the most economic solutions for adapting the functions of a product to consumer expectations. Value analysis is not a method aiming at minimizing the cost of manufacturing and delivering a product, but a procedure to eliminate needless costs (all costs that do not have a value for the customer) and simultaneously to obtain the levels of service sought by customers. It breaks the product up into simple elements in order to carry out comparisons with the competition. During this analytical procedure many methods are used (creativity techniques, market study techniques, accounting, financial, manufacturing, purchasing techniques). This is why value analysis is practised in "teams", bringing together many competencies. Value analysis, although old, remains very current because its logic corresponds to the basic steps of marketing, and can integrate the most recent techniques from the various disciplines which it brings into play (see Special focus).

The BT system provides

- A full analysis of the customer's operational requirements
- A fast comparison of different pallet handling and order picking solutions
- Optimum warehouse layout
- Accurate calculations of handling capacities
- Complete analysis of projected life cycle costs.

This system is used when a customer is contemplating a change of materials handling or is adding a new facility. The system helps the customer figure out, for example, the optimal aisle width that will accommodate the dimensions of a counterbalance lift truck, and it calculates the layout and equipment requirements to meet peak hour needs.

Birkenstock, the German shoe manufacturer decided to build a new warehouse in Asbach, Germany. An in-house consultant responsible for the procurement process for this new warehouse proposed a layout that required three lift trucks to handle the pallet movements. Using the BT system, an alternative was identified requiring only two trucks and one less operator.

Source: J.C. Anderson and J.A. Narus (1998), Business Marketing: Understand What Customers Value, *Harvard Business Review*, 76, 6, 53–65.

Deletion

The renewal of product lines requires that certain products or product lines are abandoned. For any company, the regular detection of the least profitable or non-profitable products is an important task. It relates not only to the balance and the positioning of a product line but to the potential for rejuvenating a brand.

The variety and the heterogeneity of criteria for deletion, and the effect on the management of the company and their customers make the decision difficult and often not very rational. This is especially so because decision-making frequently depends on several people with different functions who do not necessarily have the same interest in giving up a product.

There are three ways to systematically delete a product:

1. Milk the product
   It consists of obtaining as much cash-flow as possible from the product or line. Milking applies to products or lines with a declining sales volume or market share. It means cuts in the costs associated with the product (e.g., advertising) or in an increase in the product selling price without cost increase, or, by using the brand to market products or lines which are not part of the core product. An example would be bath products for perfume brands.
2. Line simplification
   It aims to restore the profitability and its development. Line simplification takes place especially in periods of growing costs and resource shortage. It offers many advantages such as

   - Cost reduction related to greater mass production
   - Reduction in stocks
   - Concentration of marketing as well as research in development expenditures.

   However, the decision to simplify a product line poses problems within the company which are caused by rivalries and group pressures. The decision to delete a product is even more difficult if

   - this product was the original product of the company
   - there is an obligation to satisfy customers in spare parts
   - there are consequences in terms of image as seen by retailers and consumers.

3. Sale of a product or a line
   Product lines or products are sold mainly for the following reasons:

   - the absence of strategic bonds with other activities of the company
   - a lack of financial resources to develop the product
   - the sale generates resources which can be used to develop other products or lines
   - the sale improves the return on investment of the capital employed
   - the market share reached by the product or line is insufficient and too distant from that of the leader.

Finally we should note the specific problems posed by returned products due to defects. The consequences of a return are generally a worry for companies: negative reactions from consumers and distributors naturally have a negative effect on the company image. Two routes are available to face product returns:

1. a passive reaction in which the aim of the company is not to undergo any more returns or withdrawals as a sanction
2. a proactive stance where the company seeks to avoid returns or undertakes action on its partners or its target customers. Prevention and management of returns is

possible and desirable. Management of defective products when acting on the information provided through each management level (production, distribution, consumption, consumers associations) can mean avoiding the most harmful consequences of product returns or withdrawals.

SUMMARY

This chapter focuses on five key elements necessary for product management: the total product concept, elements of product management, product life cycle, the management of new products, and product line management.

Specific components of a product are core product, brand name and packaging. A product is often part of a product line and should conform to standards. The core product is the physical product. A brand is a name, a term, a symbol, a logo or any other combination of these elements which makes it possible to identify the product. Different functions are assigned to packaging such as to protect the product, to facilitate its transportation and to facilitate its sale. Standards can play a strategic part by facilitating or prohibiting access to a market and distribution of a product, or by allowing a policy of differentiation. Compatibility between products and between systems is also effected by standards. A product line consists of a set of interdependent products which satisfy the same category of needs, are used together, focus on the same customers, are distributed through the same points of sale or are in the same price range. Each product within a product line is allotted a single place related to its position in the segment on which the company focuses. The life cycle is one main component of product policy. The life cycle concept is based on an analogy with biology, according to which products have a series of phases leading them from life to death. In its most traditional form, product life cycle is represented by an S curve comprising four phases: introduction, growth, maturity and decline. Product life cycle analysis shows that the specific role of the product and the services which accompany it play a role to a greater or lesser extent in the marketing-mix depending on its stages.

The management of a new product requires a process comprising four stages: discovery of new ideas, selection and evaluation of product and services, development and product testing, and launching and distribution. Ideas originate from customer experience, visits, observation of competition, idea boxes and so on. However, more systematic methods have been created to generate new product ideas such as brainstorming, discovery matrices, Quality Function Deployment and technological forecasting. Screening and evaluation methods use checklists. Once screening has been performed, tests are carried out at various stages of product development: the concept test, taste or odour test, price test, name test, packaging test, communication test, placement test, point-of-sale test and market test. Methodologies and models are used to estimate new product sales. Five categories of consumers are identified according to their speed of adoption: innovators, early adopters, early majority late majority, and laggards.

Product strategies aim to maintain or increase the product market share, to penetrate an existing market and to get out of a market. Pioneer advantages justify an innovation strategy. Less risky is the imitation strategy. Repositioning and adaptation strategies are necessary to make the product conform to consumer expectations. Value analysis is a methodology particularly effective to adapt or modify a product. Renewal of product lines and non-profitable products requires product deletion. Product deletion occurs by milking existing products, line simplification or the sale of product.

Discussion questions

1. In which phase of the product life cycle does the product play a major role among the components of the marketing-mix?
2. What are the main limitations of the product life cycle?
3. Besides the physico-chemical properties of a product, what are the other product dimensions that marketing managers should take into account?
4. What are the marketing stakes of standards?
5. What is the fundamental principle of the product life cycle?
6. What are the brand functions? Are they always fulfilled? Why?
7. What constitutes brand value? Why are brands part of a firm's equity?
8. What distinguishes an umbrella brand from a line brand?
9. How can product packaging bring a solution to consumer needs?
10. How are services a key element of the differentiation of the offer?

11. What are the specific elements of services? What are those which are the most important for the hotel business?

12. For what reasons is true innovation so rare? Define and compare innovation strategy using pure innovation with a strategy of innovation using differentiation?

13. For a firm looking for new products, what are the respective advantages of creative and technological forecasting methods?

14. How do you conduct a positioning analysis to explore innovation opportunities?

15. What are the interests and limits of the Delphi method to evaluate a new project?

16. How is it possible to evaluate the cost of entrance of a new product into an existing market?

17. What are the advantages and disadvantages of market tests?

18. When is it considered that a new product distribution curve might be best fitted by an S curve?

19. Explain what is value analysis. For what reason does it fit into the marketing foundations?

20. Under what conditions is it worth conducting an imitation strategy?

21. What methods may be used to identify product modifications in an adaptation strategy?

22. For what reasons does market clutter influence consumers' purchasing behaviour?

23. What are the differences between a positioning strategy and the other product strategies? When should it be used?

24. What criteria are used to identify products that should be abandoned?

Further reading

D.A. Aaker and E. Joachimsthaler (2000), *Brand Leadership*, New York, Free Press.

L.L. Aaker (1997), Dimensions of Brand Personality, *Journal of Marketing Research*, 34, 3, 347–346.

I. Ayal (1981), International Product Life Cycles for Industrial Goods, *Journal of Marketing*, 45, 4, 91–97.

P. Doyle (1975), Brand Positioning Using Multidimensional Scaling, *European Journal of Marketing*, 9, 1, 20–34.

J.E. Ettie and M.D. Johnson (1994), Product Development Benchmarking versus Customer Focus on Applications of Quality Function Deployment, *Marketing Letters*, 5, 2, 107–116.

J.R. Hauser and D. Clausing (1988), The House of Quality, *Harvard Business Review*, 88, 3, 63–73.

M. Lambkin and G. Day (1989), Evolutionary Processes in Competitive Markets: Beyond the Product Life Cycle, *Journal of Marketing*, 53, 3, and 4–20.

T.H. Robertson, J. Eliashberg and T. Rymon (1995) New Product Announcement Signals and Incumbent Reactions, *Journal of Marketing*, 59, 3, 1–15.

R.T. Rust and R.L. Oliver (1994), *Service Quality: New direction in Theory and Practice*, Sage, Thousands Oaks, California

G.L. Shostak (1977), Breaking Free from Product Marketing, *Journal of Marketing*, 41, 2, 73–80.

D.M. Szymanski, L.C. Troy and S.G. Bharadwaj (1995), Order of Entry and Business Performance: An Empirical Synthesis and Re-examination, *Journal of Marketing*, 559, 4, and 17–33.

G.L. Urban, T. Carter, S. Gaskinand and Z. Mucha (1986), Market Share Rewards to Pioneering Brands: An Empirical Analysis and Strategic Implications, *Management Science*, 32, June, 645–659.

G.L. Urban and J. Hauser (1980), *Design and Marketing of New Products*, Englewood Cliffs, New Jersey, Prentice Hall.

L.T. Wells (1968), A Product Life Cycle for International Trade, *Journal of Marketing*, 32, 3, 1–6.

Y. Wind (1982), *Product Policy*, Readings Massachusetts, Addison Wesley.

Advertising 9

Learning objectives

After studying this chapter you will be able to

1 Explain the role of advertising in the company communications strategy
2 Recognize the main actors in the world of advertising and explain their role
3 Analyze the theoretical foundations for advertising communication
4 Discuss the main problems concerning company advertising strategy in a European context
5 Set up a complete advertising campaign
6 Understand how the creative advertising process works
7 Set up a media strategy
8 Understand how to measure advertising efficiency
9 Explain how advertisers establish their advertising budget.

SPOTLIGHT

Omo is a brand of the Unilever group. It was launched in 1952 and was the first washing powder on the French market where it brought a revolutionary change in the life of ladies staying at home and having the habit of washing clothes by hand. Five years after its launch, Omo was used by one-third of the market, which was persuaded that "when omo is there, the dirt disappears". The introduction of the first washing machine in 1959 stimulated the competition: Bonux 1958, Skip 1959, Dash 1962, Ariel 1968, X-Tra 1971, Gama 1972. Therefore Omo was quickly outmoded, Skip and Ariel becoming the top brands. Their success originated their special adaptation to washing machine. Furthermore, Skip and Omo belonging to the Unilever group, Lever had decided that Skip was its top brand for the washing machine. However, Omo had an image of conviviality and tradition very popular among the working class.

Therefore the brand slowly declined until 1970 when Omo launched a washing machine formula 'Omo scientific' with an advertising slogan 'yes, we can'. However, this type of advertising campaign did not prevent the brand to slowly loose market share despite another more successful advertising campaign emphasizing tradition and experience. Other innovations allowed the brand to fit new trends. Therefore, Omo liquid and Omo micro were launched to fit the segments of washing liquid and contrated powder (one quarter of the market in 1992). However, the brand was still losing ground to its competitors. This situation pushes the idea to rejuvenate the brand image using an advertising campaign breaking with the traditional advertising campaign but able to transmit the message that Omo, still micro (small), was very efficient (strong) and still compatible with traditional family and speaking a language that everybody was able to know 'touti rikiki maousse costo', The message was strongly memorized (50 per cent higher than the previous spot) and extended brand penetration to younger customer segments. Furthermore, sales increased 17 per cent during the next six-month period. Advertising is one of the components a firm may use to gain value.

Introduction

Advertising is everywhere in our lives and holds an important place in our cities. Every day we rub shoulders with advertising media such as the cinema, television, press, radio, posters, and so on. Today, other methods also hold a prominent place on the advertising landscape: mailing, phoning and more modern media such as the Internet. Generally, this chapter concerns advertising in the traditional media: press, T.V. Radio, cinema and posters. Other media will be discussed in the chapter on "Direct Marketing".[1]

To perfect an advertising campaign requires specific competences. As a rule advertisers engage specialized agencies whose main role is to define, based on the results of marketing research and consistent with the marketing objectives of companies, the most effective type of advertising to use. This includes advertising creation and media strategy. These two main functions of advertising agencies will be studied in the first two sections. In the third section we discuss the problem of management control over advertising activity. However, before analysing the way in which advertising is carried out, it is important to provide some figures showing the role of advertising in European companies' communications strategies.

Advertising expenditure

The scale of advertising expenditure by companies underlines the essential role of advertising in their communications strategy.

The tables which follow indicate

- the amount of total expenditure on advertising in many countries and the advertising expenditure per capita (Table 9.1).
- the media expenditures in the world: estimation for 2004 (Figure 9.1).
- the importance of the media and the advertising industry as a proportion of GDP in countries where this industry is best developed (Table 9.2).

These data along with the two tool boxes on the advertising market and communications in Europe reveal the link between economic development, living standards and the development of the media and advertising (Toolboxes 9.1 and 9.2). This data will be completed in the following chapters with additional information concerning "new media" and in particular the Internet, which shows the tremendous dynamism of professional communications in all economically developed countries.

Table 9.1   Advertising expenditures by country

Direct Mail Expenditure

Euro million current prices	1996	1997	1998	1999	2000	2001	2002
Austria	–	–	–	1,472	1,631	1,737	1,795
Belgium	–	917	656	660	718	727	–
Czech Republic	–	–	–	151	192	230	290
Denmark	585	464	475	514	932	613	553
Finland	399	423	444	467	493	501	491
France	5,868	6,039	6,526	6,786	7,224	7,368	7,449
Germany	9,101	10,124	11,657	12,271	13,140	14,600	21,230
Greece	–	–	–	–	57	94	113
Hungary	–	–	–	134	152	186	237
Ireland	113	124	20	64	71	78	–
Italy	2,062	1,443	1,865	1,940	2,501	2,741	3,076
Netherlands	2,287	2,487	3,999	4,481	4,296	2,724	2,867
Poland	–	–	–	–	514	638	–
Portugal	30	35	38	42	54	59	–
Slovak Republic	–	–	–	10	13	37	50
Slovenia	–	–	–	–	–	8	11
Spain	1,973	2,151	2,415	2,825	3,077	3,198	3,239
Sweden	622	663	671	763	894	867	1,065
Switzerland	–	–	–	–	764	815	–
UK	3,731	5,509	5,978	7,145	7,612	9,208	9,633
Total	**26,772**	**30,378**	**34,743**	**39,722**	**44,337**	**46,431**	**52,098**

Direct Marketing Expenditure Per Capita, 2002

	Volume per capita			Spend per capita		
	Addressed	Unadressed	Total	Direct Mail	Telesales	Total
Austria	–	–	–	168.4	44.8	221.3
Czech Republic	15.4	229.0	244.4	25.9	1.9	28.3
Denmark	44.9	375.3	420.2	103.3	–	103.3
Finland	94.2	205.8	300.0	94.4	–	94.4
France	71.3	313.8	386.6	111.7	11.1	124.5
Germany	–	–	–	157.3	55.8	257.6
Greece	–	–	–	5.5	4.8	10.3
Hungary	18.1	146.9	165.0	19.9	3.3	23.9
Italy	20.5	65.2	85.8	38.4	14.1	53.5
Netherlands	90.2	639.3	729.5	151.0	25.4	178.4
Slovak Republic	18.5	55.6	74.1	5.4	2.7	9.2
Slovenia	9.5	114.1	123.6	5.4	–	5.4
Spain	–	–	–	60.8	16.9	79.0
Sweden	79.9	334.4	414.3	107.0	0.0	120.1
UK	88.6	–	88.6	66.9	82.0	163.1
Average	**58.6**	**239.4**	**239.3**	**90.7**	**33.9**	**136.4**

Source: WARC (World Advertising Research Center, research world, September 2006)

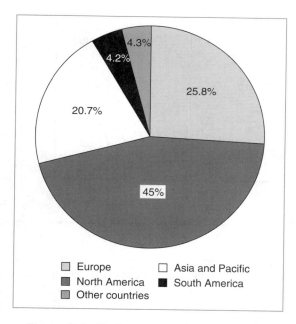

Figure 9.1 Media expenditures in the World (2004)

As well as these global aspects, we can note

- important disparities in expenditure between countries in the same zone, such as the European zone which concerns not only the global or per capita amounts, but also, as we shall see later, the respective importance of the media in each country (Tables 9.3 and 9.4).
- the "Europeanization" of campaigns, stimulated by large companies' intent on developing their brands in all world markets where they are present.

However, in spite of this tendency, it is important to highlight the differences between each country in consumer habits and media penetration which make it necessary to tailor advertising campaigns.

The objectives of communication

The general objectives of a business organization may be expressed as market share, profitability and turnover. To achieve these objectives, the organization has to define and communicate its offer for the selected markets. All marketing action contributes, at one and the same time, to the definition and the communication of the company's offer. Advertising is one of the means of expressing this offer. It is neither the only means nor an indispensable form of communication: the organization can, if preferred, use other forms of communication, sponsorship for example, and may even decide not to use advertising at all. Much depends on the communications objectives but also on the target group, the benefit to be communicated and the media infrastructure. These follow from the general objectives of marketing and can lead towards choosing, first and foremost or exclusively, advertising or other

Table 9.2 Advertising investments in proportion to GDP

Country	2004 millions (€)	04/03 (%)	Population 2004 millions (€)	Per Capita in 2004 (€)	GDP 2004 billions (€)	Ad Spends/ GDP (%)
Germany	14.481	1.8	82.3	200.0	2,099	0.78
France	9.820	4.0	58.6	167.9	1,508	0.65
Italy	8.357	6.6	57.8	144.6	1,248	0.67
Spain	5.683	4.0	41.8%	136.0	686	0.83
Netherland	3.473	0.3	16.2	214.4	433	0.80
Belgium	2.510	4.0	10.4	241.3	266	0.94
Total	46.304	2.5	267.0	173.4	6,238	0.74
United Kingdom	20.234	7.4	59.2	327.8	1,689.6	1.1
USA	143.563	6.2	280.6	418.0	10,703.4	1.1
Japan	40.730	–	126.0	227.8	4,665.9	0.6

Source: www.aacc.fr (2005).

Table 9.3 Advertising investments by media in Europe

	Newspapers and Magazines (%)	T.V. (%)	Outdoor (%)	Radio (%)	Cinema (%)	Internet (%)
Germany	62.1	26.1	4.9	3.9	1.1	1.9
Belgium	43.4	39.1	6.2	9.4	1.0	0.9
Spain	39.6	42.6	6.5	9.1	0.8	1.4
France	47.7	32.6	11.0	8.0	0.7	–
United Kingdom	54.2	30.0	6.5	4.4	1.1	3.8
Italy	38.2	52.7	2.4	4.2	1.1	1.4
Netherlands	66.0	21.6	3.8	7.1	0.2	1.3
USA	40.9	39.1	3.1	12.4	–	4.5
Japan	35.2	45.0	11.8	4.3	–	3.7

Source: IREP (2004).

Table 9.4 Advertising investments by country (1997–2003)

	1997 millions (€)	1998 millions (€)	1999 millions (€)	2000 millions (€)	2001 millions (€)	2002 millions (€)	2003 millions (€)
Germany	15,556	16,343	17,176	20,236	18,567	16,695	16,328
France	8,229	8,771	9,633	10,112	9,620	9,501	9,442
Italy	5,742	6,081	6,798	7,593	7,838	7,555	7,480
Spain	3,291	3,630	4,265	5,430	5,095	5,202	5,280
Netherlands	2,906	3,080	3,533	3,886	3,740	3,560	3,578
Belgium	1,301	1,530	1,681	2,006	1,964	2,158	2,192
United Kingdom	14,463	15,698	16,671	20,234	18,832	18,615	17,345
Total					65,656	63,286	61,645
USA	94,116	100,885	108,350	143,564	138,786	135,717	116,526
Japan	33,776	32,406	31,791	40,730	36,471	31,177	28,303

Source: www.aacc.fr 2005.

forms of market communication. For example, one of the leaders in European mail-order selling has had public relations as its priority over the years, estimating that its marketing objectives would be reached more effectively and at lower cost by using this form of communication. Different roles are generally played by advertising and by other forms of communication such as sales promotion.

The most frequent objectives of advertising communication are

- to ensure potential customer awareness of a product or brand,
- to highlight an element, a characteristic (an advantage) of a product or brand,
- to help develop an image of a product, a brand, an organization,
- to support other forms of communication (for example, promotion of important distributors).

Although it is difficult to generalize, we can say that advertising is a form of communication that is well adapted to maintaining brand or product, to attributing to this product or brand certain physical or psychological dimensions or to building an image. That is why advertising action needs time: a brand image is not built in a day. This is not the case for promotional action which can generally bring about a more rapid change in demand.

The application of communication

For each marketing operation such as launching a product, starting up an additional point of sale or extending a product line extension and so on, the organization must establish a clear communication plan which fits into the general communication strategy.

Such a communication plan first identifies the message to be reinforced: these are the communication elements to be held constant. It then determines the core message and the communication objectives to be achieved and selects from among the various communication techniques the best suited to the communication problem at hand and to the target markets to be reached. The plan then states what actions are to be taken and what resources need to be allocated.

Within this communication plan, the detail of the advertising campaign should clarify

- the objectives to be reached by means of advertising,
- the audience to be reached,
- the choice and the precise forms of media to be used (including calendars and costs),
- the means to be applied for advertising efficiency controls.

According to Dayan[2], commercial communication can be represented by the sequence indicated in Figure 9.2.

In what follows, the various steps shown in the sequence depicted in Figure 9.2 are discussed in detail. They are all based on certain psychological foundations to be outlined first.

Psychological foundations of advertising communication

The know-how of the advertising specialist is based on a range of social science theories. The advertiser works on elements of the message (forms, words, concepts, context, images and so on) having communication objectives in mind. Through this work, the specialist acquires knowledge of the use of language, signs and images, a mastery of the rules of communication and an understanding of the effects of the message on the consumer. For example, the word "flavour" can have a different sense in ordinary language and in an ad for yoghurt where "flavoured" also gives the impression of a product which is not natural and contains chemical and other additives.

Based on Freud's theory of needs, we can distinguish four types of potential effect of advertising messages on consumers. Each effect can be analyzed as a reduction in the state of tension felt by the consumer when a need arises.

1. Identification expresses the capacity of the individual to become identified with the participants in the message, either in relation to their "ideal self" or in connection with their own image as they see it (self concept). Depending on the type of person chosen in the ad (social group or reference group, age, style etc.), the individual receiving the message feels or does not feel concerned and experiences the message to a greater or lesser extent as a situation corresponding to the satisfaction of an appropriate desire within him. The use of stars, opinion leaders and the choice of actors, for example, are very important in obtaining the individual's identification with the message, and attracting him to the product on offer.
2. Projection is the "mechanism" through which the consumer, in order to diminish tension, tends to extend the behaviour beyond themselves. They bring others

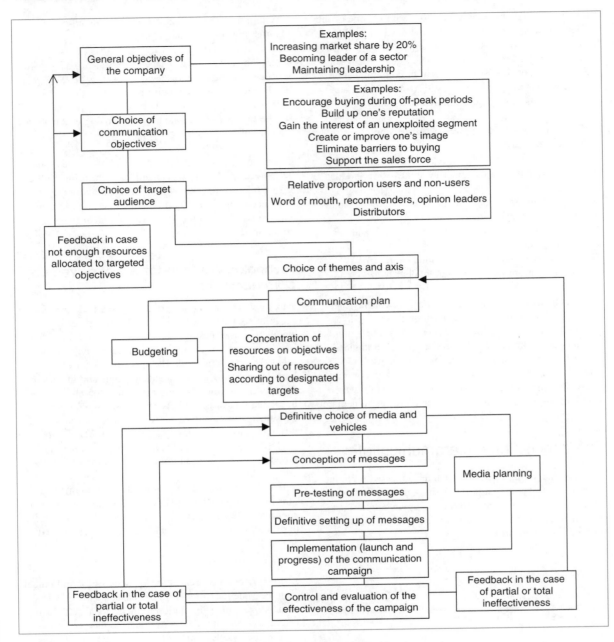

Figure 9.2 Advertising communication
Source: Adapted from A. Dayan (1986).

into the equation. Projection allows the consumer to be reassured by sharing their behaviour with others. This mechanism can be found particularly in promotional techniques or in word-of-mouth situations.

3. Transfer, widely used in advertising, is the process by which tension is transferred towards a "satisfier" object

(or situation), other than that initially envisaged. This tension is based on needs (hunger, aggressiveness, security, seduction, etc.). The advertising executive planning the communication of a product (a packet of cigarettes or a deodorant, for example) studies the consumer needs to be satisfied and tries to devise a message that portrays the product as satisfying those needs (Figure 9.3).

Figure 9.3 provokes the following comments:

- Concerning cigarettes, it is possible to play on seduction or on the fear of cancer (anti-nicotine).
- Concerning deodorant, it is possible to play on seduction or on hygiene.

4. Rationalization is the process by which the individual tries, post-purchase, to decrease the state of tension they feel (slight dissatisfaction, insecurity etc.). For example, a person who has just spent a lot on buying a car will be looking for good reasons to justify its purchase, such as: "it is an investment, expensive cars are much more reliable, they can be resold more easily", and so on. In this case, the individual is sensitive to information which confirms the behaviour. The theories of cognitive dissonance[3] or of attribution[4] may explain this process in part. The advertising agent can deliberately use those psychological mechanisms to promote products or services or to develop consumer loyalty.

Among the theoretical models offered to explain the process of persuasion, there are some which are centred on the advertising message. McGuire's model[5] based on work carried out in Yale suggests that the consumer, in order to be persuaded, must handle information across six stages (Figure 9.4).

If one of these six stages breaks down, then the consequences expected from the model may not be observed over the ensuing stages.

The cognitive response model underlines the role played by thoughts or cognitive responses produced by the consumer and which they have learned or remember, when they are exposed to persuasive communication.[6]

Therefore we would be more interested to know the contents of cognitive responses rather than how well the advertising message was learned.

Not only does advertising give rise to cognitive responses in individuals, it also brings about emotional responses, and numerous researchers and advertising executives have tried to analyse these responses: emotions, feelings, mood etc.[7, 8]

The concept of "attitude toward advertisement (Aad)", has been defined by Lutz[9] as "a predisposition to respond in a favourable or unfavourable fashion to a particular advertising stimulus during particular exposure".

The attitude towards an advertisement contains two types of antecedentss: affective reactions and other antecedents such as its perceived credibility, the attitude towards the advertiser and attitude towards advertising in general and the current state of mood.[10]

Other theories suggest that consumers may develop attitudes in ways other than the understanding and the evaluation of arguments advanced in the advertising message.

Two models suggest that persuasion could also take place based on a minimum of scrutiny of the arguments of the message: the Elaboration Likelihood Model and the Heuristic-Systematic Model.

The ELM model (Elaboration Likelihood Model)[11] suggests the existence of two means of persuasion: a central and a peripheral route. The central route works when consumers are involved and active, capable of handling information and motivated to handle it. They mobilize their knowledge and compare arguments contained in the message. An attitude results from active information processing. The peripheral route of persuasion corresponds to the principle of cognitive economy. Consumers are minimally involved with the central content of the advertising message (e.g. the product category), but may be attracted by peripheral elements of

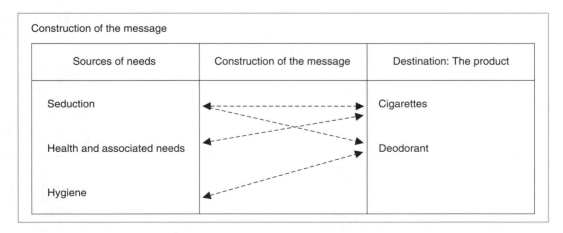

Figure 9.3 Construction of the message

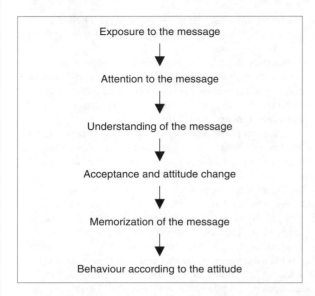

Figure 9.4 The MacGuire's advertising Persuasion Model

Source: Adapted from W.J. McGuire (1976).

the message such as the music accompanying the advertisement or the way the message is conveyed. In this case passive and widely unconscious processing of the message may take place. An attitude may develop without consumers actively processing the advertising information.

The ELM model suggests

- strategies are implemented by receivers to make their choices, taking account of their limited capacity to process information.
- situational and individual variables (whether a convenient situation or not) affect the cognitive effort put in by the receiver, such as cognitive need, personal pertinence, importance of the product, anxiety, complexity of the message, entertainment, pressure of time, assessment of the product or prior experience.

  - the importance of motivation or cognitive capacity to process information,
  - the existing ways of processing the information; for example, the confirmation of existing prior attitudes,
  - time effects of the argument following the chosen route: longer temporal persistence for the central route, stronger resistance to future undermining etc.

Petty and Cacciopo emphasize four factors that can influence the attitude of a receiver:

1. the motivation of the individual when processing the message,
2. the capacity of the receiver to process the message,
3. the type of argument used (strong or weak),
4. the peripheral elements of an advertisement: setting music, colours, speed etc.

The ELM model has been subject to a lot of criticism concerning in particular the role and level of the involvement in the persuasive process,[12] the possibility of interactions between the two persuasive routes.

The Heuristic-Systematic Model[13] distinguishes two means of handling advertising information: a systematic mode, which is based on a complete and analytical treatment of information by the receiver, and an heuristic mode, which supposes more limited processing, demanding less cognitive resources; it can thus involve simple plans or decision-making rules based on past experience. According to this second model, a subset of information would be selected, to which simple decision rules would be applied. For example, if consumers are convinced by the expert testimony in an advertisement, the decision rule which can be used to establish the consumer's attitude is, "One can trust the opinion of an expert." Decision rules would be the fruit of successful experiences and observations that are remembered. The consumer may use such rules for various reasons: such as an effort to save, a satisfactory compromise between effort and objectives, or social pressure.

MacInnis and Jaworski[14] have created a model which distinguishes three stages in the process of persuasion (Figure 9.5):

1. the antecedents to information processing, including motivation, capacity and opportunity to handle information. Motivation corresponds to the utilitarian and expressive needs of individuals. Capacity stands for the receiver's ability or competence to interpret information contained in the message. Opportunity concerns the circumstances under which the message is perceived, and whether or not they are favourable (entertainment level, incongruous elements of implementation such as unsuitable music, too rapid execution of the message, or information which does not live up to the expectations of individuals).
2. information processing depends on the attention of the individual exposed to the message. Two characteristics of this attention are taken into account: its intensity (how much priority does the consumer give to the message?) and its capacity (how much effort does the consumer give to the message?). Individuals attach more or less importance to the contents of the message itself or doing something about it, they handle the

salient elements of the message to a greater or lesser extent, have greater or lesser recourse to previous knowledge in order to categorize the elements of the message, process information contained in the message in an analytical or holistic way and react more or less emotionally to the message itself.

3. change of attitude process which means a number of things. Processes of the "halo effect", "humour effect" and "affective transfer" type correspond to the weakest levels of attention and motivation. For example, receivers who are amused are more favourable to a message even though it does not really get them involved (humour effect), they may include the message in their general attitude towards the advertised brand without specifically analysing the message (halo effect) or they may transfer their attitude concerning an emotional element of the message to the message as a whole (affective transfer). At a slightly higher level of information-handling intensity, the individual will proceed with a "heuristic evaluation", having taken a holistic view of the meaning of the message. The next level is that of "persuasion based on the message", with a shrewder analysis by the individual of the salient or non-salient elements of the message. Processes of "persuasion based on empathy" correspond to the highest levels of attention, motivation and processing

capacity, where the individual takes on the role of the person present in the advertisement (role taking) through a phenomenon similar to vicarious learning, together with "processes of auto-persuasion" where receivers exceed the elements of the advertisement to build their own scenarios around the advertised object.

The creation of the message

There are several schools of thought about the creation of advertising messages. Each advertising executive is inspired by marketing plans which they interpret with greater or less freedom. Before explaining those plans, we may observe that they all have a bearing on the fundamental issues discussed above. They assume a harmonious combination of creative ideas and the logical principles of the market communications platform.

The "classic" copy-strategy

The term "copy strategy" suggests a method of creating an advertising message which is based on several principles stemming from the experience of important American consumer goods companies, detergent manufacturers in particular. These companies have developed rules for

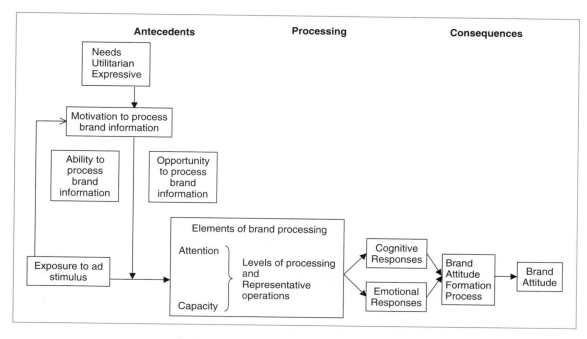

Figure 9.5 MacInnes and Jaworski's Model
Source: D.J. MacInnis and B.J. Jaworski, 'Information Processing from Advertisements: Toward an Integrative Framework', *Journal of Marketing*, 53, 4, 1989, 1–23.

elaborating the message, which are summarized in Table 9.5.

The aim of a copy-strategy is to establish the external and internal coherence of the message:

■ external coherence with the marketing strategy, the communication platform, media and vehicles,
■ internal coherence, by harmoniously combining the elements of the message.

Note that the points discussed below are mutually dependent.

The promise or axis

This is the result of marketing research studies: these indicate, for a specific target market, for the thing being advertised, the essential element to be communicated. For example, it could be a question of occupying a particular, precise position with respect to a determining belief in consumer choice (the most effective or the mildest shampoo for example). The belief and position taken are the result of marketing studies and are the basis of the communication platform. They are the foundation on which the promise is based. If this important work has not been carried out, then it has to be done by the advertising agency, which then plays the role of marketing consultancy.

The proof

The proof gives credibility to the promise by backing it up, consolidating and illustrating it. It can involve a demonstration, a testimony, a test, a presence of a substance, an agent or active principle. The justification must be credible (unless it involves a surreal or funny illustration) and in accordance with the promise.

The benefit

The benefit involves emphasizing the advantage which the consumer will gain from fulfilment of the promise, by illustrating it and sharing it. This advantage should be connected with the promise so that the advertisement attains the desired objectives. In the example above, if the advertising agent emphasizes the softness of the fabric (axis), he will then develop a more intimate relation of the benefit idea for the consumer because "to touch" concerns this kind of situation in general. This is not necessarily the case if he emphasizes the "respect for colours" axis. The choice of benefit put forward will be strongly influenced by the target market for the message.

Tone and atmosphere

Tone and atmosphere are produced by the combination of elements of the message (colours, positions, forms, sounds, situations, decor, objects, people, humour) and they should reinforce the promise and its proof. The theoretical principles of transfer and identification studied above are equally applicable. The combination of message elements creates the context for the message which strongly influences its impact. Too young a comedian, misunderstood humour, an uninteresting situation can destroy the atmosphere and be out of tone with the rest of the message, which reduces its effectiveness. On the other hand when the tone agrees with the promise made and the proof, it strengthens them and creates a style of communication which is very important for the development and support of a brand.

The "creative" copy-strategy

We shall analyse here two variants of copy-strategy said to be creative: the announcement and the creative work plan.

Table 9.5 Principles of the advertising message elaboration		
Principles	Examples of a detergent brand	
1. Claim or advertising axe	Dazzling colours	A smoother underwear
2. Proof (reason why) strengthening the claim	Colour Test (comparison with an anonymous detergent)	Presence of softening agent
3. Consumer benefit	The husband's shirt is associated as social success	Personal pleasure, sensuality, seduction
4. Atmosphere, style, form . . .	Social situation where the actors are husband, wife, friends etc.	Domain of privacy, intimacy, relations such as "husband/wife"

The announcement

An announcement is a form of copy-strategy that is less narrow than that previously described, so leaving more freedom for creativity. It is mainly based on the concept of evocation. This concept is the driving force which is going to assert, support, demonstrate and communicate the advertising promise. The example given in Table 9.6 illustrates the mechanism of this creative copy-strategy.

This message, using humour, skilfully illustrates the idea of a change of atmosphere. The "code", a distinctive element and easy to remember, is the sentence "It works" (for Vittel, it is the V sign and the mask, and for Orangina, the gesture and the words "Shake Me, shake me").

Creative copy-strategy does not necessarily require a complete demonstration. It is based on the appropriateness of the concept of evocation and the theme that is employed. Less rigorous than classic copy-strategy, it is also founded on the USP (unique selling proposition) idea and carries the risk of sacrificing creativity to originality, by diverging too much from the intended market positioning.

Creative work plan

To avoid deviations of this kind, US-based agency Young and Rubicam have suggested organizing the work of creating an advertisement according to a creative work plan. Table 9.7 shows this plan and takes up again the main stages of the development of an advertisement. The creative work plan became highly successful, and other agencies adopted it.

Table 9.6   The creative copy-strategy

The axe	Salient belief results from market research	Cut the unpleasant smells, change the atmosphere
The evocative concept	Creative idea recalling strengthening the axe, making it more credible	The escape
The theme	Concept setting up story, atmosphere, music, persons	Commercial with two convicts in their cell, after using the atmosphere deodorant they find themselves on an island with an idyllic atmosphere

Table 9.7   Creative brief

The principal fact	Summary of the marketing diagnosis (product, market, positioning, strengths, weaknesses)
The problem to resolve	To draw from the diagnosis the problem that advertising will be able to solve. The specific role of advertising in the marketing-mix
The advertising goal	The answer that advertising provides to the problem
The principal competitors or enemies	Research on directly competitive brands and products according to the goal; marketing and advertising strategy analysis of these competitive brands and products according to the goal; marketing and advertiser strategy analysis of these competitors (creation and media)
Creative strategy	Precise determination of the customer target; choice of the advertising axe (according to the copy strategy: claims, benefit, proof)
Instructions and constraints	Respect of the advertiser's instructions and constraints such as legal obligations, respect of visual or auditive elements

The "star strategy"

Many advertising people have never wanted to comply with rules of copy-strategy that appeared too strict to them. Thus, several other forms of advertisement creation have been suggested. Among these, in Europe, the "star strategy" of the French Agency RSCG (Roux, Seguela, Cayzac, Goudard) has been very successful.

The star strategy tries to transfer consistently the intended positioning of the advertising object to the elements of the advertisement. In effect, the objective of positioning may be conceived as to give a "personality" to products. In order to do this, advertising needs to communicate this personality. An agency document remarks, "the brand becomes a person. A person becomes identified, asserts himself, is loved for his or her physical appearance, character and style." So, to develop a brand, advertising objects must become identified, assert themselves and should be loved for their:

- physical appearance: what they do (performance objectives),
- character: what they are (imaginary value),
- style: what they express (implementation constants).

The following comment illustrates the idea of the inventors of the "star strategy": Their physical appearance is not a question of being beautiful or ugly. It is to possess a specific feature and to use this feature to become unique. For example, Marlène Dietrich became famous for her legs, Michèle Morgan for her eyes, Sylvester Stallone for his muscles, Coca-Cola for its bubbles and Woolite for its concentration.

The character is the second nature of a person, the only thing that is not learned. Gérard Depardieu is characterized by his force of personality, Marlon Brando was known to be the sectarian and Yves Montand became famous for his commitment. Coca-Cola's character may be expressed by youthfulness, Woolite's by seduction.

Finally, the style is the unexpected indispensable accessory of a person, the sign which has become a signal. Take Charley Chaplin's cane as an example and compare it to the rhythm of Coca-Cola or the stars of Woolite who make a big show of turning it into washing powder" (adapted from a document of RSCG).

The elements of the advertising message

An advertising message consists of a combination of various elements:

- an object which can be a person, an organization, or a product or one of its qualities;
- an argument which can involve a proof or a justification;
- a context that it is the real or imaginary place and the moment where the contents of the message are situated, creating a specific atmosphere (serious, scientific, fantastic, crazy, playful);
- a genre: a story, demonstration, incantation, parable, tale;
- a style; and
- sensory and cognitive characteristics allowing for the codification of the message.

The composition of an advertising message demands definitive work on words and images. Visual constituents such as colours, luminosity, clarity, movement, size, composition or speed, written constituents such as slogan, base line, typography, character size, text, and sound constituents such as sound, voice, tone or type of music can turn out to be determinants in increasing or diminishing the impact of a message.

Each advertising executive organizes these elements in order to build a message. Some agencies have created their own style. The agency which produced an advertisement may be recognized by the particular way the message is delivered. For example, the relation between the text and the image expresses the specific styles of famous advertising creative people such as Ogilvy, Seguela or Bernbach. Ogilvy's ads, for example, were characterized by the key presence of editorial texts emphasizing truth and the authenticity of the product.

To strengthen identification of the advertising object, the creative executive uses also elements such as the font, the graphic design of the brand or the packaging of the product which will be represented in the advertisement. For example, this is frequently the case when a reminder of the packaging of the product (pack-shot) is shown at the end of a promotional film.

Finally, other elements can be introduced, such as humour, information, narration, intrigue (a teasing campaign where the role of the first message is to arouse interest and the second to bring about a response), sex or scandal, which influence the impact of a message. Their effectiveness depends on their harmony with the set of the other elements of the message and, more widely, their fit with the target, customers, advertising objectives and media.

Trends in the evolution of advertisements

Messages are the reflection of trends in the development of the company as well as its environment. The communications environment has changed appreciably:

information overflow, market saturation and the diversification of lifestyles have substantially changed the creation of advertisements. Kroeber-Riel[15] distinguishes six major trends affecting advertising creation:

1. the topicality of the offer rather than information concerning the product: because of the limited attention paid to advertising which makes it more difficult to get a message across, "the first objective of advertising will be the topicality of the offer", understood as being "spectacular portrayal of a product so that it remains present in the spirit of the buyer". Topicality is a "necessary condition, sufficing in case of weak consumer involvement";
2. unique character rather than interchangeable profiles: the increase in competition and its internationalization make it necessary to intensify the unique character of the advertising object's profile, whether it is based on a emotional or factual quality;
3. advertising innovation more than creative self-satisfaction: advertising innovation becomes more and more important with regard to a technical innovation that is rapidly imitated: it is, for example, about the development of a new positioning instilled by a world of sensations, a new style of presentation for advertising: "In the future, advertising should innovate and try to offer reality and dreams instead of artificial, commonplace worlds, psychologically strong images and high entertaining power instead of sterile advertising inventions";
3. mental images clearly present in the mind instead of vague advertising impressions: creating concrete visual representations in the consumer's mind which arise spontaneously as soon as one thinks of a company or a brand;
4. integrated communication instead of a confusion of words and images: making the impressions left by all the vehicles of the company's communication (packaging, promotion, advertising, sales and all forms of personal contact) coherent;
5. professional advertising instead of a few discoveries: basing advertising communication on "the application of knowledge and results of research into the effects of advertising", instead of leaving free range to unbridled creativity which results in underperforming advertising.

In this context, the elements of form, notably the tone, have greater importance. Several messages play on emotions, humour, and use the testimonial of a celebrity to strengthen these elements. But there still remain numerous followers of description, demonstration and even statements from authority. Comparative advertising[16] as well as the arrival of the messages of "direct

marketing" have led to the strengthening of this tendency, giving advertising creations a more and more differentiated aspect.

As an example, a successful creative treatment which obtained a Euro-Effie award for advertising efficiency in 1997 is shown in Toolbox 9.1.

The internationalization of commercials: Standardization or adaptation?

Since Levitt[17], several authors have insisted on the need to take into account the globalization of markets. The possibility of making the same message available in different countries and cultures depends on numerous factors such as the contents of the message, the type of advertising object, the awareness of this object, standards and modes of consumption, purchase habits, and association with the media.[18]

The stakes are high. The standardization of commercials can have numerous advantages:

- saving the cost of message multiplication (different creations and different aids),
- having a consistent message for a clientele that travels a lot in different countries,[19]
- better control of communications strategy in all markets[20] and building brand-equity.

Some authors have tried to identify international customer segments having similar lifestyles and values.[21] There are numerous limits to message standardization: the result of media choices which vary from one country to another, or also to cultural, economic or statutory differences (e.g. the life-cycle stage of the product in the country) (International Spotlight).

Harvey[22] has put forward a model to assist decisions which allows for the choice between the degree of standardization and message adaptation and which takes into account six factors of influence:

- product (degree of universality of the product),
- competition (relative power of competitive forces present),
- organization (level of international experience and degree of decentralization in decision-making),
- infrastructure (similarity between the marketing media infrastructures and the agencies),
- legislation (limitations),
- culture (homogeneity in purchase behaviour, norms and values)

TOOLBOX 9.1

EURO EFFIE AWARD 1997 FÉLIX

Marketing situation

In 1989, Felix (then owned by Quaker) was a small UK brand, with 8 per cent of the market. The aim was to grow brand share in the UK to 10 per cent by 1991. By 1996 Felix had exceeded these ambitions by a huge margin and had grown to become Europe's second biggest brand. This paper will analyse the success of the brand in the UK, France and Germany, which together account for 70 per cent of the European market. (Felix, however, enjoys share of 10% + in six other countries). This success was not easily achieved. In the UK Felix was an unsupported brand with declining market share. In France the Quaker brand was Fido and had static market share. It was renamed Felix de Fido in 1991, becoming simply Felix in 1993. In Germany the brand did not exist and was launched in January 1992. We were faced with a multiplicity of tasks – to relaunch in the UK, to rename and relaunch in France and launch in Germany.

Advertising objectives

We needed to do a number of things

1. Communicate a distinctive and motivating brand proposition
2. Raise brand awareness
3. Increase brand share

The base from which we were starting was as follows.

	UK ('89)	France ('91)	Germany ('92 3 months post launch)
Brand Proposition	not est	not est	not est
Brand Awareness	39%	19%	18%
Brand Share	8%	10%	2%

Source: Millward Brown, 1991,1992, Nielsen

Creative strategy

We wanted to position Felix in a way that gave the brand a clear point of difference against Whiskas and that would be motivating to consumers. The original positioning was developed in the UK and then exported to the other European countries. We looked at what our competitors were doing and also talked to consumers. Most advertising in 1989 sought to reassure cat owners that their cat would be eager to eat the brand advertised. This approach seemed to make sense since cats are notoriously fussy eaters. However, the way in which the message was communicated appeared to be a weakness. The advertising was very rational. It relied on product shots, owner endorsement and idealised images of immaculate, perfectly behaved cats. Research told us that consumers did not identify with the cats being shown – their own cats did not look like that or behave like that. Importantly, consumers loved their cats for being mischievous and getting into trouble. We decided to position Felix as the brand that really understands what cats are like. The creative device was an illustrated black-and-white cat.

Media strategy

The initial UK budget was £250,000. Whiskas spent £8 m each year. We needed to find a way of deploying our funds imaginatively. National newspapers were chosen. They were an unused medium in the sector. We could buy small spaces often and create a regular dialogue with consumers (especially useful as catfood is a weekly purchase). We could run lots of different executions to help flesh out the character of Felix. The press buying brief was to be cheeky – like a hungry cat at meal times the press ads popped up everywhere. As the brand grew in the UK the budget grew. This enabled us to move the brand onto TV. However, the strategy remained the same – regular dialogue, targeted airtime, frequency at the expense of coverage. This led to a drip strategy, initially using airtime in one, weekly programme. This media thinking was exported to France and Germany. Felix's media buying was characterised by an unconventional approach, which made the most of funds that never came close to those of Whiskas. (Our share of voice ranges between 10 per cent and 20 per cent).

Results

Feklix's status is more advanced in the UK, and least advanced in Germany. These differences reflect the different stages that the brand is in, in terms of time since relaunch or launch, and the level of investment the brand has received.

1. Establishing a distinctive and motivating brand proposition

    We measure two key image dimensions with Millward Brown. The scores are indexed to show the extent to which the brand over-or under-achieves on that dimension.

For cats with character

	Felix	Whiskas
UK	+8	−12
France	+8	−3
Germany	+2	−1

For mischievous cats

	Felix	Whiskas
UK	+19	−20
France	+17	−14
Germany	+8	−15

Millward Brown, 1996

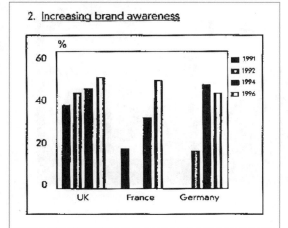

2. Increasing brand awareness

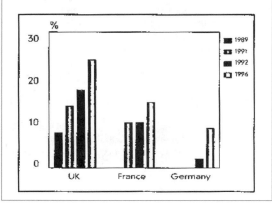

3. Increasing brand share

Is advertising responsible for these achievements?

We have explored advertising's contribution in some detail in the UK. Four pieces of evidence led us to conclude that advertising had an effect.

1. The regional differencies in Felix's share growth 1989–91 correlated with the differences in its newspaper advertising weights
2. Penetration of Felix grew faster among readers of the titles that we advertised in than among readers of other titles
3. The regional differences in the brand's penetration growth 1992–95 correlated with regional differences in TVR delivery
4. Between 1989 and 1995 there was a correlation between Felix's monthly share and the amount spent on advertising during the previous year

We built an econometric model to try and gauge the scale of advertising's contribution vs the other elements of the marketing mix. This suggested that advertising accounted for 30 per cent of the sales increase in 1989–94. Distribution increases accounted for 17 per cent, the relaunch itself for 13 per cent whilst the ongoing introduction of new variants accounted for 40 per cent of the growth.

We have not been able to conduct such rigorous analysis for either France or Germany. However, we would contend that the same factors drive the brand in these two countries. We have looked to see whether there are notable differences in France and Germany that might suggest different reasons for brand growth.

■ distribution – constant gains have been made in both France and Germany, but the scale of these gains is no greater than the gains made by Felix in the UK at a similar stage in its development

- product – it is of course possible that the product being sold in France and Germany is better than that of the competition. None of the testing data that Spillers has suggests this is the case
- price – during the time period under consideration Felix did not price-cut in any of the markets
- new variants – introduction of new variants is a key driver of sales, but Spiller's introduced new flavours and variants in all three markets (although the exact variants/flavours differ by market due to local tastes)
- competitive activity – it is possible that Felix grew in France and Germany because the competition stopped supporting their brands. This is not the case.

Whiskas, the main competitor, kept its support for the brand constant over this time period. In 1992–96 Whiskas average share of voice in France was 30 per cent and in Germany 38 per cent .

Conclusion

By the end of 1996 Felix had overtaken Whiskas as brand leader in the UK, reducing the latter's share from 50 per cent to 24 per cent. In France, Felix was only 1.3 share points behind Whiskas, having closed a 7 share point lead for Whiskas. We await the evolution of the Felix brand in Germany with eagerness.

United Kingdom   France   Germany

FELIX
Euro Effie 1997

United Kingdom

Germany

France

19
★

INTERNATIONAL SPOTLIGHT

"THINK EUROPEAN, ACT LOCAL"

Three main reasons to apply this version of the famous american formulae "Think global, act local": first no uniformization of lifestyle yet (if ever); second, existence of an "advertising culture"; and third, differences in national legislations.

1) The global village?

Common passports, a common currency, community licence plates, all these things will help us to feel and think european. But people will also sink deeper roots into their local regions as their national identities erode. In the new Europe, beign Flemish, Catalan (cf. Barcelona), Sicilian or Welsh will acquire fresh significance in terms of cultural identity and personal pride.

Newspapers know how important it is to stay close to the local market. Most "news" is national or local. Scan the pages of newspapers from five different countries and you will find different news in each: and one last but significant point: 75 per cent of the citizens of the EC neither speak nor understand any other language than their own.

As EC Commissioner Martin Bangemann has pointed out : "Europe's

2) **Advertising culture**

Surveys have been conducted to define the trends which would characterize advertising in Europe and find whether there is a pan-european advertising.

These surveys lead to the conculsion that there is none yet, for one good reason: people of the different european countries do not like, nor expect the same from advertising.

In the UK, people like advertising. There is no doubt. They are waiting for a honest and truthful publicity but they also like it to be entertaining with a touch of humour.

The French want witty ads, they want to laugh and dream, which leads the ad agencies to campaigns sometimes quite far from the product.

The Italians are a bit puzzled, divided between north and south, between serious information and creative entertainment.

The Spanish want ads to be creative and serious.

The Germans seem to be fond of severe, straight-forward advertising.

3) **Another barrier to Europe-wide campaigns is regulation**

Running campaigns across Europe is currently a nightmare for the media planner because of the existence of an exhaustive range of domestic restrictions and a variety of total exclusion zones.

For instance, all alcohol beverage advertisement is banned on TV in France, the Netherlands, Switzerland, Turkey and Norway. Austria, Ireland and the UK will not accept spirits or hard liquor . . .

Children and advertising are subject to a raft of common-sense rules drawn by countries such as Finland, Ireland and UK.

Interestingly, Germany says in its rules that toys with a war theme are restricted.

These are just a few examples of the rules and regulations which make it difficult to create a european-wide campaign.

Nevertheless, some common points in euro ads are emerging.

Source: Jacques Bille "Think European, Act Local", Jacques Bille's Conference, " Advertising in Europe in the 90's ", Conference International Advertising Association (IAA) of Budapest, October, 1999.

The media plan: Qualitative and quantitative aspects

The choice of media (cinema, posters, radio, television, press etc.) and vehicle (for television: RAI in Italy, ARD, ZDF in Germany, STV1, STV2 in Sweden, ORF1, ORF2 in Austria etc.) is a strategic decision requiring several things to be considered: whether or not the medium is a neutral factor, the appropriateness of different media to the message and to the target customers, the interaction between media, between media and vehicle, and the quality and reliability of data on vehicle. In fact, the role of the media and vehicles is to pass on the message under the most effective conditions to the designated target customers or potential customers. The detailing of the media plan poses problems of communication quality and quantity (Table 9.8).

- First the selected media should respect the message without altering it. Any vehicle in itself possesses characteristics which have a considerable impact on the advertising message (for example, time and place of reading or watching, flexibility, availability, speed of communication, etc.).

- second, the selected media should ideally cover all of the designated target customers. This poses more quantitative problems such as audience calculation and forecast, the number of contacts and the impact and distribution of contacts or cost.

The media and the message: Qualitative aspects

The relation between the medium and the message has provoked numerous debates centred on the ideas of Marshall McLuhan.[23] According to McLuhan, the role of the media is such that the message is the medium. This assertion poses the problem of the neutrality of media and vehicles. Which roles should they play? Should they be neutral vehicles of communication between the transmitter and the audience, respecting the totality of the elements communicated in the message with the least possible influence or, on the other hand, should media play a major role, through their own characteristics, appropriate to the meaning of the message itself? There is no simple answer. The interdependence between the medium and the message appears at the level of form, meaning and advertising objectives.

Table 9.8 Media advantages and drawbacks

Main advantages	Main drawbacks
Daily newspaper	
Short reservation delay	Short-lived message
Flexibility	Quality of reproduction
Credibility	
Informative advertising	
Regional coverage	
Magazine	
Audience selectivity	High cost
Long-lived message	Reservation delay
Credibility and prestige	Updating (e.g. monthly magazine)
Quality of reproduction	
Important coverage of the target audience	
Television	
Reach and coverage	
Image, sound and motion	Long reservation delay
Increasing of the brand value	Very high cost
Selectivity (according to programmes)	Risk of saturation
Repetition	
Possibility of demonstration	
Radio	
Low cost	Only sound
Flexibility	Very short lived message
Short reservation delay	Low attention
Selectivity	Risk of saturation
Repetition	Cost of film production
Fast effects	
Cinema	
Quality of image and sound	Weak coverage
High selectivity (young audience)	Low repetiton
High impact	Reservation delay
Very high attention	
Outdoor advertising	
Geographic selectivity	Difficulty to argue
Repetition	
Impact	
Proximity (for the distribution)	

Interdependence at the level of form

Each medium and vehicle requires specific treatment from the moment of the creation of the message. A message is not conceived for showing as a TV commercial. In the same way, the production technique for the message differs from one press vehicle to the other, for example from a regional daily to a weekly glossy.

Interdependence at the level of meaning

The meaning attributed to each medium or vehicle gives the message certain meanings which can alter it or strengthen it. The message will be decoded differently depending on whether it is associated with, for example, an avant-garde, traditional or scientific vehicle. Credibility, prestige, atmosphere, reception conditions (presence, reading time, activity level of the receiver) are qualities that all advertising messages seek through both the medium and the chosen vehicle. Each medium has a style and distinct characteristics within which the advertisement must be placed. Advertising context such as type and volume of the advertising and editorial context such as the subject, style, nature and form of the articles and stories have an effect on all of the advertisements.

Interdependence at the level of advertising objectives

Finally, the qualitative objectives of the communication frequently require the media to be selected and the message to be created simultaneously. Each medium has several functions that it can perform better than others. It is advisable therefore to take into account the objectives expressed in the message in order to establish the media plan.

However, the meaning of the medium changes along with its technical characteristics. While television is well suited to advertising by distributors, the same is true of the daily press, so this creates strong competition. Similarly, the appearance of direct response ads on television screens gives a new function to this medium and creates a new style of message, appropriate to the characteristics of the medium and the imperatives of direct response marketing.

Media selection criteria

To summarize, the interdependence of quantitative and qualitative objectives assigned to media makes the construction of the media plan particularly complex; in fact it entails real professional work. We can summarize the choice criteria in Toolbox 9.2.

Media and target audience: The quantitative aspects

The selection of media and vehicles into which the ads for an advertising campaign are inserted is the work of specialists known as media planners. To detail each media plan, these media planners require accurate knowledge of the audience for each vehicle. This knowledge is used to combine optimally the media and the vehicles to obtain numerous and widespread contacts among the designated target customers, while taking into account the budgetary constraints of the advertiser.

TOOLBOX 9.2

THE CRITERIA OF CHOICE OF MEDIA

- Economic criteria:
  - reach, which is the percentage of a target audience that is exposed at least once to the advertiser's message during a fixed period (usually four weeks);
  - frequency, defined as the number of times within the fixed period that members of the target audience are exposed to the advertiser's message;
  - targeting, that is, the capacity of the media to select certain individuals within the target audience;
  - life expectancy of the message; for example, messages in a daily, weekly or monthly magazine do not have the same duration;
  - cost of the media.
- Qualitative criteria:
  - use of sound: possibility of remembering a jingle, sound products (CDs, cassettes, etc.);
  - use of visual material: reminder of packaging, bringing to mind a category (perfumes, cosmetics, etc.);
  - use of movement to direct products and people, give an impression of speed, etc.;
  - use of colour, varying with the type of advertising object (food products, cosmetics, cars, etc.);
  - potential to demonstrate or present arguments (the difference, for example, between a poster and a film).
- Logistical criteria:
  - media availability, time taken to create the message (films, posters, radio commercials etc.);

- impact on distribution: consequences for shop sales, sales force; for example, poster sites near points of sale, use of local radio in the distribution zones;
- adaptation to the factual message: capacity of the medium to be present and effective in announcing an event (conventions, fairs, trade weeks, salons, special offer days etc.).
- Commercial criteria:
  - adaptation to the advertising object: kind of product (e.g. convenience goods vs industrial goods), level of customer product involvement (e.g. search products vs impulse products);
  - possibility of association with retailer advertising.
- Time criteria:
  - bursts/concentration within a specified period of time or the capacity to reach the target audience in a very short time or, on the other hand, over a longer period.
  - seasonality: certain media are used more at certain times than others; for example, a decrease in visits to cinemas, television audiences, and exposure to urban posters in summer.
- Spatial criteria:
  - interest in using regional, national, European or international media according to the purpose of the advertising object.

In fact, the development of a media plan comprises several stages:

- media strategy, which defines the media to be used as well as the distribution of the budget between them and the time schedule for their use;
- the media schedule, which entails choosing the most suitable vehicles for building the media plan;
- the choice of slots, which entails determining, taking the chosen vehicles into account, where and when the sound and vision elements of the campaign should be included;
- a posteriori control measuring results against objectives.

The audience for a vehicle

The media planner has to take into account the audience for each potential vehicle.

The audience for a vehicle represents the number of people having been in contact with this medium within a certain period. In general, this number is measured in terms of probability, that is, the potential number of occasions to see or hear (OTS or OTH) that vehicle. For example, several types of TV audience measurement compete with one another:

- the "viewer diary" used by the interviewee who regularly send records of television watched to the research company;
- the home audience monitor, a tool which measures home audience through recording when the television set is switched on;
- the individual monitor, which measures how often each individual watches television; each spectator indicates his presence through a remote control (push-button) which is recorded by the monitor;
- automatic audience measurement which records television viewing without the viewer having to intervene. This type of monitoring, known as passive, is undergoing research at the moment. Table 9.9 shows the methods of audience measurement used in Europe.

The reach for each vehicle represents the coverage by this vehicle of the designated target audience. The greater this coverage is, the more it is said, in advertising terms, that there is "affinity" between the vehicle and the target. We can thus distinguish the reach, efficiency and affinity of a vehicle (Toolbox 9.3).

- the reach scale is the classification of vehicles according to the number of people using that vehicle who also belong to the target audience (an absolute value number).
- the efficiency scale classifies vehicles according to the cost of the contact; it appears in the form of a classification according to the "cost per thousand readers" (CPM) which can be refined to CPM-TM which means the cost of reaching one thousand members of the target audience.
- the affinity scale indicates the ratio between the target audience reached by a vehicle and the total audience of the vehicle.

The detailed development of the media plan

To get the message across to the designated target audience, the media planner has to distribute the available budget between the various media and vehicles. Accordingly, as we have previously shown, the planner has to take qualitative factors into account, concerning notably the quality of contacts. For example, the impact of the message must not be confused because it is transmitted through both television and posters. This poses the problem of equivalence among media. Some media planners refuse to recognize the value of equivalence calculations. Others have put forward an experimental method allowing for this type of calculation for a campaign, according to the degree of exposure of the members of the target audience and the objectives that are being pursued (awareness, attitudes).

All media planners agree that the various functions of each medium and each vehicle need to be included in the media plan. They have to distribute their budget between media and vehicles on the basis of quantitative factors such as accumulation and duplication of audience.

Accumulation indicates for a specific vehicle the increase in reach of the target audience for the nth insertion in relation to $(n-1)$ (Figure 9.6A).

As the example in Figure 9.6B shows, an advertisement inserted into the first issue of a vehicle reaches 40 per cent audience in the designated target (u audience). The same ad inserted in the first two issues of this vehicle reaches 60 per cent of the targeted audience, or an increase in reach of 20 per cent. Three successive ads (in issues 1, 2 and 3 of this same vehicle) attain a score of 70 per cent in reach. Among those who have seen the advertisement, some will have seen it once, others twice and others three times (Figure 9.6B).

Duplication indicates the number of individuals (readers, listeners or viewers) common to two different vehicles.

Take the example of two vehicles A and B, having respectively 1 million and 800,000 readers (Figure 9.6C). Duplication is the number of individuals using vehicles A and B (hatched zone) at the same time, that is, 300,000 people. An ad inserted into these two vehicles will thus be seen once by 1.2 million readers who will only have one opportunity to see it (1 OTS), and twice by 300 000 readers (who will have 2 OTS). The net coverage, or the total number of different readers in contact with at least one of the vehicles, is 1.5 million $(1M + 0.8M - 0.3M)$ in the example above.

TOOLBOX 9.3

THE COST OF A WEIGHTED CONTACT

The basis for calculation is the cost of contact with a member of the target audience. We can calculate the cost of advertisement (Exhibit A) and the cost of the weighted contact (weighted reach).

lack reach but are low cost). We can therefore adopt a reach–efficiency scale, an index indicating the reach–efficiency relation. Such a scale leads us to adopt at one and the same time far-reaching and relatively efficient

Exhibit A The cost of advertisement

Vehicles	Audience 100% readers	Reach	Cost of advertisement (€)	Efficiency cost... Thousand readers (€)	Affinity
Vehicle No. 1	5000	3000	5000	1.66	$\frac{3000}{5000} = 60\%$
Vehicle No. 2	2000	1000	2000	2	$\frac{1000}{2000} = 50\%$

This notion can be refined by weighting different categories of people: if we assume that vehicle No. 1 is used by one million middle-ranking executives weighted 1, and two million employees weighted 0.5, and that these two categories comprise the target audience, while vehicle No. 2 exclusively affects middle-ranking executives, we obtain the result indicated in Exhibit B.

vehicles as well as those which have less reach but are very efficient: for example, let us take three vehicles A, B and C, defined thus:

A: Reach: 30% (of the target)
Efficiency: 6000£ per 1%
B: Reach: 20%

Exhibit B The cost of weighted contacts

	Weighted contacts	Cost of weighted contacts (cost per 1000 weighted readers)
Vehicle No. 1	$1000 \times 1 = 1000$ $2000 \times 0.5 = 1000$	$\frac{5000 \text{ Euro}}{2000} = 2.5 \text{ Euro}$
Vehicle No. 2	$1000 \times 1 = 1000$	$\frac{2000 \text{ Euro}}{1000} = 2 \text{ Euro}$

The reach scale favours vehicle No. 1 in the following two cases: this vehicle is used by 3000 readers in the target audience and vehicle No. 2, by 1000 readers. The efficiency scale is different: the cost of the weighted contact vehicle No. 1 is 2, 5£ (per thousand readers). It is only 2£ (per thousand readers) for vehicle No. 2.

Thinking only in terms of the efficiency scale might lead one to give preference to marginal vehicles only (which

Efficiency: 4000£ per 1%
C: Reach: 10%
Efficiency: 2000£ per 1%

These three vehicles have the same index R/E or 0.005 and are therefore equivalent on a reach–efficiency scale. We can also include affinity and produce crossed reach–efficiency–affinity scales.

No. of vehicles	% of the target audience reached
1	40
2	60
3	70
4 etc.	75

Figure 9.6A Example of audience accumulation

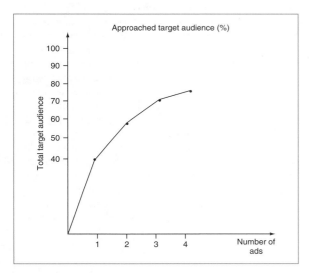

Figure 9.6B Target audience accumulation curve

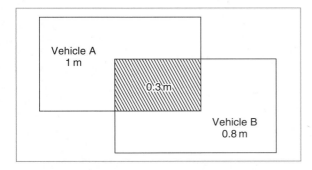

Figure 9.6C Audience duplication

The distribution of OTS (opportunities to see) or OTL (opportunities to listen) depends on the combined effects of the phenomena of cumulation and audience duplication. The percentage of targeted individuals reached once or several times is calculated for every media plan put forward. The net coverage of the target audience (percentage of people affected at least once) can be then calculated. We can thus observe, for each media plan:

- the total number of OTS;
- the average frequency which indicates the average number of contacts received by the individuals affected;
- the coverage at X OTS and more (C_x+) which indicates the percentage in the target audience affected at least x times: for example, a C_3+ equal to 30 per cent indicates that from 100 individuals belonging to the target, 30 had three or more OTS;
- the GRP (Gross Rating Point) which gives the amount of exposure to a media plan for 100 individuals in the target audience or the reach in per cent (calculated by multiplying reach by frequency for each vehicle and aggregating the ratings of all vehicles selected in the media plan).

Each of these indicators has its usefulness and its limits. For example, GRP must be complemented by indicators of variance such as C_x+ which ensures that there are not too many under- or over-exposed people. Depending on the communication objectives, the media-planner can attempt to obtain either extensive coverage or intensive frequency, or a combination of these with high frequency on certain target customers and a coverage with low frequency on the rest of the audience.

The different audience calculations of a media plan require recourse to computer technology from data supplied in each country by organizations that measure media audiences.

To these audience calculations, media-planners add two other types of consideration in order to establish the media plan: the estimation of "response functions" and the duration and pattern of the advertising campaign.

Morgensztern[24] has shown that the recollection in advertising obeys the following law:

$$S_n = 1 - (1 - \beta)n$$

Where S_n expresses the action produced by advertising for n exposures.

β corresponds to the specific memorization of the message; it expresses the intensity of recollection (rate of initial memorization of the message). The shape of the advertising recollection response curve is shown in Figure 9.7.

Concerning the duration and pattern of advertising campaigns, Zielske[25] measured memorization and memory

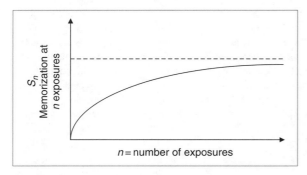

Figure 9.7 The memorization of several degrees of exposure

media-planning models. The models are based on optimization or on evaluation by simulation or by formula.

The goal of optimization models is to determine the optimal media plan according to quantitative objectives of coverage, frequency and constraints of cost and use of certain media. Proposed optimization models become more and more complex and powerful because of the number of variables to be integrated, such as prices and order size, duplication, frequency or characteristics of available television screens.

The aim of using simulation models is to compare and evaluate the impact of different possible media plans. Such models comprise a simulation of individual exposure (from files) to the media plans which can be varied and measured for each plan – that is, for example, in reach, affinity and average efficiency – by segments and C_x. Simulation models have the advantage of being flexible and quick, media-planners being able to modify their plan easily and observe the impact of these modifications on the objectives. MEDIAC, put forward at the end of the 1960s by Little and Lodish,[26] was one of the first models of this type. It has since undergone several improvements. It involves an interactive computer model which integrates numerous factors influencing the choice of vehicles, such as market segments, potential sales, the probability of exposure, the marginal response rate, memorization and memory lapse, and cost structures.

lapse in two campaigns using the same messages, identical in number with different patterns: 13 weekly messages for the first campaign, 13 messages at the rate of one every 4 weeks over a year for the second. He obtained the results reproduced below, which demonstrate that the memorization of a campaign is also connected to the pattern of advertising exposure (Figure 9.8).

The problem posed here is that of distributing the budget across time: is a constant, seasonal or periodic weight of advertising preferable during the year? How should the weight of advertising be distributed according to the communication objectives, such as to help promotion, to support a new product launch or to develop customer loyalty?

Using reach, efficiency and affinity data discussed above, media-planners may draw up several media plans where they examine performance by using

Formula-based evaluation models rely on mathematical formulae which take into account individuals' frequency of media use. The formulae are calculated from research data or more generally from sample groups and allow planners to obtain a good estimate of vehicle audiences

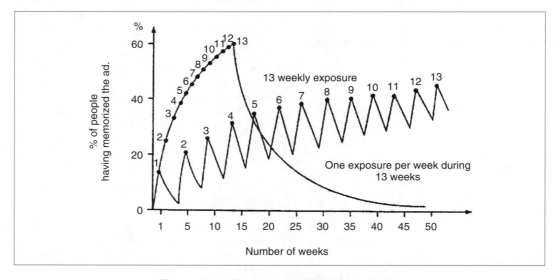

Figure 9.8 The memorization of advertising
Source: H.A. Zielske (1959).

and media-plan performance. Morgensztern's beta presentation[27] shown before gives an example of this.

Media-planners are increasingly using interactive models. Because simulation models do not contain a function of global efficiency, these models are sometimes combined with multi-criteria optimization models. But a very strong tendency to use less complex, less expensive models, allowing the planners to test multiple combinations of vehicles and to integrate quantitative elements into their choice, has been developed over the last few years due to the progress of computer technology. The quantitative media plan uses decision-support systems which integrate a variety of approaches (optimization, simulation, use of formulae).

Determining the advertising budget

Advertising budget determination is approached differently by different companies. Apart from internal costs to do with the advertiser's commercial structure, the creation, media plan and space-buying costs should also be taken into account. These three tasks can be taken on in-house by a single agency or can be shared. Agencies are usually remunerated through fees and commissions.

Central space-buying agencies totally dominate the market. Their stature is global and they are capable of selling advertising sites at a European level for international campaigns. They constitute an intermediary to be reckoned with for most agencies.

Certain important advertisers have reacted to this supremacy by creating subsidiaries in charge of media purchase and consultancy (for example Nestlé, L'Oréal or Peugeot-Citroen [PSA]).

The determination of the advertising budget frequently includes the entire communication budget of the company, integrating promotion, public relations, sponsorship and so on. We shall refer here to the advertising budget in the strict sense of advertising expenditure only, covering agency fees (creation, media-planning) and space buying.

Classic methods

There are three basic approaches. First, the allocation of the budget is made according to simple rules, generally routine, such as a percentage of sales or a percentage increase or decrease compared to the previous budget. Although these rules are open to argument, they are frequently used in certain professions. They are not based on calculations of sales elasticity with respect to advertising expenditures and can be problematic in certain cases because different products require different approaches. For example, a product about to be launched may require much more advertising than a product in a mature phase of its life cycle. Spending a fixed percentage of turnover for advertising purposes would make the launch of a new product impossible.

Some marketers determine their advertising budget with regard to competition. They try to allocate an advertising effort for their products equivalent to their competitors. This method is based either on the idea that maintaining the "share of voice" on the product helps in maintaining market share or on the principle that in order to survive on the market it is necessary to expend a certain amount on (e.g. as much as the market leader). Such methods are of limited value, however, because there is nothing to prove that there is a linear relationship between market share and the "share of voice" on a market, nor anything to prove that the volume of competitors' advertising is correct. This practice also ignores qualitative aspects, such as factors specific to the advertiser (reputation, differentiation, segments) or threshold effects.

A third way of determining the advertising budget takes into account the specific objectives of advertising in the marketing plan of the advertiser. It integrates the analysis of what budget can be afforded, the scale and growth rate of the total sales, the impact of competitor budgets, the sensitivity of consumers to advertising and so on in a complete marketing analysis. Intended positioning, market communication platform, designated target customers, the various types of cost (creation, media etc.) and the role of the other elements of the marketing mix are also taken in consideration. The problem with this rather holistic approach is its complexity which leads to a lack of precision. Sales reaction modelling, therefore, may be a useful component.

The contribution of modelling

Some authors[28] have put forward sales reaction models based on econometric methods which allow marketers to study the optimal impact of advertising or of several variables in combination, such as advertising, price and sales. Lilien[29] observes, however, that approaches to the modelling of marketing decisions which have been most successful have privileged the evaluation of alternative solutions with regard to optimization and have combined judgement and empirical data to allow for parameter setting of more realistic reaction functions.

It seems that, little by little, companies confronted with ever-increasing amounts of data and with more and more complex situations will integrate this type of decision-making aid depending on its progressively increasing accessibility to practitioners.

The control of advertising action

There are several forms of advertising action control:

■ Controls can be carried out by an agency before the campaign (pre-test) or during the campaign itself.

- Controls can also be carried out by the advertiser before the campaign to check compliance with marketing objectives or proposed budget. This is generally done at meetings with the agency. Such controls may also be executed during the campaign and after the campaign to observe its progress and to analyse its impact.
- Controls can come from external bodies such as sample group companies; independent bodies whose function is to verify the compliance of the advertising with legal regulations, or companies specialized in advertising research.

Sample group companies do advertising "freelance work", including gathering details of all insertions over a given period in the press, radio, television (surface, date, space, duration, price etc.), the advertising investments of global brand names by media and vehicles and others.

Independent institutions, such as the offices for advertising verification, comprising professionals (agencies, advertisers, media) and consumer representatives study the compliance of advertisements to the regulations (misleading, deceptive advertising) and produce recommendations, establishing a code of practice for the profession.

Before they appear, some advertisements are checked by the advertising professional bodies in order to verify their compliance to professional rules. Otherwise, the regulatory body may intervene after they appear, at the request of consumers, for example, to invite the advertiser to modify non-compliant messages or to prohibit the use of the advertisement. European directives create an increasingly important statutory framework to establish certain limits on advertising action.

Companies specialized in the practice of advertising research sell their results to advertisers.

Two types of control will be studied in this section:

1. advertising pre-tests, mainly practised by agencies, with the objective of testing the effectiveness of the creative treatment, before the campaign. It is interesting to note that there is at present a very strong tendency to shift the measures of advertising effectiveness from post-tests towards pre-tests because these can supply information before an investment is made in production and in space buying.
2. advertising post-tests, which are conducted to compare the results of the campaign with advertising objectives.

Pre-tests

The purpose of advertising pre-tests is to analyse the different elements of the message and its global impact, in reference to specific objectives assigned to the advertising communication such as the reputation of the brand name, the development of a physical or psychological characteristic or the image. Advertising pre-tests may be based on inquiry or on laboratory testing.

Techniques based on the inquiry

Inquiry techniques use an interview while people are exposed to the advertisement, or immediately afterwards. There are several forms such as the folder test, the review experiment, the split-run test, the supposed "preview" method and other forms of pre-tests.

- The folder test consists of establishing advertising registers within which different versions of the advertisement to be studied are inserted in a constant location, the rest of the registers remaining identical. These registers are subjected to samples of people who say what they have perceived, felt and understood. It thus concerns a practical form of test (the constitution of an advertising register is easy), but a little artificial because this document cannot be likened to a review.
- The experience review is a medium into which the message to be tested is inserted. A questionnaire is then administered about the impact of the message with different samples taken from the target population.
- The split-run test consists of inserting, into a back-up and with its agreement, several versions of the advertisement in the same issue distributed in different zones. Once the copies have been distributed, the impact of messages is measured either by the increase in reply coupons (if it concerns direct advertising) or by inquiries, or even at the sales level concerning consumers from different zones. The split-run test has been adapted to different media such as radio or television.
- The preview method consists of broadcasting the commercial to a public constituting a representative sample of the target audience before its commercial launch in order to test the perception and acceptance of the advertising communication.

Methods such as ADVISOR (Burke), AdVantage (GFK), Publi-Test (Research International), PRE-VISION (IPSOS), BUY TEST (TMO CONSULTING) each has their peculiarities:

- the existence or not of a sample of pre-recruited people questioned in order to verify their knowledge of the tested brand-name, their consumption or viewing habits;
- questioning a sample through a face-to-face study or by telephone, or self-completion questionnaire following exposure in an individual box;
- questioning after a real exposure situation or a laboratory exhibition;
- measurement during the exposure or after exposure to the message;
- measurement after one, two or several exposures;
- measurement of the impact of the communication alone or of this impact and the probability of purchase.

Each research company also retains its own diagnostic criteria. These are generally: the level of impact, allocation to the brand-name, the understanding of the transmitted message, approval, the image inferred in the brand-name and the product evaluated according to "image points" and persuasion (intent to purchase).

Obtained scores are compared with databases established by each research company, which allows for the estimation of the performances of the message tested against comparable messages (category of product or type of message).

Due to recent developments, brought about notably by sample group or research companies, it is possible to pre- or post-test the impact of the message on sales with distributors equipped with scanners. The sample groups can be subjected selectively (using cable television or broadcast television which are a substitute for the normally scheduled sample group's message: as in the case of Nielsen's Erim Test Sight system) to commercials concerning the same product. The impact on sales can then be analyzed by these same sample group companies using data gathered from stores in which they have scanning equipment installed. However, it is not only advertising which is tested in this case but also the other elements of the mix interfering in the choice of the consumer.

Laboratory techniques

The distinction between inquiry and laboratory techniques is less clear-cut today. As indicated above, the modern forms of pre-testing often contain commercials shown in a laboratory which then become the object of an investigation.

There are only a few techniques needing specific laboratory equipment. These are mentioned below but are little used today:

- The apparatus for measuring observations (AMO)(appareil de mesure de l'observation) consists of leafing through a review containing ads to be tested (type folder) while researchers using stop watches record time spent. The time spent in reading each ad and thus the value of the attention given to the message can be observed without the subject being aware.
- The "tachytoscope" consists of projecting a message on a screen at ever-decreasing speed (e.g. from 1/250th of second) and in studying what the subject has perceived at each projection. One can also analyse how perception is organized, in order to situate the important elements of the ad.
- The "diaphanometer" is based on the same principle but, instead of using speed, the message is blurred at first, then gradually becomes clearer.
- The eye camera consists of situating eye movement of subjects when an ad is watched or a commercial is projected. The course taken in the reading of the

message can thus be reconstructed, which allows for observation of the most eye-catching elements.
- Measures based on physiological reactions (heartbeat, electodermal resistance (EDR) are also used when considering the emotional reactions of individuals subjected to commercials.

All these measures are however used less than field research measures because they have numerous drawbacks such as set-up difficulties or difficulty in interpreting the results; for example, the measure of EDR can be an indicator of emotional intensity but it does not indicate their nature: surprise, pleasure, sadness, fear. It therefore needs to be supplemented with an interview.

Other forms of pre-testing

Other forms of pre-testing[30] exist, based, for example, on semiological or linguistic analysis. Among others, the indications of reading ease or interest for the message may be calculated. Analyses establish verb/noun relations, defining the dynamic character of the text and the principal word/additional word connections, which give the text a literary or advertising character.

Advertising post-tests

Advertising post-tests try to measure the effectiveness of the advertising campaign. This effectiveness depends on the following objectives, appropriate to the advertising communication: prompted and unprompted recall, message recognition, brand-name recognition, the attitude towards the message, the preference for the brand and the intention to purchase.

Methods of post-test have become increasingly numerous, with each organization tending to define its own forms of measurement. We mentioned in the previous paragraphs new possibilities offered by instruments such as the audiometer, or by connection with scanner data (within the framework of sample groups). We shall quote here some classic techniques: the Starch technique, the Gallup-Robinson technique, day-after recall and some more recent applications.

The Starch technique

The Starch technique comprises questioning the interviewees in order to find out which ads they saw when they read a publication. The publication is presented to the respondents and, page-by-page, the number of readers is determined who saw the ad, identified it as having been inserted by the advertiser and read it (reading at least half of the contents).

This technique is open to criticism because nothing guarantees that the interviewed person really saw the ad or that the person really saw it in that specific vehicle.

The Gallup-Robinson technique

In this technique, a sample of people is asked if they have located ads in a magazine which they have frequently read by subjecting them to a list of brand names. In this case, the magazine is not shown. Each person who says they have read the ad is then asked to describe it. Thus, one can obtain

- a raw memorization score (percentage of people saying they saw the ad),
- a proved memorization score (percentage of people who really read the ad).

The day-after recall

With television, the day-after recall uses questioning, in the 24 hours which follow the showing of a commercial, people who saw the advertising slot into which it was inserted. These people are then questioned in order to find out:

- the commercials seen by the interviewee without the person being previously informed (spontaneous recall),
- the commercials which the interviewees declare to have seen after having been previously informed (product-assisted level),
- the commercials which the interviewees declare to have seen after they have been informed of the brand-name (brand-name assisted level),
- the elements of the message which they remember.

These different techniques contain numerous variants and have been the object of new developments.

Recent post-test methods

Just as for the pre-tests, the major research companies, inspired by the above techniques, have developed their own post-test methods, known sometimes as "campaign balance sheets". Let us quote, for example, the barometer methods of IPSOS, Tri-Ad (Milward Brown) and the campaign balance sheet of Burke Marketing Research.

To test its commercials, the IPSOS company establishes a barometer display, a television-cinema follow-up, a press impact follow-up and a radio impact follow-up, by calculating various scores: recognition, allocation and approval, according to precise methodological rules relative to conditions of inquiry and treatment.

- In the case of display material, in order to establish a recognition score, the interviewee is presented with a folder into which are inserted photos of the posters, and the person is asked to say whether they saw each of the advertisements. The proportion of interviewees who saw the posters permits the calculation of a recognition score.
- Concerning the allocation score, the people who recognize a poster are asked to cite the name of the product, the brand-name or the organization which is

hidden (the proportion of correct answers is then calculated plus the rate of error: false or incorrect attributions).

- To establish an approval score, the interviewees are asked to state which posters they like.

This data, supplied for each campaign, is analyzed according to socio-demographic criteria and is then compared with standards held in a data base including

- standards for media data,
- standards for the amount of advertising investment,
- standards for socio-demographic characteristics.

Post-testing methods in advertising can be extended to other types of analysis examined elsewhere. The study of image, of sales location following a campaign, the analysis of the effects of advertising investments on the demand (modelling) are, in a wider sense, different types of measurement of advertising effectiveness. However, as soon as we extend the field of measurement in this way, we again find the classic problems concerning interaction of the different elements of the marketing-mix (what is the role played by advertising?), external effects (competitor actions, environment) or cumulative effects (effects of campaigns through time).

(i) Campaign balance sheets

Campaign balance sheets are produced during and\or after the campaign using representative samples of consumers' representative. They enable the following:

- to establish scores obtained by the campaign in terms of exposure, impact and memorization of the message;
- to determine relationships between the campaign and the improvement of scores obtained by the brand-name in terms of recall (spontaneous, aided, "top of mind" (brand-names quoted first), image, attraction, regularity and importance of purchase;
- to compare these scores with prior knowledge concerning campaigns carried out on similar product categories;
- to establish response functions between levels of exposure and an intended score for reputation or memorability;

(ii) Media-products research

The aim of media-products is to acquire a complete tool for the market analysis of convenience goods and audience qualification. Then customers can compare the results obtained from the complete set of marketing-mix variables: comparing between sample group data ("single source" concept: unique data source) and advertising audience data obtained from questionnaires on media penetration and audiometric results. Tables 9.9 and 9.10 show the principal

Table 9.9 SCQ = self completing questionnaire

	France		USA		Great Britain	Germany
Research name	Media marketing information system	Aude analyse unifiée des données	MRI (The survey of American consumers)	SMM (Simmons) study of media and markets	TGI (Target Group Index)	GVA (German Verbraucher Analyse)
Company	Secodip	Secodip/ Mediametrie	MRI	Simmons	BMRB (British Market Research Bureau)	Axel Springer Verlag AG + Verlagsgruppe Bauer....
Creation date	1980	1992	1979	1963	1968	1983
Field of the research	Adults (15 years and +)	Housewives	Adults (18 years and +)	Adults (18 years and +)	Adults (15 years and +)	Adults (14 years and +)
Sample size	11000	4560 (Secodip) 2000 (Mediamat)	20000	23000	25000	11,000 West Germany 4000 East Germany
Sample numbers continuous	4000 No	4200 Yes	9200 Yes	8000 Yes	18,000 Yes	4100 yes
Data collection method	SCQ by mail	Weekly buying SCQ	One-to-one personal interview media: SCQ Products	One-to-one personal interview media: SCQ products and TV	TV and SCQ products	One-to-one personal interview : SCQ products.
Gift	Gifts	Gifts	10 dollars	10 dollars	Gift voucher	Lottery
% Response	78.50	85	68	68	63	76
Number of questionnaires	5	1	1	1	3	1
Question...	4 or 5 hrs	30 min per week	4 hours	About 4 hours	5 hours	6 hours
Frequency of survey	2 years	Continuous	Annually	Annually	Continuous	2 years

Source: C. Fayot (1994). 'Media scann: Une avancée presse dans la recherche single source'. Décisions Marketing, 3, 3, 123–139.

Table 9.10 Methodology to measure TV advertising efficiency on TV

Company	Sample (Individuals)	Panel (Household)	Field of the research	Listening criteria
Germany				
Gfk Fernehforschung	12,000	5,200	3 years and +	to watch TV
Austria				
ORF Medienforschung	1,800	610	3 years and +	to be in the same room as the TV and to watch TV
Belgium				
CIM	1,750	630	6 years and +	to be in the same room as the TV and to be able to see the screen
CIM	1,500	600	6 years and +	to be in the same room as the TV and to be able to see the screen
Denmark				
Gallup	1,200	530	4 years and +	to be in the same room as the TV
Spain				
Sofres A.M	9,160	2,800	4 years and +	to be in the same room as the TV
Finland Finpanel Oy	1,200	475	3 years and +	to be in the same room as the TV and to be able to see the screen
Great Britain				
BARB, AGB TV, -RSMB	1,1700	4,701	4 years and +	to be in the same room as the TV
Greece AGB Hellas	2,100	700	6 years and +	to be in the same room as the TV
Ireland				
AGB Hellas	1,400	432	4 years and +	to be in the same room as the TV
Italy				
AGB Italia	7,000	2420	4 years and +	to be in the same room as the TV and watching TV
Norway				
MMI (Markeds-og Medianstututtet A/S)	1480	550	3 years and +	to be in the same room as the TV
Nederland's				
Informat	2,200	1,000	6 years and +	to be in the same room as the TV and watching TV
Portugal				
AGB Portugal	1,900	600	4 years and +	to be in the same room as the TV and watching TV
Ecotel Portugal	1,870	550	3 years and +	to be in the same room as the TV and watching TV
Sweden	1,400	1,650	3 years and +	to be in the same room as the TV and to be able to see the screen
Switzerland	4,000	1,650	3 years and +	to be in the same room as the TV and to be able to see the screen

Source: ESOMAR & CESP

media-product research systems available in four countries. New tools allow comparison of the data from an advertising campaign with purchase data obtained directly from the distribution system by means of a scanner. For example, Fagot[31] underlines "Mediacann's" original contribution which "combines quantitative scanned measurements of purchase, made by a sample group SECODIP in French homes in two market tests, with media consumption habits and various methodologies to measure the qualitative effects of the tested advertising".

SUMMARY

This chapter has demonstrated the role and objectives of advertising. Three essential tasks must be performed by advertisers:

1. to create the message consistent with the intended positioning of the object of advertising,
2. to reach the audience targeted by the message,
3. to control the efficiency and effectiveness of the advertising action.

The efficiency and effectiveness of the advertising communication depends essentially on its integration into the marketing-mix of the company and the professionalism of those who carry it out. It is up to those in charge of marketing for the advertiser to clearly establish the objectives of the communication, its main axes and the designated target audience, based on marketing research and the intended positioning. The role of advertising professionals is to create the advertising campaign and to establish a creative strategy and a media plan based on research and communication objectives furnished by the advertiser. However, this allocation of roles is not necessarily the ideal solution: in practice, it is often the case that those responsible for marketing within the company do not supply the advertising agency with a sufficiently clear and detailed base from which to work. In fact, they tend to let the agency be creative and develop a media plan without clear objectives or sufficient controls. In the same way, the use of advertising pre- and post-tests and, more generally, control over the results of advertising actions with regard to the objectives of communication sometimes lacks care.

Discussion questions

1. Gather a number of advertisements and file them according to copy strategy.
2. Gather a number of advertisements from a single business sector (e.g., shampoo, yogurt, perfume). Determine the main promises (axes of communication).
3. Consider a number of advertisements and commercials, and determine the visual and auditory codes that make them recognizable. Using these codes, test brand recognition on different individuals. What conclusions can you draw concerning the customer's purchasing process?
4. Choose a number of magazine titles and ask several persons to guess their target readership. What lessons can you draw for placing an advertisement in each of these magazines?
5. Build a media plan for a defined consumer target. For example, what media plan would you use for a brand of portable computers in order to communicate that a special deal is being offered to students?
6. Take five advertisements from a given business sector (e.g., toothpaste, perfume, yogurt). Photograph them and, using a video beamer, show such ad to a group of consumers, first completely out of focus, and then more and more in focus. Which features are recognized at each viewing level? What conclusions can you draw from this experience in terms of advertising efficiency?
7. Consult the Euro-Effie Awards on the EACA site. Pick five advertising campaigns and prepare a list of the success factors of an ad campaign.

Notes and References

1. S. Dibb, L. Simkin and R.Yuen, "Pan-European Advertising: Think Europe-Act Local", *International Journal of Advertising*, 13, 2, 1994, 1–11.
2. A. Dayan, *Marketing*, Paris, Presses Universitaires de France, 1986.
3. L. Festinger, *A Theory of Cognitive Dissonance*, Evanston, Illinois, Row Peterson, 1957.
4. F. Heider, *The Psychology of Interpersonal Relations*, New York, John Wiley and Sons, 1958.
5. W.J. McGuire, "Some Internal Psychological Factors Influencing Consumer Choice", *Journal of Consumer Research*, 2, 4, 1976, 302–319.
6. A.G. Greenwald, "Cognitive Learning, Cognitive Response to Persuasion and Attitude Change", A.G. Greenwald, T.C. Brock and T.M. Ostrom eds., *Psychological Foundations of Attitudes*, New York, Academic Press, 1968, 147–171.
7. D.A. Aaker, D.M. Stayman and R. Vezina, "Identifying Feelings Elicited By Advertising", *Psychology and Marketing*, 5, 1, 1988, 1–16.
8. R. Batra and M.B. Holbrook, "Developing a Typology of Affective Responses to Advertising", *Psychology and Marketing*, 7, 1, 1990, 11–25.
9. R.J. Lutz, "Affective and Cognitive Antecedents to Attitude toward the AD: A Conceptual Framework", *Psychological Processes and Advertising Effects: Theory, Research and Application*, L.F. Allwitt and A.A. Mitchell eds, Hillsdale: Laurence Erlbaum Associates, 1985, 45–63.
10. S.B. Mac Kenzie and R.J. Lutz, "An Empirical Examination of the Structural Antecedents of Aad in Advertising Pretesting Context", *Journal of Marketing*, 53, 2, 1989, 58–65.
11. R.E. Petty and J.T. Cacciopo, "The Elaboration Likelihood Model", *Advances in Experimental Social Psychology*, ed. L.Berkowitz, San Diego, California, Academic Press, 19, 1986, 123–205.
12. O. Corneille, "Une synthèse critique du modèle de probabilité d'élaboration", *L'Année Psychologique*, 1993, 4, 583–602.
13. S. Chaiken, "Heuristic Versus Systematic Information Processing and the Use of Source Versus Message Cues in Persuasion", *Journal of Personality and Social Psychology*, 45, 2, 1980, 241–256.
14. D.J. MacInnis and B.J. Jaworski, "Information Processing from Advertisements: Toward an Integrative Framework" *Journal of Marketing*, 53, 4, 1989, 1–23.
15. W. Kroeber-Riel, "Les perspectives d'avenir de la publicité", *Décisions Marketing*, 3, 1994, 15–22.
16. C. Pechmann and D.W. Stewart, "The Effects of Comparative Advertising on Attention, Memory and Purchase Intentions", *Journal of Consumer Research*, 17, 4, 1990, 180–188.
17. T. Levitt, "The Globalization of Markets", *Harvard Business Review*, 61, 2, 1983, 92–103.
18. N. Synonidos, C.F. Keown, L.W. Jacobs, "Transnational Advertising Practices: A Survey of Leading Brand Advertisers in Fifteen Countries", *Journal of Advertising Research*, 29, 2, 1989, 43–50.
19. R.D. Buzzell, "Can you Standardize Multinational Marketing?", *Harvard Business Review*, 46, 6, 1968, 102–113.
20. J. Killough, "Improved Payoffs from Transnational Advertising", *Harvard Business Review*, 56, 4, 1978, 102–114.
21. W.A. Kamakura, T.P. Novak, J.B. Steenkamp and T.M.M. Verhallen, "Identification de segments de valeurs pan-européens, par un modèle Logit sur les rangs avec regroupements successifs", *Recherche et Applications en Marketing*, 8, 4, 1993, 29–57.
22. M. Harvey, "Point of View: A Model to Determine Standardization of the Advertising Process in International Markets", *Journal of Advertising Research*, 33, 2, 1993, 57–64.
23. M. McLuhan (livre anglais à citer).
24. A. Morgenzstern, "Travaux et recherches sur la frequentation et l'efficacité publicitaire des media", *Université de Lille 1, Thèse de Doctorat és Sciences de Gestion*, 1984.
25. H.A. Zielske, "The Remembering and Forgetting of Advertising", *Journal of Marketing*, 23, 3, 1959, 239–243.
26. J.D.C. Little and L.M. Lodish, "A Media Planning Calculus", *Operations Research*, 17, 1, 1969, 1–34.
27. A. Morgenzstern, "Travaux et recherches sur la fréquentation et l'efficacité publicitaire des media", *Université de Lille 1, Thèse de Doctorat és Sciences de Gestion*, 1984.
28. K. Palda, "The Measurement of Cumulative Advertising Effects", Englewood Cliffs, Prentice Hall (1964) and R.P. Leone, "Modeling Sales Advertising Relationships: an Integrated Series-Econometric Approach", *Journal of Marketing Research*, 20, 3, 1983, 291–295.
29. G. Lilien, *Analysis of Marketing Decisions*, Paris, Economica, 1987.
30. B. Bertrand, "The Creation of Complicity: A Semiotic Analysis of an Advertising Campaign for Black and White Whisky", *International Journal of Research in Marketing*, 4, 4, 1988, 273–289.
31. C. Fagot, "Mediascann: une avancée presse dans la recherche single source", *Décisions Marketing*, 3, 3, 123–139.

Other forms of communication 10

Learning objectives

After studying this chapter you will be able to

1 Understand the usefulness and importance of communication methods other than advertising and sales promotion

2 Analyse the objectives and the particular role of several methods of communication: patronage, sponsorship, public relations, internal communication and lobbying,

3 Present certain specific techniques used in each of these methods of communication,

4 Measure the effectiveness of these techniques,

5 Explain the role of and the issues at stake in internal marketing,

6 Understand the essential principles involved in adopting these techniques,

7 Analyse the phenomenon of rumour and how to handle it.

SPOTLIGHT

Milka, the milk chocolate subsidiary of Kraft Jacobs Suchard wanted to link its brand Milka with family values as well as with nature. Milka first sponsored the world ski cup but was unable to use its sponsorship role in France. Therefore it decided to sponsor a new concept of ski runs for family fun and education. Ten ski resorts in the French Alps were selected. In these ski resorts, Milka used mauve signposts – the colour of the brand packaging – to brand all of the family fun and education ski runs. Sponsorship is used to communicate to the consumer the attributes that a company desires to associate with the brand.

The French retail association to which most of the major retailers belong has created a club called "lifestyles",

where members of parliament are invited for breakfasts, during which topics of general interest are discussed. Large retailers in France suffer from a poor image among members of parliament, who tend to support small shopkeepers. However, these breakfasts are opportunities for major retailers to show that they are interested in sociological trends and not only in money. During these breakfasts, which create a favourable atmosphere, they are able to communicate positive messages about their businesses because they are not asking for something, but are information providers. The French Retail Association is lobbying in this way to convince members of parliament.

Introduction

Advertising and sales promotion still represent the majority of company spending on communications. However, these two components of the mix are not the only available means of communication. The developments in the environment and in markets have necessitated the introduction and development of new methods of communication which can be combined in forms already analysed and in direct marketing, which we will study in Chapter 16. This chapter concerns patronage and sponsorship, which have been the subject of recent research, public relations, lobbying and internal communication. The forms of communication appropriate to direct marketing, such as the post, the telephone and the use of the Internet, will be addressed in the chapter on direct marketing (Chapter 16). Finally, this chapter will finish with an analysis of the phenomenon of word-of-mouth, which can profoundly affect a company's market results.

When a company is trying to achieve positioning, those in charge of communication define a communication platform which contains the major objectives and priorities, the main message to be disseminated, the targets to be reached and the principal means of communication to be used. Based on this, various forms of communication are used together, according to which specific targets have to be reached (stakeholders) and specific objectives are to be attained.

Public relations

Public relations concerns the set of complex activities aimed at creating a general spirit of cooperation within a group of stakeholders, and to establish understanding and reciprocal confidence within the company itself and between the company and its stakeholders.

The mission of public relations is to conceive and to offer to companies that need these services the means to establish and maintain good relations with the public and to inform them about matters or any questions relevant to their activities.

This mission can also, within companies, extend to personnel. The PR (Public Relations) adviser implements methods recommended by such a process and controls the results. The information which PR supplies must, of course, explain where it comes from, be objective, and limit itself to stating facts without using propaganda or commercial advertising.

This definition reveals clearly certain differences between PR and other company communication techniques, notably advertising or promotion:

- Public relations is not addressed solely to customers or prospective buyers to attempt to develop their loyalty or to persuade them to buy, but also to the stakeholders and to the section of the public concerned with the activities and functions of the company, by considering them as partners susceptible to influencing the market adversely or favourably.
- The nature of PR intervention is different from that of advertising communication. It is more a question of creating a social link, in the sense of aiming to integrate the values of the company into social life and to share these ideas with public opinion and a particular group of people. Thus, in China, PR are more effective than advertising when introducing totally new concepts because word of mouth plays an important role in the distribution of innovations.[1] Concerning credit cards, even before mentioning brands, the objective of PR is to explain the usefulness of a credit card; it is the same for breakfast cereals in a country where cereals and milk are not considered as breakfast ingredients![2]

The objectives of public relations

The objectives of PR can be very varied and concern several different types of public:

- to publicize a company action,
- to have this action understood and accepted,
- to create favourable reactions,
- to obtain the support of the target groups.

According to the International Public Relations Association, the effects of PR can be measured at three levels:

1. understanding
2. sympathy
3. support, which marks the real success of the action.

The targeted public can be within the company (staff, union representatives) or external (customers, prospective buyers, suppliers and subcontractors, public authorities, shareholders and banks, distributors, purveyors of opinion, influencers, press, etc.). For each one of these, clear goals must be established. Table 10.1 illustrates some of these goals.

This table is, of course, not exhaustive, but it demonstrates the wide range of audiences and the objectives of PR. This range requires a large variety of means adapted to each situation.

Table 10.1   Objectives of public relations

Targets	Objectives
Personnel	■ Obtain their support ■ Create favourable rumour ■ Obtain their fidelity
Clients and prospective clients	■ Increase reputation ■ Improve the image, inform ■ Explain the company's action ■ Create positive rumour ■ Consult and show them the company's interest in their opinion and claims ■ Obtain their participation in a particular action (e.g., patronage) ■ Show the company's focus on the consumer
Distributors	■ Obtain references ■ Obtain predominance ■ Have a company's action understood and accepted (e.g., modification of a product) ■ Have the distributor participate in a commercial or non-commercial company action
Suppliers	■ Obtain their cooperation ■ Ensure the security of supplies, obtain the shortest deadlines ■ Establish and confirm a partnership
Public authorities	■ Obtain aid, facilities and permits ■ React to rulings, etc.
Shareholders	■ Obtain their support for company policy ■ Obtain their financial participation (capital increase) ■ Explain a decision (buyout, public purchase offer) ■ Remove hostility to a takeover bid
Banks	■ Obtain their support ■ Increase debt and fund facilities
Press and media	■ Obtain editorial space to make the company's action known ■ Create a favourable impression of the company at editorial level
General public	■ Explain the role of the company ■ Create favourable sentiment ■ Obtain their participation
Prescribers opinion leaders	■ Obtain favourable rumour ■ Have them participate in company actions

Approaches and methods of public relations

We can classify PR action into two groups:

1. reactive actions, aimed at responding to external influences, challenges, changes in consumer attitudes, government actions, competitors' actions and so on;
2. proactive actions, intended to anticipate external influences. For example, Cogema, one of whose jobs is to reprocess nuclear waste, has set up an active PR policy to inform the public, through organizing visits to the reprocessing sites, participating in conferences on the subject and being present at environment conservation demonstrations.

There is no well-defined list of PR techniques. In this domain, the creativity of those in charge of PR and specialized agencies is applied to each situation. In the same way, PR actions sometimes overlap with other types of actions, such as sponsorship or lobbying. It seems pointless to enter into an academic discussion concerning the exact limit of the PR domain with regard to these other forms of action. The main thing is that all the actions conducted by the company become integrated into a structured approach and follow a clear strategy of communication leading to the attainment of the desired positioning. This approach can be summarized in the following way (Figure 10.1).

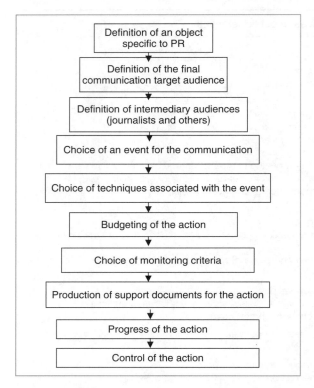

Figure 10.1 Set-up of a public relations action

Source: Adapted from J-M. Decaudin, *La communication marketing, concepts, techniques, stratégies*, Paris, Economica, 1995.

This synthesis of a PR approach gives a prominent position to three characteristics:

1. Integration: the PR of a company are connected to its communication strategy. This is an approach which becomes integrated at all levels of the company, and can concern multiple forms of action (production, social, financial, commercial and so on). Public relations can participate in the marketing action of the company and its value-creation processes. In this way, they become one of the elements of the communication strategy. In this case, they become integrated into the marketing-mix of the company and have to fit in with the other mix elements: coherence with the other marketing actions, coherence with the company's potential and its environment, coherence in time and the desired positioning.
2. Adaptation: we cannot define standard methods of PR applicable in every case. Two fundamental requirements of PR are opposed to this idea:

   ■ PR have to be renewed continuously in order to hold the interest of the targeted public

(stakeholders): the novelty effect is very important to arouse attention. It is essential therefore to find creative approaches to PR. For example, in order to launch the BMW 750, BMW offered some prospective buyers the opportunity of being met at the airport and being brought by helicopter to the test circuit. This offer was sent to the prospective buyers in a luxurious leather folder.

   ■ PR must be particularly adapted to the objectives of the company and to the targeted public. Each technique must be applied in a specific way according to the public and the circumstances. This effort at adaptation generally leads to a departure from ready-made solutions. For example, Bec, a French company specializing in public works, organized an evening at the Montpellier Opera House, where a celebrated opera singer was performing. The performance was followed by cocktails where the company members met designated targets (important clients, suppliers, members of public bodies, etc.) in a totally different framework.

3. Continuity: the set of company PR actions should contribute to the promotion and attainment of the general objectives of the company or the brand. Coherence in time and respect for the most fundamental elements of the company's positioning are choice criteria in PR operations. Each operation should contribute to the understanding of target groups about company positioning and the essential values of the company. Major sporting events, such as the world tennis tournament circuit, all host "company villages", where companies sponsoring the tournament each year invite a targeted public to attend matches and dine. This is a common blending of sponsorship operations and public relations.

Public relations techniques

Having defined these principles, the PR specialist will then appeal to a multitude of methods. The following list cites but a few:

■ information such as company newspapers, newsflashes, video bulletins, neon bulletin boards, dossiers and training periods for reception, external newspapers, telephone information or letters;
■ communication of the organizational image such as brochures, flyers, video and films of the company;
  – organized activities such as conventions, seminars, congresses, competitions, debates, open days, company visits;
  – participation in committees and work groups;
  – press relations, press conferences;

TOOLBOX 10.1

EXAMPLES OF PUBLIC RELATIONS TECHNIQUES BY TARGET AUDIENCE

Target audience	Technique
Internal	Visitors' book Company diary/press book
Public authorities	Seminars and conferences Cocktail parties and receptions Open house events Cooperation in norm-setting institutions
Socio-economic groups	Seminars and conferences Cocktail parties and receptions Open house operations
Financial analysts, shareholders and financial circles	Road show, annual report/press releases Press book Seminars and cocktail parties
Suppliers	Company diary Open house operations Technical seminars/cocktail parties
Competitors	Company diary Technical seminars Factual cocktail parties
Distributors	Company diary Open house operations Technical seminars/factual cocktail parties Press book/technical data sheets
Buyers and consumers	Company visits, chat rooms, community events Presentation of products Creation of website
Non-buyers and non-consumers	Company visits Presentation of products Creation of website Company diary Open house operations
Media and press agencies	Technical seminars/factual cocktail parties Press releases Press book/technical data sheets Annual report

Note: The fact that similar techniques can be used on several target audiences does not signify that the same action will be put into operation with regard to these targets. On the contrary, it is absolutely necessary to create specific actions for each established target audience.

- creation of events, demonstrations;
- company gifts, donations;
- support of other actions such as sponsorship, patronage, participation in fairs and exhibitions.

Toolbox 10.1 shows the relationship between some common PR techniques and the targets to be reached.

The control of public relations operations

The scale of the sums of money at stake and the objectives assigned to PR have led companies to measure the consequences of PR operations increasingly rigorously and objectively. Although not all the effects of a PR strategy can be easily measured, a certain number of indicators which partially estimate the effects of PR can be established. Naturally, these differ according to the type of operation, but it is possible to present some illustrative examples:

- opinion polls before and after the operation: difference in reputation, attitude and behaviour,
- research into image,
- editorial space obtained,
- analysis of the editorial content,
- number of enquiries, visitors, prospective buyers,
- audience achieved,
- obtaining a decision (from public authorities, for example).

In conclusion, we can say that all major companies such as IBM, Microsoft, Bayer, Hoechst and Philips use public relations. These are particularly appropriate when it is a question of influencing the people or the groups of people allowing the company to attain its objectives from the perspective of global marketing, taking into consideration all of the company's publics: customers, suppliers, shareholders, bankers and financial partners, public authorities, local government, administration, associations and so on.

Patronage and sponsorship

Sponsorship and patronage used to be considered as two different techniques in marketing communication because they concern different domains of intervention and have different goals and objectives.

An artificial distinction

Marketing literature has often distinguished sponsorship from patronage but this distinction is more or less artificial; in the medium term, their objectives are identical and consist of establishing and consolidating the company's desired positioning with respect to the targeted public.

Patronage and sponsorship are each associated with a specific domain: art, culture, social causes (cancer etc.) with patronage, and sport with sponsorship.

Sponsorship is financial support which a company (a financier) brings to a cultural or sporting activity, in return for an increase in reputation or profit based on the idea of its image. Patronage is the financial aid granted to a literary or artistic work.

Patronage and sponsorship are associated with different ends. Patronage allows for development in literature, science and the arts without recourse to any immediate advertising profit and often with a social purpose. It is like a specific form of public relations whose object should seem to appear unselfish and culturally and socially useful. On the other hand, sponsorship aims at direct

profitability due to the advertising and media feedback from the supported activity.

Finally, the objectives pursued by sponsorship and patronage do not seem to be convergent because, even if sponsorship pursues commercial objectives often linked to the brand or to the product, it is not the same for patronage, which is preoccupied rather with the institutional or company image from the perspective of society. This traditional concept has been recently reappraised.

The allocation of specific domains to each of the techniques – sport for sponsorship, and the arts, culture and social causes for patronage – becomes blurred and we see considerable overlap between these two means of communication. Today, they are considered part of an approach which considers communication by means of the event as a purpose in itself, where the choice of sector and support for the event are only one means among many to attain particular objectives. In the case of patronage, the company communicates through the partner with whom it is associated in the event, while in the case of sponsorship, it takes advantage of the event to communicate through its association with the event itself.

The generic name "sponsorship" has thus been restricted to defining a technique of communication which associates an organization, a brand or a product with a socio-culturally independent event, a sport, a group of people, an individual, an organisation or an audiovisual broadcast with the aim of attaining the objectives of marketing communication.[3]

According to this new approach, the distinction between sponsorship and patronage should no longer exist. The generic term "sponsorship" should include the development of the promotional actions whose themes are connected to sporting, cultural, humanitarian events with which the organization is actively associated. According to this new conception, promotion through action fits in as a part of the communication strategy of the company, consistent with the other constituents of the marketing-mix and concerning the intended targets, the plans to be implemented, the budgetary means, distribution of actions in time and the control of results.

Three reasons can be given for the advent of this new conception:

1. the need for the company manager to justify spending in the form of sponsorship with regard to the social objective of the company;
2. the duration of specific actions in this form of communication, which generally demands an adapted structure and organization;
3. The necessity of making the event known, which requires effort and sometimes a particular mode of communication.

The sponsorship approach

Sponsorship depends on finding an event which has testimony or proof value: it is a question therefore of "proving", by means of the event, that the product or the company possesses such and such a quality. This proof can be direct (Bridgestone and Michelin demonstrate the quality of their tyres in Formula 1 racing; Nike, Adidas, Reebok and Asics in domains such as football, athletics and tennis) or indirect (Coca-Cola for the soccer World Cup in 1998, the French oil magnate Elf sponsoring a yacht – when it is possible to create a relationship between the wind which powers Elf Aquitaine (the yacht), Elf petrol and the oil industry, aligning all forms of energy through this concept, the communications strategy of this company suddenly makes more sense than before). Individuals are less convinced when they see this relationship as an advertisement on the printed page. In this, it differs from traditional communication which generally makes reference to a dream or to fiction. The objective of this form of communication is to create an association between the event and the company, the product or the brand by stressing a transfer mechanism of attribute or affect (the favourable or unfavourable characteristics of the attributes) between the sponsored entity and the company or the product or the brand:[4] for example, Ronald McDonald and the foundation of the same name for deprived children.

However, the transfer cannot happen if interest in the event[5] and emotions are high. Using European Cup football matches as an example, Walliser[6] has shown that the most involved and emotional television audiences did not remember sponsors' names as easily as those who were less involved. The latter paid less attention to the match and, as a consequence, were more receptive to sponsors' message boards in the stadium.

It also offers the advantage of the consumer being affected by this communication in non-commercial situations: the result is a reduction in perceptual barriers in the case of an event which benefits from particular attention on the part of the consumer. We may also note that it allows for the bypassing of certain (statutory) obstacles to communication (for example, a ban on advertising).

The share of event advertising as a share of the total company communications budget in 1997 would have been 15 per cent in Italy (of which 66 per cent was for sponsorship), 6 per cent in Germany (60 per cent for sponsorship), 6 per cent in Great Britain (85 per cent for sponsorship), 5 per cent in France (75 per cent for sponsorship) and 3 per cent in Spain (80 per cent for sponsorship).[7]

The strategy of sponsorship

Any strategy of sponsorship has to be in accord with other strategies followed by the company. For example, the European strategy of LVMH, the world leader in luxury goods, is to sponsor painting exhibitions but also competitions in art schools throughout Europe.

The development of a strategy requires the definition of objectives, the choice of targets, the choice of a message, budget setting and the insertion of sponsorship in the communications mix.

Objectives

These can be commercial objectives (support of marketing strategies) or sales objectives. Certainly, the consequences can only be quantified with difficulty, notably in the short term except for some actions such as the sponsorship by Philips of the Euro 96 Football Championship, which immediately resulted in additional sales of television sets. However, according to a survey carried out by Credoc,[8] over half the consumers would be influenced by the humanitarian commitment of the manufacturer.

Sponsorship is also a means for internal staff motivation, particularly for large companies. During Euro 96, Philips organized a competition among its staff with trips to London as the prize. Numerous sponsors take advantage of important sporting events to invite their customers, to allow them to establish better relationships with the sales force or simply to reward the sales representatives during important tennis or golf tournaments, motor racing events, cycle races and football matches. As such, the associated patronage (the company completes the staff donations) or, again, the voluntary help of the employees strengthens staff cohesion and obtains a positive effect as much in the sales network as in the "internal network" (the employees of the company).

The external networks of influence or decision (political or administrative networks) are also affected by this type of action in a PR objective.

The most frequently sought objectives are undoubtedly communications objectives such as reputation, memorization, information or image. In this case, it is important to choose an activity appropriate to the profile or the expectations of the company's public (employees, general public) and to the positioning of the product and the brand. The quest for an image or reputation on the company's or the group's part is naturally the prime objective of sponsorship of the institutional type (patrimony, culture, humanitarian and social causes), whereas the improvement of the image of a product or a brand is the prerogative of sponsorship in the fields of sport, exploits or adventure. The reputation of brands and products is also a particularly sought-after objective. Through its sponsorship of football, Eurocard Mastercard was able to increase its reputation by 10 per cent. Take note, however, that sponsorship is risky when the sponsor's reputation is lower than 30 per cent.[9]

Company objectives such as to deal with urgent issues in the environment are also one of the aims of sponsorship: for example, affiliation activities (transfer of part of the selling price to the benefit of a charity; for example, the watchmakers Pion undertook to give back more than 7 euros per watch to the "red ribbon" model bought from an Association which fights against AIDS) or monetary donations. They correspond to the objectives which are more or less strongly associated with the previous objectives.[10])

If the choice of a sponsorship activity depends on objectives pursued, it also depends on characteristics appropriate to the company. It can be inspired by its logo or by its sector of activity. The computer manufacturer Bull, which chose a tree as the distinguishing feature of its logo, committed itself to environmental protection. France Telecom, whose major role is to ensure voice telephone transmission, sponsors Opera Festivals and gives support to autistic people and their families. Pharmaceutical laboratories often act in the field of health.

The identification of targets

Sponsorship allows for all types of targeting – a large sector of the public as a whole with the most popular sporting or cultural events, a mainly feminine segment with gymnastics, particular targets in some European countries with rugby, or people in a high-income group with golf.

It also allows for aiming at several targets at the same time. The existence of two types of audience (indirect and direct) increases its effectiveness. The direct audience comprises people in direct contact with the sponsored event (spectators and actors), whereas the indirect audience includes the people who follow the sponsored event in the media (television audiences, listeners, readers).

The message

The sponsorship message is based on the transfer of an attribute which is achieved between the sponsored event and its sponsor. It allows the sponsor to strengthen or improve its positioning or give it more value by adding new attributes (e.g., youth and dynamism concerning Camel with the Camel Trophy). A number of sports marketing agencies have particularly studied the values attached to each sport and to each sports star to ensure the best conformance to the values the sponsor wishes to emphasize.

The budget

The sponsor can help, financially, or again, in kind or in the form of services offered, in the form of ideas or intellectual support, or with supporting personnel. The more important the sponsorship company the higher the chance that the assistance it offers will be of various kinds. The scale of the budget is often linked to the range of interventions by the sponsor. Major brands such as Coca-Cola, Pepsi-Cola, Sony, Nike, Philip Morris, Budweiser, HSBC, and so on will be present at numerous events and occasions and dedicate substantial parts of their communications budget to sponsorship. We should note that, for certain brands of tobacco or alcohol where communication is the subject of restrictive legislation, promotion by event sponsorship is generally an excellent way of gaining indirect access to the media and reaching consumer targets.

The communication mix

To obtain maximum effectiveness, the sponsorship action must be supported and highlighted with all available methods of communication:

- advertising concerning the event, which comprises the presentation of the sponsorship action in different backup media such as the press, television and radio, through the intermediary of editorials, reports, poster campaigns and press announcements;
- public relations, such as invitations to the event for suppliers, shareholders, journalists or important customers which serve to highlight the sponsorship operation;
- co-ordination with promotional operations, such as on-the-spot activities in the form of product demonstrations, sample distribution, discount vouchers, and so on or again, activities at the point of sale with the presence of a sporting personality signing autographs, or exhibitions;
- co-ordination with internal operations, for example support between sellers or colleagues.

Measuring the effectiveness of sponsorship

The measurement of the effects of sponsorship does not generally have the same rigour as that of the other more classic forms of marketing action, such as advertising or promotion. Research work on the subject is still rare.[11] Several factors complicate the measure of the effects of sponsorship, such as the simultaneous presence of other marketing actions or the difficulty in measuring certain qualitative objectives which are sometimes very indirect and\or are fulfilled in the long term.

Measures of audience and impact in the media can be used.[12] The number of people present where the event is taking place or the number of people affected by the consequences of the event in the media are indicators of the audience, which we can qualify as a direct audience in the case of the first indicator and as an indirect audience for the second. The impact of the event can also be analysed by its audiovisual consequences (length of the TV or radio broadcast): frequency of appearance, quotation of the sponsor or patron, press spin-offs (press files); measures of reputation, image or even attitudes can be employed. But it is often delicate to isolate the event's share in figures obtained according to each of these indicators, and certain psychological effects such as lack of interest, and indirect and long-term effects do not appear clearly if these are the only criteria taken into account.

Finally, a number of survey companies have procedures to check the effects of sponsorship. For example, sampling group companies analyse televised sponsorship in the following ways: presence of a sponsor in a programme's opening or closing credits, presence of a sponsor in a pre-programme, presence of a sponsor in the form of a gift in a game. The following forms can be exploited in their analysis: concert announcements, pre-programmes, credits, integration (into the programme), games, competitions, prizes and inlays.

Available information concerns the duration of the sponsorship, the number of on-screen

appearances, the form of sponsorship, the on-screen "hourly time signal", the broadcast of supplements to the appearances.

In conclusion, it is clear that event-based communication has to be as logically planned as the other more conventional forms of communication. Sponsorship must be connected with the positioning of the brand and with all the elements of the marketing-mix, and in particular with the other forms of communication and the sales network. It must be organized by someone in charge of a specialist service integrated into the communication service of the company. In smaller companies, it can be set up with the aid of outside specialists or taken in hand by the directors themselves. Its targets, the audience, its objectives and its nature must be clarified to set the strategy (Toolbox 10.2).

Whatever the type of event agreed, a communication effort appealing to the conventional media, promotion, public relations or direct marketing is necessary. Finally, it is important to control the effects of sponsorship so as to compare them with pursued objectives.

TOOLBOX 10.2

THE TEN COMMANDMENTS OF SPONSORSHIP DEFINED BY YOUNG AND RUBICAM

1. Include patronage in the global communications policy: the virile image transmitted by the Marlboro' cowboy is compensated for by Formula 1 motor racing, which is situated in a more modern and global context.
2. Maximally exploit supported events being mindful of direct spectators but also people affected by the media, distributors, reps and personnel as a whole.
3. Share out investments usefully: in fact, one should be prepared for the eventuality where 1€ given to the sponsored entity provokes a promise of 1€ for the information that will be given concerning the event (public relations, special offers, advertising and possibly media so that they cover the event).
4. Fully understand the aimed-at targets.
5. Avoid staking everything on the result of an event, because this is of necessity hypothetical, but rather associate the image with that of the supported activity or the chosen person.
6. Maintain choices over several years because patronage acts through induction, thus apparently more slowly than an affirmative or informative advertising slogan (Elf got into sailing in 1979).
7. Always try to be specific on the chosen market (the "Paul Ricard" was sold when the increase in the number of races and French winners whetted the appetite of the public for sailing).
8. Acquire competencies concerning on the one hand, the sponsored activity and, on the other hand, the setting up of related sponsoring and communication actions.
9. Be distrustful of an increase in company awareness without increasing knowledge of its products.
10. Manage interest (do the images circulated by the chosen activity further the desired image of our brand?) and efficiency (freelancing concerning the obtained editorials, the importance of direct and indirect spectators, the evolution of reputation, image and sales following the event etc.) in the envisaged action.

Source: Adapted from a document of Young & Rubicam France in Association Française du Marketing, *Les Nouvelles du marketing*, 1990.

Lobbying or pressure group

Lobbying is the creation or use of a "lobby", that is, a pressure group. It is a word which sometimes has a pejorative connotation, because it is often associated with cronyism and bribes. The lobbyist's activity has, however, become a recognized profession which refrains from using illegal means to perform its designated tasks. Lobbying consists of privileging a particular interest such as company, association, trades union or corporation by influencing, in an indirect or open fashion, the decisions of public authorities.

The opening of economies, notably with the development of the important European market, and, more widely, the increasing importance of different types of rules in company strategy have persuaded many institutions, collectively or alone, to call on "lobbyists" to explain and to defend their economic interests with the authorities. These professional lobbyists are linked closely to administrations, such as governments, parliaments, the European Commission, ministers and advise companies on methods to be used and act in their own right to offer or adjust certain measures in the desired direction.

Lobbying differs from public relations in the sense that its approach consists of acting on a given organization to which it is close (where it "has influence") and where it knows the decision mechanisms in order to obtain or modify certain decisions controlled by this organization. Furthermore, the lobbyist exercises pressure openly. Temple cites the following example concerning the EEC:

The EEC develops economic, legal and financial rules on a large scale, but slowly. Keeping up with the techno-legal situation allows for the knowledge and estimation, in time, of the existence and contents of these measures. The "lobby" or its "lobbyist" can then use various means to bend the measure in his favour such as the secretariat of European Union technical committees (there are 273 in existence), participation in confederations or European groupings (mail order selling, farm-produce, confectionery, textiles and clothing, trade industries etc.), and the presence of outlets appropriate to Brussels. It is sometimes necessary to go as far as provoking the defeat of a bill or, more difficult still, to get a bill passed which is not on the Commission's programme. The action is sometimes more modest but equally effective, for example, in modifying just one word in a sentence to change the whole meaning. So, in the directive of July 25, 1985 on industrial responsibility, the French version fixed a franchise for the insurance mechanism, the English text spoke about threshold, which led to very important financial differences".[13]

In Washington, more than 20,000 lobbyists exercise this profession officially and in Brussels, there are more than 3000 lobbyists. Lobbying is undergoing major development in Europe. Lobbyist action is increasingly used by companies or professions, and is becoming integrated into the strategy of large companies for the markets with which they have interests. Thus, lobbying constitutes one of the company's communication methods for very precise targets which can influence the rules about how the market functions, that is, the commercial approach of the company (Figures 10.2 and 10.3).

Internal marketing and communication

Arndt[14] distinguishes three major functions of internal marketing: to inform, to develop competence and to motivate. According to Berry,[15] the objective of internal marketing is to respect and implement promises made to the clientele. It comprises giving competence, ability, tools and motivation to personnel. The internal customers should believe in the service before being able to serve the external customer.

Internal marketing and internal communication

The aim of internal communication is to cause all the internal energies of the company to converge towards its economic and commercial objectives. Internal communication is one of the constituents or one of the approaches to internal marketing, which is a wider concept: in numerous cases, internal marketing is considered as a marketing approach inside the company to make company members more convinced about projects, ideas and values which the management wishes to advance. Internal marketing would therefore be entrusted with a task consisting of directing staff activity towards favouring the development of the company.

Internal communication is an important part of internal marketing. It illustrates the function of internal marketing. For example, companies resort to internal marketing so that the employees become part of the commercial strategy of the company. The Ikea chain of furniture stores has developed a strong policy of internal communication and personnel management, based on the atmosphere and the internal environment and including management of the leadership, development and personnel promotion in order to favour the support of the employees for the desired positioning.

Objectives and means of internal communication

Most large organizations have internal communication services.

The role of these services is essentially

- to make the staff aware of what is at stake in the company,
- to build a team spirit, to strengthen cohesion,
- to establish an aura of confidence.

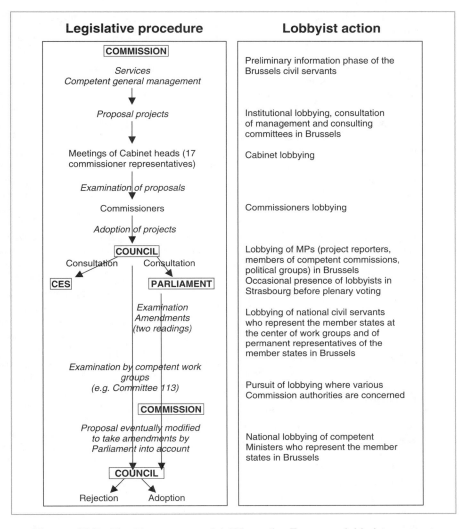

Figure 10.2 The European model: Where the European lobbyists can act
Source: B. Julien, "Eurolobbyism", *Gestion 2000*, 5, 143–155, 1990.

To know how the political system and the world of business function
To have the gift of languages and the sense of public relations
To understand the importance of a company's image and to strive to improve it
To know how to communicate
To know how to intervene at different levels (e.g., when should the Company Director be put in contact with the Minister)
To have the qualities of a diplomat
To have an important and useful address book
To be well connected (the most important point: the lobbyist does not buy or sell influence).

Figure 10.3 Profile of a good lobbyist
Source: Based on the article by J. Van Heuversuyn and J-P. Schwybroeck, "Le lobbying, une ancienne profession redécouverte", *Gestion 2000*, 5, 131–141, 1990.

More precisely, six objectives of internal communication can be distinguished:[16]

1. the managerial constituent, where internal communication appears as a management tool aimed at favouring the flow of information and making the personnel more dynamic,
2. the commercial constituent, which aims at "selling" and promoting the company both internally and externally,
3. the cultural constituent, which aims at integrating the employee into the company's culture,
4. the humanist constituent, which concerns the development and consideration of the employee,
5. political constituent – from this perspective, internal communication serves to prevent conflict and becomes an element of social strategy,
6. institutional constituent – the company being considered as a social institution, the individual having "the right to receive information concerning the lifestyle of this institution so that he can participate fully in it".

This profusion of objectives leads certain authors to question the real usefulness of this type of communication: "communication and image aim at totalitarianism in the diagnosis and change of organizations: the bulimia of tools slips here and there towards an empty sophistication of the techniques of internal communication (see cost-profit relation of transparencies, videos or internal meetings), or usury of techniques themselves (what becomes of internal radios, company newspapers or other media happenings?)".[17] As a result, internal communication can develop only in reference to overall company policies of which it is a consequence and not the inspirer.

Among the most commonly used means of communication, we can note

- induction booklets for new members,
- audio-visual company films,
- internal company billposting,
- newspapers, newsletters,
- meetings with the management, conferences, internal presentation and discussion sessions,
- training, development and motivation seminars
- direct contacts (from the management) "in situ".

In the same way, the participation of members of the company in quality circles, progress groups and company supplies also offers an occasion for internal communications.

Thus, the means are numerous and differentiated and a large number of them correspond to the objectives of people management.

Internal marketing and organization

Internal marketing appears also as a solution when authority is questioned within organizations. Influencing methods and imported marketing models have replaced top–down autocratic approaches. Internal marketing offers a valid alternative to a relation of failing or non-existent authority: when the power of coercion cannot be exercised, other types of relations must be used which resort to methods of persuasion.

The communication dimension of internal marketing functions therefore as a subtle system of rhetoric of which the admitted and explicit issues are to inculcate the values of the company and to standardize perceptions. Information is thus one of the modes for exercising power.

Internal marketing is also concerned with the organization as a system for creating and generating value where the actors render services along the lines of exchange partners (e.g., clients–suppliers), attempting to replace collective relations by inter-individual exchanges. Such a vision, which views the company as a trading area putting internal customers in contact with each other, transforms the company into a mosaic of bilateral encounters within a network of complex exchanges and poses the problem of the definition and limits of the organization (Figure 10.4).[18] It substitutes imaginary market logic denying the existence of power struggles for the awareness of rules and behaviour which legitimize, "against the market",[19] the existence of organizations! In effect, internal marketing cannot ignore power struggles which depend on resources which are more or less rare and which govern complex exchange systems.

Rumour

Rumour is one of the oldest means of communication. However, it is distinguished from the other means and media in that it is not easily mastered, it is difficult to monitor, it constitutes at one and the same time the package and its contents. It is therefore questionable to classify rumour as one of the available methods of communication available to the company in the same way as those referred to elsewhere in this chapter. In the United States, in the 1940s, "whispering campaigns" seemed to become the indispensable weapon for market conquest: they consisted of propagating rumours favourable to a product or service by people mixing with the general public in a trade show, an exhibition and so on. In this sense, rumour can be considered as a medium capable of being the object of an active step in company politics.

Certain authors underline the difficulty and danger of such a medium because of its uncontrollable character. For example, as Degon[20] asserts,

Internal marketing – form 1
- Devices: information and training in communication aids
- Transmitter: strategic summit
- Receiver: members of the organization
- Objectives: influence (persuading, getting people to join, modifying behaviour)
  integration (sharing of values)
- Context: change
- Relation to power: ambivalent

     – loss of legitimacy and re-legitimizing of the hierarchy
     – relations of influence and not of coercion
     – normalizing of representations

Internal marketing – form 2
- Devices: internal client–supplier contracts (at an entity level)
- Objectives: co-construction of internal services, sense of responsibility being given to the actors
- Context: change, decentralization of decisions
- Relation to power: ambivalent

     – theoretical inversion of the pyramid
     – lesser power of the strategic summit and the techno-structure
     – legitimacy, often increasing, of the direct hierarchy but a change in the nature of its authority from now on founded on the organizational qualities of the workgroup
     – monitoring effected by the internal client

Note: In Internal Marketing, Form 1, the company management does not take "masses" of employees into account, but rather, the sum total of individuals: internal press releases are addressed to people by name, sometimes at their homes (they do not, therefore, have the absolute status of employees). It takes place, however, through internal surveys: it is the aggregate of the opinion of individuals which is dealt with.

In Internal Marketing, Form 2, by means of contractual relations at an entity level, it is exchanges between individuals which are sought, to stop anonymity and the attenuation of responsibility, that is, in fact, to compensate for certain pernicious effects of bureaucratic organization.

Figure 10.4 The two forms of internal marketing

rumour can be the best or the worst of things. As regards its usage, it is not controllable at the quantitative level, because it would require the creation of 'opinion leaders' whose purpose would be to propagate rumour within numerous situations, a fact that remains utopian or unreliable. So the creation of rumour is not always an integral part of a communication company's performance and so much the better we would say.

We can distinguish, therefore, four elements in the constitution of positive rumour:

- The definition of an intangible message, simple and founded on real elements.
- The use of human vectors: rumour feeds on contact between individuals.
- The creation of signs: a certain number of events with symbolic value can facilitate the development of rumour.
- The use of "Evangelists": to create rumour is to have people talk about you.[21]

- Definitions of rumour have developed[22] (Table 10.2). The complexity of rumour, which renders its usage delicate if not dangerous, has been analysed by J.N. Kapferer.[23] He shows that companies also have a problem of getting rid of unwanted rumour. He also specifically cites the example of American companies suspected of having, since 1978, a large part of their capital in the hands of a very powerful sect. He shows how rumour feeds on signs, is propagated by "experts": a specialist, a holder of the keys to the reading of signs indecipherable to common people; the expert is a classic source of rumour. Authorized to make assessments, forecasts and predictions, he has an echo chamber at his disposal: people who consider him as an expert and journalists whose job is to know. Brodin and Roux[24] show clearly, through numerous examples, the important effects of rumour on markets. Noting that "when faced with this problem, companies are relatively ill-equipped and often use 'intuitive strategies' such as apathy and denial", these authors offer a certain number of strategies more adapted to preventing or responding to rumour.

Table 10.2 Evolution of the definition of rumour

Three definitions of rumour	Three periods of research concerning rumour
"Proposal linked to daily events, intended to be blunt, transmitted from individual to individual, usually rumour, without concrete data allowing for its exactitude"	The Second World War with research on war rumour: rumour concerning Pearl Harbour, for example
"Group phenomenon which gives individuals of the social body a means to alternative response which allows them to adapt to periods of change and to environmental turbulence"	The sixties with the social analysis of rumour.
" 'A legend in our times' label is a practical compromise. 'Legends in our times' represent an attempt to use traditional themes in a post-industrial context, in which 'belated capitalism' and 'sexual liberty' can be seen as conflictual vis-à-vis the rules of morality. These legends, using 'do it yourself' techniques, borrow traditional themes and replace them with a current context"	The eighties with daily rumour: for example, the rumours of tarantulas on yuccas

Source: O. Brodin (1995).

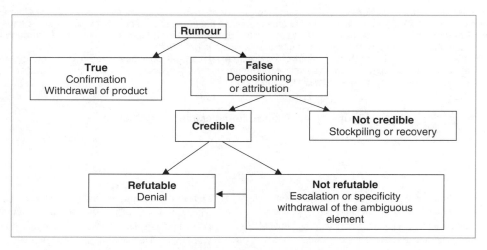

Figure 10.5 Types of rumour and choice of response
Source: O. Brodin (1995).

Figure 10.5 illustrates the choice of possible strategies:

- to carry out a "debriefing", which consists of completely dismantling the hidden sense and the basic essentials of the rumour,
- to confirm the rumour when it is well founded and, for example, to act on resolving the problem.
- to temporarily or definitively remove the product,
- to unseat the rumour through devaluing it,
- to supply new information which will "cover" the rumour by substituting itself for the negative thoughts which the rumour conveys, rendering salient the previous positive thoughts associated with the brand,
- to deny negative rumour: this denial can be more or less complete and should avoid repeating the allegation; Brodin[25] establishes the conditions in Table 10.3,
- to amplify or to establish transparency when faced with irrefutable negative rumour: the exaggeration of rumour can contribute to its disappearance by reducing its credibility; the element of ambiguity can also be removed.

Table 10.3 Set-up conditions for the denial of rumour

	Set-up conditions
Content	■ non-repetition of the rumour
	■ denial followed by refutation, show rather than declare: visual denial, tests (product test), distribution of positive information countering the rumour without specifically citing it, confident style, company engaged in the denial
	■ allocation of the distribution to a non-loyal motive
	■ avoidance of any ambiguity that might reinforce the rumour (ambiguity of reactions according to mood, for example)
	■ endeavouring to respond to the second level of the rumour (associated with debriefing)
Source	■ credible: expert, confident, pleasant and above all, independent
Distribution	■ rapid
	■ low profile, thus limited to a precise group (in this case, information to opinion leaders)
	■ otherwise wide and intense: repetition in time, combination of means (mailing, conferences, telephone lines)
	■ to all concerned target audiences: consumers, distributors and personnel in contact with the customers.

Source: O. Brodin (1995).

SUMMARY

This chapter has presented methods of communication other than advertising, sales promotion and direct marketing.

Public relations are a form of communication which fits in well with a perspective of global marketing, addressed to all "stakeholders" in the company: customers, suppliers, administrations and public authorities, financial partners, shareholders and the general public. Public relations actions have very varied forms and demand high professionalism in the definition of their objectives, the carrying out of actions themselves and the measure of their effectiveness. This usually justifies the creation of a public relations service in important companies.

This chapter has also shown the importance and role of methods of patronage and sponsorship. These two methods come together in the form of event-based promotion. This type of promotion pursues specific objectives and demands rigorous implementation where principles have been established. This type of action also calls for measures of effectiveness. Several types of measure have been presented.

The creation of pressure groups or lobbying holds an increasingly important position in the policy of companies. They may do this themselves or through their professional associations. With the development of regulation at all levels – local, national, European and world – it is important that companies make their point of view felt where regulatory authorities are concerned. The complexity of these authorities requires that real specialists, forming an integral part of the institutions, keep the companies informed of current decisions and try to influence them. Lobbying has become a method of influence much used by major corporations or professions. A lot of lobbying is directed at European Union institutions.

Internal communication also plays an important role in all types of company. It is often confused with the concept and the techniques of internal marketing. This chapter has presented links between these two concepts and has attempted to clarify the different conceptions of internal marketing. It has shown internal values and marketing's limits and has explained the principal techniques of internal communication used through posing the delicate problem of measuring their effectiveness.

Finally, rumour has a specific role in marketing communication. Rumour occurs one way or another: what is important is to acknowledge that it exists and, in particular, the possible answers for a company confronted with negative rumour. The mechanism of rumour has been analysed and several response techniques have been presented.

Discussion questions

1. Take a company and list all the in-house communication media used. What are their roles? Which targets does each communication medium try to reach?
2. Log on to websites of major corporations and compare the messages presented by their senior management. Whom do these messages address (customers, shareholders, etc.)? Which stakeholders is the company trying to reach?
3. What is the role of lobbyists? How do they operate? Taking the consumer advocacy viewpoint, discuss how stakeholders (companies, consumers, etc.) exert pressure on the authorities over a given product (such as a toy, cigaretes, or cell phones).
4. How do rumours circulate? What strategies are used to dispel them? Give one or more examples.
5. Choose a television programme such as an entertainment show or sporting event and list the sponsors' communications (stadium advertising, advertising on team shirts, winners' prizes, etc.). What are their targets or aims?
6. Look at your organization (company, university, administration, etc.) and list all corporate sponsorship or patronage activities in which it is involved e.g., sponsored teaching aids for schools. Explain the meaning of this type of communication and the value it represents for companies.

Notes and references

1. A. Delcayre, "En Chine, les RP sont un passage obligé", *Stratégies*, 954, 38–39, 1996.
2. H. Muhlbacher, H. Leihs, L. Dahringer, International Marketing – A Global Perspective, 3rd edition, Thomson Learning: London, 2006.
3. C. Derbaix, P. Gérard and T. Lardinoit, 'Essai de conceptualisation d'une activité éminemment pratique: le parrainage', *Recherche et Applications en Marketing*, 9, 2, 43–68, 1994.
4. S. Ganassali and L. Didellon, 'Le transfert comme principe central de parrainage', *Recherche et Applications en Marketing*, 11, 1, 37–50, 1996.
5. G. d'Ydewalle, P. Van den Abeele, J. Van Reusbergen and P. Coucke, "Incidental Processing of Advertising while Watching Soccer Games Broadcasts", in *Practical Aspects of Memory: Current Research and Issues*, edited by M. Gruneberg, P. Morris, R. Sykes, Wiley, 478–483, 1988.
6. B. Walliser, 'Le rôle de l'intensité des émotions éprouvées par le téléspectateur dans la mémorisation du parrainage', *Recherche et Applications en Marketing*, 11, 1, 5–22, 1996.
7. *Stratégies*, no. 1001, 28 February 1997.
8. J.M. Normand, 'Les français privilégient les produits qui respectent le mieux l'environnement', *Le Monde*, 10 janvier, 15, 1995.
9. Document interne, Young et Rubicam, journée AFM (Association Française du Marketing), 1990.
10. F. Anne and E.J. Cheron, 'Mesure de l'Efficacité du Sponsorship: une Analyse des Effets Intermédiaires sur l'Audience Directe de l'Événement', *Actes du Congrès de l'Association Française du Marketing*, 6, 121–148, 1990.
11. See T. Okker, P. Hayes, 'Évaluation de l'efficacité du sponsorship. Expériences de la Coupe du Monde de Football '86', *Revue Française du Marketing*, 118, 3, 3–40, 1988; C. Armstrong, 'Sports Sponsorship: A Case Study Approach to Measuring its Effectiveness', European Research, 16, 2, 97–103, 1988; J.L. Giannelloni, 'Contribution à l'étude du mode d'influence de la communication par l'événement', *Thèse de Doctorat és Sciences de Gestion*, Université de Lille, 1990.
12. L. Didellon, ' Mode d'évaluation et mesure d'efficacité du parrainage: une application au domaine sportif, université Pierre Mendès-France, grenoble, 1997.
13. H. Temple, 'Le Lobbying: Quand l'entreprise influence le pouvoir', Fascicule, Association pour le Développement d'une Économie de Marché, 1990.
14. J. Arndt, 'The Political Economy Paradigm: Foundation for Theory Building in Marketing', *Journal of Marketing*, 47, 4, 44–54, 1983.
15. L. Berry, 'Relationships Marketing of Services. Growing Interest', *Journal of the Academy of Marketing Science*, 23, 4, 236–245, 1995.
16. P. Détrie, 'Communication Interne: Où en sont les entreprises françaises?', *Revue Française du Marketing*, 120, 5, 77–83, 1988.
17. M. Thévenet, 'La communication interne "au-delà de la falaise" ou la recherche d'une problématique', *Revue Française du Marketing*, 120, 5, 51–59, 1988.
18. A. Seignour and P.L. Dubois, 'Marketing interne et pouvoir, Colloque 'Pouvoir et Gestion', *Collection Histoire*, Gestion, Organisation, Toulouse, Presses de l'Université, 5, 357–377, 1996.
19. O. Favereau, 'Marché Interne – Marché Externe', in 'l'Économie des Conventions', *Revue Économique*, 2, 2, 273–328, 1989.
20. R. Degon, 'La rumeur, une chance pour l'entreprise', *Revue Française du Marketing*, 113, 3, 69–71, 1987.
21. J. Doyen, 'La rumeur, menace ou outil de communication?', *Revue Française du* Marketing, 113, 3, 79–82, 1987.

22. O. Brodin and E. Roux, 'Les recherches suir les rumeurs: courants, méthodes, enjeux managériaux', *Recherche et Applications en Marketing*, 5, 4, 45–70, 1990.

23. J.N. Kapferer, 'Rumeurs, le plus vieux métier du monde', Paris, Éditions du Seuil, 1987.

24. O. Brodin and E. Roux, "Les recherches suir les rumeurs: courants, méthodes, enjeux managériaux'', *Recherche et Applications en Marketing*, 5, 4, 45–70, 1990.

25. O. Brodin, 'Le contrôle des rumeurs', *Décisions Marketing*, 4, 1, 15–27, 1995.

11 Value negotiation and personal selling process

Learning objectives

After studying this chapter you will be able to

1 Understand how culture influences behaviour at the negotiating table
2 Understand factors influencing negotiation outcomes
3 Prepare for negotiation
4 Manage the negotiation process
5 Recognize different types of personal selling
6 Describe the stages in the personal selling process
7 Gain insight into sales management decisions such as setting objectives, determining the size of the sales force, creating sales territories and route scheduling
8 Understand how companies recruit, select, train, motivate, compensate and evaluate salespeople

SPOTLIGHT

The French subsidiary of the giant company Hexal, a German pharmaceutical company specializing in generic pharmaceutical products, employs 25 salespeople. Each salesperson is able to visit each of their pharmacist customers every two months. To add more value to its customers and therefore to increase their loyalty, the company created its own Internet site in 1999. Its goal was to provide help to pharmacists. The site provided notes on each drug and class of drugs, a summary of the news of the day, offered sales of used equipment free of charge, plus free expert consulting on pharmacology, law and accounting. Since 2000, the site has enabled pharmacists to order from a catalogue of 58 patent medicines. Thanks to the Internet site, between the two visits of its salesperson, each pharmacist can now stock up with drugs instead of waiting the two months or purchasing from a competitor.

This chapter will focus both on the selling and the negotiation processes because they are intertwined. Personal selling is a process of informing and persuading potential customers to purchase products

through personal communication. Salespeople exchange value with customers. Therefore, their role requires them to match their offer to what customers are willing to pay in order to satisfy their needs. Personal selling is part of an organization's overall marketing communications. It follows that personal selling does not stand alone, but must be complementary to and coherent with advertising, sales promotion and public relations policies.

Being often the only personal contact a customer has with the company, the salesperson is also an important means of communicating the benefits of the company's products. In return, salespeople collect for the company valuable information about customers, competition and other aspects of market information. However, their task is not only to communicate value to the customers. Salespeople may create an added value over and above the basic product. Because of their liking for a salesperson, customers may be ready to pay more in a given store or to a supplier than they would pay in an exchange with another supplier.

Personal selling is executed by salespeople. Salespeople do many things. They can be simple order takers whose role is to record customer orders after an advertising campaign or a visit of a representative. However, salespeople may also be

- sellers whose role is to convince current or potential customers,
- sales engineers who have a specific competence in the field of goods they sell, combining technical and commercial knowledge,
- negotiators or business engineers combining intensive technical training in commercial, financial and psychological fields.
- medical visitors or delegates who present pharmaceutical products to physicians, or,
- sales managers supervising the activity of their salespeople

This diversity is accompanied by different types of legal status, depending on whether the salespeople are part of the company's staff or are agents for the company. External salespeople are paid by commission. They may be agents who are intermediaries acting in the name of and on behalf of the company.

The various activities of salespeople have been affected by tremendous changes in the international, competitive and technological environments. The general trend towards global business has emphasized the importance of salespeople who are experienced in international customer contact for all kinds of business organizations. As the cost of running a sales force has risen, non-specialist sales staff have become less useful. We have seen the rise of the key account manager, who is in charge of customers of vital importance to the company.

Technological changes have also had substantial effects on sales force activity. The general spread of the telephone gave birth to sales by phone and the need for telesales operators. The development of information technology (combining a computer, a telephone and a TV screen), and later of the Internet, has made it possible to consult different catalogues or directories without leaving home, to discuss online and at the home of potential buyers. This development resulted in less need for door-to-door sales. It has changed the nature of the selling job. For example, in the business-to-retailer selling job of Paris-based L'Oreal (luxury goods), electronic data interchange (EDI) and Internet use allow order taking to be automated. Therefore, the job of salespeople changes from order takers for an appointed retailer to merchandisers and managers of the sales force for this retailer. The use of an interactive CD or interactive terminals makes it possible to visualize and personalize the offer for the customer. Portable PCs allow salespeople to consult a prospects database, use price optimization programs, check their company's production capacity, planning and stocks, and sign and send contracts to their headquarters quickly. Salespeople may use these tools so as to convince potential customers of the benefits of their products and services, but they must also be trained in using those tools. This training should focus on the use of new technologies as well as on everything else that enables salespeople to improve the personalization of their offer such as financial arrangements or product adaptations.

Changing customer thinking accentuates this trend. The increased desire for leisure and better quality of life makes people seek simplicity when buying things. We now move on to discuss negotiation. Subsequently we explain basic elements of sales force management.

Negotiation

Negotiation is as old as the market economy. Marco Polo practised it. Although there are other definitions, it can be characterized by

- a perceived divergence of interest between two or more than two parties this means that a demand presented by one or several of the parties does not correspond to the proposition formulated by the other party or parties;
- no fixed or established set of rules or procedures can make it possible to solve this conflict;
- the parties create their own solution; and
- the preference of both parties to reach an agreement using discussion rather than to openly fight, to oblige one side to capitulate, to break off contact or to seek the arbitration of a higher authority.

As a preliminary step, negotiation supposes that the two parties have come into contact following an approach by the purchaser (e.g., by an invitation to tender) or of the salesperson (e.g., communicating via a phone call or mailing a list of current customers).

Negotiation takes place in a large variety of situations and therefore can be more or less intense. Using intensity as a distinguishing criterion, some people suggest that there are types of selling that need little or no negotiation. Purchase negotiations in the industrial sector are rather intensive compared to, say, transactions between a retailer and his or her customer or a bank employee and his/her customer. However, this attempt to distinguish the industrial sector from the mass consumer goods and services sectors is not as clear-cut as it may appear. Indeed, business talks between a banker and a company concerning a loan or quite simply between two individuals concerning the sale and the purchase of a used car may involve very real negotiations. The way in which commercial conditions are set seems to be a better means

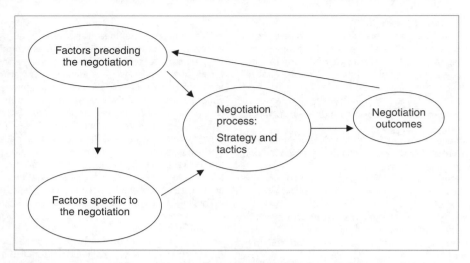

Figure 11.1   Key factors of influence on the negotiation process and its outcome

of distinguishing selling from negotiation. In selling, the commercial conditions of the exchange are predominantly fixed by the salesperson. In negotiation, they are discussed between the parties.

The outcomes of negotiation generally depend on factors which precede the negotiation, in particular the conditions of the negotiation and the process of negotiation itself (Figure 11.1). These influences will be analysed and discussed in turn. Subsequently, recommendations concerning preparation for negotiation will be presented.

Factors preceding a negotiation

The cultural background and characteristics of negotiators and the specificities of the organizations involved in the negotiation all form the environment of every negotiation. They are independent of the kind of negotiation undertaken.

Culture

Culture influences patterns of behaviour and perception as well as the values of negotiators. It acts in multiple ways on the negotiation. It affects equally the antecedents of negotiation (character traits of the negotiators) and the conditions in which the negotiation or the process of negotiation is carried out. Thus, culture influences the length of negotiation and strategies of negotiation used. Hall shows that negotiations are shorter in low-context cultures than in high-context cultures. Low-context cultures are characterized by the importance of the verbal character of a message (e.g., the proposed text of a contract). They are largely found in Northern Europe and the United States. High-context cultures attach less importance to the verbal character of a message but emphasize the importance of the communication context and thus of the negotiation. They occur in Latin America, Asian and Middle-East countries (see International Spotlight).

INTERNATIONAL SPOTLIGHT

The cultural background of a salesperson has a widespread influence on the negotiation process and behaviour. The following table contrasts Japan and China with North American and Latin American culture on selected negotiation characteristics

	Japan, China	North America	Latin America
Lawyers	Less important	Very important	Less important
A person's word	Is his or her bond	Is not to be relied upon; get it in writing	Is his or her bond
Space	People breathe on each other	People carry a bubble of private space with them and resent intrusions	People breathe on each other
Time	Polychronic – everything in life must be dealt with in terms of its own time Negotiations are lengthy A major purpose is to allow parties to get to know each other	Monochronic – time is money. Linear, one thing at a time Negotiations proceed quickly	Polychronic – everything in life must be dealt with in terms of its own time Negotiations are lengthy A major purpose is to allow parties to get to know each other
Power structure	Group decision	Group preparation of the decision, decisions are taken by decision makers	Decisions are taken by individuals
Social behaviour	Saving face is an absolute necessity. Some decisions are taken only to avoid somebody being embarrassed	Decisions are taken on the basis of cost/advantages. Saving face is secondary.	Saving face is very important. It is a matter of personal honour and dignity.
Emotions	Are valuable but should be hidden	Are not valued	Are valued very much. Negotiation may become passionate
Persuasion	Not very demonstrative, Rather quiet when thinking to be right, Respectful, patient, Modesty and circumspection are valued	Always demonstrative (even if not a true feeling), not personally involved Stay pragmatic	Emotional Flare up easily Like passionate discussions

Culture also influences the personality of the negotiators. It creates different perceptions of power and different negotiation strategies. For example, people from the United States tend to have more cooperative strategies and the Chinese of Taiwan more competitive strategies; and in Japan and South Korea purchasers have more power than salespeople and thus benefit more than salespeople from negotiation.

Organizational characteristics

Some organizational characteristics influencing negotiations are independent of the type of negotiation carried out. Others depend on the object and the situation of the negotiation. Organizational characteristics influence the result of a negotiation. Such characteristics are as follows:

■ The buying centre, that is, the group of people likely to take part in all or part of the buying process. Buying-centre members may participate actively in the

negotiation process or may intervene indirectly through their preferences (demanding a certain delivery schedule, product specification, credit terms, etc.).

■ The type of purchase carried out. For example, repeated purchase without modification will make it possible for the buyer to exert a strong influence on the final decision.

■ The role assigned to the negotiator by the organization. Role conflicts and role ambiguity lead to poor performance by the negotiator because he or she will suffer more mental anxiety or job-related tension, will be less satisfied with his or her job and therefore will be less motivated to work. Role conflicts arise when the salesperson believes that the demands of role partners are incompatible and he or she cannot possibly satisfy them all at the same time; for example, when a customer demands a delivery schedule or credit terms that the salesperson believes will be unacceptable to the production or accounting department. Role ambiguity occurs when the salesperson feels he or she does not have the information necessary to perform his or her job adequately. He or she may be, for example, uncertain about how his or her performance will be evaluated and rewarded.

■ The strategy followed by the organization and the risk it bears. For example, the sale of a product intended to be used as the central part of the production process (for example, a custom-made machine tool) generates co-operative negotiation strategies from the buyer because it generates a high risk for the company should it fail or cause production to fall below specifications.

Character traits of negotiators

The personality of the negotiators influences negotiation outcomes. Certain individual qualities appear to be especially relevant for negotiation. Indeed, a successful negotiator must have good listening ability, an interpersonal orientation (empathy) and strong self-esteem. However, the importance of personality traits for negotiation purposes varies according to negotiation strategies. Other-directedness, for example, is not appropriate for distributive strategies because other-directed negotiators are interested in and react to variations in the other's behaviour, relying upon the other to be co-operative. Such a negotiator when facing a competitive or exploitative opponent will retaliate against him, resulting in the failure of the negotiation. Other individual characteristics, not directly related to personality, may also influence the result of the negotiation – the negotiator's charm or attractiveness, his intelligence and verbal capacity, his competences based on his level of education and past experience. For example, a novice negotiator may not understand how to deal with a very demanding customer.

Some individual factors are likely to be influenced by the nature and the situation of negotiation. They are cognitive and motivational factors. Individualistic motivation means striving for a maximization of individual profit with no concern for the other party. Co-operative motivation may be defined as the search for maximization of the joint outcome. Negotiators with competitive motivations want to do better than their opponents. Individualistic, co-operative and competitive motivations will influence the strategies used in the negotiation and thus their outcome too.

Motivations interact with parties' similarities and differences in objectives. They will influence the length and the outcome of a negotiation. If one takes the example of the contract signed by Airbus with Pan Am in September 1985, it is interesting to note that it took approximately one and a half years between the first contact and the signature of the contract. This length of time was needed to solve differences between objectives. Pan Am wanted to exchange its Tristar planes for Airbus

planes. Airbus wanted only to sell its planes without taking back any Tristar planes. The final contract proved to be a long way away from both starting positions since it focused on renting Airbus planes, purchasing some for a period and holding purchasing options on some others.

Motivations are also influenced by the situation in which the negotiation takes place. Consider the example of the sale of war planes to Saudi Arabia by Great Britain in 1985: a conjunction of political factors (the simultaneous negotiations between France and Israel for the construction of a nuclear power station and a refusal to rebuild the Iraqi nuclear reactor at Tamouz with Saudi Arabian funds) and economic factors (the decrease in French imports of Saudi Arabian oil: totalling 50 per cent of French imports in 1981, and only 45 per cent in 1985) partly explain what motivated the Saudi negotiators to prefer the English "Tornado" plane to the French "Mirages 2000".

The same phenomenon occurs with cognitive factors, that is, factors affecting a person's judgement. They concern information processing, the way in which information is assessed and combined in the mind of the negotiator. For example, the weight given to some pieces of information compared to others can contribute to the formation of a positive or negative judgement towards the object of the negotiation (framing effect). If buyers tend to outperform sellers in a bargaining task where neither party has an inherent advantage, this phenomenon may be interpreted as a framing effect. Buyers view negotiations in terms of losing resources (loss) or giving up something whereas sellers view negotiations in terms of gaining resources (gain). This suggests that buyers are risk seekers and sellers risk-adverse. The more risk-seeking the negotiator is, the higher the demand will be for a negotiated settlement. Buyers will be claiming and obtaining more than the seller. This example highlights the fact that the situation facing the negotiator and in particular information cues will be strongly influenced by cognitive factors.

Conditions specific to the negotiation

Some conditions specific to a negotiation such as the goals of the negotiation and the existing power relations cannot be affected by the negotiators. Other conditions such as the number of parties and participants, audiences, time, location and physical arrangements of the negotiation may be manipulated during the negotiation.

Goals and issues at stake

A negotiation can be analysed according to the goals of the negotiators and the issues which are the object of bargaining. The goal is the idea of what negotiators would like the outcome to be (e.g., to buy/sell a car). However, to obtain this outcome, several issues are at stake. Price is a major issue but there are others also. Industrial contract negotiations may revolve around

■ specifications for the product, the process used, the performance of the product and the control mechanisms;
■ prices, formulae for price revision, discounts, premiums and penalties;
■ terms of payment;
■ delivery time and delivery schedule.

In contracts, issues are turned into clauses. The number of issues and their type affect the individual preferences of the negotiators and the strategies of negotiation used. Thus the greater the number of issues, the higher the probability of co-operative behaviour. Similarly, the greater the stake for each negotiator or the time perspective of the negotiation (long-term relations) the more the negotiator will tend to co-operate with the other party because every party stands to lose a lot should negotiations fail, and because future negotiations will allow potential retaliation if there has been aggressive negotiation behaviour.

Objectives assigned by the company to negotiators influence negotiation outcomes. For example, ambitious objectives assigned to negotiators increase their results only when the negotiators have equal or greater power than their opponents (see below). In circumstances of unequal power, setting objectives is not useful. Negotiators divert their attention from their objectives in an effort to defend themselves.

Power relations

There are various sources of power in a negotiation:

■ Coercive power can be obtained by the seller because of the uniqueness of the product in the market or because of the market structure. If the product is unique or if there is only one company likely to provide the benefit (monopoly), salespeople retain more power than purchasers. Such power inequality may have other origins.
■ Legitimate power exists when one party considers it legitimate to obey the other party. Such a power can be observed in Japan, where buyers are viewed as superior to salespeople.
■ Power can also be acquired by expertise. This is the reason why one party may invite an expert to participate in the negotiation process in order to gain influence in the negotiation.
■ Finally, the power of respect is derived from the personal relationship created with the other party. It is based on the desire to be close to or friendly with the other party, the attraction of the other party to the power holder, liking, perceived similarity or admiration. In France, the more the negotiators

perceive each other as similar, the more co-operative they will be during negotiations. US professionals on the other hand do not show this tendency.

A mixture of these types of power is likely to influence behaviour and outcomes in negotiations.

Time limit

In planning a negotiation, negotiators pay a great deal of attention to time. The closer the deadline (date or time limit) the more the negotiators tend to make concessions. So it is desirable for negotiators to be in less of a hurry than the other party. By increasing the time pressure on the other party, better terms of sale or delivery may be obtained. Moreover, when negotiators have invested a great deal of time and effort in a negotiation, they are reluctant to sacrifice the investment and to leave empty-handed.

Time has different meanings in different cultures. Japanese negotiators have a big advantage over US negotiators because they are less interested in quick action and immediate results and are more interested in long-term results. Furthermore they also need more time because they rely much more on understanding, support and consensus from the head office.

Number of participants

The number of participants in a negotiation varies. The smallest number is in an interaction between a salesperson and a buyer. Sometimes the negotiation takes place between groups of people, formed because of task complexity, the importance of the stakes or tradition. In China there is a custom of negotiating with rather big delegations, where the real decision maker may not speak up until the very end. This may seem peculiar to Western negotiators. Individuals belonging to negotiation groups can take part directly in the negotiation or may only be observers. Media, unions and political groups, for example, constitute audiences (see below) for negotiations on nuclear waste in Western Europe.

The number of participants affects negotiation outcomes as it increases the complexity of the negotiation process. Moreover, the number of participants creates social pressure. For this reason, it is desirable in a negotiation to obtain at least parity with the number of people in the other group.

Number of parties

The number of parties involved in the negotiation also influences the negotiation process. In some industrial settings, banks and governments are involved along with the negotiating companies. It is the same for mergers. If one takes the example of the merger between Swissair and Sabena at the end of 1994, it was not only Sabena and

Swissair who participated in negotiating the contract, Air France, the former partner of Sabena (who wished to be disengaged), the Belgian government and the European Commission also took part in the talks. The intervention of governments may prove particularly important in international contracts. For example, in 2001, sales of Airbus planes to several Chinese companies had to receive the approval of the Chinese government.

Audiences

All parties who observe the negotiation, or are informed about it or are affected by outcomes are called audiences. These may be, for example, trade unions, media, the community or the general public which follow the negotiation. These audiences are also groups of people who delegate negotiating power and authority to the negotiators. Negotiators are influenced by the behaviour of these audiences. For example, in 2001, when Swissair had decided to sell its French subsidiary, Air Liberté, the unions and Swissair disagreed about the buyer. Facing unions' strike threats and in exchange for the unions' withdrawal from a lawsuit, Swissair had to accede to the unions' choice.

Place of negotiation

The place of negotiation must also be considered. The party negotiating 'at home' has an advantage. Negotiating at home provides the negotiator with a certain privilege associated with greater familiarity with the location as well as a higher status because of the displacement of the other. For this reason, negotiators in general prefer, whenever it is possible, to choose neutral places located away from the home base of the parties. In addition, when the distances to be covered are large, the negotiators who travel are at a disadvantage because they may suffer from tiredness.

Negotiation setting

The negotiation setting is the physical arrangement in which negotiations take place and it is the environment through which status is communicated. More precisely, in preparing for the negotiation, the parties may decide on how the seats are laid out, what distance there is between the participants, and what decoration and furniture are selected. The setting affects the negotiation process. For example, seating arrangements side by side suggest friendship and co-operation. Parties who are competitively oriented tend to prefer to sit facing each other. In addition, the setting may change from one culture to another. For example, in Japan seats are laid out in such a way that the main negotiators do not have to face each other during the negotiation.

Negotiation process

The process of negotiation can be analysed using a strategic or tactical focus.

Negotiation strategies

There are two main negotiation strategies: the problem-solving approach and the opposition strategy.

The problem-solving approach, also called representative or integrative strategy, implies co-operation with the other party in order to avoid a conflict of interest, with the objective of jointly maximizing benefits. It stresses the importance of questioning and in particular the identification of customer needs and preferences. Once needs are identified, the salesperson seeks to satisfy them through offering a bundle of products/services. This approach seeks to satisfy the other party by considering various possible solutions while getting attractive compensation in exchange.

In contrast, the distributive or opposition strategy presumes that the parties do not co-operate. One seeks to obtain a maximum of concessions from the other party and to impose one's own solutions. Such a strategy can sometimes be observed in the sale of apartments if the purchaser tries to obtain the lowest price and the salesperson the highest price. It makes much more use of persuasion than the problem-solving approach by manipulating situational variables.

The two very different strategies of negotiation are illustrated in Figure 11.2. As the figure shows, out of 1135 sales negotiations in the banking sector, approximately half were co-operative while the

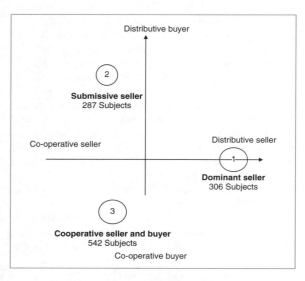

Figure 11.2 Negotiation strategies

remainder were dominated either by a salesperson or a buyer. The strategy employed will be reflected in the tactics used at the negotiation table.

Tactics at the negotiation table

During a negotiation, four phases can be distinguished:

1. making contact
2. exchanging information
3. persuading and making concessions and
4. finding an agreement.

The durations of the phases vary from culture to culture. For example, making contact takes much longer in Japan than in France, Britain or the United States.

Making contact

This phase focuses on the discussion of topics other than business. It allows for two parties to introduce themselves as well as for conversations which concern topics like family, the economy, sport or the weather. It is of variable duration, depending on culture: the French tend to take much more time than, for example, the Germans, who can be perceived as rude by the French because they tend to get to the point very quickly.

Task-related exchange of information

In this phase, negotiators provide and collect information on the target of the negotiation in order to prepare for the subsequent phases. They clarify their positions and put forward certain arguments. Information can be provided verbally or non-verbally. The tactics that are most usually employed in the verbal exchange of information are the following:

- *Commitment*: For example, "We promise to deliver this engine within the next two months and at the price originally quoted";
- *Self disclosure*: For example, "My company requires a return on investment of at least 15 per cent for the first year";
- *Questions*: For example, "Why do you demand such a high rent?"

These tactics make it possible to open the negotiation or to wait. If for example, there are many questions, it is possible to wait and study the other party. Verbal tactics will be discussed below.

Persuasion

Persuasion is sometimes completely separate from the preceding phase (as is the case in the United States) or it

may be merged with it, as happens in Japan. Some of the tactics used in the preceding phase can also be used in this phase, for example "questioning". Others such as positive or aggressive tactics are more usually found in this phase.

Positive-influence tactics are associated with representative or integrative strategies. The following are verbal tactics:

- *Promise*: For example, "If you can deliver on February 1st, I will place another order right away."
- *Recommendation*: For example, "If you keep the company name after the acquisition, then your present customers will stay with the company."
- *Reward*: For example, "This negotiation is progressing smoothly because you are well prepared."
- *Positive normative appeal*: For example, "Lowering your prices because of the new information that we have provided for you would be completely in line with common practices."

Aggressive-influence tactics are associated with distributive strategies. They are characterized by

- *Threat*: For example, "If you cannot deliver on March 1st, I will be obliged to place an order elsewhere."
- *Warning*: For example, "You may find it beneficial to preserve the name of the company after acquisition, if not you will lose your customers."
- *Punishment*: For example, "This negotiation is not progressing smoothly because you are badly prepared."
- *Negative normative appeal*: for example, "Not lowering your prices is contrary to professional practice."

These verbal tactics of influence are often associated with non-verbal communication which negotiators have to identify. Non-verbal communication takes various forms such as

- silent periods
- facial gazing
- conversational overlaps
- touching
- body language.

Silent periods, for example, are used to encourage the other party to speak and sometimes to oblige the other party to give more information. Conversational overlaps can be intended to hide a trouble, to divert the discussion. Of course, across different cultures, non-verbal communication may vary significantly. For example, the average number of silent periods of more than 10 seconds per 30 minutes of recording is 2.9 in English-speaking Canada and 0 in Brazil and Spain. Similarly, for a 30-minute period, the average number of conversational

TOOLBOX 11.1

COMPARISON OF NON-VERBAL BEHAVIOUR

	JPN	KOR	TWN	CHN	RUSS	GRM	UK	FRN	SPN	BRZ	MEX	FCAN	ECAN	USA
Silent periods	2.5	0	0	2.3	3.7	0	2.05	1.0	0	0	1.1	0.2	2.9	1.7
Conversational overlaps	6.2	22.0	12.3	17.1	13.3	20.8	5.03	20.7	28.0	14.3	10.6	24.0	17.0	5.1
Facial gazing	3.9	9.9	19.7	11.1	8.7	10.2	9.0	16.0	13.7	15.6	14.7	18.8	10.4	10.0
Touching	0	0	0	0	0	0	0	0.1	0	4.7	0	0	0	0

Bargaining Behaviour (per 30 minutes)
Source: P. R. Cateora and J. Graham (1999), *International Marketing*, Tenth Edition, Boston, McGraw Hill.

During negotiation, shall we speak to avoid silent periods? In some cultures such as Japan, Russia and English-speaking Canada it is not necessary. Is it polite to have conversational overlaps? They do not seem to be bothered about in French-speaking Canada, France, Korea and Germany. Shall we have facial gazing and how long?

Facial gazing is the lowest in Japan. Shall we touch the other? Do not be afraid to be touched in Brazil.

Such cultural differences need to be understood by expatriates or when meeting foreign salespersons. In such situations, adaptation is required. It means to be aware of culture differences and accommodate them.

overlaps is 6.2 in Japan and 28 in Spain. The average count for facial gazing is 19.7 in Taiwan and 3.9 in Japan, touching occurs 4.7 times in Brazil (see Toolbox 11.1). Not knowing and not acknowledging non-verbal behaviour may result in negotiation blunders. Therefore, understanding and adaptation are key elements for international negotiators.

Concessions and agreement

Agreement between negotiators is often the fruit of a compromise or of reciprocal concessions. These can be reached in a sequential approach or a holistic approach. If the agreement is reached in a sequential way, the negotiation progresses by successive agreements on each issue of the negotiation (e.g., price, delivery, terms of payment, standards, etc.). The sequential approach is generally preferred in the Western world.

In other regions of the world, the agreement is more likely reached in a holistic way, as for example in Japan, where concessions tend to be made only at the end of a negotiation. This may be a cause of business blunders when this behaviour is not anticipated and on one side negotiators seem never to commit themselves to anything while on the other side, sensing little progress, they may make multiple concessions.

Outcomes

In the short run, outcomes may be evaluated against the objectives of each party in relation to manufacturing and commercial conditions (see Goals and issues at stake). But outcomes must also be evaluated in relation to long-term objectives such as the maintenance or the development of a relationship with the other party. For example, it may be highly important to build a strong relationship with a supplier when seeking technology transfer. In establishing a franchise contract with a distribution partner, McDonalds will also have to establish the basis very carefully for a fruitful partnership.

One important dimension indicates whether these objectives have been achieved: the satisfaction of each party after the negotiation. Satisfaction is not simply about reaching commercial or manufacturing targets but also about the quality of the exchanges which took place between the two partners. A dissatisfied buyer will tend perhaps to return the products, to change supplier, or to contribute to negative word of mouth. A dissatisfied seller will try to avoid the customer next time or at least to minimize the input into the dissatisfying exchange for example by withholding information, reducing quality standards to a minimum or divesting resources specifically needed for that exchange.

Preparation of the negotiation

A negotiation can be extremely complex. Any negotiation requires careful preparation, to do with the selection of negotiators, knowledge of the negotiation partners, the objectives of the negotiation, the agenda, facts to confirm during the negotiation, and the setting for the negotiation.

Selection of negotiators

Negotiators must be selected according to individual character traits such as those mentioned above. These character traits can be detected by means of tests, simulation or role-playing. When teams of negotiators must be put together (because of the duration of the negotiation, its complexity, because of what is at stake or the presence of an opposing team), it is important to define beforehand the role each negotiator will have to play. For example, some will have to listen, some will have to focus on sticking to and moving through the agenda and some on the strategy behind concessions. Others will be assigned to exploit complementary but opposite roles, one acting as a hard negotiator, another as a more flexible negotiator who tends to compromise in order to facilitate the progress of the negotiation. A team includes key people such as production and technical experts, a lawyer, transport, financial and international experts, a buyer and/or a salesperson. A team leader is needed to oversee and coordinate negotiations. As the negotiation proceeds, the need for particular forms of expertise changes. For example, production and technical experts may be invaluable in exploratory and creative phases but redundant when it comes to the legal or financial aspects of the settlement.

Assessment of the partner

Before any negotiation, it is essential to be well briefed on the other parties in order to assess their objectives and obtain information which will facilitate the negotiation. Data on their financial situation, their market, their competitors and the economic situation of the market they serve is extremely valuable. Personal information such as pastimes, education and family status can be very useful in the first phase of a negotiation process. This information can be obtained from public or private organizations such as banks, or personal sources such as a network of contacts.

Clarification of objectives and potential concessions

Before negotiations start, it is imperative to clarify one's own objectives. The objectives must be constructed according to

- commercial and manufacturing issues, for example price, methods of payment, delivery and transport conditions, guarantees, after-sales service, quantities, specifications and so on
- the medium- and long-term relationships that should be maintained with the other party.

Finally, before engaging in negotiation, limits need to be specified within which the negotiation of commercial and manufacturing issues can go up to. Potential concessions and their limits must be prepared before negotiation starts to ensure coherence in negotiation behaviour. If potential concessions are carefully planned, the negotiators are able to give the reasons for each concession and thus underline their willingness to co-operate. However, fixing a minimum threshold may at times block a creative solution which would satisfy both parties. The **B**est **A**lternative **T**o a **N**egotiated **A**greement (BATNA) that a negotiator may obtain should the full objectives of a negotiation fail is the minimum threshold in any negotiation. When Volvo and Renault failed their merger negotiation in 1993, their BATNA was to continue their usual business.

Agenda and facts to confirm during the negotiation

It is quite rare for all the information to be available to negotiators before a negotiation starts. That is, certain assumptions need to be confirmed at the negotiation table. A list of this information and related questions must be drawn up in preparation for the negotiation table. For example, a penalty for late delivery, the price related to quantity or a delay in payment may be part of this list.

Each party wants to be able to impose its own agenda. A negotiation agenda is composed of the list of topics to be discussed, classified by priority order. The final agenda is in general established in a dialogue between the parties. To begin a negotiation favourably, it is advisable to start with the points which are easiest to solve.

The situation

Situational variables such as

- location
- physical arrangements
- number of parties
- time limits
- audiences and
- the number of participants

may be manipulated to gain an advantage in the negotiation. For example, outnumbering the other party to increase pressure on it, setting artificial deadlines or getting covert information on the deadline of the other party by calling its hotel to know the reservation length may be used.

Traditional selling

Just as for negotiation, selling starts with the identities of the customers. Prospecting can be done starting from address files or names provided by actual customers.

Selling also requires a preparation phase similar to negotiation (pre-approach). During this phase, the salesperson or the representative must be informed of the nature of the customer requirements and of other relevant facts such as name, education or pastimes of customers.

Some phases of negotiation discussed above are then identical for selling. However, their content is sales specific. In order to facilitate their discussion in what follows, the stages of "exchange of information related to the task" and "persuasion" will be merged into a "presentation" phase.

Approaching the customer

Four approaches are mainly used by salespeople to enter into contact with prospective customers:

Presenting themselves and the company they represent.

Although such an introduction occurs frequently, it may not attract the interest of the prospective customer and for this reason must be supplemented by one of the other three approaches.

1. Presenting the product to the prospective customer. This approach is recommended if the product is unique and likely to create some interest with the prospective customer at first viewing.
2. Informing prospective customers of the product benefits and asking whether they are of interest to them.
3. Using a reference to someone whom the prospective customer knows.

This referral approach may draw the attention of the prospective customer immediately.

Presentation or demonstration

Presentations or demonstrations are central to any sales process. They are intended to attract the customer's interest as well as to detect or identify their needs better. The product presentation proceeds in parallel with arguments to convince the prospect to buy the product. Product characteristics are central to the presentation. To try to gain the prospective customer's confidence during the demonstration, salespeople try to prove that what they say corresponds to reality. For that reason, salespeople will not only present the product, but will also use their knowledge on competition, the company and the

customer. They may even involve the customer through participation and product trial.

Two methods of presentation are mainly used.

Some salespeople opt for using a standard, learned presentation (canned sales approach). Others prefer a presentation based on knowing the needs of the prospective customer (adaptive sale).

1. The canned sales approach
   The canned sales approach supposes that the salesperson does most of the talking, the prospective customer playing a passive part, being only asked to deliver his opinion. Canned sales demonstrations tend to suppose that all buyers are identical (except when salespeople have learned to use different presentations in response to certain questions). This approach is adapted to certain specific types of sales, especially for telephone and door-to-door selling of consumer products. It has the advantages of
   - giving confidence to the salesperson,
   - using tested sales techniques that have proved to work,
   - simplifying sales training,
   - giving some assurance that the complete story will be presented.

   Controversy has arisen around this approach because it can be done without understanding the customers and may reduce the credibility of salespeople.

2. The adaptive sales approach
   The adaptive sales approach is very different in its philosophy since the salesperson initially lets the prospective customers speak about their needs, even if it means helping the customer to become aware of their needs. Once those needs are known, the salesperson is able to discuss how to adapt the offer to the prospective customer, proposing products which correspond best to the identified needs. This method requires greater competence or understanding on the part of the salesperson. That is, the salesperson must have the ability to see things as others would see them and grasp the motivations of potential customers. They must be able to process the data collected on the prospective customer quickly, which will enable them to better reflect the needs through adequate exchange offers.

The sequencing of sales demonstrations is inspired by AIDA theory of persuasion, which is based on the idea that a buyer's mind passes through several successive stages before deciding to buy: (A) attract prospect's Attention, (I) gain Interest (D) create Desire, (A) stimulate Action to complete the sale.

Objections or excuses of potential customers for not making a purchase during a demonstration are almost inevitable. They are in general welcome for they show that the prospect is interested and reveal more about their needs. Moreover, they allow salespeople to show their competence in answering. Competent salespeople know that objections have to be reformulated before arguing. The objective of reformulation is to specify the objection while distinguishing between:

- true objections
  the customer still maintains the objection by re-specifying it after reformulation,
- from false objections
  after reformulation the customer changes the objection,
- and hidden objections
  after reformulation the customer sticks to the objection without specifying it. It is up to the salesperson to elegantly propose an interpretation of the objection.

Objections may concern product, price, time or other attributes of the exchange offer. The salesperson must be prepared to react to objections relating to disadvantages of the offer and to insist on advantages. Objections related to time are particularly difficult to overcome. They are objections such as "give me a little time to think about", "I must discuss it with my family", "I must wait until pay day". Very frequently, such objections result in the loss of the prospective customer.

Closing the sale

This stage is the most delicate part of the sales process. If the salesperson fails to close the presentation by asking for the order, all the work is for nothing.

Closing depends on the detection of various signals given by the prospective customer, like asking for certain guarantees on the services related to the purchase or raising questions about conditions of payment. Five techniques are used to support this stage:

1. Make the assumption that the customer is convinced and thus proceed to the order-taking stage by asking a question such as "What address do you want it delivered to?"
2. Physically act in order to indicate to the prospective customer that it is time to place the order. For example, give him a pen or hand over the keys of the car.
3. Put the prospective customer under pressure by telling that it is necessary to buy now, because such a favourable opportunity will not arise soon again. Arguments such as the exhaustion of stocks or the existence of a waiting list are likely to create this state of pressure.
4. Deal with a key objection and then urge the prospective customer to order.
5. Use particular conditions such as an attractive price valid for a given period or a gift to push the prospective customer to order now.

Follow-up

Sales are not finished once the order is obtained. A good salesperson follows it up. This phase common to sales and negotiations is intended to avoid cognitive dissonance in the buyer. However, in sales, it is often the salesperson who ensures the follow-up, checking that the customer is satisfied, whereas in negotiations the follow-up is often ensured by people other than those who negotiated the deal, such as maintenance personnel.

Sales management

Sales management first of all concerns establishing sales objectives. Once these objectives are fixed, managing the sales force involves determining its size and deployment, as well as directing, organizing, evaluating and controlling the efforts of the sales force so as to achieve the planned goals.

Figure 11.3 summarizes the structure of the various problems raised by sales management.

Sales objectives

Objectives are fixed according to a cascade system. They depend initially on the objectives of the company, which are broken down into objectives of organizational subunits, which are reflected in marketing objectives and finally in sales objectives. Marketing objectives may be fixed quantitatively, such as turnover to be achieved, share of market to be reached, or qualitatively, such as to improve company image or service, to secure a lasting relationship with the customers and so on. The same is the case for sales objectives. The role played by the sales force and the definition of their tasks make it possible to achieve qualitative goals. For example, maintaining durable relationships will require salespeople to play the role of adviser as well as to use non-aggressive selling techniques. Quantitative sales objectives must also be specified and allocated to sales territories or product types. They will then be translated into quotas by salespeople and will be adjusted according to the potential of each territory. This cascade of objectives is not carried out only in one direction, from the top executives to the sales force. Budgeting processes often start at the sales force level, with salespeople giving their estimates of potential sales in the next period. It is best if a dialogue takes place at each stage of the process. The final objectives are only the end product of that process.

Size of the sales force

The next step is to focus on sales force size. The larger it is, the more it costs but at the same time market coverage is improved. It is necessary to find a compromise between costs and market coverage that is compatible with the resources available and the planned objectives.

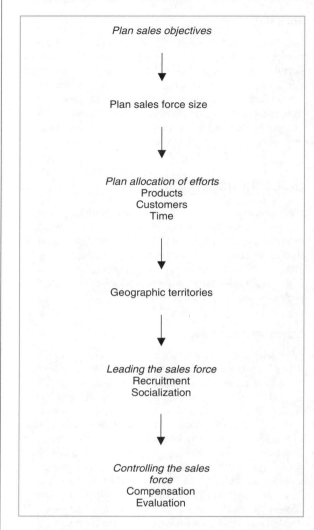

Plan sales objectives

Plan sales force size

Plan allocation of efforts
Products
Customers
Time

Geographic territories

Leading the sales force
Recruitment
Socialization

*Controlling the sales
force*
Compensation
Evaluation

Figure 11.3 Structure of sales management
problems

Various methods exist to calculate the optimal size of
the sales force. They vary in their complexity but
sometimes also rely on assumptions which are not correct
in all situations.

Breakdown approach

Past experience provides information on the average
number of customers a salesperson can visit daily. This
number can be easily converted into an annual figure and
may become an indicator of activity for a salesperson. If
the potential of prospects and customers to visit in a year
is known as well as the frequency of the visits to carry
out, it is easy to determine the number of salespeople
necessary by dividing the total number of required sales

visits by the average number of visits a salesperson can
do. To take into account differences of potential or
turnover among customers, these computations can be
carried out for categories of prospects/clients.

Past figures also provide information on the average
turnover achieved by each salesperson. Dividing the total
turnover to be achieved by the average turnover per
salesperson provides the necessary size of the sales force.
Easy to compute, each of these two methods has some
disadvantages. They do not take account of productivity
gains which can be obtained by changing the
compensation system and the commercial support
provided by the company. This method also neglects the
potential of each territory or the differences in ability
among salespeople.

Benchmarking methods

Other methods using past data do not rely on individual
company experience but on a group of companies in the
same sector. Companies taking part in a project such as
PIMS or Advisor provide information on their sales force,
in particular sales force cost. Based on that information,
the relation between the cost of the sales force and the
results obtained (e.g., cash-flow or profitability) may be
examined. The way in which results vary with sales force
cost and size can be analysed and it can be seen whether
the company's sales efforts are similar to those of
competitors.

Methods based on historical data are to be used with
caution. They assume in particular that the starting
estimates are optimal, which is obvious neither for a
company, nor for a group of companies. They rest on the
assumption that what occurred in the past will occur
again. For this reason, PIMS or Advisor methods can
prove to be dangerous during times of rapid change. This
is the reason why other methods based on operations
research have been developed. This type of method aims
to maximize profits and calculates the size of the sales
force according to, for example, the number of customers
visited, the cost per salesperson, the sales margin, the
sales potential of the sector and so on.

Sales force structure

Sales force structure is determined in line with the content
of the tasks carried out and the specific advantages and
disadvantages of each type of structure.

Structure by geographic territory

When structuring the sales force by territory, each
salesperson sells the entire product line of the company in
a territory which is allocated to that person alone. The
structure often includes a district manager in charge of
each territory, a sales manager in charge of managing
several district managers and a general sales manager.

This structure is well adapted to companies which have a relatively homogeneous range of products, homogeneous customers in terms of benefits sought, application, usage, as well as customers asking for a permanent contact.

This structure has the following advantages:

- Each salesperson has a well-defined territory. So the person can manage their own territory and, on the other hand can be more easily monitored;
- Each salesperson is living in their territory, so travelling expenses are reduced and customer follow-ups are more regular.

The major disadvantage of this structure is that it can be difficult to define territories. There may be

- unequal economic potential in the different territories, in terms of workload or sales
- Geographical reasons, customer decision-making centres that are unequally distributed geographically can prevent this kind of territory definition.

Other disadvantages mentioned for this structure include the freedom the salesperson has to make decisions about what product to emphasize and which customers to concentrate on. The territory approach could be totally inadequate should there be different customer segments with different expectations, for example with respect to information advice or after-sales service. This may be the case, for example, in the light system business where the customers may be architects, lighting system planners, electricians or retailers.

Structure by product

Product category may also be used as the basis for sales force organization. In this kind of structure, a general sales manager deals with a product or a product category. The sales manager is often subordinate to a product manager. This structure is useful for companies that have very diversified customers and products. The Hewlett Packard Medical Products Group sells a variety of products, including patient monitoring systems, operating room systems, prenatal monitoring devices and clinical information systems. Each of the four product categories has its own sales force.

The advantage of this method of sales force organization lies in the better preparation of the sales force for competitive action because of its product specialization. Its disadvantages are its

- cost
  since it is necessary to have as many sales forces as there are product categories,
- possibility of overlaps between sales forces
  the same customer may be contacted by various sales forces,

- difficulty in dealing with customers who buy multiple products
  the customer may not want to deal with several contact people.

Structure by market or customer type

Many companies structure their sales force according to customer type or market. A pharmaceutical company may have specialized sales forces for physicians, chemist shops and drug wholesalers. This structure aligns with the marketing approach and is suitable when there are markets or groups of customers that are distributed differently in geographical terms, and for whom different sales knowledge is needed.

The main advantages of this structure are the detailed knowledge of customers and the alignment of the structure with customers. The major disadvantages are similar to the product-line structure. This structure is costly. It may also cause risks of conflicts between salespeople when customers have diverse activities, making it difficult to allocate them to specific customer groups.

Mixed structures

Structures are often combined. For example, a first level structured by geographical area managed by a district manager, is followed by a second level which uses a product or market/customer structure with specialized salespeople. (Figure 11.4)

Sales territory design

Territories are allocated to salespeople in order to

- facilitate market coverage
- increase their motivation and their effectiveness
- reduce their transportation costs
- improve relationships with customers
- facilitate control and evaluation.

Sales territory design depends on the chosen organizational structure. Territories assigned to salespeople must be carefully selected. Unequal territories generate a bad climate within the selling team, territories that are too small or too large discourage the sales force, and territories that are too large cause high travelling expenses and make penetration easier for competition.

Sales territory must be easy to manage and easy to estimate. Sales territory design must take into account transportation time, and should result in roughly equal territories according to sales potential and workload.

Companies frequently establish a separate organization to deal with major or key customers (key accounts). There are different ways to organize a key account sales force. Two of them use structures mixing geographic and customer-related organisation. In the first structure, key account sales force and regional sales force are on the same level organizationally and both report to a corporate vice president of sales. In the second, both sales forces are still at the same level organizationally but report to a region manager.

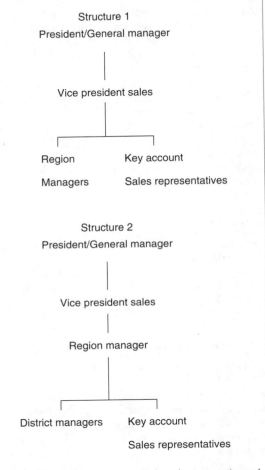

Structure 1

President/General manager

Vice president sales

Region Managers   Key account Sales representatives

Structure 2

President/General manager

Vice president sales

Region manager

District managers   Key account

Sales representatives

In structure 1 (the most common) major accounts and regular sales force are treated as equal units. They both report to vice president sales. Structure 2 is another alternative where the management of major accounts is decentralized by region. It may fit to an area where major accounts are spread on the territory.

Figure 11.4 Mixed structures

Source: J.A. Coletti and G.S. Tubridy (1987), Effective Major Account Sales Management, *Journal of Personal Selling and Sales Management*, August, 4

Equality between territories is very difficult to achieve. It can be obtained by combining geographical sectors for which statistical data exist. Various decision-making models or computer software can also be used to determine the optimal allocation of the sales force among products, customers and geographical areas (see Toolbox 11.2).

Sales force time management

Salespeople must allocate their time and efforts among prospects, customers and the company (for feedback reporting).

The allocation of time between prospects and customers is difficult to assess because of the propensity of salespeople to be more interested in actual customers. There are no easy methods of optimal time allocation.

It is also difficult to allocate time among customers and especially the time devoted to sales calls versus customer visits. Unnecessary return visits to customers should be avoided but at the same time if salespeople do not contact their customers often enough, they may miss orders. Consequently, salespeople will have to try to work out the order frequency of their customers and to rely upon their sales objectives to contact their customers.

Three main categories of tools are available for solving this problem. The first is decision models using computer optimization programs. The second is more qualitative and concerns a portfolio method prescribing a call frequency according to account potential and competitive strength. The third is a combination of these two methods and uses expert systems (Toolbox 11.2).

Travelling salespeople need to have route plans in order to avoid losing time in unnecessary travelling. Several criteria will be used for fixing the route. In addition to the optimal frequency of visit to each customer, geographical concentration of the customers, and travelling difficulties, and the residence of the representative will be taken into account. Several methods help in developing the route plan. The plan may take several forms such as spiral, clover and daisy (Figure 11.5). For example, the daisy shape makes it possible to cover a more important territory than the two others, to cover a territory regularly and to allow the salesperson to return home each day. Route planners may use also decisions models. These models employ operations research methods.

Salespeople must devote part of their time to writing daily activity reports which may sometimes be summarized in weekly reports and are synthesized in a monthly activity report. They must indicate the customers or prospects visited, as well as their characteristics (in particular orders, price, specific relevant habits, processes, relationships, etc). Using computers and modems, salespeople can also complete call reports electronically and send the information back to the office. Online databases are immediately updated and are ready to be

TOOLBOX 11.2

COMPUTER SOFTWARE AND MODELS OF SALES TERRITORY DESIGN AND SALES FORCE TIME ALLOCATION METHODS

Computer software is used for sales territory design. Car dealer territory design in a geographical area may use computer software to map customers of each dealer, to the real dealer territory and compare it to the expected territory. Based upon observed disagreement, they help to know whether dealers can handle their territory or neglect some areas (e.g., because of mountainous areas), whether areas are served by the wrong dealers and of course make the necessary adjustments.

Models such as COSTA (Contribution Optimizing Sales Territory Alignment) operate with sales response functions at the level of sales coverage units (SCU) or a group of geographically limited individual accounts. It models sales as a function of selling time, which includes calling time, as well as travel time, assuming a constant ratio of travel to calling time. The model optimally allocates the available selling time of a salesperson across the sales coverage units of his territory and assigns the SCU to territories.

Source: B. Skiera and S. Albers (1998), COSTA: Contribution Optimizing Sales Territory Alignment, *Marketing Science*, 17, 3, 181–195.

The CALLPLAN model is used to find call frequency norms for each current customer and each prospect. Call frequencies are the number of calls per effort period, which is the time period on which the allocations are based (usually 1–3 months). The model is based on the assumption that the expected sales to each customer and prospect over a response period (usually a year) is a function of the average number of calls per effort period during that response period.

The model has two phases:

1. A calibration phase in which the expected profit associated with different call policies for each customer and prospect is determined (no calls, half the current rate, the current rate, 1.5 times the current rate and a saturation rate).
2. An optimization phase, in which optimal allocation of time to customers and prospects is established.

Optimal allocation is obtained maximizing the profit with a time constraint.

Source: L.M. Lodish (1971), CALLPLAN: An Interactive Salesman's Call Planning System, *Management Science*, 18,4, Part 2, 26–40.

In Portfolio models, each account served by a company is considered as part of an overall portfolio of accounts. Accounts represent different situations and thus receive different levels of selling effort. Accounts are classified into categories of similar attractiveness for receiving sales call investments. Thus selling effort is allocated so that more attractive accounts receive more selling effort.

Attractiveness of each account is a function of account opportunity and competitive position. Account opportunity is defined as an account's need for and ability to purchase the company's product. Competitive position is defined as the strength of the relationship between the company and an account. Accounts are more attractive the higher the account opportunity and the stronger the competitive position.

Using portfolio models to develop an account effort allocation strategy requires that account opportunity and competitive position be measured for each account. Based on these measurements, accounts can be classified into attractiveness segments.

Source: R.W. Laforge, C.E. Young and B. C. Hamm (1983), Increasing Sales Productivity through Improved Sales Call Allocation Strategies, *Journal of Personal selling and Sales Management*, 4, November, 52–59.

An expert system may also be build using rules borrowed from the portfolio method rules (**If** the account sales are important **and** potential sales important, **then** attractiveness is high). These rules concern attractiveness and opportunity. The expert system includes mathematical software maximizing sales or profit with constraints on the total number of visits. It provides for each segment a level of recommended effort.

Source: H. Ait-Ouyahia (1997), Allocation de l'effort de visite: une approche à base de connaissance issue des méthodes de portefeuille et d'optimisation, *Recherche et Applications en Marketing*, 12, 3, 39–45.

---

seen by sales managers. Companies that automate call reports have a wealth of online data about customers and competition.

For example, it is possible to observe hour-by-hour price changes of competitors. The database may also provide buyer characteristics such as the type of products purchased, influential persons to talk to and so on.

Leading the sales force

Leading the sales force consists of developing a set of procedures intended to recruit, induct, train, motivate and manage the sales force. Developing a sales force means attracting qualified candidates, selecting the best, inducting to the organization, and training them to organizational standards

Route plan	Schema	Advantage	Disadvantage
Spiral		• Visiting regularity in each part of the district • Easy and quick travel back to the district headquarters	• High mileage • Topographical differences not taken into account
Clover	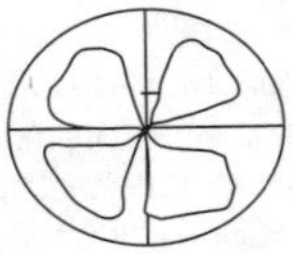	• Opportunity to be at the district headquarters every day • No hotel expenses	• Involves, sometimes, long travel • Needs a geographic centre and limited districts
Daisy	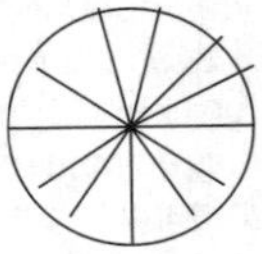	• Same advantages as clover, but also opportunity to be used for larger districts	• Same disadvantages as clover according to size limitation

Figure 11.5 Developing route plans

Recruitment

Recruitment requires, first of all, the definition of the type and characteristics of salespeople fitting the company needs. The following types can be distinguished:

- negotiators or business engineers
  who must have very good product and market knowledge and high level negotiation skills;
- missionary sales promoters
  merchandisers or consumer goods product demonstrators maintaining points of sale and advising retailers about merchandising;
- Sales promoters in services
  informing and advising key influencers or key accounts;
- medical visitors and delegates
  who engage with physicians to sell pharmaceutical products;
- salespeople
  prospecting their territory, knowing their products and those of competition, arguing, concluding the sale, following up their customers;
- prospectors
  whose function is to prepare the job of the salespeople by raising the interest of potential customers;
- order takers
  recording orders and sometimes delivering goods;

- sales manager
  fixing objectives, coordinating and controlling the activities of a team of salespeople;
- district sales managers
  supervising sales force activity under the authority of the sales manager.

The process of recruitment requires a job analysis, followed by a job description. A job description contains the following elements:

- type of salesperson,
- administrative relationships indicating to whom this person is reporting (senior sales representative, subordinates),
- duties, tasks, responsibilities of the salesperson (planning activity, sale, prospecting, job organization,
- necessary qualities (technical skills, motivation, personality),
- work skills (initiative, response to pressure, etc.).

Once this task is done, recruitment and selection objectives have to be specified. The various types of sales jobs do not require the same technical skills and individual capabilities. However, as with negotiators, two main characteristics are required for an optimal salesperson, empathy and self-esteem.

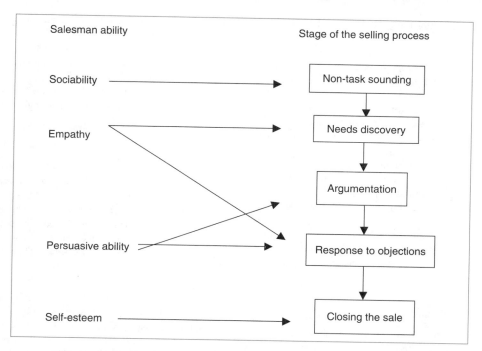

Figure 11.6 Requested abilities at each stage of the selling process

Source: S. Ganassali (1995) *L'approche intégrée des facteurs explicatifs de l'efficacité du vendeur: une application à la vente à domicile, thèse de sciences de gestion*, Université Pierre Mendès France de Grenoble.

These necessary qualities are detected by means of interviews, tests or role-playing in an assessment centre. Various qualities have different levels of importance at the different phases of a sales process. Figure 11.6 presents the phases of a typical sales process and the required capabilities of the salespeople.

Instruction and training

Selecting a sales force is an expensive operation. Once salespeople have been recruited, it is important to retain them with the organization by carefully inducting them. The familiarization of the new recruit with company history, policies and culture starts during the recruitment process and in particular during interviewing. At this stage, information on the company is provided, the products are described. Instruction continues at the time of the arrival of the new recruit by a more detailed presentation of the company, characteristics of the job and meetings with the sales team. Some companies such as Gore Associates, the world famous owner of the Goretex brand, go even a step further. Each new recruit gets a personal coach of their choice who is member of the company, helping the newcomer to get inducted as fast as possible.

Because part of the role of sales force is to represent the company and gather relevant data, their training is very important. It must focus on the following elements:

- the salesperson's role for the company,
  representation of the company in customer contacts, data collection on customers for the company, helping to retain customers, in particular solving their problems, facilitating the introduction and the consumption or use of the products of the company;
- knowledge of the company,
  its products, the competing products;
- Negotiation or sales training is carried out through classroom training,
  Classroom training involves the learning of selling skills through audiovisual materials, lectures, presentations, or case discussions, and on-the-job training,
  In on-the-job training, a salesperson learns their job by doing it. They are coached by a trainer or sales manager.
- Role-playing
  Role-playing is a popular technique used in many companies. The trainee acts as a salesperson in a simulated buying session, the buyer being either a sales instructor or another trainee.

The training of the sales force can be centralized or decentralized.

Decentralized training has the advantage of being less expensive because salespeople remain on the job while being trained; moreover it does not require the employment of a permanent group of professional trainers. While being spread out in time and absorbed on the job, the training is effective when it is well managed.

Centralized training occurs in companies which have large sales force requirements. It takes place periodically at the headquarters or at a central training facility. The best trainers may be assigned to the programs and excellent training conditions can be provided. These conditions facilitate the familiarization of new salespeople with headquarters.

The initial training must be followed up with periodic refreshers during meetings or training programmes focusing in particular on new products from the company itself or competitors.

Sales force motivation

Sales management is carried out by the senior members of the sales force such as the sales manager and the district manager. They control the activity level of the salespeople, take care that the strategy of the company is implemented and maintain a good working atmosphere. Another aim is to help with technical issues or assist in tricky sales situations. District managers, for example, can train salespeople to overcome customers' objections, or may participate in an important sales presentation.

Various factors determine how much supervision is needed. High quality, competent salespeople do not need close supervision. Newly hired individuals with below average ability and no selling experience need to be closely supervised. Geographical distribution and concentration of the sales force should also be considered. For example, companies with few salespeople, each responsible for a large territory, may find the job of maintaining close customer contact so costly and difficult as to be almost prohibitive.

The working climate partly depends on the compensation system as well as on the perceived equity of sales-force evaluation and compensation.

Compensation is the end result of multiple, sometimes incompatible, objectives such as the need to attract and keep salespeople, to ensure sufficient compensation, to control their actions and to obtain a good return on investment. Sales-force rewards are financial and non-financial.

Financial compensation

Compensation can be direct, such as salary or commission, or indirect, such as a holiday offered for the best sales performance, winning prizes in internal competitions, and reimbursing travel expenses (car expenses, restaurant, hotel). Expenses can be refunded against receipts, contractually, or up to a maximum ceiling. A certain freedom in fixed expenses can, for example, constitute an interesting indirect financial compensation since it may not be taxed depending upon the country.

Direct remuneration can be carried out according to three systems: straight commission, straight salary or a combination of both.

Straight commission

A commission is a payment for achieving a level of performance with respect to turnover or some other target. At the Singer Company, for example, salespeople are paid on a percentage of the net sales billed. The percentage varies according to the product category sold (sewing machine, vacuum cleaner or TV set). This method has many advantages. It

- encourages the salespeople, since they alone are responsible for their earnings, and
- motivates them to achieve good results since commission is directly a function of performance.
- makes it possible to control the cost of the sales force since it is related to sales.
- enables different incentives to be provided for different product categories.
  The disadvantages of this method are the following.
- While focusing only on performance, the method does not always maximize the company's profit. For example, to increase turnover, salespeople may be ready to make concessions on price.
- Salespeople consider themselves as entrepreneurs. For this reason, they are difficult to control and reluctant to keep the company fully informed.
- Earnings of salespeople are not always related to their effort. In the event of an economic downturn, for example, a reduction in commission has nothing to do with sales effort.

Straight salary

A straight salary has the following advantages:

- it provides the salesperson with a guaranteed and steady income,
- it makes it easy for management to control the activity of salespeople and in particular to assign prospecting activities which are not immediately converted into orders.

The major disadvantage of a straight salary is the absence of direct financial motivation. This is why many companies have chosen a combination of straight salary and commissions. Conditions related to various uses of

Table 11.1 Salary and usage conditions

	Conditions	Proportion of incentive (bonus or commission) to total pay
Importance of salesman's own personal skill and persuasiveness in making sales	The more	The higher
Knowledge of the company among its customers and prospects	The less well known	The higher
Reliance of the company on advertising and sales promotion	Little	Higher
Difference in quality, price or other selling points between products of competition	Little	Higher
Service provided to customer	Major consideration	Lower
Significance of sales volume as a primary selling objective	The more	More important is a high proportion
Highly technical skill or team selling	Dominant requirement	Lower proportion
Factors beyond the control of the company (national or industry trends)	Important	Relatively low

Source: R.C. Smyth (1968), Financial Incentives for Salesmen, *Harvard Business Review*, 1,46, 109–117.

combinations of straight salary bonuses and commissions are presented in Table 11.1.

Combination

A combined compensation plan includes a basic salary plus some incentive pay made up of commissions and/or bonuses. A bonus is a payment at the discretion of management and intended to take account of outstanding performance. Whereas a commission is typically paid for each sale made, a bonus, to be paid, depends on exceeding a threshold level of performance. Because of its nature, it is used only in combination with straight salary or commission. It is intended to encourage the sales force in the execution of certain tasks.

One of the most useful and powerful bonuses from a managerial point of view is the bonus on objective which is obtained only when the planned objective is reached. Such objectives may be the

- achievement of a given turnover or sales volume,
- winning of a given number of new customers,
- increase of sales margin to a particular level.

A combination of commission and salary is intended to mitigate the disadvantages of the compensation plans presented previously. The fixed part (on average, a minimum of 30 per cent) ensures a sufficient minimum income as well as motivating salespeople to make efforts to sell.

Preferences for compensation plans differ according to the sales culture. (See Table 11.2).

Other compensations

Other forms of compensation come in various guises. For example, the free or partially free use of a company car is a financial advantage. The car may be purchased or part-purchased by the company. When purchased by the company it may be used by the salesperson for the entire week or during working days only. Information circulated through the company newsletter about success in a sales contest or individual sales excellence are further examples of non-financial compensation.

Controlling the sales force

Sales management needs to check if the sales force objectives have been reached. If the objectives have not been reached, sales management needs to try to explain the deviation between target and what was actually achieved. Evaluation of the sales force thus provides information on the development of the market and competition, sales force effectiveness and a better knowledge of weaknesses to eliminate.

The evaluation rests on a periodic control exercise carried out at each hierarchical level within the sales force – sales manager, district managers and salespeople. In particular it enables cross-sectional and longitudinal performance analysis. An evaluation will be carried out for each salesperson based upon the following factors.

Quantitative criteria such as turnover, visit reports and sales statistics as well as qualitative criteria based on the judgement of the district manager or the sales manager.

This evaluation will in general be preceded by an open discussion with the salesperson on past performance.

Table 11.2 Preferences toward compensation plans in the banking industry

Plans	A	B	C	D
Plans content	100% Salary and equal split of bonus between the company's salespeople	85% Salary and individual commissions	85% Salary and equal split of commissions between salespeople of the district	100% Salary and equal split of bonus between salespeople of the district
Country Preferences				
France	5.6%	19%	38.9%	36.1%
Germany	–	51%	39%	10%
Italy	–	32%	55%	13%

Source: M. Besson (1997), *L'impact de la culture nationale sur les systèmes de rémunération des vendeurs en Europe*, thèse HEC, Jouy en Josas.
Four plans (A, B, C, D) are characterized by the importance of the straight salary as well as the way commission and bonus are allocated (either individually, split on an equal basis between salespeople, or split at the district level). French salespeople are characterized by their risk avoidance, which expresses the choice of plan A rejected by the other salespeople and by a not very frequent choice of plan B (individualized commissions). Italians share with Germans a strong will to motivate the sales force through individual commissions or bonuses. On the other hand, Italians prefer an equal split of bonuses among salespeople and the district agency, meanwhile Germans prefer individual commissions.

Control systems concerning sales-force behaviour and performance are used to determine their compensation. Control systems focusing on performance are based mainly on objective measures of performance such as turnover, volume, sales quotas, and levels of customer satisfaction. They require less management effort and control because salespeople are responsible for their own performance, which is used to calculate their compensation. One of the well-known disadvantages of this system is that it permits behaviour which can harm the future of the company; for example, emphasis on products most easily sold, or limited attention to the satisfaction of customers.

Quota systems are often used as incentive to the sales force by providing performance standards. They facilitate the control and the evaluation of the sales force starting from the analysis of the variations observed between actual performance and fixed standards.

Standards can be expressed in various forms:

- physical volume quotas
- turnover
- financial quotas like net profit quotas
- gross margin quotas
- expenses
- quota of activities related to efforts of the salesperson such as the number of prospects contacted and the number of product demonstrations carried out.

Quotas can also be fixed starting from any combination of the preceding forms. An example is the points-based method in which points are allocated to each article sold based on the priorities of the company.

Each quota system has advantages and disadvantages for the salespeople as well as for the company. For example, a physical volume quota is more encouraging than a turnover quota when prices fluctuate for reasons related to demand cycles or actions of competition. Activity quotas are intended to balance the disadvantage of physical volume quotas which may cause a salesperson to neglect any activity not resulting in an immediate sale such as prospecting, reporting, meetings internal to the company, and so on. Financial quotas sensitize salespeople to the consequences of their sales in terms of cost or profit. They seek to mitigate the tendency of salespeople to focus on products which are the most easily sold or to be interested in customers with whom they feel most at ease. Indeed, products most easily sold or customers with whom salespeople feel most at ease are not always those which are the most advantageous for the company. Margin quotas are intended to take account of this problem.

Control systems focusing on behaviour are more concerned with the sales process than with performance. Salespeople are evaluated and compensated according to a certain number of factors such as

- knowledge of the product
- quality of the demonstrations
- ability to conclude a sale
- number of accounts managed
- or number of calls carried out.

Table 11.3 Sales organization audit framework

Sales organization environment	Sales organization planning system
Extraorganizational factors Economic-demographic Political-Legal Technological Competitive Customer **Intraorganizational factors** Company organization Sales–marketing department linkages Sales–other department linkages Marketing-mix	Objectives Sales Management Program Implementation of the Program
Sales management evaluation	**Sales management functions**
Adequacy of Sales Managers Adequacy of Management Practices	Sales force organization Recruitment and selection Sales training Compensation and expenses Supervision, morale and motivation Sales forecasting Budgeting Quotas Territories and routing Sales analysis Cost/profitability/analysis Sales force evaluation

Source: T. Ingram, R. Laforge and C. Schwepker (1997), Sales *Management: Analysis and Decision Making,* Third Edition, Fort worth, Dryden Press.

Control systems focusing on behaviour lead to complex and subjective evaluations of the sales force. Their advantage is to generate behaviour that fits the strategy of the company. Salespeople tend to be better informed about the company and its objectives.

More generally, two principal techniques can be used: sales audit and benchmarking.

The purpose of sales audit is to investigate systematically and comprehensively the sales organization and environment, sales organization planning system, sales management evaluation, and sales management (see Table 11.3) to identify current and potential problems, to determine their cause and to take corrective actions.

Benchmarking is a process of measurement and analysis which compares the practices of the company with those of better performing competitors (Toolbox 11.3).

TOOLBOX 11.3

BENCHMARKING PROCESS

The first step of benchmarking requires identifying the company or sales force to benchmark. Literature search, personal contacts and industry awards are indicators of excellence and may guide the selection of the benchmark. The second step focuses on the organization's performance gap relative to benchmarked performance levels. It relies upon data gathering. The third step should identify best practices and facilitators producing the results observed during the study. Expected performance levels are established and communicated to gain acceptance. The fourth and final step requires the determination of performance goals for the process studied and the identification of areas where action has to be taken to improve performance.

SUMMARY

This chapter focused on the selling and negotiation process because they are intertwined and are sources of customer value. Commercial conditions are a basis for distinguishing sales from negotiation. In sales, the commercial conditions of the exchange are fixed by the salesperson. In negotiation, they are discussed between the parties.

The negotiation outcome generally depends on factors which precede the negotiation, on particular conditions of the negotiation and on the process of negotiation itself. Individual culture and characteristics of negotiators, specifics of the organizations involved in the negotiation all form the environment of the negotiation. Some conditions specific to the negotiation cannot be handled by negotiators (goals of the negotiation, power). Some other may be manipulated during the negotiation (number of parties and participants, audiences, time, location and physical arrangements of the negotiation). The process of negotiation can be analysed using either a strategic or a tactical focus. Two main strategies of negotiation have been identified: the problem-solving approach and the opposition strategy. These two strategies generate opposing tactics in terms of arguments, verbal and non-verbal communications, and concessions. During negotiation four phases can be distinguished: making contact, exchanging information about the negotiation, persuading and making concessions and finding an agreement. Any negotiation requires careful preparation concerning the selection of negotiators, the object of negotiation and the situation of the negotiation. Selling goes through phases similar to negotiation. However, their content is sales specific. Two methods of presentation are mainly used. Some salespeople opt for using a learned demonstration (canned sales approach). Others prefer a presentation based on understanding the needs of the prospective customer (adaptive sale).

Sales management first of all consists of establishing sales objectives. Once these objectives are fixed, managing the sales force requires one to determine its size and deployment, as well as directing, organizing, evaluating and controlling the efforts of the sales force in order to achieve the planned goals. Breakdown and benchmarking methods are used to calculate the optimal size of the sales force. The structure of the sales force is determined according to the task content and the specific advantages and disadvantages of each type of structure: product, market/customers, and geographical and mixed structures. Sales territory design is obtained by combining geographical sectors for which statistical data exist. By combining these sectors, it is possible to obtain balanced territories. A variety of decision-making models or computer software can also be used to determine the optimal allocation of the sales force among products, customers and geographical areas.

Salespeople must allocate their time and efforts among prospects, customers and the company.

Optimal time allocation between prospects and customers, and sales calls versus visiting customers is difficult to achieve. Three main categories of tools are available to help solve this problem. The first is decision models using optimization computer programs. The second is more qualitative and concerns a portfolio method prescribing a call frequency according to account potential and competitive strength. The third is a combination of these two methods using expert systems. Travelling salespeople need to develop route plans in order to avoid losing time in useless travel. Several methods help in developing the route plan. They have forms such as spiral, clover and daisy.

Controlling the sales force consists of developing a set of procedures intended to recruit, induct and train, manage, compensate and evaluate the sales force. Developing a sales force means attracting qualified candidates, selecting the best, inducting them into the organization and training them to organizational standards. Managing the sales force is carried out by the senior members of the sales force. Maintaining a good working climate partly depends on the compensation system. Rewards given to salespeople may be financial or non-financial. Direct compensation can be carried out according to three systems: straight commission, straight salary or a combination of both. Control systems relate to salesperson behaviour and performance for they are used to determine their compensation. Two main techniques are used for this purpose: sales audit and benchmarking.

Discussion questions

1. What is personal selling? How does it differ from negotiation?
2. What are the factors preceding the negotiation?
3. What are the specific conditions of a negotiation?
4. What are the two main negotiation strategies?
5. What are the three main categories of objection?
6. Provide examples of aggressive tactics.
7. What are negotiation outcomes?

8. Define BATNA, non-task sounding and task-related exchange of information
9. What are the different types of quotas?
10. What are the three methods available to calculate the sales force size?
11. On what elements should sales force training focus?

12. What are the major steps in the selling process?
13. Explain the major advantages and disadvantages of the three financial compensation methods.
14. What major factors should be taken into account when fixing the territory design?
15. How is it possible to control on a daily basis the performance of a salesman?

Further reading

H. Ait-Ouyahia (1997), Allocation de l'effort de visite: une approche à base de connaissance issue des méthodes de portefeuille et d'optimisation, *Recherche et Applications en Marketing*, 12, 3, 39–45.

E. Anderson and R.L. Oliver (1987), Perspectives on Behaviour-based Versus Outcome-Based Control systems, *Journal of Marketing*, 51, 4, 76–88.

M. Besson (1997), *L'impact de la culture nationale sur les systèmes de rémunération des vendeurs en Europe*, thèse HEC, Jouy en Josas.

N. Campbell et al. (1988), A Comparison of Marketing Negotiation in France, Germany, The United Kingdom and the United States, *Journal of Marketing*, 52, 2, 49–62.

Ph. R. Cateora and J. Graham (1999), *International Marketing*, Tenth Edition, Boston, Mc Graw Hill.

G.A. Churchill, N.M. Ford and O. Walker (1993), *Sales Force Management*, Fourth Edition, Homewood, Irwin.

J.A. Coletti and G.S. Tubridy (1987), Effective Major Account Sales Management, *Journal of Personal Selling and Sales Management*, 7, 2, August, 4.

S. Ganassali (1995), L'approche intégrée des facteurs explicatifs de l'efficacité du vendeur: une application à la vente à domicile, thèse de sciences de gestion, Université Pierre Mendès France de Grenoble.

J.L. Graham and Y. Sano (1984), *Smart Bargaining: Doing Business with the Japanese*, Cambridge, Ballinger.

T. Ingram, R. Laforge and C. Schwepker (1997), *Sales Management: Analysis and Decision Making*, Third Edition, Fort Worth, Dryden Press.

R.W. Laforge, C.E. Young and B.C. Hamm (1983), Increasing Sales Productivity through Improved Sales Call Allocation Strategies, *Journal of Personal Selling and Sales Management*, 4, November, 52–59.

R.J. Lewicki and J.A. Litterer (1985), *Negotiation*, Homewood, Irwin

L.M. Lodish (1971), CALLPLAN: An Interactive Salesman's Call Planning System, *Management Science*, 18, 4, Part 2, 26–40.

D.G. Pruitt (1983), Strategic Choice in Negotiation, *American Behavioral Scientist*, 27, 2, 167–174.

B. Skiera and S. Albers (1998), COSTA: Contribution Optimizing Sales Territory Alignment, *Marketing Science*, 17, 3, 181–195.

A. Sharma and M. Levy (1995), Categorization of Customers by Retail Salespeople, *Journal of Retailing*, 71, 1, 71–81.

R. Spiro and B.A. Weitz (1990), Adaptive Selling: Conceptualization, Measurement and Nomological Validity, *Journal of Marketing Research*, 27, 1, 61–69.

R.C. Smyth (1968), Financial Incentives for Salesmen, *Harvard Business Review*, 1,46, 109–117.

W.J. Stanton and R.H. Buskirk (1978), *Management of the Sales Force*, Fifth Edition, Homewood, Irwin.

12 Distribution management

Learning objectives

After studying this chapter you will be able to

1 Understand the role and functions of distribution
2 Understand recent changes in the profession
3 Analyse the connections between manufacturers and distributors
4 Understand the development of sales interfaces
5 Know how to set up a distribution strategy for a manufacturer
6 Understand the strategy of distributors
7 Analyse changing distribution systems
8 Analyse the internationalization of distribution

SPOTLIGHT

THE STORY OF WAL-MART

Many trace discount retailing's birth to 1962, the first year of operation for Kmart, Target and Wal-Mart. But by that time, Sam Walton's tiny chain of variety stores in Arkansas and Kansas was already facing competition from regional discount chains. Sam traveled the country to study this radical, new retailing concept and was convinced it was the wave of the future. He and his wife, Helen, put up 95 per cent of the money for the first Wal-Mart store in Rogers, Arkansas, borrowing heavily on Sam's vision that the American consumer was shifting to a different type of general store.

Today, Sam's gamble is a global company with more than 1.3 million associates worldwide and nearly 5000 stores and wholesale clubs across 10 countries. The "most admired retailer" according to FORTUNE magazine has just completed one of the best years in its history: Wal-Mart generated more than $256 billion in global revenue, establishing a new record and adding more than $26 billion in sales. The company earned almost $9.1 billion in net income and grew earnings per share by more than 15 per cent.

But it all started with an understanding of what consumers want from a retailer.

"The secret of successful retailing is to give your customers what they want", Sam wrote in his autobiography. "And really, if you think about it from the point of view of the customer, you want everything: a wide assortment of good quality merchandise; the lowest possible prices; guaranteed satisfaction with what you buy; friendly, knowledgeable service; convenient hours; free parking; a pleasant shopping experience."

"You love it when you visit a store that somehow exceeds your expectations, and you hate it when a store inconveniences you, or gives you a hard time, or pretends you're invisible."

While other discounters such as Kmart quickly expanded across the country in the 1960s, Sam was able to raise the funds to build only 15 Wal-Mart stores. Wal-Mart got the boost it needed in 1970 when its stock was offered for the first time on the New York Stock Exchange. The public offering created the capital infusion that grew the company to 276 stores by the end of the decade.

By focusing on customer expectations, Wal-Mart was growing rapidly in 11 states.

In the 1980s, Wal-Mart became one of the most successful retailers in America. Sales grew to $26 billion by 1989, compared to $1 billion in 1980. Employment increased tenfold. At the end of the decade there were nearly 1400 stores. Wal-Mart Stores, Inc. branched out into warehouse clubs with the first SAM'S Club in 1983. The first Supercenter, featuring a complete grocery department along with the 36 departments of general merchandise, opened in 1988. Wal-Mart had become a textbook example of managing rapid growth without losing sight of a company's basic values. In Wal-Mart's case, the basic value was, and is, customer service.

Ironically, technology plays an important role in helping Wal-Mart stay customer focused. Wal-Mart invented the practice of sharing sales data via computer with major suppliers, such as Proctor & Gamble. Every time a box of Tide is rung up at the cash register, Wal-Mart's data warehouse takes note and knows when it is time to alert P&G to replenish a particular store. As a result, Wal-Mart stores rarely run out of stock of popular items.

Source: Walmart.com.

Introduction

Distribution, a creator of value

Distribution is the set of operations by which a good or a service coming from the manufacturing is put at the use of the consumer or the user. Distribution systems, hitherto dominated by manufacturers, have changed considerably over the last 25 years because of multiple changes which have left their mark on what is known as "the consumption system". This system links changes to consumer attitudes with the development of distribution structures and with technological, economic and demographic changes plus social factors and influences such as the public authorities or the mass media.

For many years value was only attributed to tangible goods, not to intangible services. This is no longer the case. Distribution plays the role necessary for adjustment between producer offers and consumer demand: in this way it is a source of value creation. Geographic dispersal and the variety of consumer expectations, qualitative as well as quantitative (such as extensive brand choice, supporting products or services sold along with other products), contrast with the rationalization and the concentration of the means of production. To make products available in the quantities households want, while providing services expected by them, such as advice, finance, after-sales service, a warranty, means that intermediaries must put in place a system to fulfil consumer demand. We may consider three categories of transformation which add value to the item (Table 12.1):

1. Material and physical changes: these are operations concerning division, transport and storing of products. They are of an industrial nature.
2. Spatial and temporal alterations: they are considered as distributive functions in their own right, and consist of situating a product with regard to:

 - location: the place where the product is located,
 - batch: the homogeneous quantity of the product,

 - assortment: the list of products offered at the same location and at the same moment,
 - time: the date at which the product is made available.[1]

3. Psychological and commercial changes: these complete the industrial and distributive functions by creating balance between "the state of the upstream offer" and "the state of downstream demand".

As a result, distribution offers a certain number of advantages. It allows for a decrease in the number of transactions and for achieving economies of scale: services provided by a distributor apply to products offered by several manufacturers. In this way they can create distributor economies of scale which would not exist if each manufacturer did its own distribution.

The "distribution" function also allows for improvement in the product assortment offered to the consumer. The assortment offered by the distributors can be composed of the products of several manufacturers, thus exceeding the technical and financial constraints of each and limiting the number of products that have to be manufactured. Finally, the role of the distributor is also to respond better to the expectations of the consumers: as we shall see later, the consumer is demanding more accurate, individualized and personalized services. Taking responsibility for expected services is demanding more intense specialization.

Changes in the global consumption system have led to considerable modification of company distribution policies and, more widely, in global marketing strategies.

Locating the company globally in the production–distribution system has become a major strategic choice. At each level in this system, the functions of production and distribution are fulfilled and the different associated services are delivered efficiently. The performance of the company coupled with its situation within its environment (competition etc.) must also be taken into account. Companies may even pursue strategies of domination, although this is more likely to result in conflict. Each company strives for the most profitable

Table 12.1   How distribution channels create the utilities that reduce the gaps between manufactures and consumers

Shape and form utility	Time Utility	Location utility	Possession utility
Quantity gap Allotment Storage Packaging	**Time gap** Stockpiling Stock management Storage Financing Taking of orders Dispatching	**Spatial gap** Transport Handling Delivery	Information gap Promotion or communication of feedback information or collection of information
Assortment gap Accumulation and construction of a product assortment Construction of a product mix			**Property gap** Buying and selling Credit Payments Financing Service documents such as product adjustment, technical support, guarantee

Source: Adapted from K.G. Hardy and A.J. Magrath, *Marketing Channel Management*, Glenview, Illinois, Scott, Foresman and Co., 1988.

position, taking into account its competence and potential (financial, technical and commercial), and likely future changes. The conditions for success when faced with these strategic issues involved detailed knowledge of production and distribution systems and how they are changing.

Distribution policy has become one of the keys to the development of an effective marketing-mix: the coherence between decisions concerning prices, products, communication, promotion and services on the one hand and the choice of the distribution method and channel on the other hand is one of the essential aspects of a commercial policy. Manufacturers can no longer prepare their marketing plans in isolation and impose them on distributors: they either integrate the distribution stage into their own operations (as in the case of direct marketing, certain dealerships, franchising stores or points of sale under the trademark of the manufacturer), or they negotiate the conditions for the distribution of the product with distributors. In either case, manufacturers must take account of the appropriateness of these conditions to all the other elements of the marketing-mix.

The constant change in distribution has brought about new forms of channel organization and sales methods. Distribution companies themselves are confronted with numerous changes: changes in consumption methods combined with technical innovations concerning products (packaging, modes of transportation, conditioning, handling, automation, storage etc.), financial flows (payment by card and so on), information flows (scanned data, computerization, videotex transmissions, office automation, the Internet etc.) that are continually

modifying distributions systems. Efficiency gains brought about by the improvement of such functions as transport, logistcis or finance allow the most innovative and dynamic competitors to increase their market share or profitability to the detriment of more traditional, less creative forms of business.

Distribution has become a very wide domain which concerns not only physical goods but also services such as financial services, insurance or cleaning services and maintenance. Both public and private services should consider the problem of handling customers, users or beneficiaries: electricity supply, telephone service and medical services, aid for the handicapped or old people and so on.

Manufacture and sale have always been connected. Today, the two functions are even closer and inter-penetrated within companies. The manufacturers of tangible assets have integrated more and more non-material elements (presentation, communication, associated services) into their products. Service companies have integrated more and more direct interventions into the assembly of the end product. This inter-penetration can be seen in an increasing service orientation of manufacturing industries and by a parallel industrial orientation among service businesses.

Forecasting the most effective forms of business is as important an issue for the producer as it is for the distributor. However, no satisfactory theory or model exists in this domain. We are witnessing therefore "life-size" experiments, where, in a completely empirical way, new entrepreneurs are introducing new sales methods – like Dell with direct sales of computers. Some are successful such as certain large self-service specialty stores and hard discount stores; others are unsuccessful like certain kinds of factory shop. In any case, it is in the distribution sector that the largest numbers of companies have been created over the last 30 years (c.f. Appendixes 12.1 and 12.2: "The Distribution Systems" and "Forms of Sales).

The objective of this chapter is to provide explanations for this major phenomenon in the evolution of the Western economy. First, the changes affecting the role and functions of distributors will be clarified. Second, different analyses of the evolution of distribution channels and methods will be explained. Finally, the last part will be dedicated to distribution strategy, taking into account in turn the strategic choice of the manufacturer in distribution material and the strategic choice of the distributor. The more descriptive aspects in the discussion of distribution systems are just a part of several other aspects constituting an overview of the entire subject.

Role and functions of distribution

The role of distributors is particularly important in the case of fast-moving consumer goods: they can specialize in a type of customer expectation which will bring about the creation of specific sales methods or particular services. It would be impossible for a manufacturer to create the whole range of sales methods and desired services on its own account; on the other hand, it is generally possible for a manufacturer to diversify its offer in order to adapt it to each type of distribution channel in the strategy.

The intermediary and its functions: Classic functions in the marketing mix

The role of the distributor is less and less that of a neutral intermediary and more and more that of an active sales agent, capable of sounding out, of stimulating and of directing demand, of improving the offer and modifying conditions. The extension of the functions of the distributor is one of the landmarks in the development of the distribution function.

With the combined effects of keener competition in every sector of distribution, of technological progress which increases differentiation based on quality, the rising price of services which creates a gap with productivity, and with the increasingly subtle and varied expression of customer needs, the functions performed by distribution companies have changed.

Distributors have been able to offer new services to customers or to render the same services in a more effective or better tailored fashion; they have been able to clarify the services that they offer to customers, so putting themselves in a strategic position worthy of differentiation in the eyes of the customers, within increasingly saturated

Classic functions

- buying products demanded by customers from manufactures;
- transport of merchandise from production to consumption locations;
- breaking down of large quantities delivered by the producer into smaller lots conforming to the expectations of the consumer;
- building together assortment in a given location (point of sale) a choice of products expected by the consumer (which will depend on the nature of the point of sale);
- bulking, consisting of grouping together dispersed product lots;
- stocking of products at all intermediate levels of distribution up to point-of-sale stores;
- displaying products at the point of sale, along with associated promotional material;
- selling to consumers;
- other services such as home delivery, installation, after-sales services, finance or consumer information.

Figure 12.1   The classic functions of distribution

markets. Finally, they have changed their organization structure because of the impact of new techniques of distribution management, leading to new attitudes, structures and methods of working, requiring increasingly better training and obliging manufacturer and distributor to cooperate more closely.

What then are the functions of distribution? We may distinguish, on the one hand, a certain number of classic functions (Figure 12.1) to which "modern" functions have been added.

The modern functions of distribution (Table 12.2) go beyond the traditional functions. They do not dispute the traditional functions, but require the distributor to introduce new know-how at the technical and commercial levels. These new methods affect the meaning of distribution operations at a fundamental level in such varied domains as:

- the physical distribution of products or "logistics", thanks to containers, the use of palettes, automatic handling materials, the rationalization of storing methods, the optimization of delivery rounds, the setting up of shops, stores and so on;
- the techniques of dividing, grouping and packaging of products (packs, protective film, new forms of packaging better adapted to self-service etc.);
- sales methods: we may quote for example the generalization of self-service, including wholesalers, with the method of cash-and-carry aimed at retailers, the development of telephone selling, catalogues, postal dispatches, and electronic business;

Table 12.2 Commerce, productivity and technology

Elements of the commercial function	New technology developed by commercial companies
1. Investigation and knowledge of demand	Marketing surveys based on automatic databases set up with optical checkout readings
2. Investigation and selection of the offer	Setting up of electronic catalogues (video) aimed at member stores (Paridoc)
3. Orders and production control	Use of computer networks (Exchange of Computerized Data, EDI)
4. Production	Testing laboratories
5. Consumer information	Comparative information sheets (Fnac, Carrefour) Electronic services
6. Shipping and delivery	Cold chain Control and automatic dispatch
7. Storage and allocation	Automated platforms Vertical stocking managed by computer
8. Point of sale display	Presentation videodisc Interactive terminals Automatic labelling
9. Communication of the offer	Electronic Promotion at the point of sale Electronic services
10. Sale	Optical reading at checkout (scanning) Sales by Internet or electronic media
11. Payment/transaction	Private credit card Electronic payment (Internet) Credit
12. Services linked to use and consumption	Local informative television Electronic media

- methods of commercial intelligence gathering and action such as the use of marketing research, consumer panels, geomerchandising, set-up studies, catchment areas and product assortment studies;
- sales promotion, advertising, public relations, creation of retail brands and customer relations (development of customer departments within the company);
- store management techniques due to the development of new methods in the domains of supply and stock management, budgetary control, financial management and management of sales areas (shops, departments, shelf space). Such methods generally require the use of information technology whose progress also modifies the conditions of exploitation of distribution: for example, stocktaking, registering and payment at the checkout, development of the processes of optical scanning.

For example, most of the larger retailers such as Wal-Mart, Ahold, Tesco, Carrefour, Auchan, Casino and Leclerc use cash terminals equipped with scanners which are placed directly at the checkouts and which allow for computerized management of stock, the flow of goods and money. The same modern distribution techniques are used by car manufacturers for spare parts, and by clothing chains like Benetton for clothing distribution. In this latter case, manufacturing systems are driven by customer demand: instead of producing first and then distributing, the company produces according to what it distributes. In order to work effectively management integration is necessary, and tools of the "just in time" type are required. This method of working is widely used today in chain stores distributing fashion wear or in other industries such as computer or car manufacturing.

Concerning wholesale businesses, we can observe that besides physical and logistic functions, they can also perform

- financial functions: certification of delivery, invoicing, recovery; credit and discount actions are often added;
- information functions: wholesale companies collect information of diverse origin and transform it into management decisions which, principally through the

intermediary of stocks, aim to ensure the equilibrium of supply and demand;

■ service functions: the development of services provided by the wholesaler will, in the next decade, become one of the dominant features in the development of this function.

Manufacturers and distributors have gradually transformed their relations from simple sellers and buyers effecting transactions to a bilateral relationship setting up a real system of value creation (Chapter 1) that benefits all members of the channel from manufacturer to client.

"Trade Marketing" (Toolbox 12.1) is the expression for this approach using cooperation between manufacturers and distributors to maximize profit by minimizing needless cost and eliminating activities which do not add value. Such a system requires concerted use of modern distribution techniques, which results in shared investment between the partners in the distribution channel and coordinated organization of each service provider in this channel: manufacturers, distributors, financial service and logistics providers (Table 12.3 and next chapter on Merchandising and Logistics).

TOOLBOX 12.1

TRADE MARKETING

Trade marketing or distributor marketing is a concerted approach between manufacturers and traders involving co-operation in logistics, merchandising, information systems, and promotions. Its role is to pinpoint the needs of distributors to develop long-term relationships of trust with them. There are two types of needs:

1. economic (reduction of physical distribution costs of the product);
2. marketing (reinforcing the positioning of the brand-name through assortment, promotions and merchandising).

Trade marketing can be considered as the application of marketing to the manufacturer–distributor commercial relationship. It involves the recognition of the distributor by the manufacturer as a customer in his own right.

It requires the analysis of the manufacturer–distributor relationship, the choice of common objectives, the existence of specific structures (category managers) and the exchange of computerized data (EDI: Electronic Data Interchange).

It accompanies new practices such as ECR (Efficient Consumer Response).

Category Management is aimed at improving the partnership between manufacturer and distributor. The category manager of the product takes into account the development of a product category. He manages distributor space in a way that is understood and preferred by the customer. For example, a distributor's sales space for meat should correspond to a global offer rather than an offer which is scattered all over the sales floor. So the meat mategory includes self-service, frozen meat, traditional and ready-cooked products. A category can also include complementary needs (such as nappies alongside baby foods).

Efficient Consumer Response is inspired by just-in-time techniques. This notion appeared for the first time in 1992 during a conference of the Food Marketing Institute (U.S.). It is aimed at improving the efficiency of the supply chain at four levels:

1. optimization of supply flows,
2. optimization of the assortment,
3. optimization of promotional operations,
4. optimization of new product launches.

It requires

1. immediate acquisition of information on consumers: point-of-sale terminals, optical reading;
2. rapid transmission of acquired information in an organized form allowing suppliers and service providers (e.g. transporters, warehouse managers) to meet the demand just-in-time using systems such as EDI:[i] "the principal contribution of EDI is a reduction in delays which allows for organization of tight flows . . . based on check-out data, either with the warehouses or directly with the suppliers";
3. the creation of data warehouses stocking the information obtained from the distributors and the suppliers concerning purchases, products, special offers, store results, accessible by the suppliers[ii] and the distributors and which can be used to improve the response to the demand, in terms of stock management, shelf-space product offers, optimization of special offers, a place for category management and the introduction of new products.

---

[i] de Garets, Dubois & Paccou (1993) "Théories de la Distribution et Pratique de l'EDI chez Auchan" *Décisions Marketing*, 0, May, pp. 87–92.
[ii] This accessibility is sometimes only partial for the supplier due to the reticence of certain distributors to give all the information required.

Table 12.3   Manufacturer–Distributor collaboration in trade marketing

Domains	Actions
Logistics	Organization: just in time
Computerization	Development of computerized data exchange systems (Electronic Data Interchange)
Products	Definition of an offer adapted to the brand name, to be seen at the point of sale in terms of references and formats. Exclusive rights during the launch of a new product. Manufacture of products with the distributor's brand name.
Promotions	Joint promotion operations during a commercial demonstration (flyer including advertising for the manufacturer's products, advertising at the point of sale, ends of aisles)
Merchandising	Joint creation or concerted adaptation of a merchandising programme
Studies	Communication of global information concerning the market by the manufacturer and specific to local customer demand by the distributor. The creation of computerized databases via scanning and information handling allows for the availability of early and accurate market indications

Source: Benoun & Héliès-Hassid (op. cit.) (1995).

These in-depth modifications concerning the business of distribution have not been carried out at the same speed in all the different forms of distribution, which has led to the disappearance of some and the redefining or the emergence of others. The slow response of some distributors has excluded them from the market while others, by integrating marketing, have developed: every performed function and service rendered, be it "free" or not, has a cost for the customer. This cost is reflected in the level of prices and profit margins. Certain distributors choose therefore to perform only a few functions (discount, discount traders, certain self-service stores) with the aim of delivering the lowest prices possible, while others prefer to perform several functions and to render numerous services justifying a higher price for the "product–service" combination or "global product" (shops selling luxury goods).

Three phenomena play a fundamental role at this level:

1. the possibility of cost transfer upstream (to the manufacturers, for example, who agree to put the products on the shelves or to participate in the distributors' advertising or train their personnel) or downstream (to the customers, for example, who agree to move, store, buy in large quantities, transport etc.). For example, most large self-service stores require their suppliers to participate in advertising and promotional operations which they organize. In the same way, large self-service speciality stores such as Ikea for furniture tend to leave transport and construction in the hands of the consumer.

   Around its factory at Melfi near Naples, Fiat has gathered together 20 equipment manufacturers, which allows for the reduction of stock and the maximization of just-in-time delivery. For example, equipment manufacturers load the pallets in their own warehouse and these go directly to the assembly lines. The orders arrive every five minutes through the computer network and the bulking and despatch of parts is organized every two hours. This integration of suppliers allows for the minimization of management, transport and stock shortage costs.

2. distributor productivity in the performed function following his organization, techniques used and so on. Hard discounters such as Aldi or Lidl have also tried to maximize productivity by reducing the staff used for cleaning, shelf-space layout and checkout thanks to specific packaging techniques plus the presentation of products on pallets and staff flexibility.

3. the negotiation of profit margins between the distributor and the other members of the chain, through discount policies, for example. The principle of royalties paid by the franchising store to the franchiser corresponds to this sharing out: the franchiser, for example, takes charge of personnel training, general advertising for the franchising chain and the negotiation of supplies; in return, he requires a variable portion of the franchise turnover. Fast food chains such as McDonalds or Quick, opticians and film distribution operate according to this principle. The result is that two rival sales methods performing the same functions will be able to achieve different results depending on the combination of the elements above.

For industrial products, desirable distributor specialization is often largely the result of specialist knowledge of the intrinsic qualities of products and the more complex characteristics involved in using them. The superiority of an intermediary specialized in purely distributive functions is not such a determinant factor. It is more usual for a manufacturer to take responsibility for the bulk of these functions, assisted by providers of auxiliary services (insurers, carriers or financial institutions). In any case, as Lambin[2] notes, "this superiority of intermediaries is not inevitable. A distributor will only remain in a distribution network as long as the other partners in the exchange process judge that this intermediary exercises his functions better than they could themselves or that other institutions outside the existing system could" (Appendix 12.3 "Wholesale Business").

This last observation is valid for all goods and services, be they in industrial or in consumer markets. The most important determinant factor is the participation of the intermediary in the system of value creation for the client, both in industrial and in consumer goods.

Distribution channels and retail formats

According to Stern and El Ansary,[3] the channel is "the set of institutions which has the responsibility of ensuring the availability of products and services at a consumer level". But, as Filser[4] observes, we can distinguish, side by side with channel analysis, the analysis of the channel–customer interface. This function, ensured by the retail institutions, operates in points of sale which can be classified according to different retail formats such as hard discount, department store, supermarket or hypermarket. We will define a retail format as a set of physical and operational characteristics from a point of sale to retail, determining a store type.

The distinction between channel and retail format is straightforward: the channel concerns the succession of commercial intermediaries which transport the manufacturer's product to the customer, whereas the retail format is the distribution unit which is located at the end-point of this transportation.

The analysis of distribution channels

Distribution channel structures have been the object of numerous studies at a number of levels (see the notions of long, short, extra-short channels described later) and the number of intermediaries at each level. We can traditionally distinguish four types of channel:

1. traditional channels, where each member of the channel is independent; this is the case, for example, in the distribution of numerous traditional services such as electricity, plumbing, joinery, hairdressing services or in independent shops. These retailers or trades people are supplied by wholesalers who in turn are themselves supplied by manufacturers.
2. administered channels, where, to avoid the adverse consequences of disorganization in the channel

(absence of economies of scale, gaps in productivity, overstocking and shortages etc.), one or several members of the channel influence the other members. This can concern groups of independent traders who buy in common.
3. contractual channels, where relations between the members of the channel rest on explicit contractual bases. This is the case, for example, for retailing or franchising cooperatives; Mc. Donalds, where services is concerned, is a good illustration of this.
4. integrated channels, where a member of the channel takes over all the functions, from buying from manufacturers (or doing the manufacturing itself) up to delivery to the consumers. Ikea, which manufactures its own furniture, or Decathlon where sports goods are concerned, are good examples.

Various theoretical explanations have been offered concerning the structure of a channel: economic, behavioural and managerial approaches.

The economic approaches

Concerning economic analysis, distribution exists only because it allows the principal agents, manufacturers and customers to maximize their profit on the one hand and their utility on the other, by delegating certain functions to intermediaries who provide them at lower cost. With regard to this, Filser[5] notes three approaches:

- first, where the role of the distributor is totally determined by the producer;[6, 7]
- second, which integrates the role of economic variables such as demand,[8] the constituents of distribution cost,[9] economies of scale and other general economic indicators such as domestic income and the amount of capital invested;[10]
- third, which integrates the objectives of distribution companies: the distributors become separate agents in the development of the channel and can themselves proceed to a reallocation of certain activities in order to create change within the channel.[11]

These three approaches have created spin-off studies looking at value creation for the customer through spatial availability, batch size, delays, variety of products, product assortment, symbols associated with products, services and so on, and at concepts of channel performance measured in terms of cost and productivity. El Ansary[12] suggests the measurement of channel productivity using four concepts:

1. effectiveness with regard to the expectations of the customers;
2. equity, which is the capacity of the channel to serve all customers under the same conditions;

Table 12.4 Types of power bases available to manufacturers, distributors and buyers

Types of power base	Manufacturer advantages	Distributor or buyer advantages
Reward	Ability to offer product with low prices and quantity discounts	Ability to offer large buying volume
Coercive	Ability to withdraw product (with little loss in sales) when no comparable alternative is available to distributor or buyer	Ability to reject offer (with little loss in sales) when no equivalent distributors or buyers are available to the seller
Expert	Ability to offer superior or needed technical assistance	Ability to provide unique distribution support
Referent	Ability to offer prestigious brand name	Ability to offer image of quality retail or to serve as prestigious example of satisfied buyer
Legitimate	Contractual provision which requires to carry full line	Contractual provision which requires seller to provide warranties, repair and exclusive distribution
Persuasive	Ability to induce support via sales presentation	Ability to inform suppliers of "hot" products and special offers
Economic Scale	Ability to offer low price products	Ability to reach many accounts efficiently and with competitive prices

Source: J.P. Guiltinan and G.W. Paul, *Marketing Management, Strategies and Programs*, 2nd Ed., McGraw-Hill, Inc., NY, 1985.

3. efficiency, which is the relationship between the channel production and the implemented system;
4. financial efficiency which is the profitability of assets in the channel.

Finally, there are certain economic models which seek out the channel member who will be responsible for the essential functions of stocking and product assortment. The postponement and speculation model[13] is in line with this perspective. The postponement model allows a distribution company to improve the efficiency of its operations by redirecting the modifications of the characteristics of the product towards the intermediaries situated downstream and by delaying the constitution of stocks. Risk is thus redirected downstream (or in time). On the other hand, the distributor can accept risk by speculating: They are then encouraged to put forward modifications to the product and to establish stocks benefiting from reductions in cost brought about, for example, by large-scale production.

This set of economic approaches provides a solid basis on which to understand certain principles in the development of channels, but certain factors are neglected by these models, notably those that concern the organizational dimension and the determination of distribution companies' strategy based purely on managerial objectives. These factors are the basis for channel analyses based on the behaviour of the actors (behavioural analyses). Behavioural analyses depend on concepts such as the power of the distributors, cooperation or conflict between members of the channel.

The behavioural approaches

Studies said to be "behavioural" focus principally on the behaviour of distributors and, in particular, the appearance and resolution of conflicts.[14, 15] They are inspired by organizational theory. Table 12.4 shows the diverse forms of power held by producers and distributors by describing the advantages accruing to each protagonist for each of these forms.

Sources of conflict and the methods of conflict resolution have been studied widely. Relationships between manufacturers and intermediaries can lead to growing conflict for channel domination. In a traditional channel, each member is independent and attempts to exercise their power through the intermediary of market rules. In an integrated channel, one of the members controls the whole channel. In fact, each member of the channel, according to their power and interest, can seek to control or even integrate another member of the channel. The decision entails choosing between holding on to a supplier (or a client) and so using market forces, cooperating with this supplier (or client), or integrating this supplier (or client) into the company through merger or acquisition (hierarchical system). One finds here classic opposition between market and hierarchy developed by Williamson[16] and taken up by Mac Cammon[17]

Table 12.5 Forms of organization of a retailer's supply system

Williamson	Mc Cammon	Operational organization
Market	Traditional channel	Supply management by the point of sale or the department
	Administered channel	
	Contractual channel	External central purchasing unit (services providers)
		Cooperative central purchasing unit
Hierarchy	Integrated channel	Integrated central purchasing unit
		Integrated logistics
		Integrated production

(Table 12.5). Each solution has its advantages and drawbacks. We can observe differences in strategy between companies.

The Smartville plant where the Smart is manufactured gathers together several suppliers who work for this car manufacturer. This allows for the minimization of order and delivery times and a reduction in certain stock. The equipment manufacturers present on the site are considered to be partners in their own right, depending on the sales rate of the cars themselves. Hays supplies logistic services by being linked to Carrefour for purposes of inventory management, which allows for important logistic savings in this distribution chain. Gefco carries out transport activities for Peugeot. The choices thus made clearly demonstrate the strategies of cooperation developed by the distributors with regard to certain functions which they prefer to carry out externally. At the same time, however, a strong link is established because the service provider has made a considerable investment in the relationship and this creates commitment.

Behavioural strategies will be revisited in the concepts of generic and resistance strategies.

Generic and resistance strategies are derived from the concept of power of negotiation;[18] for a company this depends on:

- its capacity to have access (or to allow access) to the final market,
- its size,
- the diversity of its supply sources (for the distributor), or the diversification of its markets (for the manufacturer).

When this relation of power is unbalanced and moves towards complete control of one party by the other, so that one party's objectives can no longer be pursued at all, strategy becomes reactive and relies on "resistance strategies". There are three such strategies:

1. Confrontation strategy: the manufacturer and the distributor are in conflict and, generally, the manufacturer tries to resist by increasing its size or by developing other distribution methods; several producers may proliferate brand names in order to carry more weight with the distributor. The beer market in Europe, that of luxury items or food products, dominated by certain giants such as Interbrew (beer), LVMH (luxury goods), Danone and Nestlé (food products) are examples of this. The use of direct sales is another means often used by producers to avoid distributor pressure. Several wine manufacturers also use direct mail order catalogue selling or Internet selling (e.g. the "chateauonline.com" site). In the same way, certain banks or insurance companies have developed direct sales networks for their products and services (ING, Cortal, Norwich Union, etc.).

2. Cooperation strategy: a partnership (trade marketing, for example) is established between the members of the channel to optimize the management of flow and product assortments.

3. Avoidance strategy: the dominated institution tries to limit the power of the dominant institution by establishing countervailing power – very low costs which are therefore very competitive (the hard discounters Lidl, Aldi and Leader Price are examples), differentiation (through the brand or competence) or specialization (focus strategy) on a type of specific demand such as themed restaurants or shops specialized in video games or computers.

The integration of these strategies into Porter's model

The analysis of distribution channels fits well into Porter's[19] model of the forces of competition because it incorporates at one and the same time rivalry among the competitors, the power of the suppliers, that of the customers, the potential entrants and the substitute products. The usefulness of the analysis originates in the particular role of the distributor at each of these levels:

- The power of suppliers depends on the influence of the manufacturers, the distributor's desire to integrate and the desire of each agent, manufacturer and distributor to cooperate and\or to dominate.

■ The power of customers is of course very different depending on whether the customer is the distributor (for the manufacturer or for the distributor situated solely upstream in the channel) or the end consumer.

■ Potential entrants can start to compete with the weaker distributors through integration. This generally applies to foreign brand-names becoming established in the national market.

■ Companies likely to introduce substitute products are in fact new forms of distribution which are taking over the existing formats both partially and sometimes even totally. The arrival of maxi-discounters, for example, has created strong competition with certain supermarkets or hypermarkets, as well as sounding the death knell for many traditional distribution companies.

It is not surprising therefore that rivalry among distributors is based on three generic distribution strategies:

1. cost leadership,
2. differentiation,
3. focus.

These strategies will be referred to again later but it is important to note that all are based on a specific method of organizing the channel, competitive advantage being obtained as much in the structure and the optimization of functions exercised throughout the channel as in the conception and implementation of the sales interface.

We may observe that distribution companies such as "category killers" specializing in a given domain like sport, toys, clothing, electronic material, household appliances or furniture try to dominate their rivals not only through low costs but also through a strong differentiation in products. These new types of hybrid trading are becoming more and more widespread.

The analysis of distribution formats

Several authors[20] have tried to explain the development of a specific type of channel, namely retail. This is the channel within which change has been most visible. Retail formats, such as hypermarkets, supermarkets, and discount stores, local shops, factory shops and department stores have experienced radical changes, which have been often described but less frequently explained. Several theories have nevertheless been put forward.[21]

Some theories, said to be "mechanistic", seek to explain developments using a general theory of change in retailing, creating the almost quasi-automatic appearance of each new retail format. Such authors have developed "wheel" theories along with theories such as "distribution

accordion", the retail life cycle, the "dialectical process" and natural selection. Other authors have adopted a contingent approach (adaptive theories) where the evolution of distribution methods depends on several factors allied to consumer preference or distributor strategy.

The development of retail formats

The early "mechanistic" analyses of the development of retail formats have been inspired by the "distribution wheel" theory developed by Mac Nair:[22] a new retail format has appeared thanks to price differentiation, made possible by narrower profit margins. The high sales volume and the technological novelty of this format attract consumers. This success promotes the arrival of competitors. Each one tries to be different by introducing new services, which increases running expenses and causes an "embourgeoisement" of the format (wider ranges, increase of profit margins etc.). A new retail format, a new sales technology, based on low prices and low profit margins then arrives on the scene and so on.

Hollander[23] completed Mac Nair's analysis by explaining this "embourgeoisement" as a result of less attention paid to costs by the store management when the retail format is successful, through extending the product ranges because of pressure from suppliers, introducing products with weaker rotation and higher profit margins, by the tendency to raise the standard of living, which pushes shops to introduce products with higher profit margins and so on.

There is some empirical support for this theory. However, there are several exceptions and a number of new retail formats have not been based on lower prices than those of the competition but some other kind of differentiation, for example better service or wider product assortment. Mac Nair[24] himself believed that his model did not reflect all cases because it was too deterministic. However, the advent of forms of commerce such as supermarkets or hard discounters clearly illustrate this theory.

The "distribution accordion" theory is based more on product assortment width than on price. Wide and unspecialized product assortments are succeeded by narrow and specialized assortments, which are themselves succeeded by wide product assortments. This theory, developed notably by Hollander[25] from the study of American retail stores, cannot be readily confirmed either in foreign markets or even in America itself, where opposing retail formats are introduced and coexist. Nevertheless, this theory rightly indicates the importance of variety in defining a retail format and determining the success of a sales method. The present emergence of certain hard discount chains such as Leader Price who add certain quality products to their range corresponds to this second theory.

Other mechanistic processes of evolution have since been put forward:

- The dialectical model which supposes an adaptation of the retail format to competitors who have developed contrary methods. Each retail format attempts to eliminate the differentiation that gives the competitor an advantage by appropriating it in order to reap the benefits itself. Thus, a convergence occurs, a "synthesis" defining a new method.
- The life cycle model of distribution is inspired by the classic idea of a product's life cycle, but this type of model seems to be more descriptive than explanatory and suffers the same limitations as those encountered in the domain of products, such as limited predictive capacity, phase length or validity limits.
- The natural selection model[26] compares the evolution of retail formats with the evolution of biological species. Each variant is determined at its origin by a natural tendency: for some, the quality of performance, for others, price strategy. There is thus no unique model of evolution but different evolutionary processes similar to biological evolution, ageing, regression, hypertrophy and convergence. For example, ageing can be due to a variable such as the psychology of the successors due to the founder of the company, hypertrophy due to an absence of competition during a given period.

This last model is not therefore totally mechanistic but indicates clearly the adaptation of retail formats to the environment. Although it has limits – the variety of possible evolutions, for example, which does not allow for prediction – it has the merit of introducing wider analyses and mechanisms for the evolution of retail formats.

Adaptive models enable us to exceed the narrow vision of mechanistic theories. They base the evolution of distribution methods on the evolution of consumer preference. These vary in both time and space.

For instance, the niche theory explains the appearance of retail formats according to combinations of the customer's system of preferences. Each transformation of this system opens a "niche" for the definition of a new method encompassing the new combination of "price–service–variety–quality–installation–sales technology" desired by the type of given consumer. But the problem of predicting the dynamics of retail formats remains difficult because the evolution of the preference system itself depends on multiple factors in the economic, technological and sociological environments.

Finally, one more analytical model which can also be considered as adaptive seeks to explain the evolution of retail formats using company strategy itself. Constraints of management such as economies of scale, financial criteria and constraints of environment such as changing living standards, lifestyles or expectations determine the strategies of distribution companies and lead them

to define new retail formats which optimize management criteria.

Towards an integration of theories concerning the evolution of channels and distribution methods

Several arguments emerge from studying these theories, which may allow us to tackle the evolution of distribution systems. The first consists of integrating explanations relative to the channel and to the retail format. As we will show later, this integration quickly becomes a necessity as soon as we study the numerous connections between the various actors in the distribution system. Financial relationships between various groups occur at several stages in the channel. But the benefits and the need for an integrated approach are more fundamental. They are based on important interactions between the most decisive variables in the distribution system.

We can simply consider four important flows which allow the system to function (Figure 12.2):

1. a flow of products,
2. a financial flow,
3. a flow of information,
4. a flow of property.

Each of these streams is influenced by a certain number of determining factors originating in the market or the macro-environment:

- the pressure of demand such as expectations or types of needs under the influence of economic and sociological change;
- competitive pressure on each market between companies having the same type of distribution and between retail formats;
- the objectives of companies;
- technological changes which modify the conditions of flow functioning: logistics, office automation or electronic banking, either in a processing capacity or in handling speed.

The result is a system where channels and retail formats constantly interact and can undergo important modifications depending on changes in the determining factors. Each transformation of one of these factors (for example, data transmission for orders, modifications of conditions of handling and storage, or modification of customer requirements) may give rise to a modification of the structure and/or the behaviour of the companies which operate in these flows, under competitive pressure. A company which does not agree to be transformed risks being overtaken by its competitors or/and having a lower performance than the others. This has been the case of

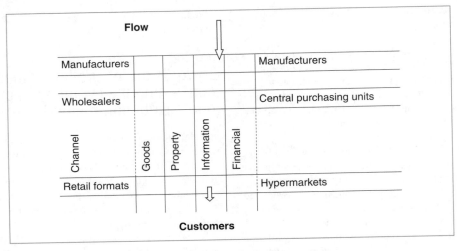

Figure 12.2   The distribution system

cooperatives in several European countries or certain types of retailers and, even more so, numerous traditional distributors controlling small shops and who either cannot or do not know how to use new sales technologies.

We can observe then either a modification of the functioning of the channel with the same actors, or changing actors such as the appearance of new type of intermediaries, new retail formats or again simultaneous transformation of all these elements. It follows that the separation of the problems of channel evolution and retail formats is not a completely satisfactory explanation. We cannot separate the success or failure of a given outlet from their integration into the distribution channel. The competitive advantages of sales formulae are obtained through better integration of the channel members. The case of Benetton, the clothing distributor, is a good example. The company notes the most successful models chosen by the customers and send orders to its factories for the upstream manufacture of items according to this choice. The retail outlet is not only the location where a pre-decided collection is distributed, it is also where successful models are decided upon.

The political economy model

The most complete model of analysis, integrating the entire set of the previous theoretical elements, has been put forward by Stern and Reve[27] under the name of the political economy model of channels. The whole channel is considered as an organization, that is to say a structure having a certain mode of operation. This organization (called internal political economy) exists in an environment (external political economy), which influences the decisions of institutions. Besides, internal political economy is in turn subdivided into an economy,

that is to say a set of structures and process of decision governing transactions, and a policy which determines the climate of transactions (Table 12.6).[28]

This table is very useful because it clearly distinguishes the two forces in interaction: the economy, which represents structures and decision-making processes such as transactional choices or performance criteria and policy which includes structures and behavioural processes such as power relations, conflict, cooperation or climate of transactions. Economic and behavioural conceptions, internal and external explanations of the evolution of the channel in relation to the environment are also integrated.

We can find a comparable framework in the pioneering work of the IMP Group (Industrial Marketing and Purchasing Group),[29] which is interested in supplier–client relations between industrial companies within an international framework and shows the importance of networks which endure and foster permanent relationships. The principles of their analysis are as follows:

- The transaction is simply one episode in the relationship between supplier and client.
- The initial client–supplier transaction requires heavy investment.
- The atmosphere of the relationship plays an important role in decision-making and in the loyalty of the partners.
- Risk is at the centre of industrial behaviour (rather than desire in the case of consumer behaviour).
- The client and the supplier interact in order to define the offer and the demand.
- Markets are networks where relations are established in a complex game between clients and suppliers and also with several other stakeholders, service providers, public or private institutions.

Table 12.6 The political economy model of channels

Political economy of the channel	Internal political economy (channel)	Internal economy	Internal economic structure	Form of transactions (market-hierarchy)
		Internal economic processes	Decision mechanisms (performance criteria)
		Internal policy	Internal socio-political structure	Relations of power and dependence
			Internal socio-political processes	Dominant sentiments (atmosphere of transactions)
	External political economy (environment)	External economy		
		External policy		

Factors influencing the choice of a distribution system

The choice of a distribution system for the manufacturer rests on numerous factors connected to its human, financial and commercial potential, its environment and its objectives. This same analytical framework can be retained for the distributor but, in that case, a certain number of specific elements must be taken into account.

The choice of a distribution system by the manufacturer

Numerous works have been dedicated to the choice of a distribution channel. This perspective seems nevertheless to be a little narrow. The choice of a distribution strategy requries not only the choice of one or several channels by the manufacturer, but also taking into consideration of the set of interactions between decisions taken at this level and the set of strategic decisions of the company. It is more a question of establishing a distribution strategy than choosing a channel or a sales method, even though these decisions are at the centre of the analysis (Figure 12.3).

Strategic objectives in distribution

The first stage consists of fixing the objectives of the company with regard to distribution. These are a "by-product" of the more fundamental objectives of the company; themselves defined on the basis of its capabilities (know how) and its mission (leading idea). Clearly a steel company conceives its distribution differently from a consumer goods company.

The company business can be defined as "a combination of satisfied needs, addressed market and applied technology" (Chapter 2). The company business, according to its level of professional skill, the type of transformation used, the length of the production cycle, the weight and bulk of products, can determine an important number of distribution decisions. For example, different types of goods such as tobacco, alcohol and foodstuffs will be the object of different forms of distribution.

The second element determining the general strategic objectives of the company is the mission which it has given itself: which type of need is it trying to satisfy? The answer to this very general question is essential because it will define in a spatial and temporal way the target customers and, consequently, the real goal of distribution. For example, the choice of a very specific target group of customers with specific needs justifies the decision in the strategic plan to build or to participate in an exclusive channel.

The general objectives of the company are fixed by the management, in line with the expectations of the owners. They illustrate at one and the same time the mission the company has given itself and the wishes of the owners of the capital. For example, an objective might be to increase turnover by 20% over 3 years, within a particular market, and achieving some specified level (10%) of return on capital invested. The choice of market depends on the mission of the company; the type and level of objectives are designed by the management: a rapid rise in capital value, growth, profitability, financial independence and diversification of risks.

Based on these general objectives, we can deduce objectives appropriate to marketing strategy and, more specifically, to distribution: territory coverage, numerical distribution objectives (number of stores holding the brand

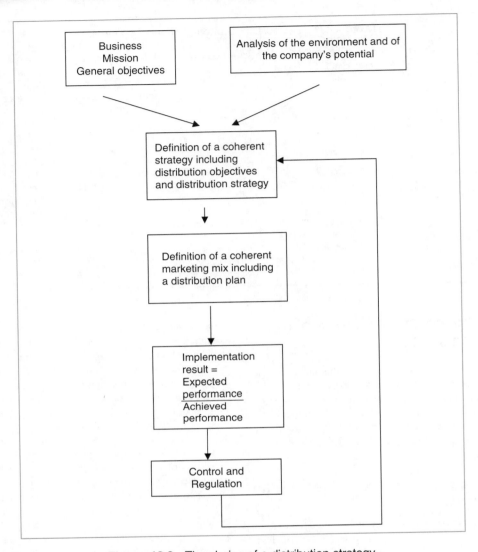

Figure 12.3   The choice of a distribution strategy

compared to the number of shops holding the product), turnover level and profitability by channel, sales method, brand name, return on invested capital.

Coca-Cola's strategy is to cover as large a part of the world as possible by entering markets at the earliest possible moment. To this end, they try to be present in all types of distribution, from the hypermarket to the automatic distributor or on the web.

Conversely, automobile distributors have tried to attain selective and exclusive distribution by arguing for the uniqueness of the product which demands numerous services such as after-sales service, security, upkeep, repairs, supplies of specific spare parts or resale of the vehicle. It seems that these justifications are insufficient, since automobile distribution is increasingly handled by other businesses, discounters or again through the Internet.

The characteristics of the manufacturer and its environment

The choice of a distribution strategy depends on a number of factors, appropriate to the situation of the company and its environment. The characteristics of the product of the business, the service provider or manufacture of consumer goods are prime factors in making the choice. In industrial marketing, it is often the case that certain types of goods need a particular form of distribution, often obliging the manufacturer to set up its own distribution network. The type of channel chosen depends not only on the type of goods but also on the type of client and, more generally, on the system of value creation for the client. If the value depends on a process of interaction, there will be a tendency to choose a direct channel. This is often the case in complex industrial services businesses requiring client participation in the setting up and delivery of the service (businesses related to research or engineering, law firms, consultants).

Several methods exist at this level: association with manufacturers of complementary goods to create units of distribution, choice of intermediaries in the specialist trade, creation or not of exclusive concessions and so on. When it comes to consumer goods, the choice of the route to market, and more widely the distribution strategy, is also related to the nature of the goods.

When the company possesses a rare and specific item or a specific market position, it is tempting to use some kind of exclusive distribution or to resort to carefully selected intermediaries. If the item requires important technical assistance, intermediaries capable of supplying on-the-spot services are better (specialized stores having a good installation, maintenance or after-sales service). When the goods are very standardized, requiring few supporting services, mass forms of non-specialist distribution may be suitable.

The nature of the company and its financial, commercial, technical and human resources are also important factors in the choice of a distribution strategy. For example, companies distributing fresh farm-produce have their own logistic needs (trucks etc.) and they have to choose intermediaries with a policy of rigorous delivery. In the same way, certain companies importing industrial goods have no on-the-spot technical facilities and have to choose intermediaries capable of ensuring technical follow-up, while local companies can ensure a complete service and choose to distribute the goods themselves. A company having a large and exclusive sales force will use a different distribution policy from one which has a network of sales representatives each covering several companies, or a company having no sales force which chooses direct marketing. The banking sector and insurance companies for example include a large variety of forms of distribution: over-the-counter, classic sellers, advisors, brokers, agents and direct selling on the Internet.

Customer types also influence distribution strategy. Their financial standing, technical knowledge, dispersal, and the services they expect influence distribution policy. When customers are private individuals, geographically scattered, and when products are standardized and need few services, the forms of self-service or direct distribution (classic distance sales, e-trade) are appropriate. In contrast, when customers are few in number and looking for technical products requiring advice and services, then more personalized forms of distribution are chosen. It would take too long to examine here all the types of customer expectations, so we will dwell solely on

the fact that the basic principle of marketing, which is the value creation for clients and other important stakeholders, plays as important a role in distribution as in production.

The characteristics of the existing distribution network also play an important role. Companies distributing the same products in several countries choose different methods of distribution because the nature of channels and methods of distribution vary by country. They can therefore choose intermediaries when these match their expectations or set up their own distribution network when no intermediary is suitable or when the one that is suitable is already working with a competitor. Catalogue selling, for example, varies a lot between France, England and Germany.

The other variables in the environment must also be taken into account when defining distribution strategies. They include political, legal, technical, social, cultural factors and so on. For example, European rules concerning price, competition, sales and distribution of goods such as tobacco and medicines still differ on numerous points, despite attempts to harmonize European Union directives, and require manufacturers to adapt their distribution policy. In the same way, the specific ways in which data transmission has developed in different countries affect the implementation of direct marketing and e-business.

Finally, strategic decisions in distribution have a direct influence on the marketing-mix defined by the company. To choose such a distribution network is, to a certain extent, the same as choosing a particular price level, type of packaging, discount or communication policy, or form of service. In the development of their strategic positioning, companies may or may not give priority to distribution: Avon based its marketing policy entirely on the system of sales by representatives. But, for other companies, the policy of distribution is a consequence of the choice made in price, product or communication. Whatever the pre-eminent element of the marketing-mix, what is essential is to be harmonized with the other marketing decisions of the company.

The definition of a coherent distribution strategy

Depending on the objectives of the company, its potential and its environment, and above all its strategic positioning, the choice of a distribution strategy is defined according to a certain number of criteria:

■ Selectivity: the company can seek the widest distribution of its product through engaging all possible types of intermediaries or, on the contrary, limit its distribution to a number of selected or even exclusive intermediaries. In the latter case, the intermediaries distribute the company's products exclusively in the product category. It may, for example, involve franchising (e.g. for textiles or domestic appliances) or exclusive concessions (e.g. for cars and industrial or agricultural technical materials).

- Power: the company chooses the form of distribution which gives it the strongest coverage of the territory. Certain very powerful distribution groups have outlets all over the territory and allow extensive distribution through themselves as sole intermediary. The coverage of a territory can thus be obtained either by a relatively unselective policy (all the possible intermediaries) or by a policy of selection of powerful intermediaries. Distributor power also affects the degree to which the supplier can gain access to end clients. This can be very important for brand-name policy. Large luxury brand-names such as Hermes, Cartier, Lacoste or Gucci will thus have a tendency to favour exclusive distribution in their own stores, whereas the more common consumer products such as Danone or Colgate will be more attracted to distribution in stores such as hypermarkets which are capable of ensuring mass distribution, even though it may be more difficult to have specific influence on the client within the framework of these stores.

- Control of the channel: a manufacturer can hope for a degree of control over the conditions of distribution (service, price, handling, advertising, promotion, merchandising) and to be able to choose the type of distribution allowing him control over these conditions. It is the case that very powerful retailing chains will carry such influence in negotiations that manufacturers are unlikely to be able to impose their own terms. There are difficulties in controlling multiple forms of distribution if an unselective approach to distribution is adopted.

  The power of the retail groups must be compared to the growing size of the manufacturers. The commercial power of manufacturers has increased mainly because of mergers between companies. These firms, having a global strategy at the outset, have placed technical, financial and human resources at the disposal of amalgamated companies which have strengthened their capacity to increase their market share and, consequently, their power in relation to their customers. The size of the principal retail groups in the world is also a kind of response to the manufacturers' power (Tables 12.7 and 12.8).

- Flexibility and convertibility: manufacturers seek to avoid over-committing themselves to a particular type of distribution for both commercial and financial reasons. They wish to keep the possibility open of developing their distribution channels in line with changes in the product range. An attempt is then made to diversify the chosen forms of distribution, so as not to invest excessively in a single distribution channel, or in burdensome technical or after-sales service. This can be pursued either by seeking to share this type of

investment with partners or by using only easily convertible investments (easy resale for other forms of business).

Aigle, a Wellington boot manufacturer, used mass distribution to increase its production strength in the 1970s and 1980s. Since 1980, Aigle has disassociated itself from its principal mass distribution brand-name "Aigle" (however, it has held on to the "Moby Dick" brand-name) and has re-positioned itself at a medium and high range level through broadening its range of textile goods. Today the brand can be found at "Aigle" points of sale and in specialized multi-brand retailers such as Decathlon (sports goods).

Dell Computer's direct sales strategy for computers and peripherals is another example of flexibility. The company can thus adapt its offering to clients without having to bear the load of the classic distributors.

In the 1970s, IBM distributed its computers through its own network. With the advent of the microcomputer, this distribution channel was no longer enough in itself and IBM entrusted individual distribution of microcomputers to intermediary companies who could guarantee this service to private individuals or other distributors.

- The competence of the intermediaries: for certain manufacturers, the choice of intermediaries capable of offering the full range of expected services such as installation, variety, spare parts, storage, commercial, technical, logistic and financial know-how and after-sales is fundamental. These aspects are very important in line with the manufacturer's choice in terms of value creation and strategic positioning. This choice is also at the centre of the strategic reflection of consumer goods manufacturers who expect, for example, excellent logistics and merchandising from distributors. Trade marketing implies a very tight link between the partners, manufacturer and distributor, in mass distribution: for example, Procter & Gamble and Wal-Mart have set up a distribution system based on strong cooperation which requires high logistics expertise on the part of both partners. We can find the same type of cooperation in industrial marketing, for example, with an important computer manufacturer such as IBM which requires large-scale professionalism on the part of its distributors.

- The delegation of functions: among the set of functions of the distributor, the manufacturer can choose to retain the functions that it knows that it will perform most effectively or which are the most profitable, and to delegate to the distributors those that they can fulfil more competently or more cheaply.

  This choice depends naturally on the appropriate situation of the manufacturer, their environment (for example, is there a distributor corresponding to their wishes?) and of their capacity to negotiate.

Table 12.7 The thirty world leaders in the distribution sector

Ranking	Name	Country of origin	Turnover 1999 (billions of euros)	Portion of turnover abroad (%)	Number of stores carrying the brand-name
1	Wal-Mart	U.S.A	162,750	13.9	3,989
2	Carrefour	France	51,946	37.7	9,061
3	Kroger	U.S.A.	45,135		3,084
4	Metro	Germany	43,952	40	2114
5	Intermarché	France	40,490*	36	3274
6	Home Depot	U.S.A.	38,250	3.7	936
7	Albertson's	U.S.A.	37,299	–	2,492
8	Sears Roebuck	U.S.A.	36,552	10.6	3,011
9	Kmart	U.S.A.	35,753	–	2,171
10	Target	U.S.A.	33,541	–	1,243
11	Tesco	U.K.	32,773	10	850
12	JC Penney	U.S.A.	31,916	0.5	4,076
13	Royal Ahold	Netherlands	31,073	69	4,000
14	Safeway	U.S.A.	30,925	17.8	1,745
15	Rewe	Germany	30,421	19.7	9,470
16	Ito Yokado	Japan	30,113	29.9	26,442
17	Edeka	Germany	29,654	2.4	11,183
18	CostCo	U.S.A.	26,847	19.1	308
19	Tengelmann	Germany	26,382	47.9	11,007
20	Aldi	Germany	25,982*	32.5	5,155
21	Sainsbury	U.K.	25,711*	13.7	845
22	Daei	Japan	25,523*	NC	8750
23	Jusco	Japan	24,576*	9.4	2,355
24	Auchan	France	23,629*	18.9	1,223
25	Leclerc	France	22,767*	1.1	850
26	IGA (Independent Grocers Alliance)	U.S.A	19,506	44.9	4,000
27	PPR (Pinault Printemps Redoute)	France	18,911	47.8	300
28	Otto Versand	Germany	18,662	49	583
29	Mycal	Japan	18,086	–	419
30	CVS	U.S.A.	18,011	–	4,098

*Estimates and data updated according to latest acquisitions and mergers NC: not communicate by the company
Source: Pricewaterhouse Coopers, LSA, No. 1678, 25/5/2000.

■ The distribution of profit margins: the analysis of distribution channels reveals that the distribution of margins among the manufacturer and each intermediary is not proportional to the value which each adds. Certain choices made by the intermediaries or even certain decisions concerning the development of a distribution system appropriate to the manufacturer are the consequence of this observation: the manufacturer arbitrates between advantages supplied by the distributors and the share of the profit accruing to them for offering their services.

■ Compatibility with other forms of distribution: it is a question of ensuring that the same brand is not distributed under different conditions or sold differently in different channels. This can create negative reactions from the distributors who are disadvantaged compared to competitors concerning price, delivery, services, credit and so on. This is the case when insurance groups who have a network of independent intermediaries decide to use direct marketing or when companies with a franchising network embark on catalogue sales. The competition set up by the distribution group which distributes services to their customers is not appreciated by the intermediaries who have not been consulted.

Toolbox 12.2 presents evaluation criteria for the manufacturer to use when choosing a distribution channel.

Table 12.8 The fifty world leaders in the distribution sector by country of origin

Country of origin	Number of companies	Accumulated turnover 1999 (billions of euros)	% Accumulated turnover 1999	Total of stores carrying the brand-name
U.S.	22	643,204	60,48	45,877
Germany	8	147,513	13,87	43,559
France	6	86,300	8,12	18,208
Japan	5	72,776	6,85	38,244
U.K.	5	50,211	4,72	5,765
Netherlands	1	31,073	2,92	4,000
Belgium	1	17,755	1,67	2,290
Australia	2	14,542	1,37	3,364

Continent of origin	No. of companies	% Turnover 1999	Total of stores carrying the brand-name
Europe	21	31,30	78,322
Outside Europe	29	60,48	87,485

Source: Pricewaterhouse Coopers, LSA, No. 1678, 25/5/2000.

TOOLBOX 12.2

EVALUATION CRITERIA OF DISTRIBUTION CHANNELS

Appropriateness to the type of distribution	– intensive distribution – selective distribution – exclusive distribution
Potential customer groups affected by the channel	– wide – narrow, targeted
Negotiating power held by manufacturer	– strong – weak
Cost of channel logistics	– cost borne by the manufacturer – cost borne by the other members
Cost of commercial contact (cost necessary to maintain relationships between the intermediaries and clients)	– high – low
Capability of the retailer to ensure the required services	– good – bad
Coherence between the distributor's image and the desired image	– strong – weak
Control exercised over the retailer	– strong – weak
Channel members' motivation	– high – low
Client solvency	– certain – doubtful
Recovery of information	– easy – difficult
Compatibility between channels	– coherent – conflictual
Amount of capital necessary (to finance the distribution)	– large – small

Distributor strategy

Distributor strategy is affected by the strategic positioning of the distribution company and on changes in the environment and the industry. Strategic choices of distributors concern their position in the channel, that is what sales methods and rules of behaviour are adopted. Finally, it is important to emphasize the internationalization of distributor strategy.

The objectives of distributors

Today, the distribution of consumer goods is dominated by major groups which first and foremost are looking for growth and profitability. In Germany, in 2000, six groups (Metro, Rewe, Tengelmann, Edeka, Aldi, Lidl) dominated the market for mass consumption goods, in France, four groups have an international dimension in this domain (Carrefour, Intermarché, Auchan and Leclerc), one group in the Netherlands (Royal Ahold) and four in the United Kingdom (Tesco, Sainsbury, Asda, Safeway).

The trend towards concentration is far from over, the objective of the groups being to achieve a critical size in global terms which will allow them to dominate the market due to their buying and distribution power. "Hostile" (without the acquired company's approval) takeover bids (public offers for purchase) in France such as Auchan's successful takeover bid concerning Docks de France in 1996 or the failed bid concerning Promodès over Casino illustrate this growth tendency.

The purpose of the group owners is to increase the value of their assets and obtain good profitability, that of the leaders being to obtain the best possible profit with regard to the assets at their disposal.

The Strategic Profit Model (SPM)[30] clearly presents the decomposition of profit achieved by a distribution company (Figure 12.4). Return on net worth depends on the rate of the financial leverage and on the rate of economic profitability (return on assets). The rate of the financial leverage is determined by the division of the total of assets by stockholders' equities, these equities representing the total amount of money which the owners have invested in the company. Therefore its main interest is to the shareholders.

Economic profitability, the ratio of net profit to total assets, indicates how well the directors are employing the assets. At the same time, it depends on the net profit margin (profit on net sales) and the asset turnover (net sales on total assets).

Distribution companies have three ways to satisfy their shareholders by obtaining a strong return on investment:

1. to increase the net profit margin (sales profitability), which can be done in various ways: by limiting variable and fixed expenses, by increasing gross profit margin through a reduction in purchase costs, through an increase in selling prices or a rise in sales volume;
2. to increase asset turnover, which can be done either by limiting invested capital or, especially, by putting it to better use (materials productivity, stock turnover and restriction of stock levels), and improvement of stock financing (longer period for payment of bills);
3. to improve financial leverage by getting the right balance between stockholders' equities and debt financing depending on the cost of capital and the profitability of the company.

The choices selected by companies concerning channels will affect each of these ratios, with large self-service stores emphasizing, for example, stock turnover, sales volume, low purchase cost of goods sold, materials productivity and the transfer of some logistic and communication costs to the manufacturer. They can also trade-off a weak profit margin against high sales, low prices with a strong asset turnover, and achieve financial leverage which ensures good profitability of stockholders' equity. However, very strong competition can bring about a drop in performance at certain levels (profit rate, rising costs, interest charges, cost of stocks, relative cost of purchases with regard to the competitors) which may render the company vulnerable. This is the case of supermarket chains such as Euromarché or Montlaur in France which have either disappeared or been taken over.

Influencing factors in distributor strategy

As an economic agent, the distributor sets a strategy, taking into account its capabilities and the changes in the environment. Several factors play an essential role: economic and demographic factors, technological factors, legal factors, competition and changing customer expectations about lifestyles.

Economic and demographic factors

Size and density of population plus disparities in standards of living bring about significant differences in household consumption and, upstream, company demand. These disparities can be reflected in notable differences in distribution networks. Northern Europe has a concentration of large self-service stores greatly superior to the countries of Southern Europe. Certain northern countries achieve very high levels of business concentration which encourages distribution companies in these countries to export their sales approach to the countries of the South, as, for example, in the case of supermarkets in Spain with brand names such as Pryca (Carrefour), Continente (Carrefour-Promodès), and Al Campo (Auchan).

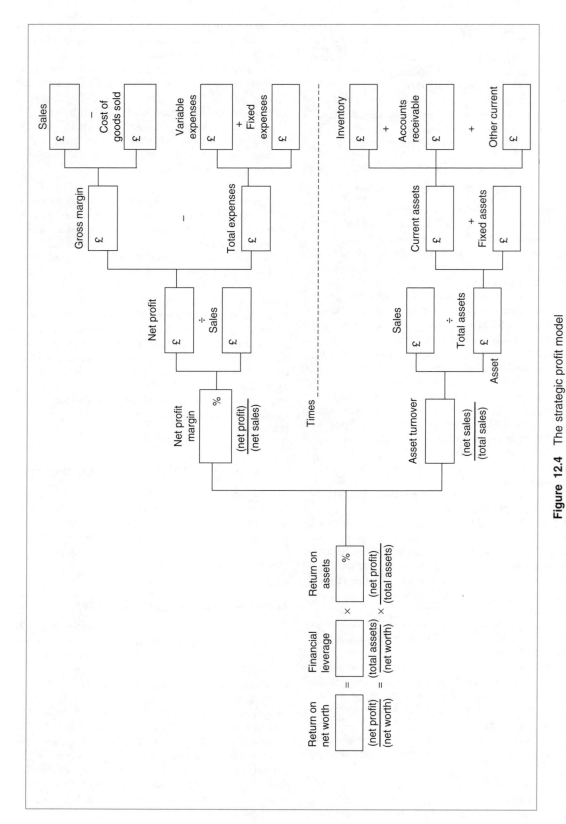

Figure 12.4 The strategic profit model

Source: D.J. Bowersox and M. Bixby Cooper, *Strategic Marketing Channel Management*, New York, McGraw Hill, 1992.

Technological and logistic factors

Distribution has undergone a veritable revolution due to changes in information systems. Next to the transactional channel, including the institutions which organize the transfer of goods among themselves, there exists a logistic channel[31] whose function is the physical distribution of products. Today this constitutes a matter of real concern among channel partners on the one hand, and between them and their service providers on the other.

The set of logistic functions has been modified by new information technology: transport operations (bulk breaking – division into groups, rounds and so on), the technical operations of physical distribution (handling, preparation of orders, reconditioning, marking of prices etc.), operations concerning management of goods in stock or in the store (stockholding and storage, management of use-by dates, treatment of orders), accounting and payment operations (invoices, payment) and management of sales promotions (coupon management). EDI coupled with the optical scanning of cash registers has profoundly changed the restocking of shops. ECR has built a strategic extension from these new conditions for the logistic function. From this point on, the control of information by a partner, whether manufacturer or distributor, concerning the whole channel becomes a major strategic issue. Some distributors wish to maintain their domination of the channel and continue to control the information; others more easily enter into partnership and are prepared to set up methods such as ECR. The joint development of EDI and ECR favours the delivery of marketing data to suppliers who participate in store management, for example in the form of suggestions regarding the product assortment. If distributors lose control of information and therefore power they may be less willing to enter into partnerships.

Today the Internet is becoming more and more widely used for distribution. Data exchange between producers and suppliers is increasingly carried by this channel. While sales to end users represents but a small part of Internet commerce, the use of this means of communication between companies is rising sharply (Appendix 12.4: "The growth of the number of buyers by Internet in Europe").

Carrefour and Nestle operate in such a manner as to optimize supplies, facilitate the introduction of new products and manage promotional actions. The setting up of an ECR system based on the transmission of information directly from checkouts thanks to scanners, allows for close cooperation between the producer and the distributor from which the client benefits: no stock shortages, lower prices and optimized choice.

The impact of new technology is very important in the industrial and services sectors. In business markets, online market places are developing, where offers and demands come together on dedicated Internet sites. The resulting competition tends to influence prices. This has led to major distribution groups organizing their own market places in which suppliers can participate (Toolbox 12.3).

TOOLBOX 12.3

ELECTRONIC MARKET PLACES

Electronic market places are electronic commerce platforms which allow for the handling of commercial operations with the aid of computerized tools. They connect buyers and sellers who, according to the type of platform, can conduct

- purchases and sales by electronic catalogue,
- tenders and responses to these tenders as well as negotiations by electronic means,
- auctions on the Internet,
- operations of the stock market type on an electronic market.

There exist

- horizontal market places, open to all types of actors, where light equipment, spare parts, second-hand material or consumable products are generally exchanged;
- vertical or sectoral places where goods relative to an industrial sector are exchanged;
- private markets linking a limited number of customers to their suppliers.

These "e-market places" have several advantages:

- cost reduction because of competition between suppliers,
- faster transactions,
- a clear and specific definition of the conditions of the offer,
- a widening of purchasing possibilities thanks to wider communication and growth in the scope of the market,
- an optimization of flows in goods and services,
- an optimization of financial and information flows.

They contribute therefore to the optimization of the whole logistic chain and to the integration of the buying, production and sales chains.

However, in practice, market places have shown certain limitations:

- some of them require computer and technological adaptations that new entrants cannot handle, in particular small- and medium-sized companies;
- they are not suitable for all types of purchases, notably for customized products;
- they can be swamped by communications between buyers and suppliers anxious to maintain good relations;
- through favouring lower prices, they sometimes contradict the classic advantages of relational marketing: quality, stability of service, trust and commitment in the transaction.

Example

Five rivals find common cause for selling

On the 3rd. of October, 2000, ABB, Alcatel, Legrand, Philips Lighting and Schneider Electric joined forces to open the first European site

for electrical installation. They intend to counter competitive start-up projects and become the leading reference point in the profession (more than 100,000 items referenced on the site with a selection of value added services included for the construction industry). The target: the two million professionals concerned by a potential market of ten billion Euros. The site should above all ensure the promotion of the five companies' brands and products; it is essentially a marketing site and non-commercial even if there is nothing in the long or short term to prevent it from becoming commercial. The five industrial concerns have united their technical expertise, are giving access to project management software, helping to set up technical dossiers, providing training courses, delivering information on normalisation, legislation, the environment, recruitment and interim duties. Globally, the site should facilitate communication between building and electrical trade professionals in the management of a building site.

Source: e+L'Usine Nouvelle, No.1, November 2000

Legal factors

Change in distribution holds consequences for other sectors of the economy. The risks of monopoly, discriminatory practices, disappearance of certain forms of traditional business because of competition, or certain manufacturers being subject to the power of distributors has led to regulatory intervention, with respect to permitted selling methods and commercial practices.

Depending on the country, legislation is more or less restrictive, which affects location and distribution policies (Table 12.9).

For example, the Italian law no. 426 passed in 1971 greatly restricted the creation of hypermarkets by conferring the right to run these shops first and foremost on cooperatives or on small pre-existing units working

together, rather than on large companies. To a lesser degree, Cadenas' law had a similar effect in Belgium.

Competitive factors

The globalization of trade, the concentration of selling power among distribution groups, the establishment of sales methods outside their country of origin, and the intervention of distributors upstream have led to an exacerbation of competition. Competition has not only taken place between retailers but also between retail formats: for example, maxi-discounters have competed strongly with the classic supermarket; specialized outlets (category killers) on a product category, offering a large product assortment (Toys'R'Us, Home Depot, Ikea, Darty) also provide strong competition for supermarkets in certain product categories.

Table 12.9 Legal disparities in Europe

	Belgium	Germany	UK	Netherlands	France
Imposed prices	No law	Forbidden	Forbidden	Forbidden	Forbidden
Suggested prices	No law	Authorized	No law	No law	Forbidden
Refusal to sell	Not forbidden	Lawful	Illegal	No law	Authorized
Resales at a loss	Forbidden	No law	No law	No law	Forbidden
Loss leader	No law	Forbidden	Controlled	No law	Controlled
Sales and liquidation	Controlled	Controlled	No law	Controlled	Controlled

Cultural factors and the evolution of consumption trends

Cultural factors, habits and buying patterns plus consumption trends do not allow for the easy duplication of a selling method from one country to another. The failure of the French hypermarkets in the United States can be partially explained by cultural factors.

Within a country, changing lifestyles and consumption patterns constitute a powerful factor in the organization of business. The rise in the level of expertise and standards demanded by European consumers, the search for quality and durability of products, established by market research companies, as well as consumer reactions to economic crises, mean that distribution must of necessity be integrated into the product offer. Category management and ECR are not only the result of logistical and technological progress, but they take account of wider consumer trends, by being quickly adaptable to customer demand or by offering "universes of consumption" corresponding to their expectations.

Two factors are of particular importance for the distributor strategy:

1. the differentiation of consumer expectations according to purchase and consumption situations and the diversity of tastes among consumers enabling strategies of segmentation;
2. the opportunity for the distributor to collect consumption information thanks to optical scanning techniques and thus to establish indispensable databases for customer loyalty programmes. Today, the major European distributors and, in particular, large retailers and specialized chains such as Le Printemps, Fnac, Kingfisher use direct marketing techniques in order to ensure better customer relationship management (see chapter on "Direct Marketing").

The strategic choices of distributors

Distributors are affected by a wide range of economic, political, and technological influences. They define their strategy according to their particular "capabilities", resources and skills, and based on an analysis of the competition and their choice of target markets.

There are several classic analytical frameworks:

- Specialization or diversification: some distribution companies possess a unique retail concept which they establish nationally or overseas. This was the case, at the outset, of Auchan, a hypermarket specialist – while other groups possessed several retail formats such as large self-service specialty stores or variety stores.

The group to which "Auchan" belongs in France is rather widely diversified (the "Decathlon" sports shop chain, "Flunch" and "Pizza Paï" self-service restaurants, participation in mail order companies with "Les Trois Suisses", do-it-yourself stores with "Leroy-Merlin", equipment rental shops with "Kiloutou", clothing stores with "Kiabi" and so on). Diversification allows for the sharing out of risk, which explains the presence of many diversified groups within the distribution sector. This type of diversification can also be explained by the search for opportunities. The broad strategic positioning of such a distributor allows for many client segments to be served with differentiated retail concepts.

- Integration or not: some distributors go as far as producing certain goods which they present under their own private label (Carrefour with Tex (clothes), etc.). A good many of them possess or are affiliated to a central purchasing unit. Some have even tried to establish "super-central purchasing agencies" combining the buying power of several central purchasing agencies to put pressure on the suppliers. Some distributors such as Wal-mart have tried to concentrate on their core business, that is store management, by cutting investment on certain upstream logistical functions. They have had to change their strategy in order to avoid stock shortages and facilitate their control of product flow up to arrival at the store.

- Segmentation or not: some companies aim at a particular segment of consumers and adapt their product/service offer and the location of their points of sale to the expectations of this segment (e.g., a shop selling luxury goods in the city centre), while other distributors try to meet all types of demand such as large self-service department stores.

The analytical framework of generic strategies supplied by Porter also applies here (Table 12.10):

- by cost,
- by the differentiation of the methods of distribution,
- by focusing on a customer segment.

But these various types of analysis are not as mutually exclusive as this framework leads us to believe. For example, the large self-service specialty stores offering discounts (category killer) concentrate on a category of products or usage with large product assortment, while at the same time competing on price. The "hard discounters" establish at the same time a differentiation and a price competition with supermarkets.

Table 12.10 Competition and trade marketing

Competition by price	Competition by differentiation

■ Optimization of information costs
  – shared access
  – real time
  – EDI
  – scanning
■ Logistic and administrative optimization
  – just in time
  – zero stock
  – direct product profit
■ Distributor
  – adapted forms of packaging
  – aiming at zero paper
■ Optimization of merchandising
  – co-managed software
■ Optimization of communication costs
  – joint creation of traffic (push/pull synthesis)
■ Financial, legal optimization
	■ Personalization of the brand-packaging-conditioning elements of the mix
	■ Supplier offer adapted to the positioning of the brand name
	■ Supplier offer adapted to the catchment area
	■ Complementary policies between the distributor brand and the manufacturer's brand
	■ Collaborative improvement of price and profit-margin strategies
	■ New promotional and communication techniques
	■ Improvement in the quality of service to the consumer

Source: M. Dupuis and E. Tissier-Desbordes (1994) "Trade Marketing: mode ou nouvelle approche des relations producteur/distributeur?" *Décisions Marketing*, 2, May–August, pp. 45–56.

In the same way, the integration strategy can have hybrid forms depending on the influence of the distributor and the manufacturer. For example, trade marketing constitutes a partnership between the manufacturer and the distributor to present simultaneously a wide assortment to customers and cooperation along the whole logistic chain in order to obtain the best service for the consumer at the lowest price. The strategy of the distributor can therefore become connected to that of the manufacturer, which poses a problem of channel domination and can limit cooperation. In practice, not all distributors are prepared to enter into the extensive information sharing that is required for this to work.

Position in the channel and choice of sales method are connected. The internalization or the externalization of functions at the retail level depends on the influence and independence of the store with regard to the upstream or downstream activities of the distribution channel: for example, what is the degree of autonomy at the individual store level for decisions such as prices, services or communication? Major distribution channels generally have very standardized retail models (Ikea, Toys'R'Us etc.); independent stores have great freedom in the construction of their marketing-mix.

The distribution approach is positioned with respect to certain central themes defining the marketing-mix and the sales approach:

■ the location and layout policy of the points of sale: size, density, closeness, framework, atmosphere;
■ the product assortment policy: number of categories of product, categories carried, presence or not of appropriate brands, the width and depth of the ranges and so on;
■ the pricing policy;
■ the service policy;
■ the communication policy.

These policies can be applied with success only if the company obtains a competitive advantage on some of them. This is possible only if the functioning of the whole channel contributes towards the creation of this advantage. Trade marketing is a means of obtaining this type of competitive advantage.

The success of a selling interface can arise either from very good control of the cost of each item sold, which is associated with a restricted assortment, or from image differentiation by means of a very wide and deep assortment. We can observe in the fact that in Europe the best financial performance is achieved either by chains specialized in maxi-discount on the European scale, or by chains running very large self-service stores such as supermarkets or hypermarkets.

The marketing-mix of the distributor

In order to implement the chosen strategy, companies have to act coherently on each variable of the mix.

- The assortment: it is a matter of determining the number of product categories sold, the width and the depth of the range, the quality of products sold and the brand policy. For example, supermarket chains have developed their strategy over the last few years by adding new product ranges such as personal computers, telephones, jewellery, perfumes, pharmacies, culture-leisure activities or organically produced products, offering their customers a new "universe" in consumption.
- The location and layout (chapter on "Merchandising"): Each distributor has its location policy in terms of size, surface and layout of the store. We may note the phenomenon of saturation of commercial hypermarkets in certain European cities which pushes retail firms towards internationalization and the organization of hypermarkets according to the purchase behaviour of the consumer – the bringing together of substitutable products (fresh pasta, deep-frozen pasta) and complementary products (tomato sauce), and the creation of real "universes of consumption", a consequence of category management.
- Services: some distributors are trying to develop mail order services, home delivery, advice, information services, consumer services and payment by credit card. A current trend is to create leisure spaces which have become known as "retailtainment" at distribution outlets where the consumer can play games, engage in leisure activities and relax. Thanks to the Internet, distributors are proliferating services offered to facilitate consumer choice, to allow consumers to obtain products more easily, to encourage them and offer promotions, and to offer them easy payment terms, with the very clear objective of developing customer loyalty.
- Pricing policy: plays a major role in competition between distributors. To cite an example:

  - the systematic presence of "best price" brands in hypermarkets or supermarkets;
  - the practice of EDLP (EVERY DAY LOW PRICING) which consists of applying low prices all the time instead of resorting to temporary promotions;
  - the development of store chains based on low prices with little variety and few services.

- Communication: distribution companies are increasing budgets for their customer loyalty programmes. This involves the use of not only classic media for developing brand awareness or for announcing promotions (publi-promotion) but also direct marketing campaigns using couponing, mailing or electronic media such as Internet.

The internationalization of distribution

Experts agree that the internationalization of distribution companies represents one of the dominant aspects of their current and future strategy. Internationalization of distribution is the result of a strategic decision: what is the targeted market (relevant market) and what is the market which is served (served market)?

The saturation of home markets in certain countries, legal constraints limiting the development of new outlets, the search for economies of scale, the decline in transport costs, the opening of borders and the relative homogenization of tastes and consumer expectation are many factors which have favoured the international orientation of distributors' strategies.

Evidence of this internationalization is given by the presence of German hard discounters in France, the extension of major national groups into Southern Europe, South America, Asia and the Orient and the development of European central agencies (Table 12.11).

E. Colla[32] notes five factors determining the foreign market entry methods used by distribution companies:

1. the degree of financial and organizational commitment of the company: direct development or acquisition;
2. the methods of collaboration with other companies – alliances;
3. the level of standardization of activities and national adaptation of the commercial offer with multinational or global strategies;
4. the direction and the type of geographic expansion through the concentration or the dispersal of initiatives;
5. the chronological order of entry in various markets (sequential or simultaneous strategies).

Existing differences between countries in the structure of distribution channels and variety of selling methods create stronger or weaker competitive conditions which can explain the success or failure of brand-name international diversification strategies. The standardization-adaptation dilemma plays a major role.

In any case, there are powerful factors in favour of the concentration of groups, in particular negotiating power and the economies of scale. On the other hand, badly controlled expansion can create an increase in coordination costs. A study carried out by the BCG[33] estimates that an "international strategy" is of value only if it combines strong local positions with global size.

Table 12.11   Wal-Mart international operations datasheet

Wal-Mart International	1629 total units Mexico (708) Puerto Rico (54) Canada (261) Argentina (11) Brazil (150) China (48) South Korea (16) Germany (88) United Kingdom (293)
History	Entered Mexico in November 1991. Entered Puerto Rico in August 1992. Entered Canada in November 1994.* Entered Argentina in November 1995. Entered Brazil in November 1995. Entered China in August 1996. Entered Germany in January 1998.* Entered Korea in July 1998.* Entered United Kingdom in July 1999.* Entered Japan in March 2002.** *Entered these countries through acquisitions. **Wal-Mart owns a 42% interest in Seiyu, Ltd, a leading retailer with over 400 stores throughout Japan.
Company trade territory	Wal-Mart serves more than 138 million customers weekly in 50 U.S. states and internationally in Puerto Rico, Canada, China, Mexico, Brazil, Germany, United Kingdom, Argentina and South Korea.
Total associates	Internationally – more than 400,000 Total Company Associates – more than 1.6 million worldwide.
Total international sales	FYE 1/31/05: $56.2 billion – 18.3 per cent increase over the previous year. Operating profit was $2.9 billion, an increase of 26.1 per cent compared to the previous fiscal year. For the month of August $4.6 billion – 11.3 per cent increase over the same period last year. For the first quarter ending 4/30/05: $14.1 billion – 12.4 per cent increase over the same period last year. Operating profit was $667 million for the quarter, an increase of 18.5 per cent over over the same period last year.

Source: Wal-Mart.com

Food distributors were subject to two main economic forces:

1. effects of scale in terms of purchasing favouring the biggest distribution groups;
2. effects of scale in logistics which favour regionally concentrated distributors. The leaders (nationally large and regionally concentrated), the challengers (regionally or nationally large) and the dominated (small in both dimensions) have developed differently.

In ten years, all the brand names which lacked scale and/or growth have disappeared

Two other factors play a major role today:

1. Size of the distribution group allows for a decrease in the costs of national advertising and for the development of better marketing and better relations with suppliers.
2. Global organization size creates substantial value for shareholders through growth.

We can therefore expect that concentration will increase because the search for global development puts companies in competition with others which are also trying to hold the strongest possible national and regional situations. It follows that takeover strategies, alliances (e.g., central purchasing offices) and the international diversification of distribution companies, such as Wal-Mart, Carrefour, Metro or Promodes, are very important.

Carrefour has been in China since 1995 and has opened many hypermarkets. Having overcome an initial slowdown which arose because of administrative obstacles, Carrefour counts on opening, with local partners, around ten stores per year in China. A little later, Wal-Mart entered the Chinese market and now operates many stores; other major groups are about to follow – Metro (Germany), Makro (Holland), Seven Eleven (USA) and Dairi & Jusco (Japan). What is at stake is becoming a leading player in this immense and rapidly developing market.

Filser[34] has shown that there are limits to the critical or optimal size of distribution groups. He observes that experience effects are not systematically linked to size (Table 12.12). In addition, he has shown that the most efficient distributors are not necessarily the biggest. Thus, Auchan which has the highest sales per unit of floor space is not the most powerful distributor in this market. In the same way, cooperatives of important national or international central purchasing units (Arci, Contact, Difra) have been short-lived. Several explanations are possible:

- The form of economy of scales curves: productivity gains resulting from the spreading of fixed assets are weak beyond a certain size (U-shaped curve).
- The supply structure: the global size of the distributor counts less than their buying and negotiation capacity in a product category. A hard discounter who buys a huge volume of one sole product will carry less weight in the eyes of his distributor than a distributor of higher global size who buys several brands in smaller quantities from numerous suppliers. In buying 600 lines, the hard discounter will benefit more from the size effect than the hypermarket buying 30,000 references.
- The size effect only plays a part if direct competitors do not benefit from the same effect. If all the distributors try to grow, the benefit of size is rapidly reduced.
- The size effect cannot be understood without taking into account the geographical concentration of points of sale. A distributor of smaller size can become an absolute necessity within a given geographical area and thus hold more negotiating power than a distributor of higher global size.

It appears therefore that the global size effect alone does not suffice to create competitive advantage. This effect can even be counter-productive and reduce the global value of the company in the case of acquisitions that cost too much (prices have a tendency to rise in a context of saturation of available real estate or restrictive legislation) or where purchased stores are poorly integrated.

It seems that the success of distribution companies must be found in the mastery of a strategy founded on strong positioning. The examples of the German hard discounters, Wal-Mart in the US or foreign hypermarket chains stem rather from this logic than from a pure logic of size.

Table 12.12 Size effect and variables of the distributor's strategic action

Variables of action	Size effect	Experience effect
Location of points of sale	Increase in the productivity of a specialized service (marketing and property)	Acquisition of competence in store location methods
Structure of the assortment	Growth in productivity of a central purchasing unit and prospecting offices for importing	Acquisition of competence in the optimization of assortment and product line structure
Price policy	Purchase volume enables better purchase prices to be achieved. Negotiation for more favourable conditions with logistic service providers	Acquisition of competence in price setting and promotional actions
Communication policy	Increased productivity in national communication campaigns. Better conditions for buying media space	Marginal effect: experience is accumulated by advertising agencies who carry out the campaigns
Service policy	Actions within the framework of each point of sale and, as a result, slight effects of scale for the company	Acquisition of competence in the construction of an adapted service offer

Source: Adapted from Décisions Marketing, No.15 September–December, 1998.

SUMMARY

Distribution is a value-creating activity. It brings about the spatial, temporal, physical and psychological transformations necessary for the consumption of goods and services. The roles and functions of distributors comprise numerous tasks to do with flows of goods and services, information and financing, the management of statutory and contractual aspects and, in particular, the ownership of goods during their transportation from the producer to the consumer.

The division of distribution tasks between distributors and producers and between different types of distributors can be organized in many ways depending on the power and interests of each contracting party.

This division of tasks has been the subject of several studies which have tried to explain:

- the different types of distribution channels enabling the transportation of products and services from the producer to the consumer. Several theories concerning distribution channels have been put forward.
- the different types of retail formats offered to the consumer.

Some more theories integrate these two approaches into a common framework. Manufacturers and distributors should each define their distribution strategies in order to ensure a competitive offer to customers. Their distribution strategies should take several factors into account – economic, legislative, organizational, technological – but above all, the different methods of relationship management between manufacturers and distributors: from conflict to cooperation or partnership. These strategies depend on company objectives, on the types of market in which they participate or on their competitive position. This can lead them to choose or combine different types of distribution strategy such as concentration, diversification, globalization and focus. The marketing-mix of the company puts into practice these strategic choices through product/service policy, points of sale location decisions, price and communication strategies.

The internationalization of distribution is a central factor in distribution strategy development. But the race for critical size does not constitute a sufficient objective in itself – other conditions are necessary if the international development of distributors is to be profitable. In particular, they must strive for competitive advantage in the aspects of location, logistics, negotiation and supplies.

Appendix 12.1

DISTRIBUTION STRUCTURE

Numerous forms of business organization exist as is indicated in the following table:

According to the length of the distribution channel	- extra-short channel (direct marketing) - short channel - long channel
According to function	- wholesale function: ensures the liaison between manufacturer and retailer (purchases in large quantities, stocks, transports, staggers) and helps the producer to avoid dealing with too many retailers, each ordering in very low quantities which creat too many transport, handling and billing operations. - retail function

According to the economic structure

- concentrated or integrated trade: businesses depending on powerful financial groups ensuring all the wholesaler's functions, generally through the intermediary of central purchasing offices and retailers
- associated trade: stores holding on to their legal independence and coming together under diverse forms (e.g. "voluntary chains" of stores associated with wholesalers' or groupings of retailers' initiatives etc.)
- independent trade: wholesale or small independent companies

According to the retail format

- Department stores generally in the city centre, more than 200,000 lines (wide and deep assortment); for example, Printemps (F), Galeries Lafayette (F), Kaufhof (D), La Rinascente (I), El Corte Ingles (ESP), Harrod's (GB).
- Variety stores: (more limited assortment, middle and bottom of the range articles, in the city centre or in the suburbs) Monoprix, La Standa (I), Woolworths (GB).
- Specialized outlets (self-service in furniture, clothing, household goods); for example, Darty (Category Killers)[i].
- Hypermarkets (sales surface greater than 2500 m^2 in France, Italy, Spain and the Netherlands but greater than 2323 m^2 in the UK and Ireland, having a wide but not very deep assortment with low prices); for example, Carrefour, Auchan.
- Supermarkets (400–2500 m^2) in France, Spain, Italy and Belgium but 400–1000 m^2 in Germany, around 300 m^2 in the Netherlands or 186–2323 m^2 in Ireland or the UK.
- Hard Discounters (about 600 m^2, very low prices, very narrow range (e.g. Ed, Aldi, Lidl).
- Small-scale supermarkets (self-service of less than 400 m^2, reduced assortment).
- Small shops (shops in the city centre, traditional or self-service shops of less than 120 m^2).
- Other forms of sale: catalogue, representatives, telephone and stallholders.

According to the legal structure

- Cooperatives (Leclerc).
- Multi-sized chain store (Casino, Carrefour).
- Association of independent stores grouping their purchases.
- Voluntary chains (Catena).
- Franchised stores (Benetton).
- Dealerships (Mercedes, BMW).

According to the structure (Rosenbloom)

- Principal structure: includes the participants who ensure the functions of negotiation, purchase, sales and the transfer of merchandise title deeds.
- Auxiliary structure: the method by which a group of distribution tasks (other than purchase, sales and deed transfers) supply services to the channel members such as transport, information systems, logistics.

(i) Certain companies using modern commercial techniques bring together, in the form of a holding, commercial companies which are very diversified in legal and economic structure, retail formats and size.

Appendix 12.2

THE FORMS OF SALE

Definitions of classic forms of sale

Traditional neighbourhood store: surface area less than 120 m^2, self-service or assisted service, which receives customers, stores merchandise and/or handles sales.

Small-size self-service store: self-service food store with a sales area ranging from 120 to 400 m^2 and sometimes also selling non-food products (5th section).

Hard discounters: self-service store with little assortment and reduced to 600 food products; discounting basic products and distribution brands (situated in town and having an area of between 600 and 800 m^2.

Supermarket: more than two-thirds of turnover comes from general foodstuffs and has a sales area of between 400 and 2500 m^2.

Large supermarket: self-service with a sales area of between 2500 and 5000 m^2 where the non-food offer is characterized by a wide but not very deep assortment.

Hypermarket: more than one-third of turnover is in general foodstuffs and has a sales area of more than 2500 m^2 (self-service).

Specialized store: food or non-food sales specializing in certain families of products.

Department store: non-food establishment, not specialized, maximum assortment and having a substantial sales area (usually more than 2500 m^2).

Variety store: same area as supermarkets, not specialized, with an assortment limited to current needs and with between one-third and two-thirds of its turnover coming from self-service foodstuffs.

Mail order or distance sales: no direct contact between the seller and buyer and which includes the dispatching of the merchandise by the seller to the buyer.

Appendix 12.3

WHOLESALE BUSINESS

Wholesale business is on the upstream side of distribution. It fulfils four types of functions:

1. logistic functions such as transport, variety and storage;
2. financial functions: certification of delivery, invoicing, recovery, credit, discount etc.;
3. functions of regulation and information by avoiding imbalance between production and retail, by playing on stocks, by ensuring the communication of information between the market and the manufacturers, by participating in the promotion of the manufacturers' products and by raising the needs of the retail dealers and the market (marketing functions);
4. functions of service: advice, training of the retail dealers, management aids, packaging and labelling.

The five trends of wholesale business

1. general trend towards concentration of companies, with more and more middle-of-the-range companies, that is to say of between 100 and 500 staff, into which smaller companies may be absorbed, while more significant wholesale businesses employ around 500 people;
2. different tendencies according to profession in that which concerns the number of establishments – a concentration of establishments where heavy products are concerned, and the opposite in ever-increasing sectors where the notion of service is capital and where the demand must be met quickly and in proximity;
3. trend towards a dichotomy between high-performance companies which are prospering and old-fashioned companies which are in trouble;
4. trend towards foreign penetration in certain branches, in general the weaker ones;
5. trend towards a common destiny between the wholesale business and the industry to which it corresponds, either for the better when there is a partnership (the thriving electricity industry), or for the worse when the industry turns its back on business (textiles, furniture).

Appendix 12.4

THE GROWTH OF THE NUMBER OF BUYERS BY
INTERNET IN EUROPE

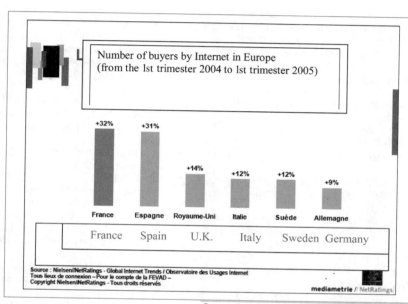

Source: (with FEVAD permission)

Discussion questions

1. Consult a distributor's website (e.g., Wal-Mart, Carre-four, Tesco) and list the functions it fulfills (both conventional and modern functions).
2. Compare a department store, a retail store, and a mail order company. For a given product (a shirt, for instance), which functions are fulfilled by the supplier, the distributor and the consumer (e.g., ship-ment, shelf filling, travel or point of sale, information, delivery, etc.)? What is the impact on the distributor's margin?
3. What are the advantages of distributor brands? What problems do these brands raise for manufacturers?

4. Consult the websites of Tesco, Wal-Mart, and Carrefour and discuss their international strategies. Compare them according to the following criteria: geographic area, store type, and store density. What conclusions can you draw?
5. Take an industry (wine or fruit, for example) and discuss the various modes of distribution. What is the impact on marketing these products? What is the role played by each agent in the industry?
6. Compare hard discounters in four European countries. Compare them to the population of their country. What are the reasons for disparities?

Notes and references

1. K.G. Hardy and A.J. Magrath, "*Marketing Channel Management*", Glenview, Illinois, Scott, Foresman and Company, (1988).

2. J.-J. Lambin, "*Marketing Stratégique*", New York, McGraw Hill, (1986).

3. L.W. Stern and A.E. El Ansary, "*Marketing Channels*", 4th Edition, Englewood Cliffs, New Jersey, Prentice Hall, (1992).

4. M. Filser, "La dynamique des canaux et formules de distribution: une approche méthodologique", Thèse de Doctorat d'Etat, Université de Montpellier (1985).

5. M. Filser, "*Canaux de distribution*", Paris, Vuibert, (1989).

6. R.H. Coase, "The Nature of the Company", *Economica, New Series*, 4, pp. 386–405, (1937).

7. G. Stigler, "The Division of Labour is Limited by the Extent of the Market", *Journal of Political Economy*, 59, pp. 185–193, (1951).

8. L.B. Bucklin, "The Economic Structure of Channels of Distribution", in B.E. Mallen (ed.), *The Market Channel: A Conceptual Viewpoint*, New York, Wiley, pp. 63–66, (1967).

9. L.P. Bucklin, "Distribution Channel: Research in Industrial Marketing", Working Paper, no. 70, University of California at Berkeley, (1971).

10. L.P. Bucklin, "*Competition and Evolution in the Distribution Trades*", Englewood Cliffs, New Jersey, Prentice Hall, (1972).

11. W. Dommermuth and R.C. Andersen, "*Distribution Systems: Companys, Functions and Efficiencies*", MSU Business Topics, 17, p. 5, (1969).

12. A.E. El Ansary, "Distribution Productivity in the United States: Analysis and Framework", *International Marketing Research Seminar*, Aix en Provence, G1–G15, (1981).

13. L.P. Bucklin, "Postponement, Speculation and the Structure of Distribution Channels" in B.E. Mallen (ed.), *The Marketing Channel, A Conceptual Viewpoint*, Wiley, pp. 67–74, (1967).

14. L.W. Stern and A.E. El Ansary (op. cit.).

15. J.C. Anderson and J.A. Narus, "A Model of Distributor Company and Manufacturer Company Working Partnerships", *Journal of Marketing*, 54, 1, pp. 42–48, (1990)

16. O.E. Williamson, "*Markets and Hierarchies*", Free Press, New York, (1975).

17. B.C. Mac Cammon, "Perspectives for Distribution Programming", in L.P. Bucklin (ed.), *Vertical Marketing Systems*, Scotts Foreman, Glenview, Illinois, (1970).

18. M. Porter, "*Competitive Advantage*", New York, Free Press, (1985).

19. M. Porter, "*Competitive Advantage: Creating and Sustaining Superior Performance*", New York, NY, The Free Press, (1985).

20. L.W. Stern, A.E. El Ansary and J.R. Brown, "*Management in Marketing Channels*", Englewood Cliffs, New Jersey, Prentice Hall, (1989).

21. M. Filser, *Canaux de Distribution*, Paris, Vuibert, (1989).

22. M.P. Mac Nair, "Significant Trends and Development in the Postwar Period", in A.B. Smith, (ed.), "*Competitive Distribution in a Free High Level Economy and its Implications for the University*", Pittsburgh, University of Pittsburgh Press, pp. 17–22, (1957).

23. S.C. Hollander, "The Wheel of Retailing", *Journal of Marketing*, 25, 3, pp. 37–42, (1960).

24. M.P. Mac Nair and M. Berman, *Marketing Through Retailers*, New York, American Management Association, (1967).

25. S.C. Hollander, "Notes on the Retail Accordeon", *Journal of Retailing*, 42, 2, p. 29, (1966).

26. A.C. Dressmann, "Patterns of Evolution in Retailing", *Journal of Retailing*, 24, 1, pp. 64–81, (1968).

27. L.W. Stern and T. Reve, "Distribution Channels as Political Economics: A Framework for Comparative Analysis", *Journal of Marketing*, 44, 3, pp. 52–64, (1980).

28. M. Filser, "Etat des recherches sur les canaux de distribution", *Revue Française de Gestion*, 90, pp. 66–76, (1992).

29. H. Håkansson. *International Marketing and Purchasing of Industrial Goods: An Interaction Approach*, New York, Wiley, (1982).

30. D.J. Bowersox and M. Bixby Cooper, "*Strategic Marketing Channel Management*", New York, McGraw Hill, (1992).

31. D.J. Bowersox, D. Closs and O.Helferich, *Logistical Management: A Systems Integration of Physical Distribution Manufacturing Support and Material Procurement*, 3rd ed., New York, Macmillan, (1986).

32. E. Colla, "Les stratégies d'internationalisation des entreprises commerciales", *Revue Française du Marketing*, 157–158, 2–3, 133–159, (1996).

33. Boston Consulting Group, cité par R. Abaté et T. Chassaing, "La concentration va-t-elle se poursuivre?", *Le Figaro*, 9 janvier, (1998).

34. M. Filser, "Taille critique et stratégie du distributeur: analyse théorique et implications managériales", *Décisions Marketing*, 15, septembre (1998).

Part IV

Value Generation Processes

Merchandising and logistics

13

Learning objectives

After studying this chapter you will be able to

1 Understand the definition of merchandising and its role within the distribution framework of product and services.
2 Explain the importance of logistics in distribution and merchandising.
3 Discuss location aspects of consumer behaviour and the implications for point-of-sale decisions.
4 Know how to manage the presentation and variety of products at the point of sale.
5 Know how to use management and control techniques concerning the product assortment.
6 Know how to promote the store and communicate its image.
7 Understand the need for good relations between the producer and the distributor and to study emerging mechanisms of cooperation.
8 Understand the main aspects of distributor logistics and, in particular, the modern forms of logistic cooperation.
9 Grasp the importance of electronic business and electronic market places in the development of merchandising and logistics.

SPOTLIGHT

ELECTRONIC DATA INTERCHANGE (EDI)

How can we know day by day, hour by hour, the success or failure of a sales promotion campaign? How should reordering be organized? How can we avoid running out of stock when there is a rush of business? Sales promotion efficiency depends upon the answers to these questions.

Sainsbury the well-known British retailer and Nestlé UK have set up an EDI system to provide answers to these questions for both companies. Based upon the Eqos Collaborator software and using Internet technology, the software allows the two partners to share information according about planning, sales forecasts and sales promotion efficiency. This EDI system allows a better, quicker and less costly response to consumer needs. Therefore it provides value to both partners as well as the consumer.

Efficient Consumer Response (ECR)

Henkel Germany (the leader in the detergent market) and Globus (a German hypermarket chain) have set up an efficient replenishment system. Before the implementation of this system, stock could reach 198 days for some products. The objectives of this system were to have the smallest order equal to a full box, have all checkouts equipped with scanning devices, and reduce the quantity of products shipped and costs of merchandise handling. The results of this partnership have been 30 per cent reduction in handling costs, increasing stock turnover and 27 per cent reduction in stock level. Globus is planning to build a warehouse to centralize its store replenishment where all orders will be sent daily. Shipments will be made daily instead of once a week. The replenishment system is a part of the ECR approach and illustrates how value can be added.

Introduction

Merchandising is the marketing activity which covers the commercial techniques used to present the product or service to be sold to the buyer under the most suitable material and psychological conditions. The basis of merchandising is optimizing the contact between the product or service and the customer, with the aim of leading him to purchase. Optimization requires the distributor in charge of this contact at the point of sale to handle the spatial and temporal aspects effectively (Figure 13.1). These aspects can be broken down into several levels:

■ The first level is that of the location of the point of sale: it can be situated in a city centre or in a suburb, either having a car park or not, near to or far from the consumer's home, with a large or small surface area, close to or far away from a competitor. The attractiveness will vary appreciably depending on these parameters. With regard to a similar trade name or a similar type of store, the choice of location in a given city is an important decision which can entail either success or failure.

■ The second level is where the techniques of merchandising address store organization, services offered, and store operations, with the aim of facilitating and increasing consumer purchases and developing loyalty.

■ At a third level, the layout and the presentation of products, whether in a city centre store or a supermarket, can strongly influence product or brand sales. Concerning brand management, the point of sale is the contact point where the consumer has personal and immediate experience of the brand. Brand presentation is for the most part based on this experience.

■ For the distributor or the producer, the choice of the product assortment displayed, its variety, the width and depth of the range, price determination for special offers and which products to push are very important decisions concerning their respective objectives of turnover and profitability. They are the subjects of negotiations that can sometimes involve high selling costs for the supplier.

The entire group of functions of distribution and merchandising cannot be done without logistics. Logistics can be defined as the technology for controlling flows

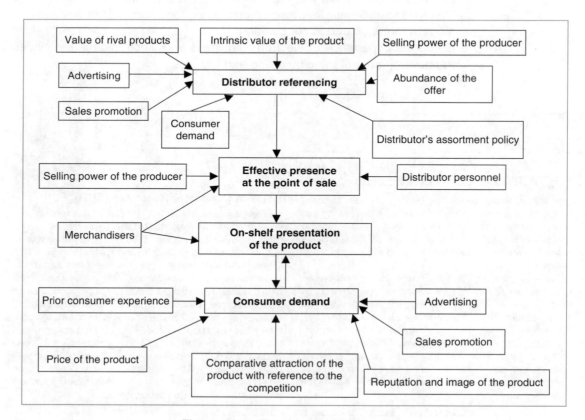

Figure 13.1   The merchandising process

(physical, financial and information) between the various actors in the distribution channel, producers, distributors and customers. It has become a key factor in competition between manufacturers and distributors. The progress made in this domain over the last 20 years, because of the impact of new information/communication technology, is considerable. The importance and the investments at stake in these functions make them worthy topics for study.[1]

Each of the above levels, location of the point of sale, its organization, the management of products (management of shelf space), will be studied in a specific section of this chapter. A fourth section will be reserved for the perspective of the producer (producer merchandising) plus the negotiations between producer and distributor, and a fifth will be dedicated to logistics.

Locating the store

The choice of the store location has been the subject of empirical research on the part of distributors and consulting companies. These studies are discussed in the first section. The second section explains the research carried out on the spatial behaviour of the consumer.

Empirical studies

Generally, the decision of point of sale location is the result of an empirical procedure. It is a question, for example, of comparing several available offers in stores, at different locations, with different prices, different surface areas and so on or, again, of choosing a location from several site possibilities. To establish these comparisons, the distributors rely on certain data and use fairly simple procedures.

Current practice consists of drawing isochronal curves around the point of sale (or its possible location) (Toolbox 13.1).

TOOLBOX 13.1

THE STORE LOCATION DECISION: AN EMPIRICAL METHOD

This method consists of drawing isochronal curves around the point of sale (or its possible location) (Exhibit A).

These curves indicate the time taken to go from the point of sale to different points on the curves. This method takes into account obstacles such as traffic lights, congested traffic lanes, canals or one-way streets. Each concentric isochronal zone bounded by curves (e.g., 5-minute, 10-minute, 20-minute curves) is then divided into sectors, according to geographic data and so on.

Subsequently, the prospective customers, the likely turnover and the market share of the store under investigation are estimated. This estimation is based either on standards calculated using data from already established comparable points of sale, for example, when it concerns chain stores, or on data obtained from external sources. The most frequently used data are

- the number of inhabitants per sector, the number of homes, their facilities and consumption plus their living standards;
- indications of disparity in consumer spending which also give indications as to the amount and the nature of spending by the inhabitants of a town, by group of products and by socio-professional category;

- results of research conducted directly with the consumers in the catchment area,
- data about prospective customers, bought or rented from specialized companies,
- the consultation of localized databases such as those created by "geo-marketing" companies which supply precise and large quantities of data concerning the inhabitants of each town or district. For example, *Mediapost*, in France, provides socio-demographic characteristics of all customers belonging to postal delivery rounds and the sensitivity of the people who live there to certain commercial offers such as money-off coupons.

This data allows for the calculation of the store's potential market. The rate of influence is the market share acquired by the store in question. It depends on the presence and characteristics of competitors within the catchment area, such as proximity, importance, assortment and commercial policy of the rival stores. The rate of evasion is the portion of spending of the inhabitants enacted outside the catchment area. On the other hand, it is necessary to consider the turnover resulting from buyers "outside the catchment area" that will be attracted by the store. The choice of location is thus linked to the spatial behaviour of the consumer.

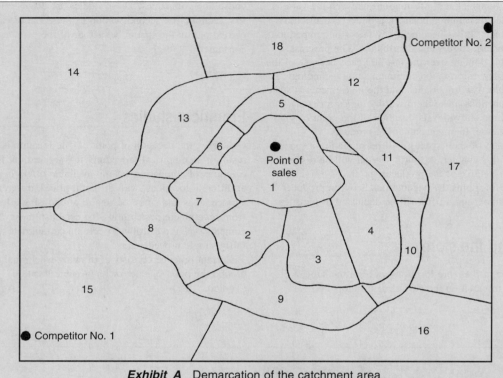

Exhibit A   Demarcation of the catchment area

The distributor divides each isochronal zone into sectors according to the geographic and socio-demographic data of the various competitors, and then, for each sector, estimates the potential market share, the potential customers and the attractiveness of the competitors.

The spatial behaviour of the consumer

Numerous authors have tried to determine the rules governing the behaviour of consumers towards businesses.

A first line of thought arises from Lancaster's[2] work on the new theory of demand. Applied to the choice of the point of sale, Lancaster's theory consists of maximizing the utility function (in the sense of the neo-classical theory) of each consumer by considering that this function depends on characteristics of the available points of sale. The consumer will choose the store which seems most advantageous to him considering his overall expectations (proximity, quality, specialization, price, approval, choice etc.)

A second trend is inspired by psycho-sociological theories concerning the consumer and rests on the contributions of the fundamental models of Howard and Sheth[3] and Engel, Kollat and Blackwell.[4] The classic concepts of the evoked set, the determinant beliefs and the

rules governing decisions are applied here to the choice of a point of sale (see Chapter on Consumer Behaviour). For example, concerning the choice of a television, the consumer can only compare stores specializing in household appliances (evoked set) and will not have recourse to neighbouring non-specialized hypermarkets. At the moment of choice, he will decide what offers the lowest prices, independent of quality: a disjunctive decision rule (the most attractive store in terms of "belief" determining the consumer's choice: price).

This second type of analysis requires accurate knowledge of the motives for using the store, such as distance, accessibility, importance and the image of the point of sale. This image itself depends on the store's marketing communications or on the distribution trade name, perception of prices, assortment, atmosphere and services provided.

Each of these motives has been the subject of numerous studies. One of the first contributions in this domain was that of Christaller.[5] The main hypothesis of Christaller's "central places" theory is that in an ideal physical space, flat with unchanging services and the consumers uniformly distributed and able to move freely, the location of the points of sale is regular and is situated at the vertices of hexagons. These vertices are geometrical centres having maximum accessibility for the inhabitants of the catchment area. The maximum distance people will travel is attained when the desire for the article becomes lower than the difficulties to be surmounted in order to obtain it.

Christaller then introduces the idea of a hierarchy in shopping centres which can be of varying levels and importance. He shows, for example, that a higher level store (more important and aimed at a larger group of customers having greater requirements) would be optimally located in the centre of the hexagon formed by six elementary points of sale (Figure 13.2), meeting more common needs. This hierarchy can contain any number of levels.

Although this theory is somewhat unrealistic due to its over-simplified hypotheses, it has inspired several works such as that of Hubbard.[6] This author suggests that the concept of distance is little used by consumers who are more inclined to argue in terms of neighbourhood or proximity.

Another well-known contribution concerning the choice of point of sale is Reilly's[7] gravitation model: the population of an intermediate zone I situated between two urban centres A and B will be attracted by each of these urban centres in proportion to their size, and in a conversely proportional way by the square of the distances between zone I and the cities A and B. This law is based on the following formula:

$$\frac{V_A}{V_B} = \frac{P_A}{P_B}\left(\frac{D_B}{D_A}\right)^2$$

where V_A and V_B express the proportion of purchases made in A and B by the inhabitants of the intermediate zone,

P_A and P_B = the population of centres A and B
D_A and D_B = distance between zone I and cities A and B.

Reilly's model was tested by several authors[8] and has been subject to criticism. The population of the city does not seem to be a sufficient indicator of the commercial attractiveness. The exponent of the value of distances has also been disputed, as well as the measure of the distance in kilometres (and not the time taken nor the consideration of the perception of the time taken). Finally, the

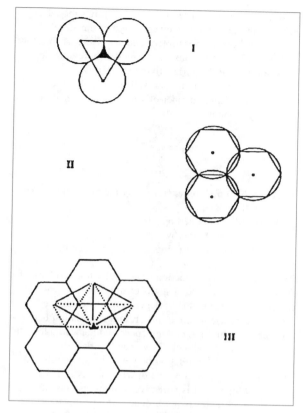

Figure 13.2 Christaller's central areas

interactions between points of sale have been studied in pairs (and not globally).

Huff[9] proposed a probabilistic model taking the size of the shopping centre and the consumer's travel time into consideration. This model allows for the measurement of the attractiveness of a group of stores (superior to 2) each compared to the other, according to the following formula:

$$P_{ij} = \frac{S_j/T_{ij}^{\lambda}}{\sum\limits_{k=1}^{n} S_k/T_{ik}^{\lambda}}$$

where P_{ij} is the probability that a consumer situated at i will go to the store situated at j,

N, the total number of stores taken into account,
S_j, the size of the store j,
T_{ij}, time taken to go from i to j,
λ, a parameter to be considered empirically for each category of products estimating the sensitivity of the consumer to distance, the sum of P_{ij} (see formula shown below) being equal to 1 (the sum of the probabilities of frequenting all the stores in the zone is equal to 1).

Several authors have tried to improve Huff's model by integrating into it the perceived image of the store's[10,] price levels, certain descriptive characteristics of the store and so on. However, making the model more complex does not generate significantly better results.

Bucklin[11] has offered a generalized model, which allows an unlimited number of variables of attraction to be taken into account:

$$A_{ij} = \frac{V_{ij}/Ci_{ij}}{\sum\limits_{k=1}^{n} V_{ik}/C_{ik}}$$

A_{ij} is the attraction exercised by the point of sale j on the consumer i.
V_{ij} is utility obtained by i by visiting j,
C_{ij} is the cost borne by i to go to j,
N is the number of points of sale considered.

The utility (V_{ij}) is a function of several attraction variables (price, sales areas, social status of the consumer), while the cost of movement (C_j) depends on distance, the inclination to use public transport and the relation between the sales area and the parking spaces. Other variables can be included in the model. Hlavac and Little,[12] for example, establish a relation between the attraction and the assortment offered by the distributor. As P. Roger[13] stresses, "this model is attractive in the sense that the number of variables is not limited a priori; however, the important problem of the balancing of the various variables remains".

Nakanishi and Cooper's[14] model is a particular case of Bucklin's model, which has the advantage that it can be estimated using a rather simple procedure (multiple regression).

Its formulation is as follows:

$$\pi_{ij} = \frac{\prod\limits_{k=1}^{q} x_{k_{ij}}^{\beta_k}}{\sum\limits_{j=1}^{n} \left(\prod\limits_{k=1}^{q} x_{k_{ij}}^{\beta_k} \right)}$$

With π_{ij}, the probability that the consumer situated in i will choose store j,

x_{kij}, value of the kth variable describing the store j for the consumer i,
n, the number of stores which the consumer i can frequent,
q, number of variables,
β_k, weighting of the variable k.

This generalization of Huff's model has been the subject of a great deal of development aimed at simplifying and improving the estimation procedure.[15] However, this type of model runs into difficulties when measuring certain variables such as image of the store.

Another trend in the analysis of consumer movement with regard to the points of sale concerns a more descriptive approach which aims principally at representing the penetration of each store within the catchment zones. P. Roger has put forward several analytical methods for the points of sale market areas using research data obtained from consumers within the commercial zones.[16] These studies allow us to limit geographically the spheres of influence of points of sale at a given time.

Today, several survey companies are developing geographic information systems which use the models and methods described above to build programmes allowing for graphic representation of the attraction zones of stores.

Finally, another type of work tries to supersede the somewhat mechanistic framework of models of attraction by introducing the experience of distributors in the point of sale location decision based on the methodology of expert systems. In this type of system, the rules employed by different experts in distribution such as store managers, heads of study, advisers in commercial installation or heads of assessment are assembled and form a database. These rules are logically combined to establish an expert computerized system. When faced with a new choice of installation, the system is capable of making a decision by using data collected on this new installation and handling this data according to the recorded decision rules.

The store conception

The attraction of a store does not depend on its situation alone. It also varies according to its image, its internal and external organization, the sales methods used along with services provided, taking account of customer satisfaction, the assortment offered and the proposed prices. In this section dedicated to the store conception, the first four points will be discussed, the definition of assortment and prices being discussed in the following section dedicated to the management of the store.

The store image

Numerous authors have tried to define a store's image.[17] While early studies on this subject were based on rather traditional techniques of measuring image, more recent research has been inspired by the methodology of positioning[18] or segmentation.[19] There is a great deal of confusion in research carried out on the image of the store. According to Hansen and Deutscher,[20] three levels of analysis can be distinguished:

■ dimensions, fundamental factors of image such as goods, services or price;

- constituents, internal ingredients of the previous dimensions such as stocks, quantities of products, for example;
- attributes, specific aspects of a constituent (e.g., such as stock shortage).

The attributes perceived by consumers arise from the set of stimuli put forward by the store, be they external such as advertising, reputation of the brand name, or internal such as structure, atmosphere, assortment, and customer types. Some studies for example have been carried out on the atmosphere of the store, the music and the people, and have tried to analyse their influence on the perception, attitudes and behaviour of consumers.

Mazursky and Jacoby[21] define the image of a store as:

- a consciousness and\or a feeling (or a cluster of knowledge and\or feelings);
- which is deduced either from a set of on-the-spot perceptions and\or of memory inputs attached to a phenomenon (in our case, a store); and
- which represents what this phenomenon means to an individual.

This definition integrates two major properties of the image. First, an image can be the result of a cognitive or emotional process, the emotional constituent being often omitted. Secondly, the process of forming the image should be understood from its definition. These authors present therefore the model for forming the image of a store (Figure 13.3).

This model compares objective reality with subjective reality. The consumer considers a certain amount of information which he gets concerning the store (left box). This information is interpreted, evaluated, integrated and is reduced to a certain number of first-level inferences, and then higher-level inferences. The result gives us a global image of the store. Lusch[22] showed how we can adapt the models for the choice of product to the model of the choice of a point of sale (Figure 13.4). An enrichment of this approach consists of integrating the image of the brand name into the choice of store[23].

The internal and external organization of the store

Primary research on store conception mainly concerns their physical dimensions: how to develop the

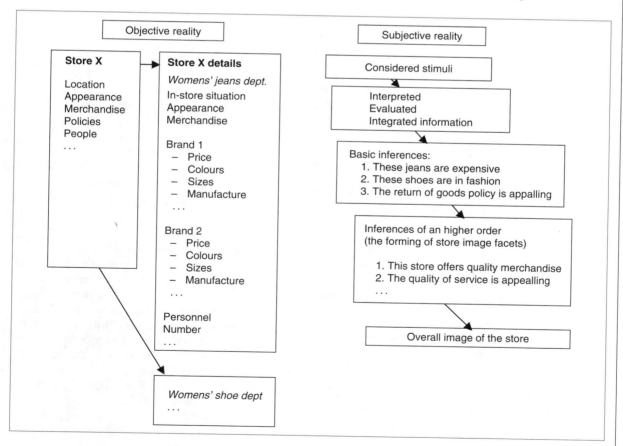

Figure 13.3 Model for the shaping of a store's image
Source: Adapted from Mazursky and Jacoby (1986).

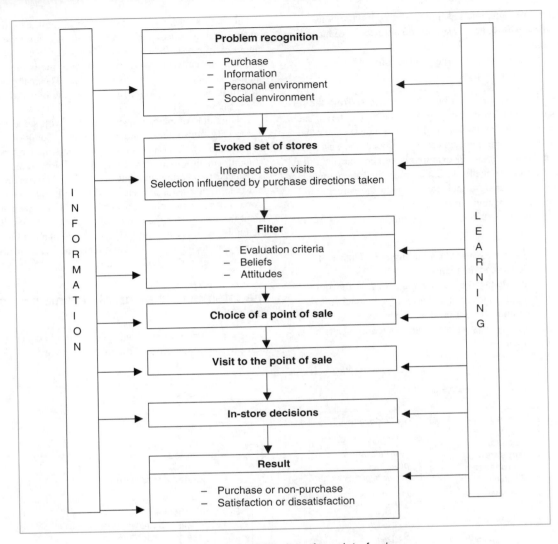

Figure 13.4 Selection of a point of sale

Source: Adapted from R.F. Lush, *Management of Retail Enterprises*, Belmont, CA, Kent Publishing Co. (1982).

surroundings (parking, access etc.), how to distribute sales areas, plot the aisles between shelves and arrange shelf space (Toolbox 13.2).

Certain rules exist for finding a balance between sales areas:

■ avoid the juxtaposition of heavily frequented sectors;
■ avoid, on the other hand, juxtaposing two lightly frequented sectors, which would create a serious "cold" zone in the store;
■ take into account the dominant direction of movement because a customer rarely moves in a contrary direction;
■ place the succession of sectors in a convenient order for purchasing.

These principles arise from studies and from the experience of distributors. They apply to the objectives of image, store productivity and are also the result of the scientific or empirical observations of in-store consumer behaviour. For example, many specialists recommend laying out continuous aisles between shelves, without side aisles which force the customer to backtrack. Ikea, a hypermarket specializing in furniture sales, has organized its stores according to this principle.

The aim is also to control the level of traffic in the different sectors of the store in order to facilitate purchases and urge the customers to pass through the "cold zones" as well, that is, those that are less frequented because they contain products with a slower purchase

TOOLBOX 13.2

PLANNING THE LAYOUT OF A STORE

A store and its various sectors may be analyzed according to the following criteria:

- need for products: does the consumer use these products very often?
- complementarity: are these types of products complementary from the consumer's point of view; for example, the "toys" and "children" sectors?
- reputation: the amount of space given to well-known brands (pre-sold brands);
- cluttering: where to place the heaviest and largest products (for example, in the "hygiene" sector (nappies for babies, toilet paper), or in a general way, the heavy products);
- handling: how to arrange the store to facilitate the handling of certain products, both by those in charge of putting the product on the shelves and by the consumers (liquids, preserves etc.);
- use: the specific equipment necessary for the presentation of the product; for example, refrigerators for fresh products.
- impulse products: where to place impulse products to facilitate their purchase and to attract the consumers; for example, sweets, perfumes, novelties.

- search products: how to facilitate the purchase, of products which require thought before purchase, such as hi-fi equipment, photography, computers and large household electrical appliances;
- atmosphere: created by the products and the layout itself (decoration, music, density of the presentation, order or disorder);
- movement: how to create movement in the store which facilitates purchase and allows customers' to optimize their purchases;
- signage: of sectors, product categories, checkouts and services;
- promotional areas: how to create and use promotional areas, such as heads of gondola and points of activity;
- surveillance: how to ensure proper surveillance of the store (theft prevention).

The importance of these criteria varies according to the kind of store and its sectors. Other criteria may be considered. For example, with regard to a "jewellery" sector, the problem of theft is of prime importance and a strongly frequented location and atmosphere, showing the jewellery to its best advantage, is advised.

---

rhythm that are renewed less frequently, such as textiles or heavy household electrical appliances. For example, it is often the case that the customer is encouraged to enter a "cold zone" to remind them of the existence of this kind of merchandise. On the other hand, sectors with faster product turnover are placed at the back of the store.

As discussed in the chapter on distribution, "category management" consists of setting up a management of products based on consumer thought processes when making buying decisions. It is a question of evoking a "universe of consumption" corresponding to the expectations of the consumers. In some cases, this type of "category management" allows in-store reorganization of products belonging to the same class such as health products, cosmetics or aperitifs. Thus, products usually presented on different shelves are regrouped in the same place such as aperitifs, alcoholic drinks, peanuts, salted biscuits or olives. Such a grouping allows the consumer to make their purchases under ideal conditions and to benefit from supplementary services. This new idea, while attractive in theory, has several constraints in practice: these groupings in the store are not easy to achieve because they impose important modifications in the structure and functioning of stores in terms of logistics, competence, heads of departments, sectors and shelf space, and in the management of products and assortment.

For example, it is not easy to present an aperitif-type environment because the management of in-store drinks requires specific logistics different from the management of biscuits or peanuts ("grocery" sector), cheeses for the aperitif ("fresh" sector) and so on. The problems of sector management and supplies thus become more complicated and have caused distributors to avoid expanding these "consumer worlds" in their stores.

Systematic studies of customer behaviour allow for the improvement of the store conception and for the distribution of sectors and gondola end bins in an increasingly profitable way. They base themselves generally on ratios quoted in Figure 13.5.

Finally, the store conception is also influenced by the marketing policy of the distribution company. The physical aspect of the store should be the expression of this. The presentation of the store's immediate surroundings such as signage, car parking, the internal and external signposting and marking, the free space area, the quality and design of the furnishings, the floor type and the cleanliness of the store can create very different atmospheres. For example, by favouring traffic, wide aisles can be perceived as being a factor of purchase comfort, and can also decrease the crowding effect and the feeling of a well-stocked store.

- Customer density in the store per zone
- Client traffic and circuit-type indexes
- Time spent per zone, shelf-space
- Index of customer density for a specific group of products

$$\frac{\text{Customer density for a specific group of products}}{\text{Number of people}} \times 100$$

- Index of attention given to a specific group of products

$$\frac{\text{Number of stops}}{\text{Number of people}} \times 100$$

- Index of handling of a specific group of products

$$\frac{\text{Number of article handlings}}{\text{Number of stops}} \times 100$$

- Index for the purchase of a specific group of products

$$\frac{\text{Number of purchases}}{\text{Number of handlings of articles}}$$

- Index of attraction

$$\frac{\text{Index of purchases}}{\text{Index of customer density}}$$

Figure 13.5   Useful data for store management

Sales methods and services rendered

Merchandising techniques are not only linked to self-service stores. Although most literature on the subject concerns stores using this sales method, merchandising principles are also applicable to other selling methods such as traditional sales with shop assistants in small shops or department stores. The essential issue for merchandising is to ensure in the best possible way the functions of distribution at the point of sale by respecting the positioning of the distributor. The functions of reception, communication, information, presentation of products, sales in the strict sense, stimulation of the customers, stocking, transportation of goods, payment, services such after-sales services, credit or delivery can be effected in different ways according to the sales methods and commercial policy of the distributor. For example, the absence of salespeople means that the functions of reception, customer information, presentation of products, sales, transport and payment are performed differently: reception will be catered for through the decor, the music, lighting, space and so on; information through products, informative labelling, communication of a "consumer service"; the presentation of products will be modified by using techniques appropriate to the self-service store (see following section); sales will be the consequence of the presentation of products in the store, promotions, internal and external communication; transport will be left to the consumer (presence of supermarket trolleys near vehicle, cash-and-carry sales), or a delivery service (paying or non-paying) will be offered to the buyer, payment will be grouped together at the cash desks where the waiting period will be longer or shorter depending on staff numbers, printing of cheques and equipment such as scanners.

The merchandising approach is closely linked to the chosen sales method. It has direct consequences for warehouse and store organization. For example, Darty, which specializes in household electrical appliances, displays the products in the store which thus becomes an exhibition area, while most products are delivered directly from a central warehouse. The size and layout of the store are a direct consequence of this choice.

Customer satisfaction

The layout of the store should develop as a result of research studies on customer satisfaction. Lucas et al.,[24] for example, have presented a grille summarizing the elements of customer satisfaction for a discount store (Table 13.1).

L.L. Berry, A. Parasuraman and V.M. Zeithaml[25] have suggested a model for measuring the quality of the service which applies also to distribution (Figure 13.6).

This model distinguishes five gaps:

- gap 1: difference between customer expectations and the distributor's perception of these expectations;
- gap 2: difference between the distributor's perception of customer expectations and their translation in terms of specification of the service such as norms;
- gap 3: difference between these specifications and the actual performance;
- gap 4: difference between the actual performance and the message perceived by the customer;
- gap 5: this series of gaps ultimately defines the difference in the total gap between expected and perceived services.

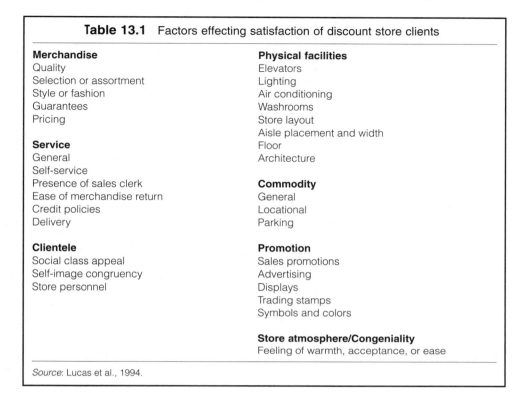

Table 13.1 Factors effecting satisfaction of discount store clients

Merchandise
Quality
Selection or assortment
Style or fashion
Guarantees
Pricing

Service
General
Self-service
Presence of sales clerk
Ease of merchandise return
Credit policies
Delivery

Clientele
Social class appeal
Self-image congruency
Store personnel

Physical facilities
Elevators
Lighting
Air conditioning
Washrooms
Store layout
Aisle placement and width
Floor
Architecture

Commodity
General
Locational
Parking

Promotion
Sales promotions
Advertising
Displays
Trading stamps
Symbols and colors

Store atmosphere/Congeniality
Feeling of warmth, acceptance, or ease

Source: Lucas et al., 1994.

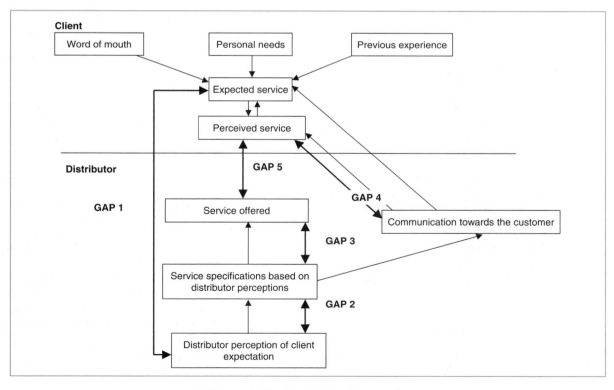

Client
Word of mouth
Personal needs
Previous experience
Expected service
Perceived service

Distributor
GAP 1
GAP 5
Service offered
GAP 4
Communication towards the customer
GAP 3
Service specifications based on distributor perceptions
GAP 2
Distributor perception of client expectation

Figure 13.6 Model of service quality
Source: Adapted from A. Parasuraman, V.A. Zeithaml and L.L. Berry, "Servqual: A Multiple-Item Scale for measuring Customer Perceptions of Service Quality", *Journal of Retailing*, 64, Spring, 1988.

Table 13.2 The five dimensions of perceived quality

Dimensions	Examples of items*
Tangibility	Their physical facilities should be visually appealing XYZ has up-to-date equipment
Reliability	These firms should be dependable
	When XYZ promises to do something by a certain time, it does so
Responsiveness	Their employees don't always have to be willing to help customers (−)
	You don't receive prompt service from XYZ'employees
Assurance	Their employees should get adequate support from these firms to do their jobs well
	You feel safe in your transactions with XYZ's employees
Empathy	It is unrealistic to expect employees to know what the needs of their customers are (−)
	XYZ does not have your best interests at heart

*First item is relative to customer expectations and the second to customer perceptions for the considered firm(XYZ).
Source: Adapted from A. Parasuraman, V.A. Zeithaml and L.L. Berry', Servqual: A Multiple-Item Scale for measuring Customer Perceptions of Service Quality", *Journal of Retailing*, 64, Spring, 1988.

In addition, the same authors have suggested ten dimensions of perceived quality of a service (Table 13.2), which can also be applied to distribution. These dimensions have then been used to create the SERVQUAL scale in five dimensions: physical supports, reliability, helpfulness, confidence and empathy.[26]

The management of products at the point of sale

The image of a store cannot be separated from the assortment which it offers. The range and management of this assortment are two essential roles of the merchandiser. They have led to the establishment of specific methods for the management of store sectors and shelf space, which range from the definition of the location and the profitability of products presented to the promotion and communication of the store's offer.

The definition of the assortment

This includes the choice of the assortment of products and brands; in particular, it is important to clarify the place allocated to the distributor's own brands.

The criteria for choice of assortment

The assortment presented by a store can be analyzed according to several different criteria:

■ The variety of products offered and, more widely, the product lines should correspond to the function which

the point of sale wishes to fulfill. The two poles of a scale which represent it should define the store as specialist or general. It is also one of the main elements for the positioning of the point of sale.

■ The width of the assortment corresponds to the range presented for a product line. Some stores offer a wide selection from bottom-to top-of-the-range products, others restrict their offer to a single level such as stores selling luxury goods, for example.

■ The depth of the assortment concerns the number of articles and references by category of the product – the greater the choice, the deeper the assortment.

Each store can be defined according to the type of assortment offered: wide and deep for department stores, narrow and deep for specialized stores, wide and shallower for supermarkets and hypermarkets, narrow and shallower for certain discounters such as hard-discounters or for certain convenience stores. Auchan in France (Al Campo in Spain and Portugal) have traditionally more product availability than Carrefour or Casino. The width and depth of the assortment also form an important dimension in the competition between hypermarkets.

The characteristics of assortment are designed to correspond to the type of target customer, the type and the positioning of the store, the size, location and convenience of the point of sale, and trade name policy. The way the assortment changes depends on changes in customer expectations and product rotation decisions. As mentioned above, where category management is used, the assortment is conceived according to the expectations of consumers and the way in which they make their buying decisions. This means that articles that were conventionally separate in the store are brought close together. Putting themselves in the position of consumers and their behaviour at the point of sale causes retailers to modify the traditional conception of assortment, and to make the "category manager" responsible for purchases, logistics and operational marketing.

For the distributor, the control of the relevance of its assortment can be managed using several criteria:

- The market share of the store in a product category: Panel data about trade names can be useful at a national level. At a local level (point of sale) special market research may be needed.
- The contribution of each category of products to the turnover and profit margin of the store (profit margin by category of product or by product).
- The rate of absolute service, which relates the number of references offered by the store to the references existing on the market.
- The rate of relative service, which indicates the percentage of customer requirements satisfied by the offered references.

For example, if the store offers 5 references out of 20 existing on the market, its rate of absolute service is 25 per cent. If these 5 references correspond to 50 per cent of demands on the market, the rate of relative service is 50 per cent.

The role of the distributors' brands

Several decades ago, a number of distributors launched products under their trade name (Casino in France, Tesco in the UK). Sometimes they produced them themselves and\or distributed them with the store's product warranty. Distributors' sub-brands then arrived, which, under a name other than that of the trade name, were distributed with prices lower than those carrying major brand names, the distributor not having the same scale of promotion expenses for the brand as the manufacturer. These were then followed by products which apparently had no brand name (for example, the "free products" from Carrefour) which allowed a distributor to offer the store's own products to customers, without any marginal advertising and promotional expenses.

Increasingly, one sees that most distributors offer products under their own brand name. This tendency has become more noticeable since the 1980s.

The nature of dealers' brands has changed. Certain distributors offer competing brands side by side with low price brands. The distributor, being generally obliged to offer the manufacturer's leading brand in certain markets and knowing the market share of this brand, puts a product on sale which is close to this product leader in several ways such as general presentation, packaging or performance (taste, enjoyment). The competing dealer brand is designed to avoid conflicts with brand leading products over direct copying (e.g., of packaging), while being sufficiently similar to make the consumer think the brands are very similar. The purpose is to capture market share from the brand leader which will benefit the distributor who has not invested in marketing communication. However, this will only work if the dealer brand is considered to be a valid alternative by the consumer. Besides, the manufacturer can defend his brand through extra communication to remove any ambiguity. It seems that supermarkets are becoming more and more oriented towards a "low price – dealer brands – brand leaders" structure. As a result, less well known brands risk seeing their market share decreasing, with only leading brands being able to defend themselves against those of the distributor. Some manufacturers have chosen to increase their turnover and have become suppliers of distributor's own brands. This phenomenon can already be observed in Great Britain and is developing in several other European countries, notably France, Spain and Portugal. Other distributors, such as Aldi, a German hard discounter, use distributor brands only.

Distributors pursue three objectives when developing their own brands under their trade name (e.g., Casino products) or under the name of brands belonging to them (Tex for Carrefour):

- The first is to increase profitability because profit margins on distributors' brands are superior to those made on manufacturers' brands.
- The second is to offer attractive prices to customers.
- The third is to differentiate the image of the trade name by offering new, original and exclusive products.

Today, distributors' brands carry with them the guarantee of the trade name and are increasingly placing emphasis on the notions of selection and quality. Besides, they guarantee to the manufacturers who supply the distributors a substantial volume of regular orders, leading to a real partnership. It is not surprising, therefore, to observe the increase in distributors' brands, since growth and profitability no longer arise readily from increasing store numbers (Table 13.3). Since 1990, across Europe, the turnover of dealers' brands has increased steadily.

Table 13.3 Private label market shares* by country (%)

	1993	1996	2000	2004
Switzerland	41.2	–	–	–
United Kingdom	37.1	42.3	42	41.5
Belgium	19.8	32.4	36.1	40.9
Germany	26.8	27.0	28.9	38.3
Spain	7.7	–	21.8	31.6
France	17.1	19.6	23.6	30.8
Sweden	–	–	7.1	25.5
Netherlands	16.3	21.4	20.5	22.5
Italy	6.8	–	12.6	15.6
USA	–	19.8	20.4	–
Portugal	2.3	–	–	–

* Market shares (volume)
Source: ACNielsen pour PLMA-www.fcd.asso.fr/FCD/pub/secteur/marques.rtf (2005).

criteria which allow for each reference to be assigned a more or less important place according to the desired objective: to maximize sales, to obtain the highest profit margin, to maximize net profit, to sell stock and so on.

Combining these three criteria follows rules which involve physical aspects of the sector as much as the principles of management.

In the case of furnishings, the height and the depth of shelves, the length of gondolas, the number and disposition of shelves allow for clusters which are more or less clear and adapted to product families. A shelf is highlighted by using a clear, clean product layout that encourages sales. Products can be packaged according to their envisaged position on the shelf: if they are high up, it is necessary for the most important aspects (brand, information, advertising etc.) to be visible for the consumer looking at them from below; on the other hand, if they are intended for the bottom of the gondola, it is advisable to place the most noteworthy aspects of the product communication on their top face so that they can be immediately spotted from above.

It is also necessary to ensure that heavy products do not require tiresome manipulation or again to place products with strong rotation in a location large enough to avoid shortages of stock. There are many such practical rules for merchandising which make the placing of products on shelves one of the determining elements of store perception by consumers. It is important to consider the effects of product presentation altogether, taking into account the visual level (bottom, middle, top of shelf), the area occupied by the product or the length the shelf space which is allocated to it, the mode of presentation of the family of products (vertically on several levels, horizontally on a single level). If certain rules seem rather general (eye level is best, "en masse" presentations, articles benefiting from clear information), it seems, nevertheless, that the distribution of products on shelf space depends first and foremost on results noted by the person responsible for each sector when he carries out regular checks. These are based on a certain number of management criteria (Toolbox 13.3).

The management of sectors and shelf space

The display and distribution of the assortment in different sectors are fundamental elements of management for the merchandiser. Several criteria apply at this level:

- The perception and attitude of the consumer regarding the point of sale are affected by the presentation and the aesthetics of different sectors. The clarity, the legibility of products and labelling, the ease of finding things and the "rhythm" and quality of the display have an important influence on visitor frequency and sales.
- The constraints of handling, re-supplying by the suppliers and distributors, the convenience of shelving and transporting products also play a major role in their layout in different sectors.
- The economic return on products varies according to their position on the shelf and the space allocated to them. Merchandising specialists have established

TOOLBOX 13.3

MEASURES OF PROFITABILITY OF THE SHELF SPACE

Several indicators allow calculation of the profitability of the shelf space of a store:

- the yield on the shelf space, which is the relation between the gross profit (equal to the gross profit margin multiplied by quantity sold) and the developed

shelf space (horizontal length calculated at a single level of the sector; for example, a gondola of 10 metres in length and comprising three levels makes 30 metres of developed shelf space),

$$\text{shelf space yield} = \frac{\text{gross profit margin} \times \text{quantity sold}}{\text{developed shelf space}}$$

- the productivity of the shelf space, which is the relationship between the turnover and the developed shelf space

$$\text{productivity of the shelf space} = \frac{\text{turnover}}{\text{developed shelf space}}$$

- the profitability index of the product, which concerns the relationship for the product of the gross profit margin rate and the rate of stock rotation to the developed shelf space:

$$\text{profitability of the product} = \frac{\text{rate of gross profit margin} \times \text{rate of stock rotation}}{\text{developed shelf space}}$$

with

- rate of gross profit margin = gross profit $\times$ 100 = turnover
- rate of stock rotation = $\dfrac{\text{quantity sold}}{\text{average stock}}$

Considering the performances of products and brands concerning each of these criteria, the store managers order a higher or lower "facing": "facing" is the number of frontal sales units offered (front row) which are visible to the customer. If shelf space falls below a minimum level, products pass unnoticed and are not sold. On the other hand, above a certain level of shelf space, sales grow less than proportionally to the increase in shelf space. Within these limits, it is a matter of distributing the shelf space in an optimal way with regard to the criteria of profitability and productivity discussed above. According to these principles, new products can only be introduced if they are backed up by substantial communication and promotion (see chapters on "Promotion" and "Advertising") sufficient to ensure an immediate demand. Under the aegis of the Food Marketing Institute in the United States and of certain important distributors, a model for calculating the real profitability of a product to a distributor has been developed, the "DPP" (direct profit by product), which tends to substitute itself for the vague notion of gross profit margin.

The DPP is clear profit (at the level of the elementary reference), by adding gross margin discounts and different bonuses to the gross profit margin and by deducting the direct costs of exploitation and handling. Figure 13.7[27] shows the interest in the calculation of the DPP, which takes into account costs really borne by the distributor and integrates all the accorded advantages, even without invoicing.

The calculation requires accurate accounting of relative costs for each article (Figure 13.8), which can be done with computer tools and scanners which directly record information about products being checked out at the cash desks using optical character reading.

The DPP can be calculated in several ways:

- The DPP in euro per unit estimates the profit obtained by selling one more unit.

- The DPP by metre of developed shelf space or by square metre per week measures the profit of a product according to the shelf space or selling surface area.

Each measurement gives information which allows for a more accurate decision about the allocation of shelf space between articles. At this level the DPP becomes integrated into computer models of shelf space management such as Apollo, Spaceman Accuspace/Accuprofit which supply computerized plans for in-store arrangements.

The DPP constitutes a particularly accurate system of information for the retailer. Most big distributors manage assortments which are so extensive that they ignore the DPP in practice and make their decisions according to the rates of net profit margins and "back" profit margins such as discounts or remissions fixed after negotiation and product rotation. Figure 13.9 summarizes the relation between the various policies of merchandising and the return on capital sought by the distributor.

Communication and promotion of the offer at the point of sale

Several forms of communication exist which promote the distributor's offer in relation to consumers.

Distributor communication

Internal communication requires that the customer visit the point of sale. In the broad sense, all of the images and sounds (messages), the store's offer and its organization contribute to building the perception and the attitude of the consumer. More specifically, internal communication

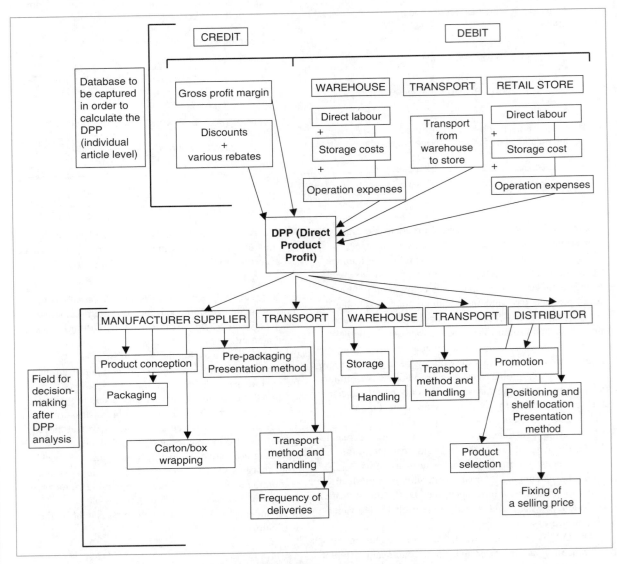

Figure 13.7 DPP: Direct product profit

can be strengthened by broadcasting sound messages, advertising at the point of sale using display units, electronic display boards, by the announcement and prominence given to promotions, by information given to customers through labelling, through product leaflets, advice given by sellers and in-store activities.

External communication concerns either the trade name at national or local level, or the shopping centre or store. This communication can be global or specific. In the first case, it is a question of passing on, generally through advertising, a message to the target group in question: the

trade name or the store. In the second case, communication aims to announce certain particular operations concerning the offer at the point of sale: a special event in a particular sector, the promotion of a particular product or special offers.

The concept of "publi-promotion" covers internal and external communications. It carries a supplementary dimension connected to the limited duration of the offer which distinguishes it from classic advertising communication.[28] The effectiveness of this type of communication has been the subject of much research notably on the memorization and the interest in messages

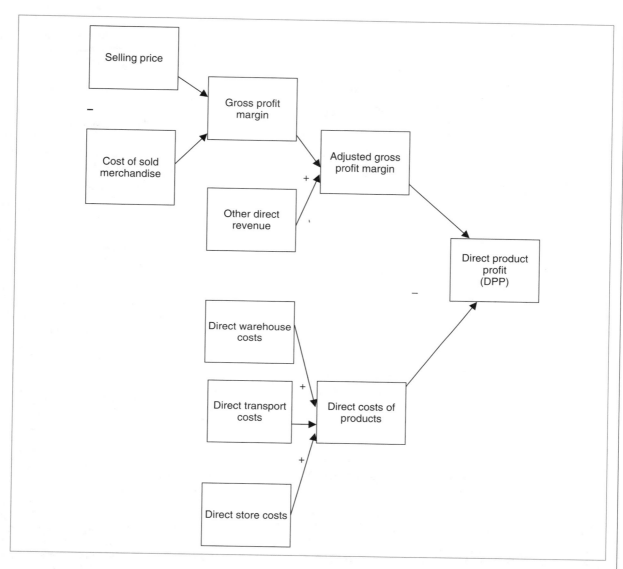

Figure 13.8 DPP structure

by type of product, nature of the media used (mailing, press, postering etc.), type of store and consumer allegiance to the store.

The promotion of products at the point of sale

Most distributors prepare a promotional plan for their store. Indeed, the abundance of special offers in distribution requires promotional operations to be planned. Certain operations concern the trade name, others the store in general, still others a sector or a category of products. Promotions can be on the initiative of the producer or the distributor or joint. The techniques used include price reductions, premiums, and end of aisles, coupons or games and depend either on the objectives of the distributor alone or on those of the producer and the distributor.

Large-scale distribution relies heavily on special offers to such an extent that their presence is one of its central characteristics. Merchandising cannot be separated from the use of special offers in the sense that these modify price policies, communication such as publi-promotion, products, stocks and the distribution of products such as end of aisle. However, the frequent use of multiple forms of promotion can be inconvenient. Consumers can become too used to it: instead of being loyal to the brand, the trade

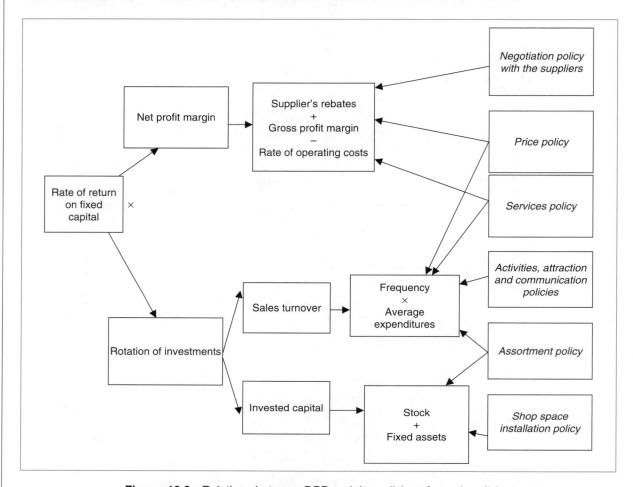

Figure 13.9   Relations between DPP and the policies of merchandising

name or the store, some consumers seek out special offers, whatever the trade name, the store or the brand. This phenomenon has been observed for durable goods such as televisions, radios or washing machines.

Thus, price promotions play an ambiguous role:

- from a positive point of view, they attract consumers to the store (mainly due to loss leaders), they allow for an increase in quantities sold and differentiate the store from its competitors.
- from a negative point of view, price promotions can help to attract disloyal customers and to damage the image of products supplied by the store (see chapter on "Pricing"). In addition, growth in sales may only be temporary and does not necessarily correspond to an increase in turnover over the long term. This is the case when the consumer has simply brought forward their purchase; the quantity remains close to what it was originally but at a lower price.

The effectiveness of promotional techniques can decline, as the consumer becomes tired of them. Today, the use of optical character reading data allows for a more rigorous analysis of this effectiveness. Panel Companies such as Nielsen, IRI-SECODIP and GfK have set up systems to measure the yield on special offers.

Merchandising and the producer–distributor relationship

Merchandising is one of the elements of the producer's marketing-mix.

Producer merchandising

The development of large-scale distribution has driven the producers of mass consumption goods to train merchandising specialists within their sales force. This can involve either "merchandisers" who have a specific role of implementing the merchandising techniques at the points of sale, or sellers-merchandisers who combine the two functions of selling and merchandising.

Producer merchandisers have numerous functions. Their basic role is to develop the distribution of products on the sales front by applying merchandising techniques to the shelf space and to the references. Merchandisers act as consultants by offering help to the distributor in the specification of optimal shelf spaces and assortment coherence. Merchandisers also have the functions of sales promoters and organizers of activities through offering promotions and promoting certain articles, informing and training managers about point of sale and ensuring the insertion and promotion of new products.

Some manufacturers carry out a store simulation for heads of department or sector allowing them to calculate their sales forecasts and profitability. Analytical models of sales data obtained from scanners are also used to help distributors with product management.

The role of producer merchandisers is necessary at several levels depending on the organization of central purchasing agencies. Some retailers forbid any in-store intervention on the part of merchandisers ("authoritarian" centres), others authorize the intervention of merchandisers but not order taking, and finally, others, the most numerous, are decentralized and allow the merchandisers to intervene at the point of sale. This decentralization can be wide and have more or less binding conditions added, such as prior referencing of the product by the central purchasing agency, negotiation of prices and discounts at a centralized level. For example, in Japan, store sellers (large stores) are paid by the producers. This may also be the case in "shop in shop" systems which consist of opening a producer sales space where the distributor is located.

The producer–distributor relationship

Over the last few years, the producer merchandising has developed markedly within the framework of trade marketing practices. Category management has led producers and distributors increasingly to integrate their management of assortments, supplies, data (data warehouse) and brands leading to a real partnership (Figure 13.10).

One of the direct consequences of the advent of large central purchasing agencies has been the modification of the negotiation relationship between producers and distributors. Frequently, a considerable part of the turnover of a manufacturer is associated with a very small number of central purchasing agencies, while the reverse is not true: for each centre, the influence of a manufacturer over its turnover is never very large. This has modified the balance of power between distributor and producer. Large-scale distributors have passed on a certain number of their costs to manufacturers, either by asking them to carry out different tasks which have been reserved for them, such as shelf filling, transport, handling, promotion, merchandising and activities, or by obtaining particular financial advantages in the form of premiums, discounts and participation charges. These side issues of profit margin are by no means unimportant and have very varied forms:

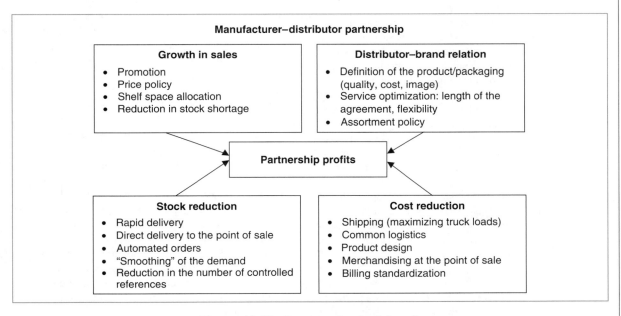

Figure 13.10 Sources of potential profit

- handshake: sum to be paid by the supplier to obtain a meeting with a buyer;
- referencing charges: sum paid to obtain a placement on shelf space;
- discount on invoices or on quantities;
- end-of-year discount: generally added to the previous discounts and can be paid by monthly or quarterly deposits from the beginning of the year;[29]
- remission for market commitment: the distributor gives an undertaking on quantities to be produced;
- remission for "good conduct": the distributor undertakes not "to spoil" prices and to ensure exclusivity;
- objective remission: the distributor receives this if he attains the assigned objective;
- range remission: the distributor undertakes to offer a complete range of products;
- "facing" remission: this is paid by the manufacturer for obtaining a more important "facing" in the shelf space;
- professional support remission: this is paid in return for promotional assistance from the store to the manufacturer;
- remission for the introduction of new products;
- allegiance remission;
- bulk remission: this is paid in return for the exploitation of warehouses by the distributor, thus alleviating the manufacturer's stock-holding costs.

Besides these discounts, a contribution to the store's advertising and promotional budgets can be requested from suppliers. Similarly, distributors can demand payment for particular placements such as end of aisles or for the presence of coordinators. Distributors can also ask for free supplies of goods or free services such as shelf placement guaranteed by the manufacturer, expenses for shelf space in return for the management and supplying of shelf space by the distributor. Finally, he can negotiate longer or shorter payment terms.

Contracts for "commercial cooperation" are concluded between the manufacturer and the distributor where mutual commitments occur concerning certain remissions and advantages explained above. The balance of power between producers and distributors strongly influences negotiation and can result in certain abuses when the producers are in a position of weakness because of their relatively small size, because their brands are little-known, because of their inexperience of negotiating with major distributors or because a very large share of their turnover depends on a single distributor.

Although European legislation forbids some discriminatory practices such as sales at a loss, remissions for no good reason, and anti-competitive practices such as agreements among distributors, it seems that the real progress of commercial negotiations does not always correspond to the wishes of legislators. There has been a transfer of certain distributor functions in distribution and merchandising to the producer, elements such as on-shelf placement, management of the shelf space, coverage of activities, or cost bearing through remissions. These practices can bring about a price reduction for the consumer, with distributors passing on a large portion of the advantages obtained via in-store prices. This aspect of the problem has had its effect on legislators because such practices can bring about the disappearance of the manufacturer that is badly affected by distributor pressure. Some European countries have taken the following measures:

- the extent of supplier discounts must be only proportional to purchase volume;
- obtaining advantages such as price, terms of payment, conditions of commercial cooperation on behalf of the supplier must on no account be the object of threats to cease stocking the manufacturer's products;
- ceasing to stock a supplier's products, or a break in stock-holding, must be preceded by written advance notice, whether the break between the two parties be partial or total.

Furthermore, to avoid resale at a loss or excessively low prices obtained due to the (forced) "cooperation" of the manufacturer, the invoice must mention any price reduction obtained at the date of the sale or provision of a service, and directly connected to this sales operation or provision of a service, with the exception of discounts not provided for in the invoice (see for example, the Galland Law of 1 July 1996 in France). On the other hand, the development of European legislation has favoured the reduction of supplier delays in large-scale distribution.

Overall, as Figure 13.11 shows, producer–distributor relations can be handled according to the two dominant approaches, either confrontation or partnership. Merchandising conditions concerning price, assortment, replacement, supply, delays or special offers are strictly linked to the wider framework which constitutes a producer–distributor relationship: companies either define a relationship based on relatively long-term cooperation which permits them to set up a policy and structures included in trade marketing; or they privilege short-term contracts. This puts particularly strong pressure at all times on prices and the set of negotiating conditions, to the detriment of certain positive effects of synergy which the trade marketing offers.

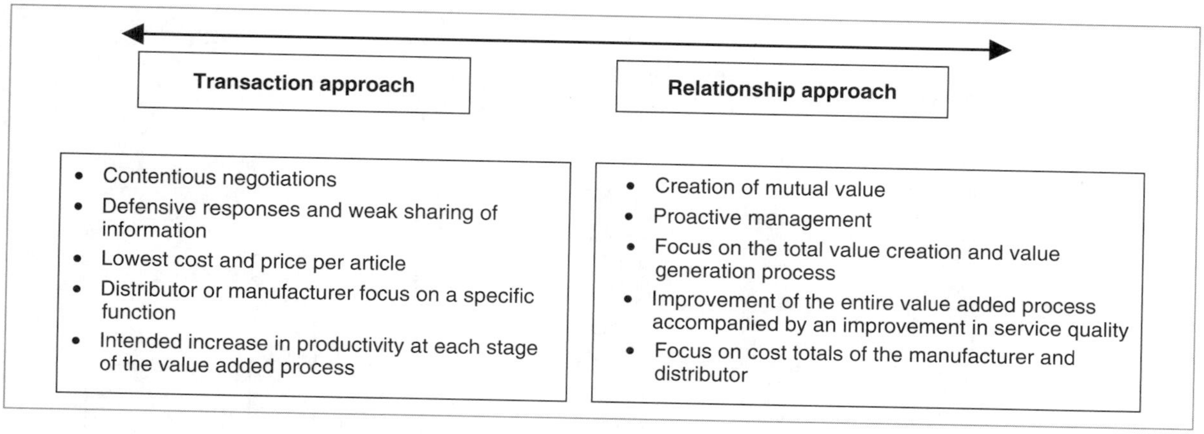

Transaction approach	Relationship approach
• Contentious negotiations • Defensive responses and weak sharing of information • Lowest cost and price per article • Distributor or manufacturer focus on a specific function • Intended increase in productivity at each stage of the value added process	• Creation of mutual value • Proactive management • Focus on the total value creation and value generation process • Improvement of the entire value added process accompanied by an improvement in service quality • Focus on cost totals of the manufacturer and distributor

Figure 13.11 Two approaches to distributor–producer relations

Distributor logistics

Logistics has become one of the key elements in the success of distribution companies. Optimally administering the different flows which constitute distribution (products, information, finance) has become a double imperative for all the links in the retailing chain between producers, distributors and service providers:

■ the imperative of productivity with objectives of minimal cost to strengthen the position of the distributor in the struggle with competitors;

■ the imperative of service in order to supply at the right time, in the right place and under ideal conditions to meet the performance expected by the customer.

The various forms of logistics

Certain ideas seen before in the chapters on Distribution figure in this matter:

■ In-store and warehouse stock management according to the "just in time" logic allows the limiting of stock-holding expenses while avoiding shortages (Figure 13.12). "Efficient warehouse response" consists of establishing a partnership between operators in the logistic chain to optimize the control of stocks and warehouses. This is possible only through using modern techniques of information management based on the exchange of computerized data.

■ The exchange of information using "EDI" (Electronic Data Interchange) principles establishes a direct link between the information systems of the different commercial partners by means of telecommunication networks. Thanks to the standardization of procedures

and documents and to the bar-code systems on products which make them recognizable and legible by optical character reading terminals, the bulk of information necessary for the handling of goods and for financial transactions such as orders, notice of dispatch, travel vouchers, product index cards, invoices is automatically transmitted, in a standard form, to each of the partners in the supply chain. Numerous advantages ensue, such as reduction of administrative costs, reduction in handling time, reduction in sending time, stock reduction and a decrease in disputes and errors. Customer service is thus greatly improved through the use of these new technologies: at any given moment, customers know the state of their orders, including when they are being transported.

Today, telecommunications are also conducted through the Internet, which tends sometimes to substitute itself for the classic telecommunication networks of data exchange for certain supply functions, notably in the search for and purchase of products. "Electronic business" is becoming an increasingly important phenomenon.

All the important European distribution chains are interested in computerized data exchange in cooperation with producers. Extranet systems are being increasingly used to build these links for the purchase and sale of goods and all the other services necessary for such operations: transport, stock-holding, payment and so on.

■ "Category management" allows for the treatment of a product category in a centralized way by placing its global in-store management under the responsibility of a category manager, the distributor[30] or sometimes even one of the suppliers who takes a leadership role.

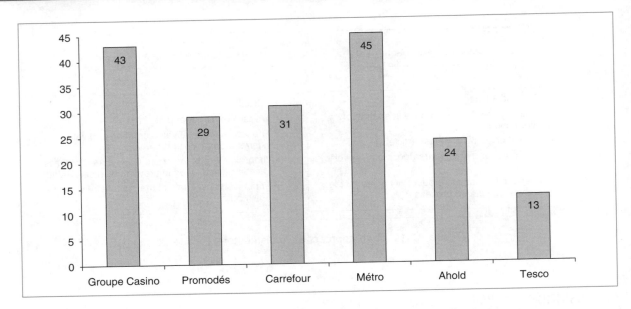

Figure 13.12 Number of days of stock in large self-service stores
Source: Adapted from LSA, 25 February 1999.

For example, Procter and Gamble would be designated as a "leader" for washing powder and would manage products in this category on behalf of the distributor.

- "Trade marketing" includes all the means used collectively by the producer, the distributor and the service providers to manage their relationships effectively from negotiation to service delivery through adopting shared methods of action, allowing greater synergy. The process of cooperation between supplier and retailer known as "Supplier–Retailer Collaboration" (SRC) has been very successful in the United States and then in Europe, following the example of Procter and Gamble and Wal-Mart. This cooperation has tended to become widespread in Europe even though certain obstacles exist, to a greater or lesser extent, in each country, as an Italian study conducted in 1994 shows (Figure 13.13).[31]
- "Efficient consumer response" allows suppliers to have direct and immediate access to the distributors' sales figures thanks to scanners at store checkouts; suppliers can thus predict "just in time" requirements and provide the necessary supplies while coordinating the tasks of the service providers and distributors themselves to this end.

The organization of logistic flows

Logistics involves the organization of the different flows mentioned above, which differs from one distributor to another.

Up to the beginning of the 1980s, the control of logistic flows was ensured by producers, either by direct delivery to stores or through regional or wholesale warehouses. Today, two different strategic options have been accepted by the industry leaders:

1. The first concerns distributors who have chosen to acquire technical installations directly, as well as transport and handling materials.
2. The second concerns distributors who prefer to use infrastructures provided by external partners.[32]

These partners are generally transport firms which have added stock control, notification and transmission of orders, order preparation, labelling and marking to the basic function of delivery.

As Paché and Colin[33] add, "delivery from the warehouse or platform depends on a combination of several orders – and so, several categories of product – into a single truck which delivers to only one point of sale. This system clearly offers a double advantage:

1. by concentrating the purchases on a few grouping points, distribution benefits from important discount on the part of the manufacturers (superior to the cost of the storing) and leads consequently to a policy of cost leadership.
2. by receiving small quantities of products daily, stores reduce their stock and can enlarge their selling space substantially.

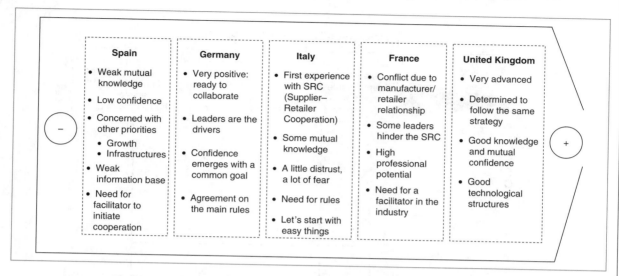

Figure 13.13 Level of cooperation between manufacturers and retailers
Source: Etude GEA Consultantia Associata

Thanks to warehouses and platforms, concentrated business thus takes advantage at one and the same time of the effects of productivity and flexibility – productivity because upstream flows are standardised, and stocks (when they are centralized) better managed; flexibility because final deliveries are better adapted to variations in demand, with less chance of a stock-out" (Figure 13.14).

The choice for the distributor consists of either internalizing or outsourcing its logistics management and, in particular, warehousing. In the Business-to-Business domain, logistics and warehouse control may bring about improved service for customers thanks to better availability of products from stock. It may also cause the company to hold speculative stocks so as to benefit from the best purchase prices. Conversely, subcontracting may lead to increased productivity and a drop in costs thanks to scale economies achieved by the company in charge of logistics. This company works for several clients and so uses facilities efficiently. On the other hand, the company giving the order loses part of its control over the marketing channel given to the subcontractor.

Electronic business and market places

Logistics management is making increasing use of electronic networks. Electronic business has numerous forms ranging from the simple presentation of the offer to the consumer on the Internet to the global management of information streams. Real electronic "market places" such as GlobalNet Xchange and CPGmarket have been created, which allow connected companies to establish trade relationships such as buying or selling, or non-trade relationships such as communication, collaboration,

handling information and payment. These market places allow transactions between providers and buyers, each buyer being able to consult a much more extended set of offers. This results in increased competition and a better adaptation of offers to demands. The purpose of market places is more than just to facilitate transactions. They offer help in determining purchase requirements, the choice of supplier, information about distribution logistics, various advisory services (tax systems, formalities of export)

There are several different types of market place. Some are administered by independent groups who thus become new intermediaries in the distribution chain, some are administered by a supplier (seller side), and others by a purchaser (buyer side). Some locations specialize in a particular activity or industry, others are horizontal and concern several activities: Etexx for the textile industry, Eu-supply for building and public works.

These market places have numerous advantages:

- They reduce the costs of purchasing products because of competition among several suppliers. In certain places, auction systems allow for the drawing up of a contract with the best provider for a type of service defined in advance by the buyer.
- They lead to a drop in administrative costs, particularly for non-strategic purchases such as stationery or general services.
- They allow for better adaptation of the product to the needs of the buyer, who is in contact with a larger number of potential suppliers.
- They speed up purchase operations and contribute to better management of logistic flows thanks to

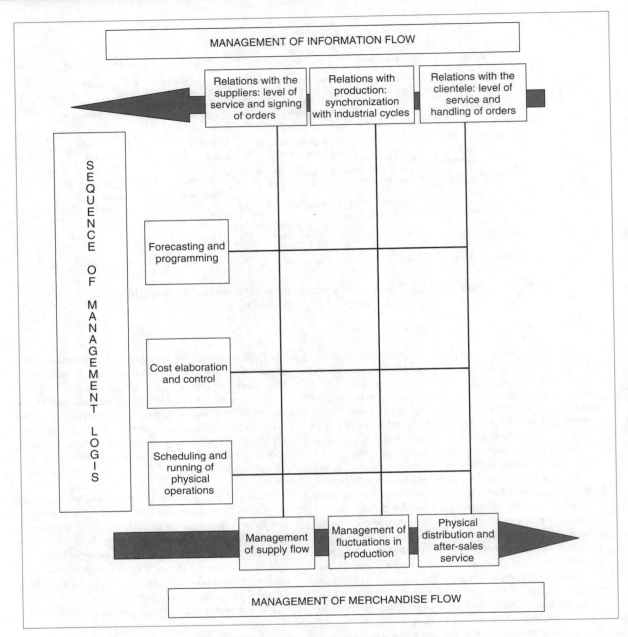

Figure 13.14 Managing the logistics process

numerous complementary services which they offer concerning physical logistics and payment.

Such market places also have several defects:

■ This method of buying does not replace the richness of personal contact. The result is that such markets are more effective where low-value products are concerned such as light-bulbs and consumable

material, rather than for specialized products requiring advice and services adapted to each client, which is often the case in B to B.

■ Market places do not allow for the establishment of customer loyalty and are closer to a transactional marketing model than a relational approach.

For suppliers, they permit much wider display of their products and services, which also helps to increase their range of customers. The resulting expansion of competition and of service provision tends to increase added value. However, a company using electronic market places can only reap all possible logistical benefits if it is capable of properly integrating its own information system with that of the market place, which requires double adaptation: technological, at an information telecommunications systems level, and organizational, concerning the adaptation of jobs, competences and procedures to this innovative type of business.

SUMMARY

This chapter has demonstrated the importance and complexity of merchandising. The problem of managing the point of sale rests on the analysis of the consumer's spatial behaviour while taking into account the specific characteristics of each store such as its importance, size, image, the nature of the trade name, the types of products and services and the characteristics of competitors.

Once the location has been selected, it is necessary to design the store by giving it a prestigious image or by respecting the existing image if the store is going to use an existing trade name, organizing it in a manner adapted to consumer requirements, providing expected services, adopting good sales methods and taking the satisfaction of the customer into consideration.

Assortment management must follow precise rules which concern both the choice and the presentation of the brands on offer. Particular attention has been paid to distributor brands which are playing an increasingly important role. Management techniques concerning sectors and shelf space employ ratio calculations which have been discussed.

The store's marketing communications are partially integrated with the communication of the overall trade name (when the store depends on a distributor trade name) but, in all cases, it is important that the point of sale carries out its own promotion aimed at consumers within the catchment area.

Relationships between producers and distributors have been subject to special analysis. Producers participate actively in the merchandising of their products within the framework of the stores. Good relationships between producers and distributors have become essential for effective merchandising. The terms of this cooperation are numerous and subject to fierce negotiation. They concern not only products, services and information but also the management of product and financial flows. These terms are presented with a particular accent placed in the final part, the link between merchandising and distributor logistics. New information technology and communications systems are again important at this stage in strategy development by production and distribution companies. The role of electronic business, with the advent of electronic market places, illustrates the profound changes which are characteristic of distribution and merchandising today.

Discussion questions

1. Take photos of a department (e.g., coffee, rice, yogurt) in three superstores operating under different names. Compare the departments: number of brands, number of linear feet, number of facings, organization of the department according to product type, brand, vertical arrangement, horizontal arrangement, etc. Judging by the differences, what conclusions can you draw concerning the consumer and the distributor?

2. Choose three types of distributors of different products (furniture, appliances, cosmetics). Consult their websites. Compare the distributors' presence (i.e., number of stores per city, trading area, etc.). How do you explain the differences?

3. Stores do not exist solely to make sales; they are also places for a consumer experience. In experiential marketing, "consumer experience is as important as product or service". Illustrate this phrase using three points of sale (e.g., haircutting salon, clothing store, cosmetics store).

4. Take a common food product, such as bread, fruit, or meat, and give a representation of the manufacturing and distribution chain, from the raw materials to the end product. Next, examine the four distribution flows (physical, product ownership, financial, information).

5. Which technologies have made it possible to increase distribution productivity over the past 10 years (e.g., scanners, automatic labeling, electronic transmission)? What is the impact on the intermediary and service provider functions?

Notes and references

1. M. Benoun and M-L. Hélies-Hassid, *Distribution, Acteurs et Stratégies*, 2ème edition, Paris, Economica, 1995.

2. K.J. Lancaster, *Consumer Demand: New Approach*, New York, Columbia University Press, 1971.

3. J.A. Howard and J.N. Sheth, *A Theory of Buyer Behaviour*, John Wiley and Sons, New York, 1969.

4. J.F. Engel, D.T. Kollat and R.D. Blackwell, *Consumer Behavior*, Hinsdale, Dryden Press, 1978.

5. W. Christaller, *Central Places in Southern Germany*, Englewood Cliffs, Prentice Hall, 1967.

6. R. Hubbard, 'A Review of Selected Factors Conditioning Consumer Travel Behaviour', *Journal of Consumer Research*, 5, 1, 1–21, 1978.

7. W.J. Reilly, 'Method for the Study of Retail Relationships', *Bureau of Business Research*, Austin, University of Texas Press, 1939.

8. Cf. for example, P. Guido, 'Vérification Expérimentale de la Formule de Reilly en tant que Loi d'Attraction des Supermarchés', *Revue Française du Marketing*, 39, 101–107, 1971.

9. D. Huff, 'Defining and Estimating a Trade Area', *Journal of Marketing*, 28, 34–38, 1964.

10. T. Stanley and M. Sewall, 'Image Inputs to a Probabilistic Model: Predicting Retail Potential', *Journal of Marketing*, 10, 3, 48–53, 1976.

11. L.P. Bucklin, 'The Concept of Mass in Intra-urban Shopping', *Journal of Marketing*, 31, 2, 37–42, 1967.

12. T.E. Hlavac et J.D.C. Little, 'A Geographic Model of an Urban Automobile Market', *Application of Management Science in Marketing*, Englewood Cliffs, Prentice Hall, 1970.

13. P. Roger, 'Description du comportement spatial du consommateur client de l'hypermarché', *Thèse de Doctorat de és Sciences de Gestion*, Lille, 1983.

14. N. Nakanishi and L. Cooper, 'Parameter Estimate for Multiplicative Interactive Choice Model: Least Squares Approach', *Journal of Marketing Research*, 11, 3, 303–311, 1974.

15. A. Bultez and P. Naert, 'Econometric Specification and Estimation of Market Share Models: The State of the Art', Working Paper 76–79, Bruxelles, European Institute of Advanced Studies in Management (EIASM), 1976.

16. P. Roger, 'Description of Consumer Spatial Behaviour: A New Approach', *International Journal of Research in Marketing*, 1, 3, 171–181, 1984.

17. Cf. for example, J.H. Kunkel and L. Berry, 'A Behavioral Conception of Retail Image', *Journal of Marketing*, 32, 4, 21–27, 1968 and P. Martineau, 'The Personality of the Retail Store', *Harvard Business Review*, 36, 47–55, 1958.

18. A.K. Jain and M. Etgar, 'Measuring Store Image Through Multidimensional Scaling of Free Response Data', *Journal of Retailing*, 52, 4, 61–70, 1976 and E. Pessemier, 'Store Image and Positioning', *Journal of Retailing*, 56, 1, 94–106, 1980.

19. M. Filser, 'Quelles Formules de Distribution pour Demain? La Réponse de la Segmentation par Avantages Recherchés', *Recherche et Applications en Marketing*, 1, 1, 3–16, 1986.

20. R. Hansen and T. Deutscher, 'An Empirical Investigation of Attribute Importance in Retail Store Selection', *Journal of Retailing*, 53, 4, 58–72, 1977.

21. D. Mazursky and J. Jacoby, 'Exploring the Development of Store Images', *Journal of Retailing*, 62, 2, 145–165, 1986.

22. R.F. Lusch, *Management of Retail Enterprises*, Belmont, CA, Kent Publishing Co., 1982.

23. M. Filser, 'La Dynamique des Canaux et Formules de Distribution', *Thèse pour le Doctorat d'Etat ès Sciences de gestion*, Montpellier, 1985.

24. G.H. Lucas Jr, R.P. Bush and L.G. Gresham, *Retailing*, Boston, Houghton Mifflin Company, 1994.

25. A. Parasuraman, V.A. Zeithaml and L. Berry, 'Servqual: A Multiple-item Scale for Measuring Consumer Perceptions of Service Quality', *Journal of Retailing*, 64, 1, 12–40, 1988.

26. Ibid.

27. J. Dioux, 'PDP, l'outil du vrai profit', *Points de Vente*, 284, 54–56, 1984.

28. G. Davies, 'Positioning, Image and the Marketing of Multiple Retailers', *International Review of Retail Distribution and Consumer Research*, 2, 1, 13–34, 1992.

29. We can fully understand that an article sold at cost price can give an appreciable profit margin due to the interplay and discrepancies in cash flow (the client paying cash, the supplier being paid at the end), and "back" profit margins such as end-of-year discounts which, paid in installments from January and placed in an account, given interesting financial returns.

30. M. Vandaele, *Commerce et Industrie, le nouveau partenariat*, Vuibert, Paris, 1998.

31. J.-M. Aurifeille, J. Colin, N. Fabbes-Costes, C. Jaffeux and G. Paché, 'Management Logistique', Les Essentiels de la Gestion, Paris, 1997.

32. G. Paché, "La Logistica Nei Rapporti Industria-Distribuzione: Il Caso Francese", *Commercio*, 41, 47–65, 1991.

33. G. Paché and J. Colin, *La logistique de distribution*, Chotard, Paris, 1988.

Pricing decisions

Learning objectives

After studying this chapter you will be able to

1 Understand the nature and importance of price
2 Recognize the constraints on a firm's pricing discretion
3 Evaluate various pricing objectives
4 Explain what a demand curve is and how it affects price setting
5 Understand the role of costs in pricing decisions
6 Understand how product characteristics may influence a marketer's pricing decisions
7 Understand how to set price using competition-based methods
8 Consider issues affecting pricing of products for industrial markets

SPOTLIGHT

In 1988, Mercedes introduced the Smart car to the market. That year, 2000 cars were sold instead of the 20,000 expected. Among the reasons for this flop was the price which was too high compared to the value perceived by the consumer.

Radical fruit, a Pepsi soft drink, has been a failure despite a careful launch. Its price was twice the average market price of soft drinks.

Pricing decisions should be taken carefully because consumers will buy only if the perceived value of the product is greater than or equal to its price.

Price is the monetary value of a product to be given away in an exchange by a company. In the exchange process, consumers will pay a monetary value in exchange for the perceived value of goods (see Chapter 1). Perceived value includes benefits such as monetary savings but also other product attributes such as saving time in supermarket shopping and cooking, product quality, convenience, freshness or prestige. Therefore, in the exchange process, price is part of the value exchanged. For example, public transportation is not used by all potential users because, despite the low price, some people find it wasteful of time.

Price is the only variable in the marketing-mix which the firm uses to capture some of the value created by the other elements of the marketing mix. Therefore it is the only source of income. All the other variables generate only investments or expenditure. For this reason, pricing is particularly important for the firm. In addition, the saturation of the markets, surplus production capacities and the standardization of functional product quality mean that price plays a more important role than ever before in the marketing-mix.

Price produces more immediate effects than the other tools of the marketing-mix. Demand and competition are generally quicker to react to price changes than to modifications in distribution, communication or product features.

Pricing must be consistent with the other elements of the marketing-mix. Indeed, it must contribute to the intended positioning of a product or a business unit. Figure 14.1 presents the approach in which pricing is integrated.

This approach is not sufficient to determine a price. It must be accompanied by simultaneous analyses focusing on five great factors:

1. objectives of the company concerning price
2. demand
3. characteristics of the product
4. competition
5. legal constraints

Their comparison will allow one to determine the price levels that will be tested before leading to a final decision (Figure 14.1).

The characteristics of these various factors and the pricing methods which correspond to them will be presented in turn. The characteristics of pricing in the industrial sector will then be discussed. It is interesting to note that pricing is also studied by means of mathematical models which integrate the influence of the various variables of marketing-mix. Because of their global character, they are presented in the chapter devoted to product management (Chapter 8).

Pricing objectives

Price plays a central role in marketing strategy. Very often pricing is the last decision to be taken with a single objective: to be cheaper than the competitors. Although optimal pricing is less interesting than looking at advertising copy, it is a key element in product positioning and product image. Therefore, pricing should be embedded in overall strategy formulation and in particular should focus on value positioning depending on the competition and the target market or segment. Once the firm's strategy is defined, pricing objectives have to be fixed.

Pricing objectives may be related to sales volume, profitability, product line, image and strategic positioning.

Objectives related to volume

Price influences the volume of the product sold. Quantities sold are often an inverse function of price. Such an observation comes from the shape of the demand curves as a function of price. Those curves in most cases have form (A) reproduced in Figure 14.2.

When the objective is the maximization of sales volume or market penetration, management will tend to fix a relatively low price. Several reasons can explain such an objective. The aim must be to

- ensure optimal use of the production capacity,
- ensure full employment of the workforce,
- obtain economies of scale or
- improve the position on the experience curve,
- occupy a position of leader in a growing market.

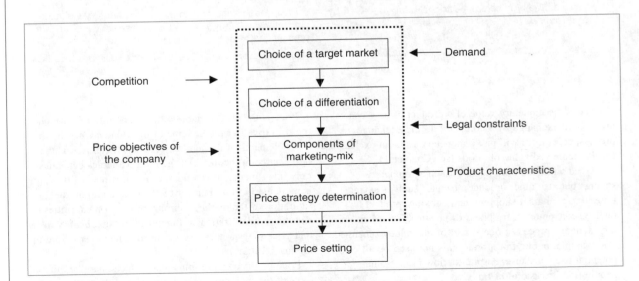

Figure 14.1 Pricing approach

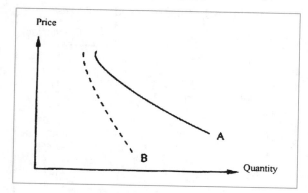

Figure 14.2 Demand curves

The influence of price on sales volume varies with the price elasticity of demand, which is defined as the percentage of change in sales volume for a change in price of 1 per cent. It is in general negative, except for certain luxury goods. In addition, elasticity is smaller when consumers use price as an indicator of quality as in the case of household electrical appliances. Low price elasticity results in a steeper curve (B) and thus a lower increase in demand (A) for the same price reduction.

Profitability objectives

Profitability and price are linked by the relation

$$\Pi = PQ - CQ$$

Π = Profitability or profit
P = Price
C = Unit cost
Q = Quantity sold

This equation shows that apparently profit is a direct function of price. However, this relation is much more complex, insofar as the price also influences the quantity sold.

The same statement can be made about unit costs. Part of unit cost comes from variable costs such as the quantity of raw materials, and part from fixed costs, allocated in the short run to the quantities sold (research and development, wages and administrative loads, labour costs, marketing expenditure, depreciation). The fixed costs thus constitute a more or less important element of unit cost depending on the quantities sold and thus on price.

For this reason, the complex relation which links profitability to price means that a high price does not always corresponds to high profitability and so it is not necessarily the case that an objective of high profitability requires a high price.

When one can estimate the quantity of products likely to be sold for one year, it is easy to fix a price which

takes into account the profitability objective. Electricity is a product category where it is possible to estimate the volume or quantity expected to be used in the following year without first knowing the price. Indeed, it is possible to calculate the price with the following formula:

$$P = V + F/Q + RI/Q$$

V = Average variable cost
F = Total fixed costs
Q = Quantity likely to be sold
I = Investment
R = Percent target return on investment

If this formula is examined, it is easy to see the danger in fixing too high a rate of profitability, which can in particular have a depressing effect on demand. A reduction in the quantity likely to be sold requires an increase in the unit price to cover the fixed overheads, which in turn is likely to involve a demand reduction.

Product line objectives

The price of a product can have consequences on its sales but also on other products of the line. Thus, price setting should aim to optimize the sales of an entire product line.

For example, the use of a discount price is intended to attract customers to the products belonging to the bottom-of-the-line in order to see them migrate either to a top-of-the-line product or, once the product has been bought at discount price, to see them buying other products of this same line. Conversely, a badly set price can generate a cannibalization effect, according to which a product of the line wins the market share of another.

Product image objectives

An image of quality or luxury is often associated with price. Setting a high price can be to maintain or create an image of product quality, of selectivity or of luxury. This relationship is important for all categories of products where customers assess quality by the price or derive social status from paying a high price, such as perfume, cars and luxury products in general.

Strategic price positioning

According to their competitive advantage (cost/price versus value) and selected markets (large or narrow), companies may choose among four strategies:

1. General price leader, using cost/price competitive advantage on a large market, such as Toyota and Nissan in the car industry
2. Specialized price leader, using cost/price competitive advantage in a narrow market, such as the 4X4 Suzuki

3. General differentiated price, using value competitive advantage on a large market, such as Renault, Peugeot and Citroen

4. Differentiated price specialist, using value competitive advantage on narrow market segment, such as Porsche and Mercedes Benz

Demand-based pricing

While setting prices, a company must take into account the sensitivity of the market to price. The customers of the company or the demand can be a barrier to price increases or price reductions.

A key influencing factor on price setting for a product is the customers' price/demand elasticity concerning the product. Elasticity indicates a change of the nature of the demand the company must take into account. In addition, a very negative price elastic demand ($E < -2$) will require a relatively low price, if the company wishes to stimulate purchases.

Elasticity can be low in the short term and high in the long term. For example, in the industrial sector, if a supplier raises its price, it may take a certain time for the customer to leave this supplier and thus decrease its demand.

Table 14.1 presents average price elasticities for various consumer goods. Data were collected and pooled for Belgium, France, the Netherlands, Germany, Denmark, Italy, Norway and Sweden.

Note the strong price–demand elasticity for detergent, jam, coffee and car expenditures (-2.009, -2.672, -2.993, -2.004). Raising the price of a detergent by 10 per cent would result in a reduction in demand of 20.09 per cent.

Table 14.1 Price–demand elasticities

Products	Elasticities
Soft drink	−1.419
Yoghurt	−1.100
Sweets	−1.982
Cigarettes	−1.224
Railways	−1.533
Coffee	−2.933
Fruits	−1.229
Electric razor	−2.469
Gasoline	−0.600
Shampoo	−1.762
Feminine hygiene	−1.405
Dish Washer	−1.692
Detergent	−2.009
Jam	−2.672
Cars	−2.004

Source: J.J. Lambin (1998), *Le marketing Stratégique*, Paris, Ediscience, p. 206.

Traditional panels or electronic panels (scanner data) allow one to measure the price elasticity of customers for existing products. It should, however, be noted that these two modes of collection do not provide identical information, elasticity showing to be greater with scanner data.

Price–demand elasticity can also be estimated for practical purposes using a procedure developed by Gabor and Granger or by conjoint measurement analysis (see Toolbox 14.1).

TOOLBOX 14.1

PRICE–DEMAND ELASTICITY METHODS OF ESTIMATION

Gabor and Granger's method consists of proposing various prices to current or potential purchasers of a product and asking interviewees at what price they will buy the product. According to the price obtained, for an existing product as well as for a new product, it is possible to draw a sensitivity curve of demand related to price. This method can be used to fix the price of a new product not far away from an existing product. In the example indicated (Exhibit A), one can thus highlight the differential of price which the market will accept, if the new product is launched (0.50 € if the price of the product on the market is 3.50 €).

The disadvantage of this method is the sensitivity to the order of presentation of the price cues, the price range used, and the absence of realism, since the respondents are not in a real purchase situation. In particular, they answer to only one stimulus, the price, whereas price is only one of the components of the product.

Expert interviews are also used to evaluate price–demand elasticity. When facing major innovations or when important changes occur in the competitive environment, it will be the only available method. It is rather simple and cheap. Its main limit is its reliance upon data internal to the company (salespeople, marketing manager, general manager). Expert interviewing involves several steps similar to the Delphi technique.

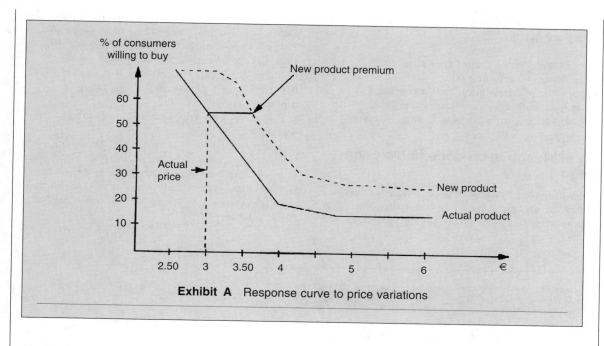

% of consumers willing to buy

New product premium

Actual price

New product

Actual product

2.50   3   3.50   4   5   6   €

Exhibit A   Response curve to price variations

- *Step 1*: Development of a questionnaire focusing on the product and price and their forecast context
- *Step 2*: Questionnaire administration to fewer than 10 experts from all levels of the company (salespeople, marketing managers, general managers)
- *Step 3*: Analysis of divergence of opinion at a meeting including all the participants and integrating the different opinions to obtain a consensus

Price tests are another alternative to expert interviews or conjoint measurement. In price testing, price is set up at different levels and its effect on market share or sales volume is observed. Tests can be performed in experimental stores or on the market. On the market, a different price is fixed in each area.

Direct selling catalogues and e-business fit particularly well to price testing.

Conjoint measurement analysis can also be used to evaluate price–demand elasticity. It is very popular and may be used for either existing or new products. This method is concerned with measuring the joint effect of two or more product attributes on the ordering of overall liking or preference. Combinations of attributes (price being one of them) are presented to respondents who are asked to rank them according to their preference. Using a conjoint algorithm, this method provides the utility function of each attribute.

Two data collection procedures are used, full profile and trade-off. Full profile requires the presentation of the whole set of combinations of attributes to respondents. Trade-off relies on a presentation of combinations of only two attributes at a time. Attributes may be verbally or pictorially described.

Example of data collection according to the trade-off method

		Lifetime length of the tyre (km)		
		40,000	50,000	60,000
Price	200	5	4	1*
	300	7	6	2
	400	9	9	3

*preference given by one respondent

Example of attribute combination according to the full profile method

Brand: Michelin
Lifetime length: 50,000 km
Price: 400 €
Type: Radial

Adaptative Conjoint Analysis (ACA) is a trade-off procedure very popular in Europe. It includes two stages: The first requests the respondent to indicate the importance of the attributes presented while the second uses this judgement to compute preferences towards the most important pairs of attributes. Attributes as well as their value levels are supposed to be independent of each other.

Choice Based Conjoint or CBC is a useful complement to ACA because this method asks the consumer to make a unique choice between the various combinations of attributes. The interviewer may reject all offered combinations. Another advantage is the potential use of non-independant attributes.

A certain number of phenomena observed about consumers have an influence on demand elasticity. They are in particular, the

- existence of an acceptable price range
- existence of a reference price
- attraction of certain prices for the consumer,
- unequal sensitivity of consumers to price,
- use of price as an indicator of quality and value.

The existence of an acceptable price range

Below a minimal threshold of price, consumers reject a product, for they associate it with bad quality. Beyond a maximum threshold, they do not buy the product, for they find it too expensive for the value they obtain. Rostand and Le Roy gave an example of such a phenomenon for coffee. The authors showed that a price increase of a 250 g package of coffee beans, from €0.46 to €0.92, in 1976, did not have any effect on demand. Another similar price increase (end of 1976, beginning of 1977) from €0.92 to €1.53 generated a large fall of consumption.

Toolbox 14.2 presents a method of determining the acceptable price range.

Such a method proves very useful to fix the price of a new product. However, by privileging price alone, it tends to move away from the real conditions of the purchase. Conjoint measurement analysis can be used to optimize price selection once an acceptable price range has been fixed (Toolbox 14.1).

TOOLBOX 14.2

COMPUTATION OF AN ACCEPTABLE PRICE RANGE

The acceptable price range is identified by means of two questions:

1. What is the maximum price you would be willing to pay for this (product or brand)? (that is, beyond what price would you feel it would not be worth paying more?)
2. What is the minimum price you would be willing to pay for this (product or brand)? (that is, below what price would you seriously doubt its quality?)

For example, let us suppose that consumers evaluate prices from 10£ to 16£. Answers to the two questions allow one to draw up the following table.

If a price of £13 is selected, the percentage of people for which this price is not too low is equal to 93, while the percentage of those for which this price is too high is equal to 2. The last column makes it possible to appreciate, for each price, the percentage of the respondents likely to buy this product. The table below makes it possible to evaluate the interest of this method, not only to study the potential demand in the price range but also to determine the acceptable price by the largest demand which is £13, price which also corresponds to the maximum turnover.

Price (£)	Number of respondents agreeing with the maximum price	% cumulated (H)	Number of respondents agreeing with the minimum price	% cumulated (L)	% of potential customers (L–H)
10	0	0	5	5	5
11	0	0	27	32	32
12	2	2	48	80	80
13	15	17	13	93	91
14	46	63	6	99	82
15	34	97	1	100	37
16	3	100	0	100	3

The acceptable price range varies according to certain characteristics of the consumers. Thus, consumers believing in a relationship between price and quality, strongly involved in the product and who do not consider price as a major concern have an acceptance range that is broader than other consumers. The existence of an acceptable price range is related to the existence of a reference price in the mind of the consumer.

The existence of a reference price

A reference price is defined as being the price which is used as a point of comparison to evaluate other prices. It can be external if it is established starting from the observation of the environment (similar prices of products, advertising, etc.) or internal if it is stored in consumer memory (last paid price, price of the last similar purchase, expected price, belief of the consumer). A reference price is either specific or consists of a price range, the end points of which are used by the consumer to evaluate the price of a product. A price is perceived as low when it is lower than the lower end point and high when higher than the higher end point of the price range.

The existence of a reference price can be used in pricing, for example, by presenting two different models of the same product with high but different prices next to each other. Such juxtaposition supports, for example, the purchase of consumers who evaluate the quality of the product based on price since one of the products (the most expensive) is better than the other.

In retailing, other methods can be used to support the use of the reference price by the consumer, and to show the importance of price reduction. They consist in particular of presenting beside the discounted price, either the regular price for the product or the percentage of discount, or the price charged by other retailers of the trade area, or even the recommended selling price of the manufacturer.

The presence of a reference price affects the evaluation and judgement of prices by consumers. The greater the variation between the current price and the reference price, the weaker will be the credibility of the offer. Vague formulations (e.g., save up to X per cent) are perceived as less valuable than precise reductions (e.g., X per cent of reduction on this model). Perceptions of the reference price are also subjected to other influences, in particular the type of point of sale or the awareness of the brand.

Psychological prices

Psychological prices can be defined as odd prices or prices fixed just below a round number (98 or 99 for example). The attraction of these prices can be explained by the focus of attention of the consumer who processes data from left to right and will use the number on the left to have an idea of the reference price. For example, a consumer assumes that a price of 98€ provides an advantageous price discount on a reference price of 100 € because the consumer is not considering the figures on the right and tends to perceive an advantage of 10 € whereas it is actually equal to 2 €. Prices of, for example, 99.95 € on the other hand may be perceived as an insult to their intelligence by some consumers.

Sensitivity to price

Not all consumers are sensitive to price differences. Those which are, tend to be loyal at certain price levels. These various preferences for price are associated with socio-demographic profiles. For example, in the food industry, high prices are the prerogative of small size households, with high incomes where the age of the homemaker exceeds 50 years. They are also related to time (for seasonal purchases like clothing or tourism) as well as different types of involvement (product, brand, activity) and of course available budget. For example, consumers involved with brands will be more sensitive to a sales promotion price of their regular brand than other consumers.

When there are customers who prefer low prices, and if the production capacity of the company is under-employed, it can be a good idea to use different prices on this set of customer groups if the company wishes to increase its market share, to avoid the possible entry of competitors in those segments or to penetrate certain foreign markets.

Different price sensitivities are opportunities for price discrimination because of the heterogeneity of the price–demand elasticity. Various strategies of price discount are then used to tackle customers who have preferences for low prices.

The discount strategy for secondary segments means selling to these segments at prices lower than those prevailing for the principal segment. Student segments, new customers or certain foreign markets benefit from this type of strategy.

The strategy of periodic discounting is intended to address the foreseeable variation (fashion, holiday periods) in price sensitivity through time. It corresponds in particular to price discounts, out-of-season or for out-of-fashion goods.

The random discounting strategy is used to attract consumers who systematically seek low prices. It consists in lowering the prices in a random way in order to attract this segment of consumers, while continuing to sell at high prices to consumers who do not seek the low prices systematically.

Price as an indicator of perceived quality

Many studies have shown that there is a positive relationship between price and perceived quality for a product. They have shown that price plays a more important role when it is the only information available and when it is associated with other information on the product (brand, store name, etc.). They also showed the complexity of this influence because of the interaction between price and this other information.

The relation between price and perceived quality is influenced by the consumers' knowledge of prices charged and their ability to detect variations between products. This varies across products, and is in particular weaker for frequently purchased products. The form of the relationship also varies with the cultural background of the respondent. Thus for syrup, there is a positive relationship between the price and perceived quality among French, while the relationship is curvilinear among Americans.

When consumers obtain information about price more easily than about quality, or when their preferences for quality lead them to take the risk of buying expensive products without being sure, the company will tend to use price as a signal of quality.

Price as a perceived value indicator

The price and the perceived quality of a product contribute to the formation of the perceived value of a product to the consumer. A brand perceived as more innovative or as a world leader in its sector can justify a price higher than that of competitors because of the perceived higher value of its products. Such an above-average price level will be more easily accepted by the customer if it is supported with arguments. In the industrial sector, an analysis of the value really delivered by the product (lower rate of defects, faster repair, longer lifespan) will be used to support the arguments of the salesperson.

Pricing and product characteristics

Product characteristics influence price fixing. The position of the product on its life cycle curve, its cost and its methods of computation, as well as its membership in a product line play a very important role.

Pricing dependent on the stage in the life cycle

The life cycle curve of a product is essential for price setting. First of all, the various stages of this curve are accompanied by changes in demand elasticity, which have consequences for the determination of price. In addition, the introduction stage poses the problem of fixing the launch price, which is fundamental for the commercial and financial success of a new product.

Price–demand elasticity varies according to the stages of the product life cycle. Figure 14.3 reproduces this development for detergents and pharmaceutical products.

For the great majority of the 43 brands belonging to the categories of products studied, one observes the following relation: $e_{\text{introduction}} > e_{\text{growth}}, \geq e_{\text{maturity}} < e_{\text{decline}}$. That is, the price–demand elasticity decreases continually starting with the introduction of the product, reaches a minimum in the maturity stage and rises thereafter (Toolbox 14.3).

Such an evolution of price–demand elasticity would suggest fixing a low introductory price and increasing the price in the maturity phase. This approach to the determination of price is called penetration strategy.

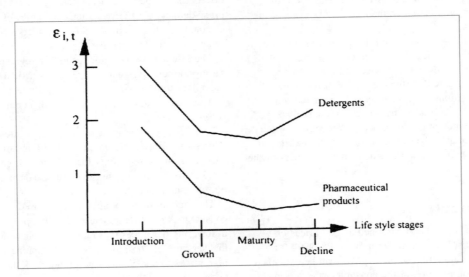

Figure 14.3 Average elasticity at different stages of product life cycle

TOOLBOX 14.3

ELASTICITY AND MARGINAL COST

In the mathematical model used, Simon shows that the optimal price for the company is a function of elasticity:

$$P = \frac{E}{(1 + E)} f(C_m)$$

E = price–demand elasticity ($E \leq -1$)
  C_m = marginal cost.
  Let us suppose a demand elasticity of -2 and a marginal cost of 30 per unit, the optimal price is 60. For an elasticity of -3, optimal price is 45. The greater the elasticity, the smaller is the optimal price.

  The ratio $E/(1 + E)$ corresponds to the marginal profit of the company. If elasticity evolves as Figure 14.4 shows it, it is rather low in the phases of introduction and growth, relatively high at maturity and decreases in the phase of decline.

Source: H. Simon (1979), "Dynamics of Price Elasticity and Brand Life Cycles: An Empirical Study", *Journal of Marketing Research*, 16, 4, 439–452.

A penetration strategy, during the launch of the new product, is used only in quite specific situations, however, which are indicated in Table 14.2. The various factors presented there explain the reasons which may push a company to quickly increase its share of the market by asking a low price. The company can also launch the product at a high price. This is called a skimming strategy. This approach is guided by factors also presented in Table 14.2.

A skimming price is close to the optimal price or profit-maximizing price. A penetration price is much lower than the optimal price.

Price setting for a new product is very important for its future. Indeed, the launch price projects a certain image (of quality in particular) in the mind of the consumer which is difficult subsequently to modify. Price setting is a delicate problem if the product to be launched is a real innovation, meaning that there is no direct comparison with existing products. Various methods can be used to determine the price in such a context.

A first group of methods uses customer surveys. Customers are asked what would be their purchasing behaviour at different price levels. These methods, like those of Gabor and Granger discussed earlier, are rather far removed from a real purchase situation since they are only centred on one of the components of the product: the price. In addition, they cannot be used for major innovations where the consumer lacks benchmarks and thus is unable to provide any reliable information.

A second set of methods measures the behaviour of consumers by simulating choice conditions. These methods comprise price tests and conjoint measurement. In price tests, consequences for market share or sales volume at varying levels of price are observed.

- Store tests
- web panels
- direct selling catalogues
- procedures such as Behaviour scan

may be used in price tests.

Table 14.2 Choice criteria of skimming versus penetration strategies

Criteria	Skimming strategy	Penetration strategy
Price–demand elasticity	Inelastic	Elastic
Share of variable unit costs in the price	High	Small
Experience curve effect	No	Yes
Ease with which competitors will enter the market	Difficult entry	Easy entry
Rate at which the consumer will adopt the product	Slow	Fast
Segment's sensitivity to price	Exists and can be taken one segment at a time	Only a mass market exists
Firm's resources to produce and market the product	Weak and restricted	Large

Conjoint measurement is very often used to fix the price of a new product. This method is used 36 per cent of the time to identify the most attractive attributes and attribute levels of new products, but 46 per cent of the time it is used for price setting.

Cost-based pricing

Costs are one of the basic components of pricing. A company that sold continuously at a loss, below cost, would go bankrupt. However, the determination of the cost of a product is not unambiguous for three reasons:

1. There are various ways of computing the cost of a product.
2. Costs are dynamic, they depend on the quantity produced.
3. Costs can be objectives to be achieved.

Price and method of calculating cost

Figure 14.4A shows the various components of variable cost and full cost.

If the company fixes its price according to variable cost (method of direct costing), it can decide to add a margin to the variable cost. This is intended to cover (part of) the fixed cost and to create a surplus. Management can allocate the fixed costs to other products and for this reason establish a price lower than the price which would have been fixed by the full cost method.

The breakdown of costs into variable and fixed costs leads to the concept of breakeven point, which corresponds to the point for which the sales cover the costs and the profit is zero. One can thus compute, for a given selling price, the number of units to be sold to reach the breakeven point.

If F = Fixed costs
V = Unit variable cost
P = Unit selling price,
the breakeven point is obtained for $F/(P - V)$

Comparing the breakeven sales volume to the market potential enables one to appreciate the profitability of the product, and how long it may take until the product becomes profitable. That is, breakeven analysis can be used to evaluate if a product is worth launching. However, the main weakness of this method is that once the breakeven point is reached, it does not provide any further information.

Associating the structure of the costs with price–demand elasticity allows one to establish the recommendations provided in Figure 14.4B.

The price of a product can also be established by the full cost method. This includes the variable costs of the product as well as a part of the fixed costs. One of the weaknesses of the pricing based on this method is allocating fixed costs to a given quantity of products sold, since it is difficult to know quantity sold in advance because the quantity sold depends on the selling price.

Price and cost dynamics

Costs are dynamic, which can affect pricing. Experience curves, for example, show that the total cost of a product decreases in time according to cumulative volume produced.[1] The simplest shape of this experience curve is the log-linear curve, which was already presented in the chapter on strategic differentiation.

The experience effect has various origins:

■ the improvement of the effectiveness of labour,
■ the standardization of products,
■ specialization in the task,

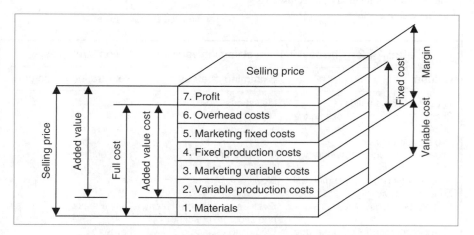

Figure 14.4A Typical structure of selling price

Demand \ Costs	High variable costs Low fixed costs	Low variable costs High fixed costs
Elastic demand Inelastic demand	Stabilize price (clothing) Increase the price (plumbing repair)	Lower the price (air line flights) Stabilize price (electricity)

Source: M. Chevalier (1977).

Figure 14.4B Price fixing as a function of cost characteristics

- innovations in processes of production,
- better use of production equipment, human resources or raw materials.

All those factors cause decreasing costs with increasing cumulative production. Experience curves do not apply to all types of product. They are important in the car industry, where the standardization, innovation process and specialization in the task are high. On the other hand, they are non-existent in luxury restaurants, where the dishes are not standardized, specialization is non-existent and the innovation process has no effect on cost.

The identification of experience curves proves rather complex because

- costs must be adjusted for inflation;
- certain components of total cost do not follow the same experience curve;
- various products share the same resources;
- the starting point for experience is sometimes difficult to identify;
- the unit of analysis must be clearly identified for the cost computation (in particular if one wants to make comparisons with competitors).

Using experience curves for pricing decisions requires a certain prudence since competitors do not necessarily have the same experience curve (a late entrant on a market can benefit from the knowledge obtained by other companies which preceded it on the market). In addition, too much reliance on these curves makes the company vulnerable to technical innovations or changes of preference in the market.

Target prices and costs

The method of fixing target costs originated in Japan. The purpose of target costs is to fix an optimal cost of a new product. This applied to the Canon photocopier at 1000 dollars. This total cost was then allocated to components

by considering them on a hierarchical basis – the functions which components fulfil for the consumer and the value allocated by the consumer to each one of them. The purpose of target costing is to integrate customer value into the product cost. It is used at the research and development and production stages and fits permanent manufacturing costs, design and value allocated by the consumer.

This method requires an exact evaluation of price and perceived value by the consumer. Packard Bell in the mid-1990s was very successful in producing less powerful but also less expensive personal computers than its competitors. After 1995 consumer preferences moved towards more powerful computers. Consumers were willing to pay a higher price. Packard Bell did not detect this change in preference until it was too late.

Pricing for a product line

Pricing for a product line is a common problem facing the marketing manager. It is also one of the most difficult to solve because of its strategic consequences for the company and of the complex relations which exist between demand and costs for a product line.

The final objective is to optimize the profit of the company for the whole product line. To set the price for a product line requires:

- choosing the product which will have the lowest price and setting its price;
- choosing the product which will have the highest price and setting its price;
- Setting the price differences which must exist between the products belonging to the line.

These choices are a function of the interdependence of the products constituting the line. Substitution and complementarily effects have to be taken into account. For example, for non-durable complementary products, and in the presence of a heterogeneous demand, such as for seasonal seats in theatre or sets of standard optional extras on cars, the company may find it beneficial to propose prices for sets of products. In this case, the price suggested is lower than the sum of the various prices of the components.

For substitutable products between which there are joint economies of scale and which are facing heterogeneous demand, the company will offer some products at high prices compared to cost (premium) resulting in a positive margin and others at rather low price – their margin will be negative. Such a practice is seen with car lines where the bottom-of-the-line is in general barely profitable but the top-of-the-line generates substantial profits. It also applies for price setting of hotel rooms and theatre seats.

When consumers are price sensitive because price determines perceived quality, and a product line has joint economies of scale, the company may use the same basic product with different names and prices. The product having the higher price is in general used to subsidize the product having the lower price or to provide margin. Such price setting is observed for the price of skis where the same basic product can be sold under different brand names and at different prices in hypermarkets and speciality shops.

When products are complementary and there are substantial differences in cost within the product line (e.g., a basic commodity and its accessories), price setting may consist of selling higher cost products at very low price (to encourage consumers to buy) and recovering the losses or the absence of margin on the other products in the line. Such a practice of captive prices can be observed for razors and blades, cameras and films, cars and spare parts. In the service sector, such a practice is carried out by means of a price with two components, a basic price and a variable usage price (price of the telephone with a basic fee and a unit phone call price). In retailing, companies practise price discounting, by lowering the price of very-well-known brands in order to attract customers who, in addition, will buy other products on which the margins of the retailer are better.

Setting the prices for a product line requires them initially to be at a level acceptable to the consumer. The price interval which separates products belonging to the same line must be sufficiently large to be detected by the consumer.[2] Pricing of a range must also take into account the existence of segments between the bottom and the top-of-the-line. Pricing can be conceptualized by means of a price rack. Figure 14.5 shows that it is inside each segment that the prices must be fixed.

For example, in France the market for toothpaste includes four segments: freshness (entry to the bottom-of-the-line), then gum, anti-tartar and finally on top-of-the-line, homeopathic. Vademecum, the least expensive brand of top-of-the-line toothpaste (homeopathic), enjoys a growth rate comparable with that of Colgate Palmolive, the least expensive toothpaste in the freshness segment. The lowest price brand of a segment

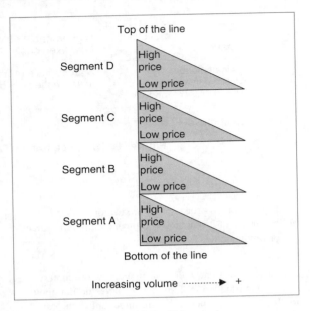

Figure 14.5 Price rack
Source: Ph. Le Corollen (1995), *Libre Service Actualités*, 1377, 16 December, pp. 90–92.

would thus be the only one in competition with the brands of the segment and not with the lowest prices of the line. Thus a drop in price of the least expensive brand of top-of-the-line affects the sales of the other brands of the top-of-the-line but also those of the segment immediately below: whereas a fall of price of the least expensive brand of the bottom-of-the-line affects only the sales of the bottom-of-the-line. This effect depends on the strength of the brands, the drop in price of a weak brand not affecting the sales of a strong brand.

Transfer pricing

A transfer price is the price fixed to transfer a good, a service or a technology between organizational units within a company. Various methods of pricing can be used which must take into account a certain number of factors.

The methods mainly employed consist in setting the transfer price between two thresholds:

1. A lower threshold which corresponds to the variable cost of production of the product (or to its direct cost) plus its transportation costs,
2. A higher threshold which is aligned with market prices.

Other intermediate methods exist such as to fix a price on the basis of full cost or on the basis of price which could be obtained from a supplier external to the company (arm's length pricing).

The lower limit allows the purchasing unit to benefit from a very low price compared to the market price and lets the selling unit absorb the fixed costs. That affects the way in which profits will be distributed between the organizational units and therefore their performance.

The objective of transfer pricing usually is to maximize the benefit obtained at the group level. So transfer pricing depends on a number of factors:

- Customs duties and taxes affect the transfer price of the products (in particular in the case of importing, the higher these custom duties and taxes the more they encourage low transfer prices);
- Profits taxes tend to make a company use transfer prices to accrue the profit in countries having the lowest taxes (tax havens);
- When organizational units are decentralized into profit centres the motivations of managers are affected by the transfer prices since the rewards (bonuses or promotions) can be based on profits. Inequitable transfer prices can generate conflict between organizational units;
- Government regulation can influence transfer pricing, for example by requiring a deposit of part of the value of the imported products for a given period (to obtain money without interest) or to impose a method of price setting;
- When a product is transferred to a joint venture and both partners share in the profits from the joint venture, it is better for the supplier to retain profit via high transfer prices than to share it with the partner.

Pricing on foreign markets

When determining prices on foreign markets, the major question is whether prices should or must be standardized – that is, if the same prices are to be applied in the various countries in which products are marketed. Because of the free flow of goods and services, this question is particularly important in the countries of the European Union.

Advantages of the price standardization

Price standardization maintains coherence and avoids parallel imports.

- **Maintains coherence**
  Standardization allows maintenance of a coherent marketing-mix necessary for a strategy of globalization. It avoids handicapping certain subsidiaries compared to others at the time of European bids to the central purchasing units of European retailing firms.

Standardization also offers the advantage of maintaining and protecting customer perception of the product on a global level when the price stands for characteristics of the product such as its quality.

- **Avoids parallel imports**
  Parallel imports (or grey markets or diverted trade) can be defined as sales of products by unauthorized channels of distribution. They are not the same as counterfeiting. If prices differ from one country to another, an authorized retailer or unauthorized middleman or retailer can buy a product in the country where it is the least expensive and resell it in the country where it is most expensive, at a lower price, competing with the manufacturer's products. For example, cameras may be bought in Japan or Hong Kong at official retailers or wholesalers. Then, they are exported to Europe or the US, where they are competing against cameras sold by official retailers.

Three conditions are necessary for the existence of parallel imports:

1. the availability of the product on various markets;
2. trade barriers (tariffs, transportation costs, legal constraints, . . .) sufficiently low so that the products can move from one market to another;
3. substantial differences in price between the various markets creating an incentive sufficient for parallel imports to take place. Those can be caused by

- monetary fluctuations (to buy in a country with a weak currency, to resell in a country with a strong currency),
- differences in demand between countries,
- segmentation strategies arising from planned price differentials which are based on different product life cycles on different markets,
- different purchasing behaviour,
- different price–demand elasticities.

Once, the European car market offered a price differential of 55 per cent for some models between the most expensive market (Austria) and the cheapest (Italy).

Parallel imports have harmful consequences for the company and the consumer:

- The development of parallel imports has an impact on retailers, who observe sales decline. They may then cease promoting the product and leave the channel.
- The products marketed by parallel import channels do not correspond to the products travelling through the approved channels of distribution for they do not benefit from the same pre- and post-purchase services. Consumers may think they have acquired the total product (service and guarantee included/understood).

- The absence of a manufacturer guarantee causes a loss of prestige for the product, if this service is refused to consumers who bought a parallel import product. If for this reason the manufacturer decides to grant the guarantee to these products, additional costs are created by this decision.

The International Spotlight presents a certain number of measures available to deal with parallel imports.

Advantages of price differentiation

Price differentiation is possible when

- price standardization leads the company to ignore important markets, supporting the entry of competitors. This may be the case if the company does not have a product portfolio enabling it to meet the needs of various countries or markets which are of interest; for example, the price of a new Renault model produced in Romania will be far below the French price level because this car is intended for sale in developing countries, a market that is difficult to penetrate because prices of the existing product line are too expensive in this market.
- price standardization corresponds to the characteristics of the markets concerned (variation in the standards of living, purchasing power, spending patterns, intensity of competition, etc.). For example, the Scandinavian

market (Denmark excluded) has prices higher than those of the other countries of the European Union in certain sectors like office supplies;
- obstacles prevent a standardized price from being set (regulation, indirect taxation, diversity of channel margins). For example, in countries where health expenditures are covered by the state, price is fixed by the state. Also different value-added taxes for the same product between countries may provide very different price levels if the company is unable to counter the effect by varying its margins.

Competition-oriented pricing[3]

Competition rests on the idea of interdependence. This means that the consequences of an action taken by a company do not depend only on its own action but also on competitor actions. For this reason, competition involves conflicts of interests leading to situations of equilibrium which are sometimes the result of

- governmental arbitration (as that occurred in France until now in air transportation)
- an agreement between the companies/countries (example: the cartel of the oil-producing countries, OPEC) or
- many implicit agreements when a company dominates the market.

INTERNATIONAL SPOTLIGHT

HOW TO DEAL WITH PARALLEL IMPORTS

A certain number of measures are available to deal with parallel imports. They are tricky to use and expensive.

- To build a communication campaign intended to alert the consumers of the potential problem caused by the parallel import products. This is expensive, but it can be most effective to preserve the reputation of the product and the network of the middlemen and authorized retailers.
- To use trademarks, packaging and different positioning in each country in which the product is sold. This solution proves very expensive, but it offers total protection. For example, in Sweden, Nescafé of Nestlé is sold claiming on its package "mildly roasted", in Italy the claim is strong taste, in France, the country of origin of the coffee is emphasized. Eating habits may also be used. In the Spanish market fat content is a competitive advantage especially for "cassoulet". Such a content is not an advantage on the French market. If the manufacturer has licensing agreements with foreign producers, this solution is impossible.

- Not providing a guarantee to consumers who do not buy the product from an authorized middleman or retailer. This solution can be expensive in terms of loss of image or reputation.
- To fix price at its lowest level or in a corridor of sufficiently narrow price so that parallel importing is not profitable any more. One practice consists of fixing, for all subsidiaries, a minimum floor price, which corresponds to the price below which no invoicing can be carried out. So this minimum price includes the potential promotions and rebates. To support the harmonization of the prices among subsidiaries, periodic controls must however be carried out.
- To repurchase the parallel imports discreetly when the company has identified the origin of the problem and is in the process of regulating it.
- To do nothing and give a guarantee for the products not acquired through the authorized channels, which makes it possible to reach new segments of customers (more price elastic) but may affect the whole authorized channel.

Competitive behaviour was first studied in economics, focusing on market structure. The essential concern was to seek the highest profitability for each market structure investigated. Market structures are specified in two dimensions: number of competitors and degree of product differentiation.

In this way, three principal situations can be identified:

1. pure and perfect competition, where many suppliers face many purchasers with undifferentiated products. None of the actors is able to influence the price level;
2. monopoly, which corresponds to a market in which one supplier faces many purchasers. The supplier plays a dominant role in price setting;
3. oligopoly, in which a few suppliers face each other in a market. The various competitors are then very dependent on each other in price setting, whether their products are undifferentiated or differentiated (the most frequent case). Differentiated products show important distinctive characteristics for buyers.

Monopoly

This competitive situation is characterized by the absolute domination exerted by the monopolistic company on the market. It corresponds to state monopolies (i.e., Railways in Spain, Italy, France) but also to new product launches.

The basis of monopoly is the existence of entry barriers for competitors to the market. Such entry barriers can be legal for state monopolies or grounded on competitive advantages like a technological innovation or the possession of a patent.

Demand and cost form the basis for price computation according to economists. They have shown that the price which maximizes the profits of the company corresponds to the intersection of the marginal cost curve (unit variable cost for the last produced unit) and the marginal revenue curve (revenue from the last produced unit). In the case of monopolistic competition, the optimal price is equal to:

$$P = (E/(1+E)) \text{ MC}$$

E = elasticity of the demand compared to the price (≤ -1)

MC = unit marginal cost

The higher the optimal price the lower in absolute value will be the elasticity, or the optimal price will be the highest when demand is not very sensitive to price.

In fact, a monopoly is free to set the price at the level which it chooses and which the market accepts. However, a company in such a situation may decide not to set too high a price for fear of government intervention or because it wishes to penetrate the market by means of a low price. Some state monopolies may set price below cost in order to make their product available to consumers who would not otherwise be able to afford it. This is the way public transport prices are generally fixed, the generated losses being covered by subsidies from various communities.

In monopolistic competition, products are differentiated by characteristics other than price (quality, company image, service, packaging, technology, physical characteristics, etc.). However, price can be used as an element of differentiation vis-à-vis competitors. But a company in monopolistic competition will initially try to exploit other factors than price. That makes it possible in particular to build brand loyalty.

Consumers who prefer a brand for other factors will be less tempted by the price of competing products.

Oligopoly

In this type of market (such as the steel, computer or car markets), the few competitors know each other and react to the actions of the others. It is thus very tricky to make price decisions because of problems raised by the evaluation of the reactions and the strategies of the other firms.

Economists first of all explained the use of price by competitors in an oligopoly by means of a kinked demand curve. Such a curve conveyed the idea that, in an oligopolistic market, prices are rather stable because a price war is regarded as undesirable because of the losses involved. In an oligopoly, any price decrease by one of the protagonists will cause an equivalent reaction by the competitors who, to avoid losing sales, will also lower their price. The quantity sold by lowering the price is then hardly higher than what it was before, because demand will be price inelastic. On the other hand, it is not the same if one company raises price unilaterally. If competitors do not imitate the price increase, the company will lose customers to the benefit of those competitors. Demand will be price elastic. The demand curve thus presents a point of inflexion at the price level currently fixed on the market (Figure 14.6).

Of course, such a situation is based upon two assumptions that appear somewhat unrealistic:

1. A low price elasticity
   A price decrease, if price elasticity is high, boosts demand and then total volume sold. Therefore a price decrease may induce an increase of the quantity sold by each competitor in the market.
2. Similar offers
   Offers from oligopolists are not exactly the same in real markets. Therefore, price variations may reflect different perceived values and therefore may not generate variation in the quantity sold.

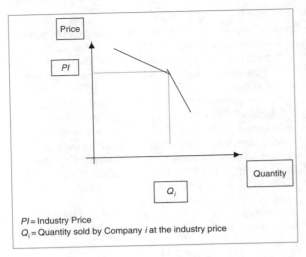

PI = Industry Price
Q_i = Quantity sold by Company i at the industry price

Figure 14.6 Kinked demand curve

PI = Industry Price
Q_i = Quantity sold by Company i at the industry price

In an oligolistic market, each competitor has part of the solution to intelligent price fixing. This is especially the case for the market leader. A constructive attitude to price is very often created by the market leader. Its role is to avoid pressure towards a price decrease and to proceed to regular price increases through price signals sent in advance. Price increase signals can also be split among competitors such as in the gasoline sector. As price increases are not popular, it might be in the interests of all competitors involved to alternatively play the role of the initiator of a price increase.

The potential for a price war should be examined with great care. Rapid price reduction may have a damaging effect. However, price wars are motivated by various factors such as

- high price elasticity
- different manufacturing costs among competitors
- very ambitious objectives
- very aggressive managerial personality

Table 14.3 illustrates various scenarios facing the company based upon cost scenarios of its products and price scenarios of the main competitor. It shows that price is mostly used by companies for an increase in price of the main competitor and an increase in costs for the company. Facing a decrease in price of the main competitor and an increase in costs for the company, companies tend to use sales promotion.

Pure and perfect competition

In this situation, never observed in practice, the buyer has perfect knowledge of the market and wants to obtain the lowest price possible. Because the customer has perfect information concerning prices of suppliers and because offers are perfectly similar, an individual supplier has no control over its price. The supplier can only accept the market price. So the demand curve for a company's offer corresponds to the curve presented in Figure 14.7.

The company cannot increase its prices because in this case, it will not be able to sell anything. It does not find it beneficial to lower its prices since it can sell all its production on the market at the given market price. Fruit and vegetable markets in producing countries (e.g., cantaloupe, peach in Spain or France) are close to a pure and perfect competition because the offer is very similar, consumers can easily check prices and there are many producers.

A company located on such a market can only exploit the quantity produced to improve its short-term performance. In the long run, to be able to change its prices, it will have to seek to differentiate its products, for example by a brand policy which may lead to pricing according to strategic groups.

Table 14.3 Percentage of respondents indicating a marketing-mix variable change as a function of different price scenarios

	Scenarios			
Price of competitor → Cost for the company →	Increase Increase	Increase Decrease	Decrease Increase	Decrease Decrease
Price	88	65	51	53
Advertising	31	51	41	41
Sales promotion	29	43	45	39
Sales force	28	32	33	24
Distribution channel	17	17	22	15

Source: V.R. Rao and J.H. Steckel (1995), "A Cross Cultural Analysis of the Price Responses to Environmental Changes", *Marketing Letters*, 6, 1, 5–14.

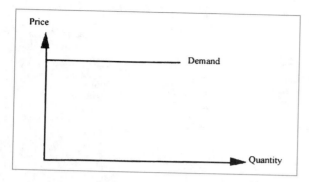

Figure 14.7 Demand curve for a company in a state of pure and perfect competition

Pricing in the industrial sector

In the industrial sector, pricing has two particular characteristics. It may be negotiated, or it maybe the outcome of competitive bids.

Price negotiation

List prices are often different from those which are really paid because variations are negotiated. Besides the effective price paid after reductions and rebates agreed by the seller, discounts because of the volume of order, and the method of payment are also negotiated. Price negotiation is necessary in numerous situations:

■ Negotiation about purchasing a unique product such as commercial property or a telecommunications satellite allows the seller to fix a price based on buyer's need and their willingness to pay.

■ In some markets, with standardized and frequently purchased products as in consumer product markets, large retailers negotiate better deals from brand manufacturers in exchange for the volume of purchases.

■ Market maturity leads to reduced product differentiation and more cost- and value-conscious customers willing to negotiate price on an individual basis.

■ Although price negotiation may occur in consumer market, such as interests for loans, price of cars, real estate as well as in the service sector (law firm, maintenance, retailing), it is in the industrial sector that price negotiation occurs the most.

In the industrial sector, effective negotiation strategies require the understanding of the balance of power between the members of the buying centre (see Chapter 7 on customer behaviour), which consists of all individuals playing a role in the purchasing. Understanding these roles is important because it allows salespeople to concentrate their efforts on decision makers. The process of negotiation has been presented in the chapter on value negotiation and personal selling process (Chapter 11).

Competitive bid

Competitive bid is an alternative to price negotiation. In a competitive bid, the buyer provides the specifications and asks suppliers for their prices. In some cases such as sales to governments or international organizations, orders will go to the lowest bidder, disregarding the value offered. In other situations, suppliers may be able to enter into discussions with buyers.

A commonly used procedure moves away from the open competitive bid and the lowest price. It consists of sending a bid to a list of suppliers selected by the company beforehand. The bids received are then analysed according to criteria like price, quality and time of delivery. The best offers are selected for further negotiations with the purchaser. The choice is then made by considering all aspects of the bid, of which price is only one criterion, related to the long-term relationship between purchaser and supplier, including cost of operation and maintenance, availability of spare parts and after-sale service. This procedure has the advantage of obtaining competitive price and of generating creative technical proposals (Figure 14.8). It results in an attractive bid which may or may not be characterized by the lowest price.

Participation in a tender requires a bid strategy. Although only one criterion, price has growing importance in the final phases of the bid. Other factors such as the relationship between bidders and purchasers have a very important role in the initial phases of the bid, allowing the possibility of engagement and collection of information during the process. Tenders are used most often to purchase equipment or on very large projects where the results can have a very important impact on the financial health of a company.

Other purchasing procedures can also be used as an alternative such as catalogue purchasing, mutual agreement, negotiated deals and the Internet.

Competitive bids make use of quantitative analysis to help managers in their examination of the implications of the data collected. Such analyses require an estimation of the probability of success according to the past behaviour of competitors and the expected profit contribution. Such estimates can be difficult to make. For example, if a company has a large excess capacity, the contribution of a bid may be quite large since many costs are already sunk. On the other hand, if winning a bid requires new capacity, incremental costs may be high and the contribution low.

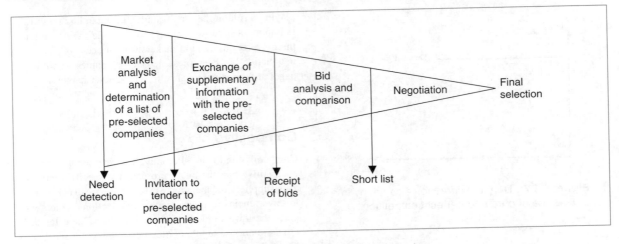

Figure 14.8 Competitive bidding procedure

Various methods may be utilized. They vary according to whether they take account of a particular competitor, last bids gained by the competitors, and of the bids gained and lost by them. To illustrate, the simplest approach will be presented using knowledge of past successes of competitors. It is based on two assumptions:

1. The existence of a constant relationship between variable costs of competitors and of the company;
2. the action of competitors will be similar to that used in the past.

The simplest approach requires the estimate of the probability of success according to the various possible bids as well as the computation of the expected profit. Table 14.4 presents the various calculations for this method.

Expected profit is the largest (optimal bid) for a price which corresponds to 120 per cent of the variable costs. At this price, the company maximizes its margin and its chances of success. However, if the company has excess capacity and wishes above all to maximize its chances of success while obtaining a positive margin, it will choose to make an offer corresponding to 110 per cent of the variable costs.

Price management

List price is rarely the price paid by the customer. Segmented pricing means that different prices are paid by different customers for the same product. Customers who are relatively price insensitive, costly to serve and poorly served by competitors can be charged more than those who are price sensitive, less costly to serve or well served by competitors. Segmented pricing uses this principle to increase sales and profitability. Different pricing tactics are developed based upon geographical pricing, discount, sales promotion and discriminatory pricing. Companies have to manage the resulting price structure because it provides many opportunities to antagonize customers,

Table 14.4 Computation of expected profits

Bid as a % of variable cost (Pr)	Success probability $P(Pr)$	Margin on variable cost $Pr - C$	Expected profit $P(Pr)*(Pr-C)$
90	1.00	−10	−10.00
100	0.95	0	0.00
110	0.65	10	6.50
120	0.50	20	10.00
130	0.20	30	6.00
140	0.10	40	4.00
150	0.05	50	2.50
160	0	60	0.00

retailers and sometimes may be in contradiction with legal constraints.

Geographical pricing decisions

Geographical location of customers has consequences for the cost structure especially because of transportation expenditures. Transportation cost is particularly important when the company is making deliveries in different countries. Price may or may not include transportation costs. Some of the main price alternatives available are as follows:

- Free on board (f.o.b.) is a price where the customer bears all costs and risks such as insurance from the time goods are placed on board a ship.
- Ex-Factory is a price where the customer is presumed to have bought the goods right at the manufacturer's factory. Therefore all costs and risks are borne by the customer.
- Cost, Insurance, Freight (c.i.f.) is a price where the manufacturer is liable for payment of freight and insurance up to the destination port.

Depending upon the attractiveness of the customer, transportation costs may be absorbed by the manufacturer.

Discounts

Companies modify their price to take into account situations such as cash payment, quantity purchase and out-of-season purchase.

Cash discount is a price rebate for the payment within a specified time delay. Cash discount aims to

- encourage prompt payment
- reduce credit risks
- reduce the cost of collecting overdue accounts

Quantity discounts are supposed to reflect reduced transportation and production costs arising from the quantity purchased. This is most common in selling to industrial customers.

Out-of-season discount is a price reduction due to a purchase of out-of-fashion goods.

Companies offer trade discount to wholesalers and retailers. Discounted prices are supposed to represent a payment for performing certain marketing functions such as storage facilities, performing personal selling services or extending credit for the manufacturer.

Sales promotions

Sales promotions include special deals, two-for-one offer, sampling, coupons and so on (see Chapter 15 on sales promotion). For a limited period of time, they are intended to

- generate new interest in an old product,
- stimulate new products trials,
- meet specific competitive situations in different geographical locations,
- enhance advertising campaign.

Discriminatory pricing

Discriminatory pricing means that the same product may be offered at different prices. Price differentials occur between customers, products, retailers and by time of purchase.

- Customers
  Some customers are more price sensitive than others and can be easily identified. For example, the price of a movie is different for students and retired people because they are more price sensitive because of their low income.
- Products
  A manufacturer sells the same product with slight modifications and charges very different prices with no differences in production costs. This practice relies upon different customer price sensitivities. In the airline industry, businesspeople are less price sensitive than vacation travellers. They value flexible scheduling. Therefore airlines charge more for regular tickets and offer discounts to customers who purchase their tickets well before departure.
- Retailers
  Retailers use the intensity-of-competition criterion to segment the location of their stores. They apply lower prices in those places where the competition is more intense.
- By time of purchase
  this is useful when the cost of serving a buyer varies with the time of purchase. For example, electricity may be sold more cheaply at night than during the day, phone calls may be sold more cheaply during the weekend or at night than during the week-day or the day. A more sophisticated version called yield management is used in the airline, cruise ship and lodging industry. It integrates not only differences in costs but also price sensitivity. It helps sellers to determine how much of their capacity they can afford to sell at a reduced price without threatening their ability to serve full price customers.

Legal and lawful constraints on pricing

A company is not always free to define its prices. Governments intervene in various ways in the price mechanism. Two major reasons lead them to regulate the prices by legal constraints.

1. The first is to control price trends, in particular during periods of strong inflationary push.
2. The second relates to the reinforcement of free competition and the regulating role of the market.

Techniques for price trend control

Although the principle of the free economy is to let the firms fix prices freely, governments are entitled to limit this when excessive price rises occur due to a strong inflationary push and when the regulation is applied for national as well as imported products (EEC court of Justice, 1979). Within the European Union, safety clauses allow governments to suspend or reduce the free movement of goods under the agreement of the European Commission (article 226 of the EEC Treaty of 1957)

The techniques of government price control depend on the speed of the price trends. In periods of high inflation, governments use rigid intervention techniques such as price freezing, price fixing, a price frame or margins fixing. In situations of relative stability, governments use more flexible techniques such as contractual policy, semi-freedom or the release on probation as regards to price.

Rigid techniques of intervention

■ Price freezes
A price freeze consists in maintaining the prices at the level reached on a given date. It was used several times, in particular for tobacco prices, in France in 2004, and in the US in August and November 1971. Previously it has been used in France very regularly for 18 years (1945–1963).
■ Price fixing
Price fixing consists in fixing a maximum price for a product or service. This limiting price is established unilaterally, without reference to the price charged at the date of application of this measurement. Prices of oil products were fixed, for example, in France in August 1990 during the invasion of Kuwait by Iraq.
■ Price frame
A price frame allows a firm to increase its selling price based upon the various increases in cost of raw materials. The administration determines, in a price formula, the elements to be taken into account and the weights to be attached to them. For example, loan interest for real estates might be a weighted function

of the wages of the building sector, steel price and cement. This technique of intervention has also been used in particular for the building industry and for the pharmaceutical industry.
■ Margin fixing
This intervention was carried out in France among distributors (wholesalers, retailers) and importers in 1982. The government either fixes the percentage of margin based on the purchase price (multiplier coefficient) or fixes the margin in relative value which is computed by dividing the absolute margin by the selling price. This intervention can be carried out product by product or in a global way. When the multiplier coefficient is used, it is easy to multiply the coefficient by the purchase price net of tax to obtain the selling price.

Example of margin calculation:

Purchase price net of tax of product $(PP) = 800 \,€$
Selling price net of tax of the product $(SP) = 1000 \,€$
Absolute margin $(AM) = SP - PP = 200 \,€$
Margin in relative value $= AM/SP = 0.2$
Multiplier $(M) = AM/PP = 0.25$
Multiplier coefficient $= 1 + M = 1.25$

Such regulation had been used in Belgium for beef and pork in 1975.

Flexible techniques of intervention

■ Contractual policy as regards to price
This type of intervention took place in France in 1966. It results from a dialogue between public authorities and representatives of each profession. Conventions, contracts, programs, fighting engagements against inflation, and so on may be the output of this dialogue. They give to companies some freedom in their price fixing, provided they do not deviate from the objectives of the government regarding price moves.
■ Semi-freedom of prices
This mode of regulation has been used in France in 1948. It allows manufacturers and retailers to freely fix their price provided that they communicate them in advance to public administration. It leaves the administration with the possibility to be opposed to the implementation of the price within 15 days starting from the intimation. Such an approach applies in particular to the pharmaceutical industry.
■ Release on probation
In this approach, companies have latitude to fix their prices, the administration not being able to be opposed to it. They must simply inform the administration of the modifications of prices which can be implemented only from the day when the administration receives the information.

Price regulation intended to support free competition

Governments or supranational institutions such as the EU have in recent times been less preoccupied with regulating prices. They are more interested in preventing companies from making formal and informal agreements to restrict competition.

Regulation intended to prevent pricing agreements or abuses of dominant position

Regulation prevents pricing agreements that restrict competition and situations in which competition on prices is limited, such as discriminatory prices, imposed minimum prices and selling at a loss.

The law prohibits cartels and abuse of dominant position. The aim is to ensure free competition (article 86 of the EC treaty of 1957). It prohibits practices such as

- building obstacles with the aim of lowering resale price or final selling price
- supporting increases or the artificial price cuts

The EC treaty provides that public authorities can regulate the prices of certain sectors (electricity, gas, transportation, motorways, books or agricultural products within the European Union) in which competition by price cannot be implemented because of monopoly, difficulties of supply or legal regulations.

The practice of discriminatory pricing restricts competition. Articles 85 and 86 of the EC treaty of 1957 prohibit differences in selling price and conditions of sale (means of payment, for example) among customers if they introduce unequal conditions to competitors (e.g, discriminatory prices between purchasers). However, discriminatory prices are justified by a corresponding decrease in the costs of the supplier due, for example, to bulk order. Refusal to sell is an illicit pricing practice involving extreme discrimination.

The EU prohibits the practice of imposed minimum prices. There is, however, an exception for the price of books in France, Germany and Austria. If the practice of imposing minimum price is illicit, the similar practice of advised prices is quite legal. This is where the producer, wholesaler or importer recommends a price to a retailer (not imposed). However, it can be prohibited when it hides an agreement or an abuse of dominant position (e.g., by hiding a concerted price increase).

Resale at a loss (resale of a product at a price lower than its purchase price) is also prohibited. This practice aims to distort competition by eliminating certain competitors. Its prohibition is meant to protect small shopkeepers from big retailers. However, exceptions exist when a company wants to align itself on competition and for

- obsolete or out-of-fashion products
- products that can be reordered at a lower price
- seasonal products
- non durable products
- clearing sales.

The regulation by the World Trade Organization and the legislation of the European Community (article 113 of the Treaty of Rome 1957) proscribe actions of dumping. Those include selling abroad at a lower price than on the domestic market and thus relate to a practice of abnormally low price. Dumped products can be countered by antidumping taxes if the three following conditions are met:

1. the dumping is manifest
2. the industry of a country of the European Community is threatened
3. there is a direct causality between the dumping and the ensuing damage

Regulation intended to protect the consumers and their freedom of choice

Legislators intervene to protect the consumer in certain cases.

- Sale premiums
  Those relate to sales which give right to premiums. European legislation is not homogeneous among countries. In France, to be permissible, premiums in products, goods or services should not be identical to products which are sold. Premiums are allowed in cash. Moreover, premiums are illicit only if they are offered to consumers. Premiums granted to retailers are permissible.
- Refusal to sell
  Refusal to sell is established when a producer or distributor refuses to satisfy the demand of a purchaser, even though the product is available, the demand conforms to regular commercial practices (the demand is not abnormal) and the sale is not regulated by law (pharmaceutical drugs). Refusal to sell is prohibited except for a legitimate reason (bad faith of the buyer, unavailability of the product, abnormal demand).
- Linking a sale to the purchase of an imposed quantity or the purchase of another product (batch selling) is prohibited. So is subordinating a provision of services to the purchase of a product (conditional sale). However, when products are presented in a single pack, batch selling is allowed.

SUMMARY

Price setting is influenced by five factors: objectives of the company, demand, competition, product characteristics and legal constraints. Pricing objectives can be clustered in three categories based on objectives related to the

■ sales volume
■ profitability
■ the product line.

They are overall goals that describe the role of price in an organization's strategy. Maximization of the sales volume or the market penetration by increasing market shares results in the fixing of a relatively low price. Its aim is to

■ ensure the optimal use of the production capacity
■ ensure full resource employment
■ obtain economies of scale
■ improve the position on the experience curve
■ occupy a leadership position in a growing market.

Profit objectives are normally set at a satisfactory level rather than at a level designed for profit maximization. Price is also set to optimize revenues on the product line. Substitution and complementarity effects have to be taken into account in price setting for a product line.

To set prices, a company must take into account the sensitivity of the demand to price. A key variable in price setting is price elasticity of demand. This is in general inversely proportional to price, except for certain luxury goods. A certain number of phenomena observed among consumers have an influence on demand elasticity. They are in particular

■ the existence of an acceptable price range
■ the existence of a reference price
■ the attraction of certain prices for consumers
■ the unequal sensitivity of consumers to price
■ the use of price as an indicator of quality and value.

The position of the product on its life cycle curve, costs and cost calculations and, the coherence of the product line have a very important role. The various stages of the life cycle curve are accompanied by changes in demand elasticity which have consequences for the price strategies followed. Two types of pioneer pricing policies are

1. price skimming and
2. penetration pricing.

Price skimming corresponds to the highest possible price that buyers will pay. Penetration price is the lowest price designed to penetrate the market.

The determination of the cost of a product is ambiguous for three reasons:

1. There are various ways of computing the cost of a product
2. Costs are dynamic, they depend on the quantity produced
3. Costs can be objectives to be reached.

Transfer pricing between subsidiaries and the existence of grey markets are specific components of price setting abroad.

Three principal competitive situations can be identified:

1. pure and perfect competition
   where many suppliers face many purchasers for undifferentiated products. None of the actors is able to influence the price level.
2. monopoly
   which corresponds to a market in which a single supplier faces many purchasers. The supplier then plays a dominating role in price fixing.
3. oligopoly
   in which a few suppliers face each other in a market. The various competitors are then very dependent on each other to fix their prices, whether their products are undifferentiated or differentiated (the most frequent case). Differentiated products show important distinctive characteristics for the purchasers.

Prices in the industrial sector are negotiated. Competitive bidding is characteristic of industrial products.

Two major reasons lead governments to regulate the prices by law. The first is to control price trends, in particular during periods of strong inflation. The second relates to the reinforcement of free competition and government regulation of the market.

Discussion questions

1. Under what conditions would a car manufacturer adopt a skimming price approach for a new product? and a penetration approach?

2. What would be your response to the following statement "Profit maximization is the only legitimate pricing objective for the firm"?

3. What are the economic stakes in transfer pricing?
4. When should prestige pricing be used?
5. What is parallel importing?
6. A marketing manager reduced the price of a brand of cereal by 10 per cent and observed a 20 per cent increase in quantity sold. The manager then thought that if the price were reduced by another 20 percent a 40 per cent increase in quantity sold would occur. What would be your response to the marketing manager's reasoning?

7. The total cost of the 20th unit produced is 900 €. The total cost of the 100th unit produced is 800 €. What is the experience curve of the product? What would be the total cost of the 200th unit produced?
8. Variable cost of a new perfume is 2.70 € per bottle of 500 ml. Advertising expenses for the year are 5,400,000 €. Selling price of a perfume bottle is 45 €. How many bottles should be sold to reach the breaking point?

Notes and references

1. Total cost of the xth unit $TC_x = KX^{1-b}$, where $TC =$ full cost, $X =$ number of manufactured units, $K =$ estimated cost of the first unit, $b =$ slope of the curve and function of experience rate $0 < b < 1$
2. If n products of the line are ordered as a function of increasing price level, the price of the jth product of the line P_j is equal to $= P_{min} \cdot k^{j-1}$, where $P_{min} =$ minimum price, $k = (P_{min}/P_{max})^{1/(n-1)}$, $P_{max} =$ maximum price.
3. Other structures such as monopsony, oligopsony or stakeholder-oriented pricing will not be discussed. For example, in stakeholder pricing, selling a new product depends on the cooperation of stakeholders because of the absence of competitors and the strong innovativeness of the product. Price setting is complex if the cost of the product is much lower than the perceived value to the consumer. A new medical treatment needs the cooperation of doctors, hospitals and insurance. Will these stakeholders agree with a high margin for the company according to the high-perceived consumer value of the treatment?

Further reading

D.F. Abell and J. Hammond (1986), *Strategic Market Planning*, Pearson Higher Education.

D. Adam (1958), *Les Réactions du consommateur devant le Prix*, Paris, Sedes.

A. Biswas, E.J. Wilson and J.W. Licata (1993), "Reference Pricing Studies in Marketing: A Synthesis of Research Results", *Journal of Business Research*, 27, 3, 239–256.

R.C. Blattberg and K.J. Wisniewski (1989), "Price Induced Patterns of Competition", *Marketing Science*, 8, 4, 291–309.

M. Chevalier (1977), *Fixation des Prix et Stratégie Marketing*, Paris, Dalloz.

B. Cova (1990), "Appels d'Offres: du Mieux Disant au Mieux Coopérant", *Revue Française de Gestion*, March–April–May, 61–63.

R.J. Doan and H. Simon (1996), *Power Pricing*, London, Free Press.

R.J. Dolan (1995), "How do you Know When the Price is Right", *Harvard Business Review*, 73, 5, 174–183.

D.F. Duhan and M.J. Sheffet (1988), "Grey Market and the Legal Status of Parallel Importation", *Journal of Marketing*, 52, 3, 75–83.

A. Gabor and C. Granger (1966), "Pricing as an Indicator of Quality: A Report of an Inquiry", *Economica*, February, 43–70.

A. Gabor and C. Granger (1944), "Price Sensitivity of the Consumer", *Journal of Advertising Research*, 4, 40–44.

A. Gabor and C. Granger (1965), "The Pricing of New Products", *Scientific Business*, August, 41–150.

E. Gerstner (1985), "Do Higher Prices Signal Higher Quality", *Journal of Marketing Research*, 22, 2, 202–215.

E. Gijsbrecht (1993), "Prices and Pricing Research In Consumer Marketing: Some Recent Developments", *International Journal of Research in Marketing*, 10, 2, 115–151.

P.E. Green and V. Srinivasan (1990), "Conjoint Analysis in Marketing: New Development with Implications for Research and Practice", *Journal of Marketing*, 54, 3, 3–19.

B. Janiszewski and D.R. Lichtenstein (1999), A Range Theory Account of Price Perception, *Journal of Consumer Research*, 25, 4, 353–368.

C. G. Kayanaram and R. Winter (1995), "Empirical Generalizations from Reference price Research", *Marketing Science*, 14, 3, part 2 of 2, G161–G169.

D.D.R. Lichtenstein, P.H. Bloch and W.C. Black (1988), "Correlates of Price Acceptability", *Journal of Consumer Research*, 15, 2, 243–252.

F. Mobley and W.O. Bearden (1988), "An Investigation of Individual Responses to Tensile Price Claims", *Journal of Consumer Research*, 15, 2, 273–279.

Y. Mondem and M. Sakurai (1994), *Comptabilité et Contrôle de Gestion dans les Grandes Entreprises Japonaises*, Paris, InterEditions.

K.B. Monroe (2002), *Pricing: Making Profitable Decisions*, 3d edition, New York, McGraw-Hill.

R.A. Peterson and A. Jolibert (1976), "A Cross National Investigation of Price and Brand as Determinants of Perceived Product Quality", *Journal of Applied Psychology*, 61, 4, 533–536.

T.N. Nagle and R.K. Holden (2002), *The Strategy and Tactics of Pricing*, Prentice Hall, Englewood Cliffs, New Jersey.

A.R. Rao and K.B. Monroe (1989), "The Effect of Brand Name, and Store Name on Buyer's Perception of Product Quality: An Integrative Review", *Journal of Marketing Research*, 21, 3, 351–357.

V.R. Rao and J.H. Steckel (1995), "A Cross Cultural Analysis of the Price Responses to Environmental Changes", *Marketing Letters*, 6, 1, 5–14.

R. Sethuraman (1996), "A model of How Discounting High Priced Brands Affect the Scales of Low Priced Brands", *Journal of Marketing Research*, 23, 4, 399–409.

R.W. Schoemaker (1986), "Comment on Dynamics of Price Elasticity and Brand Life Cycles: An Empirical Study", *Journal of Marketing Research*, 23, 1, 78–82.

H. Simon (1993), "Le Prix Optimal: un Concept Majeur", *Décisions Marketing*, 0, May, 35–45

H. Simon, F.L. Jacquet and F. Brault (2000), *La Stratégie Prix*, Paris, Dunod.

G.E. Smith and T. Nagle (1995), "Frames of Reference and Buyers Perception of Price and Value", *California Management Review*, 38, 1, 98–116

J.B. Steenkamp (1989), *Product Quality*, Assen/Maastricht, Van Gorcum.

G.J. Tellis (1986), "Beyond the Many Faces of Price: An Integration of Pricing Strategies", *Journal of Marketing*, 50, 4, 146–160.

A. Woodside and N. Vyas (1987), *Industrial Purchasing Strategies*, New York, Lexington Books.

R.E. Weigand (1991), "Parallel Import Channels – Options for Preserving Territorial Integrity", *Columbia Journal of World Business*, 26, 1, 53–60.

D. Wittink, M. Vriens and W. Burhenne (1994), "Commercial Use of Conjoint Analysis in Europe: Results and Critical Reflexion", *International Journal of Research in Marketing*, 11, 1, 41–52.

V.A. Zeithmal (1988), "Consumer Perception of Price Quality and Value: A Means End Model and Synthesis of Evidence", *Journal of Marketing*, 52, 2, 202–215.

Sales promotion

Learning objectives

After studying this chapter you will be able to

1 Situate sales promotion within the commercial strategy of the company
2 Distinguish its role and objectives with respect to advertising
3 Learn the various objectives of promotional action
4 Analyze the main vectors of promotion
5 Measure the efficiency of promotional actions

SPOTLIGHT

'Win a Donkey' was an instant win on-pack promotion linked to the cinema release of Shrek 2 and one of the lead characters, the donkey. The prize was to win a real donkey – well, actually a sponsorship of a donkey in an animal sanctuary, and a visit for all the family to see it. There were, additionally, 10,000 runner-up instant win prizes of an inflatable donkey toy.

The promotion delivered £7m incremental in sales and an increase of 60 per cent in new consumers.

PMC (Promotional Marketing Council) AWARD 2005 – United Kingdom
Campaign: Win a Donkey
Agency: Billington Cartmell Company: GlaxoSmithKline

Source: European Association of Communications Agencies (EACA).

Introduction

Amounts allocated to sales promotion and all "below the line" advertising (Table 15.1) as a share of communications resources have been steadily and appreciably increasing over the last few years. Today, this share represents nearly two-thirds of communication expenditures in most developed European countries.

The importance of sales promotion in commercial company strategy has risen considerably. This phenomenon, emphasized by numerous authors, can be explained in various ways: increasing competition, market congestion, consumer saturation when confronted with an excessive amount of advertising, trivialization of brands and products and a preference for short-term results, the requirements of new forms of distribution, and so on. This development in the promotional mix is potentially dangerous from the perspective of both general economics and the long-term results of the company. Excessive use of promotion has provoked a strong consumer and legislator reaction, and even professionals have found themselves confronted with certain negative effects – a marked drop in profit margins coupled with extreme competition. This reaction has not detracted from the increasing place of sales promotion in company commercial policy, but has served rather to ensure that it is used appropriately. However, it is difficult to establish a framework for promotional practices.

- For consumers, the attraction of some of these practices as well as their generally positive and gratifying characteristics provokes ambiguous sentiments. Consumers can be favourably disposed towards tempting promises and instant advantages, but not so happy about the temptation to spend excessively because of these promises or advantages, which may also lead to disappointment because of their short-lived or artificial aspect.
- For the legislator, it is a question of simultaneously encouraging competition and yet not interfering with commercial competition and its favourable effects on inflation and on company dynamics, whilst avoiding unfair, misleading and fallacious practices, which might damage competition and consumer confidence.

However, it is not always easy to draw the line between healthy promotional practices and negative ones.

- For the manager, promotion is a permanent temptation, since its short-term effects can be positive. The product manager, being aware of their end-of-year objectives, within the framework of budgetary control, tends to resort to promotional methods to the detriment of advertising which may have a long-term effect. However, by artificially and temporarily shifting demand towards a promotional advantage added on to the product or service, promotion can distort the development of a solid brand image. That is why companies may refuse to use certain promotional techniques (Lacoste, Hermes, Gucci etc.) which might be in conflict with their image policy.

Whichever viewpoint is taken, commercial promotion may be, as Aesop said, the best and the worst of things. This paradoxical idea is not tied in with the promotional techniques themselves: for the same operation, a similar technique (games, price reductions) may give very varied results, depending on the conditions of use. Thus, before even describing the techniques of promotional action, it is important to define the role and objectives of commercial promotion.

Very often, we assign objectives to promotion which cannot be fulfilled, or whose effects are only partially measured (with regard to the consumer and the market), or which are too restricted (the time perspective is too brief). The purpose of promotion should therefore be made clear and is dealt with in the first section of this chapter. Once the objectives and promotional policy have been defined, the marketer can choose from a large variety of techniques. The method of using these techniques in very different contexts is clarified in the second section. Finally, the third and last section deals with the various problems connected with measuring promotional efficiency.

Role and definition of promotion

Promotion is one of the most practical domains of marketing action. The term "promotion" itself encompasses numerous practices, often heterogeneous, whose field is badly defined.

Table 15.1   Definition: "above and below the line" communication expenditures

Companies communication expenditures
"Above the line" advertising
Print, cinema, TV, outdoor advertising, radio

"Below the line" advertising
Sales promotion, direct advertising, POS advertising, trade fairs, conventions, directories, Internet advertising

Comparatively little research has been done into sales promotion, in comparison to the research into advertising. The apparently simple and often blunt mechanisms of promotion, coupled with its immediate effects, may not place it on the same level as advertising which, to the theorist, may be more subtle and less immediate in its effects. This lack of sophistication is gradually being rectified and promotion today is becoming professionalized: several researchers and practitioners are now trying to analyze its mechanisms and establish its role. One of the primary consequences of this research has been to refine the definition of promotion.

The characteristics of promotion

Sales promotion is a method of marketing action used by companies or organizations, comprising the offering and communicating of a more or less clear-cut, immediate or delayed advantage to a specific target group with the aim of obtaining

- an immediate and direct modification of final demand (bring forward, increase, regulate),
- and/or an immediate modification of the behaviour of influencers, consumers (trial case), distributors or sellers, which is then passed on to final demand.

In this definition we can find several essential features of promotion:

- immediate and concrete character,
- offering a specific advantage and supplementary value to the buyers concerned,
- ephemeral character,
- exceptional and unusual character,
- connection to a product, service or sales outlet,
- origin (production, distributor) and varied targets (consumers, distributors, influencers),
- the definition of precise and measurable objectives.

Sales promotion has several aspects: a modification of the offer of products or services (in quantity, kind or quality), and\or the price of this offer plus the transmission of this modification to the target group.

Promotion and advertising

Promotion and advertising are similar in the sense that they are two vectors for transmitting the offer. Both aim to operate on the psychological motivation of individuals to promote the company's offer. So it is justifiable to include both advertising and promotion in company communications.

But, as the above definition suggests, the roles of advertising and promotion are different. Although it may be wrong to make too sharp a distinction, we may say that advertising generally tries to seduce the consumer, to lure him towards the product through modifying his attitude (pull strategy). Its objectives are long-term: it may attempt, for example, to build or consolidate a brand's profit margin. Communications with a wide audience (television, press, cinema) are preferred.

Conversely, promotion tends to favour short-term objectives and attempts to act directly on behaviour (push strategy), to use specific direct media and to modify the offer itself. These "tendencies" should however be qualified because we can find exceptions such as promotional campaigns that have very wide targets and use mass media. We should also mention the role of publi-promotion comprising media communication (posters, press, radio and so on) through promotion operations.

Promotion targets

Sales promotion includes numerous techniques which affect each agent in the commercial chain: vendors for the producer or distributor, distributors themselves (wholesalers, retailers) and consumers. It is important therefore to coordinate the set of actions undertaken by the company within the framework of the promotional campaign (special offers for vendors, distributors merchandisers and consumers). In effect, promotion can cause poor coordination in the retailing chain if a target reacts (e.g., the end client) without the others having been informed or involved. It can result in excess stock or a shortage which provokes a negative chain reaction for the company (loss of image, financial losses, vendor apathy etc.).

The role of agencies

The consequence of the increasingly important role played by promotion in the company marketing-mix, along with the variety and complexity of promotional techniques, has been the development of agencies specializing in sales promotion. These agencies play a role comparable to that of advertising agencies. They build promotional campaigns for their customers, using their expertise in the choice and implementation of techniques most suited to the objectives, and allow the target customers to access new techniques: electronic coupons, the combination of promotional and direct marketing techniques, the use of electronic media and so on.

Objectives and role of promotion

Objectives

The objectives assigned to promotional action are multiple and vary according to their target groups (Table 15.2).

The above list has the merit of describing the variety of targets and promotional effects. However, beyond their visible variety, we can find elements included in the above definition which allow us to understand the coherence of promotional techniques. Promotion aims to modify the stream of demand:

■ directly, when promotional action affects consumers or distributors and modifies their behaviour concerning demand for products or for the relevant service;
■ indirectly, when promotional action tends to change the behaviour of an agent within the distribution network, provoking behavioural modifications in buying, stock-holding or selling; this is the case, for example, when promotion is addressed to sellers in order to encourage the distributor to buy, stock or sell the promoted item so that he in turn will urge the consumer to buy that item.[1]

Table 15.2 Principal objectives of promotional activity

Objectives of promotional activity may concern

Sellers:
■ stimulate the sales force,
■ bring forward the taking of orders,
■ facilitate canvassing,
■ transform those canvassed into customers,
■ increase the number of orders,
■ contend with operations carried out by competition.

Distributors:
■ have the product referenced,
■ have orders placed with increasing rapidity,
■ widen the ordered references,
■ give an advantage to products (e.g. placement, surface area),
■ participate in the manufacturer's marketing action (promotional, advertising),
■ store or cut down on stocks,
■ introduce a new product,
■ secure the loyalty of the distributor.

Influencers:
■ make the product known,
■ provoke a favourable attitude regarding the product,
■ encourage the influencer to act.

The most common objective with promotional activity, whether direct or indirect, is to bring forward and increase short-term demand. Promotion can be used in various other ways, however, such as to increase consumer loyalty.

The role of promotion in the marketing-mix

Some promotional objectives can be also assigned to other types of marketing operations: for example, "to create an event" can be the objective of a public relations operation, "to highlight a particular point concerning brand image" can be the objective of an advertising operation. Consequently, in some cases, the real role of promotion is not easy to isolate. There are numerous interactions concerning communications policy, merchandising and direct marketing operations.

■ Concerning communications policy, promotion may be used to support advertising or a public relations operation or sponsorship. It may in this way become an integral part of the communications policy: a sample distributed to the consumer is, for example, a promotional form of communication for the product. It is, as we have indicated above, a means of communication in itself, as is all information received by the consumer concerning the product. Finally, promotional activity is often "heralded" through advertising: this is known as publi-promotion.
■ Concerning merchandising, certain promotions of the "pushing to the forefront" type for the product (e.g., end of aisle) become integrated into the merchandising policy.
■ Concerning direct marketing, promotion is frequently present in this type of operation in order to put forward a supplementary stimulus: rapid response incentive, buying more and so on.

Without being dogmatic about the definition of promotion, it is clear that the role of promotion cannot always be easily isolated within the marketing-mix. This is so because promotion can be combined with price, distribution, merchandising, communication, direct marketing, sales force, product and packaging policies. However, this affects one of the essential roles of promotion. It can become temporarily grafted on to defined policies. The flexibility with which promotional techniques can be used allows for the readjustment and improvement of these policies. We can easily find these aspects in the list of promotional objectives: obtaining of a classification, bringing forward orders, emphasizing an image factor, encouraging sales people and so on. We can, therefore, from this point on, distinguish two approaches to the use of promotion within the company.

- First, the company defines a promotional strategy by clearly fixing its objectives and the means allocated to this promotion, by defining promotional operations for a given period, the coordination between them and so on.
- Second, promotion plays a supplementary role and is used as the situation requires, often in reaction to a problem: low demand, competitor action, sales problems and communications failure. In this case, promotion has the advantage of having immediate results and is generally effective with regard to the assigned objective. However, this practice can be dangerous: it runs the risk of addicting consumers to promotional effects, and can lead to the abuse of promotional activity.

Techniques and the promotional activity plan

For several decades now we have observed an almost continuous growth in the use of promotion, and a large variety of promotional techniques are available (Toolbox 15.1).

Throughout Europe, legislators have repeatedly intervened to limit abuse. However, the imagination of professionals in the field of promotion seems to be particularly fertile and new techniques bypassing legal taboos have been put in place. The most common techniques are presented in this section along with the conditions for their use within a promotional plan.

TOOLBOX 15.1

PROMOTIONAL TECHNIQUES

1. Bonus sales

   - Direct bonus: offer of a free supplementary article added to the purchased goods.
   - Recipe bonus: bonus offer of recipe cards to all purchasers of a product.
   - Deferred bonus: offer of a supplementary advantage (bonus) subsequent to the purchase.
   - Sample bonus: offer of a sample product as a bonus.
   - Packaging bonus: transforming the packaging to make it reusable for the purchaser.
   - More-product bonus: offer of a greater quantity of the product at the same price.
   - Purchase privilege premium: offer of an article at a particularly advantageous price and promoted by a particular brand without this brand having to suffer even the slightest financial repercussions.

2. Game techniques

   - Contest: the promise of substantial winnings as a result of a competition calling for observation, shrewdness and creativity on the part of the participants.
   - Games, lotteries and sweepstakes: various forms of games of the "draw" type with a promise of winnings based on chance.
   - Tombola per store: carrying out of a draw by a producer at a given point of sale, giving a customer the right to win something without obligation to buy.

3. Price reduction

   - Money off coupons: coupon giving the right to a determined reduction on the normal price of a product.
   - Special offer: special price offered to the public over a period of time.
   - 3 for 2: offering three products for the price of two, four for the price of three and so on.
   - Grouped sales: a group of products sold at the same time.
   - Refund offer: deferred reduction on the price of a given article upon presentation of a proof of purchase.
   - Product trade-in: buying back by the manufacturer of an old product of the same brand.

4. Trial and sampling

   - Sample: reduced size product distributed freely to increase the popularity of a new product.
   - Free gift: distribution of a gift to encourage the public to perform a determined action (e.g. to subscribe to a newspaper or to visit a supermarket).
   - Free trial: offer of a trial concerning a new product without any obligation to buy.
   - Demonstration: live presentation of the qualities of a product with, if needs be, a tasting or a practical demonstration.

The techniques of promotion

Promotion can be divided into four major categories:

1. price techniques (special offers, discount coupons, repayment offers, price discount or coupons),
2. games techniques, competitions and lotteries,
3. premiums (auto paying, immediate, deferred) such as gifts and extra products,
4. trial techniques (samples, free trials).

One can add to these categories the techniques of charitable promotion (promotion associated with aid for charitable work) which have recently appeared and are growing rapidly.

Each category has evolved differently over several years. We are witnessing a general trend towards techniques based on a certain and immediate advantage compared to those offering an uncertain and delayed advantage. This preference for "certain and immediate" is accompanied by a shift towards promotions offering a financial advantage (discount, price reduction) compared with the other types of promotion.

We can also add many other techniques to those mentioned above – promoting products at the point of sale, special offers of credit and so on. Each technique can have several different versions and achieve distinct objectives in relation to consumers, distributors or sellers (Toolbox 15.2).

TOOLBOX 15.2

OBJECTIVES AND METHODS OF PROMOTIONAL TECHNIQUES

Methods		Objectives
Bonuses	Free bonus (more of the product)	To encourage buying To encourage product exposure through distribution
	Free bonuses (another product) Reuseable packaging Deferred bonus or purchase of an article at a reduced price	To encourage product trial To widen the buyer's base To increase quantities purchased To increase buying frequency
Reduced prices	Immediate reduction Refund offer Sales by batch	To increase sales To encourage trials To increase quantities purchased To encourage over-stocking
	■ multipack (same product) ■ twinned (different products)	
Coupons (reduction vouchers for the purchase of a product)	On-pack coupon In-pack coupon With-pack coupon	To encourage trials To accelerate distribution of a new product To accelerate stock rotation
Samples	Door-to-door mail drop Distribution at sales location Giving another product as a bonus in or on a packet	To encourage or bring forward the trial of a new product
Tastings Demonstrations Demonstrations	Tastings (food produce) Demonstration of operation (instant camera)	To encourage trials, to accelerate purchase To obtain immediate purchase To obtain referencing

Games and Competitions	Lotteries, tombolas Contests (concerning the public and the distribution of the sales force)	To encourage immediate sales To have the product talked about, to reinforce another communications action To stimulate the sales force and distribution

Concerning consumers, there are numerous possibilities for differentiating premiums, games, lotteries, competitions, price reductions and so on. For example, price reductions can be presented in several different ways:

- 20 per cent on the whole range,
- 20 per cent on the article of your choice,
- 20 per cent on the third article on your order form,
- 20 per cent after purchase of articles worth 100 euros or more,
- a discount coupon worth 20 per cent off list prices.

Each method of price reduction can have different effects: 20 per cent on the article of your choice can be adapted to a first order, 20 per cent on the third article is a definite appeal to loyal customers and so on. Numerous authors have tried to match each technique with the most common objectives assigned to it.

The distribution objectives of promotional techniques are considerable and numerous. They comprise two categories:

1. either to obtain a referencing by means of various actions concerning:

  - prices: launch discounts, launch couponing;
  - sales forces: competitions, premiums on new distributors;
  - action at the point of sale: animation, free setting up;

2. or the obtaining and extension of the availability of the brand due to: promotions concerning price, such as discounts on quantities or the issue of cents-off coupons according to quantities sold and stock differences.

To achieve the objectives given to the sales force, a large variety of promotional techniques can be used: bonuses, individual or group competitions, financial advantages, awards and so on. These techniques are used in multiple forms corresponding to specific objectives: competition for the best salesman with one, two or several winners, bonuses linked to global sales targets, to

products, to type of customer and so on. This relation between objectives and promotional techniques is not however systematic. Three comments are needed.

- While we can try to establish systematic relationships between each technique and each objective, we cannot assume that there is an absolutely fixed connection. Each operation is effected in a different context and requires reflection on the technique or the combination of techniques to be used. Furthermore, certain techniques can meet multiple objectives.
- Each promotional technique requires absolute professionalism. The practical conditions of its set-up are as important as the choice of the technique itself. Four characteristics allow us to classify promotion:

  1. the nature of the promotion: to give more or to ask less,
  2. the degree of certainty: certain or uncertain advantage,
  3. the delay necessary to obtain it: immediate or deferred advantage,
  4. the beneficiary of the offer: the participant in the promotion or a third person.

We may add a fifth characteristic, the effort to be agreed on by the person to whom the promotion is targeted: for example, writing, phoning, comings and goings and so on. This effort is a very sensitive variable in direct marketing promotional operations.

These five elements provide a useful framework for choosing the adapted technique by reflecting in particular on the likely behaviour of the addressee (consumer, salesman, distributor, influencer etc.).

Finally, each technique or combination of promotional techniques cannot be dissociated from the global operation to which it applies.

This coherence is situated at three levels:

1. the promotional operation itself: the different conditions of application, its set-up mechanisms, its context and its schedule;

2. the connection between the promotional operation and the other elements of the marketing operation into which it is inserted;
3. the plan of promotional action where it exists; this plan principally defines the logic of use of promotional techniques for the period considered compared with the different targets set by the company: the onset, rhythm and the importance and nature of promotional actions.

Promotion vectors

Promotion vectors comprise the product itself, the point of sale and the media.

■ The product can serve as a promotion vector through its packaging and through elements added to the product (e.g. gift tags on a bottle or elements in immediate proximity to the product such as distribution boxes for participation in games, or again, another similar product having an identical target (crossed coupon)).
■ The point-of-sale can also be one of the vectors of promotion through end of aisle, advertising material and equipment, shop windows (booksellers), supermarket trolleys, packaging bags, in-store radio, demonstration teams, catalogues about the point-of-sale, electronic communication and information terminals (intended to inform the in-shop customer in the aisle).
■ Personal media such as free media, phone cards and Internet can be of use in helping promotion.
■ Mass media, the cinema, posters, radio, press and television can also announce a promotion, stimulate the public to encourage them to take it up or participate in it and publish the results.

Promotional operations: Conditions of follow-up and definition

Some authors have tried to establish the conditions for the success of a promotional operation. Eight conditions have been suggested for the success of such an operation. A promotional operation must:

1. put heavy emphasis on serious marketing research, so that each of the actions illustrates a particular point to be emphasized;
2. affect the targeted public, who has been carefully selected;
3. be included in a campaign extending over a meaningful duration (who would expect advertising results from just one insertion?);

4. give priority to effective actions meaning clever, original or amusing actions;
5. cost must remain reasonable;
6. care must be taken in the detail and rigour of the organization;
7. the effects of promotional activity must be controlled by properly conducted studies;
8. the promotional operation must attain the goals set out at the beginning.

Other authors have added further conditions in the case of promotion to distributors.

■ Promotion must adjust to the chosen positioning and avoid simply doing the same as competitors.
■ The promotional plan must also be a coherent succession of ideas demonstrating the preferred positioning.
■ Uniformity in promotional operations, identical from one store to the next, should give pride of place to offers attributable to each shop. This implies using its own language, colours and style.

Promotional operations are not limited to one particular technique (Figure 15.1). They are effective insofar as they fit into a wider context.

The plan comprises three factors for the success of a promotional operation cited above.

1. First, as we have already seen, it is important to determine the role of promotion with regard to the other elements in the marketing-mix.[2] Promotion is more or less effective depending on sectors, marketing objectives and targets. This justifies notable differences in use depending on the activities undertaken and the product sectors (bakery, dairy, confectionery etc.), and the product life cycle (attack, support, defence promotion etc.).
2. Promotional operations are rarely isolated. They are part of the strategy of the suppliers and the distributors. That is why we cannot consider the results of promotional actions independently from results of communication strategy itself. This imperative implies that we can find coherent elements in promotion with consistent strategic principles. For example, this means that promotion must respect the graphic and visual character of the product, must not be in conflict with its positioning and be consistent with advertising strategies or distribution. It also requires that promotional effects be considered not only in the short term, but also within the framework of the marketing plan.
3. Promotional operations do not have to come down to the short-term use of a technique. Each promotional operation includes a clear definition of objectives

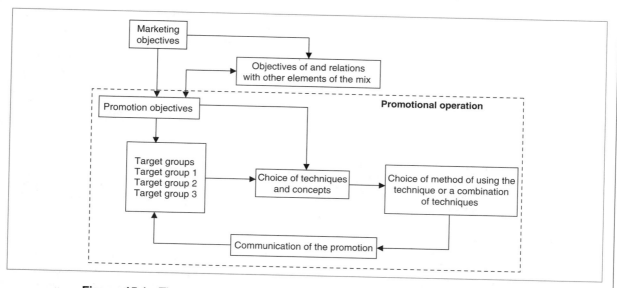

Figure 15.1   The place of a promotional operation in the value generation process

assigned to promotion, a precise definition of targets and, depending on the objectives and targets chosen, the choice of:

- the selected technique(s),
- the promotional concept itself (conception, creative support),
- the use of the technique or combinations of techniques,
- communicating the promotion to the target.

The first two elements (objective, target) are common to any marketing action. The other decisions which define the "promotional mechanism" are peculiar to promotion and involve three aspects.

1. The definition of a promotional concept means that promotional techniques need not be used restrictively. It adds a positive image of the company, which may be autonomous or linked to the advertising concept. For example, a 10 per cent discount can be transformed to "10 per cent, thank you" (for customers who have already purchased) and so on. A gift could be an anonymous gadget bought in Taiwan or, on the other hand, proof or a strong illustration of the message which the company wishes to communicate. That is why promotion, still too often used in an isolated manner, tends increasingly to integrate certain creative concepts which are leading to its development and also making it a vector of communication.

2. The method of promotion used depends on the consumer reaction we are trying to provoke. It is based on knowledge of the purchase process and encourages the use of each promotional technique in a specific way by combining it sometimes with other promotional techniques or by being part of the marketing-mix. For example, as we have shown above, a price-cutting technique (discount of 20 per cent) can be expressed in numerous different fashions (conditions of acquisition, conditions of application, length of time involved etc.). This variety in the application of each promotional technique (gift, premium and so on) allows us to obtain very different effects from the same technique. Besides, by combining the techniques, those responsible for promotion can establish plans for promotional action which can occur at different levels of the purchase process, multiplying the overall effectiveness of the promotion.

3. Finally, the communication of promotional operations can be analyzed from several angles.

It can involve publi-promotion, the objective of which is to make known the existence of the considered operation or the elements of communication contained in the promotion itself. These two aspects merge when the function of publi-promotion is not just to announce the presence of a particular promotion (e.g., "shop X offers 10 per cent in the household range", but participates in the transmission of the creative concept defined above) or when the communication vehicle is also the vehicle for the promotion (the case of a promotional announcement in direct marketing). They can also be independent when promotion is not the object of an advertising communication but, in a sense, passes on its message by itself (case of door-to-door distribution of samples, a price reduction, or animation at the point-of-sale without external advertising).

As in advertising, promotional media planning comprises four principles: coverage, repetition, efficiency and appropriateness:

1. Coverage takes into account the percentage of people targeted by the promotional operation.
2. Repetition takes into account the average number of messages to which the target group is exposed.
3. Efficiency involves estimating the cost of useful contacts (directed towards the target), as in the case of advertising.
4. Appropriateness looks at the level at which promotional communication vehicles reach the people targeted (ratio of the number of contacts within the target group to the total number of contacts).

To these "classic" criteria, which are analogous to measures used in advertising, we can add four criteria specific to promotion:

1. the depth and flexibility of the communication vehicle;
2. the coherence of image between the offer and the communication method;
3. temporal proximity, which concerns the speed of consumer response to the promotion: for example, the difference in effect between a discount coupon cut from a newspaper and the same discount coupon offered in the shelf space;
4. coverage increase: the capacity of the promotional communication to cover the target rapidly.

The promotional action plan

Proliferating promotional activity is not risk free. Companies are tempted to use promotional techniques piecemeal in order to achieve a particular objective at a given moment. Eventually, this practice will create contradictions and incoherence in the marketing activity, as well as other negative effects mentioned above. This is why it seems necessary to rationalize and to plan promotional activity. This planning may have several forms. For many companies, it is included in the classic schema of the marketing plan and, for each product or each market, is detailed as follows:

- promotional objectives,
- the target or targets,
- the type of promotion (size of the incentive, conditions for participation, distribution and consumption back-ups),
- the budget.

This first and classic conception allows one to anticipate, by product or by market, promotional pressure and to avoid excessive use. In order for the economic planning to be not too rigid, those in charge of the marketing process generally provide for a complementary promotional budget allowing them to intervene during the course of the year to accentuate certain operations and to respond to competition.

Concerning points of sale for large businesses (hypermarkets, supermarkets, shopping centres), promotional schedules are established based on regular events in the annual calendar, such as Mother's Day or back-to-school to which are added other more artificial events such as the tenth anniversary of the supermarket, store celebrations, flower festivals and so on.

Store managers register their promotional operations in this calendar, generally by putting pressure on the manufacturers so that they will participate (Table 15.3). This results in the planning of a large set of promotional operations, some affecting the whole shop, others a particular section. This planning does not exclude the presence of other forms of unplanned promotion (end of aisle, discounts, demonstrations etc.). Nevertheless, it

---

Table 15.3 Principal promotion techniques for producers and distributors

Producer promotion aimed at the consumer*	Distributor promotion aimed at the consumer
■ Lots, supplementary quantity offered ■ Samples, gifts, bonuses ■ Games, contests, lotteries ■ Coupons valid for the next purchase ■ Special prices, reduced prices, instant reduction marked on packaging, refund with proof of purchase	■ Coupons valid for the next purchase ■ Non-permanent prominent display of the product, such as end of aisle, central alley, check-out, or entrance ■ Features of promotional communication, such as brochures, shelf taker placed above the shelf-space, or promotional displays

* See also Toolbox 15.1.
Source: adapted from G. Hermet and A. Jolibert (1995), *La part de marché: concept, déterminants et utilisation*. Economica, Paris

allows for a certain amount of preparation and organization of the promotional activity.

A more elaborate form of promotional planning exists in companies that practice direct marketing, mainly in distance selling companies. These companies plan their promotional operations interactively: over a specified period, generally a full season, they prepare a certain number of promotional operations (discounts, competitions, games, gifts etc.) each of which has specific effects.

Each customer will or will not be subjected to a particular operation depending on their own reactions (responses, purchases etc.). For example, a "very good customer" will receive a free catalogue with a buying incentive (discount). If they buy something, a gift parcel will be sent, and about three weeks later, another benefit will be offered. If they do not buy, an offer of participation in a game may be sent about a month later and so on. So, customers find themselves subject to a personalized promotional process specific to their own reactions (Figure 15.2). The use of interactive planning supposes, naturally, an individualized knowledge of the customers specific to direct marketing.

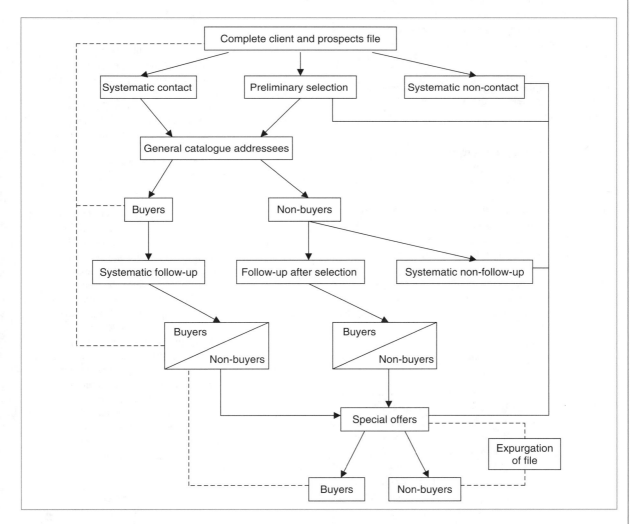

Figure 15.2 Generalization of the selection principle

Control and measure of promotional effects

The effects of promotions are generally easier to control and measure than advertising effects. The object of the paragraphs which follow is to present the principal methods used in this field and to underline their strengths and limitations.

The monitoring process for promotional effects

Sales analysis can be practised more or less explicitly (at individual locations, in distance selling companies).

When it is rigorously organized, quantities sold can be identified along with turnover, profit margins by target group, by product, by point of sale, according to the implemented techniques and the period. It can be accompanied by an estimate of the profitability of each operation, the relationship between the cost of the promotion and the surplus it generates. However, such measures are not easy to apply in each case and they have their limitations:

- Many companies do not have accounting systems that are accurate enough to supply all this data, or they consider it too expensive to collect the data.
- It is sometimes difficult to isolate the promotional effect from other effects in a marketing operation, such as the role of the sales force, other promotions offered in the same sector or advertising;
- The duration of promotional effects can be more or less easy to estimate. In the case of promotion with buying influencers, evaluation cannot focus on sales analysis alone;
- Sales analysis neglects other promotional effects such as long-term communication effects.

Distribution and consumer panels are becoming more and more reliable instruments for the control of promotional effects. The timing of the classic panels was poorly adapted to such measures, which need rapid and accurate information. With the development of optical scanning, panels are able to collect information which is frequent, rapid and accurate. In the United States, the Nielsen panel offers a service called National Scantrack, based on a sample extrapolated from the universe of supermarkets and having a turnover of more than 4 million dollars. Business customers use it principally to find out the effects of their promotions. Other services are

offered by the major panel specialists and ensure an evaluation of the effects of promotions concerning sellers, distributors or customers.

In France, IRI-SECODIP's "Infoscan" system reports on 365 shops (hypermarkets and supermarkets). It allows for promotional controls to be measured in various ways:

- the additional market share due to the promotion or to each type of promotion[3] (Figure. 15.3);
- the analysis of promotional effects according to product categories, products and brands;
- the analysis of promotional effects by consumer type, location or habit;
- the effects of promotions on new products.

Some limitations must however be acknowledged:

- The cost of the panel can, naturally, be high.
- These results concern for the greater part products generally taken into account by panel companies (mass consumption etc.).
- Some methodological problems remain: interference between promotional and other effects, interference of promotions among themselves, duration of effect and so on.
- Effects on communication are rarely taken into account.

Today, panel companies offer permanent experimental zones which, thanks to scanning techniques, enable good quality information to be obtained about promotional results. Information, in the form of scanned bar-code statements, comes from panel specialists, consumers and\or distributors. In Europe, companies such as Nielsen, GFK, and so on use this type of information obtained from "scanned" shops and\or from homes belonging to the so-called "open" zones, where the consumer is not necessarily loyal to the shops sponsoring the panel. To bridge this gap, the panel companies have also created databases from "closed" zones. In this case, it is possible to estimate the total amount spent on products by consumers from the panel, whatever their loyalty may be to a given shop. This leads to the concept of "unique database" (single source) which allows for the monitoring of the totality of a company's marketing-mix actions, in particular promotional and publi-promotional effects within the studied zone (Table 15.4).

The specific research channel allows us, in theory, to compensate for some of the previous weaknesses, but, apart from some academic research, it has to be said that they are not widespread because of the cost and time involved.

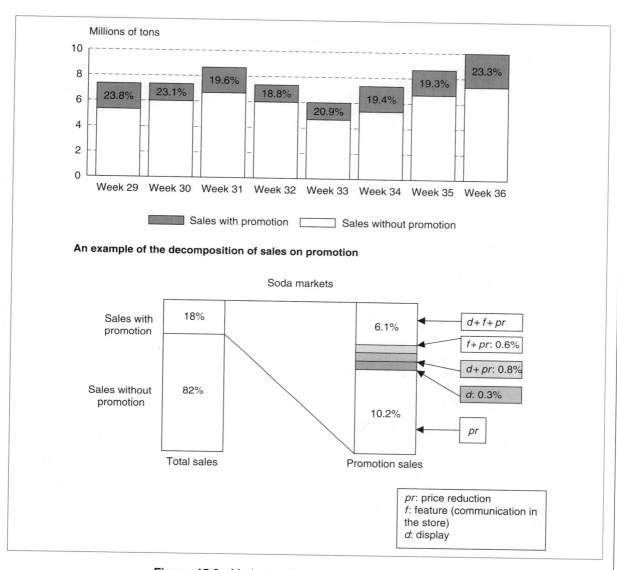

Figure 15.3 Market section with and without promotion
Source: (IRI-SECODIP Panel Infoscan)

An example of the decomposition of sales on promotion

pr: price reduction
f: feature (communication in the store)
d: display

Table 15.4	Single source data		
Sales follow-up	During given periods	Monitoring	Taking into account the characteristics
■ References	■ Hour	■ Price	■ Shop
■ Products	■ Day	■ Shelf space	■ Home
■ Brands	■ Week	■ Promotion	■ Individual
■ Categories	■ Month	■ Advertising	
	■ Year		

Source: G. Hermet "GFK document", March 1995.

In comparison, experimental studies are more common, notably in the form of tests combined with experimental plans. It is a question of testing the effects of different promotional techniques or the same technique developed using different formulations. The existence of "white zones" allows for observation of differences of effectiveness with reference to these zones and between the different methods used. One of the advantages of these studies is the possibility of obtaining results before conducting large-scale promotional operations. Other than the classic methodological problems of experimental plans, they have considerable limitations. Three limitations in particular have slowed down the use of tests:

1. Cost: it is sometimes necessary to establish as many different creative treatments as there are tests.
2. Monitoring: it requires a major presence at the point of sale.
3. Delays to the operation while the competition reacts and often observes the effects of tests.

These limits are however reduced by the possibility of conducting these experiments in association with the panel companies within the framework of the closed zones.[4]

The measure of promotional effects

Numerous studies have been carried out concerning promotional effects and more specifically concerning:

- the differential impact of different techniques depending on the objectives of the promotion;
- the effects of promotion on the timing of purchases, sales volume and the loyalty of the buyers;
- the role of promotions in point-of-sale performance;
- the impact of promotions on other products in the range and on the point of sale;
- the effects of promotions on competitors;
- the effects of promotions through time, according to the product life cycle;
- the effects of promotions according to buyer types;
- the consequences of promotions on the profitability of a particular sector.

Research on the effects of promotions can be classified into three categories:[5]

1. models for measuring aggregated data, for example scanned data at the checkout;
2. models for measuring individual data, which combine information relative to individuals and to shops;
3. models for aiding decision-making, which, as their name suggests, direct the manager towards solutions through, for example, simulation, so integrating the profitability of promotions.

Several studies have allowed for the development of measurement methods integrating different treatments of promotional stimuli, different events, modification of competitor actions, and the combination of several promotional actions and measures of effects in the short and medium terms. Analysis of research carried out on sales promotion shows that, in spite of recent progress due to the availability of more accurate and reliable data (panels), important questions remain unanswered. Blattberg et al.[6] suggest a series of 15 questions which require responses or response complements and which give several leads for future research.

1. Why do promotions create substantial sales variation for the consumer?
2. Why is sales elasticity with regard to promotions stronger than price elasticity?
3. What are the temporal effects and inventory effects?
4. How effective are forecasts of sales promotion response?
5. What are the effects of promotions at shop level and at the level of the product category?
6. What are the effects on complementary and substitute products?
7. How much of the promotions directed at distributors are passed on to customers?
8. How much sales promotion activity is wasted?
9. Do promotions have any long-term positive effect on consumer behaviour?
10. How much extra sales volume results from a retailer promotion?
11. Do promotions have an effect on the price-image of the retailer and in what way?
12. Do promotions attract extra sales for a brand beyond that of initial purchase?
13. How do consumers establish a reference price for durable goods when the product is not often purchased?
14. How does the use of a promotion designed to gain a customer influence the net current value of this customer?
15. Does promotion increase the distribution rate of a new product?

There is variation between countries. Consumer habits and differences in culture have an influence on promotional practices. It is a matter of significance in the European single market. (Table 15.5).

Table 15.5 Summary table of the principal characteristics of European legislation

	F	UK	D	I	E	B	NL	L	A	P	CH	IRE	GR	DK	SF	N	S
Gifts	▪										▪						
Grouped sales			T						T					T	T	T	T
In-packet bonuses	T		T						T					T	T	T	T
Multi-product offers			T						T					T	T	T	T
More of the product			T						T		T					T	T
Free product																	
Re-useable packaging											▪						
Bonuses linked to purchase		▪	T			T	T		T		▪			T	T	T	T
Mixed offers		▪	▪			▪	T	▪	▪		▪			T	T	T	T
Collectors	T						T	▪	▪		▪			T	T	T	
Autopaying bonus							T	▪			▪			▪			
Free lottery	T		T		T	T	T	▪	▪	T	▪	T	T				T
Contests	T		T	T	T	T	T	T	T		▪	T	T	T	T		T
Coupons			▪	T					T		▪			▪	T		▪
Reduction voucher on the next purchase			T	T							▪				T	T	T
Refund offer				▪					▪						T	T	
Animation/Demonstration																	

Authorised | T – Tolerated | ▪ Forbidden

Source: AACC Promotion

SUMMARY

Sales promotion is both a modification of the offer and a communication technique. It may play a multiple role and respond to several objectives concerning the sales force, distributors and consumers. If it is used to excess, it can have effects opposite to those desired. Companies, however, often resort to this type of marketing activity to stimulate sales teams, encourage distributors to sell their products, and consumers to buy them. In particular, promotion allows for the differentiation of the offer compared to competitors and the achievement of increased sales, winning new customers and creating customer loyalty.

Because of their variety, promotional methods can be applied to several different situations and be combined with other marketing-mix actions. This is why setting up promotional activity requires careful organization. If the promotion is launched too early or too late, and coherence between actions concerning advertising, price, distribution or merchandising is not guaranteed, not only will its effects be lessened, it will also reduce the effectiveness of the entire commercial operation. Whether or not it is considered in the general marketing plan, any promotional operation should therefore be the object of a rigorous plan of promotional action.

In the same way, the effectiveness of promotional actions should be measured for each action. The measurement of promotional effectiveness has been studied many times. Going beyond short-term and limited-period promotions has proved problematic. Nevertheless, it is important that, in spite of these difficulties, practitioners know the effectiveness of each type of promotional operation in order to reap the greatest possible benefits from this method of marketing action and to avoid problems caused by incorrect use of promotions.

Discussion questions

1. Build a sales promotion campaign for a new product in a business sector of your choice (e.g., electric shaver, toothpaste, computer, cell phone).
2. Gather one week's worth of promotional offers you receive in your mailbox. File them. Compare them. Do they have the same aims? To whom are they addressed? What methods are used for prospecting, and for developing customer loyalty?
3. Choose a department in a store (e.g., detergent, perfume). Visit three similar stores (supermarkets, for instance) operating under different names. Note down the sales promotions. Compare them. What are their aims (to encourage you to try a new product, to buy more of a product, etc.)?
4. Consult the website of a number of major service companies (hotels, airlines, etc.). Consider the specificities of the loyalty programmes on offer. What are the conditions for joining the programme, and what are the benefits? What conclusions can you draw?
5. Go to a website that compares promotional offerings and note down the differences between each offering. What are the most important differential criteria? What role does price play (elasticity)?
6. Clip a comparative table from a consumer magazine. Consider the criteria taken into account. Ask consumers about their choice of product. Add the promotional offerings of certain brands (lower price, premiums, price, etc.) to the table. Consider their impact on choice. Explain.
7. Ask three salespersons from different companies about the types of incentives they are offered: individual assistance, team assistance, bonuses for meeting targets, etc. How sensitive are they to each type of incentive? What are the advantages and drawbacks?

Notes and references

1. T.A. Shimp, *Promotion Management and Marketing Communication*, 2nd edition, Orlando, Florida, Drysden Press, 1990.
2. R.C. Blattberg and S.A. Neslin, *Sales Promotion, Concepts, Methods and Strategies*, Englewood Cliffs, New Jersey, Prentice Hall, 1990.
3. G. Hermet and A. Jolibert, *La part de marché: concepts, déterminants et utilisation*, Paris, Economica, 1995.
4. R.C. Blattberg, R. Briesh and E.J. Fox, 'How Promotions Works', *Marketing Science*, 14, 3, part 2 of 2, G122–G132, 1995.
5. P. Chandon, 'Dix ans de recherches sur la psychologie et le comportement des consommateurs face aux promotions', *Recherches et Applications en Marketing*, 9, 3, 83–109; 9, 4, 81–101, 1994.
6. Blattberg et al., Op. cit.

Direct marketing

Learning objectives

After studying this chapter you will be able to

1 Have understood the aims, role and conditions for use of direct marketing
2 Have grasped the importance of relationship marketing and the notion of CRM (Customer Relationship Management)
3 Have learned how to use the associated tools
4 Know why and how to set up a marketing database
5 Analyse and be able to use specific promotional and advertising communication techniques in direct marketing
6 Have understood the role of electronic business in direct marketing
7 Know about the main communication techniques used on the Internet

---

SPOTLIGHT

Listening to Customers Always Pays!

At the end of 2005, I became aware of a growing site and French blog: La Fraise. The site sells custom-made T-shirts with unique graphics – once a graphic is sold out, there is no reprint. The site has been a *huge* success, thanks to the blog. It is so successful that the site is mentioned as an example of what "good" corporate blogging is. The blog helped La Fraise grow and today affords three men to live from their passion.

What I specifically value in this example is the true customer orientation. What some call "customer-centric organizations" or "customer-centric marketing" is a day-to-day reality at La Fraise.

An example is that visitors are offered the chance to submit graphics of their choice to be featured in the next T-shirt collection, and the graphics that do get featured are the ones that are voted for by other visitors. What a simple and great example of "co-value creation", moving marketing from a B2C model to C2B2C model: Consumers to Business to Consumers.

And guess what? It works! The revenue generated is growing month on month to a level of over 100,000 euros in March 06 from about 35,000 about 6 to 8 months previously!

I recently visited their blog, and again was impressed: Patrice, the main manager, reviews business progress, sharing *openly and honestly* with all of us, the revenue reached month on month, the strategy, etc., thanking everyone for their support, feedback and great contribution.

Guess what? There are over 230 comments on the post! When a marketing consultant talks about engagement... this is such a great way to engage people!

The lessons:
- be passionate, share your passion
- be honest and open
- LISTEN to all
- let your customers help you, they are willing to do so if you listen to them
- stay approachable all the time

Brands, you too can do the same. Start paying attention to people visiting your brand website!

Did I buy from La Fraise? No, but I will at some point... and in the meantime, I am already a "promoter". Did you say Engagement and Word of Mouth?

by Laurent Florès, CEO, crmmetrix.

Introduction

While certain countries have a lot of experience in direct marketing, particularly the United States, in Europe this discipline has been confused with something like traditional mail order. Today, direct marketing does not limit itself to any single economic sector – it has become a form of marketing which can be integrated in the strategy of any company, under the right conditions. As a rule, companies gradually started to implement direct marketing by using just one of its techniques – mailshots, telephone, coupons and so on – in the same way as they had previously used other techniques of classic marketing. The results obtained caused most of them to use it again. The development of the Internet also opened up new perspectives. Can we then conclude that these techniques are today key elements of their marketing plan and create a progressive development in their organization and their commercial practices? This integration requires a set of conditions to be met, which are analyzed in this chapter. First, we will study the reasons for the increasing use of direct marketing, and define more precisely what lies hidden behind this particular approach. Relationship marketing and its essential constituents such as CRM will then be the object of a specific discussion. Particular emphasis will be placed on the concept of a database, the cornerstone of direct marketing. The last part of this chapter will be dedicated to direct marketing methods of promotion and communication with an in-depth look at the possibilities offered by new information technology and communication within the framework of advertising and electronic business.

Specification and definition

Although many companies are using direct marketing techniques, few have at their disposal the necessary capabilities and resources to master it. This is not the case when we consider direct marketing as a global methodology. Every business oganization is based on the creation of a multitude of contacts. They are at the origin of various data flows which pass through the company. The mastery of data flows is the prime condition necessary for successful direct marketing. The management of contacts is the key to the successful practice of direct marketing.

The EDMA (European Direct Marketing Association) has defined direct marketing as an interactive system of marketing which calls on one or several communications media with a view to provoking a measurable reaction and\or transaction anywhere. The concept thus encompasses all media activities conceived in order to establish an interactive relation with a retail dealer, a customer, a consumer or a donor.

> Direct marketing is an interactive form of marketing based on the setting up, development and use of a database which establishes personalized and incisive exchange relations at a distance between the company and its clients and intermediaries thanks to the use of specific media (catalogues, mail, telephone calls, new media of the NICT type (new information and communication technology) and/or specific use of classic media (such as press inserts, advertising slots).

Figure 16.1 Definition of direct marketing

For our part, we shall consider direct marketing in the following way (Figure 16.1).

The first element of this definition, which is accepted in most companies, is paradoxically the most innovative: it refers to the ability of the company to set up an internal system of customer management. The connection between the marketing database and the models of segmentation and positioning is generally at the centre of this type of analysis. In the same way, communication and promotion operations are directly connected with commercial file data. This requires rigorous analysis of handling mechanisms and the use of the commercial information by the customers plus reflection on the coherence of the communication.

The direct marketing methodology contains several stages, from the development of a system of customer management to the application of direct communication techniques.

The development of direct marketing

Three groups of factors explain the development of direct marketing:

1. changes in the organization of the commercial activity of companies,
2. the changing state of markets,
3. various characteristics of direct marketing itself.

Changes in the organization of the commercial activity of companies

Certain developments favour the use of direct marketing.

First of all, the simplification of sales structures, the decrease in their cost and the motivation of sales forces are finding new solutions in the use of direct marketing: we can quote, for example, the problems of customer recruitment, the creation of traffic at points of sale, choice of new sales vehicles (electronic catalogues, commercial sites on the Internet etc.) and the revitalization of the sales force. Applications developed in the banking sector, in insurance or car dealing, illustrate perfectly this type of application. For example, ING and Norwich Union are today developing totally live banking service offers and insurance. Commercial development policy (extension of canvassing activities, approach to new markets) also finds uses for the tools of direct marketing, as complements or substitutes for the arsenal of selling techniques in specific markets: industrial marketing is thus enriched with new tools that are very suitable.

We cannot consider direct marketing as an element of the marketing mix like all the others. In effect, direct marketing is just a form of marketing which is defined by a method of approach to the customer, direct (without an intermediary), personal, at a distance. It can therefore involve simultaneously a means of distribution (absence of intermediary), a means of communication (personalized at a distance), a sales method (express, without sales force) and, more widely, a marketing approach where the individual customer is a personalized target.

A "customer–solution" relationship is substituted for the classic "segment–product" relationship (Table 16.1).

The individual replaces the segment or is a segment of one person or company. And because we can "treat" each person or each company as a customer target, it becomes possible to personalize the offer in order to present the solution preferred by each customer.

Thus, direct marketing can be considered as a particularly suitable marketing practice when customer needs become more varied and more complex. During the last decade, changes in business and in society have taken a direction that reinforces the development of this form of marketing. The 1990s were generally defined as the era of globalization. It was also the era of individualization and, consequently, that of direct marketing. In most large European countries, the share of communication in "below the line"[1] advertising media, which roughly cover direct marketing media, has greatly exceeded that of major traditional media. Germany has the widest market for direct marketing ahead of the United Kingdom and France (Table 16.2).

Direct marketing also allows finer segmentation and strengthens the personalization of commercial contacts in the search for better differentiation with regard to competition. It becomes an increasingly effective means for setting up market entry barriers by allowing the rapid development of awareness, of the image of a company and the development of customer loyalty. For example, companies using television campaigns in direct marketing have viewed their popularity rate developing appreciably in the space of just a few weeks (Tables 16.3 and 16.4).

Direct marketing also allows for rationalization and a greater rigour in the management of products. It is characterized by the creation of very detailed marketing plans mainly inspired by procedures of management control such as operational cost accounts and performance indicators. Thus, equivalence can be improved between the commercial investments of the company and the nature of its products and its customers.

Thanks to direct marketing, companies have new internal and external vehicles at their disposal, necessary for the establishment of direct communication with their markets. In the same way, numerous more accessible services, advertising space or media, appear, such as private channels, new supports such as Internet or postal services, and offer wide development perspectives to companies.

Finally, direct marketing allows firms to obtain immediate tangible results that correspond directly to sales imperatives and are increasingly directed towards the short term.

The influence of the state and development of markets: relationship marketing

The development of customer behaviour, company organization and information system as well as available media and distribution structures increases interest in the use of direct marketing. Two factors seem to be particularly significant.

The basis for direct marketing is a precise "characterization" of current and prospective customers generally leading to returns on investment superior to those obtained with classic techniques. This is particularly true for increasingly narrow and competitive markets. The smaller the customer base to be served, the more justified direct marketing techniques seem to become. This would, for example, be the case for a manufacturer of industrial scales trying to reach a specific customer segment or, in a totally different context, a local authority looking for foreign investors.

Table 16.1 Classic marketing and direct marketing

Classic marketing	⊠ Market (global) ⊠ Segments (differentiated) ⇐---- ⊠ Segment (concentrated)	⇨ Product
Direct marketing	⊠ Solution ⇐----	⇨ Customer or prospective client

Table 16.2 Total direct marketing, € million

	1993	1994	1995	1996	1997	1998	1999	2000
Austria	–	–	970	884	993	1,052	1,101	1,151
Belgium	–	–	–	–	917	656	660	718
Czech Republic	–	–	–	–	–	–	151	192
Denmark	427	452	554	585	463	475	515	535
Finland	330	343	372	399	423	444	466	493
France	4,139	5,115	5,364	5,868	6,039	6,526	6,786	7,177
Germany	7,373	6,954	8,181	9,101	10,124	11,657	12,271	13,140
Greece	–	–	5	–	–	–	–	57
Hungary	–	–	–	–	–	–	134	152
Ireland	81	90	100	113	124	20	64	71
Italy	1,704	1,782	1,926	2,062	1,443	1,865	1,969	2,641
Netherlands	1,676	1,897	2,124	2,287	2,487	3,999	4,481	4,296
Poland	–	–	–	–	–	–	–	514
Portugal	19	23	26	30	35	38	42	47
Slovak Republic	–	–	–	–	–	–	10	12
Spain	1,657	1,742	1,844	1,973	2,151	2,415	2,825	3,024
Sweden	523	545	577	622	663	671	1,012	1,197
UK	1,932	2,708	2,847	3,731	5,509	5,978	7,145	7,612
Total	**19,862**	**21,650**	**24,891**	**27,655**	**31,372**	**35,795**	**39,629**	**43,031**

Source: FEDMA (Federation of European Direct Marketing) "Survey on Direct and Interactive Marketing Activities in Europe", 2001.

Table 16.3 Direct mail: spend and volume per capita Summary of spend and volume per capita, 2000

	Direct mail volume per capita			All DM spend per capita (€)		
	Addressed	Unaddressed	Total[1]	Direct mail[1]	TS	Total[2]
Austria	90.1	455.4	545.5	142.1	–	142.1
Belgium	106.7	–	106.7	68.9	–	70.2
Czech Republic	12.1	58.4	70.4	17.4	1.2	18.7
Denmark	44.5	369.2	413.7	100.4	–	100.4
Finland	97.3	207.3	304.6	93.1	–	95.3
France	–	–	382.8	108.7	9.9	121.0
Germany	78.4	188.6	267.1	108.3	36.7	159.9
Greece	–	–	–	4.6	0.8	5.4
Hungary	10.5	109.2	119.8	13.0	1.6	15.1
Ireland	30.0	61.6	91.6	12.4	6.5	18.8
Italy	26.0	–	26.0	32.5	10.9	45.8
Netherlands	96.6	582.8	679.3	148.2	120.1	270.8
Poland	–	–	–	8.6	4.7	13.3
Portugal	19.6	36.5	56.1	4.7	–	4.7
Slovak Republic	1.3	7.0	8.3	1.6	0.4	2.2
Spain	–	–	21.8	66.9	9.8	76.7
Sweden	74.7	324.3	399.1	121.2	–	135.1
UK	78.2	–	78.2	56.6	66.8	127.7
Total[3]	**78.6**	**245.1**	**199.7**	**68.8**	**27.4**	**97.7**

Notes:
1. Includes catalogues where available.
2. Includes Internet data where available.
3. Totals calculated on all available data, excluding populations of countries for which no data are available.
Source: FEDMA (Federation of European Direct Marketing) "Survey on Direct and Interactive Marketing Activities in Europe", 2001.

Table 16.4   Direct marketing interest

Motivation for those making the offer	Contribution	Consumer interest
– minimization of stock – "just-in-time" – ability to react and make a decision – creation of customer loyalty	speed personalization	satisfaction reduction in time lost more adapted offer less anonymous offer
– creation of customer loyalty – possibility of fixing errors – ability to react	interactivity (two-way communication) performance control	possibility for dialogue better adjustment of the offer on demand
– reduction of fixed costs	resource sharing	possibility of lower prices "complete offer"
– creation of customer loyalty	intelligence, expertise	better consideration of the need
– increase in turnover	profitability	

On the other hand, direct marketing offers the possibility of bypassing certain obstacles such as the presence of excessively powerful distribution partners or the high cost of media which makes them inaccessible to certain companies.

Direct marketing is being increasingly used today in domains where techniques of mass marketing dominated before (Table 16.5).

In the first case, direct marketing comes as a back-up or in combination with traditional marketing methods such as sales promotion, public relations and sponsorship. We can consider that any complex (meriting explanations) or high emotional value (allowing a narrower, friendly relation) product can find added value in a more personalized, social and, consequently, more enduring relationship. In the second case, the development of direct marketing in the industrial domains or Business to Business ("B to B") are obvious signs of the adaptation of this form of marketing to companies, where each customer is a particular case (a particular business) and where the proposal of a personalized offer (a solution) is more acceptable than that of a standard product.

Finally, when customer demand becomes very complex, direct marketing supports a personal on-the-spot sales method. It is, then, a tool for developing customer loyalty and a support for sales force actions.[2]

Confronted with increasingly competitive markets, today companies tend to build customer loyalty through developing and maintaining relationships which we will refer to as "relationship marketing".[3]

Relationship marketing provides a double transformation of the transactional concept of exchange:

1. A temporal transformation, where the exchange is no longer considered as short-term but as extended in time. It includes the development of confidence and commitment

Table 16.5   Opportunity in direct marketing

Very little direct marketing	Mass standard products	Weak involvement, Weak added value
Supplementary or compounded direct marketing	Mass products	Strong commitment "Complex" and/or "Friendly" to Added Value (e.g. press, wine)
Quality domain of direct marketing	Products + services Complex individualized products Services	e.g. games sector, games, property, computers, hi-fi ... office equipment, packaging, computer material e.g. trips, hotels, museums ... credit cards, insurance
Direct marketing + sales force	Products as "Solutions"	Business to business Industrial products Complex services

of the partners in the relationship as far as the implementation of common systems. For example, business partners may share information systems such as their database or their Computer Aided Design tools or, again, may closely cooperate in the establishment of common services and procedures linked to total quality management.

2. A spatial transformation, aiming to substitute a relationship of an organic nature for the contractual approach dominating transactional relations. Such an organic relationship can integrate several actors in the exchange, leading to a network[4] of closely interacting people or businesses. For example, the German consulting company Hyve helps manufacturing firms, such as Audi, to establish international relationships with highly involved customers via the Internet, who actively contribute their experience and "expert" knowledge to the development of new products.

Direct marketing is part of this trend because it allows for the development and enrichment of the supplier–customer relationship. The creation of a customer database allows for more acute and pertinent knowledge of customers, facilitating customer loyalty. In a way, it "solidifies" the relationship by nourishing it, using new information technology which allows for interactive and personalized communication.

Influencing factors inherent in direct marketing itself

Three factors can be highlighted at this level:

1. Direct marketing offers a vast possibility of tests, spending controls and measure of efficiency, which differentiates it from other methods of sale or communication. Furthermore, the budget necessary for the implementation of a direct marketing operation is comparatively low (at least in the short term), which constitutes a real incentive for any company in search of new approaches.

2. The set-up speed, flexibility and secrecy with respect to competitors are other attractions of direct marketing which justify its practice in numerous cases.
3. New information and communication tools based on Internet technology have provided new directions and possibilities of direct marketing which we cannot fully measure yet.

All of these factors have caused many companies to use more and more direct marketing.[5] When they no longer see direct marketing as a form of action foreign to their overall marketing plan which simply allows them to carry out a short-term limited operation, but, rather, they intend to modify their marketing plan to integrate direct marketing, then we can assume that they have really understood the contribution of this method. This can cause them to use classic marketing techniques in a different way, leading them to apply their research and databases differently, along with their handling, decision and control methods.

Customer relationship

All managers agree on one principle: it is much cheaper to hold on to customers by satisfying them than constantly to win over new customers from competitors. The current customers are the best advocates for the company, brand or trade name on the market. So, the regular customers, the subscribers or the members of the network find themselves propelled towards the heart of the organization and contribute directly to the company's success. Knowledge of customer motivation, measures of quality received from services, estimates of satisfaction, programmes for the development of customer loyalty, answers to enquiries or handling of possible complaints thus become of the greatest importance. Therefore, "CRM" applies tools and specific techniques, derived from classic direct marketing, applied with particular effectiveness because of new information and communication technology (Toolbox 16.1).

TOOLBOX 16.1

TOOLS OF CRM

Customer Relationship Management uses numerous tools for the purpose of developing customer loyalty. These tools frequently use software packages which can automate a certain number of tasks and means of telecommunication, in particular the Internet, with or without interaction between company members and customers.

The following list is not exhaustive:

- "Marketing" applications such as:
  - "data warehouse" and "data mining" management,
  - application of these tools to the company ("data mart"),

- customer segmentation,
- generation of lists of prospective customers for a targeted campaign,
- listing of all the products and their characteristics,
- management of loyalty programmes,
- personalization of offers,
- management of campaigns and media (fax, phone, mail shots, e-mail, promotional offers, etc.).

■ The management of customer service:

- precise identification of the customer (surname, first name, address, phone number).
- purchase background,
- taking charge of and following-up of customer orders,
- follow-up of complaints,
- planning and management of after-sales service,
- follow-up of customer loyalty actions,
- closing sales.

■ Sales management: often in the form of a programme of Sales Force Automation (SFA), which includes:

- management of sales reps' agenda and contacts,
- management of opportunities,
- sales forecasts,
- management of commissions,
- generation of offer proposals,
- management of sales reports,

- management of sales statistics,
- sending of messages and information via mobile vehicles (palm, mobile telephones).

■ The management of customer relationships on the Internet,

- personalization methods and tools,
- automatic proposals according to past customer reactions,
- management of communication channels (mail, Palm pilots, Wap, push media etc.).
- management of phone calls and "Call Centres",
- phone management of incidents,
- management of various services offered on the Internet, information services, advice, payment, additional offers.

■ A necessary integration.

All these actions require interface work between:

■ interacting computer solutions (compatibility of software packages and information systems (see databases),
■ software packages and telecommunication tools,
■ the organization of tasks and workstations by means of company services,
■ interface with the management and telecommunications systems of customers and suppliers.

The organization of this system of information and marketing action has led to the appearance of "database marketing" (marketing based on databases), "data warehouses" (data storing), "data mining" (data processing), "one-to-one" marketing (individualized marketing) and the use of the Internet.

In managing customer relationships, it is important to avoid providing negative value to customers, that is, costly elements of the total product for the company which have no particular worth for the customer in the short or long run. It is as important as avoiding excess value, that is, providing customer value which goes significantly beyond the value the organization receives in exchange. A particular tool, the estimation of the lifetime value of a customer ("customer's lifetime value"), continually updates the current and expected financial flow from each customer during its relationship with the company. It helps to manage customer relationships in a balanced manner that is financially profitable to the firm.

The commercial database

The point of departure for any direct marketing approach is the construction of an operational client file. It allows

the company to carry out analyses which help define the target customers for direct marketing operations.

The conditions of use of commercial data

In order to establish personal contact with its customers and prospective clients, an organization has to have some relevant information which allows it to effectively contact them. In practice, few companies really possess these elements.

The implementation of a customer file corresponds in this situation to the setting up of a list supplying the name, address and possibly the phone number of a group of current or prospective customers. In spite of the ubiquity of computers which renders this work easier, this aspect remains relatively important. It is a question, for example, of defining memory stores, data updates, format standardization, storage capacity and the use of efficient procedures. These problems arise systematically when the basis for this work is an accounting file, established by sales and not by customer. Setting up a simple operational customer file requires considerable investment which concerns general information management within the company. For example, automatic transfer from the accounting file to the customer file requires the integration of data processing systems.

Indispensable for prospecting new clients, such customer files are also needed for direct marketing. But they are not sufficient. A direct relationship with a customer will in fact be only really effective if it is personalized. The file must contain external and internal indicators which allow estimation of the opportunity of turning a given offer to a (potential) customer into a sale. Customer files should therefore have pride of place in the "commercial database" or "customer database" integrating a large number of behaviour variables.

A "customer database" includes, in a more or less aggregated form, the description of all commercial contacts established with the customers as well as their responses.[6] A given group of external elements (socio-economic indicators, addresses and so on) may enrich this description (these elements are generally the only ones available on prospects).

Today, there is a large quantity of data available, whether it stems from production file data or business connections such as correspondence, phone or Internet-obtained contacts. Companies have real "data warehouses" at their disposal, where they store all available data before it is transformed, aggregated, completed or simplified to become useful within the framework of the commercial database which originates from this data warehouse. Tracking down the most relevant data and handling this with a view to commercial action is called "data mining". Customers are selected and classified. Their value is estimated. Their reactions to specific company actions are monitored, and customer loyalty is followed closely. For this type of activity, statistical techniques of data analysis are applied very extensively. The methodology of extraction and analysis of data contained in a database (Tables 16.6 and 16.7) constitutes a special expertise sought after by companies, such as AT&T or American Express, which already possess large databases.

Large mail order companies possess this type of expertise which constitutes the bases for a customer management system. This customer management system can be defined as a number of interrelated answers to very simple questions:

- Who? (identity, socio-demographic characteristics)
- What? (nature of purchased products)
- Where? (home, business environment)
- How? (order, payment method)

Table 16.6   Examples of variables to be contained in a database

Identifier	Name and address
Demographic characteristics	Age, sex, profession, marital situation, number of children and so on.
External enrichment	Geographic and social characteristics concerning residence, area, community (geotypes). Belonging to a "socio-type" or "socio- style" and so on.
Customer background	Last purchases, frequency, loyalty.
Order method	Mail, Internet, telephone, stores, television.
Purchased products	Newness, recency, frequency; amount of purchases, payment method.
Behavioural data	Customer status (multi-mail order or not), propensity to order, typological assessment.

Table 16.7   Storage levels of data in "La Redoute's" database*

Level 1	Customer addresses plus essential indicators for telephone selling and direct contact (e.g., in-store)
Level 2	Used for the customer segmentation and the setting up of a customer profile. Turnover, number of orders over the last season and habits are listed. It is the only level which is not accessible in real time.
Level 3	La Redoute's contacts concerning the customer, dates and types of despatches and customer actions (dates and times).
Level 4	Customer background, minutely detailed. Only the previous few months are retained. Older details are stored in another file.

* La Redoute is the French leader in catalogue sales.

■ Why? (price, presentation)
■ Following what? (commercial pressure, links with previous purchases).

Building a database requires one to retain the nature and periodicity of data. The storage method and usage method must be defined (Figure 16.2). The basic element of any database is commercial contacts. These contacts are generally documented in an order form which provides highly structured and rich information around which numerous company activities revolve.

The set of data made available by recording, organizing and managing customers relationships allows for the selection and implementation of a sales approach. The approach selected depends on what we know about the customer's situation (details of the latest orders or those in hand, the nature of the commercial actions undertaken

etc.). Thanks to this information, it is possible to react quickly to customer demand, define offers of products and services adapted to the customers' particular expectations and to have direct and personalized relations with each of the customers. The objective of a commercial database is not just the development of short-term sales through improved customer relationship management, but also the building and monitoring of customer loyalty. Thus, a database serves numerous classic marketing goals Figure 16.3 such as:

■ the definition of customer "profiles";
■ identification of criteria discriminating between customers and non-customers, sensitive or not to company offers;
■ determination of attractive offers adapted to various customers profiles;

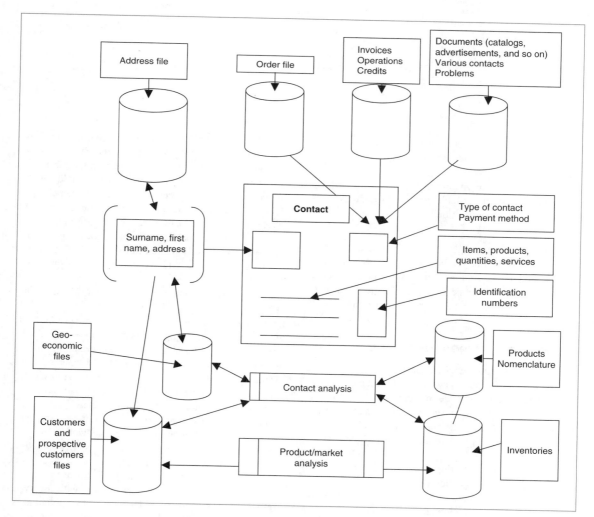

Figure 16.2 Organization of data flows

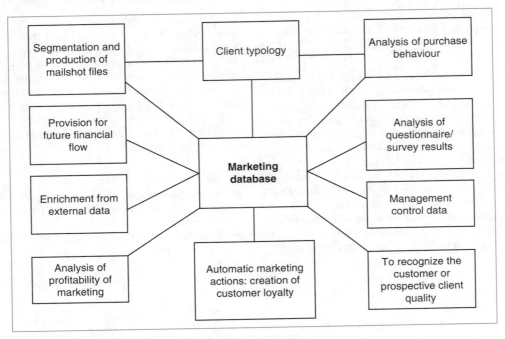

Figure 16.3 Marketing database = Profit centre

- update of selection criteria for priority prospective customers and the definition of actions to be carried out;
- monitoring the development of business with each customer based on available data on customers' reactions to company actions.

Using these different aspects, good practice in direct marketing is based on producing widespread research and numerous models whose aim is to allocate the commercial resources of the company according to the quality or the sales potential of its customers or prospective clients.

The use of a commercial database

The creation of a commercial database is the first phase in the development of direct marketing within the company. This database contains an accurate identification of the customers and prospective customers, an indication of the offers which have been made and the results obtained (purchase, request for information, absence of reaction, etc.).

Proceeding from observation and analysis of customers' reactions to decision and action presupposes the implementation of a system of handling and control of the entire set of recorded commercial data. This system is characterized by models which transform the mass of

available data within the company to real information, more limited in extent, allowing for the choice of offers and type of action to be implemented on the market. One such model is the most frequently used method for segmentation called "recency-frequency-monetary value" (RFM). "Recency" varies according to the date of the last purchase made by a customer. We can more or less assume that the probability of repurchase by a customer in a company is directly related to the "recency" of their last purchase. Frequency, which is the number of purchases during the reference period, can be considered as an implicit measure of the appropriateness of the company offer to the expectations of the customer. Recency and frequency can be compared with the turnover obtained with a customer over a given period (monetary value). Some companies are able to calculate an approximate margin for each customer (the "RFM+M" method) (Tables 16.8a and 16.8b). It is thus possible to establish a classification of customers based on one of these criteria or on a combination of them all. This classification remains essentially a management tool: it represents a basis for the differentiation and personalization of customer contacts.[7] However, it presents only something of a caricature of customer activity.

Generally, a measure of "potential" (for example, in terms of orders or turnover) is associated with this type of segmentation (Figure 16.4). The size of this potential is at one and the same time related to the level of sales pressure

Table 16.8a The "RFM+M" method

Order period	Order period	Order period	Order period	RFM+M Method
T − 4	T − 3	T − 2	T − 1	
1	0	1	1	**R**ecency (has ordered at least once)
2	0	3	2	**F**requency
100€	0	150€	150€	**M**onetary Value (amount)
10€	0	15€	20€	**M**argin

Table 16.8b Segmentation by activity profiles

Order period				Frequency	Recency
T − 4	T − 3	T − 2	T − 1		
+					
	+			Only ordered once	
		+			
+				Nothing over two periods	No order during the preceding period
	+				
+		+			
+	+	+			
	+	+			
+		+	+		
	+	+	+		
+	+	+	+	Loyal customer	
+		+	+		Have ordered last year
			+	New customer	

the company is ready to develop and to the probability of customer response, estimated from the RFM variable. In effect, it is possible to calculate a set of probabilities from these variables and allocate each customer to a given "potential" group. Thus, each group has different expected activity levels (measured in volume or value) and sees itself being allocated investment according to its potential.

For example, during a period of low activity, an increase in sales pressure from promotional activities aimed at previously defined groups of potential customers allows for an increase in activity. Continuously updating the indicators of customer response during the same period allows for perfect correspondence between customer quality and the commercial efforts of the company.

Real personalization of contacts with customers can only be achieved when considering less aggregated and more qualitative elements, such as the characteristics of the products bought. In fact, these elements are the result of customers responding to the information issued by the company. Combining these elements results in another model of customer classification. This describes all or some of the products and services offered according to their characteristics: the product itself (such as size or material), the product category (such as textiles, or household material) or some of its properties (such as presentation method or on sale). Thus, the description of individuals can be enriched by a succession of presence-absence indicators (called sometimes "tops") for each of these characteristics. These indicators are very useful for the selection of customers, the personalization of offers, the determination of the content of these offers or their mode of presentation.

Purchase indicators usually concern the objective characteristics of products such as size, material or colour. They can be used in the supply chain management. These purchase indicators are frequently enriched with a more subjective analysis of the customers' perceptions of the products on offer. New segmentation of customers according to different "consumption patterns" becomes possible. It can be integrated into an analysis of the offer in terms of handling and use of information by the customers (Table 16.9).

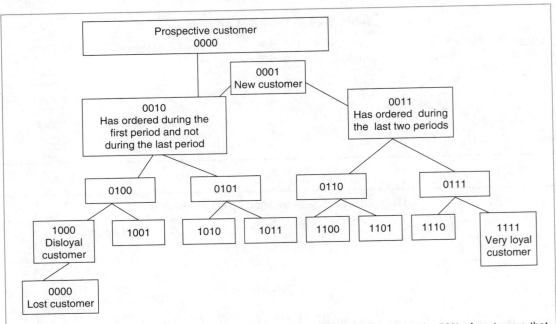

Commentary: For each profile, we can calculate the transfer probabilities: for example, 50% of customers that ordered during the first period (0001) ordered again during the second period (0011). 60% of the customers that ordered during two periods ordered again during the third period (0111) and so on. Thanks to these transfer probabilities, it is possible to calculate a "probability" for each segment (1111, 1110, 1101, 0011, 0001 etc.) to buy again during the future period and the company can adapt its direct marketing expenditures according to these probabilities.

Figure 16.4 The recency profiles

Table 16.9 Different types of approach to a client for a direct marketing database

Quantity-activity approach	RFM model
	Market share = penetration × loyalty rate
	Mark-up rate
Type of activity approach	Purchase indicators, shelf-space indicators
	"Pattern of consumption" indicators
	Client styles (e.g. pioneers, followers, early majority, etc.)
	Purchase methods (concomitance of purchase indicators: for example, purchase by card – household appliances – request for extension of guarantee)
External data enrichment	Combination with external files qualifying the client, such as magazine subscriptions or credit cards.
	Exploitation of external databases using addresses or first names. Complex internal analyses.
	Typologies and combinations extracted from databases linking different kinds of variables such as types of documents frequented, types of purchase, sensitivity to special offers, first names, "geotypes" or age.
Use of earlier classification in order to predict	Establishing the probability of amounts, nature and dates of purchase

Databases are generally analyzed by means of statistical methods such as cluster and discriminant analysis, which create groups of customers with identical profiles. They allow the analysis of behaviour, for example, by relating the purchase of a product with other data concerning customers and helping to determine the probability of purchase. Analytical methods have been considerably improved over the last decade. They include analytical methods such as neural networks:[8] these work in a way similar to the human brain and permit the handling of numerous problems in the analysis of customer behaviour.[9]

Companies such as Consodata and Calyx-Claritas in Europe have created consumer databases by sending several million questionnaires to households. These questionnaires contain more than 150 questions based on five criteria: socio-demographic, purchase (places, amounts, frequency, intentions), consumption (type, brand, volume, preference), equipment (environment, leisure, car, financial), lifestyles (sport, leisure activities, culture, media, holidays). Several million individuals have been recruited. These "mega-databases" allow the companies to sell numerous services to their business customers:

■ analysis of company files in comparison with the "mega-database": augmentation of addresses by new information and profile studies;
■ address location for prospecting;
■ sharing of information obtained from questionnaires inserted in customer packaging;
■ putting addresses and information collected during the year at the disposal of companies subscribing to the inquiry;
■ consumer analysis by geographic sectors for customer targeting ("geomarketing").

Communication in direct marketing

The creation, development and maintenance of personalized business relationships between a company and its customers constitute the basic objectives of direct marketing. Not only are the means of communication specific, such as mail-shots, phone or electronic, but the objective of communication is also different from other forms of communication, notably advertising: immediate action. In effect, the ultimate purpose of direct marketing communication is to make the prospective customer fill out a form (an order form or information request) and to send it to the company by telephone, mail or the Internet.

Consequently, direct marketing communication and promotion techniques are specific. Originally reserved for specialized companies, they are being increasingly used by companies with traditional distribution networks such as manufacturers of luxury goods, cars, computers and air-conditioning but also by car rentals or hotels. The limits of their use have been extended.

In direct marketing, some things are absent from the company's offer: atmosphere, greeting and personal contact. One must compensate for this with clever message composition. The presentation of the product, the selling message, the instructions to the customer to "act now" and the layout of the order form become crucial ingredients. When the offer is reduced to the presentation of a product or products using vehicles such as leaflets, catalogues and press advertisements, you have to get the text, visual elements (drawings, photographs) and sound messages (phone) right. The quality of customer contact is inextricably related to the professional handling of these issues. In the same way, credibility, confidence and loyalty can only be obtained by understanding purchase behaviour. Adequate decisions are based on intensive data gathering and analysis relative to business relationships. Their implementation has to set up the means of communication and promotion likely to attain the objectives of direct marketing: to make the consumer react quickly by provoking a response, namely filling out an order form or asking for information. In order to achieve this the direct marketers organize promotional campaign plans that distribute customer actions in space (across segments) and in time (first offer, re-launch, development of customer loyalty).

In effect, each direct customer contact is characterized by a number of tangible and intangible processes and results. For example, mailings may lead to purchases, and raising confidence may increase customer loyalty.

Before detailing the set-up mechanisms for the various techniques of promotional action, an accurate analysis of their objectives seems necessary. Their conditions for use need to be clarified. This will be done in what follows. Subsequently, the techniques specific to direct communication will be presented with a focus on the most recent Web techniques. Their specific role and effectiveness will be explained.

The objectives of direct promotional communication

The objective of using the entire set of media in direct marketing is to promote a "direct" relationship between a company and its customers or prospects. The initiators of the contact can be the company, when it makes an offer, or the customers, when, for example, they send an order form, call the company or visit the home page on the Internet. Such contact serves as a basis for establishing a real communication process between the company and its potential customers. A communication process, to become enduring, must take the form of a loop where any action leads to an action in response, and any exchange induces another one (Figure 16.5).

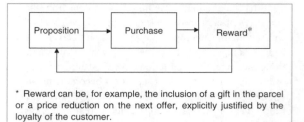

* Reward can be, for example, the inclusion of a gift in the parcel or a price reduction on the next offer, explicitly justified by the loyalty of the customer.

Figure 16.5 The logic of mutual response

Thus, the objective of the techniques of communication and promotion implemented in direct marketing is to persuade customers to accept the company's offer and to act. It is then up to the company to thank the customer (development of customer loyalty) by offering an incentive which increases the attractiveness of a new offer to follow.

Compared to traditional sales promotions, promotional actions in direct marketing rarely limit themselves to immediate incentives but try to establish a relationship of trust, a sort of "implicit contract", the result of which should be the development of customer loyalty. Certainly, some sales pitches will suggest several reasons to buy immediately, but this type of argument has a particular context such as the pleasure in the offering, surprise, choice and seriousness. Furthermore, it takes into account the specific mechanisms of distance buying which permit a period of reflection and a comparison between offers. Promotional elements must be formulated according to the decision-making processes. For example, they generally demand active and rapid participation on the part of the customers so as to involve them – to scratch (scratch-card), cut, read, phone or push buttons. These gestures constitute a first step towards acquiring the order. Apparently trivial, they cause the consumer to gradually become engaged in the buying process. The choice of a particular promotion technique is made not only according to the chosen customer segment, but also according to the type of media used by those customers.

Although price promotion, often aggressive and expensive, is still very much in use, direct marketing users implement promotional actions which tend to establish stronger personalization of the company–customer relationship. We also know that there can be improper use of promotion. For example, excessively aggressive promotion can unfavourably influence purchase behaviour, may lead to postponement of purchases while customers wait for a special offer and may produce the perception of unreliability or depreciation in value of the offer.

The specific objectives of the offer can be to bring about a first purchase, to increase use of the main catalogue, to increase the average number of orders, to react to a competitor, or to attain sales objectives. Each objective justifies a particular choice of promotional action. For example, a "sweepstake"[10] tends to accelerate orders. If a particular incentive is added, such as rapid ordering (doubling of potential gain if response in eight days), acceleration of orders is greater. On the other hand, a contest can slow down the arrival of orders because of the response-time factor or the need to consult somebody with greater expertise. These effects of acceleration or slowing down can be used to modulate the rhythm of orders according to production patterns.

The techniques of direct promotional action

Most direct marketing offers contain invitations to home inspection, free trials or free samples. These elements associated with the offer have a double role: to stimulate and to motivate the prospective customers but especially to minimize the perceived risk. The three techniques examined in what follows are characterized by a "pure" promotional aspect comprising incentives alone. It is about price reduction, free gifts, games and lotteries. A large number of other techniques exist but it is not our aim to present a complete list here. Rather, the three most common techniques will be discussed. This will be sufficient to demonstrate how promotion becomes integrated into direct marketing.

Price reduction

Whether they are in value or percentage terms, promotions based on price reduction constitute the most widespread promotion technique in direct or classic marketing. The effectiveness of this method depends on the "saving" sentiment which has always been a strong purchase motivation.

This form of incentive is very simple because it is systematic and only needs certain items to be bought. This simplicity is a good means of making prospective clients more aware of a particular offer (e.g., newspapers or magazines which offer subscriptions without price reductions are few in number) or of creating a centre of attention concerning certain products in a range (new products, products in everyday use which initiate the customers to distance buying etc.). Nevertheless, many things can limit interest in discounts. If used too much, discounts progressively distort consumer behaviour, by causing a systematic search for special offers, the expectation of a special offer, the loss of awareness of the notion of a normal price, and the establishing of the promotional price as the reference level for future purchases. These medium-term negative effects contribute to delaying or suppressing customers' orders when they find prices too high because they are not on special offer or because the mark-down is not considered sufficient.

This type of phenomenon is now well known. However, it is a good idea to underline its importance in a context of direct selling. Direct marketing requires a large amount of information to be presented to the customers through specific vehicles (letters, catalogues, Internet). In this context, many companies are hesitant to use price reduction in too brutal a way: because it tends "to cannibalize" the rest of the message, to transform it into a simple "price" offer to the detriment of other information. The increase in sales obtained in the short term does not compensate for long-term negative effects. This is why direct marketing companies are trying either to avoid the excessive use of price promotion or to combine it with other techniques which lessen the drawbacks attached to it.

The short-term effectiveness of price reduction and especially competitive pressure nevertheless make the use of reduced price inevitable on certain markets. Thus, the real "discount war" in which certain companies are engaged is to the detriment of the companies that are caught in a vicious circle. That is why many companies have tried to rid themselves of this system by choosing a more solid positioning at a strategic level such as speed, quality, up-market and rarity and by privileging the use of other promotional techniques such as free gifts.

The gift

Although it can be differentiated, for example by size of order or time elapsed, price reduction is characterized by its anonymous, impersonal, even purely commercial aspect. On the other hand, a gift is of a more intimate, emotional and playful nature. Thus, many offers in direct marketing are accompanied by free gifts, "surprises" or premiums.

The main interest of the gift lies in its relational and emotional character. Furthermore, it also has numerous technical possibilities for personalization. However, whatever its nature, it is not the gift itself which is most important, but the way in which it is offered. The gift is generally a means of provoking or anticipating a purchase decision (by making the promise more attractive), of increasing the volume of purchases (when additional gift systems are connected to the quantity of purchases) and thanking the customer for developing their loyalty.

However, the gift is rarely the essential motive for purchase. Unlike price reduction, it is not necessarily connected to the purchase – many companies offer gifts which have little direct sales link. It must thus be considered as a testimony of interest shown towards the customer. The company which offers the gift must show care in choosing it in relation to the image which it wishes to give of itself and its customers. The means of presenting the gift has to be based on real creative communications work. Besides, the choice of a particular gift requires a certain number of conditions to be taken into account:

- At a technical level, it should be light, not cumbersome, solid, easy to store and manufacture (to avoid possible problems of re-supplying) and easy to pack.
- At a commercial level, it must be useful, easy to photograph, have a satisfactory life expectancy, be credible and, if possible, exclusive (cannot be found in stores).

The nature of the present, its originality and presentation strongly influence the obtained results. Therefore, various tests on the customer target group of the promotional action may need to be carried out before making a choice (a particular object can be badly perceived today and give very good results in the near future, and vice versa). Although often used, this type of action may seem limited. The need for active participation in the exchange process by the customers generally requires recourse to other promotional techniques such as competitions and games.

Contests and games

The effect of promotional actions is in many cases limited by their weak financial incentive or their commonplace nature (in particular price reductions). To create a motivating event for customers or the various partners of the company requires the presence of a more substantial and more attractive stake. The technique of contests and games meets this condition. Unlike the previous techniques, it generally constitutes the main object of the offer.

A contest is in a general sense an event at the conclusion of which it is possible to classify the participants. This classification is carried out according to answers given to a set of questions. Although less and less appreciated by many customers[11] (so much so that major mail order companies no longer practice this form of promotion), this technique is still used, by replacing traditional intellectual questions by questions about the organizing company, its products or services. The circumstances surrounding the setting up of a contest thus concern the launch of a new product or service, the opening of a point of sale, the organization of a network and so on, and allow the company to make a customer target aware of the characteristics of its offer. In each case, responses require only a minimum of effort on behalf of the participants but require them to manipulate a certain amount of information of a commercial nature and improve their knowledge of the company offer.

The simplicity of such contests allows them to be considered as games of chance. Apart from their technical characteristics, they can strengthen the effectiveness of the general company communication plan.

Their effect on sales is undeniable: they lead customers to look for extra information, but above all they play on the rather widespread belief that the chances of winning increase when the customer places an order (which is false and in most European legislation, forbidden by law).

However, the number of winners being by nature very small, several participants may resent not having won (even though their responses were correct!). To limit such effects, it is usually necessary to make provision for a consolation prize for each loser, which appreciably increases the difficulty of this technique.

Games of chance

The degree of difficulty of certain contests represents an important constraint to wide participation. The intervention of chance in the determination of the results of a game thus constitutes the best means of not making it too selective and no longer looking for effort on the part of the participants.

The sweepstake is a form of promotional technique which depends on this principle. The winners are designated by a preliminary drawing of lots (a "pre-draw") whose results are communicated to the prospective customers by a participation coupon which is sent to them. If the draw has designated them among the winners, they just have to return this coupon to know exactly (and to receive) what they have won. Another process ("post-draw") comprises organizing a draw on the basis of participation coupons which have been returned, and is then a game of chance.

The operation of this technique demands expertise: choice of prizes, the draw, management of correspondence, and includes different types: "everybody's a winner" (consolation prize), "early bird" (supplementary winnings for a response given within a certain period), "advanced postcard" (preliminary announcement of the game and its prizes) in how they are presented (guaranteed by a celebrity which strengthens the credibility of the game, a list of the most recent winners etc.). The most important aspect is personalization which laser printing processes have greatly simplified.

Sweepstakes, forbidden in several European countries, give rise to strong disapproval from consumer associations or even from some direct marketing professionals. The quality of customers gained by this method can be low (weak average order quantity, higher rate of outstanding payments). Besides, we may question the impact of games on the perception of the offer and the image of the organizer by the participants. There has been a strong decline in the use of sweepstakes over the last few years, following the condemnation of certain companies who misleadingly used this technique by playing on ambiguous presentations of the possibilities of winning.

Consequently, it is advisable to test and carry out qualitative research in order to judge the real consequences of games and to have a better grasp of how to set them up.

If classic advertising communication can only be pre-tested with difficulty in real use situations, direct marketing offers the possibility of tests which permit improvement of its form and content. This is why all these techniques are the subject of reflection and continuous creativity effort on the part of companies which use them.

The use of tests

In general, tests aim to allow a selection to be made between different offers or to confirm a particular offer by subjecting it to various evaluation criteria. These are generally concerned with the impact of the offer on sales (easy to measure in this context), and the overall effectiveness of the communication (memorability, comprehension etc.). In the first case, it is enough to reproduce the well-known split-run[12] procedure (either in its original context, the press advertisement, or through several different mail shots). In the second case, we use usual methods of research and measurement of the qualities of a message. These tests allow for the progressive improvement of the effectiveness of offers and "direct" company messages.

The effectiveness of a direct offer is generally estimated from three angles:

1. with regard to its definition: is it preferable to offer "a 20 euro reduction for 100 euros of purchases" or "40 euros for 200 euros"?; "two free books and two at 30 euros" or "four books for 30 euros"?
2. with regard to the differences in return which can be obtained: what is the supplementary return to be had with a gift (or a particular gift)?
3. with regard to the selected customer target group: does the offer appeal to the target customers?

■ In spite of conditions favourable to testing, these are rarely conducted rigorously according to a methodological plan. For example, the conditions of exposure to messages are not sufficiently thought through. The effective use of tests is associated with their methodology, just like advertising tests. Many tests are concerned only with the form or presentation of messages, and not with the global offer. It is important to test the offer itself along with its coherence within the communications strategy of the company and the other elements of the marketing-mix. Being aware of this problem, some large companies build real "campaign plans" where promotional operations are planned according to customer segments, customer reaction and major additional aspects of the company's marketing-mix: types of communication, offers produced and potential distribution problems (e.g., predictable congestion at the order dispatching centre).

The integration of direct promotional action techniques into market communication strategy

The short-term effectiveness of promotional techniques, in a world of increasingly fierce competition, has become important. It is dangerous to use it as the only instrument of the marketing strategy of a company. Only the conditions under which the company operates on the market will determine the appropriateness of promotional methods. Direct marketing promotion techniques must be considered as one solution among many, according to the specific objectives of the company. They must be integrated as an element of its overall marketing strategy. The use of direct promotions does not constitute a strategy in itself but simply a method of marketing action. They are very often looked on as being independent, as a supplementary method of obtaining more orders. In fact, they can be more useful in the long term when they intervene after an accurate analysis of customer decision-making processes and determination of the communication strategy which results from it. These actions can thus help to stimulate demand at a particular moment and in the desired direction, while at the same time not being in conflict with the other messages of the company. The flexibility and adaptability of promotional techniques allow one to differentiate the offers according to different customer segments to be reached. Their contribution to the overall marketing strategy of the company is then clear and their negative effects are reduced.

To establish a personalized and durable business relationship demands an intense process of communication, covering all of the following stages: prospecting, negotiation, sales, control and follow-up. This sequence of stages is standard marketing practice. The techniques of direct marketing, besides requiring the particular infrastructure described above, have come to act as a substitute for, or a complement to, the classic techniques of communication throughout the entire process. Direct promotions cannot be inserted or excluded from market communication plans. Only a general communication platform can allow one to determine the proper mix of classic and "direct" communication techniques. From this perspective, the still common barrier between the media plan and "direct" communication plan should not exist, if we refer to the rules of coherence between marketing actions, defined by the basic concept of the marketing mix. The result is a communication platform comprising the central message, the major communication objectives, the specific messages for each customer segment and the specific media and advertising vehicles for each customer segment and each message.

The combination of promotional techniques of the in-store reduction voucher type and direct marketing techniques are becoming increasingly common. Certain companies such as Catalina have offered programmes to American supermarket chains which constitute a database of the best customers (frequent shoppers) based on optical reading systems and offering advantages such as vouchers, gifts or discounts.

The concept of the market communication plan envisages the manner in which the different types of operations can be combined according to selected customer target groups and the reactions of these customers during the campaign. The plan is drawn up in four steps[13] (Figures 16.6–16.9):

- The first comprises analysing the sales accounts of previous seasons or years in order to determine the seasonal profiles and establishing, period-by-period, sales by product.
- In the second stage, communications are created in time for the following season according to the targeted customer segments.
- Based on past experience, the objective of the third step is to establish results expected in terms such as quantities sold, average number of orders, frequency of orders or transformed prospective clients.
- At last, the fourth step consolidates earlier data in the plan, period by period.

Direct marketing media

The practice of direct marketing is regularly enhanced with new media or vehicles. It would be vain to attempt to draw up an exhaustive list and to delineate where each of them should be used. We shall discuss two more limited issues having a wider conceptual and methodological reach:

1. the use of classic media within the framework of direct marketing,
2. the place and the methods of communication on the Internet.

Classic media

Four principal media will be studied here: direct press media, mailing, phone and television.[14]

Press media and vehicles in direct marketing

Out of all the various press media on the market, magazines hold a key role. This arises from several constraints:

- To achieve the desired value of presentation quality, specific advertising space may be required. This space is not only sometimes difficult to obtain, but may also be expensive, for example space on covers. The use of covers sometimes poses the problem of reluctance on the reader's part to mutilate the magazine),

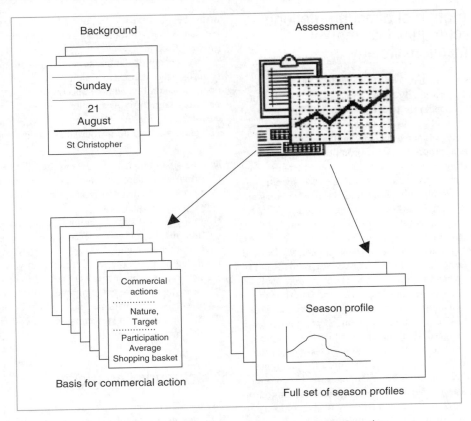

Figure 16.6 The different stages of a commercial action plan
Stage 1: Assessment

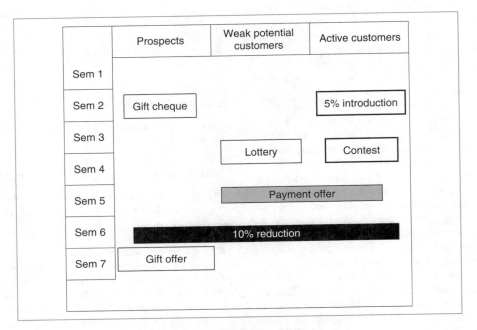

Figure 16.7 Stage 2: Commercial plan

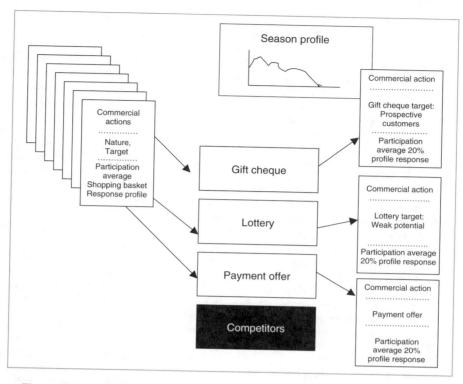

Figure 16.8 Step 3: Choice of basic profile and similar historical background operations

	Base: Projected turnover	Action 1 Projected additional turnover due to action 1	Action 2 Projected additional turnover due to action 2	Action...	Total by week
	(000€)	(000€)	(000€)		(000€)
Week 1	1,000				1,000
Week 2	1,000	50			1,050
Week 3	1,000	500			1,050
Week 4	1,000	700			1,500
Week 5	1,000	200	100		1,700
Week 6	1,000	50	300		1,300
Week 7	1,000	–	–	–	1,350
Week...					–

Figure 16.9 Step 4: Direct marketing plan

- If a lot of presentation space is needed, print media may be rather costly.
- Related to space there may also be layout problems. Where can the advertisement and the reply coupon be situated?
- The ability to produce inserts which offer a better return are reduced and there are difficulties in producing split runs.

Nevertheless, certain arguments can be put forward favouring the "press" media, such as the emergence of press vehicles which allow for increasingly accurate reader analyses resulting in more effective customer target selection, the scale of vehicle circulation and knowledge of their reading conditions.

The development in vehicle numbers has been very important over the last few years. New possibilities to reach increasingly precise customer targets through the media are now at our disposal (improved vehicle selectivity) with better-known and more distinctive characteristics. It is easy to have all the known data about these vehicles such as the age, sex, location and socio-profesionnal group of readers and to proceed a priori to a selection according to the objectives and analyses of the company. Feedback can be obtained in terms of orders or requests for information. In effect, the sensitivity of different readerships to diverse types of product or service offers can be measured rapidly and simple surveys, carried out on new customers, enable useful comparisons to be made; for example, between their profile and that of all the vehicle readers, or the profile of customers obtained by other means, or again, the profile of all customers. When results obtained due to these comparisons are systematically recorded, they make it possible to undertake valuable time-series analyses. Accumulated experience while adding and comparing analyses also improves market knowledge.

Whether it is to reach a well-specified customer target group or a very wide public, in many cases the desired number of contacts can be reached through the medium of the press. Direct marketing specialists are well aware of changes in magazine readership and follow this closely because the profile of the readers can change very rapidly.

Finally, knowledge of reading circumstances such as time of day, week, time spent or the number of times the magazine is read is very useful. Certain circumstances are more favourable to purchase than others. In this respect, analogies between the reading of a magazine and that of a mail order catalogue can be established. For example, concerning these two vehicles, a peak of return of coupons or orders can be observed at the beginning of the week.

A vehicle is selected for the greater part according to its success in terms of responses. This criterion is valid for all direct marketing media. However, the responses on press ads, measured by the number of returned coupons, are generally rather modest. Weak response, whether it concerns qualification, that is, request for more information, or sales must be compensated for by the size of the profit margin obtained on each product. This encourages the use of the response criterion for relatively highly priced products. We may also note that the indirect effects on the image of the company must be taken into account in the appreciation of results, both at the levels of awareness and at that of reader perception.

An improvement in response can be obtained by synchronized use of direct marketing tools. For example, highlighting a phone number can increase the rate of response from 10 to 30 per cent. The value of advertisements and press-inserts depends above all on the content and the form of advertisements and on the quality of the marketing methods which they express (Toolbox 16.2).

TOOLBOX 16.2

THE ACHIEVEMENT OF DIRECT MARKETING ADVERTISING

The aim of the ad in direct marketing is to make the customer or prospective client react as quickly as possible. Before completing the act of purchase by signing the order form, the customer follows a process of learning which can be designated simply with expressions such as "AIDA" (Attention, Interest, Desire, Action) or more explicitly according to the hierarchy of the effects of communication: Exposure, Attention, Understanding, Attitude, Behaviour. This theoretical process tends to guide the customer towards one of the following acts: to cut out, write, "address" or phone.

To facilitate the completion of the process, some recommendations can be made.

- clear, realistic presentation of the product or service;
- simplicity of the offer and its benefits which should be immediately understood;
- overview of the product or service in term of function and benefit;
- clarity, colour contrast;
- creation of breaks and gaps in the presentation corresponding to different ideas in order to avoid dullness, for example, by using differently placed words or a change of typeface;
- repetition of arguments;
- incentive to purchase such as promotion, premiums, competitions;
- response facility in terms of location of the coupon, clarity of instructions or payment conditions.

Mail shots

Mail shots are the most basic of direct marketing media. Their role remains very important and their conception follows precise rules.

A direct marketing medium par excellence, intimately linked to "mail-order selling", mail shots are characterized, besides their personalized aspect, by flexibility of use. They generally comprise from five to six basic elements:

1. the envelope in which they are inserted,
2. a letter,
3. a leaflet,
4. an order form,
5. a reply envelope,
6. various commercial documents.

Their main objective is to attract an order. But they can also respond to other motives. For example, they are used "to qualify" prospective clients, to prepare the work of the sales force and to serve as a means of re-launching or starting up a more extended process of communication.

The effectiveness of this medium depends first and foremost on the availability of adequate data. It is desirable that these data should be personal and contain reliable information about the first name, surname and addresses of potential customers. The offers only work well if they are really personalized. Personalization will make the prospective client remember the address and tone of the mail shot employed.

Mail shots have many advantages:

- First of all, they can be applied to numerous situations and be combined with other forms of communication.
- Their effectiveness can be accurately evaluated: most replies to mail shots occur within the three weeks following their dispatch. However, in the B to B sector, their "life expectancy" can be much longer.
- They contribute to the augmentation of company data: an analysis of the reply rate in terms of nature, origin or spacing out over a period helps to complete the company's "customer" database.
- Finally, mail shots provide an excellent means of testing offers at several levels: the customer target segment can be verified and refined, the form can be improved at each dispatching and the content can be modified (Toolbox 16.3).

TOOLBOX 16.3

THE CONCEPTION OF A MAIL SHOT

There are many constituents of a mail shot. At least, there is an envelope, gatefold, order form with reply coupon, a letter or a discount voucher. Each document must be created according to a certain number of principles. However, all mail shots have a relatively simple purpose: to make the customers react, that is, to lead them to open, read, fill in, write a cheque or to indicate their credit card number and return. Each document plays a precise role in this process. For example, the envelope should cause the addressee to open it at all costs. Therefore, before opening it, the addressee must be able to discern the contents of the message or at least must be intrigued. This effect can be obtained by respecting the following four rules:

1 The correct personalization of the address. A badly spelt name discredits an offer.[i]
2 A clear indication of the name and the address of the sender. This is indispensable in order to benefit from special postal rates.
3 Mention on the envelope of precise and selective incentives, relative to the offer contained in the message such as "Pay less taxes!" , "Do you really like flowers?".
4 Use of elements distancing oneself from rival mail shots either intriguing or tempting the addressee (teasing).

The processes of envelope printing offer wide possibilities of giving them a character suited to target customer expectations. For example, envelopes may take official, artistic, serious or unexpected aspects. Manual franking, although expensive, can strengthen the impact of a mail shot by giving it a less commercial and more personalized aspect. At this level, the use of a sorter is often useful because this person can pool dispatching and control postal rules as well as offering numerous other services such as sealing, labelling, adding protective film, printing and laser publishing.

The objectives of the letter are to present the offer, allow memorization and especially to make customers act or obtain a reply. Rules concerning the development of direct selling copy are numerous and often controversial. They correspond to the classic selling method: to minimize the perceived risk for the prospective customer (physical, financial, psychological and social) and to maximize expected satisfaction.

The act of distance purchasing presupposes that this principle be scrupulously respected and sustained by a rigorous demonstration by means of concrete facts which the target customer cares about. This meets the expectations of two important principles of direct communication: attraction and demonstration.

The editing of a letter requires detailed knowledge of the targeted customers, both their expectations and their interests, as well as in the vocabulary used (especially if it is technical). The content of a letter is judged according its first paragraph. The power of persuasion of the first argument must arouse interest. In the same way, it is advisable to underline certain elements of the text, to highlight certain key paragraphs, and to use a postscript "head or end of page objective". Tests have shown that this is read in the majority of cases, sometimes even before the body of the text.

The production of such a document again uses basic principles of written communication such as clarity, simplicity, conciseness and logic but differs in some respects from classic letters, as the following analysis shows (Exhibit A).

[i] Some professionals prefer not to add indications on the envelope so as not to give it an overly commercial character. This obliges the addressee to open it in order to discover the contents. So we can see that different approaches exist.

Exhibit A How to write a good letter

Rule	Illustration
Prepare your letter	"You know exactly what you have to say, how you are going to say it and in what order"
Make provision for a slogan	"Sum up in a few words the most important aspects of your promise and of the offer
Carefully choose your first paragraph	"Give preference to your first offer"
Develop all your arguments	"Develop absolutely all the advantages of the product or services you are offering"
Give proof	"Look for all the necessary means of reassuring your reader concerning the authenticity of arguments"
Look for possible restraints	"Anticipate questions and give the correct response"
Edit your text	"It is always possible to cut and condense without losing key ideas"
Be personal	"Give the reader the idea of familiarity, that you are aware of his taste, problems, aspirations and so on"
Give your page an interesting look	"Make provisions for tabs, use italics and annotation margins"
Use simple words	"Have your letter read by a 12-year-old child. Replace what he or she does not understand"
Use short sentences	"The ideal is to have one idea per sentence"
Put keywords at the ends of sentences.	"The best way of highlighting a word is to place it at the end of a sentence"
Use link words between paragraphs	"This is how; That is why. In addition. And, of course. In fact. But, above all. Better still"
Be enthusiastic	"You should be really pleased with the product or the service that is offered"
Give the signatory personality	"Give the signatory an image of honesty, credibility and likeability"
Finish your letter with the same promise as at the beginning	"End your letter by repeating the promise" (key idea at the beginning)
Insist on a prompt reply	"Encourage the reader to react quickly" (time limit, stock limit, additional gift etc)
Carefully choose the signatory	"As a rule, the highest position in the company"
Be objective	"Head or end of page objective, often read first"

Phone

Direct marketing by telephone is very different from the use of advertisements or mail shots. The difference is so marked that telephone marketing is sometimes wrongly considered as a form of marketing in its own right.

At first, many companies used the telephone only to reduce the cost of making field sales visits. In several companies, however, the change brought about by the use of the telephone has called many aspects of its functioning into question, such as commercial organization, communication strategy, information and training systems.

Without sufficient preparation, the use of the telephone creates many problems.

The media discussed above provoked the customer to react. This reaction could only be estimated in terms of probability. The telephone is a medium which is directly interactive. The exchange which the other media attempt to create through reductions or reply coupons is established from first contact. This immediate interaction of the telephone explains its strong relevance to direct marketing. A rapid means for the creation of a contact between the company and its potential customers, the telephone has other advantages also: it is flexible. A campaign can be intensified or cut back at will. It is selective, which is particularly useful in the industrial environment where specific individuals in an organization need to be addressed. In addition, the telephone is complementary to other media which is important for re-launch, preparation or testing purposes. And it is highly controllable. It is a testing tool par excellence. It is consequently well adapted to prospecting – that is, the quest for new customers – and to following-up current customers which can be standardized and intensified by the use of phone.

However, three essential limits can reduce the usefulness of telephone calls: the technical difficulties of putting them into operation, the anonymity of the caller and especially the lack of control over a phone conversation due to insufficient training of sales people in this particular technique.

It is not sufficient to have a connection and a receiver to make this tool into an integrated medium of communication and sales management. Numerous conditions must be fulfilled. The first condition is to analyse the relationship of the organization with its customers, suppliers, service providers, intermediaries and other important stakeholders and the traffic and use of information related those stakeholders within the company. This aspect is fundamental, even though it may be necessary to adapt the degree of formality of this research to each type of company. The most important results will judiciously determine the management of phone calls made and received by the company. Responsibility, training, negotiation, accompanying documents, file creation and management depend on the quality and quantity of contacts with stakeholders as well as internal information needs. It is nevertheless frequently the case that the elementary rules of management for this medium are not handled rigorously. So, it is better, for example, not to give a phone number to customers if no procedure for the management of calls has been defined and if these are met with negative or delaying replies of the type: "Hold on for a few minutes, we don't know where he is, maybe you could call back later."

Both in the making and in the receiving of calls, stakeholders expect to have competent communication partners. Therefore, these people have to be available and informed. Besides, when the telephone is used before or after an on-site visit, the phone message must be consistent with the overall perception which one intends to give the stakeholder. This requires the integration of the "telephone" medium into the mix of the company. The content of the call in terms of information, service or arguments as well as its form in terms of voice, tone or presentation need to be consistent with all the other contact points between the organization and its stakeholders. To this end, it is necessary that phone call be prepared and administered according to tested techniques.

For this reason and also to facilitate large-scale operations, for example "general public" operations necessitating the use of a switchboard of sufficient volume, telemarketers or sellers and specialized firms offer advantages of professionalism. Such call centre companies specialize in making, handling, receiving and analysing calls for their organizational customers.

When the use of the telephone as a medium becomes very important and frequent, the integration of a specialized service to administer calls can be justified (improved consistency with the entire set of company commercial actions). This decision depends on the size and activity of the company coupled with the role this direct marketing tool will play.

The phone can also be used by the customers to complain. Customer complaints must be dealt with rigorously because it is known that an adequate reply is a source of customer satisfaction and increases their loyalty. The handling of complaints is one of the most important aspects of CRM. Today, in each company using CRM programmes such as the banks, insurances, telecoms, distribution, car rental firms, airway companies and also many industrial companies such as data processing companies (Dell, Compaq, IBM or Apple), capital or semi-finished goods, a call centre has been installed to help customers and reply to their complaints.

Good use of the telephone for direct marketing purposes requires a certain amount of training on both sides, personnel as well as stakeholders of the organization. Customers and other stakeholders need to be familiarized with this new form of communication which is often a break with habit; on the other hand, the sales force, procurement people, market researchers, service technicians or complaint handling personnel must be trained in the use of the phone. The introduction of this medium is, therefore, often progressive because of the time necessary to acquire the specific know-how required.

By means of the telephone more than anywhere else, the power of negotiation and the force of negotiation occurs through perfect mastery of the voice, articulation and language which are the main elements of identification for the correspondents: intonation and words are substituted for gestures. According to specialists, "everything can be heard on the telephone: the smile, good humour, credibility and so on".

Although the basic principles of phone negotiation are similar to those of classic negotiation, some important differences remain: the meaning of certain words can be cumbersome and the simplicity and logic of the argument must be evident. It is not possible, as in the case of the written word, to go back on what has been said. Therefore, the basic principles of direct marketing can be found in phone negotiations: to inform the partner precisely, to furnish proof and arguments, for example, concerning cost, delays or references, to insist on the advantages to be had from the offer. To establish a confident atmosphere is often the key to success in negotiation. In the absence of tangible evidence concerning the reality of the proposed offers, there is a risk of not being able to convince communication partners. When decisions cannot be made immediately, a frequent occurrence in organizational buying, the offer must be strengthened by trying to reassure the receiver. To compensate for the drawbacks of the telephone, notably the impossibility to visualize and confirm the quality of the offer, it is wise to rely on other direct marketing media. Documentation may be sent as well as samples. Free trials or visits to reference sites may be offered. It is to this end that vehicles offered recently through IT (the Internet in particular) are often used.

Television and teleshopping

Television can be used in many ways in direct marketing:

- advertisements in the form of direct marketing and inviting the viewer to get information or make an order either by writing to a given address, phoning a telephone number or contacting the company by fax, or the Internet;
- teleshopping programmes where the products presented are offered to the viewers in an off-line mode. That is spectators, having no particular needs, watch the programme and react only when interested;
- teleshopping programmes chosen by viewers according to their particular requirements thanks to cable and satellite television, allowing them to interact with the provider and thus to choose from the various offerings.

The development of teleshopping is very inconsistent across Europe. It is generally much less significant than in the United States. It reaches wider (less specific) customer segments such as older people or the young, and concerns certain types of products. They are mostly unusual with strong added value, such as in the areas of keeping in shape, health, food supplements, luxury goods, fancy goods or do-it-yourself.

Other IT media

Advertising on the Internet and Electronic Business

Multimedia technology allows for the combined use of text, image and sound. Direct marketing uses a number of these tools: the CDROM and ICD (Interactive Compact Disc), fax, electronic mail and the Internet. Overall, these different means of electronic business should develop considerably, in particular in the industrial goods sector. Many companies such as Dell or Amazon.com have found a means of being continuously present on foreign markets, presenting their offers to professional and\or individual buyers and doing business with them.

The integration of multimedia within marketing strategy seems inevitable and will favour the practice of electronic business.

Advertising via the new electronic media

There are several approaches to on-line advertising: the banner and the "micro-site", and "rich media" which include a wide variety of formats (see glossary in Toolbox 16.4).

The banner

The banner constitutes the great majority of advertisements which can be viewed today. It continues the idea of the press insertion or display, in the sense that it appears according to the Internet user's navigation. It is a rectangular frame containing an image, generally in .gif or .jpg format, and text displayed at a given place on an HTML page. There can be up to 90 possible banner dimensions. Standard dimensions have been defined by the IAB (International Advertising Bureau).

The aim of banners is to reach the customer target group in order to deliver the message and to be clicked on to create interaction. Their main objectives are to build up awareness and to generate contacts.

Web banners have the following characteristics:

- They are placed on a site in return for a fee or other equivalent such as the sale of space or a partnership.
- They affect Internet users visiting the editorial site.
- They are useful to the Internet users and their repeated use is a means of ensuring their effectiveness.
- They can change because it is possible to modify the message or the graphics of the banner, or have its display assessed.
- They are interactive and other sites can be visited just by clicking.
- They are all the more effective when they are situated on well-targeted vehicles with a strong audience. In this respect the classic media-planning rules in advertising can be applied.

The banner can also exist in the form of a "micro-site". In this case, the banner is no longer a link to the advertiser's site, it becomes instead a separate site. The user does not leave the site they are visiting for that of the advertiser.

TOOLBOX 16.4

GLOSSARY FOR INTERNET ADVERTISING

IP address: Address allocated to all computers connected to the Internet. A computer can have a different address for each connection.

Clicks (number of) (ad clicks): Number of times a banner or an advertising object has been clicked on, measured from the page of origin.

Clickthroughs (number of): Number of registered effective clicks, that is the number of clicks that brought about the complete downloading of the destination page. Remark: It is sometimes used wrongly in place of the click.

Cookie: Small file, following a page use, placed on the user's hard disk by the site server. It allows for the collection of data concerning user navigation behaviour. The user can refuse the installation of cookies on his disc or eliminate them after consulting the site.

Cost per thousand pages with viewed advertising:

Cost of buying advertising space on a site, based on 1000 pages containing advertising which have been viewed. This indicator estimates and compares the advertising rates of the various sites according to the number of pages containing advertising which have been viewed. It has become the reference indicator for the marketing of the advertising site. (Rate of clicks = Number of clicks/number of exposures).

Duration of consultation by visit: The sum of the duration of the consultation of each of the pages comprising a visit. Two notions should be distinguished: time taken to transmit the desired page and time chosen to consult the page.

Exposures (number of) (ad impression): Number of times an advertising object is totally downloaded to the user computer.

Hits (number of): Number of times various files are referred to which constitute a page, or more often: one or several HTML files, one or several text files, one or several image files, one or several sound or video files. This indicator, useful from a technical point of view, is not relevant from a marketing point of view, and on no account constitutes an audience indicator.

Hosts (number of): Number of machines which are connected to a site. Several users may use the same machine.

Internet user: Anybody who has used at least one Internet function (Web, FTP, chat, forum, mail) over a defined period.

Logs: Information appropriate to the administration of servers and which registers the number and characteristics of administered hits. The logs are recorded in four types of files: transfer log files; error log files; repository log files; agent log files.

Memory cache: Disk space allocated to the navigator (browser), and allowing them to fulfil, on the user computer and without other settings, the same role as a proxy server. The effects are identical to those of the proxies: absence of audience measurement by the principal site, without a particular procedure.

Geographic origin of consultations: Not always possible to determine. Usually, when they are available, the IP user address or additional procedures (data bases, language of the navigator) are used. Electronic addresses with the ending ".com" do not correspond to a guaranteed geographic origin.

Pages visited with advertising (PAP) (number of): Visited Pages, on which appear one or several advertisements (banner or advertising objects, icons). The counting of the viewed pages, when it is carried out exclusively on site, gives the real number of pages viewed with advertising.

Page: Multimedia document consisting of files delivered by one or several servers, and presented in the browser window of the user. Files are laid out within one or several frame(s) (visual subdivision of the page). The loading of a new file within one or several frame(s), following user action, is considered as a change of page.

Viewed pages (number of): Number of times a page is totally downloaded on the user machine. We distinguish online from offline pages viewed. Pages viewed online correspond to pages originating directly from the main server (site) without intermediate buffering. They are counted at the server level. Pages viewed offline come from memory cache or proxy servers. They are viewed by the users but are not counted in the site log files.

Pages viewed per visit (number of): Average number of pages viewed per visit on a site and over a defined period.

Ad request: During an editorial page request, recourse to all the advertising objects intended for this page.

Page request: Action of the Internet user aiming to view a page on their computer.

Server: Material and software solution used to exploit online services by ensuring data access.

Ad Server or Banner Server: Campaign management software (from programming of advertising objects to online statistical follow-up). This management is carried out independently from that of the editorial pages. The ad server allows for the dynamic insertion of advertising objects (at present mostly banners or advertising bands) in prescribed spaces on the editorial pages. It also offers customer-targeting possibilities.

Proxy server: Server relay allowing a supplier or an access intermediary to store the most frequently requested Web sites.

Session user: Interval of uninterrupted time between the moment the user begins and terminates an online consultation with their browser. Several visits to different sites can correspond to a unique session.

Site or Web site: Technically speaking, the set of addresses used to locate files (or URLs=Uniform Resource Locators), gathered together under the same domain name. Concerning marketing, it is the set of URLs for which the publisher exercises their content responsibility. This URL can be localized on one or several sites, in the technical sense of the term. (Example: a press site containing two technical sites: one concerning the publisher and an archive site concerning a person receiving benefits. The user does not notice that they are changing sites – other than in the domain name.)

Visit: Set of pages viewed on the same site during the same session. Current practice considers that an absence

of consultation of new pages on this site exceeding 30 minutes terminates the visit.

Visitors: Individuals who consult the same site over a defined period. The total number of visitors takes into account the duplication of the number of visits. Without individual identification, it is at present almost impossible to define the visitor technically.

The banner is directly linked with a database which handles information given by the visitor. The Internet user can enter an e-mail address to get information about a product or take some other action without leaving the visited site.

"Banner exchange" is a technique of exchange between two sites which agree to inter-advertise for purposes of attracting prospective customers. The effectiveness of each site depends on how well matched the two linked sites are. Several banner-exchange networks such as "Link Exchange" are currently in operation.

"Rich media"

The concept of "rich media" constitutes a generic expression which corresponds to many types of advertising.

Interactive banners containing a hypertext link to another site can be animated, integrating audio and video sequences into the message. Some banners have a limited life expectancy. They disappear from the screen after a certain lapse of time.

Today different zones can contain things such as data fields, pop-up menus, radio buttons or checkboxes. Barnes and Noble have used this technology to create boxes which enable one to search the catalogue. For example, by typing "Shakespeare", Internet users will be taken directly to the corresponding list of works by the author.

"E-mail advertisements" are boxes which allow the Internet user to enter an electronic address and automatically receive information by mail.

Most of the newer technology can be integrated into a zone by coupling several different effects (sound, video) without affecting download time:

- Animated demonstration; for example, a banner for an automobile site where the Internet user can select the model, colour, accessories, shape of bumper and so on.
- Updated zone: updated in real time. For example, this kind of zone can reflect the progress of a football or tennis match.
- Printing zones: the Internet user can print out a commercial document detailing the characteristics of the product listed.
- Game zones: certain advertisers have developed banners containing interactive games.

- Extendable bands: the principle is to combine the lightness (cluttering and display speed) of a classic banner with the content of a micro-site. The initial banner is displayed for a short time and invites the Internet user to obtain further information by clicking a "more info" button. When the Internet user activates this button, the size of the band increases and can cover most of the page. Internet users can repeat the operation until they get to a purchase form. This type of technology permits the creation of real marketable banners.
- Double window (pop-up window): this technique displays a supplementary window which appears on top of the page visited by the Internet user. The double window offers the advantage of transferring the user to a site while keeping the original site open.

Direct mail

D-mail (or express-mail) consists of sending mail ads in the form of text messages directly to an Internet user, a customer, prospective client or partner through his mailbox. There are several options such as:

- Private mailing-lists offer Internet users the possibility of registering of their own free will, in order to receive information from an advertiser directly to their inbox.
- "Mailbox" services encourage Internet users to subscribe to their mail services in order to obtain advantages in the form of samples, special offers, services, free products or previews.

Files established in such a way can be bought or rented by companies.

The advantages offered by d-mails are the following:

- Investment is low compared to classic mailing. Transmission and production costs per unit are very low, and reproduction costs are nonexistent.
- The ad can be perfectly customer targeted.
- The sending of mail is immediate and without spatial constraint other than the understanding of the languages in which they are written.

- The level of response can be superior to that of paper mailing because the same channel is used to receive the message and to respond. It can achieve better results than classic mailing when it is well targeted.
- Responding is simple. It can be immediate without the constraint of posting, looking for an address or supplementary costs.
- Efficiency can be easily measured and d-mail is one of the most effective advertising methods on the Internet. Twelve to eighteen per cent response levels are commonplace!

On the other hand, "d-mail" can have another form: the non-customer–targeted bulk mail, sent from databases bought from a list collector. This d-mail is called "bulk mail", "spamming" or simply "spam". This inexpensive practice is intrusive and can be blocked by Internet users. An advertiser who pollutes the letterboxes of Internet users risks a deterioration of their image. Some software packages allow Internet users to counteract spam (Cybersitter, AntiSpam, Dead letter, E-mail remover or again Spam Eater).

Mail shots would seem therefore to be a tool for the development of user loyalty. To be effective, they should be careful by planned:

- To be accepted by the people to whom they are addressed, by being customer targeted or by having their advance agreement. Personalization facilitates acceptance by the receiver but does not guarantee it.
- To remove people from the list if they wish to leave.
- To contain a real incentive.
- Not to be repetitive: to have short life expectancy.

Push media

The push technique, also known as "broadcasting" or "web casting", "pushes" information towards the consumer. The consumer thus receives information directly without having sought it. It is important that this information be customer targeted and personalized. Frequently, the targeted persons have declared their willingness to receive the type of information which is sent to them by the company. Each time new information appears, it is automatically transferred to the Internet user's mailbox.

Newsgroups and forums

"Newsgroups" are "free" spaces for communication between Internet users who meet online to discuss a particular subject. The company can create its own newsgroup or "forum" with regard to its products, services it offers or other subjects more or less connected to its activity, such as sponsored events, information on the newsgroup theme. A sporting brand, for example, may give information to the consumer on their chosen sport. It

is important therefore that these newsgroups and forums be controlled by a moderator in order to avoid loss of control. This form of customer communication requires an efficient and effective follow-up and results are not guaranteed. That is why certain firms prefer not to use it.

"Pay-per-sale"

There are banners or hyper-links placed on a commercial site which take the visitor directly to the site of the advertiser when the Internet user clicks on the link or banner. If this results in a sale, the banner owner pays a commission to the site of origin. This mechanism can work well if the site of origin is well suited to the customer target, highly frequented and if the "pay per sale" offer acts as an incentive. These conditions are difficult to fulfil.

Distribution lists

Distribution lists allow Internet users to exchange messages with each other after registering on a list which draws up an inventory of all emails. These lists can be limited or reserved to certain Internet users according to criteria established by the list initiator. The company can create its own distribution list to promote its products or services as well as its activity. It is also advisable to make provisions for a moderator. A company can also negotiate in order to place the offer on an existing list. It is important that the form of this offer be understood as a real opportunity by those listed so that it is not seen as intrusive.

Interpage advertising

Interpage advertising is an advertising slot inserted between the entrance to a site and full access to its content. It allows advertisers to maximize use of the Internet user's memory about a product, brand or site address through maximum exposure. The advertisement occupies the full screen or window for a few seconds. This advertising slot can be animated and have sound and is imposed on the Internet user. It cannot be clicked on. Thus, it comprises pure exposure aimed at awareness and memorization. The user cannot "quit" this advertisement and is, of necessity, exposed to it. A variant is the flying ad which moves across the screen to catch the Internet user's attention. A good example is Homer Simpson running after a doughnut on the home page of an important American press site.

Page backgrounds

The background of an HTML page can also serve as an advertisement for a company or a brand. For example, Disney used it for the launch of the film "The 101 Dalmatians" by presenting information concerning back-up sites on a white background spotted with black to give a "Dalmatian" impression. The background is not click-able. It is thus primarily a means for companies to obtain reputation and memorization of a product or an event.

Advertising effectiveness on the Internet

The effectiveness of communicating with potential customers in the Internet may be controlled in various ways. The marketer may, for example, register the number of times a Web site has been consulted, the number of "clicks" on an advertising banner, the time spent on a site or the effectiveness of the communication in terms of purchase and sales. Some companies specialize in the analysis of connections and marketing of commercial Web servers. Others have tried to adapt the sample group technique to Web use by installing software or a sort of black box, on user hard disks to learn about their mode of Internet use. For the purpose of measuring communication effectiveness, three types of indicators can be distinguished.

Indicators of editorial audience

Such indicators may be the number of online pages visited, the number of offline pages visited, visits, the number of visitors, the number of pages viewed per visit, the geographic origin of visits (pinpointed by the nationality corresponding to the electronic address of the user or by identification of the access provider), the duration of each visit.

Indicators of advertising audience

Such indicators may be the number of on-site pages visited containing advertisements, the cost per 1000 pages with advertising visited online, which is the cost of buying advertising space on a principal site based on 1000 pages with advertising visited online. This indicator allows one to estimate and to compare the advertising rates of the various sites according to the number of pages with advertising visited.

Indicators of advertising efficiency

Such indicators may be the number of clicks, the number of pages with advertising and the rate of clicks. The measures known as "site centric" take into account visits to sites, such as the number of hits or visited pages, by means of log files, cookies, markers (see glossary in Toolbox 16.4). "User centric" or "consumer centric" sample groups are based on Internet user samples and allow one to distinguish the number of visits per site from the number of Internet users. They can contain more complete information on Internet users but pose problems for measuring how often a site is visited. As there are numerous sites in existence, a very large number of sample groups would be needed to work out how often less consulted sites are visited (Figure 16.10).

The audience measuring service of Nielsen/ NetRatings collects real-time data coming from more than 178,000 Internet users in the world. The sample in the United States comprises 57,000 individuals who have Internet access from their place of residence and 8000 from their workplace. Some 100,000 individuals all over the world will soon join the current panel members. These panels represent the largest Internet media-measuring sample in the world. Just like the TV Mediamat panel, these panel members are given points which allow them to choose gifts from a catalogue.

Nielsen/NetRatings use a technology capable of measuring simultaneously Internet use and the associated advertising exposure. This is done using a software installation, a sort of black box at the panel member home.

Site audience is expressed by the number of visitors (or cumulative audience) and coverage. Repeated data as well as audience progress are also supplied. By adding other tools (banner tracks), e-Ratings give 'advertising banner click' data and record the clicks of the panel members. The rate of clicks can thus be analyzed according to socio-demographic criteria.

Figure 16.10   An example of audience measurement

The integration of electronic communication in the marketing strategies of companies

Several remarks can be made concerning the integration of electronic communication in the marketing strategies of companies:

- Just like the use of other media, the use of a network of electronic communication is not enough to ensure the success of a business. The use of information technology must be integrated into the marketing strategy. Methods of integration still remain widely underestimated and provide fertile ground for research.
- In the same way, the marketing-mix of a business organization is profoundly modified by the use of electronic communication media. The services offered are different. New service possibilities such as training or discussion forums arise. Prices may be differentiated, new forms of advertising can be used and the distribution of information is changed, for example, by the options of downloading new software packages or updates destined for the customers. At this level also, advertising and promotional techniques are subjected to numerous tests and experiments.

Electronic business

Electronic business is for the moment only in its infancy (Tables 16.10 and 16.11). But this type of business will internationalize direct marketing (Figure 16.11); (Toolbox 16.4). This tendency is particularly obvious in the B to B sector. But it is also developing where individual customers are concerned – households equipped with computer and IT capabilities. The dismantling of commercial and legislative barriers as well as the fast-growing distribution of IT capabilities should ensure progressive but constant development in this type of business and create new marketing practices most of which have still to be invented.

Table 16.10 Internet/Online expenditure, € million

	1993	1994	1995	1996	1997	1998	1999	2000
Austria	–	–	4	–	–	–	–	–
Belgium	–	–	–	–	–	–	–	–
Czech Republic	–	–	–	–	–	1	5	13
Finland	–	–	–	–	–	–	1	1
France	–	–	–	–	6	12	64	144
Germany	169	205	614	1,023	1,278	1,227	1,329	1,227
Hungary	–	–	–	–	–	–	2	6
Italy	–	–	–	–	–	–	29	140
Netherlands	–	–	–	–	–	7	20	39
Slovak Republic	–	–	–	–	–	–	1	2
Spain	–	–	–	7	12	20	72	–
Sweden	–	–	–	–	–	–	56	123
UK	–	58	60	77	131	185	237	260
Total	**169**	**263**	**678**	**1,107**	**1,428**	**1,454**	**1,822**	**1,967**

Source: FEDMA (Federation of European Direct Marketing) "Survey on Direct and Interactive Marketing Activities in Europe", 2001.

Notes: No information is available for other countries. German data includes *bildschirmtext*, and methods of calculation changed in 2000.
Sources: DDV, AIDIM, DMSA, FECEMD, DMA UK, IAB.
Although the Internet is now a reasonably well-established medium in Europe, measurement of internet DM is still variable, and only 11 of this survey's participants were able to provide figures. These data are distorted by variations in definitions and monitoring, most noticeably the inclusion of *Bildschirmtext* in German figures, a form of videotext which accounts for most of this figure. Other estimates put the German market much lower (for example, the IAB figure is € 93.8 million, a 76 per cent rise on the previous year), and the UK is in fact the largest Internet market amongst these countries.

Despite these methodological problems, it is clear from these figures that the Internet is still a fast-growing sector, particularly in smaller countries. All of this year's new participants saw at least a 50 per cent growth in Internet spend (Czech Republic grew from € 0.7 million to € 1.4 million) as did Belgium, Finland, France, Italy and Sweden (and probably Germany). The more mature markets – most obviously the UK – saw slower growth. Overall, growth in countries where both 1999 and 2000 figures are available was around 12 per cent.

Table 16.11 European Online Retail Revenue by Country, 2000–2006 (estimate)

Country	Euro (million)						
	2000	2001	2002	2003	2004	2005	2006
Germany	2,376	4,865	9,245	15,320	23,785	33,838	44,547
UK	3,158	6,353	11,069	16,236	22,069	29,012	38,995
France	614	1,460	2,935	5,036	7,932	11,379	15,445
Italy	272	658	1,510	2,939	5,085	7,884	11,164
Switzerland	230	581	1,223	2,119	3,431	4,973	6,392
Sweden	359	697	1,244	2,055	3,130	4,447	5,928
Spain	124	285	666	1,277	2,306	3,709	5,401
Netherlands	456	825	1,372	2,088	3,024	4,096	5,329
Denmark	164	341	657	1,131	1,758	2,547	3,517
Belgium	118	331	652	1,103	1,755	2,548	3,490
Austria	180	356	625	1,030	1,630	2,390	3,365

Table 16.11   (Continued)

Norway	178	315	619	1,046	1,623	2,344	3,259
Finland	126	228	393	641	982	1,395	1,901
Portugal	17	44	115	239	448	756	1,157
Ireland	26	63	144	284	494	770	1,095
Greece	8	17	51	125	262	476	772
Luxembourg	7	15	31	55	89	132	188
Total	**8,413**	**17,435**	**32,547**	**52,723**	**79,803**	**112,695**	**151,982**

Source: Forrester Research.

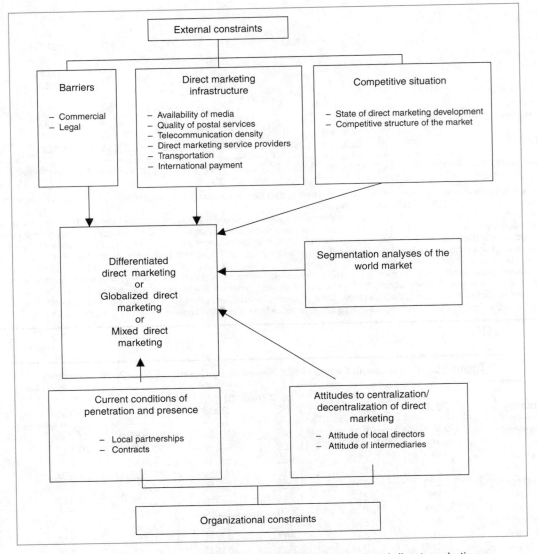

Figure 16.11   Schema guidelines for choices in international direct marketing

SUMMARY

This chapter has discussed the role and nature of direct marketing. This not only amounts to techniques of communication or promotion at a distance but also constitutes a global, personalized and interactive approach to customer relationships including market research, joint product innovation and selling. It is a modern approach to markets which involves the exploitation of new information and telecommunications technology. All of the marketing processes of an organization are affected by direct marketing: from the determination and selection of which markets to serve, to the creation and generation of value for stakeholders.

The increasing desire for the personalization of offers to consumers and ever more intense competition in markets have favoured the emergence and extension of this type of marketing which puts customer relationships first. The management of customer relationships mobilizes multiple approaches of information technology and communication in order to develop customer loyalty. Effective and efficient direct marketing depends on the creation and exploitation of commercial databases listing information about the identity and the behaviour of customers. The development of such databases requires sound technological and business know-how. The handling of data results in a multitude of operations for the purpose of prospecting potential customers and developing their loyalty.

Communication and promotion in direct marketing can be carried out using classic media such as press, television or radio or by resorting to means of communication such as the phone, mail shots, TV ads or the Internet. We are witnessing a very important development of direct marketing action. Its use is becoming increasingly attached to the framework of a real strategy of personalization and development of customer loyalty which affects all the variables of the marketing-mix and justifies the title of CRM, customer relationship management.

Notes and references

1. It is very difficult to measure the real development of direct marketing. Data from institutes whose objective is to measure the "above the line" media expenditures show a major development in "below the line" media which includes expenditures effected outside classic media vehicles (thus, in part, expenditure effected on specific direct marketing vehicles (telephone, mail shots etc.) but this is a very restricted concept of direct marketing.

2. E. Gummesson, "The New Marketing – Developing Long Term Interactive Relationships", *Long Range Planning*, 20, 4, 10–20, 1987.

3. F.R. Dwyer, P.H. Schurr and S. Oh, "Developing Buyer-Seller Relationships", *Journal of Marketing*, 61, 2, 11–27, 1987.

4. D. Iaccobucci, *Networks in Marketing*, London, Sage Publications, 1996.

5. E. Ronan, *Integrated Direct Marketing*, New York, McGraw-Hill, 1988; E.L. Nash, *Direct marketing: Strategy, Planning, Execution*, New York, McGraw-Hill, 1986. P.L. Dubois and P. Nicholson, *Le Marketing direct intégré*, Paris, Chotard et Associés Éditeurs, 1987.

6. We cannot deal here with the legal problems linked to the setting up of an ever more rich and complete consumer database. The law in this domain has greatly evolved in Europe taking into account worries over consumer liberty. Appendix 1 takes up again some fundamental guiding principles concerning the dispositions present in the laws of EC countries.

7. See M. Filser, "Méthodologie d'élaboration d'une typologie de clientèle en marketing direct", *Revue Française du Marketing*, 126, 57–66, 1990.

8. P. Desmet, "Comparaison de la prédictivité d'un réseau de neurones à rétropropagation avec celle des méthodes de régression linéaire, logistique et AID, pour le calcul des scores en marketing direct", *Recherche et Applications Marketing*, 11, 2, 17–29, 1996. A. Ainslie and X. Drèze, 'Le datamining et l'alternative modèles classiques-réseaux neuronaux', *Décisions Marketing*, 7, janvier-avril, 77–86, 1996.

9. It is not possible to deal with the application of the neural networks to direct marketing here, as it has not been sufficiently developed yet.

10. A sweepstake is a lottery where the draw has taken place before communication to the public (pre-draw): the winning numbers have been drawn beforehand. It only requires the entry form to be sent in to discover what has been won. This type of lottery cannot be accompanied by a purchase obligation.

11. However, some sectors (particularly the press) still show great interest in it in order to create customer loyalty and to win over new clients.

12. Split-run methods and, more generally, pre and post testing have already been dealt with in the chapter on "Advertising". They can be adapted to direct marketing messages.

13. Adapted from G. François, "Prévisions et animation commerciale dans la vente par correspondance", *Revue Française du Marketing*, 126, 67–79, 1990.

14. It is impossible to analyze here all the direct media such as catalogues, CDs, diskettes, cooperative-mailings (grouped mail shots) and so on.

Appendix 16.1

MAIN LEGAL PRINCIPLES IN EUROPEAN LEGISLATIONS

Under the aegis of the European community, the legislation of different European countries concerning the establishment and the use of data files is becoming more uniform.

Several legal principles are prominent in this uniformity:

- To ensure the protection of privacy and personal or public freedom:
  For example, it is advisable to make sure that information used in the automated treatments is adequate, relevant and not excessive with regard to the ends for which they are registered. Information relative to racial origins, political, philosophical or religious beliefs, trade-union membership, health, sexual habits of individuals, malpractice and condemnations should not appear in reports, except in statutory cases which are strictly restrictive in this respect.
- To protect one's identity:
  The identification of the individual by a code common to different files, notably to those of the administration, could facilitate uniformity and interconnection. It is important to survey and strictly limit use and interconnection between administrative and private data. It is a question of protecting the individual from threats on privacy, reproduction of files and the numerous possibilities of data processing and telecommunications.
- To guarantee peoples' right to data access and the right to preliminary information:
  Consumers have the right to information held by the administration or private companies about themselves.

Faced with the computer which can record, store, gather and diffuse information, individuals must be able to protect their private life from administrative controls, economic interests and motives for medical or sociological research. The right to access gives each person the ability to know about the existence or not of personal data in an automated or manual file and, if they wish so, to have it changed. The exercise of this right allows individuals to control the correctness of data stored on their account and, if necessary, to rectify or erase it.

Control by individuals of the data which concern them presupposes on their part awareness of the file content in which it is listed. This right to preliminary information conditions the exercise of other rights such as the right to access or to oppose. It is demonstrated by:

- an obligation to inform when data is collected. During the collection of subject data, the person must be informed about the compulsory or optional character of answers, the consequences of not answering, the addressees of information as well as the existence of a right to access.
- the transparency of automated handling.
- To benefit from the right to oversight: the individual must be able to benefit from a right to oversight by a time limit for conservation of name-specific data stored in computer memory in order to avoid definitive labelling of individuals. This right to oversight is essential for the most dependent and most vulnerable individuals: children, patients, job seekers, criminals who have served their sentences and so on.
- To be able to exercise a right to opposition and rectification: everybody can decide for themselves on the use of personal data and thus have the possibility of refusing to appear in certain files or to refuse the communication of personal information to a third party. There are various forms of expression of this right to opposition:

  - the refusal to respond to non-compulsory collection of data;
  - the need for written consent for the handling of sensitive data such as political opinions or religious beliefs;
  - the power to require the elimination of data contained in commercial files or of mail-order sales;
  - the possibility of demanding the granting or marketing of information.

The right to opposition contains two limits:

1. Its exercise is subordinate to the existence of justifiable reasons;
2. It does not exist in many public sector processes.

The right to rectification constitutes a complement to the right to access. Each person can correct errors which have been made on the occasion of the communication of personal information. So, in the case of inaccuracy, they can insist on this information being rectified, completed, clarified, updated or erased.

Discussion questions

1. Take a service company (e.g., retail store, restaurant) and create a possible structure for its customer database.

2. RFM analysis is one of the basic principles of data mining. How would you apply it to a restaurant, record store, phone service provider, or theatre? For each business, what is the impact of applying this segmentation using a database?

3. Take several mails you have received in your mailbox. File them according to aim (i.e., prospecting or developing customer loyalty, awareness, encouraging larger orders, etc.). Analyse each of their features (text, address, phone number, website, envelope).

4. What are the advantages and drawbacks of direct-mail advertisements, telephone marketing, and e-mail marketing when it comes to creating familiarity for a new product?

5. How do you measure the attrition rate of a customer database? How can you minimize that rate? What efforts can you make to cause a database to grow despite the loss of some customers?

6. How do you measure the efficiency of a mail marketing campaign compared to an e-mail marketing campaign?

7. Describe the "multi-channel" approach for a given service (e.g., airline, hotel, car rental). What are the benefits and dangers of such an approach?

Index